Maud Powell

PIONEER AMERICAN VIOLINIST

PIONEER AMERICAN VIOLINIST

By

Karen A. Shaffer

and

Neva Garner Greenwood

Foreword by Yehudi Menuhin

The Maud Powell Foundation — Arlington, Virginia

Iowa State University Press — Ames, Iowa

FRONTISPIECE:
Maud Powell, about 1911. Neva Garner Greenwood Collection.

LIBRARY OF CONGRESS CATALOGUING-IN-PUBLICATION DATA

Shaffer, Karen A., 1947–
  Maud Powell, pioneer American violinist.

  Discography: p.
  Includes index.
  1. Powell, Maud, 1867–1920.   2. Violinists—United
States—Biography.   I. Greenwood, Neva Garner.   II. Title.
ML418.P79S5   1988   787.1'092'4 [B]   87–28121
ISBN 0–8138–0989–4 (alk. paper)

To
The Memory of
Neva Garner Greenwood
and
to
My Family

Contents

Foreword

AS I READ THE PAGES OF THIS BOOK, A CURIOUS RE-IDENTIFICATION OCCURS: I
redefine myself as both an "American" and a "violinist." It is a recognition of certain attitudes and qualities, an approach to the future,
which mark the land of our birth and which we share — despite the
fact that our musical culture was, as it had to be and still is up to a
point, nurtured in Europe; in Maud Powell's case, as in that of my
first great teacher, Louis Persinger, from a rich broth of German and
English, Belgian and French influences.

Intellectually and aesthetically I was deeply influenced by that
dynamic and beloved literary figure Willa Cather, as well as by the
musicianship, sense of taste, style, and sheer exuberance of Maud
Powell's artistry. These two great ladies reflected the vital, ardent,
confident, and unburdened Americanism of my formative years. They
were forward-looking, innovative, yet self-disciplined. Thus here I
have rediscovered two, one might almost say maternal, influences
from the land of my parents' choice rather than from the land of my
origins — influences environmental rather than hereditary.

When I consider Maud Powell's enthusiasm and passion for helping the wounded soldiers in the First World War and her innumerable concerts for the troops, and then reflect on my own experiences
during the Second World War; when I read of her endorsement of
osteopathy and compare my own penchant for the so-called "fringe"
medical practices; when I consider her faith in and loyalty to American composers (I think of Roy Harris, of Copland, of Bloch, Ross

Lee Finney, Bernstein, and many others), I am made conscious of the path I have pursued in her image as a violinist and musician, and a warm feeling of fellowship, of fraternity, fills my heart. And when I read of her concerts in all the towns of the United States which I know so well from childhood and from my own touring of nearly sixty years, I realize that I must have inhabited fairly often the same hotels she stayed in. When I read of her friendship with Sir Edward Elgar, of her understanding of the German classics, of her European formation, the reader will understand why in all modesty I feel a human and professional kinship with this extremely sensitive and strong woman.

I was four years old when I began to play the violin, the same year in which Maud Powell died. As a child of five I heard her recordings, and her silvery sound of greatest purity became a guiding inspiration to my ambition and formed the image I had of a graceful lady, poised and beautiful as she played my chosen instrument. I like to think that she bequeathed a legacy to me: the very truth she had lived and died for and her commitment to her violin, to her music, and to humanity.

YEHUDI MENUHIN

Preface

THE NAME OF MAUD POWELL, ONCE KNOWN IN VIRTUALLY EVERY AMERICAN household, has faded from public memory into the recesses of past and forgotten history. It seems strange that one whose life and art were once legendary should slip away without our noticing. Did her fame slip away because she was a woman, because she was an American, because she died at a relatively early age, because technological advances displaced her recorded art from public hearing, because she lived before radio and television? Surely all of these are contributing factors, but perhaps there is a more fundamental reason. Could it be that she simply shares the fate of other violinists whose art was revered in her day? How many people today really understand the importance as performers of such violinists as Camilla Urso, Joseph Joachim, Eugène Ysaÿe, or even Fritz Kreisler? Surely it is few who remember the American-born violin soloists Arthur Hartmann, Geraldine Morgan, Francis MacMillen, even Albert Spalding.

Perhaps our ignorance about Maud Powell, as well as other great masters of the bow, stems from the fact that the history of violin playing has been preserved primarily through an oral tradition handed down from master to pupil through the years. The oral tradition was singularly important before the era of recordings. Violinists passed on to each other the memorable personal traits, style, technique, and musical interpretations of violinists whose art they had personally witnessed or about which they had learned from their own masters. Some knowledgeable persons, Henry C. Lahee, for example, wrote down these observations and from time to time published articles or books about the key figures in the history of violin playing.

Although there has been some excellent recent scholarship in which the history of classical violin-playing has been reviewed, there is no comprehensive treatment of the development of violin playing in America during the nineteenth and early twentieth centuries. The subject is not generally formally taught in American universities and music conservatories. American violinists and other string players graduate knowing little of their own cultural history. Composers they know, but they know much less about performers of the past unless the performers were prominent composers as well.

This serious dearth of scholarship concerning violin playing in America begins to explain our ignorance of Maud Powell. Further contributing to this lack is the fact that throughout our history some of the most influential teachers in America have been trained primarily by Europeans and hence have passed on to their pupils only the European oral tradition. We have lost sight of the important American figures in the development of violin playing in America. The greatest American violin virtuoso of the nineteenth and early twentieth centuries, Maud Powell, did not teach individual pupils, and this circumstance further explains the missing American links in the historical chain.

Because of our nature as a nation of immigrants, the history of violin playing in America is a complexly woven fabric combining homespun yarns with the color, refinement, and variety of European and, more recently, Asian textures. For this reason, the thread of the American history of violin playing is difficult to trace. It is no wonder that until now no one has taken it upon himself to spin out the tale. My good fortune was to find that it becomes comprehensible when seen through the life of Maud Powell.

I confess that I began the task of writing this biography in ignorance. I have had to discover the hard way that the American-born Maud Powell was one of America's most significant musical pioneers. It was with wonder that I began to realize that she was America's first great master of the violin. The more I learned, the more my wonder grew as I realized that her noble art and exemplary life both inspired and pointed the way toward America's development of its own musical culture. It was with astonishment that I eventually concluded that the history of violin playing in America cannot be grasped without an understanding of Maud Powell's pivotal influence as an artist and as a human being.

Here, then, is an important story revealing our musical heritage, an understanding of which is vital to the enrichment of the American musician's art and that musician's ability to make a real contribution to our culture. It is with humility and hope that this biography is offered as a first step toward the reclamation of our rich, though obscured, heritage and as a source of inspiration to present and future generations of American violinists, fulfilling what undoubtedly would have been Maud's wish had she lived to express it.

The story of how this biography came into being is a story of two individual dreams which fused into one through the shared love, labor, and joy of two people. Although it is only now apparent, Maud Powell's influence has been at work for many years, leading us inexorably to bring forth the story of this great-souled artist's life.

Maud Powell inspired the dedicated musical life of Neva Garner Greenwood, whose original research gave the project its beginnings. A gifted musician in her own right and a thoughtful and inspiring teacher, Neva often told me of her fabled journey in a Kansas City streetcar carrying, along with her violin, two large framed pictures of Maud Powell and Fritz Kreisler, the ideal models for a promising young violinist in the 1920s. Growing up at a time when Powell's name was legendary, she remembered her violin teacher mourning the artist's early death with repeated expressions concerning the warmth and beauty of her tone. Although Neva Greenwood never heard Powell play in person, she was deeply impressed by these early images of the great violinist. Neva once confessed that "I have had [Maud Powell] on my mind practically my whole life."

Years later, the mother of one of Neva's pupils, Laura Adams Woodside, rekindled this early interest in Powell by telling her of Maud's association with her own grandfather, New York critic William B. Chase, near whose family homestead in New Hampshire Maud had built a summer home. Maud Powell was part of the Chase family lore. Aroused by Laura Woodside's enthusiasm, Neva visited Whitefield, New Hampshire, around 1974, and thus began her great adventure in tracking down Maud Powell.

Neva Greenwood toured the country and wrote hundreds of letters seeking people and places associated with Maud and subsequently accumulated the largest collection of Powell memorabilia in existence. She managed to talk with those few still living who had known Maud Powell personally, including Maud's first cousin Mabel Love. She found other relatives who could and did graciously provide important family information and photographs.

Sadly, few of Maud Powell's personal possessions, letters, and memorabilia remain. Most of them were scattered upon her death, since she had no children and her husband died not long after she did. However, Neva Greenwood found a wealth of information in the music journals of Maud's day. Thanks to Powell's eminence in the musical world and her accessibility to the press — as well as her own facility with the pen — her activities and thinking were fairly well recorded in print.

In Neva's original research, which was largely concluded by 1980 due to her ill health, she was encouraged and assisted by her devoted husband Joseph Greenwood, with his trusty typewriter, and by her daughter Elizabeth, an unflagging supporter of the project. Her daughter Nancy, with her husband Frederick Brooks, also proffered helpful advice and encouragement.

In 1980, Neva Greenwood brought the results of her original research to me and asked that I write the biography of this American artist. Neva and I had met for the first time when I, a college freshman, shyly appeared at her studio seeking my very first violin lesson. I soon came to share her love for the violin and its discipline and to understand her intrigue with the instrument and its possibilities. Moreover, I grew to love and respect her for the intelligence and caring she so uniquely combined with her musical gifts.

I shall always be grateful for the friendship which our mutual love for the violin nourished through the years. Through this friendship, my life has been graced with music and through her, I first experienced the pure joy that comes with music-making in an intimate setting. Through this friendship, my lifelong ambition to write a biography has been realized. That such a great human spirit should be the subject of that biography has given me endless joy and satisfaction. It has been the delight of my life to write the life of Maud Powell as well as a deep honor and privilege.

While the biography has brought me deep-seated joy, it has also required personal sacrifice. I began to supplement Neva's research and write the biography a year prior to becoming counsel to a congressional committee in 1981. Writing a book in conjunction with a full-time job required isolation from friends and family. Every week-end and every evening was spent with Maud. Violin lessons and prac-tice eventually had to be abandoned altogether; social engagements were turned down. Faithful friends who did come by or who heard from me inevitably were put to work on some Maud-related task. My family's desires to see me were not very often fulfilled. When they were, my parents and my brother and his wife were set to work proofreading, lending editorial judgments, and, after the Founda-tion was established, my mother even stuffed envelopes and attended to bookkeeping while my brother wrote a computer program for the mailing list. My father gracefully performed essential major home repairs and outdoor work so I could concentrate on Maud. I am grateful for his standing offer to provide financial support to meet my personal needs if necessary which enabled me to do my work on Maud with a sense of security and peace of mind. For all their help and for their love and loyalty, I am most grateful. I am especially grateful that my mother has shared my interest in and enthusiasm for Maud and my sense of adventure in our travels together in search of Maud Powell. I was the fortunate heir to her musical and literary bent which from my birth she began to pass on to me. I rejoice that, in a sense, Maud Powell has brought us all closer together in spite of the diminished amount of time I have had to share with them.

The task facing me was imposing. The deep intertwining of Maud Powell's life with the history of violin playing in America required that that history be told together with Maud's own story to reveal her true significance. All of this had to be recreated from scratch since there was no previous biography and there is no comprehensive, author-itative work on violin playing in America in existence. Such an enter-prise is inevitably laborious and time-consuming because it must be so painstakingly put together. The task required of me a great deal of personal research and study, growing into a fascinating and mov-ing intellectual and spiritual journey which employed all my creative powers. When combined with my discovery that to know Maud Powell is to love Maud Powell, the biography became an immensely ful-filling labor of love. My personal sense of Maud's presence, prodding me and looking over my shoulder as I was writing, pervaded and surmounted the isolation and pain of the creative process with a sort of heartwarming revelatory dialogue as I thought out and vicariously relived the events, actions, thoughts, and emotions of her life. Adding to my sense of fulfillment was the warm comfort of sharing with Neva Greenwood the results of my writing, from which long, satisfying conversations ensued, drawing us ever closer to one another.

In 1985, during the last year of Neva Greenwood's life, I left my position with Congress and devoted all my energies to rewriting a voluminous manuscript, thanks to the perceptive encouragement of award-winning author Christopher Hope, which was reinforced by Trudy McMurrin, at that time director of Southern Methodist University Press. Six months later, I emerged from nearly total isolation with a new manuscript.

By that time, although we did not know it, Neva was suffering from a terminal illness. In March 1986, she read the completed manuscript. By May 1986, she was so ill that she could not attend violinist Jody Gatwood's superb performance of the Dvořák violin concerto in Maud's honor, with the McLean Orchestra. Although she was the venerable age of eighty, her considerable intellectual powers and interest in all life were only slightly diminished by deteriorating health. Hence, her death in June came as a shock. The realization that Neva Greenwood would never see the published book was heartbreaking. We had been friends for twenty years.

The Maud Powell Foundation was born as a result of a groundswell of loving appreciation for Neva Greenwood from her friends. Their contributions led to the establishment of a memorial fund to further publication of the book and incorporation of the Foundation, which had long been a dream of mine, to administer it. As a result of donations by countless friends and family members of Neva Greenwood's and mine and Maud Powell's, Maud's biography is being published under the auspices of The Maud Powell Foundation in cooperation with the Iowa State University Press, which, thanks to its thoughtful director Richard Kinney, took a real interest in the manuscript late last year.

Publication of this book largely has been made possible through the prescience, enthusiasm, and benevolence of Trudy McMurrin, a gifted editor, who almost intuitively understood Maud's significance from the start, who had the grace to share my enthusiasm, and who has generously given me important encouragement over the last three-and-a-half years. Throughout my work on this book, Trudy has continually chided me about the exuberant enthusiasm for Maud Powell which my writing reflected. It had always been my intention to allow Maud to speak for herself, above all. Yet my awe of her and enthusiasm often got the better of me. At my urging and hers, Trudy patiently excised (almost) all my superlative adjectives from the manuscript so that Maud could reveal herself as the great human being she was.

Although duly chastened, I sense, happily, that I am in good company. The reader will notice that those who personally witnessed Maud Powell's performances repeatedly described her as tall and statuesque in appearance. In fact, her physical height was approximately five feet three inches, probably about average for a woman of that day. But her dignified bearing and the manner in which she held her head and violin (up, not down like a "criminal," as Dancla instructed her), combined with the aura which surrounded her, gave Maud a presence that was larger than life.

The singular beauty of this book is due to Trudy McMurrin's keen eye and sound judgment. In a labor of love, with only token compensation for all her work, her gracious acceptance of the responsibility for handling all editorial and publishing details has turned our fondest hopes into a wonderful reality. For this, she has my abiding thanks and warm affection.

Through it all, Maud Powell has been the guiding light for all our labors. In fact, I believe that Maud's spiritual presence has shadowed my personal search for her. Who can explain my blindly stopping in front of the only remaining structure in Peru, Illinois, (Maud's birthplace) which had any association with Powell, the Maze family home, where she had in fact stayed overnight in 1908, and which stood as the Maze homestead even before Maud's birth? How was it that on the only day I forgot to take my camera with me and we were going for the first, and so far as I knew, only, time to the Henry Ford Museum where Maud's Guadagnini rests, my mother discovered a color photograph of the crest on the violin's tailpiece in the museum shop's 1986 calendar (better than any I possibly could have taken)? How can I express the strong sense of Maud's presence which moved me to tears as I walked through the streets of "dear old Leipzig," where she had studied? How did it happen that the very day that Neva Greenwood and I met the American violinist Aaron Rosand in Baltimore to talk about Maud Powell, we were notified that Maud's Tourte bow was for sale?

Aaron Rosand discovered that Maud Powell's spirit still lives within that bow, which came into his possession in 1985. Long fabled in the W. B. Chase family as "the charmed stick" because it has perfect balance, the bow released its magic in his masterful hands. As soon as he began to play with it, he could not put it down, so beautiful was the tone it produced. "The Magic Bow," as he refers to it, has brought a new dimension to his playing, including a new singing tonal power and vitality. Fittingly, this poet of the violin gave a beautiful recital in Chicago's Orchestra Hall on April 26, 1987, commemorating the 120th anniversary of Maud's birth, which was witnessed by thirty warm-hearted citizens from Peru, Illinois.

On that same journey, I was at last able to hear Maud's favorite violin, her Guadagnini, played at the Henry Ford Museum. Thanks to the gracious efforts of Bruce Simpson, I heard speak the instrument which had been Maud's truest voice and in which her spirit still dwells. By some magical serendipity which I have come to expect in my Maud Powell adventures, Mr. Simpson played bits of the Bruch G minor violin concerto. How could he have known that that music had been running through my mind from the outset of the trip and was in fact the concerto with which Maud had made her debut? I had experienced something similar when Aaron Rosand privately demonstrated Maud's bow for my mother and me. Just as I began to request that he play part of the Sibelius violin concerto, which Maud premiered in America and so dearly loved, he began to play it. I never got the composer's name out of my mouth.

It has become perfectly clear to me why the critics always raved about Maud's tone, for the violin is full-throated and sings with a rare brilliancy and warm, golden quality, rather like sunrise over the Grand Canyon, and the bow doubles in fullness the tone that can be achieved with other bows. That is all apart from her superb artistry.

Maud Powell's spirit stood among those few who gathered together in a small room in Gstaad, Switzerland, on August 23, 1984, to commemorate her birthday. Honoring her was Yehudi Menuhin, who, born in America nearly a half century after Maud, I believe to be her true heir in mind, in spirit, and in mastery of his art. As he and I exchanged toasts in her honor, Maud's presence was truly palpable.

As deeply moving was Yehudi Menuhin's tribute to Maud Powell on March 5, 1986, celebrating the centennial year of her debut during his recital in Chicago's Orchestra Hall. No one present will soon forget the graceful words he spoke from the stage and his entrancing rendition of Powell's transcription of "Nobody Knows the Trouble I See," the last piece that she ever performed on stage. Heightening the excitement of the evening, forty-seven cheerful people from Peru, all wearing Maud Powell buttons, traveled 200 miles round-trip under the intrepid leadership of Nancy Chadbourne Maze to witness the event.

No artist has given as generously of his time and energy as has Yehudi Menuhin to ensure that the legacy of Maud Powell can be reclaimed by all Americans as their own very special heritage. His gentle indulgence and openness to adventure allowed me to lure him into sharing my love for his distinguished predecessor, about whom he had known from early childhood. I shall always be grateful for his perception of Maud's historic importance as a violinist and human being and for his personal encouragement and interest in the biography's fulfillment. Yehudi Menuhin's deeply personal and touching tribute to Maud Powell in the foreword is a humble and graceful testament to the power of one life to move another, though it be equally as exalted in its guiding light.

On behalf of the late Neva Greenwood and myself, I would like to extend thanks to more people than can be mentioned here. Therefore, I have tried to express our thanks through the notes wherever possible as well as in the formal acknowledgments. We are indebted to countless dedicated librarians, to relatives and friends of Maud Powell, and to many others who so willingly gave of their time to furnish the information which has enabled us to bring Maud Powell back to life. Further, we are indebted to the Board of Directors of The Maud Powell Foundation and all its supporters for making publication of this book possible and to the Iowa State University Press for its part in the publication process and for ensuring its widest possible distribution.

I am certain that Neva, who also suffered from the isolation imposed by her research for this project, would have wished to express her gratitude to her family and friends for their support and understanding.

On a final personal note, I am deeply grateful to my family and friends, who gave freely of their moral support and practical assistance. Both family and friends suffered my seclusion from normal social intercourse with a loyalty and indulgence for which I am truly grateful. I especially wish to express my heartfelt appreciation for my friend Melissa Pittard, whose faithful friendship eased me through the heavy burdens and enriched the joyous moments of the last years of this project.

Finally, Neva and I have been grateful to Maud Powell, herself, who has been the living inspiration for all our labors.

ARLINGTON, VIRGINIA   K.A.S.
OCTOBER 1987

The Modern Violin-playing Tradition

The tradition of Corelli: a teacher–pupil genealogical tree illustrating Maud Powell's artistic heritage (dotted lines indicate influence). With acknowledgment to Margaret Campbell, whose diagram for *The Great Violinists* has been altered slightly to more fully reflect Maud Powell's artistic development and is used with permission.

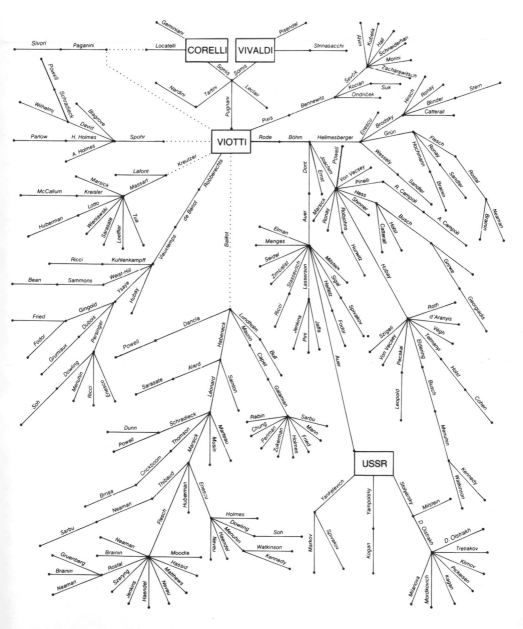

1

Pioneer Heritage

I must study Politicks and War that my sons may have liberty to study Mathematicks and Philosophy. My sons ought to study Mathematicks and Philosophy, Geography, natural History, Naval Architecture, navigation, Commerce and Agriculture, in order to give their Children a right to study Painting, Poetry, Musick, Architecture, Statuary, Tapestry and Porcelaine.

—*John Adams to Abigail Adams, May 12, 1780*

MAUD POWELL WAS BORN ON AUGUST 22, 1867, in a two-story brick house in Peru, Illinois.[1] The house stood overlooking the Illinois River as it meandered through the green and golden valley and the bustling little town of Peru which hugged the shore along the river's banks. Situated on the gentle bluffs directly north of the local chair factory, at the intersection of Bluff and Adams streets (1112 Bluff Street), the house's simple appearance belied its sturdy structure. Its foot-thick walls fashioned of brick reflected the uncertainty of frontier life, but its structure also symbolized the determination with which Peru's early settlers had set down roots in that untamed land.

Maud's heritage and that of her parents, William Bramwell Powell and Minnie Paul Powell, was bound to the historic settlement of the West. Theirs was a pioneer heritage forged from spirits which dreamed dreams as large as the land itself and matched each dream with heroic courage, determination, intelligence, and nobility of spirit.

Maud Powell was born with the same extraordinary passion, integrity, and vision which characterized her forebears. It was fitting that she should be born in the heartland of America at the opening of the long period of peace which followed the calamitous Civil War, for her life would symbolize and give rise to a new stage in the growth of the United States. Maud Powell would become one of America's greatest artists and the nation's foremost pioneer in music. But on that particular day in August, the residents of the little town of Peru went about their business as usual, unsuspecting of the extraordinary gift which had been given them that day.

Just outside of town and for miles beyond, farther than the eye could see, stretched fields of grain—corn, wheat, oats, and barley—broken here and there by a homestead and generous stands of trees. The land was rich, richer than perhaps the French explorer Joliet suspected when he first traveled by canoe up the Illinois River in 1673. Glaciers had evened the virgin land and in their final retreat enriched it with deep and fertile soils which overlaid generous deposits of coal, oil, fluorspar, stone, and other minerals. Connected by a network of rivers which laced through the prairie toward the Mississippi, the state of Illinois was perfectly situated to become the crossroads between East and West, North and South, once the Northwest Territory was opened for settlement.

The hopes and later prosperity of Peru's early settlers were founded on the bounty of the land.[2] In conjunction with its sister village LaSalle, Peru's location between the navigable portion of the Illinois River and the terminus of the Illinois and Michigan Canal ensured its rise in commercial importance in the 1840s.

Walking along Water Street, following the lines of the river, one could get caught up in the commotion surrounding the arrival of mail boats from Peoria and cargo vessels from the Mississippi and the changing of horses at the stagecoach stop. Commerce with the South in the 1840s involved the exchange of sugar, molasses, cotton, and light manufactured goods for grain, leather goods, and ice. Boatyards grew up along the river to serve the ice industry. The center of town was crowded with shops and offices reflecting the trading fare of the day. The town boasted a saloon, clothing and furniture stores, tobacconists, and grocery and dry goods shops.

The construction of the Rock Island passenger and freight depot indicated the commercial importance of the increasingly prosperous town. Boarding houses arose nearby to accommodate the newcomers who arrived seeking work in town or land they could farm. The Federal Land Office, the U.S. Express Company, and the First National Bank were prominent in facilitating commerce and promoting growth.

The Post Office was run by the local druggist, who advised his customers on the best remedies for their ailments and, aside from the newspaper, provided the primary source of news in town.

Farmers from as far as eighty miles brought the wheat and corn harvest to the mill at the foot of Putnam Street or to the brewery nearby and returned home, their wagons laden with merchandise from town. Blacksmith and carpenter shops were plentiful. The hardwood forests supplied the lumberyards and sawmills, while the earth's clay supported the brick factory in Peru. Brick and frame two- and three-story structures heated by wood-burning stoves housed the burgeoning community. The buggy factory, glass and bottle works, plow works, pork house (packing plant), zinc furnace, hide and leather merchants, and cooper shop were all evidence of the discovered treasures of the land. Farther up on Water Street, in the west end of town, coal was mined to support two coke ovens and the blacksmith and carpenter shops.

Most of the town's dwellings were situated on the gentle sandstone bluffs which rose above the town, overlooking Water Street and the Illinois River. To one of these homes, William and Caroline Paul brought Maud's mother, Minnie, upon the death of her parents in LaSalle in 1849.

Minnie's natural father, Peter Bengelstraeter, born in 1805, had been a hard-working and ambitious man who had accumulated a small fortune as a wire drawer in "Rhenish Prussia" in his native province of Westphalia.[3] A determined man, once he set his mind on emigrating to America, he could not be swayed to change what he considered his destiny. His wife, Wilhelmina Potthof, whom he had married on May 22, 1835, shared his determination and ambition.[4] Peter's brother and sister and the Potthof family believed that the young couple had been induced by "seductive writings and bad people" to embark on so dangerous a journey.[5] Feelings ran so high within the family that there were no farewells when Minnie's parents left forever the beautiful valley of Lösenbach near Lüdenscheid where Minnie and her four siblings had been born.

The Bengelstraeter family made their way to New Orleans by the summer of 1849, where they were welcomed by German friends. The new arrivals then journeyed by steamboat up the Mississippi and Illinois rivers to LaSalle, where Peter had arranged to purchase a farm for gold. But the deal was never to be completed. Peter and Wilhelmina, along with their oldest and youngest children, were among the hundreds of dead claimed by the black cholera that followed a disastrous flood which swept through the Illinois valley that summer.

Dying and unable to speak English, Wilhelmina motioned to the attending physician that he should take care of her surviving children: William, ten; Wilhelmina (Minnie), six; and Henrietta (Kitty), four.[6] Peter and Wilhelmina Bengelstraeter died within an hour of one another during the first week in August and were buried in unmarked graves.

Dr. Ruben B. Landon and his wife took the children in and then arranged for William to be cared for by a family named Smith, Minnie to be adopted by William and Caroline Paul of Peru, and little Henrietta, of whom they had become fond, to remain as a member of their own family.[7]

Minnie's adoptive father William Paul, born in Scotland in 1807, was one of the successful early merchants of the city, to which he had come in 1843.[8] This vigorous man was known for his honest business dealings, perfect decorum, and unfailing courtesy. His wife Caroline was a very well-educated woman with a keen interest in social questions.[9] While he was active in the establishment of Peru's first public schools, she was a physician who actively employed her skills in the community.

Minnie Paul grew up with high spirits and an irrepressible love of music.[10] She always claimed she had Hungarian blood, with a gypsy soul, and it was not so hard to believe if one gazed into her lively black eyes and got caught up in the abandon with which she danced. Her famous daughter once responded to a question about her ancestry: "Through my mother I have inherited real Gypsy blood, I am sure. My mother was a German, but she must have had Hungarian ancestors. I remember her once saying when she heard a band of strolling players, 'I could follow them.' She meant it. She was a Gypsy, and so am I. I always think of that remark of hers when I play the final movement of the 'Wieniawski concerto.' "[11] Minnie's vivacious charm made her a popular figure in Peru, and she enlivened the life of the community as an accomplished pianist and gifted amateur composer.

Peru's population was 3,000 when it was incorporated as a city in 1851. The city hall, built in 1855, was the site for concerts and appearances by such well-known singers as Adelina Patti and Jenny Lind. Musical German residents organized choral groups such as the Maennorchor, established in 1863. Public celebrations were brightened by the Philharmonic Society, a seventy-member mixed chorus and orchestra, the Mozart Club, and the Northwestern Lightguard Band, composed of brass and reed instruments. Concordia Hall and Garden was the early scene of stage productions, concerts, and dances.

Peru mustered its share of volunteer Union soldiers during the Civil War, always mindful that Abraham Lincoln and Daniel Webster, the most prominent spokesmen for preservation of the Union, were native sons. And Minnie Paul was chosen by the ladies of Peru to present the members of the volunteer company with a beautiful silk flag.[12] But Peruvians did not permit war to interfere with progress in civic matters. In 1858, the town's 3,652 residents supported seven public schools. Four years later, Maud's father, William Bramwell Powell, was appointed school superintendent to direct the system's needed reorganization and expansion.[13] He arrived in June of 1862.

Peru was to be the proving ground for this thoughtful man's first experiments with innovation in education. Bramwell Powell believed that education should improve not only the economic circumstances of people's lives but the aesthetic ones as well—that it should build character as well as knowledge and understanding. A man of high purpose and moral character, his life was guided by John Wesley's rule for Christian living, taught him by his parents:

> Do all the good you can,
> By all the means you can,
> In all the ways you can,
> In all the places you can,
> At all the times you can,
> To all the people you can,
> As long as ever you can.

He pursued his vision with a kind of missionary zeal characterized by faith, intelligence, dedication, and discipline mingled with tenderness, traits which were a part of the heritage which he transmitted in turn to his daughter Maud. William Bramwell Powell was the son of two extraordinary individuals, Joseph and Mary Powell.

Born around 1800 in Shrewsbury, England, near the Welsh border, Joseph Powell was a deeply religious man, drawn at an early age to the teachings of John Wesley, the founder of Methodism.[14] John Wesley and his brother Charles inspired a spiritual revival which spared England from the political revolution that might have been spawned by the pitiless conditions under which laborers and their families lived and worked during the industrial revolution of the mid- to late eighteenth century. These "warm-hearted" Methodists were doctrinally tolerant, stressing personal religious experience, universal salvation by faith, and practical ethics. The concomitant establishment of schools and health clinics, in addition to meeting houses for worship and religious study, was a practical manifestation of the strong social consciousness which became a hallmark of the Methodist tradition. John Wesley preached in the open air to reach the poor industrial classes effectively abandoned by the decaying Church of England. He personally appointed lay preachers from among the common people, men and women who God had touched, to sustain wherever possible the work he began. Wesley's extraordinary organizational skills—the underpinning of which was the formation of a democratic alliance between lay persons and clergy—as well as his personal inspiration, nurtured both the popular appeal and phenomenal institutional growth of Methodism throughout England.

Joseph Powell, a well-educated young man by the standards of the day and a tailor by trade, had gone to London to seek employment. There, among the Methodists, he was recognized for his personal qualities and licensed "to exercise his gifts in the Methodist Episcopal Church so long as his doctrines, practice, and usefulness comport with the discipline of said church." His wife, Mary Dean, born in Hull, England, on November 11, 1805, was also devout and well educated, and with their marriage in Birmingham on January 31, 1828, she became his life-long partner in Christian service.

More inspired to preach than to ply his trade, Joseph Powell was lured by the opportunity offered by the New World to preach and at the same time minimize his financial reliance on tailoring by taking up land. In 1784, John Wesley had given his blessing to the establishment of the American Methodist Episcopal Church. From the Methodist centers of Baltimore, New York, and Philadelphia, the co-founding Methodist bishops Francis Asbury and Thomas Coke began appointing itinerant preachers to spread the Word to people living in rural areas and frontier villages as America began its westward expansion.

In 1830, with hopeful hearts, Joseph and Mary Powell sailed with their two small daughters from Liverpool to New York City. Their prayers were answered when Joseph was commissioned to be a Methodist circuit rider, and over the next twenty years the couple migrated steadily westward toward new frontiers. Joseph Powell was driven by the need to preach to those who were in need of his message, and he would never be content to settle where established churches and modern cities had developed.

Moving west, the Powells became very much a part of the historic moral and physical struggle which formed the events leading to the election of Abraham Lincoln in 1860 and the Civil War which followed. They had arrived in a country already being torn by sectionalism. The South's most fervent spokesmen could see the power of the South giving way in Congress with the westward migration which brought new states into the Union and with the increasing moral pressure against slavery. Joseph Powell, a handsome and magnetic speaker, took part in the debate over slavery, even as he and his family swelled the numbers of hopeful settlers moving into the heartland.

While following the canal route west across New York State, Mary Powell gave birth to two sons, John Wesley (Wes) in Mount Morris in 1834 and William Bramwell (Bram) in Castile in 1836. But the family did not linger in New York, since Ohio offered the opportunity Joseph Powell was seeking. There, where the people were converting the wilderness to productive land, Joseph could vigorously persevere in his ministry and buy farm land to sustain his growing family, thereby minimizing his reliance on the tailoring trade.

The Powells established a home base in the largely Welsh frontier community of Jackson (250 people), with the purchase of land and construction of a frame house in 1838. As a Methodist circuit rider, Joseph was required to ride alone on horseback through miles of virgin wilderness to reach settlements where he would preach and lead revival meetings. Such a life required a rare blend of courage, self-discipline, hard work, intelligence, common sense, devotion to duty, health and vitality, humor, patience, generosity, and loving-kindness. Not surprisingly, the Methodist circuit rider became one of the most important civilizing influences on the American frontier.

Joseph rode throughout the rich Ohio country, bringing books and papers, news of the latest agricultural and mechanical advances, and the word of God to the inhabitants of the frontier villages along the way. The Powell family expanded to eight children—Martha, Mary, Wes, Bram, Lida, Nell, Walter, and Juliet. Left alone for weeks at a time while Joseph rode circuit, Mary schooled their children on the Bible and Shakespeare, Webster's *A Grammatical Institute of the English Language*, and American and English literature and history. While the Powells instilled in their children a sense of discipline, industry, and devotion to duty, the purchase of a piano increased the family's delight in music-making and hymn-singing, also vital elements in the Methodist tradition.

Joseph, with his stern discipline, boundless energy, and religious orthodoxy, and Mary, by nature gentle, kind, and devoted to service to others, became community leaders, respected and loved by those who felt their influence. The Powells entertained prominent participants in the religious and political life of the state as well as the community. Conversations were wide-ranging and brought young Wes and Bram into close contact with the realities of their times and the issues of the day. Slavery, religion, and politics were central to discussions with such guests as George Crookham, the local naturalist and community leader, Professor Charles Grandison Finney of Oberlin College, Salmon P. Chase, the leader of the Liberty party in Ohio, and Joshua Giddings, Whig representative in Congress.

True to the teachings and beliefs of John Wesley, Joseph Powell preached against slavery throughout southern Ohio and did his best to shelter his family from the backlash of the pro-slavery element. After the Methodist Episcopal Church formally split into South and North over the slavery issue in 1845, Joseph Powell joined the Wesleyan Connection which had broken with its parent in 1843. He was assigned to Wisconsin at his request.

In Wisconsin, their father's absence from home and deeper concern for the "fertilization of his spiritual acres than with the soil and crops of his quarter section," left Wes and Bram, aged twelve and ten, with the management of the wheat farm. Bram later attributed his professional success to the rigorous discipline of the land.

Joseph's interest in the establishment of a Wesleyan college and seminary in Wheaton, Illinois, twenty-five miles west of Chicago, led to his election in 1853 to the Board of Trustees of the Illinois Institute. There, Joseph oversaw the training of men and women in Christian service while continuing to ride circuit for his faith. Bram and the younger Powell children attended the Institute, later reorganized under the Congregational Church as Wheaton College in 1860, one year after Wheaton's incorporation as a city. Joseph and Mary Powell, in harness to their faith to the end, died on March 12, 1870, and December 28, 1871, respectively.

While he was growing up, Bram had drawn close to his older brother Wes during their father's frequent absences.[15] Since the days when they had managed the wheat farm and driven the wagons into town through rough country, and sometimes even rougher crowds, Wes often had set an example or prepared the way for Bram. Rejecting the ministry for which Joseph Powell gladly would have paid the educational fees, Wes had set off to earn his own way to a natural science education through teaching. In 1854, eighteen-year-old Bram accompanied him to Decatur, Illinois, where Wes assumed a teaching position at Emerson School on Long Creek. There, both youths pursued advanced private instruction in Latin, Greek, some mathematics, and natural science.

Bram listened as his brother held evening geography classes in the one-room schoolhouse. Ingeniously combining his love for his subject and for music, Wes taught his pupils the state capitals, mountain ranges of the world, and rivers in Europe and Asia to the tunes of popular songs. The course was enormously popular and its content long remembered, and Bram never forgot this remarkable demonstration of a teacher's power to make learning of useful subjects fun and so interesting that pupils would desire to learn more and so acquire a genuine love of learning.

With his arrival in Peru in 1862, Bram was eager to launch his own experiments in education. Unlike his brother Wes, Bram was quiet and shy, but he still commanded the attention of the townspeople with his obvious intelligence and strikingly handsome appearance, his broad mustache and sensitive eyes somewhat belying his serious manner. No doubt Minnie Paul, gifted in her own right and attractive with dark curly hair and bright black eyes, quickly determined to work her charms on him. On May 28, 1865, with the conclusion of the Civil War, Bram, twenty-eight, and Minnie, twenty-one, were married, their intelligence, spirit, and mutual love for music forming a bond which would be severely tested by the painful separations necessitated by their daughter's extraordinary musical gifts.[16]

Many years after the birth of "Minnie Maud" in 1867, Minnie would write without exaggeration of her daughter's propitious beginnings in the sturdy brick house on Bluff Street, "Of the families who lived on the high bluff overlooking the Illinois River, that of her parents ranked among the most intelligent, thoughtful and refined."[17]

2

Aurora

Happy is the home that is filled with song, where boys and girls sing the melodies of the people, and where they make these melodies more musical with the violin, the piano or the flute; for to music is consigned the purest joy.

—*John Wesley Powell*

THROUGHOUT HER YOUTH, MAUD'S MOTHER had longed for a musical career, but her dreams fell victim to the times. For a woman, a career was out of the question.[1] Yet Minnie was clearly talented as an amateur composer and pianist, and her husband shared her love for music and sympathized with her unrealized dreams.

While expecting her first child, Minnie determined that its musical development would not be thwarted and accordingly fastened her hopes on the child through whom her ambitions were to be realized.[2] Maud later spoke of the importance of her career to her mother and of her mother to her early musical development: "My mother . . . is musical, but her talent whatever it might have been with cultivation remained undeveloped. She often said to me, 'I have achieved through you what I was never able to do myself.' It was my mother who, so to speak, first 'tried music on me' to find out if I was musical."[3]

Although Minnie had "determined that her first *son* should be a violinist," the birth of a daughter did not deter her ambition. In those days, the violin was not commonly played by women because the awkward playing position was thought to be unladylike. Maud recalled, "My mother was not to be balked by such a trifle. As soon as I was old enough, a baby violin was put into my little hands."[4]

[11]

Formal instruction on the violin and piano would wait for Aurora, Illinois, where Bramwell was summoned in 1870 to assume the duties of superintendent of the East Side public schools.[5] Located forty miles west of Chicago and incorporated in 1857, Aurora, the City of Lights, physically straddled the Fox River.[6] In the island in the middle, the town erected its city hall in 1868, creating a symbolic link between the two sides of town.

The Powells moved into a comfortable but modest home which still stands at 16 West Street, and Maud soon became familiar to the neighborhood children as a "very little girl—quick, lively—with a mass of ringlets flying about her head and face."[7] Under her mother's instruction, the precocious youngster could play small pieces on the piano by the age of four. Bram and Minnie chose Professor G. W. Fickensher, the head of the district music department, and his daughter Emma to instruct their daughter on the violin and piano, respectively. Maud remembered: "I began music study . . . when I was seven, not with the violin, but with the piano: I always had a predilection for the piano; I love it and it has retained a little place in my musical life. . . . About six months after beginning piano, the violin was started."[8]

The neighborhood children soon began to see Professor Fickensher, his violin tucked securely under his arm, regularly round the corner into West Street and disappear into the Powell home. This short, wiry, bearded German was not a virtuoso, but he was a good musician and he loved the violin, making violins and violin varnish in his own workshop when he was not teaching. What he knew, he knew correctly and well.

Fickensher soon realized that his student's talent was unusual. One of Maud's earliest childhood friends had the impression that both he and Maud's father harbored secret ambitions for her from the time she was five years old and that she was ever trained in that direction. She recalled that Maud was a "lovely girl, in appearance and disposition, very friendly, cheerful and full of fun, but in a way led a rather secluded life. . . . She was very much interested in her studies and music, and while popular with her schoolmates, she did not mingle a great deal with the general youthful activities."[9]

The careful guidance of her parents was critical to the development of Maud's musical gifts. Their love for music, coupled with their understanding of the importance of discipline and hard work, formed the basis for Maud's early routine: "The earliest fiddleistic struggles I seem to remember very little about. To get up at 6:30, practice an hour before breakfast, or to come home from school to practice another hour before supper seemed perfectly natural and right, because the habit had been formed. Mother's word was law."[10]

Maud attended the Center School, a four-story brick structure which towered over the town. Professor Fickensher regularly appeared in her classroom for a half-hour's instruction in music. Recalling her beloved teacher years later, Maud reflected, "He lived to a ripe old age, and in those 85 years I know he never harmed a living thing either in thought or deed. How well I remember the lessons in his little room at the Center school building, the German lessons which I postponed learning till the last minute, and the fiddle lessons which I studied most dutifully."[11]

Customarily, Professor Fickensher accompanied Maud home for her private violin lesson at the close of the music period. On one rare occasion Maud rebelled, trudging down the long corridor with the professor leading her by the hand, her feet stomping and dark curls shaking in remonstrance all the way. Coming out of the superintendent's office, Maud's father took a hand in restoring her to her better behavior.[12] Maud reflected, "Life even at that time had for my small self a stormy side. How many tears did I shed because the 'small boy' had an irrepressible desire to guy me as I trudged through the streets with my violin-box! And how I sometimes rebelled against the long hours of practice! . . . Sometimes too, being a pioneer girl violinist, I smarted under a few burning glances of disapproval even from my elders, but this antipathy to a progressive idea soon wore away leaving only smiles of pride and encouragement."[13] Through it all, Maud's deep inner attraction to the violin remained as irresistible as it was intangible.

Although somewhat isolated by her routine, Maud was an affectionate girl and lavished much of her affection on her brother Billy, who was four years younger than she (born October 13, 1871) and the perfect companion for play.

Maud's parents ensured that she received a well-rounded education and the necessary physical exercise to remain a healthy and well-balanced child. She played with such abandon that one former playmate vividly recalled an image of her as a "daring youngster of eleven, hanging from a hammock rod by her heels, dark curls falling over her flushed, laughing face."[14] A tomboy at heart, Maud exercised daily, rolling a hoop—with her left hand. Her father promised her five dollars if she would roll the hoop for a certain period each day and never use her right hand. The idea was to protect her bow arm so that the muscles would develop only in conformance with her violin practice. Looking back on her early years, Maud said, "My father was one of the most advanced educators of his day, and he had no intention of permitting me to have a one-sided education."[15] He was careful to apportion three, and as she grew older, four hours a day as sufficient for her musical studies.

Her parents guided her musical development with steady hands, attending her lessons and overhearing her practice.

> . . . my father was deeply interested in music, and of course, in my progress. He watched it carefully, especially from the mental side; he saw to it that I understood what I was doing, that I learned how to memorize and had incentives to do it. After I returned from a lesson he would ask, "Well, what did you do today?" "Oh I have a new piece, or a concerto," as the case might be. "Are you going to learn it by heart?" "I don't know, maybe." "Well, if you learn it by Christmas you'll get a five dollar bill." That was only a few weeks away, but I made it a point to be ready at the appointed day to play that concerto from memory to my father and so secure the coveted reward.[16]

Mrs. Powell explained, "Realizing the great advantage of being able to play before an audience without the use of notes, her parents at first bribed the little musician to memorize everything she learned."[17] Eventually, it became natural for her to play everything from memory, learning all her music by heart as she was taught it.

Maud's parents exposed her to Aurora's musical events and involved her in their own participation in the musical life of the community, from church music and local singing groups to chamber music within their own home. Maud said, "I heard all the music I possibly could hear; [i]n fact, music was part of my life."[18]

As far as the Powell family's involvement in church music was concerned, Maud grew up in the Methodist tradition which, in addition to imbuing her with a deep-seated personal faith, a missionary spirit, acute social consciousness, and an appreciation for democratic principles, endowed her with a rich musical heritage. The Methodist congregation was a singing congregation with a vast repertory of original hymns. John Wesley's *A Collection of Psalms and Hymns*, published at Charlestown, South Carolina, in 1737, was one of the first hymnals in the English language for use in public worship. His 1780 *Collection of Hymns for the Use of the People Called Methodists* contained verses written by both John and his gifted brother Charles.

Charles Wesley's overriding contribution to the Methodist tradition consists of his innumerable hymns—bright, cheerful, optimistic, and simple, resounding with praise and joy—set to bounding rhythms and endearing melodies, vigorous marches, or the dignified harmonies of a Bach chorale. Many of his hymns were set in the classical music tradition, based on music by Bach and, later, by Mendelssohn, Spohr, and Weber. Others were set to lively and well-known traditional tunes. They all brought into the Methodist movement the cheering and uniting element of concerted praise.

Growing up in the Methodist Episcopal Church, Maud undoubtedly felt the uniting power of the joyful singing of well-known and beloved choruses from early childhood. The power of music to move, to inspire, to bind people together in loyalty and affection surely made an indelible impression on the young musician.

Aurora was an unusually musical town and provided other important opportunities for Maud's musical development. Like hundreds of other little towns in the West, it traced its musical beginnings to the early settlers who first carted a precious violin or the family piano across the old Northwest Territory to their new homes in the level plains of Illinois. Hymn-singing and religious song services in private homes and later in the First Congregational Church typified the first community efforts at organized music. The most elaborate musical performance up to 1860 was *Queen Esther*, a cantata, in which a visiting Kentuckian led an Aurora cast. The First Methodist Episcopal Church installed the first pipe organ in 1871.

The pride of the growing community was the completion of the Coulter Opera House in the 1870s. Its distinctive architecture marked the edifice as a fashionable as well as a favorite gathering place for all of Aurora. The stage was christened with the Adelaide Phillips Company's rendering of the *Barber of Seville*. The hall's wooden orchestra seats and luxurious padded balcony seats were crowded with the town residents on that occasion. The Aurora Light Guard Band frequently gave Grand Promenade Concerts in the handsome house, and the colorful Scandinavian violinist Ole Bull appeared there in 1872. The illumination at the main intersections of city streets with the novel brilliance of gaslights made evening concert-going in Aurora a special treat.

It was at the Coulter Opera House that Madam Camilla Urso, a violin virtuoso of the first order, appeared during the 1870s. Maud, then about seven years old, remembered her appearance there with reverence.[19] Urso's playing ignited a fire within her that served as her inspiration throughout the rest of her life. "She first showed me what it was I wanted to do — what all my crude scrapings might become."[20]

Born in Nantes, France, in 1842, the daughter of a Sicilian flutist and a Portuguese singer, Camilla Urso was a prodigy who studied with the Belgian master Massart at the Paris Conservatoire. Brought to America by her family in 1852, she began concertizing and until her death in 1902 was one of the best-known violinists in the United States. Appearing in the great cities of Europe and America, she is said to have played divinely with a magnificently big, round, and singing tone. She toured extensively in America, playing in small towns as well as large, convinced of the importance of bringing classical music to the uninitiated as well as to sophisticated audiences. New York critic Henry E. Krehbiel conceded her the rank of one of the foremost of living violinists: "In her case, the idea of sex, which so often obtrudes itself and modifies critical judgment, is never thought of . . . she does not play like either a man or woman, but like a sound, noble, earnest and inspired musician."[21] Maud responded to her playing as if summoned to awaken to the gift that was within her own soul.[22]

Shortly thereafter, in 1874, young Maud performed during one of the "delightful" receptions which the Powells hosted for the public school teachers to foster unity of spirit. Maud's father affectionately lifted his daughter onto a stool, lightly presenting her to the gathering as a violinist. Visibly pleased, the little girl began to play, astonishing the assembled listeners: "Her execution, tone and expression were remarkable for so small a child."[23] Maud's father mused, "I am almost convinced that Maud possesses an unusual love and an exceptional talent for music and if so I intend to do all in my power to advance Maud in that line." Although undecided, he appeared to favor the violin over the piano since it seemed to him to be his daughter's first choice.

Music was not the only area in which this kind and prescient man advanced his daughter's education during this period, for she received the full benefit of his innovative ideas on education. Powell's notable accomplishment in Aurora was the introduction and working out in the classroom of his own theory of how to teach children to speak, read, and write proper English. His departure from the educational methods of the day, which had turned the approach to education on its head, was radical.[24] Rote learning, excessive memorization, drilling, and mechanical routine, high-toned reading matter, and the use of the rod all centered learning around the authority of the teacher. The energetic Powell rejected the rod outright as an inducement to learning, favoring instead the development of interest and enthusiasm through the lure of things worthy to be loved. "Make your schools attractive and interesting to the children, and they will be filled," he adjured his fellow educators. "[T]he school exists for the child and not for itself."[25]

For him, all teaching began with "a loving appreciation of the way the child learns."[26] Bram concluded that a child learns best from personal experience (as opposed to rote learning) and then devised a new teaching approach based on that premise.

Fundamental to that approach was his view that command of the English language, in speaking, writing, and reading, is absolutely essential to learning as a lifetime process. He further viewed the ability to think methodically, to organize one's thoughts on any given subject, as the key to learning how to express oneself clearly with proper English. Bramwell chose as his vehicle for development of these skills "subjects of thought . . . presented to the child first through the senses. He must be made to know through original channels of information."[27]

Maud's father advocated teaching music in the same way, approaching it first as an aural experience, introducing the forms only after the aural grasp became evident. Well in advance of his time, he insisted on music in all the grades, believing that "nothing in the course of instruction, besides civics, takes a child into a mutuality with nature as music does. It leads him to see the dependence of man upon his fellow-man in society; it teaches him to realize himself as a part of a composite whole, and leads him to understand and appreciate the value of others in society."[28]

Above all, Bramwell Powell's view of education was broadly conceived and farsighted. It required "self-imposed purposive activity on the part of the child . . . induced . . . by a broad, intellectual, thoroughly-planned leading on the part of the teacher." Obtaining knowledge was to be secondary to the creation of an intellectual approach or attitude toward learning "characterized by intellectual alertness or interest, intellectual exactness or accuracy, and intellectual control or a cultivated will."[29] His ideal was to make "school life a continuation of and a delightful adjunct to a cultivated home life."[30]

Obviously, Maud did not exaggerate in the slightest when she indicated that, with her father, it was impossible to have a one-sided education. Her father's ideal classroom for the child encompassed all the world:

> The work of the primary school in all branches is to fill the child's subconsciousness with richness. Take him into the fields; take him to the riverside; take him to the hillside, to the mountain top, to the zoological park, to the museum, to the birds' nests, to the tea-kettle where the vapor is, to the icehouse, to the cars, to the railroad station; take him out and let him fill himself with experience. Do that in everything you teach, and do not fail to do that in music. Do not go to the music book; go instead to the child's knowledge of music, his own singing of the beautiful songs he has learned to sing correctly. Then, in music as in literature, in the fourth and fifth grades of school you will have your pupils singing music as now we have in the fourth and fifth grades our children reading literature.[31]

Both Maud and Billy became known for their original and independent minds and the forcefulness and facility with which they expressed themselves in speech and writing. From the beginning, their minds were trained to see broadly, clearly, and deeply so that they developed an unusual and precocious understanding of the world and people around them which in turn deepened their own sense of self and development of character.

Maud reflected: "I experienced the refining influence of a sweet home-life, surrounded by books, music, flowers, pictures and gentle home pleasures, under the moral guidance of broadminded parents, and meeting constantly people of culture and refinement."[32]

While in Aurora, Maud's father became nationally known for his educational ideas, and he traveled throughout the country to speak at conferences on education and to conduct teaching institutes. Consequently, a steady stream of educators from across the country visited the Powell home to learn of Bramwell's educational approach in Aurora. Many school systems adopted his textbooks, while his books on teaching methods were introduced extensively into the curricula of normal schools throughout the United States.[33] By 1874, Powell was nominated by his peers for the office of superintendent of public instruction in the state in recognition of his work.

Although filled with a strong sense of purpose and enthusiasm for his work, Maud's father remained a shy man, more comfortable with action than with words. Increasingly in demand as a speaker on education, the slight, keen-eyed figure with auburn hair betrayed his native timidity in the rather sharp, nasal quality of his voice and hesitating manner of his speech.

The guests who frequented the Powell home contributed to the stimulating intellectual atmosphere within which Maud and her brother grew. Mrs. Powell's support for women's suffrage occasioned long, earnest conversations with Susan B. Anthony and other leaders of the movement, who shared Mrs. Powell's ambitions for Maud.

The frequent visits of Bram's brother John Wesley to their Aurora home were always a treat for the whole family.[34] Wes and Bram were as close as brothers could be. Both followed the ideal their father had preached, "The world is my parish." But while their father had preached religion, Bram preached education and Wes, science, and they each revolutionized their respective fields.

Bram's quiet nature and innovative mind were the perfect complement to Wes's talkativeness and his eagerness to expound on his latest discoveries and theories. As the first white man to travel the one-thousand-mile length of the Green and Colorado rivers through the forbidding walls of the Grand Canyon, Wes could lay claim to the bold and adventurous spirit of the explorer. But he more than matched the daring of his adventures with the boldness of his scientific theories, his tremendous physical bravado supported by a supple, rigorous mind, the breadth and depth of which seemed limitless to his colleagues.

His interest in physical geology, anthropology, and ethnology was matched by his interest in education, philosophy, and music. His pioneering efforts in many of these fields had lasting influence. The one-armed Civil War hero emerged successfully from his exploration of the canyon in 1869 with a small party of men (sure death for any man, it was said) only to further astound the scientific community with the novel and provocative view that the canyon had been formed as much through uplift of the surrounding rock as from the erosive action of the water on the canyon walls—a theory which has been confirmed since then. It was this intrepid explorer who, on that expedition, first immortalized his favorite niece by naming a tributary which flowed into the Green River at Desolation Canyon in Utah "Minnie Maud Creek."

Bram was as intrigued with his brother's scientific theories as Wes was with Bram's innovations in education. In their long discussions, they swapped theories to which they had given birth as excitedly as fathers brag about their newborn children. Maud took it all in as she grew, loving the stimulating intellectual atmosphere within her own family.

As early as 1876 the young violinist began to play publicly. She made one of her first appearances at a charity concert held in the First Methodist Episcopal Church. But Maud remembered her real debut as an impromptu performance:

> My first public appearance was at a picnic before I was nine years old. Instead of watching the dancers or joining them in their pleasure, I stood with critical ear eagerly watching and listening to the violin player in the little rural orchestra. During an intermission, I boldly faced this wonderful man who could play waltzes and polkas and, telling him of my ability to pay the violin, demanded of him his instrument that I might play him a tune. He refused at first, but finally let me take his violin and then I played him a little composition in which occurred pizzicato effects and harmonics. I was the observed of all observers among the dancers and onlookers, who listened in wondering silence. When I had finished, their extreme enthusiasm completely overcame my bravery so, suddenly frightened, I ran to my mother.[35]

By the age of eight, Maud was playing Mozart sonatas with her mother at the piano. By the time she was nine, Professor Fickensher found he could teach the young violinist no more. With characteristic integrity, he advised further study with William Lewis of Chicago.

Lewis had been a violin prodigy whose cellist father had been his first teacher.[36] Born in 1836 in Chulmleigh, Devonshire, England, he became at ten the soprano soloist in the Exeter Cathedral in London. While there, he pursued his violin studies with the best masters. He came to America with his parents in 1850 and settled in Bellevue, Ohio, where he worked his parents' farm. In 1862, Lewis settled in Chicago, eventually accepting a position in Root and Cady's Music House and engaging in solo and orchestra work with the Philharmonic Society. The enterprising Lewis reputedly garnered some violin instruction from such masters as Theodore Thomas, Henri Vieuxtemps, and Henri Wieniawski when they appeared in Chicago. When the great fire of 1871 destroyed one third of Chicago, the Root and Cady concern dissolved. Undaunted, Lewis established his own firm, the William Lewis Music Company, which thrived on the sale of sheet music and musical instruments, while its proprietor continued to build up a considerable reputation as a concert artist and violin teacher.

Since Maud's progress on the violin and the piano were parallel, she studied piano with Agnes Ingersoll, an associate of Lewis's in chamber music. In 1875, Lewis had organized the Chicago Quintette Club which would grow in five years into the Chicago Chamber Music Society. Agnes Ingersoll, with Emil Liebling and other early Chicago musicians, was among its first members. From this woman Maud learned to reverence that which is "best and ideal" in music. She said Miss Ingersoll used to give her "pretty things" to play, including a "book of duets with simple counterpoint in the second part which delighted my soul."[37]

The weekly journey to Chicago and the expense of lessons required sacrifices, but Mrs. Powell wrote, "[T]he ambition of making their daughter an artist having taken possession of them, her parents let nothing stand in the way of success."[38] Since they could not afford to escort her, Maud made the forty-mile trek to Chicago by train each Saturday for her lessons alone. The young violinist did not seem to mind. It was an adventure! She eagerly mounted the steps of the Burlington Northern railway car with violin case in hand and her music roll under her arm. Emerging from the Van Buren Street station, she walked to 152 State Street, where Lewis and Ingersoll had their studios. The happy child darted in and out among the pianos with her ball while waiting for her lesson. Chicago was a tremendous city of 335,000 by then, bristling with trade of the grain harvest and cattle herds, supported by the portage offered by the Great Lakes and the raw power of the railroads.

Lewis soon realized that this nine-year-old's talent was exceptional, and within the first year of his instruction she made public appearances playing duets with her teacher. Later in that same year, the gifted youngster made a six-week tour of Illinois, Michigan, and Wisconsin with the Chicago Ladies (probably vocal) Quartet. It was on that tour that the public first acclaimed her as a prodigy. Of this period Maud could only recall, "To play with my teacher was a joy."[39]

Maud delighted in discovering Lewis's eclectic interests. He was a scholar of music history, knowledgeable about world affairs, and an expert connoisseur of violins. More importantly, Maud found her new master's style of playing irresistible. She described him as an "unfettered" player, without much refinement of technique, but extremely "rugged."[40] "To William Lewis, a man of genius who played the fiddle because he couldn't help it, I owe much of my vigor and freedom of style. Nor was I obliged to undo or remodel habits or methods when I went abroad."[41] Lewis (to whom Maud "owed the most") was a "natural player, a born genius, who was, of course, very careful and painstaking with me." He "gave me a splendid start."[42]

Another fine musician who influenced Maud's early development was Edwin A. Stein. An organist whose father was a professor at the Leipzig Conservatory, Stein had received his music education in Germany. He came to Chicago from Dresden, but ill health had forced him to seek the quiet of a small town. In Aurora he played the organ at the Universalist Church. In the early days of the Coulter Opera House, he conducted the theater orchestra and taught music. Upon Lewis's advice, the Powells engaged Stein to teach Maud music theory, harmony, and composition. As Maud recalled, "I was taught harmony and musical form in direct connection with my practical work, so that theory was a living thing to me and no abstraction."[43]

During the 1880s, Stein built up a local orchestra. One of its former members declared, "It was a serious thing to belong to Stein's orchestra, for it meant study and application under the great leader."[44]

Maud joined the Stein Orchestra as a first violinist and was given the honored seat as partner to the concertmaster, Dr. E. B. Howell. She practiced with the orchestra once a week, taking her place among her adult male colleagues with her feet dangling from the chair. Her extreme youth "caused her to be looked upon with much pride by her townspeople who showed their interest and good will by many little presents, frequent verses dedicated to her, and by complimentary concerts."[45] Nicknamed the "Child of the Regiment," Maud found that "to play in the local orchestra of sixteen or more pieces was an ecstasy of delight."[46] She later observed that "Association with the director Mr. Stein, a man of excellent musical understanding and of strong individuality, was of inestimable value as a formative influence."[47]

Maud's solo opportunities increased with Stein. He had built up a chorus along with the orchestra and on March 24, 1880, Maud "assisted" in a chorus and orchestra concert with a performance of de Bériot's Concerto No. 1. On May 4, 1881, Stein's Orchestra gave its "First Annual Concert" at the Coulter Opera House. The way to the opera house that evening was illuminated by electric lights, as Aurora was the first city in the nation to completely light all its streets with electricity.[48] Inside the hall, the stage was filled with four first violins, four second violins, one viola, one cello, one bass, one clarinet, two cornets, one trombone, and timpani. The Stein Orchestra's rendition of works by Suppé, Koelling, Wilhelm, Sullivan, and Weber was interspersed with zither and voice solos and by music by the Plain family orchestra. Maud played *Lucrezia Borgia* by Hauser.

In addition to her appearances with the orchestra, Stein often asked Maud to play at church song services where he played the organ. With Stein at the piano, Maud also performed in concerts in other Illinois cities, like Evanston, where the audience applauded with both hands and feet to emphasize its approval. Sometimes she went with her father's vocal quartet to a neighboring town and played some violin solos. Maud fondly remembered the "church services at which I sometimes played, (and oh, my agony when my dear old dad sang a wrong note in the tenor part of the quartet!)."[49]

Although she was hailed in Illinois newspaper reviews as "one of the wonders of the age," rivaling the Hungarian violinist Eduard

Reményi, and a brilliant career was predicted for her, Maud never seemed to be spoiled by her concert appearances.[50] Indicative of her attitude was her statement, "To play in an occasional concert was interesting, except that I hated the grand clothes necessary for those occasions. . . . [E]verybody was so very kind to me, only it was a burden to my soul to have to wear all the fine toggery and be decked out like a prize rabbit."

For her early appearances, Maud wore simple white frocks with sashes or blouses and skirts, but later something more pretentious was required of her: "I can still see it and experience the sensations that overwhelmed me when I wore it. I am certain that I never played worse in my life than when garbed in that wonderful 'creation.' There was a bright red plush skirt, quite full, over which was draped a much shirred yellow silk 'drop,' the collar was square, in imitation of a décolleté neck and there were bits of lace in every imaginable spot. This skirt came below my knees and I wore high yellow boots and bright stockings of the same shade."[51]

Maud's partner in Stein's Orchestra, Dr. Howell, often played chamber music in the Powell home. With Maud at the piano, Howell on the violin, and Charles Van Liew on the cello, Maud savored the trios of the old masters. Maud's mother enjoyed the sessions as much as anyone. The cellist sometimes felt "lost in the shuffle." He came to view Mrs. Powell as a woman of "heroic ambition and determination." When his notes started running "flat and squeaky" one afternoon, "she came over beside me and told me to 'get up there'—and I got— a little more acceptably at least." Reflecting on Maud's musical training, Van Liew said, "All during her musical training, in the years when any girl might naturally have longed for some forbidden pleasures at times, that mother's artistic heroism . . . was back of her."[52]

After four years of instruction with William Lewis, Maud's teacher advised her parents that she should go to Europe to continue her studies. He had prepared her as best he could, laying the foundation for a secure technique and large repertoire. Lewis, together with Stein, advised study at the Leipzig Conservatory with Henry Schradieck.

On June 1, 1881, the town of Aurora sponsored a testimonial concert, billed as Maud Powell's Farewell, in the Coulter Opera House. The concert was given by Stein's Orchestra and featured Maud as the violin soloist playing the *Adagio* and *Finale* to Ferdinand David's Concerto No. 4. More was demanded of her, so it is likely that the youthful violinist played Drdla's *Souvenir* as an encore. She then performed "Home Sweet Home" as the closing selection. Her rendition was described as "unforgettable." "Tears seemed to drop from her bow as she skillfully drew it across her instrument. I venture to say that few, if any, ever heard it played with more feeling."[53] Mothers reportedly wept and even some fathers' eyes were moist when she lifted her bow from the strings for her final bow. The people of Aurora gave her a snake bracelet of Roman gold with ruby eyes which became a precious keepsake. She wore it whenever she returned to Aurora to play as a gesture of appreciation for all that the town had meant to her.[54]

The next day, Maud crossed the street to the home of one of her closest friends, Matt Shoeman, a good-natured drayman. The concert the night before had been a resounding success, netting a fine sum of money. That afternoon, a dignified committee headed by Professor Stein made its way to the Powell home to present the purse. Instead of being in the expected place when they arrived, Maud was up on the roof of Matt's house watching him repair a chimney. "When the two pals spied the sedate committee approaching, Maud hid behind Matt until the men had entered her home; then she hustled down the ladder and made for her own back door."[55]

The necessity of European study at that time in order for a talented musician to become a finished artist should not be underestimated. The United States did not then have music conservatories that ranked with the venerable institutions in European capitals. If Maud's talent was to be developed to its fullest extent and opportunities for a career as a solo artist were to be opened to her, European study was imperative.

For the Powell family, this development meant painful separations. Bram would have to remain in Aurora at his post—and give up the house on West Street—to provide the necessary funds, while Minnie took Maud and Billy to Europe. Maud's parents could have refused to proceed, but in a sense there was no real choice. Both Bramwell and Minnie knew that the course which they had chosen even before Maud's birth had become a destiny to be fulfilled.

Just before their departure, the Powell family called on their friends and neighbors to bid them farewell. A teacher recalled Maud's father smiling and saying, "When Maud returns, we expect her to be a fine violinist." But Maud's mother quickly interjected, "She must be better than a 'fine violinist,' she will be a second 'Camilla Urso.' "[56] At the age of thirteen, Maud was on her way to Europe to study with the best masters in the world.

Maud, about seven years old.

Top, Maud's parents, William Bramwell and Wilhelmina (Minnie) Paul Powell; *bottom,* Maud's birthplace at 1112 Bluff Street, Peru, Illinois (no longer standing).

Top, Maud, about age three; *bottom left,* Maud's brother, William Paul Powell, age six; *right,* Maud, about age five.

Maud's father, at left, and uncle Major John Wesley Powell, Wheaton, Illinois, 1865.

Early inspirations: *top left*, Camilla Urso; *right*, Wilma Norman-Neruda (Lady Hallé); *bottom*, William Lewis, Maud's violin teacher in Chicago.

Top, drawing by Maud of "South Gate," on "Liberty" Street (?); *bottom,* Joachim's graduating class, Berlin, 1885, with Maud seated in the second row at the far right, Henri Ern standing fourth from the left.

Maud's European masters: *top left*, Henry Schradieck; *right*, Joseph Joachim; *bottom left*, Charles Dancla; *right*, composer Max Bruch.

Maud as a student in Leipzig, 1882.

3

Leipzig, 1881–1882

*Frankly, I say to you that "the game is not worth the candle,"
unless your music is a part of your very fiber, your breath of life.
If you love it thoroughly, love it objectively . . . and cannot be
happy without it, then go ahead. But you wouldn't have needed
me to decide for you, if that were the case; you would have been
impelled by something within, regardless of advice or a thousand warnings.*

— *Maud Powell*

MAUD HAD LOOKED FORWARD EAGERLY TO THE VOYAGE to Europe, but as
she parted from her father, sadness mingled with her sense of excitement and anticipation. Her youth did not shield her from understanding that this interruption of their happy family life was for her
sake alone. She must fulfill the trust that had been placed in her. In
her heart, she knew it was the right course. In fact, for her it was the
only course. Music was "part of her fiber," her "breath of life."

Mrs. Powell's thoughts must have drifted to her parents as the
ship steamed toward the land of her birth. As they passed the white
cliffs of Dover, young Maud probably thought of her father and his
parents who had sailed from England in search of a new life. She had
roots in the Old World which she would rediscover and transmute
through her violin playing.

To ease the transition, Maud, her mother, and Billy apparently
were escorted to Germany by American friends, including William
Lewis. They arrived in Leipzig by July 8, 1881. On July 22, Mrs.
Powell wrote to her sister-in-law: "I have realized more fully the last
two days how far away from home and friends we are, as —— party
left us to visit Berlin and Dresden. They return tomorrow and remain

a few days here, on their way back to Liverpool, from whence they sail . . . for home. When they are gone 'for good' I shall feel like a ship without a rudder."[1] Apparently Maud's father was due to join them for a brief time in the near future, a comforting prospect for Mrs. Powell.

Maud's mother reported further, "We are situated as pleasantly as one could expect in such a benighted country."[2] She had settled them in a boarding house considered "the best in the city." "[T]hat was saying very little" in her estimation. She complained that the beds were composed of "feathers, fleas and dust" and what is more, the beds had not been changed in the two weeks since their arrival. She had to become accustomed to a change of bed linen only once a month, table linen once a week "no matter how soiled," and towels once a week. Her astonishment was capped with her declaration that "[Y]ou are not sure of your own napkin either."

She was pleased to discover that the food was "quite United States in style." But her thoroughly puritanical upbringing did not prepare her for the freedom with which beer flowed at all hours of the day. "Indeed I believe beer is the staple article of food and the principal source of amusement with the Germans. Everything else is thrown in as extras."

The three Powells occupied two rooms with high ceilings and hardwood floors covered by a rug in the center. The walls were frescoed and calcimined and in the corner towered a white porcelain stove about nine feet tall which would provide heat in winter. Maud's mother immediately rented a piano and bought some plants to put in their windows, following the local custom. They had been amazed to find that almost every window up to the fifth floor was ablaze with the color and fragrance of blooming plants. With the delivery of the piano, it was home.

Maud began taking lessons in German and was amused by the gymnastics with which they all tried to make themselves understood, especially since their landlady could not speak English. They all studied diligently and seized every opportunity to speak the language. They made it a rule never to leave a shop without having made themselves *verstehe* (understood). After a time, Maud was speaking fluent German. She remembered, "I was only thirteen years old and got used to the German culture very quickly. Unfortunately, it was not that easy for my dear mother."[3]

The cultural transition was eased somewhat by the presence of eight American conservatory students who lived in the same boarding house. Through them and American acquaintances made through letters of introduction, the Powells learned of the best places to visit and the scheduled musical events. Maud formed a lasting friendship with Geraldine Morgan, who had come from New York with her mother to study with Schradieck.[4] There is contradictory evidence concerning the presence of the American Nettie Carpenter and her mother in Leipzig for the same purpose.[5]

After an hour of practice and their customary breakfast at eight a.m., the Powells regularly set out to explore their new surroundings. They soon got used to walking four or five miles a day and finding their way around the city. They were charmed to find that a respite from the hard granite pavement could be found in a number of parks, even within a block of their lodging, where they could hear "the best of music" every day of the week. Mrs. Powell noted wryly, "and of course the inevitable beer is here also." But she found that "one soon gets accustomed to seeing the men and women sitting together and taking their beer, and one very seldom sees any drunkenness, so the habit does not impress one as being odious." It pleased Mrs. Powell's free spirit to find that "Ladies are allowed to go everywhere alone here, even to the opera, which begins at six and closes about nine."[6]

The Powells first glimpsed the Leipzig Conservatory when they attended the closing concert of the term. They were not, however, prepared for their disappointment when they discovered that the building was ugly. Somehow, it was like a cruel trick; the incongruity of studying the highest and most beautiful of arts in a building devoid of any artistic inspiration was painful to contemplate. To Maud and her mother, the structure looked like an old warehouse outside (which, in fact, it had been) and inside it was "not much better." Mrs. Powell described the building:

> Everything is so dingy, dusty and worn. The first flight of stairs are of stone, and one experiences a curious feeling to climb the same stairs that all the old masters have passed up and down. These stairs are very much worn; in many places they have been filled with cement, and even pieces of stone have been set in. The concert room is small and stuffy, with long wooden benches, and the stage

extending across the end of the room without any curtains, or anything in fact except a piano and common chairs to furnish it. It is quite evident that elegant surroundings are not looked upon with favor when work is to be done.

Maud's initial shock began to wear off as soon as she was seated in the concert room and the students began to play. One of the performers was John Rhodes of Philadelphia. At the age of seventeen or eighteen, he was Schradieck's best pupil, considered even better than August Wilhelmj, a prominent virtuoso. Mrs. Powell said he was the finest player she had ever heard. Afterward, she presented the young performer with a letter of introduction. When Rhodes later called on the Powells, he played for them. Then he insisted upon Maud playing. As her mother recalled, "He . . . appeared very much astonished when he listened to her, and when she got through was very enthusiastic in his praise, saying she was far ahead of any of the young ladies at the conservatory (if only he could have said of anyone there, how much better I should have liked it)."[7]

Apparently it was not at all certain at this point that Schradieck would accept Maud as his pupil. No final prior arrangement could be made because he needed to hear her play before passing judgment, and that could only be done in person. Therefore, it must have been with some trepidation that Maud and her mother, armed with letters of introduction from her American teachers, set out with John Rhodes to meet Henry Schradieck.

The choice of Maud Powell's teachers in Europe was critical to the full development of her capabilities as a violinist. It is fortunate that her parents were so aware of the need for a well-rounded education in music as well as in general, because Maud's broad musical training laid the foundation for the remarkable wholeness of her art.

There were several schools of violin playing which predominated in Europe at that time.[8] If one were to be able to interpret the works of the European composers authoritatively, exposure to these schools of violin playing was essential. One reason for this was that the violin literature had been composed primarily by or for men who were themselves violin virtuosos. Therefore, it was imperative to study their style of playing and to gain insight into their musical interpretations. That meant learning the different techniques used for bowing, fingering, and phrasing music of different styles and periods, besides learning the peculiarities and subtleties of rhythm, melody, harmony, and temperament which characterize each musical style. To approach this music, it was also important to absorb the cultural atmosphere of the different European countries in which violin music and playing had evolved; beginning with the Italian master Arcangelo Corelli (1653–1713). Although violin playing had been carried on long before, Corelli's distinction was to sum up the developments in violin-playing during the high Baroque period and raise it to a new level of dignity and expressiveness. He created a style of composition suited to the nature of the instrument and full of future possibilities upon which later violin masters could build. From him radiated the development of the Italian art of violin playing from which all other schools of violin playing were derived.

A century later, his artistic descendant Giovanni Battista Viotti (1753–1824) laid the foundation for a new style of violin playing which dominated the early nineteenth century. While residing in Paris from 1782 to 1792, he transformed the French violin school of Leclair and Gaviniés through his style of playing and composition. Significantly, Viotti ushered in the new age of modern violin playing with his use of the modern bow (designed by Louis and François Tourte) and a Stradivarius violin which together produced a richer and more brilliant tone than that produced by previous violinists. Viotti's influence was so powerful that the major European schools of violin playing emanated from his example as passed on through Spohr (Germany), Kreutzer (France), Baillot (France), Robberechts (Belgium), Rode (Austria, Germany, Russia, Hungary), and Pixis (Bohemia).

Naturally, Viotti's descendants developed variations of their own on Viotti's style. Through the generations, separate "schools" of violin playing could be identified by particular aspects of technique or interpretation or even of violin composition. Of course, there were many instances of cross-influences and syntheses among the different schools, as exemplified by two of Maud's masters, Henry Schradieck and Joseph Joachim.

Arriving at Schradieck's home, the Powells were led inside to a tall, handsome man who wore a full beard, his wavy hair swept back and falling just short of his collar. His youthful appearance and kind but quiet nature could make one forget the fact that he had been playing the violin for thirty-one of his thirty-five years and had already acquired a remarkable reputation as a virtuoso and teacher.[9]

Born April 29, 1846, in Hamburg, he began violin studies with his father at the age of four. He made his debut at five, playing Beethoven's Violin Sonata, Op. 17. In 1853 he was sent to Brussels to study with Hubert Léonard, at that time the greatest exponent of the Belgian school. Schradieck won the conservatory's second prize in 1857 and first prize in 1858. In 1859, he journeyed to Leipzig to study with Ferdinand David, one of the finest exemplars of the purely classical style.

At eighteen, Schradieck became a violin professor at the Moscow Conservatory. While there, he lived in the home of its director and founder Nicolaus Rubinstein, who, with his brother Anton, became a close friend. He knew Tchaikovsky, learned much about violin playing from Ferdinand Laub, and also knew violinist Henri Wieniawski, who made Rubinstein's house a sort of headquarters. After six years as concertmaster for the Russian Musical Society, he was appointed concertmaster of the Gewandhaus Orchestra in Leipzig, directed by Carl Reinecke. At the same time, Schradieck succeeded his late master David as teacher at the Leipzig Conservatory.

Upon hearing Maud play, Schradieck readily agreed to teach her. Reporting to her sister-in-law that he only "takes the most advanced" pupils, Mrs. Powell was relieved. Formal entrance examinations were to be held in August, but the term would not begin until October.

The date of the entrance examinations was formally announced and Maud soon found herself before an audience small in number but intimidatingly renowned for its wisdom and experience.[10] She was introduced to this jury of faculty members: Schradieck, Hermann (harmony), Carl Reinecke (ensemble playing), A. Reckendorf (piano), Alfred Richter (music theory and composition). Maud played the music she had prepared, sight-read music chosen by the jury, and then from the back of the room, named the notes played on the piano. Upon her acceptance, she was given a tour of the building while her guide recounted the illustrious history of the institution of which she was now a part.

The Leipzig Conservatory owed its remarkable beginnings to the happy confluence of musicians in Leipzig in the 1840s.[11] Through the unselfish exertions of Felix Mendelssohn-Bartholdy, the conservatory opened on April 2, 1843, the first institution of its kind in Germany. The faculty was composed of a brilliant set of musicians: Robert Schumann (composition and piano), Ferdinand David (violin), Moritz Hauptmann (harmony and counterpoint), Christian Pohlenz (voice), and Carl Becker (organ).

This musical circle over which Mendelssohn presided had its beginnings in Leipzig in 1835, when the twenty-six-year-old composer, conductor, and pianist was appointed conductor of the Gewandhaus Orchestra, then one of the most distinguished in Europe. Within a short time, he met Clara Wieck and Robert Schumann and introduced Chopin and Moscheles to his new friends during their visits to his home. Mendelssohn enticed his friend Ferdinand David to become concertmaster of the Gewandhaus Orchestra in 1836 and later a faculty member of the conservatory. David had been a pupil of Spohr, who, through the influence of Viotti and Rode, had founded the classical "German" school of violin playing. David's violin artistry and friendship would become the inspiration for Mendelssohn's Violin Concerto in E Minor.

In his turn, David drew Hauptmann into the faculty to teach theory of music, as Hauptmann had been his own instructor in Berlin. Mendelssohn likewise persuaded Moscheles, Beethoven's pupil and Mendelssohn's own beloved piano instructor, to join the faculty in 1846. The twelve-year-old violin prodigy Joseph Joachim, who arrived just at the time the conservatory opened, was quickly recognized and brought into Mendelssohn's musical circle. David was destined to teach Henry Schradieck, Joseph Joachim, and August Wilhelmj, the first two of whom would in their turn become Maud's teachers, thus binding her forever to the grand heritage and noble tradition of the German school.

As Franz Liszt, Hector Berlioz, and other significant musicians were welcomed into this circle (Wagner alone was excluded), Mendelssohn and his friends gave an impetus to the musical life of Leipzig which continued to flourish during Maud's day.

The jury had been impressed with this young girl's command of her instrument and her perfect pitch. She was more advanced than her deceptively small frame had led them to believe. They ranked her among their most advanced students and placed her in the corresponding classes. They soon confirmed their original opinion of her talent when within three weeks of the term's opening (October 4, 1881), Maud was chosen to play in the traditional Friday evening student concert.[12] These were given only by the best pupils, and it was considered a high honor to be invited to play. The concerts were notable for their artistic quality and were always well attended by the students at the conservatory as another vehicle of learning. Clearly, Maud and her new master Henry Schradieck were of one accord from the beginning.

As with most great musicians, Schradieck's talents and interests seemed limitless. His art, through his masters Léonard and David, represented a fusion of the Franco-Belgian and German disciplines. Schradieck the virtuoso with dazzling technique could enthrall his audience with works by Wieniawski, Vieuxtemps, and Ernst, while Schradieck the intellectual artist could probe with the keenest sensitivity and understanding the depths of Beethoven and Bach. There was a universality about his art that gained stature from his regard for the traditions of the past and from the remarkably strong personality that gave his playing a majesty and charm all its own.

Schradieck was in fact a modest man, retiring in nature and more suited to the intellectual challenge of teaching and the intimacy of chamber music than to the life of the virtuoso. He frequently played the great violin works he was teaching for his pupils privately and with his ensemble classes he sometimes took the leading part. The students believed that he knew practically all the Beethoven quartets by heart and was capable of conducting from memory all of the Beethoven symphonies.

He did not school his pupils in any "method," but sought to reveal to the student his own artistry. His aim was to develop in each student habits of deep introspection, of critical technical and artistic analysis of his own work that would enable him to adapt or invent for himself technical material that would strengthen the weak places in his equipment and enable him to work out his own musical artistry. "The mental insight—that is the most important of all!" was Schradieck's most characteristic expression during a lesson.

The master spared no effort to bring forth each student's full capacity. The length of a lesson was measured by the work to be done, not by the clock. He never accepted anything less than a pure and beautiful tone, demanding that virility, breadth, and color characterize violin expression. The slightest slip in bowing or fingering would be instantly noted and played by him in correction, proceeding from his infallible and seemingly inexhaustible memory.

The choice of Schradieck as Maud's teacher could not have been more fortunate. She felt that her master was a kindred spirit, and she said that from him she learned musicianship.[13] Her "extraordinary" talent and capacity for growth surprised him as the weeks slid by. He had to admit that this slip of a girl had captured his imagination and was taxing his teaching powers more than he could at first have believed possible. Teacher and pupil formed a bond known only to kindred souls, and forever after, Maud would write to her beloved master and he would attend her concerts whenever he could.

Although Maud's study in Leipzig resulted in a greater expansion of experience than she had expected, the strong, healthy youngster worked tirelessly and thrived. She had "abundant grit" and never relented in her efforts until the music in her "inner ear" was perfectly transmitted through the violin to which she gave her total commitment.[14] Even at that early age, she possessed a rare depth of character. One person who knew Maud personally while abroad observed: "Maud . . . played in several large concerts in Leipzig, with the most flattering success; and yet she was not flattered. A child of remarkably good sense, a true artist in soul, nothing of the kind could spoil her, while she felt herself but a crude beginner on an instrument of infinite capabilities."[15]

She rarely minded making personal sacrifices for the violin, but her free spirit did rebel when she was forced to give up favorite outdoor activities. Upon her return from European study, she told an Aurora friend of her fondness for rowing a boat and driving a spirited horse, and then explained that these sports ultimately had to be given up for the sake of her hands. Maud eventually gave up skating as well. She took further precautions by never holding a book in her left hand on a day when she was going to play a concert. In recompense, the resourceful artist did find a way to enhance her natural vigor safely with exercise by taking up swimming and dancing. In "Fiddle and the Fiddler" she said dancing was especially alluring to her: "It is such a natural thing to do . . . I can't understand why everyone who plays does not dance. Why, if you have a desire to express rhythm with your hands, shouldn't you have the same desire to express it with your feet? But dancing in America is not everything that it might be. There is too much of the decided 'tum, tum, tum' to it. In Vienna it is an art."

Her mother's presence was both comforting and helpful, allowing Maud to concentrate wholeheartedly on her studies.[16] When they went shopping together, Maud took a book along with her. While her mother looked over garments, Maud studied but was on hand to try them on.

Perhaps more importantly, Mrs. Powell acted as Maud's protector and advocate, a role which was nerve-wracking and demanding, for it required both discretion and vigilance. Maud's mother bravely faced unexpected duties as an alien in a foreign land:

> I was quite startled one day at receiving a summons from headquarters to appear on a certain day and pay my taxes. I considered it the better policy to put in an appearance promptly, as police regulations are so strict in this country. So in company with an American who had been through the mill, I started off for new fields to conquer. After turning many a corner, and going through some queer places, we finally found the number. Although my conscience was clear enough, I mounted the stairs with some trepidation, and entered the awful presence. As usual, I had to give the full name of the "other half" of us; all that he ever has been, is, or expects to be, etc., etc. To the question of what I was myself, I answered, "nichts" (nothing), which rather went against the grain, but under the circumstances it was quite convenient to be nothing, as thereby I had nothing to pay. Last year our landlord had extra heavy taxes to pay, because some of his boarders neglected the tax collector's summons. I tell you the Germans who go to America and become what would here be called rich, and then grumble about taxes, had better come back here to refresh their memories as to how they were taxed before they went to America. Why it is something fearful the way they are taxed; all because of their immense army. The standing army numbers about 800,000, while the reserves swell the number to between two and three millions of men.[17]

A "delightful ride" through the countryside with other Americans on one "perfect" autumn day could not assuage Mrs. Powell's feelings of alienation: "As we drove through the Rosenthal, . . . I could not avoid a shade of sadness. The foliage of the trees had been changed by the frost, and the falling leaves reminded us of a long winter to come among strangers in a strange land. I looked for brilliant colored leaves to press, but found none. The maple does not grow here."[18]

In the countryside, Maud and her mother saw women leading a hard life. Even on Sunday, women and girls were at work in the fields digging potatoes, aided by clumsy tools and vehicles, even using cows where an American would have used a horse or an ox. Clad in the simplest clothing and great, ill-fitting wooden shoes, the women earned ten cents a day and board. "As one might readily suppose," Mrs. Powell noted, "the women are not graceful after years of the hard out-door toil and exposure."[19] She believed that "it would be safe to say that not one potato could be found in that field when those women left it, for such rigid economy, is practiced here in everything."

The presence of the other American boarders was comforting, but the return to America of one whose health had broken down in the damp climate was disquieting. Mrs. Powell commented wryly, "I only wonder that we don't all get sick."[20]

While Maud reveled in her work and surroundings, her mother shouldered the heavy responsibility of ensuring that her daughter was afforded every opportunity to grow and advance in her art. Maud once talked about the suffering which these burdens imposed:

> I tell you that any mother who has a talented daughter has my full sympathy. It is difficult enough for the daughter to spend all her youth concentrating her thinking and energy only in this direction and to practice six to eight hours a day and her poor mother is always there. She has to hear each line again and again until she goes to the dear [expensive?] professor for an hour lesson. If I think about Leipzig, I can still see three mothers accompanying their daughters to their music lessons. My mother was one of them, a Mrs. Carpenter, another one. Here we were, sometimes the three of us sitting next to each other, afraid that one of us could be set back or might not get as much attention because she was a foreigner.
>
> If there was a concert in which the daughter was a participant, the mother had to worry about everything—the dress and the fitting and the fear—what they call stage-fright—as if she were playing herself. And then, there is the program, and maybe the first name is not correctly printed or her number is not in the right place on the program or maybe the next morning the reviews are not good enough. It is dreadful, just dreadful, for the poor woman.
>
> Well, I tell you, my own mother had a nervous breakdown [much later]. Her nerves are still not as good as they should be now [after

1904]. . . . And another one of the above-named women had to spend five months in a psychiatric institute. Who finally pays double for all the fame of a talented daughter? The mother of course![21]

Naturally, there were rewards. Mrs. Powell's ability to serve as Maud's accompanist enlarged the intimacy already existing between mother and daughter. These two musicians could take in with relish the musical atmosphere which surrounded their lives, knowing exactly what they were about, and share it all with a keen wit, a wink, and a nod which transmitted the understanding of shared experience.

In November, Maud and her mother attended a rehearsal of Beethoven's Sixth Symphony by the Leipzig Gewandhaus Orchestra. Conservatory students were allowed to attend the rehearsals, which were as good as the concerts, free.[22] The Gewandhaus tradition of playing standing up and of opening the season with Beethoven's First Symphony and closing with his Ninth added to the musical lore of the city.

The Gewandhaus was a surprisingly small hall, oval in shape, with a gallery all around and finished in white and gold. On either side were niches filled with handsome urns. Over the stage was a plaster medallion of Mendelssohn. The seats ran lengthwise facing a center aisle, obliging the audience to look sideways toward the stage.

Schradieck, the concertmaster, loomed head and shoulders above his eighty colleagues. Mrs. Powell and Maud were fascinated to "watch with what ease he draws the bow, while others appear to work so hard."[23] Mrs. Powell observed: "Herr Reinecke is leader, and it is interesting to watch him, for he appears to feel every note. He is getting to be quite an aged man but to witness his playing the piano and see how nimbly his fingers move over the keys, you forget his age." Maud's mother was thrilled with the performance of the Pastoral Symphony, reporting, "I never before heard anything so affecting."

The Gewandhaus Orchestra served as the opera orchestra in the Stadt (State) Theater. One could hear an opera there almost every other night, with stage plays on alternate evenings.

But for Maud, the importance of Leipzig was symbolized by St. Thomas Church, where Johann Sebastian Bach had played the organ more than a century earlier (1723–1750). There, the Powells attended a performance of Bach's B minor Mass in November. Although they went early, every seat was taken; but they "managed after much squeezing and some 'cheek' to get a standing place in the gallery, directly opposite the organ which gave us a fine view of the audience, the orchestra and singers."[24] As the music progressed, they tried to visualize Bach sitting on the same seat which was then before the organ.

Maud and her mother were amazed at the universal draw of music for the citizens of Leipzig. All classes of people attended some of the best concerts. She often saw people attending concerts who looked like they could ill afford the price of admission, yet who evidently were willing to sacrifice much in order to hear a good concert. Overall, the quantity and quality of music available in Leipzig at generally nominal admission prices was intoxicating to Maud's musical blood. She later wrote, "When I went abroad I fell right into the foreign way, loving the new impressions and sensing the artistic atmosphere at once."[25] For Maud, this was the answer to the question so frequently asked of her while she was in Europe, " 'Why do you come over here to finish your studies; why not continue in your own Country?' "[26] In 1896 she wrote: "Excellent teachers and the best of music are to be found in America, and pupils can secure the best instruction in the world in this country. But the musical atmosphere is lacking. To get this, to be surrounded by busy, ambitious fellow-students, to escape the home and social duties, to have no mistress save art, to hear more music—not better music but more and at less cost—in short, to be in a musical atmosphere conducive to profitable work, and much of it, the student must go abroad."[27]

Exhibiting a trait especially characteristic of the Powells, Maud treated the world as her classroom, seeking to learn from every experience. She later advised other violin students to follow the same path in learning to play the violin: "To hear a master in his art is indeed a liberal education and of value equal with daily instruction and practice. To hear even a mediocre performer is sometimes valuable as a lesson in what not to do. Music of all grades, classic, romantic and popular and of all nationalities, German, French, Russian, Scandinavian, etc. should be heard and played, to secure catholicity of taste. Of course, the greatest amount of time must be given to classics, for above all must a love for the best and purest be inculcated."[28]

The gifted violinist studied piano under Reckendorf and participated in ensemble and orchestra playing (which Schradieck and Carl

Reinecke directed) with the other conservatory students. She later reflected: "The training derived from ensemble practice is of inestimable value. The performer's sense of rhythm is thus developed. She learns to yield herself to other instruments, and the relation of one instrument to another, while her intonation becomes more acutely correct and she in every way gains in courage and consequent facility of expression."[29] Maud had the advantage of hearing her master perform in the Gewandhaus chamber concerts and even the great Joachim perform with his quartet.

She easily grasped the principles taught by Hermann in harmony classes and Alfred Richter in music theory and composition. Her creativity overflowed into the margins and on blank pages of her harmony notebooks, where she skillfully sketched "striking faces, illustrations of amusing incidents seen on the street, or while traveling, and bits of woodland scenes appealing to her sense of the beautiful."[30]

The energetic youngster won favor with her instructors for her pluck and manifest musicianship. For Christmas, Hermann presented her with some of his compositions and some of his manuscript. Schradieck favored her with a call at the boarding house, an unusual compliment as he seldom made social calls. His inability to speak much English caused the Powell family to "air [their] German to the fullest extent, which is a hard thing to do and at the same time be sociable," Mrs. Powell merrily related. "[H]owever, he spent much time with us, so we concluded it must be very entertaining to listen to our poor German."[31]

These kindly calls and the musical festivities (including Joachim's appearance in the New Year's Day concert at the Gewandhaus) helped to pass the holidays and ease the threesome's longing to be reunited with Maud's father and home. The Powells attended Wagner's *Tristan und Isolde* during this time, and they were soon to hear Anton Rubinstein, pianist, and Hans von Bülow, conductor, at the Gewandhaus.

Maud settled into the new term in January feeling rested and eager for the work. She was immediately scheduled to play in a quartet at the opening concert. Billy resumed his schooling at a public school for boys while Mrs. Powell and Maud tried to perform the necessary social amenities.

A hunting visit by the king of Saxony created a stir in Leipzig, prompting Mrs. Powell to report that "it would take something greater than a king to put Americans in such a flutter."[32] While out walking, Mrs. Powell and Billy suddenly sighted the American flag at the consulate amid the city's display of the many German flags. Billy threw his hat into the air and yelled "hurrah," an action Mrs. Powell confessed relieved her feelings although everyone looked at him "as though he were a wild animal."

Soon thereafter, Maud and her mother attended a ladies' "coffee" given by a German teacher of languages during which the two had to remain polite and keep their Yankee sentiments firmly in check. Between servings of cakes and coffee, the ladies did "fancy work," "tongues keeping time with the fingers." Both the king of Saxony and the American consul got "their share of attention" during the conversation. Since the talk was all in German, Mrs. Powell reported, "I looked volumes, and necessity made me very discreet in my language." After three hours, the Powell women "bid Frau W. good bye with the conviction that gossip is not purely an American trait."[33]

By July 1882, Schradieck reluctantly admitted that he had no more to teach Maud, whom he had come to cherish as his pupil. Maud was to perform with orchestra for the first time in Leipzig as her final bow to the conservatory. Although she had dreamed of playing at the Gewandhaus before a great audience, the full implications of her fulfillment of that dream suddenly came rushing in on her. "Conscious nervousness overcame me first when I rehearsed the first time with orchestral accompaniment. . . . I broke down, wept, went home in disgrace, but came back the next day to pull through triumphantly."[34] Although we do not know what she played, two reviews survive which may have related to that performance:

> Miss Powell's playing, which was marked by charming development of tone and exact intonation, was faultless even in the most delicate notes, did not make a single deviation from accuracy in bowing, and indicated at the same time remarkable depth of emotion.
> — *Musikalisches Wochenblatt Leipzig*

> Steady bowing, pure intonation, and tasteful rendering, are proof of great talent in Miss Powell, a violinist who is still a child.
> — *Leipziger Tagablatt*, Leipzig[35]

Although the official records note that Maud left the conservatory in October 1882, her final examinations were completed by July.[36] Schradieck reported, "Miss Powell not only has an extraordinary talent but also the highest degree of aspiration and application, and therefore the progress she has made in the one year of her studies here is really surprising." Hermann agreed with him. Reckendorf reported on her piano playing: "Was extremely dexterous in playing piano and made very nice progress. Before leaving she played Moscheles Op. 85 and Kalkbrenner Op. 52 as well as easy sonatas of Haydn and Mozart briskly and with beautiful musical understanding." On her theory of music and composition examination, Alfred Richter wrote: "Very industrious and assiduous. Shows for her youth a surprising understanding. Has rather good knowledge of theory of harmony."

Maud graduated from the Leipzig Conservatory with a first grade diploma. Afterward, she said her experience in Germany instilled in her a reverence for art and recommended the training to others: "It is in Germany, to my mind, that the embryo musician will secure the best musical foundation. There she will acquire breadth and virility of style, earnestness of intention and truth of sentiment."[37] Clearly, through her master Schradieck, she had absorbed the best of the German school of violin playing and had become a part of that tradition. What remained to be studied was the refinement and polish of the French tradition.

4

Paris, 1882–1883

It would be endless to attempt a Description of this Country. It is one great Garden. Nature and Art have conspired to render every Thing here delightful.

—*John Adams*

THE KALEIDOSCOPIC COLOR AND CONFUSION OF PARIS, created by a mélange of some two million residents from all parts of the world, was both exhilarating and intimidating on first impression. The French language was alluringly musical, and the expansive boulevards, gracious architecture, and welcome intervals of green pleased Maud's artistic eye.

If the inner musical life of Paris matched its outer raiment, then Mrs. Powell's judgment that her daughter should benefit from the refinement of the French art of violin playing would be justified. Her judgment was never in any danger of contradiction. The musical life of Paris was exceedingly rich during that period and nowhere was this more in evidence than at the Paris Conservatoire. The names of Dancla, Alard, Massart, Franck, Massenet, Saint-Saëns, Dubois, and Delibes graced the roster of faculty members in keeping with the brilliant history and rich traditions of that institution.[1]

When Maud Powell arrived to seek admission in 1882, the number of applicants had reached 764. Although founded in 1795, the Paris Conservatoire had not admitted its first female violin student, the eight-year-old Camilla Urso, until 1850. The entrance examinations were highly competitive and extremely rigorous for the few vacancies which arose each year.[2] The age fixed for admission was between nine and eighteen for the violin and piano departments. An applicant was required to perform three pieces of her own choice. In addition, she was expected to play a concerto movement chosen by the faculty. Then she had to play from a faculty member's manuscript at sight with only three mistakes per page. The competition was especially difficult for foreigners since only two were allowed admission in each class of twelve. Worse, the official tally showed that there were eighty-eight candidates competing for six vacancies in the violin classes, and three days would pass before she knew the results.[3] Maud said later that the days before the entrance examinations were the most anxious of her entire career.[4]

On her arrival at the Conservatoire on the appointed day in mid-October, Maud was escorted through the long, dark corridor that led to the examination hall by a seemingly indifferent usher.[5] The ancient building at 15 Faubourg Poissonnière had been a military barracks before it housed the Conservatoire, and the corridors exuded a dank and musty odor which added to her discomfort. The concert hall, small, spare, and uncomfortable, did little to dispel the gloom which seemed to permeate the entire building. Rectangular in shape, long and closed in on all sides, it had a high ceiling partly made of glass. As she mounted the stage and turned to tune her instrument, Maud could discern a long baize-covered table at which sat a number of solemn-looking gentlemen who would judge her aptitude for study at the Conservatoire. Among these faculty members were Ambroise Thomas, the Conservatoire's director, and Charles Dancla, the eminent violinist.

Once she began to play, her nervousness disappeared. To her delight, the hall made up for its distressing appearance with remarkable acoustics. As she breezed through the last test, she could hear the jurors murmur among themselves and glimpse smiles of satisfaction beneath the row of mustaches and beards before her. One man's eyes betrayed his deep interest and anticipation as she stepped down from the platform. Dancla broke tradition in his excitement, sending her a note in advance of the official notification congratulating her on being the first considered favorably among all the applicants and informing her of her assignment to his class.[6] Maud later said, "I remember that I was passed first in a class of eighty-four at an examination, after only three private lessons in which to prepare the concerto movement to be played. I was surprised and asked him [Dancla] why Mlle. —— who, it seemed to me, had played better than I, had not passed. 'Ah,' he said, 'Mlle. —— studied that movement for six months; and in comparison, you, with only three lessons, play it better!' "[7] On October 25, 1882, Maud Powell was officially enrolled in the Conservatoire Nationale de Musique et de Déclamation.[8]

Charles Dancla was a diminutive man of sixty-four years, whose fine facial features were capped with a bald dome and animated by large, bushy eyebrows and a perfectly proportioned mustache.[9] Indeed, there was very little about Dancla that could not be said to be well-proportioned. It was a fact that the outer decorum of his dress and general appearance simply reflected the delicate balance and taste which characterized his inner sensibilities. Maud's new master was, above all, an artist, and unmistakably of the French school. As far as she was concerned, he was the personification of French art. Donald Jay Grout provides a concise statement of the French tradition which Dancla so well exemplified:

> The specifically French tradition is something essentially Classical: it rests on a conception of music as sonorous form, in contrast to the Romantic conception of music as expression. Order and restraint are fundamental. Emotion and depiction are conveyed only as they have been entirely transmuted into music. That music may be anything from the simplest melody to the most subtle pattern of tones, rhythms, and colors; but it tends always to be lyric or dance-like rather than epic or dramatic, economical rather than profuse, simple rather than complex, reserved rather than grandiloquent; above all, it is not concerned with delivering a Message. . . . A listener will fail to comprehend such music unless he is sensible to quiet statement, nuance, and exquisite detail, able to distinguish calmness from dullness, wit from jollity, gravity from portentousness, lucidity from emptiness.[10]

Dancla's personal history revealed how thoroughly steeped he was in the French tradition.

Dancla's musical soul was shaped by the greatest French masters from the beginning of his life at Bagnières de Bigorres in the Pyrenees, where he was born on December 19, 1818. Before he was ten, he played concertos of Rode and Kreutzer as well as a trio by Baillot at a charity concert. By 1828, his father was persuaded to seek Rode's blessing for his admission to the Paris Conservatoire. Rode, who had been one of Viotti's greatest pupils, embraced the youngster and wrote for him letters of introduction to Kreutzer, Baillot, and Cherubini.

Rode, Baillot, and Kreutzer had been among the first generation of violin professors at the Conservatoire Nationale de Musique et de Déclamation when it was organized under the directorship of Sarrette in 1795. These three violinists compiled and edited *Méthode de Violon*, which comprised a part of the *Méthode du Conservatoire*, prepared jointly by the faculty of the Conservatoire as a means of uniting the school in its early days. The study literature written by Rode, *24 Caprices*; Kreutzer, *42 Etudes ou Caprices pour le Violon*; and Baillot, *Art du Violon*, during their tenure at the Conservatoire laid the technical foundation for modern violin playing.

While Rode was the only one of this trio to study directly with Viotti, both Baillot and Kreutzer were deeply influenced by him. Baillot, under whose tutelage the young Dancla was placed, was considered the last representative of the great classical Paris school of violin playing before Paganini's influence held sway. Although deeply impressed by de Bériot (who fathered the Belgian school) and Paganini in 1830, Dancla remained thoroughly within the French tradition as taught by his master and had become known by Maud's day as the finest exemplar of the old French school of violin playing.

For Maud's master, his selection in 1857 as a member of the Conservatoire's faculty was his greatest honor as an artist. To him, teaching was a sacred trust which required the strictest artistic integrity, a role for which he was admirably suited and which he performed with unfailing sensitivity and grace. In his memoirs, Dancla expressed his teaching ideals:

> The professor . . . must certainly carry in his teaching an individuality and artistic initiative . . . but he must not forget the great principles, which were his masters' legacy, which he must conserve in his turn in their grand lines and transmit to his disciples. . . .
>
> Teaching is a gift, in music, in painting, in literature, and I think that to conserve the tradition, a certain force of conviction, of character, is required, given the nature of man, whose tendencies are on the whole independent.[11]

As Maud grew to know her master better, she found him to be a rather sad little man whose career, while successful, had been plagued by numerous disappointments—often the result of the intrusion of politics into art.[12] Yet Dancla happily counted among his friends and colleagues some of the greatest violinists of the century: François

Habeneck (1781–1849), a pupil of Baillot who taught Alard (Baillot's successor at the Conservatoire) and Sarasate; Hubert Léonard (1819–1890), the great Belgian virtuoso and teacher (pupil of Habeneck) who taught Schradieck, Marteau (1874–1934), Thomson (1857–1931), and Marsick (1848–1924), who would in turn teach Enesco, Flesch, and Thibaud; Joseph Massart (1811–1892), a pupil of Kreutzer and Dancla's colleague, who taught Marsick, Kreisler, Urso, and Wieniawski (1835–1880), who in turn taught Ysaÿe. This then was Maud Powell's heritage as transmitted by Dancla and to some extent by Schradieck through Léonard.

In Dancla's class, there were thirteen pupils, five of whom were female, including the seventeen-year-old American Nettie Carpenter, who had been admitted to the Conservatoire in 1879.[13] Each student was required to study solfège (the art of sight singing, designed to train the ear) and harmony and play in the orchestra. Albert Lavignac (b. 1846) was the newly-appointed professor whose educational works on *Solfèges* (in six volumes) were responsible for completely reforming the teaching of the discipline. Harmony was taught by Théodore Dubois (b. 1837), who, similar to Lavignac, had distinguished himself at the Conservatoire by taking successive first prizes for harmony, fugue, organ, and, in 1861, the Prix de Rome for composition. The Conservatoire's records indicate that Maud was excused from participation in the orchestra and also from piano instruction.[14]

From the beginning, Maud's new master took a special interest in her. He knew instinctively that her intelligence and spirit and advanced command of her instrument set her apart from her classmates. Consequently, the Conservatoire's prohibition against faculty members giving private lessons for remuneration did not deter him from giving Maud private lessons, gratis, in his home.[15] The lessons lasted about an hour and a half and were entirely independent of Maud's Conservatoire instruction. Dancla was preparing her immediately for the concert stage, working on repertoire.

Maud had brought from Leipzig and America a style of playing remarkable for strength, spirit, and accuracy. Under Dancla's tutelage, she enhanced these qualities with softness and lightness of touch. While under Schradieck she had explored the depths of the Austro-German composers, under her French master she gained fluency in the great Franco-Belgian literature. Maud explained her period of instruction under Dancla this way:

Dancla was inspiring. He taught me De Bériot's wonderful method of attack; he showed me how to develop purity of style. Dancla's method of teaching gave his pupils a technical equipment which carried bowing right along, "neck and neck" with the finger work of the left hand while the Germans are apt to stress finger development at the expense of the bow. And without ever neglecting technical means, Dancla always put the purely musical before the purely virtuoso side of playing. He was unsparing in taking pains and very fair. Dancla switched me right over in his teaching from German to French methods and he taught me how to become an artist, just as I had learned in Germany to become a musician. The French school has taste, elegance, imagination; the German is more conservative and has, perhaps, more depth.[16]

Predictably, among the works Maud studied with Dancla were those of Viotti. In her master's estimation, Viotti's music best exemplified the French tradition because of its "nobleness of thought, grandeur and elevation of style, expressive and charming melody."[17] As his master Baillot had before him, he venerated Viotti as the true head of the French school of violin playing and did all in his power to preserve the purity of that tradition. Dancla thought Viotti's music most admirably suited for instruction of the student because "it was he who, by the admirable division of the bow, supplied to the technique the incomparable means of coloring the style and accentuating the musical thought."

Dancla also found the works of the seventeenth- and eighteenth-century Italian masters—Corelli, Tartini, Locatelli—which had laid the foundation for the French tradition, to be useful in the development of technique, style, and musicianship. He chose certain works of the Viennese composer and violinist Joseph Mayseder to develop a limpid tone and elegance and purity of style and the finales of concertos by Viotti, Rode, and Kreutzer to develop a variety of bowing and expression. Admiring the violin artistry of the closely allied Belgian school, Dancla taught his pupils the compositions of Wieniawski, Vieuxtemps, and de Bériot.

With those for whom he had no real artistic affinity, Dancla still mustered appreciation for their technical accomplishments and passed on what he learned from them. For instance, Dancla had never forgotten hearing Paganini play, although he was only thirteen at the time. "His violin still sings in my ears," he noted in his memoirs. Of Paganini's technique, the French master observed:

> Some artists have said that Paganini was a dazzling meteor who left no trace of his path. I dispute the validity of this opinion as erroneous and unjust, because to-day, as then, Paganini has rendered a great service to intelligent violinists, who have gained inspiration by novel effects once peculiar to him. . . . I believe that outside of the works of Bach, Tartini, Locatelli, Campagnoli, and other ancient and modern works especially contrived for enlarging the play of the fingers, it is necessary to study seriously the studies of Paganini, which are masterpieces, a very monument of the art of violin playing. . . . In spite of the abandon which Paganini gave to a phrase, he was exact in his delivery of a measure.

In his estimation, only Vieuxtemps approached the finger ensemble achieved by Paganini which, to Dancla's mind, "was so indispensable in obtaining sureness of intonation." Of his friend Dancla observed, "Vieuxtemps was a virtuoso in the best meaning of the word; his style was large, of clear sonority, powerful, transparent, perfect in intonation; his bowing was supple, his staccato was pure, . . . everything was united in him, and he was a remarkable composer."

Maud's master chose de Bériot's bowing style as a worthy model for his students. While Dancla admired the elegant and irreproachable bearing of de Bériot as well as the purity of his tone, he observed, "His style was of a rare exactness, and his bowing was remarkably supple." What he had learned about bowing from observing de Bériot he taught his American protégée.

Maud found that her master laid great emphasis on bowing as the key to violin expression: "The bow in the hand of the artist is the singing voice; the proper pressure on the string produces the emphasis and the 'unexpected' [*l'imprévu*] which gives all the color and charm to his style and which impresses and transports the listener. The intelligent artist understands that with a beautiful tone, he must always and before all seek to *speak well*, and to put the eloquent authority of his bow in the service of the work which he interprets, in penetrating above all the true character of that work." Maud's playing would be notable for a beautiful singing tone with a "speaking" quality which made the music deeply moving. Clearly, Dancla's teaching pointed the way toward the full development of her own artistic gifts.

In addition to technique and style, Dancla stressed the need for painstaking intellectual analysis of and "mental insight" into a composer's music. For him, *intelligent* musicianship was the hallmark of the great artist and the highest tribute this French master could give. It was a trait he found characteristic of Maud's playing.

In Maud's view, Dancla's attention to technical detail, always in the service of a musical ideal, and his artistic balance between the bounds of tradition and the individual genius of the performer (combined with his ability to convey to his students an understanding of these delicate interrelationships) allowed him to stand without peer as a teacher of the violin. Through the keenly sensitive and observant artistry of Charles Dancla, the promising American violinist absorbed the finest technique and artistic refinement of the great French tradition.

Maud came to cherish the modest little man who shepherded her through this period of study and claimed that of all her European masters, Dancla was "unquestionably the greatest as a teacher."[18] The respectful formality and air of dignity and discipline which prevailed at the Conservatoire did not inhibit the development of a close friendship between master and pupil. Once Maud's career was launched, she always made special plans to visit with Dancla, and he rarely missed an opportunity to hear her play in Europe. His expression of disappointment on one unfortunate occasion when her crowded schedule did not permit a visit with him touchingly exposed the depth of his attachment to her.[19]

The Powells had settled themselves in comfortable accommodations on the Rue de Clichy, just up on the left from the Trinité Church and not very far from the Conservatoire and the Madeleine Church where Théodore Dubois played the organ.[20] Maud's mother related that Maud "quickly became known in the American Colony, and her acquaintance with many prominent musicians, artists, literary people and others, dates back to the year so profitably spent in the French Capital. Among others was the [Philadelphia] Artist, A. G. Heaton, who painted her portrait, which was afterwards on exhibit at the Academy of Design. At times, Miss Powell played at private houses among the American Colony, and among the Parisians."[21]

Their residence was not far from Montmartre, which had become the fashionable meeting place of such French "Impressionist" masters as Monet, Renoir, Manet, Dégas, Seurat, and the American Mary Cassatt, who studied under Dégas. In 1880, the sculptor Auguste Rodin received a commission from the French government for the doors of a proposed new museum of decorative arts. Meanwhile, in sculptor Frederick Auguste Bartholdi's studio, construction was proceeding on France's centennial gift to the United States, the Statue of Liberty, already six years overdue.

In Paris, as in Leipzig, Maud sought to grow in every respect possible and to learn from every experience. The family practice of self-education was strongly ingrained.[22] Musically, as in every other way, Paris obliged her.

At the Salle Favart, the Opéra-Comique was in the midst of an outstanding era in its history, staging the world premieres of Bizet's *Carmen* in 1875, Offenbach's *Les Contes d'Hoffmann* in 1881, Delibes' *Lakmé* in 1883, Chabrier's *Le Roi malgré lui* in 1887, and Lalo's *Le Roi d'Ys* in 1888. Although the Opéra Comique outshown the Grand Opera during that period, nothing could usurp the latter's place as the business and musical center of Paris. The opera was housed in a magnificent structure designed by Charles Garnier, opened in 1875, covering three acres on Rue Auber not far from the Powells' living quarters on Rue de Clichy. Charles Lamoureux conducted the orchestra in operas by such composers as Saint-Saëns, Rossini, Thomas, and Gounod. Ballet premieres at the Palais Garnier included *Sylvia* (1876) and *Namouna* (1882).

Many ensembles performed in the Conservatoire's concert hall, but the orchestra organized by the Société des Concerts du Conservatoire was considered "incomparable." Dancla soloed with this orchestra, and Maud undoubtedly went to hear him. He also had his own quartet, which Maud must have heard as well.

The Société des Nouveaux Concerts, established by Lamoureux in 1881, presented during its lifetime the most distinguished list of premieres, especially of French music. It was one of the richest periods of French composition, and many composers, including Franck, Delibes, Dubois, Thomas, Saint-Saëns, d'Indy, Gounod, and Massenet, were closely associated with the Conservatoire and thus were known personally to Maud. Her lifelong interest in and promotion of new music can be traced in part to her youthful experiences in Paris.

Dancla introduced his promising pupil to the drawing rooms of Paris, which through their connection with the Conservatoire provided a valuable setting for the outlet and public appreciation of students' talents. One American correspondent who heard her reported: "Maud Powell is indeed a 'virtuoso.' Aged fifteen, this charming young lady promises great things with her violin; the *brio* with which she executed a *Marche Militaire* by Léonard, will not be easily forgotten. She afterwards delighted her audience with a *Reverie* by Dancla, proving herself a thorough musician in soul as well as technique."[23]

One person who came to know Maud personally in Paris related: "I soon grew to respect the slender slip of a girl, in short dresses and long curls, who, usually silent and always modest and retiring, sat opposite me at the *Pension* table. She had an expression of thoughtful, earnest determination beyond her years and hardly comporting with the glowing tints and soft contours of her round, young face. I have never known so studious and diligent a girl." Surprised that Maud forsook the pleasure of parties in favor of violin study, this person acknowledged, "Yet she was not merely a violinist by any means. We found that she was a good [word illegible] thorough musician—playing the piano very well, and reading the most difficult music . . . easily . . . ."[24]

As early as January 24, 1883, at the mid-year examination for which Maud played Viotti's eighteenth concerto, Dancla had evaluated his pupil's progress, noting carefully in his report after three months of study, "Mlle. Powell, age 15.4, 1st year of study, intelligent nature, hope for the future of this student."[25] Of his other pupils, none seemed so far advanced except Nettie Carpenter, whose four years under his tutelage enabled him to note with more surety that she would become a "true virtuoso."

At the conclusion of six months of study with Dancla, Maud approached the great Belgian violinist Léonard (who had taught Schradieck) and requested his guidance on her career.[26] After listening to her play, the master advised her to spend a year concertizing in England. Dancla concurred. Her technique was secure and her style clearly that of an artist reflecting, although not exclusively, the "exquisite finish and polish, grace, smoothness and delicacy" of the

French tradition, while at the same time retaining the firmness and breadth and the almost virile vigor which had always characterized her playing.[27] On April 25, 1883, the records indicate that Maud Powell withdrew from enrollment at the Paris Conservatoire after only six months of study.

5

England, 1883–1884

I am a part of all that I have met.

— Alfred, Lord Tennyson

ARRIVING IN LONDON, MAUD, HER MOTHER, AND BILLY SETTLED into a pension in Portland Place, near the American consulate, where a number of well-connected and influential Americans lived. The poet James Russell Lowell was at that time the United States Ambassador (1880–85), and like other Americans who made their way to England during that period, he left his mark on the literary, musical, and diplomatic life of London. Queen Victoria, who was within four years of her Golden Jubilee, said of him, "During my reign no ambassador or minister has created so much interest or won so much regard."[1]

Maud was introduced into the musical circles of London, aided by letters of introduction given her by Léonard in Paris:

> My studies abroad were broken by a year of concert-playing in London. I was then in my early 'teens. A musician in the pension in Portland Place where I lived, introduced me to an ambitious young manager, a woman, who, when she heard me play, sent me out with a little concert company. I do not remember much about the business details, but I remember I did get my modest fee and I believe that the manager made some money too. I became acquainted with George Henschel and other distinguished musicians through that charming and gifted woman, Mrs. George B. Carpenter, mother of our distinguished and well-known composer, John Alden Carpenter.[2]

Through friends, the young violinist also met Alfred, Lord Tennyson, who was raised to the peerage while Maud was in London.

It was not unusual for a young artist to try her musical wings in England. Then, as now, English audiences were known for their critical ear and conservative taste, and the power to discern the authentic performance from the superficial. Disdain for anything less than genuine, honorable contact with the music they heard caused them to cut to the quick any artist who dared affect pretension.

By tradition, English audiences were especially attuned to vocal music, perhaps owing to their great literary figures. Certainly the influence of Handel's operas and oratorios and Purcell's theater music had shaped England's early musical inclinations. England had no long tradition of producing great violinists. Then too, after Purcell, with the coming of Handel, the thread of native English composition had been lost, to re-emerge in Maud's day with the works of Elgar.

The arts in England were boosted by the patronage of the nobility. The Prince of Wales was frequently seen in the royal box at Covent Garden, and his efforts on behalf of British composers and artists in particular were notable. His desire to provide for more comprehensive music education led to the foundation of the Royal College of Music, which he opened on May 7, 1883, soon after Maud settled in London. Jenny Lind-Goldschmidt was among the faculty and George Grove was its first director. (Grove became best known for his *Dictionary of Music and Musicians* [1879–1889] for which Maud, at his request, eventually wrote an autobiographical sketch.) During the same week, the Prince announced the knighting of both George Grove and Arthur Sullivan.

Opera was thriving in London during this period. Arthur Sullivan and his colleague William Gilbert were regaling London audiences with some of their wittiest and most popular comic operas. In 1881, the Savoy Theatre had opened with *Patience*, a satire on the aesthetic movement led by the Irish poet Oscar Wilde, followed by *Iolanthe* in 1882. *Princess Ida* was produced in 1884, while Maud was in London. The Savoy was the first theater in the world to be wholly lighted by electricity at a time when the merits of electricity were still being hotly debated.

In May 1883, the first month that Maud was in London, the Royal Italian Opera produced such standards as Verdi's *Aida*, with

Adelina Patti, and Gounod's *Faust*, with Pauline Lucca, at Covent Garden. Meanwhile, Alberto Randegger, the conductor for the Carl Rosa Company, under whose direction Maud played that year, was attempting to establish a national school of opera.[3]

Hans Richter, who had conducted *Tristan und Isolde* for the first time in London in 1882, was due to premier *Die Meistersinger* at the Drury Lane Theatre. The Viennese conductor's fame in England arose from his having shared conducting duties with Wagner himself in a series of Wagner Concerts given in Albert Hall in 1877. In 1879, Richter had instituted his own series of concerts in which he conducted a one-hundred-piece orchestra each season (May–June). These "Richter Concerts" excited much attention, chiefly for the maestro's knowledge of the scores of Beethoven and Wagner, which he conducted from memory.

During this period, it was common form for solo singers and solo instrumentalists to appear in the same concert, whether with orchestra or in recital. As a result, the fifteen-year-old violinist appeared with some of the finest singers of the period, including the versatile tenor Edward Lloyd and baritone Charles Santley, who had toured England with the great violinist Wilhelmj a decade earlier.[4]

With a voice especially noted for its range and beauty, Edward Lloyd had reached a position of great importance as an oratorio singer and recitalist. Brought up in the English choral tradition through the choir at Westminster Abbey, Lloyd provided for the young American a stunning example of the force and beauty of that tradition. According to contemporary authorities, the quality of Santley's voice was "remarkable for richness or sonority" and his "power of varying the tone-colour," but beyond these was "the informing spirit of energy finely held in control."[5] Famous as an oratorio and concert singer, he was closely identified with the part of Elijah in Handel's work by that name.

Maud's association with many great singers during this time served to enhance her already notable singing tone, phrasing, and use of tone color. By closely observing these singers, she learned to let the music breathe, so that melodies flowed out of her instrument as if she were in fact singing. Already, critics were noting that the violinist with the "marvelous skill and mastery of technique," who "has a fine penetrating tone and a full fourth string, particularly excels in cantabile passages, which require deep expression and sympathy."[6]

The American violinist Louis Persinger would one day say of her playing, "Wherever there was a phrase to be 'sung,' Mme. Powell's violin simply rang with melody."[7]

As she began making her way in England, London critics noted that Maud played with "admirable taste, precision, correctness, and feeling."[8] One London critic reported: "Miss Powell's command . . . is simply astonishing in one so young. In smoothness, depth, and evenness of tone, her playing would compare favorably with the experienced artist of mature years, while she has with these important qualities all command over the technical difficulties of the instrument."[9] Another wrote that the young artist "made a marked impression, her performance being particularly accurate and brilliant; she played with a long sweeping bow, good intonation, and the double stopping was perfect."[10] Maud was "rapidly becoming known as a brilliant and accomplished player" according to one critic who confessed that it was "difficult to realize her extreme youth while listening to her vigorous interpretation of the good and interesting morceaux she presented to the public."[11]

Repeatedly, Maud was asked to play at the private mansions of the nobility in London until she became quite the rage in that milieu.[12] Twice she was commanded to appear at Kensington House before the Prince and Princess of Wales and the Princess Louise, Marquis of Lorne, and others of the royal family.[13] She even had to decline one invitation to play for the Prince because of a previous concert commitment.[14] And it was reported that she played for Queen Victoria during that busy year.

Throughout this period, Mrs. Powell's concern for her family remained active and constant. Through correspondence with Bram, she agreed that it was time young Billy, who would be twelve in October, received the benefit of instruction under his father's supervision. On September 8, 1883, Maud and her mother settled Billy aboard a steamer at "Queenstown," and he arrived in New York harbor nine days later.

Mrs. Powell was keenly sensitive to the strains the family's separation had placed upon her marriage. She often thought of Bram's loneliness, living in a rented room without his family, to say nothing of her own longing for the comfort of his presence. For this reason, she was glad to send Billy to his father and constantly urged her sister Kitty to visit Bram whenever she was in that part of the country.[15]

Maud toured Scotland in September, which reminded Mrs. Powell of her adoptive father, William Paul, for whom she had a deep and abiding affection:

> We left London last Friday [September 21, 1883], enjoyed the ride up here [Glasgow] exceedingly, though it was a long one — ten hours. We came alone and landed here at 10 p.m. in the rain, so that we felt rather forlorn. I thought of Father all the time after getting into Scotland, and was reminded of Scott's descriptions of scenery constantly as we passed crags, brawling brooks, hills covered with heather and capped with dense mists, bogs, dense woods, and as wild, grand views as anything Scott has described. When we passed through Dumfries, dear to the heart of the lovers of Burns, got a glympse of old Sweeheart [*sic*] Abbey, that is, the ruins which are covered with ivy. . . . I have sent Father some [heather] to remind him of "Auld Lang Syne". . . . [16]

Mrs. Powell and Maud visited Paisley, a few miles from Glasgow, where father Paul had been born. Within two months of their visit, with an ocean between them, father Paul died at the age of seventy-six.

Maud was scheduled to play a concert the day after they arrived in Glasgow. The young artist, who had just turned sixteen in August, wore no cosmetics or jewelry but gathered some heather to wear on her dress. Her mother chronicled her daughter's triumph that evening: "Maud played Saturday night to nearly three thousand people, and quite captivated their hearts by playing a selection of old Scotch airs. They applauded after each air, and then were so quiet instantly that you could have heard a pin drop. When she got through they fairly stormed till she gave an encore. The papers this morning give her the honours of the evening."

In November 1883, the Popular Concerts opened its winter season in London. Begun by the pianist and conductor Charles Hallé (b. 1819, Westphalia), the Popular Concerts had evolved into chamber music sessions held on Saturdays and Mondays in the Royal Albert Hall and St. James's Hall. Maud and her mother would have attended as many of the Popular Concerts as they could. The young violinist undoubtedly was excited to see Madam Wilma Norman-Neruda, later

Lady Hallé (1838–1911), lead the quartet which played regularly at the Monday series.

Madam Norman-Neruda, who played Ernst's Stradivarius violin, came from the distinguished Neruda family of violinists and had begun to play almost as soon as she could walk.[17] As a prodigy she excited much attention in Vienna with the extraordinary power of her bow, the deep sentiment of her cantilena, and her facility of execution. Her first appearance in London in 1849 was a sensation. In 1864 she married a Swedish musician named Ludwig Norman but continued her concert career. When she returned to London in 1869, she played with the Philharmonic and in the winter took her place as first violin at the Monday Popular Concerts. She thereafter returned to England each winter and spring season, playing at the Popular Concerts as well as in the Philharmonic, Crystal Palace, and Manchester concerts.

At the Popular Concerts, Madam Norman-Neruda headed a string quartet with Louis Ries (violin), Ludwig Straus (viola), and Alfredo Piatti (cello). These superb players were frequently joined in chamber music by the Russian pianist Vladimir de Pachmann, Edward Lloyd, Charles Santley, and Charles Hallé, who married Madam Norman-Neruda in 1888, after the death of her first husband.

Charles Hallé shared the conducting duties for these chamber music sessions with Sir Julius Benedict, who was well known for his versatility as a composer and his abilities as an orchestra conductor and pianist. Born in Stuttgart, he had settled in England in 1835 and was regarded by his colleagues as one of the most eminent of the foreign musicians since Handel to come to England. In 1850 Benedict had accompanied Jenny Lind to the United States, directing most of her concerts there. Maud appeared as soloist with orchestra under his direction during the 1883–84 season, prompting critics who heard the performance to call her a "young artist of decided promise."[18] One who had been watching Maud's progress wrote, "We have no hesitation in repeating that this young artist is now one of the most promising violinists before the public."[19]

Rivaling the Popular Concerts were the London Ballad Concerts, which featured vocal interspersed with instrumental music. Dr. Frederic Cowen, conductor and composer, frequently composed popular songs for these concerts that were sung by such artists as Edward Lloyd,

Charles Santley, Carlotta Patti, and Antoinette Sterling, with all four of whom Maud appeared in this or other forums.[20]

Two of these singers exemplified the growing English–American cultural connection. Antoinette Sterling was born in New York City in 1850. It was said that she possessed, even at an early age, a voice of extraordinary range which later developed into a contralto of great richness and volume. Her first appearance in England was in 1873, with Sir Julius Benedict conducting a Covent Garden Promenade Concert. Remaining in London, she became known as a ballad singer and was a popular favorite.

The Italian-born (1840) Carlotta Patti had made her debut in 1861, in New York City where her father had been manager of the Italian opera. Patti was known as a concert singer of the lighter class who possessed a pleasant and remarkable facility of execution which made her a great attraction at the Promenade Concerts. Her more famous younger sister, Adelina, had made her debut in New York as well, in 1859. She became a renowned prima donna who toured the United States frequently throughout her career, without missing a season at Covent Garden.

Maud also appeared with another singer who furthered the English–American connection. When Maud first met him in 1884, Georg Henschel had just relinquished his post as the first conductor of the Boston Symphony Orchestra, which had been formed in 1881. He had returned to make his home in England, where he earlier had impressed London audiences with his rich baritone voice and the "artistic intelligence" with which he rendered songs by Handel and Schubert. He was to give innumerable vocal recitals with his wife, the American soprano Lillian Bailey, whom he had tutored. Henschel gained fame as a voice teacher, succeeding Jenny Lind-Goldschmidt at the Royal College of Music in 1886–88.

Maud had been introduced to Henschel through her Chicago friend, Mrs. George B. Carpenter. Her son John Alden, whom Maud knew then as a seven-year-old schoolboy, would become a distinguished American composer after receiving his formal education at Harvard and studying composition with the British composer Edward Elgar, who was now just getting started. Elgar's *Intermezzo*, an early composition, was premiered in December of 1883 by Stockley's orchestra in Birmingham, where it received public acclaim.

The cultural cross-breeding was not limited to musicians alone. Henry James reached his most productive period of writing while residing in London, completing *The Portrait of a Lady* in 1881. During this period, James's writings focused on the impact of European culture on Americans traveling or living abroad.

Meanwhile, the American painter and etcher James Whistler, whose assimilation of Japanese art styles helped lay the foundation for modern art, was also in London during this time. Maud was destined to perform in his famous Peacock Room. American painter John Singer Sargent was thriving as a portrait artist in his adopted London home. In 1904 Sargent would be commissioned to paint a portrait of the masterful Hungarian violinist Joseph Joachim, who was to figure prominently in Maud's future.[21]

Early in 1884 Maud went on one last long tour of Britain, this time with the noted soprano Jose Sherrington.[22] At Newcastle-on-Tyne, Maud played in a "Grand Popular Concert" in aid of the organ fund of St. Dominic's Church. Members of the nobility and church dignitaries crowded into the church to hear performances by some of England's leading soloists. In the reviews that followed, Maud received greater and more enthusiastic attention than any other member of the company. Her performance of the Andante and Scherzo movements from a David concerto was given in "splendid style" and "loudly applauded, and an encore enthusiastically demanded, to which, however, the lady did not respond." Later on, Maud played another "exquisite violin solo." Finally, she rendered a concerto by de Bériot. At the conclusion, she was "forced at length to yield to the wishes of the enraptured audience, and gave an encore."[23]

The young American returned to London at the end of February 1884, in time to hear Norman-Neruda's farewell for the season as she performed the Razumovsky Quartet in F by Beethoven at the Monday Popular Concerts. Coming to take her place was Joseph Joachim, who was at that time the "greatest of living violin players."[24]

Considered the premier quartet player up to that time, Joachim had played each spring in the Pops Concerts since 1865, each year steadily raising the standards of the music to be heard.[25] Joachim opened his appearance with the Pops on February 25, 1884, by leading his colleagues in two sextets by his friend Johannes Brahms, whose music he widely championed. He also played a Bach unaccompanied sonata.

In March, Joachim was joined in the Pops Concerts by Clara Schumann. The public flocked to hear them, and it was reported that St. James's Hall was not large enough to accommodate the people seeking to hear the two play works by Robert Schumann and Brahms.[26] For their first concert, Joachim led one of Dvořák's quartets in honor of the Bohemian composer's first appearance in London, where he was to conduct his own works with the Philharmonic on March thirteenth.

No doubt Maud and her mother made every effort to hear Joachim play in London before their planned return to America. At this time, Lady Hay offered to write a letter of introduction for the young violinist, which she could present to the great master.[27] Joachim's position as music director of the Hochschule in Berlin and his renown as a teacher and artist made his judgment and advice highly valuable to aspiring young artists.[28]

The letter presented, Mrs. Powell related what happened: "Hearing her play, he pronounced her talent of the highest order and said he was gratified to discover, not another prodigy, but an embryo artist with wonderful talent. . . . Urged by Joachim to come to Berlin to study with him, it was decided that she should remain another year in Europe, believing that a year spent under Joachim's most masterful guidance, would be a great advantage to her both artistically and professionally."[29] Maud remembered, "I shall never forget my joy when he told me that he would take me into his class at the Berlin Hochschule, but that I must come over from London at once to go through the form of examination."[30] That spring, the promising artist packed once more and set off for her last round of formal studies with one of the greatest masters of the century.

6

Berlin, 1884–1885

A teacher affects eternity; he can never tell where his influence stops.

—Henry Adams, 1907

WITH THE ADVENT OF JOSEPH JOACHIM IN 1868, BERLIN HAD EVOLVED INTO Germany's primary music center, a distinction which had formerly belonged to Leipzig. It seems impossible that the influence of one man could have been so great, but Joachim was no ordinary individual. His gifts as a violinist were remarkable at an early age. Born June 28, 1831, in Kittsee, Hungary, Joachim was a child prodigy with extraordinary depth.[1] When yet a boy, he studied with Joseph Boehm, who made him thoroughly familiar with modern French technique as represented by Kreutzer, Baillot, and Boehm's master Rode, which enabled him to gain "unlimited command over technical difficulties in music of any style."[2]

The young violinist presented himself to Felix Mendelssohn in Leipzig in 1843 as an artist in his own right at the age of twelve. After examining him, Mendelssohn concluded that Joachim did not need the conservatory or a teacher in violin playing. He advised Joachim to work alone and play before David from time to time. In addition, Mendelssohn himself played regularly with the boy and served as his advisor in musical matters and as a father in his personal life. In Mendelssohn's intimate musical circle, Joachim met and made music with Robert and Clara Schumann, Franz Liszt, and Hector Berlioz. He was further influenced by Ludwig Spohr, considered to be the direct heir of Viotti and Rode and the founder of the German school of violin playing.[3] Spohr (1785–1859) was the master of Ferdinand

David and noted for his singing style and the breadth and beauty of his tone.

With David, Joachim, like Schradieck, explored the music of Bach, Beethoven, Mendelssohn, and Mozart, as well as the concertos of Spohr.[4] David instilled in both Joachim and Schradieck a reverence for unaccompanied Bach and the Beethoven concerto, for which Joachim became famous as the most faithful champion of the nineteenth century. Further, David's love for the Beethoven quartets enhanced the youth's earlier exposure to these masterworks.

Joachim's debut at the Leipzig Gewandhaus was rapidly succeeded by his first appearance with the Philharmonic Society of London. On May 27, 1844, he played the Beethoven concerto with Mendelssohn conducting, immediately winning English acclaim for his beautiful tone, musical maturity, and intelligence. At the age of thirteen, he took his place among the acknowledged masters of the world.

As with his musical taste, Joachim's character developed along classical lines, exhibiting an earnestness of purpose, kindliness, and forbearance which mark the well-governed individual.[5] He also developed a thorough dislike of superficiality, whether in art or in human beings, and distrusted show of any kind.[6] Reflecting on his character, Maud observed: "When I compare his quiet, staunch, upright way with the diplomatic manners of the present day, when promises are easily made and easily broken, I cease to marvel at the amazing respect and affection in which the 'dear old man' was held. The adoration he inspired in England was truly wonderful, and indeed hardly less in Germany. I always associated in my mind as three giants of the old school — Theodore Thomas, Hans Richter and Joseph Joachim. All three stood for the noble, the true, and the simple in character as well as art."[7]

Through these character traits and his insistence on rendering truthful service to his art, Joachim became a great moral power in the musical life of the nineteenth century, the force of which endured into the twentieth century, revealing itself in the approach of performer and audience alike to music.

Before Joachim, the use of the modern bow (begun with Viotti) and the rise of a new freedom of expression in music (Romanticism) had lent themselves to the appearance of violinists who indulged in the new technical possibilities of their instrument while frequently losing sight of the quality of the music being rendered.[8] The word "virtuoso" acquired a tarnished connotation suggesting technical prowess and showmanship rather than excellence in the service of a higher art. Reflecting on this type of performer, Maud observed: "The old days of virtuoso 'tricks' have passed—I should like to hope forever. Not that some of the old type virtuosos were not fine players. Reményi played beautifully. So did Ole Bull. I remember one favorite trick of the latter's, for instance, which would hardly pass muster to-day. I have seen him draw out a long *pp*, the audience listening breathlessly, while he drew his bow way beyond the string, and then looked innocently at the point of the bow, as though wondering where the tone had vanished. It invariably brought down the house."[9]

Paganini (1784–1840), of course, became the symbol for this type of violin playing, although his antics were backed by a musical understanding of which many people subsequently lost sight.[10] As classical music, formerly written for private audiences among the nobility, became the province of the general public, audiences demanded opera transcriptions and bravura pieces from masters of the piano or the violin. The showmanship of Paganini and Liszt crowded from public view the older, timeless masterpieces of Bach, Haydn, and Mozart. Beethoven was not accepted. Virtuoso performers were expected to produce their own works to please the insatiable appetite of the crowd for something new.

Although Joachim had acquired all the technical facility of Paganini, he played the violin not for its own sake, but in the service of a musical ideal.[11] Technique was subordinated to the musical message. He became known for his ability to combine "in a unique degree the highest executive powers with the most excellent musicianship."[12] His performances of the Beethoven concerto were noted for these qualities, and by 1859, Joachim was recognized in London for the new standard he embodied as an artist.[13]

After the death of Robert Schumann in 1856, Joachim and Clara Schumann, a formidable pianist, both at odds with the "new music" of Liszt and Wagner, concertized together and apart, increasingly gaining widespread recognition and appreciation for their musical point of view.[14] By the latter half of the nineteenth century, Joachim and Clara Schumann could attract audiences with more serious programs, combining the older masterpieces of Bach, Beethoven, and Mozart with newer works by composers like Brahms and Schumann.

Works were rendered in their entirety, a format not previously tolerated, and further, were performed from memory. Joachim also played the unaccompanied sonatas of Bach publicly, thus reviving the greatest of all works for the violin.

In Germany and England especially, Joachim, through his quartet and solo appearances, cast his spell over audiences, educating them to the point where they would not accept a lesser standard of repertoire and execution from any performer. This was largely his achievement.

In 1868, Joachim was offered and accepted the post of professor of violin in the Berlin Hochschule für Musik, of which he became director upon its reorganization in 1875. He immediately dedicated his full energies to organizing the school, conceiving it as an institution devoted to teaching musicianship above all. Breadth of tone, purity of style, broad, free bowing, a rational technique—always subordinated to the service of the music—and a reverence for the classics were the guiding principles of the Hochschule.

By the time Maud came to know him, Joachim was fifty-three and was to his pupils the veritable "grand old man." He was tall, with a splendid physique, and his leonine head lent a certain nobility to his bearing. Between the gray hair and bushy gray beard, kind brown eyes could be detected peering through large glasses. But he always pulled off his spectacles before playing in a manner which revealed how deeply he saw into a work. In all, Joseph Joachim was an imposing figure.

When she arrived at the Hochschule on Potsdamer Strasse for the examination, Maud found herself amid a crowd of young men and women of all nationalities, many of whom had studied with famous masters and were now seeking to study with the greatest master of the violin world. Most of the Americans were at a disadvantage since they generally began the violin too late, while continuing the full public school curriculum which detracted from the concentration serious violin study requires. Some professors at the Hochschule did not expect much from "wild" America since it had no musical life in their view. But Joachim was known to like Americans.

Maud was spared the discomfort of her peers over the examination procedure. She would not have to wait three long, anxious days to know her future course. Her more settled nerves and inner assurance enabled her to meet her new master on more human terms:

When I arrived at the Hochschule the morning of the examinations, I found that the boys were to play first and later the girls would be put thru their paces. I sent in my card to Dr. Joachim to the horror of the whole room full of prospective pupils. He came out presently, and with the kindest manner explained that I would be heard immediately after the lunch hour, and that my turn would have order of precedence over all the other "girl fiddlers." Sure enough, I was called into the long, bare, terror inspiring examination hall, ahead of the other girls, many of whom had been waiting for hours. I was put thru the tests of violin and piano playing—absolute pitch and sight reading, at the end of which the gray haired ogres, who had been surrounding me, sat down at the long table and began scribbling while Dr. Joachim came up to me and said: "You will please come to my class on the first Monday morning after the opening of school. In the meantime, you will have to get your papers and class hours from the secretary." He was kindness itself and true to his word.[15]

Foreigners were rarely admitted to the Hochschule under the age of sixteen, nor were they given free tuition. Female students had gained the right to compete for admission only a decade earlier.[16] Acceptance was based on talent, training, and prospects for a career in music. Many were told that they must study a year or two privately before trying again for admission to the Hochschule. Even those who were admitted might not study directly with Joachim. To be with Professor Joachim once every two weeks was a great honor and once a week was even a greater honor. "[T]o be assigned to his instruction immediately on entrance to the Hochschule was well-nigh maddening to the great number who did not go."[17]

Not only was Maud, now sixteen, immediately assigned to weekly lessons with Joachim, but for her Joachim himself waived "the six month registration rule and the preparatory class drudgery experienced by most young pupils."[18] Further, she at once began the study of concertos instead of studies and exercises and soon was playing with orchestral accompaniment, an indication of her new master's high opinion of her artistry.[19]

Because Joachim's aim at the Hochschule was to teach musicianship first of all, his pupils were trained for careers as teachers, quartet players, concertmasters of orchestras, and the like, but not necessarily for careers as solo artists.[20] Over his lifetime, he personally coached some four hundred pupils, but very few became virtuosos like Maud Powell.[21]

Two of Joachim's weaknesses as a teacher affected this outcome. First, although he always illustrated his meaning with bow and fiddle, providing (in Maud's words) a "shining example," he could not or simply did not orally explain technical points to his students. Secondly, he failed to see or acknowledge the true value of the Franco-Belgian compositions of Henri Vieuxtemps and Henri Wieniawski as vehicles for the development of violin technique, including tone and the singing style essential to the cultivation of a solo artist. The latter omission was often cited as the explanation for the predominance of virtuosi from the Franco-Belgian school in the late nineteenth and early twentieth centuries.

For Joachim's counterparts of the Franco-Belgian school, to play the violin was to delight as much in the artistry of the execution as in the music itself. Their music virtually celebrated the instrument. Such notable violinists as Vieuxtemps, de Bériot, Sarasate, and Wieniawski, who thrived during the nineteenth century, composed music for the violin which unabashedly combined a wealth of melody with the requirements of technical virtuosity. This music is so well suited to the violin that the instrument is made to revel in melodic charm, elegance, and grace, as well as virtuosic style.

In contrast, the classical and romantic repertoire for which the German school was known was largely composed for certain violin virtuosi (Kreutzer, Clementi, Bridgetower, David, Joachim) by composers who were not themselves violinists (Beethoven, Mendelssohn, Schumann, Brahms, Bruch). There were notable exceptions, like the violinist-composer Ludwig Spohr—whose music owed much to Viotti's influence through Rode, and who founded the German school of violin playing—and of course Bach and Mozart. Understandably, these composers were concerned more with musical content than with violin technique, although the latter was always taken into consideration. This approach conformed with Joachim's musical predilections. (Joachim was not purely a classicist, however. He had a romantic temperament, which explains his attraction to the music of Brahms, in particular.) Thus, he chose to explore with his students the profound musical depths of the Austro-German literature above all else.

Although he knew well enough the music of Vieuxtemps and Wieniawski, with whom he had been friends, he steadfastly refused to teach or perform their works, primarily for their lack of musical depth.

Maud came to revere her master and happily gleaned from him the best he had to offer. However, unlike a good number of her companions, she brought to her study with this violin giant a perspective all her own which enabled her to balance his instruction with the teachings of her previous masters and her own experience. She soon observed: "Joachim was a far greater violinist than teacher. His method was a cramping one, owing to his insistence on pouring all his pupils into the same mold, so to speak, of forming them all on the Joachim lathe."[22]

In a broader context, Maud expressed her view of the problem:

> Of course, all artistic playing represents essentially the mental control of technical means. But to acquire the latter in the right way, while at the same time developing the former, calls for the best of teachers. The problem of the teacher is to prevent his pupils from being too imitative—all students are natural imitators—and furthering the quality of musical imagination in them. Pupils generally have something of the teacher's tone—Auer pupils have the Auer tone, Joachim pupils have a Joachim tone, an excellent thing. But as each pupil has an individuality of his own, he should never sink it altogether in that of his teacher. . . .
>
> It was no doubt an advantage, a decided advantage for me in my artistic development, which was slow—a family trait—to enjoy the broadening experience of three entirely different styles of teaching, and to be able to assimilate the best of each.[23]

One had to have his technique well in hand to benefit Joachim's instruction.[24] Maud had come to Joachim at the right time in her training. As she mounted the steps to his home on the fourth floor at 17 Bendlerstrasse for her private lessons, she could enter his studio with confidence in her technical equipment. She did not find octaves difficult and harmonics she always found easy. But for a time she did have trouble with the staccato bowing:

> Perhaps it is because I belong to an older school, or it may be because I laid stress on technic because of its necessity as a means of expression—at any rate I worked hard at it. Naturally, one should never practice any technical difficulty too long at a stretch. Young

players sometimes forget this. I know that *staccato* playing was not easy for me at one time. I believe a real *staccato* is inborn; a knack. I used to grumble about it to Joachim and he told me once that musically staccato did not have much value. His own, by the way, was very labored and heavy. He admitted that he had none. Wieniawski had such a wonderful *staccato* that one finds much of it in his music. When I first began to play his D minor concerto I simply made up my mind to get a *staccato*. It came in time, by sheer force of will. After that I had no trouble.[25]

It was in the matter of bowing that Joachim stood most accused of fitting students into his own mold. He was constantly reminding his students that "Bowing is the soul of violin playing," and his assistant teachers followed through by perhaps too devotedly teaching his method.[26] When asked about his bowing technique, Joachim responded that it had probably originated with Viotti and descended thence to Rode, to Boehm, and to himself. Of other violinists who used the method, Joachim named Vieuxtemps, de Bériot, Laub, and Ernst, and he suspected that Wieniawski and Paganini also obtained their great effects by employing the same technique.[27] Since Dancla had taught Maud de Bériot's "wonderful method of attack," her bowing was already sufficiently supple and clean to meet Joachim's standards. The secret was in the strength and flexibility of the thumb.

Above all, Joachim was a "great adviser, a former of style, and a master of interpretation" who spared no effort to endow his pupils with the same understanding and insight which had caused him to revere the music of the great masters.[28] They need not see the work exactly as he did, but the students should learn to think for themselves and to probe the depths of the greatest compositions with understanding.[29]

Whether in the privacy of his home or in the classroom with its thick doors and walls from which no sound escaped, the great master would often walk the floor, violin in hand, and pour out in marvelous revelation the music of Bach, Beethoven, Mozart, and Mendelssohn. His playing was a lesson in itself, for it revealed with stunning simplicity his absolute devotion to his art, brooking no affectation or sham. Each time he played Bach, it was with a freshness and spontaneity which made the music come alive. Joachim always achieved a big tone and played broad chords with an organ-like effect. Looking like a legendary Norse king with flowing gray locks and his violin tucked under his chin, his fingers fell like iron on the fingerboard, infallibly in tune, while his bow arm summoned the grand, noble tone from the depths of his instrument.

Joachim's energies could wilt students who labored to please him during a lesson. While kind and sensitive to his students' personal problems, he could be terrifyingly forthright in his musical prescriptions. Joachim told one pupil that his technique "made him ill," there was so little behind it.[30]

It was no secret that it took talent and industry to win over the "old man." Combined with her extraordinary intelligence, these traits soon made Maud one of Joachim's favorites. Within three months of her entry into the Hochschule, a photograph of Maud with her classmate Madge Wickham, which they gaily had presented to their master on his birthday, could be seen among his possessions.

The confidence Maud evinced in the photograph had been amply justified by Joachim's own judgment. He had already confirmed the special artistic affinity between master and pupil by presenting her to the Berlin public in a performance of the Beethoven concerto with the Berlin Philharmonic, which he conducted.[31] Maud's master could have bestowed no greater honor on his pupil.

Among her classmates, nine women and five men, Maud quickly became known for the rapidity with which she grasped a new work and her "abnormal" powers of memorization.[32] She memorized everything in her path—scales, etudes, and masterworks alike. And nothing she memorized escaped thorough analysis by her keen intellect, not of the violin part alone, but of the piano or orchestral score, if at all possible.[33] Throughout her studies abroad, she found her habit of memorization, formed in early childhood, to be of inestimable value for its discipline and its obvious musical rewards. In later years, she advised other young students: "The student should learn to memorize her music. Her repertoire will thus be always available. She will, when not confined to the printed sheet, give more thought to the content of the music and its reproduction, thus learning to play with greater freedom and authority. The pleasant effect on the listener will also be enhanced. Moreover, should the student go to Europe for further study she will certainly command greater respect and attention than she would were she a 'slave to her notes.' "[34]

Throughout her studies, the young American continued to play gypsy-like, with fresh verve and abandon, qualities all her own and which no amount of discipline or training could wholly suppress from her style. Joachim always expressed wonder at the temperamental quality in her playing until he heard the legend of Maud's "Hungarian" ancestry. From the moment of that discovery, her Hungarian master understood the artistic kinship he felt with her and addressed her in endearing terms as his "little American cousin."[35]

Respected and loved though he was by students and teachers alike, Maud could see that her master was a lonely man. After three years of painful separation, 1884 marked the year of his divorce from his wife of two decades, the contralto Amalie Weiss. Worsening the effect, Brahms's attentions to Amalie in an attempt to mend the breach strained the two men's long-cherished friendship.

The relationship between Brahms and Joachim was already legendary. Brahms had written his violin concerto for Joachim in 1878, with Joachim deferentially suggesting changes to make it more violinistic, improving it musically in the process.[36] The concerto's first performance was on New Year's Day in 1879 at the Leipzig Gewandhaus, with Joachim playing the solo part and Brahms conducting.

Undoubtedly, Maud studied this great work under Joachim, reveling in the majestic beauty of its melodies and the gypsy-like fire of its finale. Critics at first called it the concerto *against* the violin, and even the great Belgian violinist Eugène Ysaÿe said he could not make his violin "sing" while playing it (an opinion he later revised).[37] Even Joachim had jokingly advised Brahms that the concerto was "unplayable" due to its great technical difficulty, although he implicitly understood its musical worth.[38]

The concerto was clearly ahead of its time, representing an organic fusion of the developments in violin art since Beethoven and Paganini. Brahms adroitly took advantage of the freedom made possible by Paganini's technical advances but subordinated them to the service of the music in a concerto conceived along symphonic lines, a development initiated by Beethoven. With her innate musical genius, Maud not only understood this work, she mastered it well before it gained public acceptance. She may also have met Brahms, who, though living in Vienna, came to Berlin occasionally.

With her old Leipzig friend Geraldine Morgan of New York, Maud participated in the full round of classes at the Hochschule in theory, music history, ear training, and piano, as well as ensemble and orchestra. Classes in ensemble playing were emphasized at the Hochschule, with Joachim frequently leading the sessions just as he invariably conducted the Hochschule student orchestra. Students had before them the additional example of the Joachim String Quartet.

Joachim was by all accounts the greatest violinist to devote himself to quartet playing during the nineteenth century. Formed in Berlin in 1869 and lasting until Joachim's death in 1907, the Joachim Quartet was one of the most remarkable ensembles ever created.[39] It was said that the four players understood each other as if they were governed by one will. When Maud heard them play at the Singakademie, Heinrich de Ahna played second violin, Emanuel Wirth, viola, and Robert Hausmann, cello (all were teachers at the Hochschule). For Maud, the Joachim Quartet was one of the most splendid features of Berlin's rich musical life.

Each evening Berlin offered a rich diet of musical events. The opera could be seen every night of the week presenting Wagner as well as Rossini. Concert artists came in a steady stream, including the graceful violinist Pablo de Sarasate and the regal Clara Schumann. The Singakademie's annual production of Bach's *St. Matthew Passion* was not to be missed, along with the concerts of the young Berlin Philharmonic which had been formed in 1882.

Music was taken as seriously as the "inevitable" beer to which Mrs. Powell had to accustom herself again. The American colony continually worried over the corruption of its young female students amid foreign customs, while Mrs. Powell serenely observed her daughter's steady and forthright character continue to build around a fundamentally healthy and sound inner core.[40]

Maud herself was a student of character as much as of music and quickly discerned what was genuine in the personalities which surrounded her. Maud met and formed a friendship with the German composer Max Bruch, who was at that time the director of the orchestra at Breslau. He had toured America in 1883, conducting performances of his more important instrumental and choral works, so he and Maud undoubtedly found much to talk about.

Joachim and Bruch had been friends for many years. Bruch had dedicated his first violin concerto, in G minor, to the violinist, who premiered it in 1868. As with all of Bruch's violin concertos, Joachim advised the composer on writing the solo part. Their congenial collaboration resulted in one of the most popular concertos in the violin literature and one of the most adroitly suited to the nature of the instrument. Maud studied this masterpiece under Joachim's guidance, reveling in its expressive, lyrical style so fitting for the violin, its rocking rhythms and its full, sonorous orchestration.

She chose this concerto for her performance with the Berlin Philharmonic in March 1885, which marked the conclusion of her studies with Joseph Joachim. She had, within a year's time, met her master's highest expectations, and he took great pleasure in pronouncing her a finished artist. He invited her to make her formal debut with the Berlin Philharmonic. With her master on the podium, Maud summoned all the artistry that had been developing within her through eight years of study and played Bruch's brilliantly conceived concerto with great intelligence, rendering the lyricism and power of its line with deep feeling and manifest musicianship.

Her master finally told her "to go home and play out her heart." But so intensely had she been influenced by the great violinist that it would take her six years to throw off her mental control and reserve and to really be able to play herself out to her audiences.[41] Time would be needed to integrate the intense intellectual discipline which had been required to control her technique and interpretations with her emotional and intuitive response to the music. Only through the integration of brain, hand, and heart could she make her art her own and present it naturally, freely, and authoritatively as an integrated whole flowing out of her own nature. Joachim, and her other teachers, had provided her with the needed intellectual and technical training. He knew that she would have to find her own way through experience to the artistic truth she sought. On the appointed day of her departure for America, Joachim met his protégée for one last bear hug and presented her with his photograph, which he had affectionately inscribed, "To, his talented, industrious and dear pupil, Miss Powell, in remembrance of Josef Joachim."[42]

Maud, at the time of her American debut, 1885.

Top, 1898 portrait of conductor Theodore Thomas who called Maud his "musical grand-child"; *bottom,* two composers whose violin concertos Maud premiered in America: *left,* Peter Ilyich Tchaikovsky; *right,* Antonin Dvořák.

left, Anton Seidl, who conducted Maud's American premiere of the Dvořák violin con-
to; *right,* Walter Damrosch, who conducted her American premiere of the Tchaikovsky
in concerto; *bottom left,* American composer Amy Cheney Beach, who dedicated her
nance, Op. 23, to Maud; *right,* Maud in 1894.

Top, Maud in the 1890s; *bottom left*, her father; *right*, her uncle John Wesley Powell. *Facing page*, painting by Stanley Meltzoff of the founders of the National Geographic Society at the Cosmos Club, January 13, 1888. Maud's "Uncle Wes" is standing near the center with his hand on the globe; her father is on the left, third from Wes's right, bending over with his hand on the table pointing to a document; Maud's uncle A. H. Thompson, geographer, is standing farthest to the right, and her cousin Arthur Powell Davis is standing second from the left.

..THE..

Maud POWELL

STRING QUARTET

MISS MAUD POWELL, First Violin.

JOSEPH KOVAŘÍK, Second Violin.

FRANZ P. KALTENBORN, Viola.

PAUL MIERSCH, Violon

Maud at home in the early 1890s; the drawings on the wall may have been hers.

Maud in 1892.

7

Theodore Thomas's Musical Grandchild

*There is no thought to be taken about precedents,
for there is no precedent.*

—Francis Bacon

*Not I, not any one else can travel that road for you,
You must travel it for yourself.
It is not far, it is within reach,
Perhaps you have been on it since you were born and did
not know, . . .*

—Walt Whitman

IT WAS SPRINGTIME IN AURORA, A PERFECT TIME FOR A FAMILY REUNION.
Those who knew Bramwell Powell had never seen him happier. On
April 19, 1885, he had returned from New York with his wife and
daughter. He could not take his eyes off his Maud; his little girl had
been transformed into a young woman. Charles Van Liew, who used
to play the cello with Maud, noted that she was "looking her best."
"She had a splendid figure, moved with spring and vivacity, and her
cheeks were becomingly plump and rosy."[1] If the father could hardly
recognize his daughter as a result of her physical transformation, he
could find great comfort and satisfaction in the fact that she remained
unaffected in manner—simple, modest, vivacious—her sense of humor
and keen sense of fun still intact.

Bram's friends said he "counted nothing as lost that enhanced . . .
[his daughter's] culture and widened her powers.[2] In this, his wife
was at one with him. Maud's parents could embrace each other feeling that their daughter's gifts and her development of them had
justified the sacrifice they had made to further her musical promise.

At the behest of the people of Aurora, gratified by the honest efforts she had made and proud of her success, Professor Stein scheduled a "musical welcome" in Maud's honor for May 11, in which she would appear with a variety of local artists. Through music, Maud could thank the many family friends in Aurora for their support and dispel the skepticism about her abilities that underlay the fuss that had been made over her return from study abroad. Maud responded to the gesture with a note, part of which read: "I am very glad to be at home again. The warm greetings and generous appreciation you give me, are a source of great pride and much gratification, for I have desired first, to please and satisfy my friends. I return to Aurora, as a child to its dear home, . . . happy to be among those whom I love."[3]

More than a week before the concert the Coulter Opera House was sold out for "the grandest affair of its kind ever held in this city." The program was light. Stein's Orchestra played "Home Sweet Home" as the audience eagerly awaited the young violinist's appearance: "With firm step and the perfection of youthful grace she walked upon the stage, with a self possession which many an older artist would fain acquire. Opera glasses were leveled and the eyes were satisfied, the magic bow was drawn and harmonies from another world delighted the ear."[4]

Maud rendered Sarasate's technically demanding *Faust Fantasie* with breathtaking ease and perfection. She stood with "willowy grace, bending over her beloved instrument with the soulful eyes of an artist," and when she released the final notes the audience shouted and applauded its approval, showering her with floral pieces which she smilingly acknowledged. She then played Nardini's *Larghetto*, Zarzyki's *Mazurka*, and Dancla's *Bolero*. One reporter wrote: "The star of the evening was Miss Maud Powell, tall, graceful and girlish. There was about her a dignity that comes of a life decorously spent and native gentility combined. She was of Aurora, and Aurora determined to show its pride and appreciation of her four years of patient climb up the rugged steps of art to fame and we might almost say, perfection."[5]

The violinist had won over her hometown, according to local critics: "The large audience, many of whom had come with suspicious ideas that her talents were greatly over-estimated, applauded to the echo, and none of them departed with any other idea than that they had been in the presence of an artist of wondrous capability." Maud made the listeners feel that they were in the presence of a "human being who has great gifts and who dedicates them to the uplifting of his fellow man."[6]

Maud soon journeyed to Chicago to seek out her former teachers William Lewis and Agnes Ingersoll. The crucial question now was how to launch her career. There was only one answer. She must play with an orchestra conducted by Theodore Thomas. Maestro Thomas stood at the pinnacle of classical music in America and as a conductor was hardly equaled abroad. The history of classical music in America is inextricably intertwined with the life of Theodore Thomas, so great was his ideal and so fully was it lived.[7]

Born in 1835 in Hanover, Germany, Thomas was a violin prodigy when he arrived in America with his family at the age of ten. When the Italian Opera Company was formed in New York, he played among the first violins and taught himself how to develop a singing tone by studying the technique of such singers as Jenny Lind and Henrietta Sontag. In 1852 the completely self-educated Thomas was made concertmaster of the orchestra, then under the direction of Luigi Arditi, and at the age of twenty-two, he became the company's permanent conductor.

By 1854, Thomas had been elected a member of the Philharmonic Society of New York, and for thirty-six years his name was associated with this orchestra, first as a violinist and later as its conductor. From 1855 to 1868, Thomas also led the Mason-Thomas String Quartet, and by 1859 he was regarded as America's most accomplished violinist.

When he was twenty-seven, Thomas found that he could not be satisfied with the standard set by the New York Philharmonic, that the field of quartet music was too restrictive, and that the opera, which he conducted, was not wholly congenial to his nature. There was only one thing for him to do—create his own orchestra. With the formation of the Theodore Thomas Orchestra in 1862, he dedicated himself to conducting, determined to raise his audiences and musicians alike to an appreciation for the highest form of classical music.

It was a goal not easily attained. The public of the period was used to programs filled with miscellany designed solely for entertainment, programs characterized by a hodge-podge of vocal and instrumental numbers. Thomas's aim was to accustom these same audiences to purely orchestral music, the highest expression of which was the symphony. He discovered soon after organizing his orchestra that he could not sustain public interest in a complete symphony. Instead, he had to offer music of the lightest character compatible with his standards, which meant that he could present only one movement of a symphony sandwiched in among opera overtures and waltzes to lighten the fare.

Theodore Thomas was an autocratic conductor who demanded the best from his men, expecting their full devotion to their work — a standard he likewise demanded of himself. He did everything in his power to protect his players and look after their welfare, paying their salaries out of his own pocket when necessary even when, following the Great Fire of Chicago in 1871, it meant financial ruin for him.

He raised the quality of their performance to the highest in America — and eventually beyond standards set in Europe — by keeping his men playing together all year and by drilling them until they played with perfection. He was the first to compel the string sections to bow every work uniformly, insisting that the phrasing with the bow was critical to the quality of sound the orchestra achieved. Steinway Hall on Fourteenth Street became his orchestra's permanent home when it opened in the winter of 1866–67.

In 1867 the self-educated Thomas went to Europe to take the measure of himself, his standards, his goals, his techniques. Thomas met Berlioz in Paris and then Dvořák in Berlin, where he heard Joachim play Beethoven's violin concerto. Thomas was surprised to find himself ahead of the first European musicians in conducting, and he had little to learn in quartet and solo playing even from Joachim. The trip confirmed him on his course, giving him new confidence. He was further fortified with new ideas for attracting audiences to his concerts through the irresistible melodies of Johann and Josef Strauss.

Thomas was now a master program-builder. His New York Summer Night Concert programs were at once attractive and educational to the public. He divided each program with two long intermissions. The first part was composed of short, brilliant pieces, during which latecomers were settled. The second part featured symphonic movements and classic gems, presuming the audience to be settled down and receptive. The third part featured marches, waltzes, and pieces with rich orchestral color and strongly marked rhythms, rejuvenating the audience with high spirits and sending them home happy.

Thomas said, "What our over-worked business and professional men most need in America is an elevating mental recreation which is not an amusement."[8] This he provided for them, rarely presenting the same program twice and giving performances which met the highest standards, rising above the mediocrity that he claimed was the "curse of art."

After the 1868–69 season, Thomas gave up the unremunerative winter concert season in New York in favor of a tour schedule which at first included the larger cities of the East and Midwest as well as smaller ones along the route. Between 1869 and 1891, Thomas traveled a "Musical Highway" several times a year, thereby becoming the educator in classical music of a nation. He nowhere dropped his standards, forcing all his audiences to reach for something that was above them collectively.

By 1870, Thomas could give a whole symphony for the Summer Night Concerts in New York, although he did it only occasionally. This progress encouraged him to use the centennial of Beethoven's birth to render a Beethoven program in each city along the "Highway." For most cities, it was a first.[9]

From the beginning, Thomas persistently presented to American audiences new music not previously performed in the United States, and sometimes not even in Europe:

> The people cannot read new scores for themselves, as they read new books, it is therefore one of the missions of a symphony orchestra to perform for them the current musical literature. . . . As for the American composers, the only way in which to develop composition in our own country is to play the works by American writers side by side with those of other nationalities, and let them stand or fall on their own merits. I do not believe in playing inferior works merely because they are American, nor rejecting good ones because they are not foreign. Let our composers realize there is a standard to be reached before they can be recognized, but that if they do reach it, they will be certain of equal recognition with writers of other nations. They will then have an incentive to produce the best that is in them and will produce it.[10]

In March of 1873, the appearances of Anton Rubinstein, pianist, and Henri Wieniawski, violinist, in the United States enabled Thomas to present a program which for the first time met his personal standard.[11] In Chicago, Rubinstein played Beethoven's Piano Concerto in E-flat and Wieniawski played his own Concerto No. 2. Rubinstein described his experience with the Thomas Orchestra to William Steinway, the piano manufacturer:

> I shall take away with me from America one unexpected reminiscence. Little did I dream to find here the greatest and finest orchestra in the wide world. I have been in Munich, Brussels, Amsterdam, London, Paris, Vienna, Berlin, and all the great European art centers, but never in my life have I found an orchestra and a conductor so in sympathy with one another, or who followed me as the most gifted accompanist can follow a singer on the piano. There exists but one orchestra of sixty or eighty men which plays so perfectly, and which is known as the Imperial Orchestra of Paris, and was created by a decree of the French Senate in the days of the first Napoleon and they are engaged for life. They may have twenty or more rehearsals for one performance, to insure absolute perfection, and they play as perfectly as the Thomas Orchestra, but unfortunately, they have no Theodore Thomas to conduct them.[12]

Theodore Thomas and his orchestra first came to Chicago on a permanent seasonal basis with the opening of the Chicago Summer Night Concerts in 1877. These concerts were held in the Interstate Industrial Exposition Building near the railroad tracks on the Lake Front of Michigan Avenue, opposite Adams Street, until 1888. Eventually, in 1891, Thomas fulfilled his dream of a permanently endowed orchestra in that Midwestern city. He found the people of Chicago "openhearted, generous, and enthusiastic" and claimed that "Chicago is the only city on the continent, except New York, where there is sufficient musical culture to enable me to give a series of fifty successive concerts."[13]

The Chicago Summer Night Concerts enhanced the friendship between Theodore Thomas and William Lewis. Hence it was natural for Lewis to introduce his protégée to the great conductor. Maud recalled: "My introduction came to Theodore Thomas through 'Billy' Lewis, my Chicago teacher. It seemed impossible to make an appointment with Mr. Thomas as Mr. Lewis' letter was disregarded. I reported this to Mr. Lewis, who straightway wrote another and a stronger letter to Mr. Thomas, in which I understand some strong language was used. Mr. Lewis said 'damn it' he must hear Maud Powell; that he,

William Lewis, was not the person to recommend anyone to a man in Mr. Thomas' position, whose talent was not worthy of the introduction."[14]

Unknown to Maud and her teacher, Thomas had embarked on a transcontinental tour from Maine to San Francisco in April, and he might not have received the letters until later. Maud waited with increasing anxiety as Thomas's reply was delayed: "At the time I finished my studies abroad and returned to this country . . . girl violinists were looked upon with suspicion, and I felt that I had a hard road to travel in my native land."[15] Many another young woman would have retreated from her ambition right then, but Maud Powell was no ordinary lady. It was inconceivable to her that anything or anyone could stand between her and her artistic destiny. With her mother, she went to New York City and found her way to Steinway Hall to face the man who stood at the doorway to her future:

> I determined to take matters into my own hands. I walked into the hall one morning where the rehearsal was being held with my violin under my arm. When it was over, and before the musicians had dispersed, I walked up to the great leader. My heart was in my throat, but I managed to say pretty bravely, "Mr. Thomas, I am Maud Powell, and I want you to give me a chance to play for you." His big heart was touched, I suppose, for he nodded his head, reached out his hand for my score, and called the musicians together. I knew it was a crucial moment in my life—a girl only eighteen [seventeen] daring to be a violinist and demanding a hearing of the greatest orchestral leader in America! I had brought the score of the Bruch Concerto, and it is not difficult to do one's best when one knows every note of a concerto backward. When I had finished, Mr. Thomas engaged me on the spot for his next concert.[16]

She was booked to make her American debut with the Thomas Orchestra that summer in the Chicago Summer Night Concert Series.

It seemed as if half of Aurora turned out for the Summer Night Concert on July 30, 1885. Chicagoans turned out in force as well. One critic noted that "a considerable number of musicians and musical people" had been attracted to the concert by the announcement of Maud Powell's debut. The word among Chicago's music circles was that William Lewis's protégée had returned from study abroad with the great Joachim's warm endorsement. William Lewis and the Powell family were seated in front for the concert, which the press would describe as "made memorable by the debut of the promising young American violinist, Miss Maud Powell."[17]

The first division of the concert featured the Overture, Air, and Gavotte from Bach's Orchestral Suite in D, Schubert's Unfinished Symphony, and the Prelude to Wagner's *Tristan und Isolde*. The second division began with Beethoven's Coriolanus Overture. Max Bruch's Violin Concerto in G Minor was next. Maud appeared as a "tall, graceful figure" with a "sweet, though firm and expressive face."[18] The seventeen-year-old violinist was received with warm applause as she lifted her violin to her chin with "perfect confidence."

The conditions under which she played were hardly ideal: "A solo violin in a 'Union Depot' . . . has enough to contend with in the size of the place and the heat of the evening without the too-officious help of escaping steam, tooting whistles, ringing bells, and the 'chough, chough, chough' of departing trains—all of which came out in full force last night. . . . Add to these the babies crying, also turned on in the softest passages of the music."[19] Intonation was also a problem for Maud. It was a hot July evening and humid breezes coming off Lake Michigan blew through the open-air hall, demoralizing her gut strings.

The Bruch concerto had been played so rarely as to be "quite strange" to her listeners. However, the critics for the *Chicago Tribune* and the *Chicago Daily News* were familiar with the work. The *Daily News* critic noted: "She played the adagio with fine expression and remarkable purity and sweetness of tone. The finale requires a broad style of playing which it is natural that Miss Powell should not yet have acquired. Its difficulties of execution were, however, overcome with skill and apparent ease. Her bowing is very graceful and her stage presence is unusually pleasing."[20]

The *Chicago Tribune* critic observed that "Miss Powell has an excellent bow, good execution, a large tone, for so young a player, and much sentiment."[21] Her playing created a "favorable impression" and her work as a whole was "full of promise." Her performance was greeted with "prolonged and flattering" applause. Upon reflection, the *Chicago Daily News* critic observed: "She is a young girl of remarkable talent and a commensurate amount of application and perseverance. These qualities are all that is needed to give her a place in the front rank of American violinists."[22] The Chicago *Inter Ocean* pronounced her a "worthy successor of Camilla Urso."

Maud later discovered that William Lewis, "the dear man," had sat dissolved in tears as she played the Bruch concerto with a mastery beyond his reach. An Auroran observed that she played the concerto "with complete mastery of its difficulties and a full understanding of its depth and beauty."[23] Even then, she was said by the musician and writer Gustav Kobbé to have played with a "large solid tone and a technique which was finished without being finicky." "Classical repose, romantic tenderness, grace, esprit and great technical nerve," all were points in her style which she could bring into play whenever the composition demanded them.[24]

Above all, Theodore Thomas glowed over her success: "At the close of that concert—my debut in America—Mr. Thomas came to me with his two hands full of greenbacks. He handed them to me, saying, 'I want the honor of paying you the first fee you have earned as an artist.' "[25] Theodore Thomas christened the young American his "musical grandchild" and engaged her as soloist for the New York Philharmonic's first concert of the 1885–86 season in November.[26]

The history of the New York Philharmonic illuminates the early struggles for symphony orchestras in the United States. When the New York Philharmonic Society was founded in 1842, there was no responsible music director, with predictable consequences. The standard of performance was inferior and the programs consisted of a hodge-podge of compositions, ranging from symphonies to inconsequential pieces, incongruously thrown together. Because the Philharmonic concerts were infrequently given (three the first season and only six per season by the twenty-seventh season), the musicians took other engagements just to make ends meet. This meant that rehearsals were haphazard, with orchestra players coming and going as they pleased.

When eighteen-year-old violinist Theodore Thomas was elected a member of the Society in 1854, the orchestra still lacked leadership. A decade later, when Thomas established his own orchestra in New York, the Philharmonic suffered greatly from the competition of the superior ensemble. Thomas's impact on New York's cultural life became painfully evident when financial necessity drove him to give up his "Symphony Soirées" during the 1869 winter season in favor of the "Musical Highway." However, in 1872, he heeded the pleas of New Yorkers and returned to the city once a month for a concert while maintaining his "highway" schedule.

By the spring of 1877, the Philharmonic's fortunes were so low that the Society offered the conductorship to Thomas without any conditions, and he accepted. This arrangement ironically resulted in his becoming his own most successful rival in New York. He deliberately set out to make the Philharmonic series the most important concerts, giving second place to his own. In 1880, Thomas removed the rivalry by giving a lighter series of concerts with his orchestra, the Thomas Popular Concerts.

In order to perfect the New York Philharmonic, he drew from the ranks of his private orchestra, assuring constant engagements for the greater part of its members, which also conveniently placed them under Thomas's direction year round. These same musicians then were employed in the New York Philharmonic, the Brooklyn Philharmonic (which Thomas conducted from 1866 to 1891), and the Thomas Orchestra. Brooklyn and New York choral societies were also founded under his direction. Hence, New York's classical music life was dominated by the artistic prowess, inspiration, and tenacity of one man.

Thomas's musical stature was evident in his lowering the concert pitch of the orchestra by nine-sixteenths of a tone in 1881. After long consideration, Thomas decided to align American orchestras with the reformed German pitch or the "normal diapason" adopted by a French government commission twenty-five years before. The action required every instrumentalist in America to buy a new instrument or adapt his old one to the new pitch, as well as requiring instrument manufacturers to conform. That the musical world followed Thomas's lead was ample testament to his influence.

To play with the Thomas Orchestra or the New York Philharmonic under Thomas's direction was to arrive as a musician. Not only had Maud Powell played with the Thomas Orchestra in Chicago, she was to be introduced to New York audiences and a number of other important Eastern cities under Thomas's baton.

A Friday afternoon public rehearsal always preceded the New York Philharmonic's Saturday evening concert in its season series of six concerts. Maud was anxious as she arrived at the Academy of Music on November 13, 1885. She had discovered that her Guarnerius violin, chosen for her by Joseph Joachim, was disabled. Learning of her plight, one of the orchestra members generously loaned her his own Guarnerius, which Maud gratefully played.

Besides Bruch's G minor violin concerto, the program featured Weber's *Euryanthe* Overture, Arnold Krug's *Symphonic Prologue to Shakespeare's Othello* (a new composition), Dvořák's *Scherzo Capriccioso*, Op. 66, which the orchestra was playing for the first time, and concluded with Beethoven's *Eroica* Symphony No. 3. The November 14 concert was hailed by the critics as a flawless performance, in which the 115-member orchestra presented with "utmost dignity and worthiness that art which makes us understand how heaven is a possibility." The Philharmonic, at its opening concert of the season, was recognized as "far in advance" of any other orchestra in the United States, and it was greeted appreciatively by a "large and brilliant" audience.

Maud Powell won the "final stamp" from Henry E. Krehbiel, the Nestor of New York critics, that day:

> It is seldom that a woman is honored with an invitation to play a violin solo at a concert of the Philharmonic. Such an invitation, when it is justified by the performance, is an introduction to the first rank of interpretative artists in this country. In the case of Miss Maud Powell, the distinction was well bestowed. She is still a very young woman and has her home in the West. By last night's performance she established a right of domicile wherever good music is cultivated. She is a marvellously gifted woman, one who in every feature of her playing discloses the instincts and gifts of a born artist. She has not reached the height of her ability by any means but her accomplishments are already so bright that they challenge the application of the severest standard from one who would pass judgment upon her. She plays with a conscious ease and reposefulness that is astonishing in one so young. Without great warmth, she yet exhibits a fine intellectual grasp of her music and is able to hold the interest of her listeners for every bar. Technically her management of the bow is more finished than her stopping, but the latter is remarkably firm and correct. Few violinists have been heard here in recent years whose intonation was as free from fault as Miss Powell's. Her occasional slips in this respect are uniformly in the high positions of the G and D strings, or in double-stopping. Her tone is not fully developed and is wanting in dignity and suavity, but is ample in quantity for all purposes. It is delightful to meet a young American artist who has in her the ability to give so much present plea-

sure, and who promises so much for the future. . . . If she maintains the standard she set for herself last night, she will win the
abiding favor of the New York public, and her future career will be
watched with warm interest.[27]

The critic for the *New York Sun* seemed also to grasp the significance of the debut: "[Miss Powell] displayed every qualification of a
true artist—repose, dignity, discretion, talent, and study. Her bowing is vigorous, her tone marvelously sweet and clear, her sentiment
healthy and genuine. . . . [T]he impression left by her debut in the
Philharmonic was that Miss Powell has a great artistic career open
before her—one justly earned, which will surely be honorably
maintained."[28]

Uncle Wes and his wife had joined Maud's parents and brother
Billy in New York for the concert, swelling the family celebration.

8

The Powell Family in Washington

*All the emotions of the human spirit are coined into song.
Song is the reservoir into which all human feelings are poured,
and it is the fountain from which all human feelings may be
drawn.*

—*John Wesley Powell*

MAUD WAS IMMEDIATELY SWEPT INTO A SERIES OF ENGAGEMENTS with Theodore
Thomas. Engaged as a soloist with his orchestra for two years, at a
"very large salary" ($150 per performance), she appeared with the
Brooklyn Philharmonic and toured with the Thomas Orchestra, meeting with much success everywhere. Mrs. Powell took up "the road"
with her daughter as Maud began the life of a virtuoso. It seemed
natural in a way, after all that had gone before. Maud, who had
turned eighteen in August, was comforted by her mother's presence.
She needed someone to handle the details of living while she concentrated on her art. Gowns for performance and traveling clothes
had to be selected, cleaned, and pressed, interviews juggled, meals
arranged, and countless other matters given meticulous attention.
For someone to dedicate her life to the requirements of living in
order that another may pursue art requires a sacrifice that only love
can make, and Mrs. Powell readily made that sacrifice. In a sense, she
was driven by her own repressed ambitions. As Maud's reputation
grew, there was vicarious satisfaction in being able to live for and
through her daughter.

These were the rewards. But the price was nonetheless high. While
understanding the necessity of the sacrifice, Maud felt deeply the
pain it inflicted on each member of her family. Her sensitivity in this

[87]

regard may have added impetus to her innate inclination to work hard at her art, for she was notably unsparing of herself in her devotion to excellence in performance. In her article "The Price of Fame," styled as advice to aspiring violinists, Maud's writing poignantly reflects her awareness of her family's care in her behalf:

> Did my mother ever tell Aunt Jinny how I became a violinist? It is a serious confession. The family was broken up when I was taken abroad. Father, fond of home and adoring his wife and children, was left homeless, wifeless, childless: his part to work, work, work and send the monthly check regularly across the seas to pay for lessons, music, concerts, clothes and board. Four years of study abroad, and then the return. But separation was still necessary, for the concert field had to be "worked" from the East, and father's work lay elsewhere. The son and brother went home to his father, but his education was continued without home or mother influence. There were fifteen years of homeless life for all of us: then the nervous strain of professional life, with its incessant travel and irregular hours, proved too much for the brave little mother. She went back to her husband and planned a home life anew. But who shall say, after fifteen years of separation, with estranged habits and interests, that home was ever quite the same again?
>
> Then the question arises: Shall a girl go abroad and fight the battle alone? Not you, my dear, nor any other American girl! And why not? Because she is too far from home, in a land where her independence, her freedom of speech and manners are misunderstood and misinterpreted; where the temptations are more numerous and different from those at home; where her youthful and American unafraidness, and the consciousness that there is no one from home to see and judge, will assuredly lead her into difficulties. Or if, on the other hand, my little American girl is of the guarded, cautious sort, she will have to be so doubly discreet in her behavior, being alone, that her poor little nature will be dwarfed and repressed, her self-expression will suffer from self-consciousness, and her art will not grow and flower as it ought.
>
> I once heard Mrs. Theodore Thomas say that an artist should have a companion, besides a manager and a maid or valet, to keep the career a-going. Can you bethink you of a relative or friend who will go abroad with you—someone who loves you well enough to sacrifice all her own interests for the sake of your career?[1]

Just after Maud's return from Europe, her father was appointed superintendent of the public schools of the District of Columbia, effective July 1, 1885. Washington, D.C., had been his brother's base of operations since 1872, two years after Congress funded the United States Geographical and Geological Survey of the Rocky Mountain Region with John Wesley Powell in charge. Although Bram's appointment came as a surprise, his national reputation as an educator had won him the position. Greeting the news with regret mingled with pride, Aurora's board of education and teachers presented him with a fine bronze statue of Dante. Fifteen of Maud's Aurora girlfriends took her on a picnic and afterwards had their photograph taken professionally, which they then presented to her. The Powell family moved to Washington in the latter part of August.

Bram was assured that he would have exclusive authority to make the reforms he advised were necessary, but his brother warned him that the nation's capital was a conservative southern city fraught with political intrigues. A congressional committee had oversight authority for the administration of the public schools, a fact which could not be ignored without disastrous consequences.

Undeterred, the new superintendent plunged into the work. While he pronounced the schools quite good in some respects, he found that much of the educational approach was backward, relying too heavily on mechanical routine. Reformation of the teaching body was required in order to introduce a new approach. With characteristic energy, he met with the teachers individually and in groups and enlarged the scope of the city's normal school, assuming much of the instruction load himself.[2] One who observed his methods noted, "His peculiar strength lay in his personal force, in the clearness and definiteness of his plans, in his indefatigable industry, in the quiet enthusiasm that pervaded his life, and in the absolute faith which he always manifested in the possibilities of the teacher."[3]

In Washington, all Powell's ideas and his work in Peru and Aurora would come to fruition. In addition, the greater visibility of his new position enhanced his authority when speaking before the meetings of the National Educational Association and the American Academy of Political and Social Science held throughout the country.

The companionship of his brother eased the loneliness caused by the long absences of his wife and daughter. There was additional comfort in the growing bond between father and son. As Billy recalled,

"Father and I were very close friends and companions during all those Washington years."[4] Billy's growing interest in literature and writing forged a further special bond between the two.

Whenever they could be together, Bram and Wes sharpened their minds on each other, elaborated on their latest theories and visions, laughed over their difficulties, and reveled in the peculiar excitement and comfort experienced by twin spirits engaged in changing the perceptions of the world in education and in science. Both possessed original, prophetic minds which lured them to propound and implement ideas far ahead of their time. In Washington, each one involved the other in his enterprises.

Ever since his first expedition down the Colorado River in 1869, Wes had been coming to Washington to garner financial support and supplies for his explorations and studies from the politicians and the military. He moved easily in Washington circles, gaining important backing for his enterprises from Ohio Congressman James A. Garfield and from Joseph Henry and Spencer Baird of the Smithsonian Institution. As Wes's work expanded, his influence grew.[5] In 1885, when Bram arrived, Wes was at the height of his powers.

Wesley Powell's observations of the West's unique physical characteristics led him to believe that its arid lands could not be settled in the same fashion as the rest of the country. He knew that the popular slogan "rain follows the plow" would lead settler families inexorably to disaster and tragedy. Further, the unfettered exploitation of the timber, grasslands, and mineral resources threatened to undo the natural balance that made the lands tenable by man. For these reasons, he advocated protection of the public domain, the reservation of minerals, and the conservation of renewable resources and of water for irrigation in order that the lands might be used for the benefit of all the people.[6]

As one of the first to examine personally the western lands and to see them with an understanding born of extraordinary powers of observation and thought, Powell chose to tame the political and economic drives to exploitation through illumination of facts about the West. Only with a proper understanding of the characteristics of those lands, based on scientific facts, could enlightened political and economic decisions be made about their use. Although he endured withering political and personal attacks from members of Congress, he pursued his mission with integrity and vision.

A man "electric with energy and ideas," Powell was responsible for organizing the study of the western lands of the United States in every facet — geology, topography, water resources, native Indian population. He was the driving force behind the unification of the geological and geophysical surveys into what became the U.S. Geological Survey, headed first by Clarence King in 1879, followed by Powell himself in 1881. His advocacy of water conservation led to the belated establishment of the Bureau of Reclamation, while his concern for the study of the arts, institutions, languages, and opinions of the native Indians led to the immediate organization of the Bureau of Ethnology, which Powell himself directed under the auspices of the Smithsonian Institution until 1902.

In the 1870s and 1880s, Wes either founded or participated actively in numerous professional organizations designed to promote the discussion and dissemination of scientific ideas and knowledge. As might be expected, there gathered around the magnetic Powell some of the brightest and most far-sighted men of the day.

The Powell brothers were the prime movers in the foundation of the National Geographic Society, formed in 1888 for the "increase and diffusion of geographic knowledge." Best reflecting the universality of Wes's interests was his founding of the Cosmos Club, dedicated to the advancement of the members in science, literature, and the arts. In this he was joined by Washington's intellectual elite, including Henry Adams and Clarence Dutton, who had become familiar figures in Wes's parlor on Saturday nights when friends lingered, thoroughly absorbed, through wide-ranging discussions of science and letters.

Wes's investigations into Indian linguistics led to a firm friendship with Melville Bell and his son Alexander. The Bells had come to Washington in 1880 to do their pioneer work with the deaf through establishment of the Volta Laboratory. Wes had a standing invitation to the "Wednesday evenings" held by Alexander Bell, during which a small circle of men gathered in conversation on any subject of interest. Alexander Bell had invented the telephone in 1876 and organized the Bell Telephone Company in 1877. The Powells felt at home with this enterprising and inventive man and induced him to join in founding the National Geographic Society.

One of Wes's closest friends was Samuel P. Langley, who arrived in Washington in 1887 to succeed Spencer Baird as Secretary of the

Smithsonian. In May and November of 1896, Wes witnessed Langley's steam-driven aerodromes prove the practicability of powered flight on the Smithsonian's grounds.

Wes had his own literary evenings which were considered to be "a feature of life in the capital." Joined by friends with widely-ranging interests, Powell could hold forth in the company of such persons as Edward Everett Hale, the famous orator, advocate of reform, and chaplain of the Senate; Hamlin Garland, the dean of American novelists; the sociologist Lester Ward; W. J. McGee of the Geological Survey; Henry Adams; John Hay, a distinguished public servant and Adams's closest friend; and Alexander Bell. Such company was eminently suited to the man who had the temerity to read the works of Scott, Tennyson, and Longfellow aloud to his companions on his second exploratory venture down the Colorado River through the Grand Canyon.

Wes's home on M Street became the hub of family gatherings. His sister Ellen had married A. H. Thompson, one of Wes's most able assistants in his geological work, while sister Martha and her husband John Davis came to Washington in 1891 upon Davis's election to the U.S. Congress. Bram, Ellen, and Wes lived near each other, and each Sunday two of them would call upon the other.

Maud vacationed with her family during the summer months, reviewing new music and practicing her repertoire for the coming season. Her closeness to Billy and the sustenance and inspiration she drew from natural beauty are apparent in the vignettes of family life found in her letters during the summer of 1890.[7]

> "The Highlands"
> June 21st, '90

Mamma and I came down to Washington yesterday and were immediately escorted by my father and brother to this charming country place. Shall not work much the next two weeks, as my brother wants me to give my time to him before he makes his Western trip. This is the loveliest spot imaginable—large breezy rooms, broad piazzas, beautiful lawn on one side, a forest of old trees are another, four tennis courts on a third and a glorious view from the fourth; hammocks, a croquet ground, etc. etc. One *ought* to succeed in having a good time! *nicht wahr?*

Shall have to get a piano up from the city before I shall be content, though.

> Haverhill, N.H.
> July 24, 1890

I have a whole big house to practice in which one of the inhabitants, not living in it herself, has thrown open to me. There are glorious views of the mountains from many of the windows which are really inspiring. Pray excuse my scrawling hand. My brother is at my elbow urging me to quit writing so that I can go out to play tennis with him.

> Pittsfield, Mass.
> Aug. 30, 1890

I too, have been holding sweet communion with Nature this Summer and feel that I have gained purity and nobility in my art in consequence. The mountains are the place to get new life and inspiration.

Whenever Maud came to Washington, Uncle Wes arranged for his favorite niece to give a private recital in his home for the family and their closest friends. Always in high spirits, Uncle Wes delighted in the fact that his niece could command attention in a crowd as well as he and meet his good-humored antics with the perfect aplomb of a veteran artist. On one occasion, another of Wes's nieces recorded: "Uncle Wes teased the ladies until Maud said unless he behaved himself and stopped acting like a bad boy, she would put away her fiddle."[8]

9

Maud Powell on Her Own

*. . . the mind of an artist, in order to achieve the prodigious
effort of freeing whole and entire the work that is in him, must
be incandescent, like Shakespeare's mind. . . .*

—*Virginia Woolf*

*Artistic growth is, more than it is anything else, a refining of the
sense of truthfulness. The stupid believe that to be truthful is easy;
only the artist, the great artist, knows how difficult it is.*

—*Willa Cather, 1915*

MAUD AT ONE POINT WROTE FEELINGLY OF HER INNER STRUGGLES DURING THE
early years of her career:

The unhappiest period of my life was perhaps after I returned
from my studies abroad. I missed the student life, the sound of
music all about me, the talk of music and comparing of ideas with
fellow-students. I missed the architecture, the parks, the organized
life of well-governed cities. In fact I was miserably homesick. I felt
lost and was like a rudderless ship. I was only sixteen [eighteen],
but had made my bow as a professional violinist with some distinction under Theodore Thomas' baton at the New York Philharmonic,
so must henceforth stand on my own feet artistically.

Many were the times when I longed to seek advice in both a
musical and a business way, but I was morbidly shy and foolishly
proud, so I pegged away alone, often wondering if I were on the
right track. These years of uncertainty were six or eight. I practiced
and studied a good deal. All the time I tried to keep a level head. I
sought inspiration wherever I could find it and tried to cultivate
taste.

I read more than I have ever had the time to read since. People thought me cold. But despair was in my heart, and I wondered constantly if I was a fool to keep on. I doubted my talent (at times), I doubted my strength and endurance, I doubted the ultimate reward of my labors. Yet I kept on, simply because of the "something" within that drove me on. I had a reverence for art—instilled into me in Germany—and I had the real artist's yearning for self-expression. And so I passed through the dark years and gradually came into my own.

I believe the successful outcome was a matter as much of character as of talent. Through all, in spite of praise or censure, whether just or unjust, I kept a certain poise of self-judgment and self-criticism. I have ever sought artistic truth according to the light that has been given me. Whatever conviction carries with my work *is* because it has been developed and *is* myself.[1]

During the sweep of engagements with Theodore Thomas, Maud had had little time to reflect on the future course of her career. In the years that followed, she grimly confronted musical conditions in her beloved country.[2]

To better understand America's cultural position at the time, it should be noted that up to 1885, only a relatively small number of Americans had been exposed, and those only intermittently, to the highest examples of the European art of violin playing.[3] Among the best-known violinists who had toured in the United States after 1843 were Ole Bull, Henri Vieuxtemps, Eduard Reményi, Henri Wieniawski, Emile Sauret, August Wilhelmj, Pablo de Sarasate, and Camilla Urso. Among these, only Urso concertized steadily in the United States.

Throughout Maud's career, from 1885 to 1920, there were few American violinists with whom she might be compared. After Maud, the much younger Chicago-born Albert Spalding (1888–1953) was the most notable American violin soloist of the day, perhaps followed by the Philadelphian Arthur Hartmann (1881–1956), who was a good friend of Maud's. Among American male violinists who gained distinction, and whom Maud undoubtedly knew, were Francis MacMillen (b. 1885) and Maximilian Pilzer (b. 1890), both Joachim pupils; Edwin Grasse (b. 1884), a pupil of Thomson; Eddy Brown (1895–1974), a pupil of Hubay and Auer; Theodore Spiering (1871–1925), a pupil of Schradieck; Max Bendix (b. 1866), concertmaster and assistant conductor of the Thomas Orchestra; Louis Persinger (1887–1966), a pupil of Ysaÿe; David Mannes (1866–1959), who founded a music school in New York; and Sam Franko (1857–1937), who studied with Joachim and Vieuxtemps. Franz Kneisel (b. 1865 of German parentage) made his career in America from 1885, when he became concertmaster and solo violinist of the Boston Symphony Orchestra.

The finest violinists of the day were generally Europeans, many of whom toured in the United States in the 1890s. Among them were the Russian Adolf Brodsky, from 1890 to 1894 concertmaster of the New York Symphony under Damrosch; the Belgian masters Martin Marsick (1895–96), Emile Sauret (1895–96), César Thomson (1894–95 and 1896), and Eugène Ysaÿe (1894–95 and 1897–98); the Bohemians Carl Halir (1896–97) and Franz Ondříček (1896–97); the French master Henri Marteau (1893–94 and 1897–98); and the German violinist Willy Burmester (1897–98). A very young Fritz Kreisler (b. Austria, 1875) toured the United States in 1889 and then did not return until 1900.

Camilla Urso (1842–1902) and Lady Hallé (1839–1911; U.S. tour 1898–99) were the most prominent international women violin virtuosos in Maud's day. Besides these, in the early days of her career there were few women artists with whom Maud's skills might be compared. Teresina Tua — an Italian violinist exactly Maud's age, who had won the first prize for violin playing at the Paris Conservatoire in 1880 — toured in the United States in 1887. The American Nettie Carpenter was also heard in the United States in the late 1880s. Geraldine Morgan, Maud's close friend in Leipzig and Berlin and the first American to win the Mendelssohn Prize, returned to New York in 1892 and made a fine debut with the New York Symphony.

While Europe produced such artists as Gabrielle Wietrowitz, Marie Soldat-Röger, Mlle. Irma Sethe (Mme. Saenger-Sethe), these rarely played in the United States. Born in 1866 in Germany, Wietrowitz had studied violin with Joachim, winning the Mendelssohn Prize twice. After a brilliant European concert career, she assumed the leadership of a female string quartet in England around 1898 which rivaled any of the male organizations. In 1901 she settled down as a professor at the Berlin Hochschule. Marie Soldat (b. 1864, Germany) was also a pupil of Joachim and a Mendelssohn Prize winner. She had made her first important appearance performing the Brahms concerto with Hans Richter conducting. She began to devote herself more to chamber music in the early 1900s, forming the Soldat Quartet with three other students from the Berlin Hochschule—a group which engaged the interest of Brahms. The noted authority Henry C. Lahee reported that Maud Powell was considered to be the equal of Soldat and Wietrowitz in "tone, technique and interpretative power."[4] Irma Saenger-Sethe (b. 1876, Belgium) won first prize at the Brussels Conservatory in 1891 and later was favorably compared with Lady Hallé.

These, then, were the violinists with whom Maud's skills could be compared during the first decades of her career.

During the 1886–87 season, Theodore Thomas cut back drastically on his orchestra engagements, retaining only the regular concert series of the New York and Brooklyn Philharmonic societies, while he embarked on a disastrous attempt to establish an American opera. There were only two other professional symphony orchestras in the United States, the Boston Symphony and the New York Symphony. Then, too, the New York Philharmonic's season, which lasted from November to April, consisted of only six subscription concerts. Beginning in 1887, the Boston Symphony had a twenty-concert season at home from mid-October to mid-March, in addition to a few performances in New York and, later, in Baltimore and Philadelphia. The small number and short seasons of the country's professional orchestras made engagements difficult for an artist to obtain— and doubly difficult for a female soloist since women players were barred from professional orchestras.

Making matters even more difficult, artist management was in its infancy, recital circuits were not established, and there was a lack of sponsoring organizations and experienced concert managers throughout the country. When Maud made her debut, there were only two professional managers in New York City (possibly the only ones in the country), L. M. Ruben and Henry Wolfsohn. Ruben was reputedly the first professional artist manager in America. Although he predominantly acted as agent for many foreign opera singers, he was considered to be one of the best and most indefatigable managers for musical artists in general. Some of the better-known American artists under his management were Fannie Bloomfield-Zeisler, a pianist friend of Maud's who was considered to be of the first rank, and Mary Howe, a soprano and composer from Washington, D.C.

Wolfsohn (b. 1847), who had studied piano and voice, became a manager in 1879, and his story reflects the concert conditions near the time of Maud's debut. His career had been launched at thirty-two, when the celebrated violinist August Wilhelmj, who had found that no one individual had the country-wide connections necessary for the planning and execution of a financially sound United States tour, sought him out in Chicago and requested that he undertake the management of his American tour.

Wolfsohn settled in New York in 1881, formally launching the Wolfsohn Musical Bureau three years later. Ruben, who was the sole impresario in New York at that time, warned Wolfsohn that there was not enough business in the city for two! However, Wolfsohn built up an excellent business, justifying his long-held faith in America's readiness to appreciate high-quality musical offerings. He went abroad to lure European artists to the United States, with much success. By 1901 he was managing some of the greatest artists of his time, among them violinists Thomson, Wilhelmj, Marteau, and Kreisler; pianists Joseffy, Rosenthal, de Pachmann, and Bloomfield-Zeisler; and singers Lilli Lehmann, Campanari, the Henschels, Lillian Blauvelt, Clara Butt, and Marchesi—most of whom Maud Powell knew personally. By 1894 Maud was also under Wolfsohn's management, although she began with Ruben.

Major concert halls were beginning to appear with the support of groups of private citizens led by individual philanthropists. Although Philadelphia's Academy of Music had been built in 1857 and Cincinnati's Music Hall in 1878, the Auditorium in Chicago, designed by Louis Sullivan, was only completed in 1889, the Metropolitan Opera House in 1883, New York's Carnegie Hall in 1891, and Boston's Symphony Hall in 1900. New York was the performance center of America's classical music life, although Boston was the country's intellectual center.

In these times and under these conditions, Maud took great comfort in Theodore Thomas's friendship and support. If he were prejudiced against women in any field, it was the same prejudice he attached to men who did not meet his standards: "I do not care for so-called 'pretty women.' What I admire is character and intelligence."[5] Thomas called Maud's work "legitimate playing," recognizing as he did the solid musical foundation behind her brilliant technique. Maud described their relationship matter-of-factly: "Theodore Thomas liked my playing (he said I had brains). . . . All through the earlier part of my American career I had the secure satisfaction that Mr. Thomas was watching my development, standing sponsor for my talent and lending a helpful hand occasionally with a real engagement. That early experience with orchestra—still in my teens—was of invaluable help in all of my future work."[6] But she could not make a career exclusively out of playing with Theodore Thomas.

In 1887, Maud set out to conquer Boston. The influence of three prominent figures was widely felt in that citadel of the arts: Henry Lee Higginson, Mrs. John L. Gardner, and John Knowles Paine. Higginson, a wealthy Boston banker, had personally endowed the Boston Symphony Orchestra in 1881 to "play the best music in the best way," thereby making it the first permanently established orchestra in the United States (Georg Henschel was its first music director). John Knowles Paine, a composer and teacher at Harvard since 1862, was the educator of a generation of composers whom Maud came to know personally and whose music she promoted.[7] Mrs. Gardner, a highly flamboyant and intelligent woman, had become Boston's most ardent promoter of literature, painting, and music, and in her commodious home gathered the artists and celebrities of the age, a good many of whom Maud came to know: Oliver Wendell Holmes, James Russell Lowell, Henry Adams, Henry James, Owen Wister, Charles Eliot Norton, Arthur Foote, Edward MacDowell, Julia Ward Howe, Oscar Wilde, Nellie Melba, Wilhelm Gericke, Charles Martin Loeffler, John Singer Sargent, and Ignace Paderewski.

In Maud's first Boston recital, given on her own initiative, her qualities were noted with satisfaction by the critics although she arrived there "entirely unheralded." Her appearance with Madam Hastreiter, an opera singer, fell between that of two other violinists, the Belgian Ovide Musin (1854–1929) and the Italian Teresina Tua.

A critic observed that Musin's ability to play bravura pieces matched any violinist outside of Sarasate and Wieniawski and that Tua was on the road to virtuosity and popular success. However, he drew a firm line between their musical qualities and those of Maud Powell. He called Maud the "most musicianly of the young lady violinists, whose playing is of the clean-cut classical school, and who deserves the highest praise of every one who desires to see real music replace fireworks on the violin."[8] Her choice of the Gade violin concerto ("the dullest concerto we have recently heard") "could not hide her really artistic powers." (Maud's performance of the concerto, written in 1880 by the Danish composer Niels Wilhelm Gade, may represent her first attempt to introduce a new composition to the United States.)

The young violinist carried a letter of introduction from Theodore Thomas to Wilhelm Gericke, the conductor of the Boston Symphony since 1883. Gericke engaged her to play the Bruch concerto with the seventy-five-member orchestra on March 5, 1887. Gericke (b. 1845) was the first great disciplinarian of the Boston Symphony, a regular drill master, reflecting his Austrian origins. In 1885, he engaged as concertmaster Franz Kneisel, a German violinist who distinguished the post until 1903. The nationality of the orchestra's conductor, concertmaster, and most of its musicians, like that of the New York Symphony, the Thomas Orchestra, and later the Philadelphia Orchestra, demonstrated that America's higher musical culture was largely imported, chiefly from Germany and Austria.

The presence of the standing-room-only audience on the night of March 5 was attributed to the excellence of the program offered — Schubert's "Unfinished" Symphony in B Minor, Brahms' *Hungarian Dances*, Liszt's symphonic poem *Les Préludes*, and Bruch's Violin Concerto in G Minor. The next two days' reviews indicate that Maud Powell conquered Boston that evening:

> Her playing of the Bruch concerto made a hit at once. Her tone is singularly large, warm and rich, her bowing and her finger work excellent and her phrasing artistic. . . . She is strong, straightforward and hearty, rather than a graceful or poetic, player, and gives evidence of true artistic feeling and appreciation. She was warmly received by the audience, and well won her reception.
>
> — *Boston Evening Transcript*

> Her style has almost a masculine breadth and is full of character, and yet there is much of the delicacy and refinement naturally associated with the violin playing of her sex. She has an easy, graceful stage presence, which predisposes the hearer in her favor. . . . Her playing of the beautiful adagio movement was full of sentiment and feeling, and the violin sang the leading theme with fine expression. The finale was given with splendid freedom, the solo instrument standing out with all desired prominence. Miss Powell gained an enthusiastic recognition of her sterling abilities, and richly merited the applause. . . . The orchestral accompaniment has never had such a brilliant performance as on this occasion, and it is very rarely

the . . . soloist appears to be so completely en rapport with the players of the band.
— *Boston Herald*

Maud's "easy, graceful presence and quiet manner" hardly prepared the critics for the "great degree of strength and vigor" with which she played. One critic wrote, "She must have frightened the first violinists just behind her. . . . Such breadth of tone, such boldness of attack, and such clear double-stopping are seldom heard."[9]

For all Maud's success in Boston, the difficulties she encountered in breaking down the prejudices against a woman violin virtuoso took their toll in those early years. Within one year of her death in 1920, Maud reflected on the sex-based barriers which she had had to overcome:

> When I first began my career as a concert violinist I did pioneer work for the cause of the American woman violinist, going on with the work begun by Camilla Urso. A strong prejudice then existed against women fiddlers, which even yet has not altogether been overcome. The very fact that a Western manager recently told Mr. Turner [her manager] with surprise that he "had made a success of a woman artist" proves it. When I first began to play here in concert this prejudice was much stronger. Yet I kept on and secured engagements to play with orchestra at a time when they were difficult to obtain.[10]

Early in her career, this prejudice affected her manner of playing the violin: "The fact that I realized that my sex was against me in a way led me to be startlingly authoritative and convincing in the masculine manner when I first played. This is a mistake no woman violinist should make. And from the moment that James Huneker wrote that I 'was not developing the feminine side of my work,' I determined to be just myself, and play as the spirit moved me, with no further thought of sex or sex distinctions which, in art, after all, are secondary."[11]

Perhaps at no point do Maud Powell's inner personal qualities and resources become more evident than in the years following her return to America. What contemporary critics called her "instantaneous success" as an artist did not prevent her from seeing that appreciation of her art in America was in its infancy. Outside of the cities along the "Highway" Theodore Thomas had cultivated, and even within those cities, were vast numbers of people who knew little of classical music. If these people were to participate in America's cultural growth, they would have to be sought out and patiently lured to new levels of music appreciation. Further, it was clear that one could not sustain a career solely on solo work with orchestras. She would have to utilize whatever forums were open to her for the propagation of her musical message.

As she contemplated her future career, Maud soberly assessed the possibilities in her own country, knowing that her sex was against her from the start and that she would pretty much have to "go it alone." The possibilities for the companionship of musical colleagues were centralized in a few large cities. Adding to her feeling of isolation, in her mind, at least, marriage and a career could not be combined.

The mantle of Theodore Thomas and Camilla Urso was heavy indeed. It would be a lot easier to return to Europe where the groundwork for appreciation of her art had already been laid, where it had been ingrained in the culture for centuries. No doubt there she would find ready acceptance. But Maud Powell was never to turn away from a task waiting to be performed, and the one that had fallen to her— to educate a nation, like her father, uncle, and grandfather before her—was a challenge certainly in keeping with her quintessentially American pioneer spirit. Lesser spirits might shrink at the prospect, but Maud Powell's was indomitable. While contemplating writing Maud's biography after her death, Godfrey Turner reflected: "If any young woman could really know what Maud Powell suffered for her art, she would not go into the game."[12]

In a sense, anyone with a gift for violin playing and application to the work might achieve the technical perfection for which Maud Powell was especially noted. Indeed, during her lifetime, other women violinists such as Kathleen Parlow, Geraldine Morgan, and Nettie Carpenter would achieve probably comparable skills, but Maud was always in a class by herself. Even among her male virtuoso contemporaries, she was a special artist, ranking with Kreisler and Ysaÿe.

It was character that made the difference in her art. Maud was forthright, open, and kind, and her violin playing conveyed these traits to the audience as clearly as the articles she wrote or the handclasp with which she greeted friends and strangers alike. There was a special intelligence, energy, and vigor in her playing, reflecting the brilliancy, optimism, and enthusiasm with which she met life. But just as she knew laughter and love and could make her audiences experience these emotions, she knew enough of pain and suffering to make her violin weep. As a youth all these emotions and traits were hers, and as they were broadened and deepened with experience of life her art reflected her growth as a human being.

If self-education and independence of mind can be considered to be markedly American traits, there was something particularly fitting about Maud's calling herself from the beginning an American player out and out, seldom referring to her education abroad. She once said, "The real education begins when you commence to work by yourself."[13] From the time she first appeared on the concert stage in the United States until her death, not a year went by that the critics did not note new growth in her violin playing, particularly in the breadth of her style and in the remarkable depth of her musical understanding.

The completion of her formal education simply meant for Maud that her real education was about to begin. What her teachers had given her were various approaches to the study of music and violin technique. They had given her insight into *how* to study; she now took the best from each and synthesized it with her own ideas until she molded her own approach. As she reflected:

> I do not believe that a pupil should remain too long under the guidance of teachers. Ordinarily eight years of uninterrupted work will suffice. As the budding artist develops in mind and character, independent study, together with the technique already attained, will secure an individuality of expression. By means of incessant mental and physical effort the technique or mechanism of the art will become so much a part of the performer that she will be able to give unhampered thought and attention to the meaning and mood (that is, to the interpretation) of the composer's work. The growing artist must give her individuality of expression every opportunity for development. Work independent of the teacher will tend to the cultivation of a critical judgment, while the performances and interpretations of others will assume a new and personal interest. She will watch her own work more closely, experimenting with awkward passages and difficult phrasings, learning thus how and what to select in order to achieve the best.[14]

She believed that the essence of success was "the determination to *excel*; a bull-dog instinct to stick grimly, ferociously to one's task, and not let go except with one's life."

During "the dark years," she practiced six or eight hours a day, usually with intermissions. She could easily practice for two and a half hours "in perfect self-forgetfulness, walking up and down the room," a habit her mother sometimes found tedious. "Can't you sit still for a little while?" Mrs. Powell would plead, but to no avail. "She is up again in a moment." For Maud, the movement eased the tension caused by the physical strain in playing the violin. Then too, it was natural for her to respond bodily to the music as she played. She found that it was hard not to do it on the stage. "The tendency is to walk about. There is a great strain in playing. There is the physical effort in standing and holding the arms raised, and then the position of the fiddle held up against the neck under the ear, vibrating against the vocal chords. Sometimes I get entirely out of breath."[15]

She understood the importance of a secure technique, constantly striving for technical mastery of her instrument which she could then bring to the service of music:

> Violin mastery or mastery of any instrument, for that matter, is the technical power to say exactly what you want to say in exactly the way you want to say it. It is technical equipment that stands at the service of your musical will—a faithful and competent servant that comes at your musical bidding. If your spirit soars "to parts unknown," your well trained servant "technic" is ever at your elbow to prevent irksome details from hampering your progress. Mastery of your instrument makes mastery of your Art a joy instead of a burden. Technic should always be the handmaid of the spirit.[16]

The security of her prodigious technique was remarkable throughout her life. Although she had been a prodigy who played with the intuition, instincts, and abandon of a born artist, her father's influence prevented her from suffering the after effects of purely intuitive playing. Maud learned from the beginning to play with a conscious understanding of the physical means by which technical requirements were met, and this spared her having to undo or remodel the habits she had formed prior to her study in Europe.

Maud drew an interesting comparison between talent and genius in advising young girls of the pitfalls to be avoided while learning the violin:

> Talent allied to intelligence and determination is not to be despised. It is sufficiently rare, but it is not that God-given divine fire we call "genius," a gift accorded only to the elect! Genius is a law unto itself: it surmounts difficulties over which mere talent must plod step by step. It "arrives" and cannot explain its methods. But, unfortunately, genius often lacks the balance-wheel of common-sense. It falls by the wayside, consumed by its own fire. Talent is more sane and, I may add, achieves where genius fails.[17]

In addition to her great technical skill, Maud's intuitive feeling for music was buttressed by a strong intelligence which she trained on the score, so that a profound intellectual understanding undergirded her interpretations of the violin literature. Like her father, she believed in learning from the original source, not from someone else's conception of it. Her musical interpretations defied classification as being of the Berlin school or of any other school in particular. A fellow violinist and long-time friend of Maud's observed, "From the first Miss Powell followed her unerring instinct and, while well taught, she reasoned out her own conclusions."[18]

She could not have designed a more thorough reasoning process for herself or one more calculated to result in an entirely original and individual conception of the works she performed. Study of the piano score or the orchestral score as well as the violin part was of great importance to preparation of any work. Her own facility on the piano was of invaluable help to her in this endeavor:

> Every violinist should play the piano. You will be at a great disadvantage if you cannot study your repertoire from the piano score. You will lose much by not being able to play accompaniments for others. What can you get out of a new composition—say a quintet, if you can look over only the violin part? If you play the piano, the complete score is yours. The piano is a useful servant. True, it is a poor mechanical contrivance of wires and ivories, but it is a library. The whole literature of music is yours, symphonies, operas, quartets, songs, et al., if you play the piano.
>
> A student must also study the theoretical, structural part of music—harmony, counterpoint, form and composition. Without these, you play without comprehension, memorizing by rote, phras-

ing parrotlike. You trust a little to taste, but more to luck. When reading a new composition, you do not know where the second theme begins, you are in a wilderness when you reach the "development," and fail to anticipate in time that you are coming to the "recapitulation." The thing is a muddle to you, structurally and harmonically. How can you convey anything of the composer's meaning to others if you know nothing of it yourself? You will be at a loss in chamber music. Indeed, you will get small chance to join others in that delightful work when they discover your superficiality.[19]

Before learning any new composition, Maud would get its structure well in mind, then analyze its different parts and knit them together, keeping in mind their relative bearing upon each other. All this work was done away from the piano and violin. Only then would she play the piece over in its entirety, either from the piano score or with an accompaniment to the violin. From this exercise, she would get an impression of the whole and its continuity. She would then let the work sink deeply into her consciousness. Her interpretations were then worked out mentally, away from her instrument.

The intellectual insight which each of her teachers had stressed enabled her to recreate each work at will and thus to infuse each performance with the spontaneity and improvisational qualities which breathe life into music. Her art was great because it was wholly her own, as violinist Edith Winn wrote:

Many women violinists, some American by birth, have come and gone. Maud Powell distanced them all, mainly because she allowed nothing to interfere with her conception of great works, no not even a creed or a school. Others played as taught, and were mere reflections of some great teacher. She used her brain in working out principles, and when away from the master's hand was able to make her future sure and successful by her own intelligence and superior musicianship. No one worked harder to perfect and add to an extensive repertoire. While others were content to be mere virtuosi, she was bent on being a broad musician and a truly educated woman. There were books on her table; there were thoughts in her mind of woman's work in all lines of activity; she felt the world's needs in the larger sense.[20]

Playing the violin is like writing one's signature; both reveal the identity of the person. One observer noted: "To hear her practice is a

great privilege. It prepares one for the broad conception, the absolute freedom and sincerity which marks all her performances. She
wanders to and fro, from one room to another, graceful, confident,
and unconfined. The woman herself is so gracious, so wholesome,
and so charmingly enthusiastic, that one cannot help but bow to her
sovereignty."[21] Maud's playing reflected her fundamental humanity,
and to these qualities audiences responded. The crest for her stationery, inscribed with *Esse quam videri* ("To be rather than to seem"),
reflected her belief that her art must be large enough to encompass
all life:

> A musician must study humanity before he can accomplish big things.
> I believe that all the master musicians were inspired psychologists,
> just as Shakespeare was in literature; that they had a wider human
> understanding vouchsafed them than is bestowed upon most men,
> because they had a message to deliver. But I believe they would
> never have realized the greatness of their missions, nor have attained
> to the true heights of their genius if they had not retired into them-
> selves and tested their knowledge by the experiences of their own
> souls. The results are incorporated in their works, and it is the
> interpreter's task to read and deliver the message correctly. And so I
> would that it were possible for all of us before we attempted to
> sound the depths of these inspired beings to retire into solitude,
> and study music by studying ourselves. It would make us better
> musicians.[22]

As Edith Winn observed, "Her imagination and humanitarian sympathy gave vitality to her conception of all works of all periods, but
she always felt the influences of achievements in war, science, philosophy, invention, political aspects too, as closely affiliated with
music."[23]

While the "dark years" broadened and deepened her human sympathies, Maud's abiding faith in and unquenchable enthusiasm for
her art brought her through, a stronger and more highly developed
person. Her "tenth rule" on practicing reflects the importance of
inner conviction: "*Love your instrument as yourself.* But love your art
more than either. Keep the fires of enthusiasm burning. Nothing
was ever accomplished without faith and enthusiasm."[24] The obliga-
tion she felt toward her fellow human beings helped to fire her imagination and enthusiasm: "The possibilities of mankind is the thing
which countless ages have striven to solve, and why does the young

artist not rise to his opportunity to add a little light to this superb problem? He has it within him if he will only seek for it, and he has no right to spend the time and energy that is necessary for a musical education, and then neglect to do so."[25]

These were the profoundly idealistic wellsprings of Maud Powell's life, and it was said that from the time of her debut forward she "created forever new standards of violin-playing," not only in America, but abroad as well. Her art both synthesized and transcended the artistic developments in Europe and provided a new conception of violin playing—one born of lofty ideals and rooted in originality of conception, developed largely independently of external influence. Maud Powell's transfusion of the American spirit into the age-old European traditions was a revelation to the musical world and made her legendary among violinists.

With the appearance of Maud Powell from 1885 on, Americans were to have their first opportunity to hear regularly a violinist of the first rank whose versatile musicianship allowed her to communicate with authority to her listeners the essence of any musical work, regardless of its style or period. And America was ready to receive what she had to teach. It was only appropriate that this thoroughly American artist would serve as the first great model for American violin playing. She had a nation to educate and perhaps no one was better equipped, more wholly prepared as a human being and as an artist, to perform that task.

10

Music and Musicians

*It's a complex fate, being an American, and one of the respon-
sibilities it entails is fighting against a superstitious valuation of
Europe.*

　　　　　　　　　　　　　　　　　　　—*Henry James, 1872*

*For masterpieces are not single and solitary births; they are the out-
come of many years of thinking in common, of thinking by the
body of the people, so that the experience of the mass is behind the
single voice.*

　　　　　　　　　　　　　　　　　　　　　　—*Virginia Woolf*

As she made her way in the musical world, Maud sought out music
and musicians to expand her own musicianship. In the fall of 1887,
she signed a three-year contract with New York manager L. M. Ruben.
Under his management Maud embarked on a prolonged "Western"
tour for the 1887–88 season about which very little is known except
that she did return to Aurora to perform in January. Theodore Thomas
also engaged her to perform with his orchestra at the Chicago Music
Teachers' Convention on July 6, 1888, where she was accorded "a
brilliant ovation" amid the "wildest enthusiasm." She was booked to
perform in Europe beginning in late summer.

　　By the time she appeared at the Oberlin Conservatory of Music
in Ohio, on March 9, 1888, her reputation had been well established. Musicians of the Conservatory, which had been founded in
1865, listened to her with high expectations which were "more than
realized." Although her finished technique and genuine musical feeling were noted with approval, her "wonderful tone, such as you don't
hear everyday" thoroughly enchanted them. They had not expected a

woman violinist to be capable of such breadth of tone and admitted their surprise as well as delight in hearing her produce "clear, full sonorous tones." They were equally amazed by the "surprising power" with which she played the finale to the Bruch concerto and the "wonderful delicacy and smoothness" of the passages in double stops in the Andante to the Mendelssohn concerto.[1]

Maud's recital programs, with piano accompaniment, had already begun to reflect her musical standards and her interest in educating her audiences. In addition to the Bruch and Mendelssohn concertos, she played Saint-Saëns' *Introduction and Rondo Capriccioso*, a sampling of Wagner's work through Wilhelmj's transcription of *Die Meistersinger*, a Chopin *Nocturne*, and even a *Caprice* by Ogarew. Thus, in one concert Maud gave aspiring musicians a good sampling of music of different styles and periods. Although it was a time of intense personal study and self-education, Maud had already begun her life work as the educator of a nation. She returned to the Oberlin Conservatory almost yearly at the request of the teaching faculty, who recognized in her an exquisite model of violin playing and musicianship for their students.

For two years, Maud absented herself from New York while she toured, studying scores, learning the art of dress and programming, reading books, developing her technique, and broadening herself, experimenting all the while. When she returned, it was to give the first movement of the Tchaikowsky violin concerto with Anton Seidl (b. 1850, Hungary), the conductor of the Metropolitan Opera who also conducted the "Metropolitan" orchestra in symphony concerts.[2] After serving as conductor of the Leipzig and the Bremen operas, Seidl had come to New York in the same year that Maud had made her debut. A close associate of Wagner in Bayreuth, he is credited with conducting the first performances in America of most of Wagner's operas between 1886 and 1889. Seidl was to succeed Theodore Thomas as music director of the New York Philharmonic in 1891. In this and his Metropolitan Opera post Seidl continued until his death in 1898.

The concert held on April 6, 1888, in Chickering Hall, marked the first time any portion of the Tchaikovsky concerto had been played with orchestra in the United States. Tchaikovsky had composed the concerto in 1878 for his violinist friend Yosif Kotek, who advised him how to make the concerto more violinistic. While the composer waited patiently but expectantly for his friend to perform the work,

Kotek balked at its difficulties and the concerto languished, unperformed. Disappointed, the Russian master re-dedicated the concerto to Leopold Auer, the renowned violinist at the St. Petersburg Conservatory in Russia, in the hope that he would give the work its first hearing. But Auer pronounced the work impossible to play (a judgment he later revised, playing it in November 1893, and then teaching it to all his pupils, including Heifetz, Elman, Zimbalist, and Parlow, who played it throughout the world).

Without the composer's knowledge, the Russian violinist Adolph Brodsky gave the world premiere in Vienna on December 4, 1881, with Hans Richter conducting. It was probably a poor performance. There was only one rehearsal, and the parts were filled with so many mistakes that the orchestra played the entire score *piano*, so that if anything went wrong it would be less noticeable!

The critics tore the work apart. Eduard Hanslick scathingly described the concerto as "music that stinks in the ear" in which the violin is no longer played but "torn asunder" and "beaten black and blue." Reading of the performance, the composer immediately wrote his thanks to the violinist and, in gratitude for his braving such criticism, transferred the dedication from Auer to Brodsky.

Despite Hanslick's critical epithets, Maud recognized that Tchaikovsky's spontaneous outpouring of melody and dancing rhythms was enormously appealing music. Maud's affinity with the concerto's Slavic passion and unabashed tunefulness probably convinced her that it was worthy of the attention of music lovers in her own country. It was a daring move on her part, knowing the potential for severely critical reviews that might inhibit the full flowering of a career well launched but still in its infancy. Perhaps the risks were lessened somewhat by the warmer reception given Brodsky's continuing championship of the concerto in Europe. However, because the work required the development of new technique, it was still a novelty in Europe and remained so to the turn of the century, when Maud herself played it in England. Some indication of the concerto's imposing nature from a nineteenth-century perspective can be derived from the fact that even Joachim did not attempt to play it in public, although he was known to have practiced it.

American interest in the concerto was heightened by the fact that the twenty-year-old artist's career was being followed closely by New York critics. After chastising Maud for her "seclusion" from

New York audiences, one critic's attention to her progress almost overshadowed his review of the concerto:

> Though we expected much of her, we were agreeably surprised to see that she surpassed our most sanguine previsions. Her selection was a very difficult one, and her excellent technique was tested to its utmost, but came out victorious; her bowing was large and even, her tone full and clear and sweet, though powerful, she plays with calm assurance and in a thoughtful and artistic manner, without any of the affectations of dash and childish ingenuousness, which the different young lady violinists we have lately heard seem to think indispensable. Miss Powell is without dispute the best of the young lady violinists of today. . . . Tchaikovsky's concerto was much admired and is a very interesting work; we regret that Miss Powell did not play the whole of it . . . [W]e hope that she will soon give . . . this concerto in its entirety.[3]

Among Maud's most valued letters was the one she received from Anton Seidl after the concert: "Beautiful as the concerto is, your splendid playing made it even more so."[4]

Ten months later, on January 19, 1889, Maud returned to New York to the Metropolitan Opera House to present Tchaikovsky's entire concerto for the first time with orchestra in the United States. Walter Damrosch conducted the New York Symphony in the performance. His father, Dr. Leopold Damrosch, had founded the New York Symphony Society in 1878, and it rivaled Theodore Thomas and the New York Philharmonic in giving new compositions their first American or even world performances.[5]

Maud's performance was hailed by the critics as a "brilliant achievement." Although the audience loved it, the "formidably difficult" work itself received mixed criticism, the first movement receiving highest praise for its combination of strength and coloratura passages. While the gracefulness and beauty of the second movement was noted, the critics added that it lacked "depth or breadth." The last movement was dismissed as "somewhat dry and uninteresting in both subject matter and treatment." The *New York Times* review indicates that Maud served Tchaikovsky's music well:

> Miss Powell's playing was not faultless, but its defects were pardonable, while its excellences were such as to entitle this lady to a very high position among female violinists. Her reading of the work was uncommonly intelligent; in fact, it was a wholly just and adequate

exposition. Her style was full of masculine power and of superb spirit. Her attack of the chords at the opening of the theme was so bold and certain as to chain the attention at once, and her entire handling of the movement was devoid of anything tentative or timid. She played the long and difficult cadenza with a roundness of tone, a brilliancy of bowing, an accuracy of stopping and a tastefulness in phrasing that were simply masterly. It was a treat to hear a woman play the violin so well, and only congratulations are to be offered to the lady. The repeated and warm recalls of the audiences were thoroughly deserved.[6]

In the 1890s, Maud continued to gain in artistic stature, bidding "fair to fulfill her early promise." When she played the Mendelssohn concerto with Theodore Thomas and the Brooklyn Philharmonic on January 17, 1890, one critic noted, "Her performance was distinguished by great clearness of design and, especially in the second movement, by dignity of style and elevation of sentiment."[7] The growing musician's performance of the same concerto four years later led one critic to write: "Miss Powell is a born artist, too conscientious to resort to trick for the purpose of capturing applause, and, being an artist, her moods are so variable that if one listens to her a hundred times it is only to come away, not only with gratification, but also puzzled to know how and by what witchery she contrives to render so varied the interpretation of the same work. She executes the Mendelssohn concerto as no other violinist in America can."[8] Backing her art were the intellect and spirit which Maud revealed in her program note:

> The popularity of the Mendelssohn Violin Concerto is deserved. Its spontaneity, its bubbling vivacity, its faultless contour will keep it young for all time. Romantic in spirit though classic in design, as Mendelssohn music is, this violin work is manifestly a most perfect expression of his genius and seems destined to go down in history as his masterpiece. Its appeal is to the old and young alike, to the musician and to the layman, and all conclude that while it may not equal the Beethoven Concerto in nobility and exaltation of spirit, it may be regarded, nevertheless, as the most perfect violin concerto ever written.[9]

Maud made many friends among the musicians of New York, contact with whom helped to expand her own musicianship as well as theirs. Among them were Frank G. Dossert, Henry Holden Huss, and Harry Rowe Shelley, all native Americans who were striving to compose as well as to perform and teach.

Frank Dossert was born of French parents in Buffalo, New York. He succeeded to his father's post as organist of the Buffalo Cathedral at fifteen and became especially noted as a voice teacher, a gift inherited from his mother. In 1882, he became the organist and music director of St. Stephen's Church in New York. His studio for teaching voice, piano, and composition was based in Carnegie Hall by the turn of the century. Eventually, he became music director of the Paris Conservatoire International d'Opéra et de Chant. His American wife was a mezzo-soprano, concert artist, voice teacher, and linguist. Together they established a private studio in Paris in conjunction with his New York studio. With Dossert, Maud experimented with organ accompaniment to the Bach sonatas for violin and harpsichord and tried out new music which he obligingly sent her from Europe.

Dossert came into international prominence with his Mass in E Minor, composed in 1888 and dedicated to Pope Leo XIII in honor of his golden jubilee. It was sung in Liverpool, Paris, Vienna, the principal cities of the United States, and at Saint Patrick's Cathedral in New York. Then in April 1892, the young American composer directed his Mass in St. Peter's on Easter Sunday with the pope celebrating. News of the event infused new hope into the struggling school of American composers. The sometimes awkward efforts of early American composers had been dismissed by their European counterparts: "In Europe we look upon America as an industrial country — excellent for electric telegraphs, but not for art."[10]

The paradox facing the American composer was that the European classical music tradition was at once his heritage and alien to his experience. Almost of necessity, American composers were trained by Europeans at home or abroad. They could either compose completely within the European tradition or attempt to develop a new "American" music, adapting European forms and techniques to create an art reflecting the American character and experience. Some American composers' attempts to write within the European tradition were of excellent quality, such as the violin sonatas of Mrs. H. H. A. Beach and Arthur Foote and the compositions of Horatio Parker and Edward MacDowell. The 1926 American supplement to *Grove's Dictionary* observed: "It is not . . . the absolutely original quality of American composition before 1900 that arrests attention —

except the remarkable work of MacDowell—but the fresh, ambitious, thoughtful and confident spirit that animates it." Here was a start, but the development of uniquely American music was still more difficult, requiring a synthesis which was largely beyond the Americans' reach before the twentieth century.

As Americans devoted themselves to pioneer life on the frontier and later to unparalleled agricultural, commercial, and industrial growth, the song of their struggles welled up from the earth—raw and unrefined, naive, boisterous, unselfconscious, optimistic, boundless, imaginative and free—as varied and complex as the immense land itself. To transform American folk art into a cultivated art required not only synthesis but time as well. Henry James described what was required for development of the American writer: "[The] moral is that the flower of art blooms only where the soil is deep, that it takes a great deal of history to produce a little literature, that it needs a complex social machinery to set a writer in motion. American civilization has hitherto had other things to do than to produce flowers, and before giving birth to writers it has wisely occupied itself with providing something for them to write about."[11] But in time, Emerson's interest in development of a truly American culture flowered with the robust poetry of Walt Whitman and Carl Sandburg, and the humor of Mark Twain and evocative fiction of Willa Cather: bold, imaginative, full of life; while in painting there emerged the peculiarly American scenes, colors, and brush strokes of Winslow Homer, Frederic Remington, and George Bellows.

As for music, in which the means of expression are so much more difficult to master, sophistication came more slowly. The raw materials were there, in the Indian's chant, the colonist's hymnody, the African slave's rhythmic melodies. Besides these, the indestructible melodies of Stephen Foster, including "Oh, Susanna" and "Old Folks at Home," and sheaves of patriotic hymns, marching tunes, and stirring songs spawned by the Civil War were uniquely American but were not successfully transfused into the classical music tradition until the advent of Charles Ives (1874–1954). Music required more time to incubate.

It must be remembered that the institutional foundations for classical music in America were being laid between 1860 and 1920—during Maud's lifetime.[12] Music conservatories began to appear only after the Civil War. One of the first was formed by the Peabody

Institute in Baltimore in 1860 (completed in 1868). The Oberlin Conservatory was established in 1865, followed in 1867 by the New England Conservatory of Music in Boston, the Cincinnati Conservatory, and the Chicago Musical College. In 1869 the Philadelphia Musical Academy came into being, followed by the Cleveland Conservatory in 1871, the Detroit Conservatory in 1874, the College of Music in Cincinnati in 1878, the New York College of Music in 1878, the Cleveland School of Music in 1884, the National Conservatory of Music in New York in 1885, the Chicago Conservatory in 1885, the Northwestern Conservatory in Minneapolis in 1885, the American Conservatory in Chicago in 1886, and the Toronto Conservatory in the same year. The Institute of Musical Art in New York, which merged with the Juilliard Foundation in 1926, was not founded until 1904. New York's Mannes Music School was founded in 1916 by the violinist David Mannes, and the San Francisco Conservatory was established in 1917.

Due to Lowell Mason's efforts in the 1830s and those of later educators like Bramwell Powell, music became a part of the public school curriculum in the United States, and institutions for higher learning built on that development. Musical instructors had been at Oberlin College since 1838, and at both Yale College and the University of Virginia since 1849. After 1860, other significant appointments were made, beginning with John Knowles Paine (whose orchestral music was the first to demonstrate a complete grasp of the symphonic idiom) at Harvard in 1862. Harvard established the first full professorship in music in 1875, followed closely by the University of Pennsylvania, Yale University, and others. In 1876 the Music Teachers' National Association was founded, followed by the Music Educators' National Conference in 1907.

Maud understood the difficulties facing the American composer, for she saw clearly the outlines and trends of history.[13] But she coupled her insight with characteristic optimism for the future of American music and did her best to encourage American composers.

By 1890, Maud had formed a lasting friendship with Henry Holden Huss, born in Newark, New Jersey, in 1862. A fine pianist, he studied first with his father and then at the Munich Conservatory, graduating in 1885. He composed a great deal of instrumental music, including a piano concerto, violin and cello sonatas, a piano trio, and even a string quartet at Ysaÿe's request.

For Maud, he would compose a violin concerto, dedicated to her, as well as *Romanza in E* for violin. In a letter to Dossert, she draws a comical picture of an evening of concert-going with Huss in June 1890. The occasion was the opening of the new Madison Square Garden with Eduard Strauss and his Imperial Court Orchestra. Fifteen thousand people gathered to hear the "Waltz King of the World":

The last music I heard in New York (it would be more correct to say *tried* to hear, for the hall was so vast that the proper effect was lost) was the much advertised Strauss orchestra and their military and very angular director. He is simply ludicrous to look at, with a bow-arm to make a violinist's eyes ache. However, he infuses a marked individuality into his band, more in the way of splendid rhythm and elastic rubatos than anything else. Mr. Huss, who was my escort, afforded me much amusement for he seemed positively miserable listening to "dance-tunes." His impatience was comical to see. I am afraid I said one or two rather mean things at the time in order to vindicate my own keen enjoyment of the sprightly and swinging rhythms.[14]

Maud kept an observant eye on the developments which were to shape the coming season:

I was to have gone on a three months tour with [Eduard] Strauss and his orchestra but the contract was broken as Strauss' physician forbade his undertaking the extra work of conducting my accompaniments, on account of his growing ill-health. It seems that the heat in N.Y. has nearly prostrated him and that he has lost fifteen pounds of flesh. More than one foreigner finds on visiting America now-a-days that he can't pocket the shekels without some hard work. I suppose our N.Y. season will be very full again this year. Ondříček the violinist will be over and I fancy Scharwenka will make an American tour. He has been over here this Summer reconnoitering and who knows, perhaps he will transfer his Conservatory to the soil of the United States.[15]

Xaver Scharwenka (b. 1850) was a German pianist renowned for the beautiful quality of his tone, "rich, round, soft, yet great, and singing." In 1881, he had opened his own conservatory in Berlin, which after 1893 was known as the Klindworth-Scharwenka Conservatorium. Maud read his actions clearly, for the Scharwenka Conservatory of Music opened its doors in New York on September 28, 1891.

Earlier, European instruction in America had been furthered by
Henry Schradieck's arrival in Cincinnati in 1883. Overburdened with
duties in Leipzig, Maud's former master had accepted an appointment as conductor and violin teacher at the Cincinnati College of
Music, a post he retained until 1889. He settled permanently in the
United States around 1894, serving as principal violin professor at
the National Conservatory in New York until 1899, when he went to
Philadelphia. There, he taught at the South Broad Street Conservatory, and after 1912 he was affiliated also with the American Institute
of Applied Music in New York.

The arrival of such masters as Schradieck and Scharwenka was
well timed, as Americans were, by the 1880s, becoming economically
and culturally capable of receiving the training European musicians
of the first rank had to offer.

Despite the Strauss cancellation, in early 1891 Maud hastily scribbled a note to Dossert indicating that she was "desperately busy."
She had organized a string quartet, "which takes much time," while
preparing new works for her solo engagements. All she could see
ahead of her was "a confused mass of work, work, work."[16]

Little is known of this quartet, although it was probably the second professional female string quartet to be formed in the United
States. The earlier Eichberg Quartette had been formed in 1878 by
pupils of Julius Eichberg, the first director of the Boston Conservatory, and continued into the 1890s.

Maud was preparing for the American premiere of Saint-Saëns'
Violin Concerto No. 2 in C, composed in 1879, as well as the world
premiere of Harry Rowe Shelley's violin concerto, to be given less
than two weeks apart. She played the former with Theodore Thomas
and the Brooklyn Philharmonic on February 14, 1891. The concerto
was hailed as a "good specimen of the sound and many sided musicianship of Saint-Saëns."[17] While the critics for the *Times* and the
Tribune simply noted that she "played in her usual style" and in an
"exceedingly intelligent and tasteful manner,"[18] the critic for the
Musical Courier of February 18 wrote:

> Maud Powell has made great strides in her art lately, as everyone
> knows. She plays now with a color and warmth that have hitherto
> been absent. I am not enough of a Saint-Saëns fanatic to admire
> everything he has done, consequently I cannot praise without stint

the second concerto that Miss Powell played at the last Brooklyn Philharmonic concert. But how she did play it!

The cadenza was delivered in a manner that stamps Miss Powell as an artist *hors ligne*.

If I were a conventional music critic I would speak of more ripeness of conception, &c., but being an everyday truthful mortal I confess at once that Miss Powell was the master of the work from the outset; it did not master her.

Maud had known Saint-Saëns in Paris and had once described him as "the intellectual, the witty, the eccentric, the widely travelled and widely read, the critic, composer, virtuoso, pedagogue, commander of the Legion of Honor, Dr. Mus. Ox." She frequently played his *Introduction and Rondo Capriccioso*, describing it to her audiences as a "wonderfully clever" piece which would "probably stand the test of time as well as anything he has ever composed." She further observed: "Written in real violin idiom, with rhythmic charm and of crystalline clarity of material it has long been a prime favorite with violinists."[19] She played this piece at Seidl's Fourth Sunday Concert in the spring of 1891 "in the most finished manner, and showed her easy, elastic bowing, beautiful tone and vigorous style." The Hungarian violinist Reményi was in the audience that night.

Shelley's concerto was given on February 23, 1891, in a concert devoted to American composers at the Brooklyn Academy of Music under the auspices of C. Mortimer Wiske. Wiske had attracted much attention with his decision to devote an entire concert in his Brooklyn series to American works. Maud probably had met Shelley (b. 1858, Connecticut) in New York, since he was the organist of the Church of Pilgrims in Brooklyn. Known as a composer for piano, organ, and orchestra, but chiefly as a songwriter, he composed his only violin concerto in Switzerland in the summer of 1890 and dedicated it to Maud Powell. While Shelley's concerto was one of the few compositions presented which received favorable comment, it fell short of having lasting value. The *Times* reported on February 24 that although the concerto contained "some good melody," the orchestral part was "weak and without color." However, "the work was beautifully performed by Maud Powell, whose tone was strong and brilliant and whose bowing was vigorous."

The concert as a whole was excoriated by the critics, including Henry Krehbiel, who wrote:

Truth compels the confession . . . that the American composer never suffered half so much from neglect as he did from attention at this concert. . . . After nearly two hours of painful endurance the strongest impression that could be carried away from the concert was that it was the urgent duty of the Manuscript Society, or some other body of American musicians, to appoint a guardian ad litem or next friend to sue out a writ of injunction against Mr. Wiske if ever again he should undertake to patronize the American music in the way of a National concert.[20]

Assistance for the American composer was coming, in the form of Dr. Antonin Dvořák. In 1892, the fifty-one-year-old Bohemian composer agreed to become the director of the National Conservatory of Music in New York. He was to head a faculty comprising such musicians as Victor Herbert (conductor, composer, and cellist), James G. Huneker (pianist, musicologist, and music critic), Horatio Parker (composer), and Raphael Joseffy (pianist). Dvořák's appointment was hailed as a symbol of America's readiness to excel in the development of its own musical culture, as it had in agriculture and industry.

When Dr. Dvořák arrived in New York in late September, New York critic H. E. Krehbiel pointed to the composer's background and accomplishments as particularly fitting to the American character.[21] He had risen from humble peasant origins in his native Bohemia to world renown by virtue of native talent, tireless effort, and persistence in the face of adversity—and without formal education in composition. Here was a European appropriately fitted to guide American composers toward original creative effort. Dvořák had a very clear idea of his mission in America. He said, "I came to discover what young Americans had in them, and to help them to express it."[22]

It was the age of "national" composers, among whom Dvořák was foremost.[23] He gave his music a distinctly national flavor by drawing on native folk melodies for the wealth of melody, color, and rhythm which characterized his works. Nationalism was the means by which composers of those countries whose tradition had been dominated by the Austro-German influence sought to throw off that domination. Of these composers, Dvořák and Tchaikovsky remained largely within the mainstream of the German romantic tradition, while others such as Grieg, Smetana, Sibelius, Nielsen, and Elgar composed within a more distinctly national idiom. It was Dvořák's individuality and originality of invention within that tradition which drew American attention to his observations and counsel concerning their own dilemma.

The American composer needed to be freed to expand Old World forms to accommodate the expression of the New World. In order to accomplish this, Dvořák adjured American composers to turn to the folksongs of America for inspiration, a movement for which another Powell pioneer was laying a foundation. Maud's aunt Juliet Powell Rice, a pioneer in the teaching of folk music, transcribed many Indian songs into standard notation as an outgrowth of her interest (as well as that of her brother Wes) in ethnology.[24]

Dvořák believed that Negro and Indian melodies must be the real foundation of any serious and original school of composition to be developed in the United States.[25] He convincingly demonstrated what could be done by composing the Symphony *From the New World*, which was premiered by the New York Philharmonic with Anton Seidl conducting in Carnegie Hall on December 16, 1893.[26] The young American composers got the point and many, such as Arthur Farwell, Henry F. Gilbert, Charles Wakefield Cadman, and Cecil Burleigh, consciously followed his advice. All of these composers Maud knew, and in keeping with her American sympathies, she championed their works by playing them throughout the country on her annual tours.

If she had not made his acquaintance in Europe, Maud met the Bohemian composer shortly after his arrival in New York. She was eager to give his Violin Concerto in A Minor its first performance in the United States. The violinist found its sustained flow of melody, harmonic richness, and rhythmic vitality enormously appealing music, a judgment, however, her former master Joachim did not share.

Dvořák had composed the concerto in 1879 in response to a commission by Joseph Joachim, possibly at the urging of Brahms. Even after the composer altered the completed score to suit the great violinist, Joachim remained dissatisfied, and the music languished in his hands without a hearing. Two years later Dvořák terminated the agreement with Joachim and offered the first performance to his countryman Frantisek Ondříček, who gave the premiere in Prague in 1883.

Planning to introduce the concerto first with piano on her forthcoming tour of Ohio, Maud sought out the composer for his advice. It would be doubly valuable since Dvořák himself played the violin. Upon hearing her proposal to premiere the work, the normally reticent man with a furrowed brow, a high forehead looming above large, searching eyes, warned her that Joachim had once said the concerto was too difficult for any woman to play. Undeterred, Maud proceeded to play the concerto for the composer. When she finished, he arose in great delight to congratulate her, proposing puckishly that he "should write to Joachim at once that he had found a woman who could play his concerto perfectly."[27]

In her recital at Oberlin Conservatory on November 18, 1892, Maud brought her "deeply musical temperament" and "almost unlimited technical skill" to bear in "well-balanced proportion" to reveal the concerto's "great beauty and worth."[28] Its qualities were "at once deeply felt" by her musically literate audience which immediately ranked the work next to the Mendelssohn and Bruch concertos. The listeners further appreciated the violinist's "gift of making one see and feel the beauties of the composition, and forgetting the presence of the performer." Her appearance on stage was called "unconscious grace itself," an allusion to Maud's complete absorption in the music once it began. Upon completion of her tour, Maud returned to New York triumphant, reporting to Dvořák that his concerto had been received everywhere with the "greatest enthusiasm."

When the time came to premiere the concerto with orchestra, Maud again sought the composer's guidance. The work was to be performed on April 7, 1894, in Carnegie Hall. The New York Philharmonic was to be conducted by Anton Seidl, Theodore Thomas's successor and a good friend of Dvořák. It was a busy season for Maud, but she prepared the work carefully. In a hastily-written letter to her friend Henry Holden Huss dated March 4, she reveals the thoroughness with which she prepared for the performance:

> I have heard from Mr. Bergner who says he cannot help me in the violin matter. Do you think my Amati will be overpowered? To be sure the tone is not heroic but is it so small that it sounds crushed and overwhelmed in a vigorous work vigorously orchestrated and vigorously accompanied? You heard it at [illegible] Hall—tell me your impression. You spoke of the G string jamming—that I can eliminate to a great extent by a slight change of interpretation—but more power I cannot give it. You know Seidl's tendency—to spell vigor with a big "V"—and you know too how resonant the orchestra is in Carnegie Hall. Did you hear me play there with Van der Stucken just after the Arion European trip? You could judge somewhat by

that though of course the Philharmonic orchestra is larger than that Stucken had.

I hope I am not bothering you too much. I shall be very grateful to have you give me your frank opinion.[29]

The violinist's painstaking preparation produced worthwhile results, according to the next day's *New York Sun*: "Miss Powell's rendering of Dvořák's concerto deserves nothing but the highest commendation. It was a praiseworthy effort from every point of view, distinguished by purity and beauty of tone, facile fingering, skillful bowing, and a masterly command of the intellectual requirements of this elaborate piece of writing, which is a most valuable addition to violin literature." At the concert's conclusion, Dvořák found his way to the artist's room to give her his personal thanks for her beautiful performance.[30]

11

Worlds Apart

No one can love a symphony or an opera who does not first love song.

—*John Wesley Powell*

AS SHE ATTEMPTED TO EXPAND APPRECIATION FOR HER ART throughout America, Maud performed in every forum open to her, touring on her own or even with bands or singing societies. While she often gave recitals wholly on her own, assisted only by a pianist, she sometimes appeared with a great singer like Lillian Nordica. Combinations of artists were still common as traveling concert troupes, because it was felt that the smaller towns along the route needed variety in order to draw audiences and sustain their interest. Maud's touring experiences with the Gilmore Band and the New York Arion Society reflect the contrast between the musical atmosphere at home and abroad.

THE GILMORE BAND TOUR

When Maud began her tour with Patrick Gilmore and his band in the spring of 1891, the distinguished band leader, born in Ireland in 1829, was the ripe age of sixty-one.[1] Gilmore's irrepressible love for music and enthusiasm for life on a grand scale had given him the gift of perennial youth, leading some observers to remark that he always looked like he had just popped new out of a bandbox!

No other name was more closely associated with the rise of bands and band music in America than that of Patrick Sarsfield Gilmore. While bands had always been associated with military units in America's history, the invention in Germany around 1815 of valves for cornets, trumpets, and horns had provided these instruments with a flexibility which enabled bands to develop into vernacular counterparts to the symphony orchestra. It was on this technical development that Gilmore capitalized when he arrived in Boston in 1859, a cornet virtuoso, and began to reorganize the Boston Brigade Band. In his hands, the thirty-two-member band became a professional concert-giving and dance-playing organization known as Gilmore's Grand Boston Band.

During the Civil War, Gilmore became bandmaster for the Union Army, during which time he organized his first large festival concert.[2] Upon the conclusion of hostilities, he organized the National Peace Jubilee, an immense extravaganza which was destined to bring him lasting fame.[3] In 1873, he became director of the band of the Twenty-second Regiment of New York. It was this band which he developed into probably the greatest in the world, without peer from 1880 until Gilmore's death in 1892.

Gilmore was a first-rate musician who loved classical music as well as popular tunes. He composed such enduring patriotic songs as "Columbia" and "When Johnny Comes Marching Home Again" and had a good deal of the classical literature arranged for band. While the genial Irishman primarily sought to please his audiences, he also attempted to instill in them an appreciation for the classics, contributing in his own way to musical progress in America. Gilmore further advanced music appreciation by giving copies of selections played by his bands to other bands that he encountered in his travels.

His artistic standard was a high one, leading him to seek out professional musicians of the greatest talent for his band. One of his associates said that "all of his players, the elite of the musical profession and artists from all musical countries, were the greatest players on their respective instruments."[4] No band could rival Gilmore's for the smoothness, flexibility, and precision of its playing, nor for its wide-ranging repertoire. Classical music arrangements were kept as close to the original as possible, regardless of the difficulty of execution. Even though he was a severe drillmaster, his men said it was a pleasure to play for him.

Following the example of Theodore Thomas, Gilmore and his band toured the country annually. His name had become synonymous with excellence in programming, combining showmanship and variety with quality. Consequently, his concerts drew large, enthusiastic audiences.

Gilmore achieved a perfectly balanced band of brass and woodwind instruments by maintaining a ratio of two woodwinds to one brass. He often argued with orchestra conductors that a band of one hundred players, properly chosen, could play the great classical music as effectively as a symphony orchestra. It was with such a band that Maud Powell was invited to tour during April and May of 1891.

The Gilmore Festival Tour of 1891 featured seven soloists. Reflecting the times, Maud was the only instrumentalist, while all the rest were opera singers: the great tenor Italo Campanini, Ida Klein, Louise Natali, Anna C. Mantell, Spigaroli, and Sartori. Seventy-five concerts were to be given in less than two months on a grueling tour that began in the East, probably in April, and then moved west to Chicago and back to New York in May. As might be expected, the programs featured a potpourri of opera selections, orchestral music, popular music, and a variety of violin pieces. Chicago critics called the performances of Campanini and Powell the "artistic features of these concerts."[5]

On May 3, Gilmore's tour reached the half-way point with a concert at the Lenox Lyceum in New York. This scheduling provided Maud with an opportunity to meet Tchaikovsky, as Carnegie Hall's inaugural concert was given two days later with Campanini and the first American appearance of Tchaikovsky, who had come to conduct his *Marche Solennelle*.

By May 15 and 16, 1891, Maud and the Gilmore Band were in Chicago for three concerts. The band played with the "dash and spirit, the technical accuracy and . . . the furious tempo which have made Gilmore's band famous." After every number at least one encore had to be given.[6] Chicago critics were particularly interested in the young violinist, since they claimed her as their own:

> Miss Powell is making rapid strides in her art, and at the present rate of advancement the time is not far distant when her position among the foremost of the world's lady violinists will be assured. Her playing possesses great breadth and virility, combined with the delicacy and poetry expected in a woman of refinement. The tone she produces is full of warmth and soul, while the expression and intelligence characterizing her work show the presence of the feu sacre which vitalizes and glorifies all it touches. Last evening Miss Powell played Sarasate's *Faust Fantasie*—a work bristling with difficulties of every description—with splendid effect, winning a double

encore, to which she responded with an Etude and Moszkowski's *Serenata*.[7]

While in Chicago, the artist met with a couple who looked in on her for a family friend in Peru. Describing Maud as a "beautiful girl, with large brown eyes and a fine complexion," the lady wrote that her "sensitive face is that of an artist and all her movements are graceful." The musician spoke freely about her professional life, stating plainly that she did not think she would ever marry, as it would "interfere with her career." Maud's visitors further reported, "She is said to be kind and generous, especially to young violinists, and to have a devoted circle of friends."[8]

By May 31, 1891, the touring company was back in New York to kick off Gilmore's series of concerts at Madison Square Garden. Maud's last performance with Gilmore was given there on June first. In another year, he died on tour in St. Louis on September 24, 1892. Two days later, John Philip Sousa's newly-founded band played its debut concert at Plainfield, New Jersey. The first number was Gilmore's "The Voice of a Departed Soul." Said to have been more popular than the president of the United States during his lifetime, Gilmore's hold over the public seemed undiminished even after his death. In 1906, more than 12,000 people attended a concert in his memory in Madison Square Garden given by John Philip Sousa and Gilmore's successor, Victor Herbert.

THE NEW YORK ARION SOCIETY TOUR

When the New York Arion Society toured Austria and Germany for the first time in its history, Maud Powell, "the famed American violin virtuoso," was chosen to accompany the group.[9]

Founded in 1854, the Arion Society was a musical club whose primary purpose was to promote *mannergesang*, the German part-song for men's voices. The existence of a number of these societies throughout America did much to promote popular musical culture in a country where the piano, sheet music, and song were the most popular forms of entertainment. The continual influx of German-speaking immigrants into the United States during the nineteenth and early twentieth centuries supplied fresh enthusiasm for these clubs. Frequently they reached a high degree of professionalism, and in New York, at least, the Arion Society even provided choruses for the first professional productions of operas like Wagner's *Tannhäuser* and *Lohengrin*.

The artistic standards were notably high in the Arion Society due to the high calibre of the voices, the dedication of the members, and the quality of leadership provided by Frank Van der Stucken, who had succeeded Leopold Damrosch as director in 1884.[10] Born of German and Belgian parents in Texas in 1858, Van der Stucken had received his musical education abroad and had been encouraged as a composer by Grieg and Liszt. He was an advocate of new music, especially by American composers, and his concert of American compositions at the Paris Exposition in 1889 won him election as an "officier d'Academie." In 1895 he was appointed musical director of the College of Music in Cincinnati and conductor of the new Cincinnati orchestra. His excellence as a conductor prompted the great Belgian violinist Ysaÿe to remark that he was "exceptionally gifted" and "most attentive" in leading that "magnificent orchestra" in a 1905 concert.[11]

On June 25, 1892, the sixty singers embarked on the steamship *Wieland* for their tour, which included the cities of Hamburg, Berlin, Leipzig, Dresden, Vienna, Munich, Stuttgart, Heidelberg, Frankfurt, Wiesbaden, Mainz, Bingen, and Cologne.[12] The two instrumental soloists were pianist Franz Rummel and Maud, who was escorted by her mother, as always during these years. Frank Dossert was a member of the chorus.[13]

Arriving in Hamburg on July 10, 1892, the Arions were officially received with "music, cheers and hearty greetings." Their first concert was scheduled for July twelfth.

Throughout the tour, Van der Stucken had arranged to employ the local professional orchestras to accompany the chorus, but because of the season, the musicians' vacations often frustrated his plan. In Hamburg, the resourceful conductor had to engage a military band. Under Van der Stucken's patient but strict leadership, the musicians performed satisfactorily even though they had not kept up their string instrument practice.

More than 3,000 people, including Hamburg's elite, a host of Americans, and hundreds of singers from local societies, crowded into Ludwig's concert house in St. Pauli for the concert. Arnold Krug, the composer and conductor; Julius von Bernuth, director of the Philharmonic and the Hamburg Conservatory; the director of the

Steinway factory there; and Henry Schradieck, who was then professor of violin at the Hamburg Conservatory, were in the audience.

The Arions fairly took the audience by storm, and when it was Maud's turn to perform, the men smiled inwardly, anticipating her impact on the unsuspecting crowd. One of the chorus described her appearance for the *Musical Courier*: "Miss Maud Powell was the first soloist and a most powerful and pleasant surprise to the Hamburgers. They evidently had not yet heard of the *facile princeps* [the acknowledged chief] among the American violinists, but they were by no means slow in appreciating her. She played the Bruch G minor concerto with her wonted finish, beauty of tone and exquisite musical feeling and she was overwhelmed with applause."

The Arions were greeted with a "marked crescendo" of enthusiasm in Berlin. Representatives of numerous singing societies officially welcomed them and sent them on their way amid the "hurrahs of the Berliners." A string of 125 carriages, all adorned with American flags, took them through the principal streets of the city to their hotels.

Again left without an orchestra, they had to substitute the band of the Third Regiment of the Guard of Spandau, who were found to be incapable of playing the accompaniments to the Bruch violin concerto and the Liszt E-flat piano concerto. Both Maud and Rummel therefore had to forego playing with orchestra.

The Arions impressed the musicians and critics in the audience, who admitted that they had never heard "a gathering of dilettanti sing with so much artistic unity and conception."[14] Everything was "refined, polished and yet strong." Dressed in white with gold shoes, Maud performed Saint-Saëns' *Introduction and Rondo Capriccioso*, to which the audience of ten thousand responded with enthusiasm, demanding several recalls.

It is probable that Joseph Joachim was in the audience that night and that Maud and her mother visited with him during their brief stay in Berlin. Max Bruch was present, adding to Maud's disappointment that his concerto had had to be omitted.

The Arions were greeted by cheering crowds when they arrived in Maud's "dear old Leipzig" late in the evening of July thirteenth. The enthusiasm at the concert there was even more pronounced and spontaneous than it had been in Hamburg and Berlin. Maud "created a furore with the Bruch G minor concerto, and later on with the Nardini *Larghetto* and Sarasate's . . . *Zapateado*." She was in "grand form" that night, no doubt energized by her return to those beloved surroundings.

By the time the Arions arrived in Vienna, one member reported, "all of us were pretty broken up." "Traveling on the American plan, even when you can command a special train, is more than fatiguing, if you cannot at the same time enjoy American comforts," he commented. But their reception in Vienna overshadowed everything they had witnessed up to that time and quite overwhelmed them. Word of their excellence had preceded them from city to city on the tour, until in Vienna they were received like gods. Although it was nearly midnight, and they were more than an hour late, a crowd of 800 was on the station platform to greet them. They were hailed as the "Knights of the Holy Grail of German Song."

In spite of their weariness, the Arions knew that in Vienna they must reach the highest artistic standards because they had a rival "worthy of their mettle in the celebrated Viennese Mannergesangverein." "[E]verybody was bound to do his level best or die." As a result of their efforts, members of the Vienna singing society declared that a number of the choral performances "could not be equaled, let alone surpassed." In the home city of the notorious critic Eduard Hanslick, the critics praised the Arion performances without stint. The audiences were deeply stirred, applauding furiously, and at the end showing their enthusiasm with "handkerchief waving, hat throwing and acclamation so hearty and so outspoken" as to amaze and overwhelm the performers.

A large part of their success in Vienna was attributed to the two soloists.[15] At the first concert, Maud "created a perfect furore with the Bruch G minor concerto, the Chopin nocturne in E flat and Sauret *Farfalla*," and she had to play a number of encores. The next day, the Vienna papers unanimously declared her the greatest living lady violinist. One of the Viennese critics had much to say about the twenty-four-year-old violinist's appearance:

> Maud Powell promises to be a star of the first rank. She has a very impressive technic and a tender touch. She plays with a smooth bow which gives the violin a golden, rich tone that only a real artist can produce, an artist like Maud Powell. Her melody is singing; it is as

lovely as her appearance. A well-shaped head is placed on a very delicate figure, a figure which only sways with particularly graceful movement. Her repose and distinguished appearance comport with her serious countenance which is accentuated by her dark, thick eyebrows. A strong will speaks out of this woman's face, which tells you that she is a hard-working person, a real American, purposeful and determined. She plays in the same way. When she finishes her playing and realizes the enormous applause, a smile comes to her face and she becomes a simple young girl. The Bruch concerto was in all movements excellent. In the piece for violin and piano, the Chopin nocturne in E flat, she was not quite as perfect in the staccato. In the Sauret *Farfalla* she tried to make up for that. But with an unforgettable intimacy and softness, she played *Crépuscule* by Massenet. Against a violinist like this, Mr. Rummel had a formidable task before him in attempting to match her performance.[16]

For the second performance, the orchestra, specially brought together for these concerts, arose as the young violinist entered the stage, a highly unusual compliment, which she returned by playing Mendelssohn's violin concerto "gloriously."[17] When she completed that masterpiece, the "audience arose as one man" and "surged forward to the stage, applauding and shouting."[18] The audience simply would not stop applauding although she returned to the stage repeatedly. Maud recalled, "When I played there they stood upon their chairs and applauded; they came down to the front and gathered around me; they kissed my hands and my skirt, and I was glad to get back to my hotel to escape them."[19] But she could not escape until she had played two encores, including her own transcription of Massenet's "gem of a song" *Crépuscule* (Twilight).

The Viennese public, which was known for its high standards and which had heard all the greatest violinists of the century, manifested its esteem for Maud's artistry by presenting her with baskets of flowers. The ribbon on one was engraved: "Möge immer wie in Wien— dir verdientes Lob erblüh'n" (May your success bloom like the flowers in Vienna). The critics, in reporting her "enormous success," exclaimed that "with Maud Powell, there is a new shining star on the American musical horizon."[20] At a luncheon held in the Tonhalle with about 300 people present, Dr. Jacques, a silver-haired, high-ranking mem-

ber of the Reichstag, spoke for all of Vienna when he raised his glass
in a toast to the Arions:

> But I may not speak solely of the songs. I also have to include
> the exquisite instrumental performance, particularly the accomplish-
> ments of this blessed girl, out of whose miracle violin a whole sky of
> poetry, of most delicate feelings, and with it a downright victorious
> mastering of all technical and material aspects, emerged.
>
> A Jeanne d'Arc of music is what I would like to call Miss Maud
> Powell, because under her guidance and participation it can only go
> upward from triumph to triumph. A musical defeat where she rules,
> is an impossibility. . . .
>
> If you had sung your songs on the ocean to the dolphins, or if
> they had heard those violin tones of Miss Maud, they would have
> nestled against your feet and would have allowed you to ride on
> their backs, as according to Herodot's legend, the delphic of Arion
> did.[21]

News of the success of the Arion tour was cabled along the route
to the New York papers, and even English musical journals reported
its progress, noting that the group had in its company "one of the
best American violinists."[22]

After its triumphant return to America, the Arion Society gave a
charity concert in Carnegie Hall October 30, 1892. Maud performed
Bruch's G minor concerto with fresh "freedom and buoyancy" and
Saint-Saëns' *Introduction and Rondo Capriccioso* with "verve and
abandon," the critics noting the improvement in her playing:

> Miss Powell is fulfilling the promise of her first appearances. It
> is a genuine pleasure to watch the growth of such a sincere and
> studious artist. Her performance of Bruch's G minor concerto last
> night was noble in the breadth and dignity, not only of its tone,
> but of its sentiment. There was depth in the first movement, repose
> in the second, and vigor in the third. Its technical excellences were
> supplemented by those of the lady's playing in the Saint-Saëns
> *Introduction and Rondo Capriccioso*. In the two numbers, Miss Powell
> demonstrated that she is going forward in her art to the high place
> which has been confidently predicted for her.
>
> — *New York Times*[23]

Despite the praise she received in her own country, Maud found
the return home difficult. The differences between the European and
American audiences in their response to music were notable, and

that affected her playing—although it was not noticeable to the critics:

> I have never had anything to complain of in American audiences. . . .
> They have always been very kind to me. But an audience here is
> quite different from an audience abroad. An American audience
> cannot give way. Perhaps they are not sure of themselves, though
> that may not be true of a musical audience. But there is a certain
> Puritanism about Americans; they cannot give way and allow their
> feelings full sway. It is the same with a player. One of the first
> things an American musician has to learn is to let himself go, to
> throw himself out. It is that certain Puritanism. And there is some-
> thing in the climate, too. Foreigners speak of it. When I came home
> after my trip abroad with the Arion Society I felt the difference
> immediately. I played the same music and I was surrounded by the
> same old friends, but I could not play.[24]

Ever after, the violinist remembered the Arion tour as her greatest triumph, the warmth of the people engraved on her mind and
heart forever, "the people . . . most enthusiastic, standing on their
seats and waving their handkerchiefs, and crowding down toward the
stage to be nearest me as I played."[25] The Arions made Maud an
honorary member of the Society.

12

Musical Visions of the New World

Chicago was the first expression of American thought as a unity.

— *Henry Adams*

BY 1890 THE EAST NO LONGER DOMINATED American economic life. Pittsburgh's factories were turning out an entire third of the world's output of iron and steel, and middle-America's grain, gleaned by McCormick's reaper and then his reaper-thresher combine, was feeding a growing populace. Chicago, with its one million people in the heartland, was the hub of the nation. It was poet Carl Sandburg's "Chicago":

> Hog butcher for the World,
> Tool Maker, Stacker of Wheat,
> Player with Railroads and the Nations' Freight Handler;
> Stormy, husky, brawling,
> City of the Big Shoulders. . . .

These cocky Chicagoans, who laid claim to Maud Powell, were now ready to bid for parity with New Yorkers in cultural attainments as well as economic stature.

The musical life of New York was rich and varied. The level of audience appreciation rivaled that of Boston, but the New York Philharmonic remained an unendowed orchestra. When prominent Chicagoans led by Charles Norman Fay approached Theodore Thomas with a plan for a permanently-endowed orchestra in Chicago, they assured him that he would have his own orchestra and an opportunity to concentrate solely on his art. Thomas delightedly accepted the offer.

Following the model set by its Boston counterpart, the Chicago Symphony Orchestra was to have a twenty-week season, giving two concerts a week. Sixty men were drawn from the Thomas Orchestra in New York, while thirty others were selected from the resident musicians of Chicago. As a result, the newly constituted orchestra included many of the best musicians in the country.

New York was stunned by the announcement of Thomas's departure but rallied enough to show its appreciation and affection for the leader during his farewell concerts. Thomas asked Maud to participate in the last concert of the Thomas Orchestra, held on April 18, 1891.[1]

Immediately after his appointment as music director of the Chicago orchestra, Thomas was also appointed music director of the World's Columbian Exposition, to be held in Chicago during the summer of 1893 commemorating the four hundredth anniversary of Columbus's discovery of the New World. Perhaps no other American city could have been more expressive of the energy, vision, and freedom of the world Columbus had opened to European eyes.

Daniel H. Burnham's architectural plan envisioned the most eminent architects of the nation creating a city of exhibition buildings surpassing anything the world had ever seen. Each firm was given the freedom to design within the classical style a temporary exhibition structure. Works of art by the finest painters and sculptors of the day, including Mary Cassatt and the American sculptor Saint-Gaudens, adorned these structures. Frederick Law Olmstead, the landscape architect of New York's Central Park and the grounds of the nation's Capitol, was commissioned to plan the waterways, islands, and landscape features of the Exposition and the general layout of the buildings. The result was a great "White City" of unsurpassed beauty.[2]

If art and architecture were to be represented on such a high plane, Theodore Thomas determined that the music inside the buildings would match them.[3] Two principles formed the basis for the music program Thomas envisioned. First, he would make a complete showing to the world of the musical progress of America, both executive and creative. Secondly, he would show America the music of the world, as exemplified by European nations. To perform this music, the Thomas Orchestra became the Exposition orchestra, enlarged to 114 men and extended to include two large military bands. Thomas formed an Exposition chorus of 1,000 voices and a Children's World's

Fair Chorus of 1,200. Visiting organizations which gave performances at the Exposition included three American symphony orchestras, a string quartet, and bands and choral societies of every description.

The finest American composers could designate which of their works they wished to have performed, and two were additionally commissioned to write compositions for the occasion. Seven out of twenty-one compositions were selected for performance, including at least two by women composers, Miss Margaret Lang and Mrs. H. H. A. Beach.

Thomas managed to entice nearly every eminent American musician as well as a number of prominent Europeans, such as Dvořák, Paderewski, and Saint-Saëns, to participate in his grand scheme (Brahms, Massenet, Tchaikovsky, and Joachim declined). In approximately 200 concerts given in a three-and-a-half-month period, 125 of which Thomas conducted personally, he succeeded in giving an exhibition of music of every school, nationality, and period on a scale that had never been heard before in the United States.[4]

Maud Powell took her place among some of the world's greatest musicians at the Exposition. She was the only woman violinist to appear in these concerts and served as the representative American violinist. Under the baton of the great conductor, the young artist appeared twice, on July 18, 1893, playing the Bruch G minor concerto, and on August 4, 1893, playing the Mendelssohn E minor concerto. The *Musical Courier's* review of the July 18 performance in the July issue revealed the remarkable growth in her musicianship:

> The whole program was an undiluted pleasure, the orchestra seeming to be in the noblest mood, Thomas in his very best vein, and Miss Maud Powell fairly eclipsing all former efforts ever heard from her. . . . It is hard to know where to begin to praise Miss Powell, for nearly every tone she played was full of meaning. She has improved beyond what was supposed to be the limit of her powers; her tone is pure and noble, her bowing grace itself, and her conception of the concerto was equal to that of any of the great violinists whom I have heard perform this noblest of Bruch's solo works. . . .

A plaster cast of Maud Powell's right hand was made by Warren B. Davis for display at the Exposition.[5]

Maud's participation in the World's Columbian Exposition had another dimension. She was a member of the Advisory Council of the Women's Branch of the World's Congress Auxiliary on Music. In this capacity, it appears that she was involved in organizing the Women's Musical Congress that was held during the Exposition.

Throughout Maud's life, the women's suffrage movement was a vital force for positive social change in American life. It was a movement in which her own family was deeply involved. Maud's mother was active in it as Maud was growing up, and her aunts Ellen Powell Thompson and Mary Powell Wheeler were nationally-known suffragettes who worked closely with those indomitable pioneers Elizabeth Cady Stanton and Susan B. Anthony.

Perhaps more importantly, the principle of intellectual equality was an assumption from which life in her family proceeded. After all, Maud's Aunt Emma Dean had shared in Uncle Wes's explorations of the West and was the first woman to climb Pikes Peak. It was Mrs. Powell's determination to break the "piano syndrome" with her daughter that brought the violin to Maud's hands in defiance of convention. Maud once related a family joke: "I inherited my music from my mother and my brains from my father."[6] The joke met with a quick rejoinder from her mother: "Yes, and that makes us both angry, for I consider that I have some brains and her father thinks that he knows something of music." Both of Maud's parents rejected the stereotypes which attached to gender, insisting on the healthy development of the whole human being.

Maud once reflected on the impact these early influences had on her career:

> Raised in an atmosphere charged with the then radical spirit of woman suffrage it is perhaps surprising that I did not come sooner to a realizing sense of the importance of the question. . . . As I grew older my studies absorbed my time and strength. Yet, through my girlhood years there persisted an undercurrent of thought that urged me ever onward — to try to prove that a woman could do her work as thoroughly, as capably and as convincingly as a man. Indeed throughout long years I fought my battle against prejudice, even as Camilla Urso — revered be her memory — fought the battle before me. In my early days, the names of Mrs. Cady Stanton and Susan B. Anthony were household words. I remember with affection the gentle, honest nature of that good woman "Susan B." who took a real interest in my future career, even giving me my first nest-egg, a gold sovereign, toward buying a "Cremona" violin. Both women

wanted the little American girl to show the world that a woman could "fiddle as well as a man."

Years passed. The battle of life and the persistent struggle toward an ever higher artistic goal consumed my energy. Curious as it may seem, a public life was foreign to my nature. It seemed to take all my courage to pursue my own little path toward recognition, leaving no surplus vitality to be devoted to the big general cause of "woman's rights." I honestly felt that I was doing my share toward advancing the cause by developing to the utmost the talents that nature had given me. I believed that sheer force of example would raise standards and fire enthusiasm in other girls, and that on the heels of equipment and efficiency, success would follow. I knew that equal suffrage was right; but that other women had greater gifts of speech and of disposition to work actively in the cause than I, I felt sure.[7]

Maud might have been a leader in the suffrage movement had events taken a different course, but she was first of all, above all, an artist. Music was in her blood and if she were to speak for women, she would speak through her chosen instrument, the violin. She would dissolve all prejudice by performing with such perfection that the critics' pens would be drained dry with praise, leaving no ink for criticism. And she would take up the pen herself to encourage and educate women, especially, in the art of violin playing. From the earliest days of her career, articles by Maud Powell began to appear in music magazines with advice on how to practice and the attributes essential to a violinist — "musical talent, health, and application!"

Keenly aware that her example was inspiring countless girls to take up the violin, as Urso's had sparked the development of her own talents, all her life Maud did everything humanly possible to make clear to these aspirants that violin study was not to be undertaken lightly. A career as a violinist was only for those with powers "absolutely above the average." She knew only too well that the glamor of the stage too frequently hid from view the labor, courage, physical strength, and persistence required to become a violinist of the first rank.

The Women's Musical Congress, held July 4–6, 1893, gave Maud the opportunity to speak on this topic and to be with a number of her musical colleagues and friends. Mrs. George B. Carpenter chaired the event, while such distinguished women as Lillian Nordica, the

American opera singer, Rose Fay Thomas, wife of Theodore Thomas, Camilla Urso, and Maud delivered papers to the assembly of 1,500 persons. The papers and the examples set by the individuals giving them provide some insight into the work and status of women in music.

In an address entitled "Women of the Lyric Stage," Nordica pointed to the need to study in Europe but recommended that girls take with them business-minded chaperons of good character. Born Lillian Norton in 1859, this world-renowned prima donna had received her early training at the New England Conservatory of Music and rounded out her education in Milan, where she changed her name to sound foreign — a common practice for avoiding the prejudice against American-born musicians.[8]

Mrs. Thomas spoke on "The Work of Women's Amateur Musical Clubs." These clubs could be found in towns of all sizes across the country, their members actively sponsoring and participating in music programs, promoting young artists, and bringing the best artists to their locality. Mrs. Thomas's enthusiasm for the work of these clubs led, as an outgrowth of the Musical Congress, to the formation of the National Federation of Music Clubs, an organization which contributed significantly to the growth of musical understanding in America.

During her lifetime, Camilla Urso was more than a fine violinist who did much to extend the appreciation of the American public to classical music; she was as well a strong spokeswoman for opening the music field to women on an equal basis. In her address "Women Violinists as Performers in the Orchestra," she pointed out that women instrumentalists were fully equal to their male counterparts, noting that they were often more diligent and accomplished than men. She observed that a woman generally had to be better than her male counterpart in order even to have a chance to compete with him. Urso then went on to advocate the opening of theater orchestra jobs to women as well as positions in professional symphony orchestras.

Theodore Thomas had hired a female harpist for the Chicago orchestra during its first season, but women players were mostly excluded from orchestra positions until the 1930s, and even then, opportunities remained slim.[9] Musicians' unions, by largely barring women from membership, further retarded their entry into orchestra positions.[10] These barriers, and the increasing numbers of women

players, led to the formation of numerous women's orchestras throughout the United States.[11]

Urso recognized that women violinists' options were limited mostly
to solo playing or teaching, both less preferable lives than that of the
orchestra player. Urso had found her life as a solo violinist a difficult
one. In her last years, she was reduced to playing in vaudeville shows
because she had not amassed any retirement funds, and she refused
charity. Reluctant to recommend such a life to any young woman,
this courageous violinist reckoned the cost: "My life is made up of
hard work, and under the circumstances I should say to young girls
who are thinking of becoming professional violinists, 'Don't.' Solo
playing and teaching are all that are open to women violinists now-
a-days."[12] She made this statement in 1893, at the age of fifty-one.

At just half Urso's age, Maud was more optimistic about the
future of women violinists. The paper Maud delivered to the Congress, entitled "Women and the Violin," encouraged women to play
the violin but warned that its mastery requires both discipline and
devotion. The speech (a version of which was published in 1896 in
The Ladies' Home Journal) was a rare instance of a concert artist
setting forth a detailed prescription to be followed by anyone desir-
ing to pursue serious violin study. Maud gave her impeccable advice
on the path to violin mastery with violin in hand, using the instrument to demonstrate certain points.

Maud said that a child must begin violin study early, between six
and nine years of age. From piano lessons started six months before
the violin the child would most easily learn the rudiments of music,
such as the "tone intervals in scale and melody combinations" and
the "simpler time values." As the child advances, she should be given
training in music theory to attain both musical knowledge and mental discipline. A good instrument and bow are "absolutely essential,"
in her view, to enable good tone production and to train the ear.
The best instructors are desirable at all periods but "indispensable"
at the beginning.

She stressed the importance of daily practice imbued with a
"healthy, hearty spirit." Practice requires "regularity of hours combined with intelligent, thoughtful effort." Two or three hours a day
are sufficient for the young pupil, four hours for the older worker,
plus one or two hours of ensemble playing. Maud carefully prescribed different body stances for practice and performance, recom-

mending that the weight be on both feet equally during practice, but more on the right foot for solo playing.

Hearing as much good music as possible performed by the great violinists would help develop catholicity of taste and technical awareness. Practice in front of a mirror and ensemble playing sharpen one's critical listening facility. The latter enhances one's sense of rhythm and facility of expression. Maud also emphasized the value of memorizing music.

She urged young violinists to go abroad to study in Europe's artistic atmosphere. She warned, however, that a student should not remain too long under the influence of teachers. A violinist needs to work independently of a teacher in order to gain individuality of expression.

Maud both opened and concluded her speech by encouraging women to study the violin. In her view, the small number of successful women violinists was not because "woman is endowed with a poorer quality of talent than man," but due to the fact that "she rarely takes up . . . the violin with the intention of making of it a life work." To regard it as a temporary occupation to be abandoned after marriage and children signified "a lack of earnestness and thoroughness, and of intensity of purpose, essential to the achievement of success and vital to its accomplishment."

Maud argued that women were "especially qualified by nature to be interpretive musicians" due to their "fine sensibilities," "keen intuitions," and sympathetic natures. Further, she pointed out, the violin "is not only the most perfect of all instruments, ranking second only to the human voice, but it is also the most graceful, both in itself and its manipulation." But Maud stressed that a violin student must have the "requisite musical talent together with adequate physical endowment," including perfect health, strength, and endurance. Not only was the concert stage "open to them as to women singers" and the field of instruction "naturally theirs," but women as amateur musicians had an important role to play in raising musical standards across the country. In this way, Maud summoned women to the service of "the divinest of all arts — music."

On July fifth, during the second session of the Congress, Maud joined Amy Cheney Beach in the premiere of the *Romance*, Op. 23, which Beach had composed for the occasion and dedicated to Maud. These two friends must have taken special delight in the occasion.

Both had been child prodigies, were of the same age, and had made their debuts with Theodore Thomas in the same year. More importantly, they shared spirits of broad-minded intellectual inquiry, industry, and enthusiasm for their art.

Beach was a leading representative of the late nineteenth-century Romantic style cultivated by Chadwick, Foote, and others of the Boston school; yet she had no formal training as a composer and never studied abroad. In 1885 she was well launched as a concert pianist; however, her marriage in that same year, at eighteen, to Dr. H. H. A. Beach, a prominent Boston surgeon, had slowed her development in that direction. Her husband encouraged her to focus on composing instead. Although Amy Beach had received some training in harmony along with her piano lessons, what she learned about composition she learned on her own. This woman eventually mastered every form of composition from the symphony to the simple song.

Her *Gaelic* Symphony, Op. 32, was the first symphony composed by an American woman and was premiered by the Boston Symphony Orchestra on October 30, 1896, with Emil Paur conducting. She wrote a violin sonata, Op. 34, which was premiered in 1897 by Franz Kneisel (concertmaster of the Boston Symphony), with the composer at the piano, and played in Paris in 1900 by Ysaÿe and Pugno. She was equally successful in producing her Mass in E-flat and her Piano Concerto in C-sharp Minor, Op. 45.

Beach's works were characterized by technical mastery, spontaneity, and originality—all traits crystallized in the *Romance* written for Maud Powell, described as "graceful though difficult of performance." Those who heard it played that day by the pianist with the large, smiling, blue-grey eyes and blond hair and the violinist with the dark, curly hair and expressive face were never more convinced that "there is no sex in music." The "beauty and grace" of the composition and the "faultless interpretation by the brilliant composer and artist" were proof enough for those auditors. The audience "cheered to the echo" when the piece was completed, and the performance had to be repeated. During the encore, the thrill was heightened when the manuscript fell from Maud's music stand, but "the beautiful thread of melody moved on and on, for Miss Powell had made it her own in every sense."[13]

The Maud Powell String Quartet, 1894–1898

Instead of crouching more and more over the instrument as so many violinists do when in the heat of virtuoso execution, Maud Powell seems to grow taller and statelier, lifting her inspired bow on high, like some Sappho of old holding her golden lyre up against a glowing sun.

— *Review from Minneapolis, Minnesota*

MAUD POWELL BEGAN AN ENTIRELY NEW VENTURE IN 1894. She formed her own professional string quartet with three male colleagues, something no woman other than Lady Hallé in England had ever done.[1]

She chose Dvořák's protégé from the Prague Conservatory to play second violin. Josef Kovarik, an American born of Czech parents, was first violinist in the Seidl Orchestra and a violin professor at the National Conservatory of Music. For violist she chose Franz Kaltenborn, a first violinist in Seidl's Metropolitan Orchestra and a member of the New York Philharmonic who had been a member of the Schandt-Herbert String Quartet. The cellist was Paul Miersch, born in Dresden and educated at the Munich Conservatory, who had been appearing as a soloist in the United States for a number of years.

First-class professional string quartets had been a rare phenomenon in America up to this time, probably because such ensembles require a high degree of sophistication from musicians and audiences alike. One of the earliest quartets of any quality was the Mason-Thomas Quartet which Theodore Thomas had led in the early part of his career. Perhaps the only quartet to reach the same level of professionalism was the Kneisel Quartet in Boston, formed in 1885, and possibly the earlier Eichberg Quartette.[2] Still, in America, the Kneisel Quartet was heard mostly in Boston and the larger musical centers such as New York, Philadelphia, and Baltimore.

Maud was motivated to form a string quartet by her love for chamber music and her desire to share with a broader spectrum of Americans "the most beautiful literature of all."[3] Formed with the backing of the Redpath Lyceum Bureau, the Quartet had five solid weeks' booking, playing every night, wherever lyceums were to be found throughout the United States. This arrangement fulfilled Maud's desire to reach audiences largely removed from the main cultural centers. The lyceum was a prominent nineteenth-century forum for adult education, offering small urban and rural communities lectures, debates, concerts, and other forms of educational and cultural activities not otherwise available to them. The addition of single engagements booked through her new manager Henry Wolfsohn meant that the Quartet's first season was to be very full.

The first appearance of the Quartet was in the chamber music room at Carnegie Hall on October 26, 1894. In making this important appearance, Maud, at twenty-seven, must have been aware that in the history of the instrument few violin virtuosos of her calibre had ever devoted themselves to ensemble playing. Lady Hallé and Joseph Joachim were notable exceptions.

The formation and leadership of a quartet demands qualities of give and take, a sense of balance and a perspective which are not always easily developed by the virtuoso used to solo work. For this reason, Maud strongly recommended for students the cultivation of chamber music skills, through which she believed true musicianship is developed. Leadership of the Quartet provided an outlet for Maud's latent talents as a conductor, since women were barred from conducting professional orchestras. (It was claimed that the men in the orchestra would not stand to have a woman conduct them, nor would the public accept the spectacle!) She once frankly admitted that, had she been a man, she would have been a conductor rather than a virtuoso.[4]

The auditorium was full for the first concert and the audience appreciative of the ambitious program: Mozart's Quartet in D Minor, Smetana's quartet *Aus Meinem Leben*, and Maud's friend Christian Sinding's piano quintet. The *New York Times'* review, however, reflects the difficulty of finding musicians in America at that time capable of forming a first-rate string quartet, and the critic chided: "Miss Powell is too excellent an artist not to have realized . . . that her new quartet was not yet all that it might be."

The fault lay less with the optimism of the leader than with the inexperience of her colleagues. While the violist's qualities as a "serviceable orchestra player" were noted, his quartet playing was "extremely crude and colorless." The second violinist was found to be an "accurate player" but "quite devoid of style." Finally, the cellist had "a little more style than is necessary." This critic went on to observe:

> As for Miss Powell herself, she proved to be an excellent quartet player, keeping well within the bounds of modesty and yet holding the balance of power in her hands. To her credit, too, must be set down the excellence in ensemble work which was reached in some parts of the evening's performance. . . . The promise of the new organization was revealed in [a number of] passages, and it is only fair to hope that in time its entire work may reach the level of the best playing of last night.[5]

The Quartet was scheduled to play two more concerts at Carnegie Hall later in the season, by which New York critics would mark its progress. In the meantime, the musicians' extensive tour included such cities as Newark, New Jersey, Boston, New Bedford, Holyoke, Lynn, Salem, and Lowell, Massachusetts, as well as Troy and Elmira, New York, and Aurora, Illinois.

Although the programs the Quartet offered in the small towns along the route were somewhat miscellaneous in character, they were not inartistic and brought to these people a quality of music rarely heard outside the large cities. The program in Elmira, for example, featured the allegro vivace movement from Mendelssohn's Quartet in D Major, Grieg's *Saltarello*, and also *Gavotte*, *Angelus*, and *Presto* by Bazzini, Liszt, and Haydn, respectively. Other artists, usually a singer or local chorus, sometimes appeared with the Quartet, whose members also performed solos from time to time.[6] For its concert at Vassar College, the Quartet offered more substantial fare, including Haydn's Quartet in D Major and Grieg's Quartet in G Minor, as well as Maud's solo rendition of Bach's unaccompanied Violin Sonata in E Major.

The Quartet returned to New York for its second concert at Carnegie Hall on December 4, 1894. Henry Holden Huss assisted as pianist. The program included Dvořák's Quartet in C Major, Op. 61, Grieg's Sonata for Piano and Cello, Op. 36, and Beethoven's Quartet in F Major, Op. 59, No. 1. The critics found that the ensemble had improved, noting the skill and delicacy with which the difficult and involved Dvořák quartet was played, and especially the careful shading, accuracy, and precision which marked the last two movements. The Beethoven quartet was rendered with the same attention to detail and good ensemble work as the Dvořák. Maud was recognized as "unquestionably a very successful leader," while the Quartet was said to deserve recognition for its excellent musical character.

The last New York concert was given on January 3, 1895. By then New York audiences and critics had heard the great Belgian violinist Eugène Ysaÿe, who was then making his first appearances in the United States. Unruffled by what other artists might have considered stiff competition, Maud led her Quartet in a program of works by some of the greatest masters—Haydn's Quartet in D Major and Brahms' Quintet in B Minor, Op. 115, with assisting clarinetist Carl Reinecke—while she played Bach's unaccompanied Violin Sonata in E Major.

Before a fair-sized audience the Quartet performed admirably. While the *Times'* critic still noted some shortcomings, he commented that the work of the Quartet had improved so much that "there is every reason to hope that the organization will continue its labors next season." And the masterful playing of Ysaÿe in the city had not diminished the critic's estimation of Maud Powell as an artist.

> Miss Powell has proved herself to be a scholarly and energetic leader, with an intelligent comprehension of chamber music playing. If anything had been needed to demonstrate the fullness of her artistic equipment as a soloist, it would have been supplied by her performance of the Bach sonata last night. She played it with superb vigor, breadth, and authority. Her mastery of the technics of her instrument was never displayed to better advantage, and her intellectual grasp was notable.[7]

The Quartet's season probably ended in March or April of 1895. Some sources indicate that the Maud Powell Quartet continued to exist until 1898. In any case, by May 1895, Maud was in Oberlin again for a solo recital which included Goldmark's Suite for Violin and Piano, several movements from Bach's unaccompanied Violin Sonata in E Major, and Lalo's Concerto Russe in G Minor, which Maud premiered in America (possibly that season). This time, Ysaÿe and César Thomson, another gifted Belgian violinist, had preceded her, but that fact did not diminish Oberlin's appreciation for her art:

> Miss Maud Powell came last Friday evening and gave one of those delightful recitals which have endeared her to the Oberlin music lovers. Her programs are always choice and full of novel and varied elements, her personality is most charming, and her playing that of a finished artist. In fact, as a recital giver, it is doubtful if she has a superior among resident American violinists. Her feeling is deep and truthful, and her versatility remarkable. Her playing is strong and impassioned where force and brilliancy are required, at other moments exquisitely tender and pathetic. There is never a hint of feminine lack of vigor, and her ability to sustain her energy through a long and arduous program is a constant source of surprise to those who hear her. She seems constantly to grow in technical facility and in breadth and refinement of tone. Her performance Friday was a veritable triumph, for in an atmosphere of such suffocating heat that sitting in the hall was a distress and hand-clapping a painful labor, she nevertheless made her audience forget discomfort and inspired an enthusiasm that increased steadily to the end. Considering the fact that we have had such supremely great violinists as Ysaÿe and Thomson with us this season, Miss Powell's success was an extraordinary achievement.[8]

14

Missionary for Music

*Dazzling and tremendous how quick the sun-rise
  would kill me,
If I could not now and always send sun-rise out of me.*

— *Walt Whitman*

BESIDES PLAYING WITH THE RESIDENT ORCHESTRAS in all the main cultural centers, Maud had toured throughout the country every year, particularly the Midwest, giving recitals in small towns as well as the larger cities. By 1898, she was credited with having given more recitals in the United States than any other native violinist. She knew the country as few others did, and she believed deeply in America's cultural future.

Everywhere she stopped, she made an effort to meet the local musicians, seeking them out to discuss music with them and to discover the musical attainments of the town. Her interest was great and her curiosity insatiable. She probably knew every musician and music promoter of any consequence in every place she played. When she was not playing a regularly scheduled concert, she could be found promoting musical growth in some other way—by encouraging young students in their studies or by meeting with and advising local music clubs or orchestras. Edith L. Winn, one of these young students, described their first meeting:

> Maud Powell was vitally an American. There was something unusual in her handclasp. . . . [I]t was more than a firm, warm greeting. Rather was it energy, genius, if you will call it so, vitalized by character. . . .

[148]

Maud, who cleverly autographed the date February 17, 1897. The score is the opening measure of the Bruch G minor violin concerto with which she had made her debut.

This page, Maud in 1897 and the colleagues with whom she was ranked: *left*, Belgian violinist Eugène Ysaÿe; *right*, Austrian violinist Fritz Kreisler. *Facing page*, Maud's conductors: *top and bottom*, *left*, Sir Henry Wood and Hans Richter, with whom she performed in England; *top right*, John Philip Sousa, with whom she toured Europe; *bottom right*, composer Camille Saint-Saëns, who conducted Maud performing his B minor violin concerto in England.

Facing page, Maud in Europe: *top,* with soprano Estelle Liebling on tour with the Sousa Band, 1903; *bottom,* with John Philip Sousa on tour, 1903 or 1905. *This page, top,* "Sunny," H. Godfrey Turner, Maud's husband and manager; *bottom,* Maud Powell logo devised by Sunny and painted by Maud. The quotation is from an English critic.

MAUD POWELL

" THE ARM OF A MAN
THE HEART OF A WOMAN
THE HEAD OF AN ARTIST "

STEINWAY PIANO USED

MGR. GODFREY TURNER, NEW YORK

MAUD POWELL

Facing page, top right, advertisement devised by H. Godfrey Turner; *left,* Maud on her South African tour, 1905; and, *bottom,* in a rickshaw, which conveyed her to concerts "in my evening dress, valuable fiddle in hand," in Pietermaritzburg and Durban, South Africa. *This page, left,* photo of Maud in 1904, autographed April 1905 to a saxophonist in the Sousa Band; *top right,* composer Jean Sibelius, whose violin concerto Maud premiered in America; *bottom,* Wassily Safonoff, who conducted the premiere.

Maud in 1905.

I first met Miss Powell in the early nineties. She was tall, graceful, thin, lithe, with dark eyes that looked straight into mine, with rare enthusiasm. Her fine brown hair waved back from a low forehead. Her smile was like that of one who has boundless optimism. . . .

At the time I first heard Miss Powell play, in a college town near Pittsburgh everything seemed very vague to me. I had little money for a career and less health. Miss Powell inspired me to high endeavor. I whispered my eager desire to go to Berlin to study, and dared mention the name of Joachim as a possible teacher.

"Don't think of him," said Miss Powell, as she caught up the train of her bright red dress (she wore brilliant colors in those days). "Joachim is too busy to teach you. Go to Jacobsen. He is careful of details. But do not narrow yourself down to a mere school. Study in various schools, and get the viewpoint of many good teachers." . . .

In two years time, my dream came true. . . . Then I learned how Maud Powell had worked, and how proud the teachers at the Hochschule were of her achievements.[1]

Focusing her sights on her musical mission, Maud largely ignored the fact that touring was physically costly. Traveling conditions were appalling. Timetables were always geared to the speed of the technology, not to the pace of human life. Visits with friends while on tour were planned around train schedules. Once Maud sent a message to an old Aurora friend scheduling a meeting in the afternoon since she was "resting after two nights on the train and with the prospect of turning out at 4:25 tomorrow morning."[2]

During the October-to-May touring season, rail cars were often overheated and extremely stuffy, while on many occasions they were also overcrowded, filled with bad odors and crying children. Train travel was hazardous as well, the wooden cars heated by kerosene stoves, while the science of controlling their movements by telegraph was often subject to spectacular demonstrations of fallibility when trains collided head-on. In further injury, rail passengers were blanketed with soot as the locomotive belched thick black smoke on its way.

Hotels offered a variety of accommodations, clean and unclean, overheated and unheated, with bath and without. Then too, conditions for washing clothing were extremely variable, and rooms sometimes were hosted by bedbugs.

The quality of hotel food required the traveling virtuoso to develop a stomach impervious to assault. Once, at a large hotel in Texas, the food was so bad that Maud could not eat. Returning to her room, she exclaimed indignantly to the elevator boy, "This is positively the worst hotel I have ever been in!" Unperturbed, the boy replied, "Yes, madam, that's what everybody says."[3]

Traveling with a violin was not always easy, for the instrument required extra handling care during long journeys. While on tour in 1897, Maud sent her violin carefully packed in its case and enclosed in a coffin-shaped pine box to the express office:

> I soon followed to attend to addressing the package and to give directions for shipping. To my dismay, the clerks knew nothing of such a box as I asked for; I thought my beloved fiddle was lost. It could not be found anywhere until after minutely describing the box, giving its dimensions and other peculiarities by which it might be identified, a sudden gleam of intelligence came into the clerk's face, and disappearing, he soon returned with the box across his arms. "We had it on ice," he whispered sympathetically.[4]

The American virtuoso early developed into a recitalist *par excellence*. In Oberlin in 1893 she presented a program which included Beethoven's *Kreutzer* Sonata, the Bach *Chaconne* for unaccompanied violin, and Franz Ries's Suite for Violin and Piano, Op. 34, along with shorter works by Nardini, Wieniawski, Schubert, Brahms, Sarasate, and Ernst, bringing home the fact that she could play any piece of music from the Baroque to the modern with authority, style, and great beauty. Her imagination and humanitarian sympathy gave vitality to her conception of works of all periods and styles. In the days before recordings, these special endowments enabled her to be one of the most powerful educational forces for music in America, and she was determined to use her gifts for this purpose.

Maud never played down to her audiences, but she never bored them either. Like her father in his teaching, she would rather entice them with things worthy to be loved than bully them into learning something new. Maud was a master at programming, as was Theodore Thomas, from whom she received some advice:

> The main thing . . . is for the artist to get his audience into the concert hall, and give it a program which is properly balanced. Theodore Thomas first advised me to include in my programs short,

simple things that my listeners could "get hold of"—nothing inartistic, but something selected from their standpoint, not from mine, and played as artistically as possible. Yet there must also be something that is beyond them, collectively. Something that they may need to hear a number of times to appreciate. This enables the artist to maintain his dignity and has a certain psychological effect in that his audience holds him in greater respect. At big conservatories where music study is the most important thing, and in large cities, where the general level of music culture is high, a big solid program may be given, where it would be inappropriate in other places.[5]

Maud managed to make her music appeal to people in all walks of life. In one city, a prominent newspaper editor told her that he never missed one of her concerts, even though he was not musical. He felt there was a literary quality in her work which appealed to the layman. "Do you know, I liked that," Maud mused, "because I would enjoy doing my country good culturally if I could. It is nice to have that faculty, even though it be in ever so small a degree. Please the public without lowering your ideals is my belief. You have to make your public feel you are above them, if only a trifle, because the minute you stoop to them they sense it, and they do not like it."[6]

Her experience with one small-town audience sometime after 1906 confirmed her belief that almost any audience could appreciate classical music as long as it was performed with the warmth of human sympathy and musical understanding: "I remember having many recalls at El Paso, Texas, once, after playing the first movement of the Sibelius concerto. It is one of those compositions which if played too literally leaves an audience quite cold; it must be rendered temperamentally, the big climaxing effects built up, its Northern spirit brought out, though I admit that even then it is not altogether easy to grasp." Then again, the same piece of music might be received differently in different cities. Maud reported that "the Sibelius concerto caused adverse criticism in New York when I played it, while in El Paso, San Diego and a number of other Western cities, I played it about a dozen times and it was very well liked."

Edith Winn commented:

I have never known Maud Powell to cheapen her art, nor to play badly. She played in her concerts in the South and West the same programs as in New York and Boston. The public did not know her by a few miniatures, some little gems good enough in themselves, but misleading to students who realize little concerning the great amount of solid material to be studied. She had a large and varied repertoire, constantly changing as it were. She played in Oklahoma as in New York—the great literature of the violin. That was to her a mission. And thousands heard her, while many young women awoke to the earnestness in the art she loved. She, more than anyone in America, has created, abetted and inspired the American girl violinist.

In later years, Winn spoke to the artist about the good she was doing by playing at so many schools and colleges all over the country. Maud replied simply, "I must carry a message as long as I am able." As her later manager Godfrey Turner explained to Winn: "She accepts engagements at small colleges or for Women's Clubs because she wishes to carry inspiration to the people who do not ordinarily hear artists of her rank. It is a sacred trust with her, and she will continue to do it as long as she can."

People who heard Maud Powell play remembered the experience for the rest of their lives. One reporter in the small Minnesota town of Winona expressed his awe at "the magic wonder of her performance. . . . ":

> How can she produce those miracles of sound? Does she infuse into the wood of the violin some emanation from her own soul? Is it the cords of her inner being that we hear vibrato instead of the strings she seems to play upon?
>
> Between what an ordinary person can do and the feats of a genius like Maud Powell the gulf is immeasurable.
>
> There are plenty of men and women who can fiddle. Some can even make music flow from the strings, but there never are more than two or three persons in the world at the same time who can work the miracles she can. Sometimes she frolics with impossibilities, evoking unheard of beauties with light quick strokes of the bow that almost elude the eye in their facile deftness. Sometimes she draws it over the strings as softly and slowly as twilight falls thru the tinted robes of angels on a cathedral window and always whatever she does, there flows from the violin an unbroken stream of perfect melody.[7]

Some pointed to her legendary "Hungarian blood" as responsible for a certain warmth of temperament, gypsy-like in fervor, which was one of the distinguishing characteristics of her art, serving to "human-

ize a technique which was almost too perfect." One music observer
in New York commented:

> It is impossible to speak of her unenthusiastically, for she unites
> all the charm of a beautiful and graceful woman to musicianship
> that holds one enthralled. Apollo and Juno seem to have conspired
> in her composition, and the result is a high priestess who draws
> worshiping thousands to the temple. . . .
>
> She possesses all the qualities that go to make up the ideal vio-
> linist: sound musicianship, masculine virility coupled with femi-
> nine delicacy, a highly poetic intensity, and a tone that draws almost
> hysterical plaudits from her hearers. . . .
>
> It would be a very cold gathering, indeed, that could resist the
> Tchaikovsky or the Beethoven violin concertos as played by this art-
> ist. Her tone is so exquisite, her mastery so brilliant, and her inter-
> pretative intelligence so beautiful—ah, she is an artist![8]

People who knew Maud Powell believed that her mind and spirit
were "charged with the light of elemental truth." W. J. Henderson,
a distinguished New York critic, wrote: "She is a blood descendant
of Spohr, and when she tucks her fiddle under her chin, she makes a
solemn reverence before the altar of music and officiates as a priestess
in the temple."[9]

The irresistible quality of Maud Powell's performances stemmed
from her deep, unselfish devotion to her art. In giving young people
advice on "What One's Art Should Mean," she wrote:

> Long before a girl of the right caliber has completed her studies, she
> should have received the baptism of her vocation—the words "fame"
> and "greatness" should have disappeared, to be replaced by truth
> and art. She must be a worshipper of the thing itself. Her ambition
> should no longer be to excel but to deliver the message of the musi-
> cian. Her own greatness should count for nothing beside the great-
> ness of her art. It never occurs to me to ask myself if I have achieved
> greatness or fame, but I do realize with a thrill of wonder and
> delight that after long, long years of praying and fasting in the tem-
> ple, I am able to deliver the message of my art to hungry and thirsty
> souls.

By the turn of the century, New York audiences and music critics
rivaled their Old World counterparts in sophistication. The cosmo-
politan character of the city made it a natural center for the arts,
drawing students and professional musicians for study and work.

Where once those artists who came from Europe sought only America's gold, they now sought her critical acclaim as well. Audiences and critics alike reverenced art, and they were no longer tolerant of virtuosity without musicianship. American critics were known for their unconventionality and frankness as well as for their irreverence for performers and severity of judgment. If there was a great deal of individuality and a certain literary quality in the reviews by New York critics, it could be attributed to the breadth and variety of their typically American education and experience.[10] The leading critics of the day included Henry E. Krehbiel (*New York Tribune*, 1880–1923), Henry T. Finck (*New York Evening Post*, 1881–1923), William J. Henderson (*New York Times*, 1883–1902; *New York Sun*, 1902–37), Richard Aldrich (*New York Tribune*, 1891–1902; *New York Times*, 1902–37), William B. Chase (*New York Evening Sun*, 1896–1916; *New York Times*), and James G. Huneker (various journals, 1891–1921). Krehbiel was ranked first by Europeans and was called the "Dean" of American critics.

Maud knew all these critics and appreciated their function. She recognized Krehbiel and his colleagues' eagerness to further classical music in the United States and to educate Americans to ever-higher standards of performance and appreciation. Her encouragement of American composers was especially endearing to these critics, who recognized Maud's significance as a violinist. She was their ideal model of a great American artist, not only in the perfection of her technique and her eminent musicianship, but in the high ideals which guided her life and work as well.

When, rarely, a critic noted a fault in her playing, she wrote him her thanks for his "kindly suggestion" and instantly set about correcting the difficulty. It was New York critic James Huneker's comment, early in her career, that she was not paying enough attention to the feminine side of her playing that determined her to be just herself and play as the spirit moved her.

By 1898 the New York critics had heard nearly every significant concert artist of the day from Europe and America. They were discerning with respect to the relative merits of violinists, and Maud had to face the inevitable comparisons.

Before 1894 and the advent of Ysaÿe in America, Maud's rendition of Wieniawski's *Russian Airs* stood comparison with Wieniawski's own. Playing the music with "a degree of excellence seldom equalled," her rendering of the variations in harmonics "vividly recalled Wieniawski's playing of the same."[11] Although Maud had never heard Wieniawski play, her musical insight enabled her to recreate the composer's vision with authority.

The Belgian master Eugène Ysaÿe represented for Europe what Maud Powell represented for America—a new standard of violin artistry which accomplished a synthesis of the several schools of violin playing up to that time. Both artists had a similar command over the instrument, universality of repertoire, and depth and versatility of musicianship. Europeans noted that Maud's playing suggested Ysaÿe, while Americans measured Ysaÿe against the standard set by Maud Powell.

Ysaÿe had toured the United States in 1894 and returned for a second tour in 1897–98. In 1898, the two artists were in New York at the same time and undoubtedly enjoyed hearing each other play. On January 30, Maud and Xaver Scharwenka played Beethoven's *Kreutzer* Sonata at an Aschenbroedl concert organized by Victor Herbert.[12] Ysaÿe and the French cellist Jean Gerardy attended, along with other prominent musicians. The critics were delighted with the performance, which was given with "rhythmical swing, spirit and technical perfection."[13] It was the best since that given by Schradieck and Joseph Gittings in Brooklyn: "Many a respectable work of genius would have sounded tame after the perfectly delightful manner in which Miss Powell and Xaver Scharwenka revealed the ever young, fresh and delicate mysteries of the *Kreutzer Sonata*. It is not every day that this familiar yet unhackneyed masterpiece gets played as these two artists played it, and there was no mistaking the impulsive sincerity of the applause which followed each movement and occasionally broke in between sections." Maud also played a quintet for soprano, violin, horn, cello, and piano by Bruno Oscar Klein which had an exacting violin part. The *Times* critic W. J. Henderson noted that Maud "showed herself again one of the most competent of our ensemble players."

The American violinist played Bruch's D minor concerto twice in fifteen days at a Seidl Waldorf-Astoria concert on February 3, 1898, and then with the New York Philharmonic on the eighteenth. The next day's reviews of the first concert reflect the pride Americans took in this American artist:

Miss Maud Powell played Bruch's second violin concerto so well as to obliterate the best impressions made by some of the foreign artists who have played that work here. . . . It would be difficult to talk within reason and say too much in praise of Miss Powell's playing. We cannot recall a time when she displayed such superb dash and spirit, or when she or anybody else played with purer intonation. It was a performance that could be measured by Mr. Ysaÿe's performances at the Philharmonic and Symphony societies, but by nothing else that New York has heard in the department of violin playing this year.

— *New York Tribune*

Miss Powell has been from the outset of her career a very serious and devoted artist. She shows evidences of growth, and her performance yesterday, perfect in intonation and instinct with all the larger impulses of true musicianship, was the most satisfying exhibition of violin playing that has been given this season.

— *New York Times*

As the *Commercial Advertiser* asserted, "Miss Powell . . . [demonstrated] that she is a much better violinist than many men of far greater pretensions that come over here to win American dollars." And the *New York Evening Post* asked: "What need of sending to Europe for Ysaÿes and Marteaus when we have such great artists at home?" The excitement continued in the reviews of the second concert:

It is difficult to speak of Miss Powell's performances yesterday without seeming to run to hyperbole. But it is a joy to praise such playing. Miss Powell produced from her instrument a big, vital tone that was simply inspiring. In the involved passages she played with a freedom, a dash, a certainty, which were most invigorating. In the difficult high positions her intonation was absolutely accurate and her tone remarkable in its purity. But it was in the artistic revelation of the content of the work that Miss Powell shone. Her intellectual grasp of the composition was complete and her exposition of its emotion masterful. She played with immense passion, yet with perfect balance and with beautifully prepared moments of elevating repose. In short, her performance was absolutely noble and crowned her with laurels which will not fade.

— *New York Times*

If there is one especial characteristic to be noted in her playing it is temperament. She is the very embodiment of it, yet has it so well within hand that it never runs away with her. She threw into the not particularly exalted concerto a marvelous fire and intensity that raised it to an unwonted high plane. In her hands it became a living thing, fairly glowing with richly hued colors. Miss Powell has a superb, big sonorous tone, full of brilliant solidity. Her stopping is flawless. There was no scratching or scraping, but a luscious mellowness that makes a very strong emotional appeal. Her style is finished and graceful, with a masculine virility. . . . As an encore she played a movement of a Bach sonata in a most admirable fashion. She succeeded in keeping the rigidity of the classic form while bringing out all the beauties of the work in such a way that there was no stiffness or palpable restraint.

— Commercial Advertiser

Miss Powell played superbly, and was applauded to the echo, achieving as fine a triumph as has fallen to the lot of any solo performer at a Philharmonic meeting this year. Her success, indeed, was even more emphatic than it was when she played the same composition at the Astoria, about ten days ago. The applause which called her again and again to the stage was a sincere tribute of appreciation, and to still it she at last played in a masterly manner the prelude to the sixth of Bach's solo sonatas — that in E major.

— New York Tribune

With her gifts as a violinist well recognized in America, Maud resolved to return to Europe for extended tours. As she headed for her European adventure in the spring of 1898, it was fortunate that the accolades were so fresh, for it would take all her legendary grit to overcome the initial reserve of the English people and the European prejudice against American violinists. It would be like starting all over again.

15

Conquering Europe, 1898–1900

*Far better it is to dare mighty things, to win glorious triumphs,
even though checkered by failure, than to take rank with those
poor spirits who neither enjoy nor suffer much, because they
live in the gray twilight that knows not victory or defeat.*

— *Theodore Roosevelt, 1899*

MAUD POWELL CLEARLY DID NOT NEED TO GO TO EUROPE to enhance her
reputation at home as many of her compatriots did. It was the lure
of the musical atmosphere abroad which drew her there. Eager as she
was at just thirty years of age to learn and grow with every new experience, the fresh stimulus would add depth and breadth to her art.

Perhaps it was fitting that Maud, hailed as America's finest violinist, a symbol of America's cultural potential, should set out to
conquer Europe the same year the United States came of age as a
world power in the Spanish-American War of 1898. While the United
States had much to learn about the subtleties and possibilities of
power, its European neighbors were not slow to recognize the presence of a new force which must be included in future political calculations.

England at last embraced its offspring as a necessary and natural
ally, encouraging the United States to accept dominion over the Philippines, Wake, and Guam to hold the balance of power in the East.
Henry Adams looked on as his friend John Hay, then Ambassador to
the Court of St. James, was summoned home by President McKinley
to shoulder the responsibilities of Secretary of State in 1898. With
Germany helping to "frighten . . . England into America's arms,"
Adams mused, "He could feel only the sense of satisfaction at seeing

the diplomatic triumph of all his family, since the breed existed, at last realized under his own eyes. . . . "[1]

It was the end of the Victorian order. While external life continued to progress and benefit from the practical inventions of the age — the telephone, the electric light, and even the automobile, which made an occasional appearance — underneath, the old order was dissolving. Scientific discoveries were radically changing the Newtonian notions about the universe which had enabled life to proceed with some certainty during the nineteenth century. If Henry Adams haunted the Paris Exposition in 1900, it was because he sensed that something in the old framework had collapsed. In his view, the dynamo had come to replace the Virgin in human hearts.

In 1897, J. J. Thomson in Cambridge discovered the electron, upsetting all former notions about the stability and predictability of the substratum of the universe. Marie Curie defined and isolated polonium (radium f) in 1898, the first discovery of a radioactive element. Although Einstein was still a student, it would be only a few years (1905) before the initial presentation of his special theory of relativity, which postulated the equivalence of mass and energy expressed in the famous equation $E = MC^2$.

With the death of Victoria in 1901, King Edward VII would strive mightily to keep the inner turmoil of Europe from exploding during this transitional age. But war machines continued to build as Germany and Britain expanded their far-flung empires. While Victoria pursued the Boer War (1896–1902), the Kaiser's military men were observing the organizational sleight-of-hand that enabled Barnum and Bailey to move a circus as if it were an army.

While he juggled with other kings for peace, Edward continued to cultivate the arts, bringing a vital and forceful presence to bear in the cultural world. Maud Powell would do her part to obtain European recognition of America's cultural attributes.

There really was little difference at the end of the century between the musical atmosphere of London and that of New York, Boston, or Chicago. Many of the same world-class musicians could be found making appearances on both sides of the Atlantic — Ysaÿe, Paderewski, Busoni, Hofmann, Gerardy, Nordica, Melba, Schumann-Heink. Maud, who was accompanied by her mother, felt at home in London because of the transatlantic exchange and because they both could be reunited with musician friends who did not often cross the Atlantic. Among these were Joseph Joachim and Georg Henschel and his wife Lillian Bailey.[2]

Through such connections, Maud found new opportunities to perform, even though her English manager (connected with Wolfsohn) let her down. Mr. Vert, who also managed the Richter concerts, largely left her on her own—alone and unheralded. In spite of this handicap, she began making her own way in London—to the delight of American music observers there.

It was not an easy task. London was content with appearances by the finest European violinists. Such masters as Sarasate, Brodsky, Nachez, Thomson, and Sauret were in evidence, as well as Ysaÿe, Joachim, and Lady Hallé. Ysaÿe had found a second home in England as had Joachim before him. He was lionized in the same way, receiving the Philharmonic Society's Gold Medal in 1901 as had Joachim earlier. While Joachim still dominated the Popular Concerts, his counterpart Lady Hallé, edging toward retirement, took up permanent residence in Berlin in 1898, returning nevertheless to London each season to continue the Pops, and touring America during the 1898–99 season.

With the erection of Queen's Hall in December 1893, London concert offerings had expanded to include the Promenade Concerts given by the Queen's Hall Orchestra, under the direction of Henry J. Wood, the Sunday Concert Society series, and the Symphony Concerts instituted in 1897. All these were in addition to the London Philharmonic Society series and the Richter concerts in which Hans Richter conducted the Queen's Hall Orchestra.

For all that, one American observer reported that London was not hearing the quality of programming and performance to which Americans, in New York and Boston at least, were accustomed. The London correspondent for the *Boston Transcript* hoped that the visits by the American singer Blauvelt, violinist Powell, and pianist Bloomfield-Zeisler would dispel the "insular notion" that Americans lag as far behind in music performance as "they really excel it."[3]

The American violinist surprised those who heard her for the first time in Europe. One particularly unprepared critic who heard Maud play in London in December of 1898 reported:

> Yesterday afternoon at the small Queen's Hall Miss Maud Powell gave a violin recital which, we own, surprised us. Although she was

rather barbarously described on the programme as the "eminent American violinist," we were beforehand neither aware of her eminence nor of her nationality. She came to us without preliminary puff or anticipatory paragraph, and thereby she astonished us the more. She has an extraordinary masculinity of touch. It was with difficulty that we could trace throughout her whole recital one element of femininity or one hint of that which we have always associated with what is soft or tender in music. She impressed us by sheer muscular strength, by immense forcefulness, and by a tremendous self-assurance. Lady Hallé has strength, but it is veiled by the wonderful velvet quality of her tone, as it were sheathed in a womanliness of feeling and of soft-expressiveness. Miss Powell's strength is of an utterly different order. It is straightforward, piercing, frank, and shoulder-high. There is no compromise about it; it goes straight to the point; and is immediately convincing. It follows naturally that she addresses herself less to the emotions than to the intellect. She has one quality, however, which gives to her playing a peculiar satisfactoriness; she has a most true ear.

Many great players — we have one particular player of great eminence in our mind — in spite of their command over their instrumental resources, in spite of their instrumental intelligence, . . . sometimes err in point of absolute truth of ear. Miss Powell in this respect never once went astray. She played with masterly precision three movements from Bach's Sonata in E major, and in Bazzini's brilliantly commonplace *La Ronde des Lutins* she was no less than superb. Yet, as we have already implied, she does not touch the heart. It is rather the head that she induces to admiration than the feelings that she leads into the ways of exuberance. Even the Massenet *Crépuscule*, sentimental though it is to the verge of sickliness, won that pathos she gave it by a withdrawal from rather than by an insistence upon its most essential qualities. In a word, Miss Powell has a very particular individuality, which is quite engrossing from the points of view which we have indicated. She has a marvelous technique, a wonderful accomplishment, and she has a fine self-confidence. She may go very far indeed.

— Pall Mall Gazette[4]

Not every critic registered such surprise. Within a short interval, the American artist gave a concert for a full house at the small Queen's Hall. She gave Rust's Sonata in D Minor a "highly intelligent reading" and observers noted the remarkable "virility of tone and assurance of rhythm rarely found . . . amongst women players." Still, when she launched into Wieniawski's *Faust Fantasie*, everyone in the hall marveled at the "astonishing technique of the American artist."[5]

Maud was beginning to catch musical London's attention, but she was very much dissatisfied with her progress during her first season there. Overcoming a certain provinciality toward American violinists as well as bias against women players—in spite of Lady Hallé's universal acclaim in the British Isles—required courageous and dramatic action. Maud met this exigency with characteristic resourcefulness:

> When I went to England to live, . . . I gave my initial recital in London, which did not do a scrap of good, except that the three line criticisms were good, although practically lost in a mass of other mentions of concerts. At any rate, managers knew I was on hand and the musicians became aware of my presence. I had a few letters of introduction which brought me [a] few engagements, but I felt that I was not getting on and would never get on in conservative England unless something extraordinary happened. I went over to Berlin, gave a recital, and while there played the Second Concerto by Max Bruch to the composer himself, whom I had met when I had studied in Berlin as a girl. I apparently pleased him very much, whereupon I ventured to ask him for a card of introduction to Dr. Hans Richter, who held the most important post in England, conductor of the Hallé Orchestra in Manchester. Armed with this I returned to London, called up my nice, conservative, reliable old manager, Mr. Vert, who had never taken more than a perfunctory interest in me, told him I wanted to meet Dr. Richter and that I had this card from Dr. Max Bruch. Richter, who was not in town and would not be, and was too busy to see anybody when he did come, turned out to be coming incognito to Mr. Vert's office the next morning. An appointment was made and I, an artist with a reputation behind me, swallowed my pride and went down to Mr. Vert's office and played parts of the Tschaikowsky and the Beethoven Concertos for the distinguished old man himself. His eyes glowed and he said: "You shall play either the Tschaikovsky or the Beethoven at one of my concerts in the autumn. It depends upon what the concertmeister, Mr. Brodsky, decides to play. If he plays Beethoven, you play Tschaikovsky and vice versa." Well, I played my Tschaikovsky and according to the local music critics I made a sensation. After that it was all easy sailing in England, and continental work followed that.[6]

When Bruch heard her play his D minor concerto, he enthusiastically exclaimed that she had played it as well as Sarasate, for whom it was written, and with infinitely more *Leidenschaft* (passion).[7]

In Berlin the plucky American appeared at the Singakademie on March 19, 1899, where she was warmly appreciated by the German critics. One described the event:

> Among the audience . . . , doubtless more than half represented the American colony, which had . . . turned its back on the great Ysaÿe to do homage to one of its own artists. We venture to say that those present met with no disappointment. Miss Powell played the Tartini Sonata in G minor (Didone abbandonata), three movements from the Bach Solo-Sonata in E major, two solos of Lalo and Ogarew and the Wieniawski Faust-Fantasie. . . . [T]he celebrated violinist upheld her reputation. . . . The performance was perfect. Her whole style of interpretation is governed by the presence of an exceptionally sensitive and deep musical nature. Her thoroughly artistic and refined temperament shows itself in every phrase and her work upon this evening was a great credit to America.[8]

Even the *London Musical Courier* reported in May that she had achieved a "well-deserved success" in Berlin. More interesting was its comment about her style of playing: "Though a pupil of Joachim, Miss Powell's style is that of the Belgian school. She has breadth, wealth of tone, colour, fire, and brilliancy. Her conception is noble and virile, and her execution faultless. She is moreover, ripened by years of public playing and by hard study by herself. True individual progress must come from within. Miss Powell suggests forcibly Ysaÿe, and in many respects she is not far removed from that great master."

With her mother, Maud returned to London for her encounter with Richter and then spent the summer in Buxton, giving light concerts and learning to ride a bicycle. Her appearance with Richter and the Hallé Orchestra in Manchester was scheduled for December 7, 1899.

The Manchester Orchestra was popularly known as the Hallé Orchestra since Sir Charles Hallé had been its conductor from its inception in 1857 until his death in 1895. Richter, who resided in Vienna, had accepted the permanent conductorship in 1897.

Arriving in Manchester, Maud renewed her friendships with baritone Charles Santley, who also was to perform, and with Adolph Brodsky, who had been concertmaster of the New York Symphony under Damrosch (1890–1894). Brodsky, who had first performed the Tchaikovsky concerto, had become the concertmaster of the Manchester Orchestra in 1895. Surprisingly, it was only the third time the Tchaikovsky concerto had been performed at these concerts. The critic of the *Manchester Guardian* reported:

> Miss Powell did not yesterday indulge in any technical display of the non-legitimate kind, we are not aware that she ever does so; but she is, nevertheless, the most sensational violin player that we have ever heard. She cultivates a kind of demoniac style, laying about her in a continual frenzy where there are rapid or complex passages to be played, and where, as in the opening part of the canzonetta forming the middle movement of the Tschaikowsky concerto, there is only a simple melody to be brought out, her tone is, with the aid of a mute, made weird and witch-like to an extraordinary degree. The basis of this peculiar style is an astounding technical facility. Even the most formidable passages in the concerto came out with a rip and a snap that were always eloquent of the performer's fiery energy, correct musical ear, and thorough grasp of the composition.[9]

Maud made her first appearance with the Liverpool Philharmonic Society in response to the need for a substitute for Lady Hallé, who had been scheduled to appear March 6, 1900.[10] Established in 1840, the Liverpool Philharmonic was conducted by Dr. Frederic Cowen, who had succeeded Sir Charles Hallé in 1895. The concert was viewed as of "considerable importance" because it introduced the American violinist, who "fairly took the audience by storm." Playing Saint-Saëns' Concerto No. 3 in B Minor, which Maud called a work of "unusual beauty and classic lucidity," the critic reported that "from the outset it was apparent that the newcomer was a veritable magician of the bow."[11] Finding in Maud Powell "a worthy substitute indeed" for Lady Hallé, he observed:

> The concerto is more than a show piece, it calls for a display of the highest artistic attributes as well as of executive skill. And there is no direction in which Miss Powell is not highly accomplished. She is . . . an artist to the fingertips, and her magnificent performance of the exacting music served to rouse the enthusiasm of the audience to an unwonted degree, resulting in a double recall. Later Miss Powell played three movements from Bach's Sixth Sonata unaccompanied, and here the audience were able to gauge still better

how talented a violinist she is. The demand for an encore was quite undeniable.[12]

Thereafter, Maud Powell was proclaimed "the Lady Hallé of America," and Cowen promptly engaged her for the next season. For that concert on December 4, 1900, Maud played Bruch's D minor concerto along with the English composer Coleridge-Taylor's *Gypsy Song* and *Gypsy Dance*.

Throughout 1900, the American violinist concertized extensively on the Continent as well as in London and the English provinces, her reputation growing as she played. She even spent a portion of the summer in the Ardennes at Spa, Belgium, playing in several concerts at the Casino with the contralto Helen Niebuhr.

In London, Maud often joined friends in chamber music programs and participated in charity concerts as well as concerts given in the private mansions of the nobility. During the week of November 3, she gave two recitals in London prior to her twenty-concert tour of the British Isles. She was being carefully watched by music connoisseurs. After "putting her powers to the test" with three movements from Bach's E major sonata, an eminent critic reported that she "played the several movements with facility, musicianly phrasing and high intelligence." At the same concert, her performance of Hubay's *Fantasie Hongroise* was called "marvelously clever," revealing "extraordinary mastery over her instrument." A storm of applause forced her to respond with encores, including Bazzini's *Rondo*, which was received with "rapturous delight." This particular observer concluded that the "great charm of Miss Powell's playing is her pure, limpid, singing tone."[13]

Before her return to America at the end of the year, English critics recalled the great violinists that they had heard—Vieuxtemps, Wieniawski, Joachim, Sarasate, Ysaÿe, Sauret, and the latest arrival, Kubelik, the "Paganini of 1900." Then they observed: "But besides Lady Hallé there are few women who have ever attained a great position in this special branch of music. America has, however, produced a very fine violinist in the person of Miss Maud Powell. . . . A brilliant and virile player, Miss Powell is invariably paid the compliment of not being judged from the standpoint of women players, but from that of excellence as a musician with the technique and strength of a man."[14]

As she returned home, one of the best music critics in England tipped his hat to the lady, writing, "Miss Powell came, played and conquered."[15] To seal the compliment, she was invited to make her debut with the Philharmonic Society of London in June of 1901.

16

Turning Point, 1901

Art! Who comprehends her? With whom can one consult concerning this great goddess?

— Beethoven

MAUD'S RETURN TO THE UNITED STATES LATE IN 1900 came at a difficult time of transition for the family. In 1894, John Wesley Powell had resigned as director of the U.S. Geological Survey although he remained director of the Bureau of Ethnology. He was weary of wrangling every year with Congress over the Survey's appropriations and weighed down with the increasingly painful stump of his right arm. For more than twenty years he had matched wits with his detractors who attacked him personally in order to subvert the realization of his ideas. His integrity and vision, backed by the facts recorded by the Geological Survey, slowed the exploitation of the West as short-sighted politicians like Senator Stewart of Nevada used the power of Congress to attempt to hound him out of office. Powell had built the Survey into an institution which would endure to carry out his vision well beyond his lifetime.

With the formation of the Bureau of Reclamation in 1902 according to principles he had suggested, Powell's plan to conserve and release the West's natural wealth for the benefit of the American people was on its way to belated fulfillment. He died on September 23, 1902, with this satisfaction.[1]

Bramwell Powell's career paralleled that of his brother Wes.[2] Unorthodox in his educational approach and obdurate in his determination to reform the Washington, D.C., school system, Bramwell steadily became more controversial. He discarded the examination and drilling methods which had forced children out of school pre-maturely.[3] In the single-minded pursuit of his ideals, Bram discharged admittedly incompetent teachers who had political connections. He daringly required teachers to go to the Smithsonian to learn of nat-ural history and to the seat of government to learn first-hand of its functions and operation. Finally, Senator Stewart, who disliked the Powell brothers, chaired a Congressional investigation of the District's schools between 1898 and 1900.

The Congressional committee judged that the schools were improp-erly organized and that the teaching of nature study and science interfered with drilling in spelling, reading, writing, and arith-metic.[4] But Bramwell Powell and the parents in the community knew better. The tests thrust upon the students in these subjects by the investigators showed worthy results. More importantly, Powell had succeeded in making learning attractive to children and in reaching larger numbers of them for longer periods of time than ever before. He had brought the parents along with them by inducing active parental interest in the education of their children. Above all, he had succeeded in educating the whole person, not just in training the intellect.[5] At a school board meeting on June 27, 1900, Maud's father spoke eloquently in his own defense:

> Those results for which the Senate committee instituted search, the power to "do sums," to spell all the words properly and to use punc-tuation marks correctly, under my supervision we have made subor-dinate, not incidental, and the higher things, manhood, courtesy, obedience by self-control, without punishment of any description; power to do, willingness to make the effort, continuity of purpose and strict integrity in representing work, all that make for that higher citizenship which every patriot would have characterize our nation-ality, for these that I have sought to make the chief characteristics of the schools of the capital, the Senate committee made no inquiry.[6]

The community which had felt the dedication and love which this distinguished educator poured into all his work appreciated his efforts. Nevertheless, by an act of Congress, Powell and the entire school board which had backed him were dismissed. The school board reluctantly accepted Bramwell's resignation, effective July 1, 1900, approved his report on the District schools, ordered 5,000 copies printed, and adopted a resolution of thanks to Maud's father which reflected the esteem in which he was held.[7]

Maud found her father unbowed by his Washington experience. Eager to further education in new ways, he was sent to the Philippines in 1901 to investigate its school and textbook needs.

While there, he contracted malaria. When he completed his mission, he returned to Mt. Vernon, New York, to live out the rest of his days, which ended on February 6, 1904.

Maud's mother finally "gave up the road" in 1901 as a result of a "nervous breakdown." We have no more information on Mrs. Powell's illness except that she did recover and lived a reasonably active life until her death many years later. Undoubtedly, however, the strain from all those years of touring and looking after her daughter's needs as Maud's schedule grew more and more demanding had finally taken their toll. She attempted to pick up the pieces of a long-abandoned home life with Bram in Mt. Vernon, with what degree of difficulty will never be known. Maud seemed to indicate that Bram and Minnie had grown apart through the years of separation and were much like strangers to one another. The presence of Billy in the household may have tempered the difficulties, if it could not wholly dispel them.

Maud was welcomed home by an eager New York audience which gathered in Carnegie Hall for her first appearance with the New York Philharmonic in more than two years. Emil Paur had succeeded Anton Seidl as conductor upon the latter's death in 1898. Maud played the first movement of the Beethoven concerto and the Rimsky-Korsakov *Fantasia Concertante on Russian Themes* on January 11 and 12, 1901. She probably had met the Russian composer while he was conducting in Brussels during the previous year. The *Fantasia* was composed in 1886 but had not been performed in the United States. Strangely enough, Maud had not previously played any part of the Beethoven concerto with the New York Philharmonic. But to her, Beethoven was an old friend: "The name of Beethoven inspires reverence in the soul of every musician. With the possible exception of Bach he was the mightiest of the mighty in music."[8]

Maud's first appearance after her return from abroad followed by one month Fritz Kreisler's debut in Carnegie Hall (December 7, 1900), when he played the Bruch G minor concerto with the New York Philharmonic. However, the presence of the great Austrian violinist did not lessen the New York critics' interest in or esteem for

Maud. The thoughtful *New York Sun* review is typical of the reception for her concert:

> Miss Maud Powell returns to her native land after an absence of several years, a noble artist for whom the dignity of her art and its serious proclamations are of more importance than bewildering virtuosity. The technic is there; the tone, once too strenuously masculine, is now tempered to a grateful [fitting] sweetness, while the purity, the dazzling technical mastery are all potent witnesses to this young woman's intense artistic devotion. She has broadened and she has mellowed, and, best of all, she plays her instrument like a woman, and does not ape the so-called "grand manner." The reading . . . of the Beethoven concerto was subjective, yet detached from all feminine cloying sentimentality. Miss Powell has brains, and she uses them. Dignity, musical emotion well modulated and a perfect mechanism were the qualities exhibited in this number. Her tone color is richer and more versatile. The run of octaves in the amazingly difficult cadenza [Joachim's] had the effect of a piano glissando—so smooth, so sequential were they.
>
> —*New York Sun*

The reporter for the *New York Tribune* concluded: "Miss Powell played the fantasia with splendid dash and vigor where they were required, and lovely sentiment when opportunity offered. Eight or ten recalls were her reward, and finally she silenced the glad clamor by playing the slow movement from a Bach sonata [*Chaconne*] in a pure and refined classic style."[9]

The conductor Emil Paur wrote Maud a note of appreciation: "Your beautiful and masterful playing still rings in my ear."[10]

Concert life had been steadily improving in the United States since Maud had made her debut. The first two decades of the new century would bring even more progress with the formation of more professional orchestras, the presence of more high-calibre concert artists, and improved concert circuits.[11]

The formation of orchestras was often the result of the accumulated efforts of women's music clubs over the years. The women of the Thursday Musical Chorus, formed in 1892, could claim a great deal of credit for bringing the German musician Emil Oberhoffer (1867–1933) to Minneapolis and providing the musical atmosphere and support for the Minneapolis Orchestra's formation in 1903. The Thursday Musical had engaged Maud Powell for recitals almost annually in the 1890s, and after the orchestra was formed, Maud performed with it under Oberhoffer's direction.

The board of directors of the Cincinnati Orchestra Association was composed entirely of women who had run the orchestra's affairs since its first season, beginning in January 1895. The Association had been formed to break the city's fifteen-year dependency on the Cincinnati College of Music Orchestra. Frank Van der Stucken, the Cincinnati Orchestra's conductor until 1907, presided over ten afternoon and ten evening concerts each season. The orchestra was reorganized in 1909 under the direction of the young Leopold Stokowski (b. 1882), who came to the United States in 1905. (Maud Powell would perform under Stokowski's direction with both the Cincinnati and Philadelphia orchestras.)

In other cities, the efforts of industrialists and philanthropists—often backed by their wives, who formed the working committees to get things moving—resulted in the formation of new symphony orchestras. The withdrawal of Theodore Thomas and his orchestra from giving regular concerts in Philadelphia after 1891, together with the community's desire to produce opera, spurred the formation of the Philadelphia Orchestra in 1900. The Orchestra Association, comprising three hundred men and women prominent in social and artistic affairs, was organized with the aid of women's committees from towns and cities contiguous to Philadelphia.

The Orchestra Association engaged the German conductor Fritz Scheel, who had been Hans von Bülow's assistant in Hamburg, and sent him *abroad* to recruit an orchestra. Not surprisingly, most of the musicians recruited were German-speaking. When the London-born Leopold Stokowski took over the Philadelphia Orchestra in 1912, rehearsals were still being conducted in German because Scheel's successor Karl Pohlig was also a German. Since Stokowski spoke German, he continued the custom for a short time, but eventually dropped it as being ridiculous.

By the 1907–08 season, the orchestra was giving twenty afternoon and twenty evening concerts in Philadelphia and further influencing the region's musical growth by giving concerts in such cities as Trenton, Harrisburg, Wilmington, Baltimore, and Washington.

The incentive for the Pittsburgh Symphony Orchestra's formation was steel magnate Andrew Carnegie's gift to the city of a building, dedicated in 1895, to house a library, an art gallery, a museum, and a music hall. The orchestra's first concert was given on February 27, 1896, and in the following years it gave thirty-six concerts in Pittsburgh each season and toured such cities as Cleveland, Buffalo, Toledo, Detroit, and Toronto.

In a great groundswell of cultural activity, these cities' experiences were repeated throughout the country, and other notable orchestras began to take their places in the musical life of America.[12] The major orchestras toured, thereby expanding their influence, and were engaged for summer music festivals in such places as Cincinnati, Nashville, Norfolk (Connecticut), Albany (New York), Syracuse, and Worcester (Massachusetts), for which Maud was often a soloist.

After 1900, the number and quality of visiting artists from abroad also increased markedly.[13] Among the most notable Europeans were Ysaÿe, Kreisler, Jan Kubelik, and the French master Jacques Thibaud.

Among the American violinists was Albert Spalding (Chicago, 1888–1953), who made his first appearance in America in 1908 with the New York Symphony. He had received his training in Italy at the Bologna Conservatory and from Lefort in Paris. The American violinist Louis Persinger (1887–1966) returned to the United States in 1912 after studying under Becker in Leipzig and then with Ysaÿe in Brussels and Thibaud in Paris, making his debut with the Philadelphia Orchestra under Stokowski. The Canadian violinist Kathleen Parlow (Calgary, 1890–1963) made her American debut in late 1910, performing the Tchaikovsky concerto with the Russian Symphony Orchestra. Leonora Jackson (Boston, 1879–1969) made her New York debut in 1900.

Among the Russian pupils of Leopold Auer was Mischa Elman (1891–1965), who made his sensational New York debut playing the Tchaikovsky concerto with the Russian Symphony Orchestra on December 10, 1908. Another Auer pupil, Efrem Zimbalist (1890–1985) settled in the United States permanently in 1911, marrying in 1914 a friend of Maud's, the famous soprano Alma Gluck. Jascha Heifetz arrived later, in 1917. Auer himself (1845–1930) came to the United States in 1918, near the end of his life.

Maud Powell knew or heard all of these violinists, and a good many of them made an effort to hear her perform.

Among Maud's friends in the musical world could be included many of the great opera stars of the period, most notably the Americans Lillian Nordica, Louise Homer, Geraldine Farrar, Emma Eames,

Alma Gluck, Lillian Blauvelt, David Bispham, and Herbert Wither-spoon, Clara Butt, Nellie Melba, Ben Davies, Enrico Caruso, Riccardo Martin, Marcella Sembrich, Ernestine Schumann-Heink, Luisa Tetrazzini, and George Hamlin. Among pianists, she was a close friend of the American Fannie Bloomfield-Zeisler and certainly knew Teresa Carreño, Ignace Paderewski, Vladimir de Pachmann, Katherine Goodson, Ernest Hutcheson, and Leopold Godowsky. She probably also knew Moriz Rosenthal, Josef Hofmann, Ferruccio Busoni, Raoul Pugno, Olga Samaroff, and Ossip Gabrilowitsch. Among cellists, she was a close friend of May Mukle and probably also knew Pablo Casals, both of whom toured in the United States before 1920.

Maud's 1901 tour reflects the changes in America's musical atmosphere and concert circuits as well as her own artistic growth. Between January and May she was booked to give more than fifty concerts with the leading orchestras and in recital throughout the country. On this tour, most of her appearances with orchestra followed performances by Fritz Kreisler, providing an opportunity for comparison of the two artists. In one particular instance, in a New York recital Maud happened to play the same piece Kreisler had a month earlier and the critics praised her as before.[14]

Maud's return to Oberlin, after five years' absence, provides another basis for comparing her with other great violinists of her day. The demanding program she chose reflected her delight in contrast and her love of both old and new literature: Tartini's sonata *Didone Abbandonata*, Saint-Saëns' Concerto No. 3 in B Minor, three movements from Bach's E major sonata (unaccompanied), and five shorter works by Coleridge-Taylor, Bazzini, Schubert, Brahms, and Hubay. Her discerning audience noted that while her playing had always been "pure, firm, and poetic," she had "gained remarkably in brilliancy and depth of feeling" so that "she may stand unchallenged amid such a peerage as Marteau, Adolf Brodsky, and the never-to-be-forgotten Ysaÿe."[15]

The Oberlin review also enables us to evaluate Maud's tone coloration, since it particularly emphasizes this aspect of her art. One of the important aspects of Kreisler's playing was his beautiful golden tone, which is attributed to his use of an intense, but varied, vibrato which he applied to passing as well as sustained notes and in rapid as well as slow passages. The technique was distinctly different from Joachim's, in which vibrato gave life only to sustained notes. Kreisler himself said that the technique had originated with Wieniawski (1835–80), who had "intensified" the vibrato in such a distinctive manner that it became known as the "French vibrato." Ysaÿe (1858–1931), who ushered in the twentieth-century approach to violin playing, had advanced the technique further. Maud, who was constantly compared with Ysaÿe and only a decade younger, clearly had developed a similar technique. Reviews and recordings as well as testimony of those who heard Kreisler, Powell, and Ysaÿe play indicate that the differences in their art were more personal than technical.

John Maltese, a violinist and noted record collector whose extensive collection includes the recordings of Joachim, Sarasate, Kubelik, Auer, Marteau, Ysaÿe, Powell, Kreisler, Elman, Zimbalist, and Spalding, views Maud Powell's technique and artistry as the bridge between the old and modern schools of violin playing. The old school represented by Joachim, Dancla, Schradieck, and Sarasate, was characterized by limited use of vibrato and audible slides from position to position, sometimes more as a result of technical requirements than musical expression. Maud was trained in the old school and from an early age had all the technical equipment required of a virtuoso; but unlike Kubelik and Auer, she continually refined her technique in keeping with new developments in the art. Her intelligence and keen powers of observation enabled her, through her own experimentation and her observation of other violinists, to develop new ideas for refining her playing. That there was noticeable improvement in her technique and growth in her musicianship from year to year is borne out by the repeated testimony of critics in their reviews.

Apart from *refining* her technique, the noted Puerto Rican violinist José Figueroa observes that Maud pioneered the development of *new* violin technique when she gave the American premieres of the Tchaikovsky, Dvořák, and Sibelius violin concertos. Each work presented unprecedented technical difficulties for which Maud had to develop her own *original* solutions which placed her in the forefront of technical developments.[16]

Equipped with an "amazingly efficient" technique which her recordings of Sauret's *Farfalla*, Sarasate's *Zigeunerweisen*, and the Finale to Mendelssohn's E minor violin concerto reveal, Maud developed, Maltese observes, a vibrato geared toward the modern style at a time when Leopold Auer eschewed vibrato. Maud's recordings reveal that her vibrato grew more controlled through the years and that she used it discriminately to make her playing ever more expressive. Stressing the importance of consciously controlled vibrato, she advised students not to "overdo" the vibrato and to vary it in keeping with the period of the composition. ("Don't use the same vibrato in an eighteenth-century composition that you would use in an intense, dramatic, modern piece.")[17]

Maltese points out that Maud also used slides discriminately so that their use was purely a function of musical expression, not of the technical necessity of changing from one position to another. Some slides were of the old school, but they were meaningful in that day, in keeping with tasteful musical expression of the time.

Maltese concludes that Maud Powell was always advancing the art of violin playing and maintained a terrific technical facility "equal to anyone." Among all the violinists of her day, her recorded art stands out as musically stunning and satisfying, technically immaculate and refined, and endowed with a spiritual quality which demands his "attention, respect, and love."[18]

Affirming this view, Albert Moglie, the noted Washington, D.C., luthier and nonagenarian, when asked to compare the technique of Ysaÿe, Elman, Kreisler, and Powell, whom he heard in person after 1910, declared that Powell's technique was "much the same" as theirs. Despite seventy intervening years, Moglie still could describe the electrifying effect of a Powell recital given in New York's Aeolian Hall in 1914: "It is very hard to forget it. It seems to me it follows you." Without hesitation, he said, "She was the greatest of her days; no question about it. She was one of a kind." "And if she were playing today?" I ventured. "Same thing. Never change!" he replied emphatically.[19]

The fact that Victor chose Maud to be the first instrumentalist to record for its prestigious Red Seal label and repeatedly signed her to make recordings until the time of her death—and that these recordings were world-wide best-sellers—also indicates that she expressed the height of violin-playing in her time.

The review of the 1901 Oberlin concert points to the fact that Maud was continuing to refine the purity of tone and rich tone coloration which had always characterized her art:

Miss Powell plays with the air of a master. Her tone is firm, pure and sonorous, her technic facile and unobtrusive, her interpretation subtle and always poetic. There is an abundance of variety and contrast in her tone-color itself, from the rich, glowing "ultra-violet," to the clear, bell-like flageolet tones of which she is such a master. In the lovely pastoral movement of the Saint Saëns concerto she obtained a tone so liquid and fragile as to suggest an idealization of the oboe, such a shepherd's pipe as one might hear of a summer's day in fabled Arcady. In somber moods, no less than in delicate, she made the tone-color in itself highly expressive. The Tartini [sonata], which under so many hands is mere dry bones, she played with true poetic insight into its lofty melancholy, and made every measure consistently expressive of the sorrows of the fated Dido. Moreover, in this composition she showed the broad rhythmic sweep and strong molding of phrases which cannot be got by striving after, but is a gift from the gods.[20]

The Pittsburgh Symphony Orchestra was in only its sixth season when "America's leading violinist" played with it the Saint-Saëns Concerto in B Minor. Maud's friend Victor Herbert had become the permanent conductor in 1898. With Herbert on the podium, the violinist's performance was reportedly "beautiful in the extreme."[21]

That season, Maud also played the Saint-Saëns Concerto in B Minor with the Cincinnati Symphony Orchestra conducted by Frank Van der Stucken. Since the early founding of the Cincinnati Conservatory of Music in 1867 and institution of the biennial Music Festivals in 1873, under Theodore Thomas's direction, Cincinnati had been prominent in the arts. The city's critics, now highly respected, received Maud in the following vein:

Miss Powell has advanced herself to the front rank of violinists, and among the many eminent soloists heard during this season easily ranks first. To speak of technic is, of course, superfluous. . . . Miss Powell's playing is characterized by a wonderfully clear, broad tone, brilliancy, decisiveness and perfection of detail. It is, however, the musicianly understanding and the intellectual conception of her work that adds to Miss Powell's playing the elements of greatness. It is not playing for matinee audiences nor for impressionable persons of either gender, but for the musician, the thinker and the artist. Encores, of course, and after that more encores, compelled Miss Powell to appear several times on the platform.

—Cincinnati Enquirer

At the Peabody Conservatory in Baltimore, the "famous and ever popular violinist" presented a recital that included, in part, the Tartini Sonata in G Minor, three movements of Bach's Sonata in E Major (unaccompanied), Wieniawski's *Faust Fantasie*, and Saint-Saëns' *The Swan*. The program gave wide scope to her extreme versatility, according to the critics, but the Bach "received a rendition nothing short of stupendous."[22] "Again and again she was obliged to respond to the applause, especially after the Bach movements, which she played in a manner rarely heard," one reviewer reported.[23] Her art had deepened since this audience had last heard her: "Her tone, always wonderfully pure, has grown broader and more soulful, and to her wonted repose is added a new fire and vigor."[24] Critics noted the complete sympathy between Maud and her accompanist Harold Randolph in the Beethoven Sonata in C Minor, which was "noble in conception and impeccable in execution." Providing another example of America's musical progress, the American-born and trained Randolph was the director of the Peabody Conservatory, where he had been a student, and he was also an established concert pianist.

Of a similar program given before the Wednesday Morning Musicale in Nashville, the critics commented, "Though she exercises perfect artistic restraint, the fire of her soul flashed forth at times with an effect that might be called electrical." Maud's performances created "the fascination which comes when high emotional feeling has the fullest mechanical resources at command for its expression."[25]

Maud arrived in Boston in April to give a recital as well as to play with the Boston Symphony Orchestra. The recital included the Tartini sonata and probably was much the same as those she had given earlier on this tour. Boston critics were known for the severity of their judgment and so it is of particular interest to read how they received Maud after several years' absence.

> It has been some years since I heard Miss Powell play. I had remembered her as an excellent violinist, but hardly as the distinguished artist I heard on Saturday afternoon. Miss Powell is now easily a virtuoso on her instrument, in the fullest sense of the term, moreover, she plays with a vehemence of emotional expression which is almost sui generis. Its intensity does not seem to be in the least factitious, it is not merely a matter of grand style; it is genuine emotional heat, applicable to the grandest as well as to the less

noble work. There were passages in the Tartini sonata that fairly made you quake. Note, too, that this expressive vehemence is not applied at random; its employment is governed by a very sure musicianship, in perfect good taste. Neither is it all of the same unvarying sort; there was an intensity in Miss Powell's delivery of Coleridge-Taylor's . . . lovely Gypsy Melodies which was of a very different sort from the profounder passionateness shown in parts of the *Didone abbandonata*.

—Boston Evening Transcript

Miss Powell has grown steadily in artistic stature until few of her sisters can claim reasonably to be her peer. Of women who have visited us of late years only Lady Hallé is to be named with her in the same breath. Miss Powell has reached her goal by honest and honorable means. Her own natural gifts, her genius for indefatigable and intelligent work have placed her in this proud position. She has not put her strength in press agents with Sackbut and psaltery and high sounding cymbals; she did not use sex or her nationality to boost her into a place she did not deserve. Her one great friend and helper has been her indisputable talent. It would be an idle compliment to say that she plays like a man for she plays better than many men. It would be misleading to say that she plays like a woman, even though the possession of the . . . sentiments and gentler emotions was thus implied. Miss Powell plays like a true artist, who knows all emotions and passions, but is not mastered by them. . . .

—Boston Journal[26]

On April 12 and 13, 1901, Maud joined the Boston Symphony Orchestra, with Wilhelm Gericke conducting, for a performance of Tchaikovsky's violin concerto. One reporter noted that the marked cordiality of the large audience, manifested in enthusiastic recalls, made amends for a long-postponed lack of appreciation. The *Boston Journal* critic Philip Hale wrote that "few violinists have shown here . . . as keen a sense—of the value of rhythm as was shown by Miss Powell last night. The performance proved that the eulogies pronounced on her in foreign capitals were not hysterical, and that she must be ranked among the leading violinists, irrespective of sex or nationality."[27]

On April 19 and 20, Maud appeared in Chicago to perform the Tchaikovsky concerto with Theodore Thomas and the Chicago Symphony. Maud had written to him, "I am looking forward, oh so eagerly, to playing with you once more!"[28] He granted her her first choice of the three concertos she proffered.

The Boston reviews served to heighten the expectations of the Chicagoans, who, according to the *Chicago Tribune*, greeted her with a full house and "abundant applause."

> . . . Miss Maud Powell . . . yesterday did some violin playing the equal of which has not been heard here in many a day. Nothing the year just ending has offered in the violin field has equaled in artistic completeness the work she did yesterday, and this statement is made with full recognition of the array of able performers who have been heard here during that period [including Kreisler]. The Boston critic [who wrote] . . . that Miss Powell "must be ranked among the leading violinists, irrespective of sex or nationality" can but be said to have spoken praise that was in every way just and merited.
>
> She is a player who asks no critical indulgence because of her sex. Her playing is virile with a virility that is of the masculine, and not of the feminine type—there is a wide difference between the two—and the listener is at no time permitted to note anything that in point of conception or tonal power is other than masterly.
>
> The Tschaikowski concerto was played with a breadth of manner that told of absolute supremacy over all technical difficulties, and with a dramatic intensity, an authority, and a poise that belong only to the "grand style" of performance.
>
> It was an artistic achievement to be long remembered and cherished. An encore was insisted upon and granted in the form of a truly splendid delivery of the Sarabande and Bourree from Bach's B minor suite for violin alone.[29]

One critic noted that Maud Powell's appearance had been the artistic high point of the year because the solo playing was "of the first order of art" and the artist, together with her beloved friend Theodore Thomas, inspired the orchestra to play with finer ensemble "than happens more than once or twice in a season."[30]

While in Chicago, Maud visited another old friend, William Lewis, and gave a private recital for his class. It was her last visit with this beloved master, for he died the following year.

As she sailed for Europe in June on the steamer *Augusta Victoria*, Maud could reflect with great satisfaction on the most successful concert tour she had made in her own country. America's musical growth had enabled her to perform with more professional orchestras and to be received by her countrymen with greater appreciation than ever before, developments which augured well for the future.

At Home in Europe, 1901–1902

God calls you to be eagles, and to fly from sun to sun, over continents.

— *Henry Ward Beecher*

THE PHILHARMONIC SOCIETY OF LONDON, FOUNDED IN 1813, had a long and venerable history of association with the greatest composers and artists.[1] In its eighty-ninth year, the Society was giving just seven concerts per season, from February through June. The soloists featured in 1901 included the pianists Busoni, Carreño, and Sauer and violinists Franz Ondříček, Lady Hallé (playing the Mendelssohn concerto), and Jan Kubelik (playing Paganini's D major concerto). Maud Powell was the only other violinist to appear.

In the first portion of the June twentieth concert, Leopold Godowsky, the masterful Russian-Polish pianist who now lived in America, made his first appearance with the Society, playing Brahms' Piano Concerto in D Minor, Op. 15. Maud appeared during the second half, which featured Edward Elgar conducting the first performance of his *Cockaigne* Overture.

It seemed "strange" to the critic of the *London Times* that this was Maud's first appearance with the Philharmonic. He wrote that "she has long deserved the honor." Dr. Frederic Cowen conducted her performance of the Tchaikovsky concerto, still a relative novelty in London. It had first been played in England by Brodsky, at a Richter concert in 1882, and was better known in the North, where he continued to perform it.

The large audience gathered in Queen's Hall heard the American violinist perform with "great dignity, brilliant execution, and true musicianship." She rendered the canzonetta "with exquisite taste," and although she had to stop to tune in the middle of the cadenza which follows it, the *Times* reviewer declared that the interruption had no serious effect on the music. Repeatedly recalled by the audience, Maud refused to yield to demands for an encore.

From June of 1901 to December of 1903, Maud made London her home and concertized steadily in Europe and the British Isles. Her association with other artists was one of the features of life in London she valued most. Ysaÿe and Busoni gave a recital together the same evening that Maud played with the Philharmonic Society, and Kreisler made his London debut that year at a Richter concert on May twelfth.

Maud made frequent appearances on the Continent during these years, including engagements with the Lamoureux Orchestra of Paris and the Leipzig Gewandhaus Orchestra. Following her performance with the Philharmonic Society, she began an extensive European tour, arousing great enthusiasm wherever she played. She played three times at the Casino concerts in Spa, Belgium, in August, and in September she played Saint-Saëns' B minor concerto with l'Orchestre Philharmonique in Scheveningen, Holland. The *Journal des Etrangers* wrote: "Miss Maud Powell is one of the most remarkable violinists we have ever had here, and I speak from a lively memory. She possesses, besides a rare mechanism, a power of expression that is full of life and warmth and decided individuality. She throws her whole soul into her interpretations." The critic for the *New Courant* of Rotterdam said that her bowing reminded him of Wieniawski.[2]

Maud also toured Germany, Italy, and France in 1901, and she included the music centers of Bohemia, Denmark, Austria, Hungary, Poland, and Russia in her tours of Europe during the next two years. Throughout her long sojourn abroad, Maud's reception in the press was much the same everywhere:

> In Paris: "Gives her a place in the ranks of the world's greatest artists" — *Figaro*.
> In Liège: "One of the world's greatest violinists" — *La Meusa*.
> In Berlin: "Ravished with her warm tone, fluent technic and pure style" — *Vossische Zeitung*; "A violinist of the very first rank" — *Tageblatt*.

In Vienna: "A beautiful singing tone and amazing virtuosity" — *Neues Wiener Tageblatt.*

In Prague: "Achieved a triumph. . . . Stoical repose and an amazing command of nuance and dynamics" — *The Bohemia.*

In St. Petersburg: "Genius for musical interpretation . . . . marvelous sense of rhythm" — *Petersburger Zeitung.*

And in Warsaw: "silvery tone, dazzling technic, warmth of temperament" — *Kurjer.*

In the *Irish Times* Maud was regarded as "A distinctive unit among the big multitude of seemingly perfect violinists who flood the present-day market."

Back in Liverpool, she was "Magnificent. . . . ranks with the foremost of modern performers on the king of instruments" — *Liverpool Courier.*

And in London, according to *The Times*, there was "Nothing but praise to be said of her . . . exquisite taste and faultless execution."[3]

The American artist always spoke enthusiastically of playing for Russian, Polish, and Hungarian audiences. When in their presence, Maud played with an "unconscious abandon and a nervous tensity of feeling." She felt that this environment magically aroused all the "gypsy" elements of her musical soul.

During this period Maud became well known to London audiences of the Queen's Hall Orchestra, the Saturday Pops, the Erard, Broadwood, and other concert series. In the English "provinces" she was exceedingly popular. She had regular engagements with the Liverpool Philharmonic, the Hallé Orchestra in Manchester, the Scottish Orchestral Concerts in Glasgow, Edinburgh, Dundee, and elsewhere, the Foxon concerts in Sheffield, the chamber concerts in Nottingham, the Gloucester Festivals, and Maud is even reputed to have played in Westminster Abbey. The American violinist frequently played for royalty, including the Viceroy of Ireland at the Viceregal Lodge in Dublin, Princess Louise of Battenburg at Kensington Palace, the Dukes of Cambridge and Edinburgh at concerts of the Royal Amateur Orchestra in London, and for Lady Warwick at Warwick Castle. Maud also performed under Nikisch, Colonne, Steinbach, Safonoff, Weingartner, and Richter, the great conductors of the time, who were familiar to London audiences.

In January of 1902 she was in Manchester, possibly for her performance of the Beethoven concerto with Richter and the Hallé Orchestra. At thirty-four, Maud was at the top of her profession, and so she was obliged to respond to interviewers' persistent questions about how she had got there. One such interview reveals her natural manner, straight thinking, and forceful speech as well as something of the price she had paid for her art:

"What I should like to hear from you is some account of the struggles which a young artist has to face in attempting to gain a footing. As you know, there are dozens of colleges turning out more or less competent young men and women by the hundred, and each of these youngsters imagines that he or she is going to take the world by storm. He has only to sit down and the letters and telegrams will come of their own accord."

"Yes—I myself should like to say something on that point; it's a matter I feel very strongly about. The certainty of achieving Fame which most musical students possess is not only pitiable, it is pitiful. When I see a young girl striding along with a violin-case in one hand and a roll of music in the other, my heart aches for the sorrow and disappointment she will have to go through. Concert playing is no career for anyone unless he have powers absolutely above the average. And even then it is one of the most disheartening professions a girl can possibly enter. A man like Kubelik can get as many engagements as he wants, but Kubelik is a technical giant, and I am not speaking of giants. I am speaking about the ordinary run of violinists, pianists and vocalists of whom there are scores. An artist has to *seek* engagements: they rarely come to him. He has to obtain letters of introduction to managers, he has to introduce himself sometimes, and if he gets terribly snubbed, well, it's all in the day's work, and he has to put up with it. People say 'there's always room at the top.' So there is, but how many people get there? Not one out of every five hundred. A man or woman may become fashionable, but who understands fashion and who is able to fathom its strange eccentricities? I know very well that it is extremely unpopular for a successful artist to talk in this way; he is generally accused of being anxious to avoid future competition by discouraging young aspirants; but, believe me, I speak right from my heart when I give Punch's advice to those about to marry—'Don't!' It doesn't pay; and not only that, it is the most heartrending profession in the world. Take my own case, for instance, I am no longer in the first flush of youth—in fact I've been before the public a fair number of years, but *I haven't saved a cent*! I simply can't. Artists are supposed to dress well both on and off the concert platform; they are supposed to stay at the best hotels when travelling; and they are supposed to keep up appearances in a thousand and one little ways which I needn't trouble to explain. Added to all this, an artist is really only a child—he doesn't understand the value of money because he receives it in fairly large sums after half-an-hour's work, and he spends it as quickly as he gets it. Not one artist out of twenty is a good business man: it isn't natural that he should be. The artistic temperament is all against it. The artist's life is a hand-to-mouth existence; anything between £200 and £20,000 a year may be made from it, but the prizes are few and far between. And of late years another difficulty has sprung up. It is not only extremely hard to obtain engagements, but at certain concerts one is expected to pay for one's appearance, and (*mirabile dictu!*) there are actually a large number of men and women who are willing to do this. The ambitious sons of wealthy bankers gain an entrance to certain concerts merely by the length of their purse. Of talent they have little, of money they have a great deal—so that is how the trick is done. They put a premium on mediocrity, and concert managers begin to expect really able artists to sacrifice sums of money just for the sake of appearing once or twice at their concerts. I am glad to say I have never paid a cent for any one of my appearances; I would rather starve than encourage a system which is ruining the prospects of so many talented men and women."

Here Miss Powell would have sighed if she had been that kind of person; but instead of sighing she spoke in a high passionate voice, and looked as if she would like to emphasize her remarks by vigorous thumps on the table with her fist. She is a woman who feels intensely; you can see it in her face. She has suffered because she has not been afraid of the world. She has fought it and conquered it. . . . We both looked at the clock simultaneously; there were three minutes left.

"Quick!" I exclaimed. "Let me have something of English music. What do you think of Elgar?"

"Oh—Elgar is the English Richard Strauss—the greatest composer we have, or, at all events, the man who will eventually become the greatest composer. He is the musician in whom I am most interested here in England. He has something much more than talent; 'genius' is not too big a word. And Richard Strauss is the greatest musician alive. He has wonderful technique, tremendous depth of thought, and a soul that is neither afraid nor ashamed to feel. At least, that is how he appears to me, don't you know."[4]

Maud had met Strauss in Europe. He was one of those European composers who owed much to Theodore Thomas, who gave the first performance of his Symphony in F Minor in New York in December of 1884, before the young composer had gained any real recognition in Europe. By the turn of the century, he had composed *Also Sprach Zarathustra* and *Till Eulenspiegel*, and he had gained recognition as an excellent conductor. Maud included in her repertoire his Violin Sonata in E-flat, which he had composed in 1888. In a program note she reveals her perceptions about Strauss:

> Richard Strauss is the most successful of living classical composers both from a popular and financial point of view. He has fought his way doggedly and has lived to enjoy the financial fruits of his genius. He is the supreme example of the tendency of the modern school, the tendency to juggle with technical knowledge with a fiendish facility. He knows the temper of the public and is past master of the advertiser's art of arousing the public's curiosity. Many of us think he has perpetrated the operas of Salomé and Elektra as huge jokes, his tongue in his cheek meanwhile. If not, he is a colossal musical degenerate. The E flat Sonata is one of his earlier works, and may be considered very beautiful. It has a wholesome, amiable spirit while disclosing a truly extraordinary technical efficiency on the part of the then youthful composer.

Maud had become acquainted with other composers on the Continent as well, including Engelbert Humperdinck, who had composed his masterpiece, the opera *Hansel and Gretel*, in 1893. He called her "an artist of distinction" after hearing her play.

In England, Maud formed close associations with both Edward Elgar and Samuel Coleridge-Taylor. Coleridge-Taylor was of Afro-English descent, born and educated in England, studying violin and composition at the Royal College of Music. When Maud discovered him, the young composer was teaching at Trinity College, London. Maud had performed his *Gypsy Dance* and *Gypsy Song* in America on her last tour there, underscoring her willingness to promote the works of new composers.

Maud appears to have recognized Elgar's importance in freeing British music from the German influence which had predominated since Handel's time. Elgar was the first Englishman since Purcell (apart from Arthur Sullivan) to gain an international reputation as a composer. Richard Strauss was particularly impressed after a German performance of Elgar's oratorio *The Dream of Gerontius*, composed in 1900.

When Maud was invited to lead the quartet for the Saturday Popular Concert on February 8, 1902, the *London Times* reported that musicians who had watched her career were excited by the announcement. For English musicians, Joachim and their own Lady Hallé had established the standard which must be attained to be ranked among the greatest musicians. Virtuosity as a solo artist was not enough; the true test of a violinist's merit lay in his or her ability to exhibit consummate musicianship in string quartet playing. At last, English critics were to have their chance to see how this pupil of Joachim measured up in the same forum in which the great master still held forth each year. The *Times* reported on February tenth:

> Miss Powell has long been favorably known to concert-goers as a highly-accomplished violinist of the modern school, and though her reputation as a soloist is high, it is not every first-rate soloist who makes an efficient quartet leader. Save for a slight want of decision in attack, which might easily have come from lack of sufficient experience in playing together with her colleagues . . . and an equally slight deficiency in quantity of tone, there is nothing but praise to be said of her performance. None of the charming freshness of Haydn's quartet in D from opus 64 was lost, and her share in the combined practical exposition of Dvořák's theories on the use to be made of what he imagines to be Indian and negro melodies as propounded in his so-called American quartet in F, op. 96, would surely have satisfied the theorist himself.

The Popular Concert, which also featured the pianist de Pachmann, was one of the best attended that season. The *London Musical Courier* reported that Maud asserted herself as an artist of "unmistakable talent and power" and that in both quartets "she displayed the necessary qualities for a leader—firmness, excellent tone, and, wherever expedient, delicacy and restraint." She treated with "breadth and dignity" her solo rendition of an étude by Fiorillo and then rendered a "vivid and brilliant performance" of Paganini's Caprice No. 24, the technical difficulties of which "she surmounted with grace."

Not all of Maud's concerts went so smoothly. Arriving to play in the last of Miss Marie Foxon's chamber concerts held in Sheffield, Maud found her luggage had gone astray and, to her dismay, there was no alternative but to appear on stage in her traveling costume. This misfortune, however, did not prevent her violin playing from being the artistically outstanding feature of the concert. The *Courier* reported that she played with "magnificent abandon" and "perfection of technical ease and finish." Paganini's Caprice No. 24 was rendered with "expert double stopping" and "a display of virtuosity that could hardly be excelled," for which the artist was recalled with "unmistakable warmth." The latter performance earned her the title "The Lady Paganini" from the critic of the *Sheffield Independent*.

Maud was a popular figure in English circles. Her genial, outgoing disposition won her many friends, and she treated England as her second home, enjoying its traditions and participating fully in its social life and responsibilities. Typically, in March of 1902, she played in a concert benefiting St. Mary's Training Home for Girls, which had been founded by the late Mrs. Gladstone.[5]

The now-elderly Camille Saint-Saëns was also a familiar figure in London. Maud had known the affable, witty musician since her days at the Paris conservatory.[6] By November of 1902 the irrepressible composer had conducted several of his compositions at the Philharmonic Society's concerts and at the last two London Music Festivals. He invited the American violinist to join him in a performance of his Concerto in B Minor in London. After the performance, he wrote her: "Magnificent. You have style and the passages in octaves which you have added are most effective."[7] That Maud had added new notes to his concerto which he accepted with approval indicates the security of her musicianship—especially since Saint-Saëns, in a conflict with Nadia Boulanger, had expressed strong contempt for women who dared to compose.[8]

Musical life in London centered around the Queen's Hall Orchestra and the numerous concert series in which it was engaged. The Promenade Concerts were essentially a very old series which had languished for some years before the enterprising manager Robert Newman engaged Henry J. Wood to conduct the series in the new Queen's Hall in 1895. Through this series, the thirty-two-year-old Wood was credited with revolutionizing public appreciation for orchestral music. In 1902 the compositions which the Queen's Hall Orchestra presented for the first time in London included works by Tchaikovsky, Mahler, Franck, Fauré, d'Indy, Sibelius, Sinding, and Smetana—an indication of the brilliance of the period.

The young conductor, who had introduced the public to Tchaikovsky's first two symphonies during the previous fortnight, asked Maud to play the Tchaikovsky concerto on September 10, 1902. Afterward, Wood declared: "Miss Powell plays the Tschaikowsky concerto better than any other living violinist."[9]

Hardly more than a week later, Wood tapped Maud to substitute for Beatrice Langley, who was to have played a Mozart violin concerto on September nineteenth. Maud played Beethoven instead, and Joseph Bennett, the distinguished critic for the *Daily Telegraph*, whom Maud counted among her friends, wrote that the violinist interpreted Beethoven's "noble concerto . . . in a reverent spirit, paying heed to both the emotional and intellectual sides of her task."[10]

On November 9, 1902, the Sunday Concert Society sponsored a special performance in Queen's Hall to celebrate King Edward VII's birthday. Maud was invited to play the Tchaikovsky concerto and Elgar to conduct his *Coronation Ode*, composed that year. Under the direction of Arthur Payne, the program was as follows:

> God Save the King
> Coronation March—Saint-Saëns
> Violin Concerto in D—Tschaikovsky
> Coronation Ode—Elgar (composer conducting)
> Homage March—Wagner

It was extraordinary for an American to be asked to participate in such a concert. While it is uncertain whether the king himself attended, there is no doubt that the choice of soloist would have pleased him. The musically erudite king had previously "commanded" the American violinist to play before him. He reportedly exceeded the bounds of perfunctory court enthusiasm after her performance, calling many bravas and applauding vigorously. The thoughtful Edward commemorated the occasion by later presenting Maud with a beautifully modeled diamond pin in the form of a violin.[11]

Stars and Stripes Abroad, 1903

. . . words were never so eloquent as the heavenly music of that incomparable band.

— *Columbus [Ohio] Dispatch, 1901*

ALTHOUGH SHE HAD ACQUIRED A SLIGHT BRITISH ACCENT after so much time in England, Maud Powell was, as one critic happily observed, as "American as the 'Stars and Stripes Forever!' " Perhaps for this reason, John Philip Sousa asked her to join his band on its third European tour during the first half of 1903. She had all the attributes necessary for a Sousa soloist: indisputable artistry, beauty and grace, and a winning stage presence.

It might seem strange that the protégée of Joseph Joachim and Theodore Thomas would consent to tour Europe with a bandmaster. But Sousa was not just an ordinary bandsman; he was a musician of the first rank and Maud Powell recognized that fact. The points in Sousa's character and musical genius which made him a warm friend of Theodore Thomas were the same ones which bonded Maud Powell to him.[1]

Sousa (1854–1932) had grown up playing and loving the violin as the "queen of instruments," but his early professional experience in theater orchestras had convinced him that neither the violin nor the orchestra was the vehicle for his life's work. Shrewdly assessing the fast pace of American life and the consequent necessity for variety to attract and retain interest, this gifted musician chose the band over the orchestra for its versatility of instrumentation and repertoire. And he chose consciously to entertain rather than to educate, for it was the delight of his life to please an audience. He saw it as his mission to "lift the unmusical mind to a still higher form of musical art" by first reaching "every heart by simple, stirring music."[2]

Sousa perfected Gilmore's concept of balanced instrumentation, artfully blending woodwinds and brass, first as leader of the U.S. Marine Band (1880–92) and then as master of his own band.[3] With this instrumentation and his insistence on oneness of tone from his players, Sousa often boasted that his band was superior to any orchestra. He once said, "In dynamics, I never heard any orchestra that could touch us."[4]

In keeping with his desire to "make a music for the people, a music to be grasped at once," Sousa wrote music of nearly every description, from operettas, suites, and humoresques to his famous marches.[5] He fulfilled his stated mission largely by combining on his programs his own stirring music with his own brilliant transcriptions of the classical literature for orchestra into the band idiom.

Always eager to discuss the classics with learned musicians like Thomas, Sousa possessed a broad knowledge and deep understanding of music. Revering Bach as the greatest composer and Wagner as the "Shakespeare of music," Sousa regularly included transcriptions of their music and that of Tchaikovsky, Richard Strauss, and Dvořák on his programs. He liked to say that Thomas played Wagner, Liszt, and Tchaikovsky in the belief that he was educating the public, while he, Sousa, played the same composers' works in the belief that he was entertaining the public. Sousa had played an important role in educating the public to a greater appreciation for music of all types. Like Thomas before him, he played the classics in remote areas where no symphony orchestra had ever been heard. He was playing Wagner's *Parsifal* ten years before it was performed at the Metropolitan Opera.[6] It was Sousa who was largely responsible for introducing ragtime to Europe at the turn of the century and who later contributed to the international acceptance of jazz.

The bandmaster's test for the worth of any piece of music was whether it was "inspired" by a higher power.[7] Sousa's own marches were written with the conviction that they should "make a man with a wooden leg want to step out and march."[8]

In Europe, bands were highly developed by the time Sousa first toured there in 1900. Yet to Europeans Sousa's band was a wholly new phenomenon. The German press likened the band to a tremendous organ, while the French compared it to a great orchestra.

Sousa's choice of musicians was critical to the quality of his presentations.[9] One violin soloist remarked that appearing with Sousa's band was "being one artist in front of a whole band full of them!" Indeed, the entire band was composed of virtuosi, many of whom had played under Gilmore. Sousa made it a point to feature soloists on practically all instruments, providing his bandsmen with greater opportunities than they could have had with anyone else.[10]

Sousa regularly engaged a female singer and a violinist to tour with him in the United States and abroad. For both the 1903 and 1905 European tours, Sousa chose as soloists the brilliant coloratura soprano Estelle Liebling and Maud Powell, "that remarkable violinist" whom he called "one of the best-loved soloists in America."[11]

While Maud was a veteran artist of thirty-five on the 1903 tour, her twenty-two-year-old companion Estelle only recently had been launched in Europe on what was to be a brilliant career as a prima donna.[12] The young American-born singer came from a distinguished family of musicians in Germany and America, and she was due to make her American debut in the 1903–04 season at the Metropolitan Opera as Musetta in *La Bohème*, with Caruso as Rodolfo.

The European tour of 1903 was exceedingly strenuous, even by the touring standards of that strenuous day. Leaving New York harbor on Christmas Day 1902, the band arrived in Liverpool and then proceeded to London for its opening performance on January second in Queen's Hall. It was the first of 362 concerts to be given in thirty weeks in thirteen different countries. Fifty-two concerts were given in London alone, and none of the programs was repeated.

Averaging two concerts a day, both band and soloists were expected to perform at their peak. The soloists always played with band accompaniment, often Sousa's own transcriptions. He amazed all his auditors with the delicacy of the band accompaniments to such monumental works as the Beethoven and Mendelssohn violin concertos, which Maud played on the tour. Sousa always insisted on the inclusion of certain favorite violin pieces in his program repertoire. Among these were Saint-Saëns' *Introduction and Rondo Capriccioso* and Wieniawski's *Faust Fantasie*. If Sousa felt particularly inventive one day, he might dash off a piece and hand it to his violin soloist for the evening's performance. Maud also included in her tour repertoire such selections as Sarasate's *Zigeunerweisen*, Handel's *Largo*, a Fiorillo *Etude*, Vieuxtemps' *St. Patrick's Day*, Ries's *Adagio and Moto*

Perpetuo, a Paganini caprice, and Bach's *Air* on the G string. *Caprice on Dixie* for unaccompanied violin was composed for her by Sousa cornet soloist Herman Bellstedt, Jr., and Maud proudly proclaimed the work "quite worthy of Paganini."[13]

So many shorter selections were required because of the way in which Sousa compiled his programs. Each program generally included nine selections, with two or more encores after each one. Programs started exactly on time, when Sousa mounted the podium wearing his white kid gloves and gave the signal to the navy-blue–uniformed bandsmen to begin. Sousa went from one number to another with no more than a twenty- to thirty-second pause in between. Encores were generally begun within five to ten seconds.

Sousa shrewdly placed the violin solo late in the program (generally the eighth selection), after many Sousa marches had been played. Their expectations satisfied, the audience then was settled down enough to appreciate the violin performance.

As a conductor, Sousa was thoroughly convincing in his delivery of a work. Stepping onto the podium, he underwent a transformation; he became the "thing that I am conducting." His emotional involvement in the music and his unusual control over his musicians made every Sousa concert a moving experience. One of the bandsmen described playing with Sousa: "He was a small man, not a dashing-dapper-dan who could tower over us. And he had a kind, little old pipsqueeky voice, not a big boomy voice to shout out commands. But when he stepped on that podium, something happened. I can't explain it; it just happened. We knew we were playing with the immortals, and no one could touch us."[14]

A gentle man of sterling character, Sousa treated his musicians well. Maud once said that Sousa never failed to pay his men in full no matter what his losses, and he paid them well.[15] He did not fraternize with his men, but he understood them well enough to know when his advice or an encouraging word or quiet assistance with a personal problem was needed.

On tour he kept his female soloists largely apart from the men in the band, for the sake of propriety. (He also feared that he would lose his soloists in marriage to his bandsmen.) Maud and Estelle were treated to first-class hotels (a different hotel from the men's) and dinner each evening with Sousa himself and his wife. The band leader's wry wit and engaging conversation on any number of subjects in which he was well versed — poetry, American history, law, national and international developments, and questions current and vital — made him a genial companion.

Sousa's strictures did not prevent Maud from becoming personally acquainted with the "boys in the band" nor with their English manager H. Godfrey Turner. The son of a famous English journalist, Turner was connected with the management of the Empire Theater in London. His gift for seeing the funny side of life endeared him to her as the tour proceeded on its grueling schedule. Maud and Turner had at least one friend in common, the dancer Adeline Genée. Beyond this, we know little of how their friendship began.

The band's schedule included innumerable towns throughout England, Scotland, Ireland, and Wales, in many of which Maud had played before.[16] Consequently, she was received by these audiences as a well-known favorite. Reviewers commonly reported that Maud Powell was accorded "the heartiest reception of the day."[17] Like Sousa, she had a flair for charming an audience, which endeared her to the great band leader. In Dublin, as Maud returned to the stage for an encore, a small boy sang out from the gallery, "Something Irish!" Laughing, Maud turned to Mr. Sousa and whispered "*St. Patrick's Day.*" At its conclusion, of course, the applause was deafening.

Maud's appearances with the Sousa Band only seemed to enhance her hard-won reputation in England. Her performance was often acclaimed by critics as the highest artistic achievement of the entire program. Sousa frequently endured the congratulations of English critics for securing the services of "so excellent a violinist as Maud Powell." The London *Standard* review is typical: "Consummate skill. . . . technic and style absolutely without flaw. The artist simply revelled in ever varying intricacies and brought out the full beauty of the music with grand effect."

One English critic who heard Maud for the first time on the Sousa tour, wrote:

> For a violinist of Miss Maud Powell's class I have been looking out for a long time. She has power of a very rare order. This power comes not from striving, or with the polishing of technic. It is the magnetic soul-influence which sets every note that comes from the strings aquiver with emotional fire. It is long since I drew more satisfaction from a violinist than I drew from Miss Powell's playing. Her technic is not to be disparaged by any means; indeed, both her

hands are highly developed. Add her tone to her technic and you have a perfect artist. I don't demand that anyone shall play with purer, sweeter, more soul-filled tone the stream of melody which makes the Andante movement of Mendelssohn's Concerto than did Miss Powell.

Early in the tour, the company was pushed to the limits of its endurance. On January 18, the band gave a matinee concert in the Shakespeare Memorial Theatre at Stratford-on-Avon. That evening, they played at Leamington, at which point a "normal" touring day would have ended. Instead, the company proceeded to Warwick Castle as Lady Warwick had persuaded Sousa, over the objections of his manager, that a concert at midnight was a sensible idea.

A fierce storm arose that night. Although the band members arrived without mishap, the same could not be said for the music. The concert was played entirely from memory. Afterward, the Sousas, Maud, and Estelle Liebling went to a well-deserved supper with the Earl of Warwick and his guests.

As a favorite of King Edward, Sousa received a royal summons for a second command performance at Windsor Castle on January thirty-first.[18] Two performances in Manchester had to be canceled in order for the company to comply. They reached the Royal Borough by special train shortly before nine o'clock and then proceeded immediately to the Waterloo Chamber to give the concert.

Eighty people were in the audience, and in addition, the king had invited the band of the Scottish Guard to sit in the gallery. The distinguished gathering included the Prince and Princess of Wales, Prince Charles and the Princess of Denmark, Prince Christian and the Princess of Schleswig-Holstein, as well as the American Chargé d'Affaires, Mr. Henry White, and his wife. At the king's request, Sousa departed from the printed program and led the band in stirring American marches and ragtime. Arthur Pryor's trombone solo reportedly pleased the king immensely, as did the singing of David's *Thou Brilliant Bird* by Estelle Liebling and the performance of Sarasate's *Zigeunerweisen* by Maud.

The king's request for the American national anthem at the conclusion of the program gave Sousa a chance to display his legendary showmanship. He instructed his men to play "The Star-Spangled Banner" and then to go into "God Save the King," beginning just as softly as possible and then gradually growing louder. With the band and guests standing, Sousa watched the king's expression change as his own national anthem swelled the hall. It was a diplomatic masterstroke. Shaking the American band leader's hand, the king warmly expressed his pleasure in the concert, after which they went in to dinner.

Maud had helped make the concert a particularly memorable one for the youngest member of the band. Just nineteen at the time, Jan Williams remembered: "Maud took a liking to me because of my youth and my talent. When we played for the King of England she helped to arrange for me to be positioned in an advantageous spot in the band." At the age of ninety-four, he wrote, "What impressed me most about Maud was her kindness in helping me get professional attention in the music world in spite of my youth."[19]

The tour of the Continent was no less arduous than that of the British Isles. Beginning April 19 in Paris and ending June 7 in The Hague, the tour included cities in Russia, Poland, Bohemia, Scandinavia, and Western Europe.[20] The band and Maud, both already familiar to Continental audiences, were particularly well received in Europe.[21] In St. Petersburg, the company played before Czar Nicholas II, and the local *Herald* declared that "Miss Powell brought us very near the artistic holy of holies by her beautiful violin playing."

The tour with Sousa was clearly a personal triumph for Maud, with the violinist almost stealing the show from Sousa everywhere they played, according to the local press notices. Although Maud's mother later indicated that this made Sousa "jealous," the man's infinitely good nature, integrity, and appreciation for genuine artistry must have overcome any feelings of rivalry.[22] Certainly Maud had become a great favorite with the band members:

> At our last concert, at Blackpool, just before sailing for home, the boys gave me an ovation. When I finished my number — the Saint-Saëns Rondo, which they accompanied beautifully — they applauded, shouted and the drummer clanged his cymbals. The audience caught the meaning of it all and joined in vigorously.
>
> Afterwards, when the band bade me good-bye, they made speeches: "enjoyed every note of my playing," "honor to be associated," "privilege to know" etc. Two men said simply "God bless you" and one man broke down altogether. It all touched me deeply.

Sousa kissed my hand and said: "You have held your own right up to the last note."[23]

Thereafter, Maud considered the Sousa band tour one of her proudest achievements.

The band sailed for New York from Liverpool on July 31, 1903. Sousa told reporters that he was delighted with the tour, calling it the most successful he had ever undertaken. Indeed, some observers believed that with the possible exceptions of President Grant, Admiral Dewey, Mark Twain, and President Theodore Roosevelt, no American had been received with greater acclaim in foreign countries than John Philip Sousa.

Maud remained in the "old country," spending her vacation with friends in Ireland. In the autumn, she resumed concert life, fulfilling engagements throughout the British Isles and in Berlin, Vienna, Warsaw, and Holland.

A Sunny Partner

*Let woman then go on — not asking favors, but claiming as a
right the removal of all hindrances to her elevation in the scale
of being — let her receive encouragement for the proper cultivation of all her powers, so that she may enter profitably into the
active business of life. . . . Then in the marriage union, the
independence of the husband and wife will be equal, their
dependence mutual, and their obligations reciprocal.*

— Lucretia Mott, 1849

MAUD RETURNED TO AMERICA ON JANUARY 8, 1904, and immediately
embarked on a tour of the country which included performances
with the symphony orchestras of Boston, Cincinnati, Chicago, St.
Louis, Philadelphia and Pittsburgh. During that year, she announced
her engagement to be married to H. Godfrey Turner, the genial
manager of the Sousa tour. At the same time, she made it clear that,
unlike most women artists, she had no intention of giving up her
career — a pronouncement that naturally met with the approbation of
the musical world of two continents. More importantly, the companion with whom she had chosen to share her life was fully in accord
with her plan to continue her work, having resolved to devote his
whole life to Maud as her manager and friend.

The marriage question had always been a difficult one for Maud.
She naturally yearned for the comforts of domestic companionship,
but at the same time she understood that her love for the violin
excluded all but the most unusual partners. From the beginning, she
knew that the choice was marriage *or* a career. For a woman, a combination generally was not considered possible. It was reported by an

Maud in 1908.

This page, top, Maud in traveling costume about 1907; bottom, Mrs. Davenport-Engberg, conductor of the Bellingham Orchestra, and Maud, Bellingham, Washington, in 1912 or 1913. Facing page, top, The Maud Powell Trio, 1908–09, l to r: Maud, May Mukle, Anne Mukle Ford; bottom, the Trio on tour, 1909, l to r: Anne Mukle Ford, unidentified person, Maud, May Mukle.

Maud in 1908, testing the acoustics of her new home (*below*) "The Cedars" in Great Neck, Long Island.

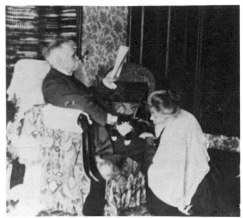

Top left, Maud's mother and brother Billy at her parents' home in Mount Vernon, N.Y., probably between 1904 and 1908; *right,* Maud's parents at home with the family cat, probably between 1900 and 1904; *bottom,* Maud and her first car, a Ford, in front of her Great Neck home.

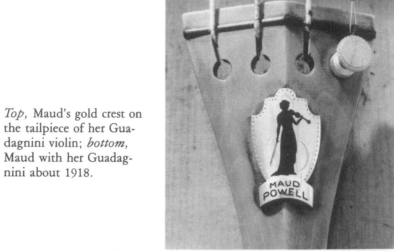

Top, Maud's gold crest on the tailpiece of her Guadagnini violin; *bottom*, Maud with her Guadagnini about 1918.

Maud's favorite violin, labeled: J. B. Guadagnini, Turin 1775.

Photo of Maud in 1909, autographed to Katharine Howard, a pianist.

Auroran that Maud had once given up "one she dearly loved" for her art.

In 1908, she reflected on the risk a woman took in deciding in favor of a career as a concert artist: "It is a difficult question — too difficult to answer by a simple yea or nay: — Shall you become a great artist and have the multitude at your feet (if you are lucky), or shall you marry the faithful and honest Dick, live a life of humdrum domestic felicity and suffer ever after with a gnawing sense of defeated and thwarted ambition, a bitter 'might-have-been'?"

Pointing out the need for a very real talent, health, strength, a good physique, character, will power, courage, and determination, "stick-to-itiveness, with an inexhaustible fund of patience," she asked young female aspirants, "Do you love your music more than anything else in the world?" Then she wrote of the sacrifices which this love must transcend.

> You must expect to sacrifice something in the way of general education if you are to become an artist. Madame Camilla Urso once told me that she never learned her ABC's until after she had mastered her scales. And I was taken out of school and carried off to the Leipsig Conservatory when I was only [thirteen]. If you want to become a great instrumentalist, you must class yourself with the acrobats and toe-dancers, who train, train, train, from childhood on; always, everlastingly and unceasingly. How you are going to stand that hard labor, with your delicate frame and sensitive makeup, I don't know. And were you as strong again as you are, I should still say, "Not strong enough for the fight." . . .
>
> And tell me, when you are thirty or thirty-five, and one day admit to yourself that you did not know what you were talking about when you declared in your early twenties that you were never, never, never going to marry, but intended to devote your whole life to your art; when your heart and your head and your art cry out for a fuller life and broader sympathies, and you feel that you have come to a standstill in development — then what are you going to do? Dick by that time will have turned his heart elsewhere, or if not, what right have you to marry him, with your high-strung nerves, your self-centered life of study and travel, your habits regulated to the demands of a critical public and not a bit adapted to a home career? . . .
>
> And it is a question whether many women would consider it worthwhile anyway, considering that they lose their childhood, miss

the school companionship and social life of early womanhood, and live always a life of training and restriction. There are the hours of practise, the careful diet, the keeping in physical trim, the constant self-denial in the matter of social pleasures, late hours, shopping expeditions, or the many things one likes to do and may not, because of harming the hands or stiffening the muscles. They say Liszt never carried even an umbrella, for fear of dulling the sensitive responsiveness of his precious fingers. Mme. Urso told me, years ago, that I must never take a needle in my hand, for the same reason.

Frankly, I say to you that "the game is not worth the candle," unless your music is a part of your very fiber, your breath of life. If you love it thoroughly, love it objectively (so few women do that), and cannot be happy without it, then go ahead. But you wouldn't have needed me to decide for you, if that were the case; you would have been impelled by something within, regardless of advice or a thousand warnings.[1]

Maud must have struggled mightily with her emotions before agreeing to marry Turner. Only his lifelong experience as a theater manager in England and his extreme geniality made the decision in his favor possible. His family was deeply involved in the theater. His sister Ethel May Turner, an actress, had married the actor Percy Marshall. Their son and Turner's nephew Herbert G. Marshall became a well-known actor in England and America.

It was especially important for Maud at long last to have a deep-seated friendship with someone who understood the "Bohemian world and world of art" and who could both comprehend and ease the peculiar loneliness inherent in the life of a celebrity. Maud once expressed her affection for friends of her family in Peru and Aurora in the deepest terms because they had known her and her parents before she became famous. Her interrupted home life had prevented her from forming the sorts of childhood and adolescent attachments which so often last a lifetime. The life of the virtuoso further militated against the formation of close friendships as there was so little time in which to develop trust and to grow. As she once confided to a Peruvian, although she could claim to have friends in almost every city, she deeply felt the lack of friends who cared for her for herself alone.

In Sunny, Maud had finally found someone whom she could trust to love her for herself and who could also serve as a loving ally, entering wholeheartedly into her life as a virtuoso.

It was unfortunate then that Maud's mother opposed the match, ostensibly because Turner, who was born in London and had served in the English army in the first Sudan campaign, was a "foreigner."[2] Although he took out naturalization papers in America even before the wedding, apparently some discord surrounded the circumstances of the private ceremony. Sadly, the couple were married with no family members present on September 21, 1904, at the Vail farm near Pawling, New York, where Maud had been vacationing. A minister from nearby Patterson, New York, officiated. Turner was forty-four and a widower; Maud was thirty-seven.[3]

Because she had been performing under her own name as a professional for some twenty years, Maud did not give up her name after her marriage, nor did Turner expect her to. Instead, she adopted the prefix "Madam" before her name as an acceptable compromise.[4] In further concession to her career, she wore a gold wedding band on her right hand, keeping her left hand facility unencumbered for violin playing.

Godfrey Turner was as industrious as Maud and well equipped to handle his wife's engagements. Henry Wolfsohn, Maud's manager at the time of her marriage, apparently assisted Turner in setting up an agency of his own in New York, where he engaged young Edna Speier as his secretary. Devoted to the Turners, Miss Speier would become as much a part of their lives as if she had been truly family.

Turner was full of original ideas for promoting his wife's career.[5] He originated the idea of using Maud's silhouette as an advertising trademark on her programs, advertisements, and stationery. To the silhouette Turner added a logo penned by an English critic, "The Arm of a Man, The Heart of a Woman, and The Head of an Artist." His many advertisements for Maud Powell were unfailingly clever and amusing, as was the cable address the two adopted, "Catgut, New York."

Perhaps Godfrey Turner's most endearing trait was his infinitely good nature — his resourceful and original mind attuned to the humorous side of life. His humor was just the tonic Maud needed to counter the stress inherent in the life of a touring concert artist. He would do anything to make Maud laugh, often "cutting up" with her brother Billy, frequently through photography, which all three enjoyed.

Among the couple's friends, Turner soon earned the nickname "Sunny Jim" or just "Sunny" because he looked like the Sunny Jim whose face appeared in breakfast cereal advertisements. Godfrey accepted his nickname cheerfully and used it in signing his letters which, according to their critic friend Henry T. Finck, would "bubble over with humorous sallies."[6] The nickname stuck more because of his fun-loving character than his appearance. His sunny disposition led Finck to say that he was the "funniest Englishman I have ever met."

Unfortunately, humor alone could not relieve the nervous tension which Maud constantly combated, particularly during long concert tours. "I have always suffered more or less from the torments of nervousness. Fortunately the worst moments of nightmare are those immediately preceding the first entrance upon the stage, for, once lost in the music, nervousness readily turns to inspiration."[7] Then too, violin playing was physically trying. As Maud explained, "It twists the left arm around snake-fashion; it kinks the spine a trifle, compresses the chest, and throws all the exercise upon the right arm. . . . The closeness of the sound and the vibration to the left ear also tries the nerves."[8] She constantly sought remedies for her condition from physicians whose advice was sometimes more dangerous than the illness itself. Once, however, she consulted a wise German-American doctor who recommended exercise to relieve the tension, as this interview reveals:

> "Making beds is fine exercise for feminine musicians," declares this greatest of women violinists.
>
> "Still," she observed, adjusting a stray lock of black hair with the end of her diamond-studded bow, "still, I don't know that I'd recommend it for a house maid or a farmer's wife. But for the multitude of women that haven't the good fortune to be kept well by a reasonable amount of active exercise about their homes—for women with too many servants, women with too much society, or with club duties, literary or artistic pursuits to occupy their minds and tantalize their nerves—there's nothing better than simply making beds.
>
> "I know because I've tried it, and I've tried the more pretentious, fashionable and expensive cures as well. When I got back from England, some time ago, I was a wreck—simply a wreck."

The intonation of this statement was that of some scarcely-breathing graduate from a Siberian prison, but the speaker was so fresh, youthful and energetic—so comely also, as every concert-goer knows. . . .

"I was, really," she protested. "I was a well-nigh perfect ruin as to nerves. I went to a German doctor in New York whom a friend recommended. 'So?' he exclaimed, when I told him that I might as well be buried at once.

"Then he asked if 'the fraulein had beds ge-made.' No, she hadn't; certainly not. 'Aber the fraulein should the beds make—all of them in the house, not one only.' Well, I went home and made beds and kept making them; and it did me a hundred times more good than tablets, motorcar-ing, the rest-cure and the Riviera."[9]

Maud had been based in New York City since the 1890s, so she and Sunny shared an apartment in The Knickerbocker at 117 West 95th Street. We do not know if Maud had been living there prior to her marriage, but it is certain that the couple enjoyed considerable domestic felicity. For most of their meals they ate out, with the exception of breakfast and Sunday luncheons. Maud enjoyed cooking from time to time and recipes for some of her favorite dishes occasionally appeared in the newspapers. Although she had a maid, Maud loved doing things about her home and filled it with the many beautiful objects she acquired on her tours throughout the world. Her own sketches and photographs of many composer and artist friends graced the piano and walls, while books and music overflowed various desks and cabinets. Above her music cabinet containing orchestra parts for various violin concertos hung one of F. S. Dellenbaugh's paintings of the Grand Canyon, which he had first viewed as a member of John Wesley Powell's 1871 expedition. The piano's presence was essential to Maud's happiness: "I must always have my piano near me; a room or a house without a piano is sadly incomplete. One feels lost without that instrument; how immeasurably our homes would lose if pianos should be absent!"[10]

By 1915 Maud and Sunny had moved their studio to Gramercy Park, where absolute quiet reigned. "I must have it," the violinist explained to a reporter. "I can work here without being disturbed by sounds from without, and that means much in this great city."[11] There, Maud once gave a memorable concert for her mother, her brother Billy, and her cousin Mabel Love, because she had learned that Mabel had never had a chance to hear her play. Mabel remembered that she played "a long time" and it was "lovely."

Although they retained their studio in Manhattan, in 1908, Maud and Sunny built a two-story frame house in Great Neck Hills, Long Island, which they surrounded with trees. Located at 31 Hillpark Avenue, "The Cedars," as it was christened, became their legal residence and a permanent home for Maud's mother and for Billy, who was in the publishing business and would soon become an editor for Commerce Clearing House Legal Division in New York City. Maud and Sunny spent time at The Cedars mostly during the summer months. Its location near Little Neck Bay enabled them to relax by sailing their yacht *Cremona* or skimming through the water in the launch they merrily dubbed *Fiddle-Dee-Dee*. These sojourns were a tonic for Maud's nerves, although she could never escape music completely, as the "surf ripples forward and back in diatonic scales— unlike the wind, which manifests itself chromatically."[12]

It was comforting as well as handy for Maud to have a companion with whom she could work out the myriad details attendant upon concert life. For example, the matter of dress, which was obvious and standardized for male performers, required thoughtful consideration by a woman violinist. Sunny argued that "the dress suit is the solution," but failed to persuade his wife to adopt it, even in modified form.[13] For all the problems elegant gowns presented, Maud really believed that no other attire was appropriate for maintaining the dignity and beauty expected of a female concert artist.

Maud resented the time required to deal with dress, however, and eventually found "a treasure of a couturière," who bought and planned everything for her. Indicative of her distance from the subject at times when the matter was being handled by others, the artist described one of her gowns as made of "some sort of white material, I really don't know what it is called."

Few descriptions of her gowns survive, but Maud did love red and its variations and the textures of silk, satin, velvet, and brocade in her concert attire. For one appearance, her gown was described by a male critic as "a striking non-union suit cut out of pink mesquite netting well below the waist line, and out of airy, fairy, creamy stuff above." This fashionable dress lacked only a "Paris hat and pompadour."[14] On another occasion, she wore "a wonderful dress of spangled white chiffon, cunningly draped over many tones of red, so that it shaded from the waist down from white through palest pink to deep red at the foot." In the towns of the Midwest and South, Maud, always sensitive to her audience's taste, was careful to dress more conservatively.[15]

With her usual perspicacity, Maud understood that her outward appearance affected the audience's reception of her art. In her 1908 article "How Fashion Invades the Concert Stage," Maud wrote that "dress plays almost as important a part in the concert as the talent itself." She always believed that the "professional woman owes it to her public to dress fashionably" and that it was "absolutely essential that she have a certain style and individuality in the selection of her gowns"—particularly those worn before a critical audience.[16]

The selection of fabrics and trimmings, the planning of suitable styles, and then the "long weary hours of fittings" consumed much valuable time because the violinist's gowns were fashioned to be comfortable as well as stylish. It was "absolutely imperative that there be perfect freedom of movement and that the completed gown be easy in every part." A graceful train could be managed easily through the use of cleverly hidden weights and heavy cords.

The brilliant lights of the concert hall and the absence of background or scenery revealed every line and showed the defects of one's costume more plainly than was the case in the theater. Hence, Maud knew that an artist's dress "must not be too conspicuous or it will detract from the recital, which is not a dressmaker's exhibition, but a programme of classical music and nothing she wears should be too brilliant or inharmonious with the hangings of the hall." If one dressed in bad taste, the violinist observed, the "audience's sense of discomfort somehow projects itself across the footlights."

When Maud was scheduled to appear in an unfamiliar hall, Sunny would observe and report to her the colors of the hangings and the general effect. "If the predominant shade is red or some other brilliant hue, I select a white gown or one of a delicate tint of yellow. On the other hand, a new room with much white plaster and few decorations save palms and potted plants causes me to appear in a warm red costume or similar bright combination."

Maud always insisted that her hair be "becomingly dressed so as to give a good shape to the head." It had to be "comfortable and well pinned" so that "no strand or hair pin detaches itself." Shoes had to be "easy yet in the latest fashion, harmonizing with the gown and . . . in perfect condition." She rejected the "extreme heel of the French type."

Maud occasionally was known to scour the city for a particular ornament or jewel as a special addition to a concert costume and then forget it in the excitement of the evening. She admitted that "clothes are a bother, yet a blessing and each faded gown recalls happy days and pleasant people in all parts of the world." Despite all the long hours and attention her concert gowns required, Maud declared that she had no regrets and concluded that the result was "well worth all the time and trouble."

Once the season's tour schedule was set and all arrangements were made, Sunny frequently went on tour with Maud, leaving the capable Edna Speier to handle affairs in New York. In effect, he replaced Maud's mother, a fact which may have provided the deep-seated cause for Mrs. Powell's resentment—even though she had long since given up "the road." Indicating how important they were to each other, Maud once commented that both she and Sunny "hate it alone."

They never had children together, although Sunny had a son by his previous marriage who eventually settled in New York. (Nothing else is known about him.) Maud consciously chose not to have any children in order to continue her career, although it was a form of fulfillment which she idealized, and she always expressed regret that she had never been a mother.

In all, Sunny's presence was a godsend. Maud's marriage to him was one of the single most important events in her life, truly freeing her to present her art to the American people in all its wholeness.

A Succession of Fiddles

Music is freighted with joy and sadness, with hope and fear, with courage and cowardice, with glory and shame — it is freighted with all emotion; and how does the form of sound become informed with feeling?

—John Wesley Powell

Maud Powell tucked her violin under her chin and touched with its quivering strings almost every octave in the unuttered language of the human heart.

—Review from Charleston, West Virginia

BEFORE HER RETURN TO AMERICA IN JANUARY 1904, Maud purchased a beautiful Joseph Guarnerius del Gesu violin from W. E. Hill and Sons of London on December 14, 1903. She paid £600 for it, which was generally the highest value placed on such an instrument at the time. The violin bore the famous del Gesu inscription with the date 1731, and it had once belonged to the Viennese violinist Joseph Mayseder.[1] Prior to its purchase by Hill's, the instrument had been in the Crawford collection in Edinburgh for fifteen years.

The Crawford collection was famous for having in its possession one instrument in particular, the "Messiah Strad" or "Le Messie."[2] Crafted by Antonio Stradiveri in 1716, it was one of the most perfectly preserved Stradivarius instruments in existence. It was the last instrument in Mr. Crawford's collection, but nothing could tempt him to sell it. However, he had agreed that should he ever decide to let it go, he would give Maud Powell the first opportunity to purchase it.[3]

Since Maud had made her first acquaintance with a violin as a child, the succession of fiddles she possessed had increased in quality as her talent expanded. She began with a half-sized violin purchased for ten dollars, advanced to a full-sized instrument under Lewis's instruction, probably studied abroad with a violin made by Georg Gemunder of New York in 1869, and returned to America with a Guarnerius chosen for her by Joseph Joachim. From 1890 forward, she played an Amati dated 1635, which had been loaned to her by E. J. Delahanty of New York.

There is hardly a relationship which is more personal than that between a violinist and his instrument. Maud always referred to hers as a "fiddle," a term of endearment which she explained by saying: "But I should feel that it was almost an insult to call my dear old fiddle a violin. To say 'fiddle' is like using the familiar pronoun of the Germans 'du,' 'thou.' " The word "fiddle" also took her back to the "cozy ranch cabin where everything is in touch and tune with nature." It recalled the first time she heard the *Arkansas Traveler* played by a "ruralite" on a "wheezy box." Maud once described how she developed intimacy with an instrument: "The space of time during which 'my new violin' becomes 'my dear old fiddle' may or may not be agreeable. There are the new colors to be learned and the new possibilities to be discovered. It is exactly the same process through which one would pass in developing a mere acquaintance into a dear friend."[4]

The Mayseder Guarnerius brought Maud endless pleasure and soon earned from its new steward the appellation of endearment. The player and the instrument were well matched, for Joseph Guarnerius (1698–1744) had managed to combine intense brilliancy with concentrated power in the tone of his instruments, to bring out the full range of which generally required a powerful player.[5]

In her appreciation and care for her instruments, Maud had come a long way since her student days. Dancla had taught her how to care for her violin. When she first came to him for a lesson, he called her attention to some resin he found on her instrument and wrote her name in the dust, but in telling the tale Maud asserted that "he never did that for me but once."[6]

A few years after she purchased the Guarnerius, Maud wrote an article in which she gave students impeccable guidance on the care of the violin. She prescribed methods by which the instrument and its strings should be cleaned and stressed the importance of keeping the instrument at an even temperature with just the right amount of humidity. Extraordinary circumstances required extraordinary care.

Many a time, when traveling at night, in zero weather, I have put the violin case under the blankets in my berth, as carefully as though it were a live thing. On one occasion my train was delayed nine hours by a blizzard. The steam pipes froze—so, very nearly, did the passengers—and all that day I kept the violin wrapped in blankets, much more worried over it than about myself. I was to give a recital that night, and only arrived in town at eight o'clock, but when I walked on the stage at ten minutes of nine, I found the violin in a splendid condition, thanks to my care.[7]

Maud subscribed to a "golden rule" theory in caring for her violin: "Our climate, with its sudden changes and its extremes of both dryness and sodden humidity, is unfavorable to both artist and instrument. Both live in a state of too constant tension and resistance. Take care of yourself—health is valuable above all else—but don't forget to take care of your instrument. It will reward you for your pains. Treat it like a tender human being, and invite its soul—and your own."[8] Like most artists, Maud thought of her violin as a living being because it was so much an extension of her own soul. Through it she expressed her innermost spirit, and its responsiveness to her every nuance of feeling made it vibrantly alive in her hands. Consequently, her advice concerning the choice and care of a violin reveals her deep sympathy for the instrument:

It is not well for a beginner to use a poor instrument. But he need not use the best. It would be brutal to put a very fine instrument into the hands of a novice who did not know how to use or care for it. There is a certain way of using the fingers and bow; it must not have too much heat and the strings must be kept in good condition and must be kept clean. A violin is sensitive, and if one part is not in good condition all will suffer from sympathy.[9]

She was careful not to overwork a fiddle in her possession. She believed that a "good violin that is overworked comes as near having nervous prostration as is possible for an inanimate thing. It is tired all over and in every part; it loses all its energy of tone and expression and becomes useless for good work." As a result, she did not always practice on her concert instrument, but neither did she practice on a second-rate one. In her view, the latter course resulted in the ear losing "its power of detecting delicate shades of color and the hand its power of bringing them into being."[10]

On May 5, 1905, Maud purchased from J. & A. Beare of London a violin crafted by Joseph Rocca in Genoa in 1856.[11] Along with his teacher G. F. Pressenda, Rocca (1807–65) is considered the finest Italian violinmaker of the nineteenth century. His instruments possess a very rich tone and great carrying power. This particular violin was modeled after a Stradivarius. Maud used the Rocca almost exclusively during her concert tour of South Africa in 1905.

Around February 1907, Maud discovered almost by accident the instrument with which she was to have her greatest love affair. It bore the label "Joannes Baptista Guadagnini, in Turin, 1775." Ernest N. Doring, a noted luthier in New York, called it "a magnificent specimen, with full coverage of brilliant red varnish." Doring was with John Friedrich & Bro. in New York when in 1926 he certified that the violin was a genuine example in all essentials.[12] It was made during the last and best period of the Italian luthier's career. Maud purchased the violin from the New York luthier Oswald Schilbach for $4,000.[13]

Maud's Rocca violin became the companion to her Guadagnini and not the beautiful Guarnerius. Maud gave up the Guarnerius because she could not play the two violins interchangeably.[14] They were quite different in size, tone-production, and shape. The Guadagnini was smaller than the Guarnerius, leading the diminutive violinist (approximately five feet three inches tall) to remark, "Then my hand is so small that I ought to use the instrument best adapted to it, and to use the same instrument always."[15]

In commenting to an interviewer on the quality of various instruments, Maud defended her choice of the Guadagnini:

> Do you know . . . that the fine "Strads" and "Amatis" of the world have almost reached tone bottom, and that the Guadagninis and Bergonzis are about the only instruments of today that have good, solid bodies? Not long since I was playing one of the most famous of all Strads. It had cost its owner $15,000, and he was insanely proud of it. As I started to bow gently, its tones startled me with their strange, weird beauty. Then they excited my nerves, and I began to draw heavily across the low strings, when to my positive shock, tone power and beauty suddenly vanished. The quality had gone, heaven knows where, and I was scraping bottom.[16]

The violinist loved the Guadagnini for its healthy wood and whole-souled responsiveness to her every command. The purity of the tone it produced, capable of soaring easily over the orchestra, and its perfect responsiveness throughout every string position and register were its most endearing traits. Although the tone of her Guarnerius was deeper, coming more from within the instrument, Maud commented that "all in all I have found my Guadagnini, with its glassy clearness, its brilliant and limpid tone quality, better adapted to American concert halls."[17] She concluded: "Guadagnini is the fiddle for my work. It is in perfect preservation and the atmosphere of neither steam-heated trains nor zero weather seem to affect it. If I had a Strad in the same condition as my Guadagnini the instrument would be priceless." It was to her "the one perfect thing."

When Maud spoke of the Guadagnini, her delight in its qualities indicated how perfectly matched were the instrument and the artist:

> "You simply can't appreciate how beautiful an instrument this is. . . . Look at its big broad chest under the bridge. No hollow, caved-in consumptive lines there that tell of the 'one-lunger.' Then listen," rapping the wood with her knuckles, "do you hear that strong, healthy ring? This fellow never knows what it means to be frozen, husky and hoarse; he's a big, lusty boy, whom I do love to thrash and beat black and blue, so different from the other violin in the box there, which is best likened to one of those gentle, many-mooded women of the world, who become stubborn, and, for the sake of peace, must be cajoled and cautiously wooed."[18]

Maud once played under circumstances which confirmed her belief that her Guadagnini had a living soul. The "concert" was given in a forestry building in Oregon in the presence of a few friends. When she saw it, Maud was irresistibly drawn to play her violin within the embrace of this veritable log cathedral. She quietly proceeded to the north gallery and began playing Fiorillo's study for unaccompanied violin with its organ-like effects. One of those friends who was present wrote:

> We who were at the remotest corner of the great building were overwhelmed with the dominant power and soul-swamping impressiveness of the composition, the artist who played it and the wonderful acoustics of the house built of logs. When its last crescendo

arose and echoed and re-echoed through the nave of the cathedral of the logs we were silent, the little audience was awe stricken.

Then she came down to the main floor . . . and the strings of that inspired Cremona commenced singing soft and low, dear old *Traumerei* . . . . She played it with a mute and the tones were no more than whispers, but in the farthest end of the great building every note was distinct and clear.

Miss Powell . . . said it was as though the soul of the violin were speaking to the rugged primal soul of the mighty logs and had acknowledged at last its fellowship with the forest. That was the eerie feeling that we all had. The violin was uttering the call of the wild, was pouring out its soul. All the pent-up melody of that old Cremona . . . seemed to come forth in a plaintive croon song. The long dead frondage of the long dead wood monarch seemed to rustle and whisper hopeless love songs and, as the cadences died away, the heart of the violin seemed to break as breaks the heart of one who sees a loved one die. Then the vast room was still, still as the silence of dead melodies and we felt moved to speak in whispers and walk on tiptoe.

Only the wholesome smiles of Maud Powell, the genius who had set this spell upon us, served to bring us back. . . . [19]

By 1910 the Guadagnini was valued at $15,000 while the slender, magical fingers which made it sing were insured for $50,000 from "all possible risks."

In addition to her violins, Maud had several priceless bows.[20] In her possession was the "Kreutzer" bow, made by the French master François Tourte, who perfected the modern bow, for the violinist whose name Beethoven immortalized. Maud also played with a bow made by French bow maker François Nicolas Voirin, who fundamentally altered the Tourte bow design and whose bows were characterized by lightness, balance, and grace.

Another essential part of Maud's artistic equipment was her instrument's strings. When her career began, violin strings were made of gut and were therefore very susceptible to changes in the weather— making intonation something of a gamble as the music progressed— and to breaking due to the tension caused by bow pressure. Eventually, experimentation with metal led to the steel E string and the silver, copper, or aluminum-wound gut G, D, and A strings.[21] In musical circles, much controversy surrounded the introduction of metal strings, engendering heated debate over the differences in tone quality achieved with metal-wound gut versus gut strings.

Maud was always experimenting with new strings, seeking brightness and clarity of sound as well as durability. Not surprisingly, she was one of the first to adopt metal strings and used a silver G string as early as 1904. By 1907 Maud had resorted to a metal E string, and in explaining the circumstances she expressed the frustration which the matter of strings caused serious violinists:

> Strings? Well, I use a wire E string. I began to use it twelve years ago one humid, foggy summer in Connecticut. I had had such trouble with strings snapping that I cried: "Give me anything but a gut string." The climate practically makes metal strings a necessity, though some kind person once said that I bought wire strings because they were cheap! If wire strings had been thought of when Theodore Thomas began his career, he might never have been a conductor, for he told me he gave up the violin because of the E string. And most people will admit that hearing a wire E you cannot tell it from a gut E. Of course, it is unpleasant on the open strings, but then the open strings never do sound well. And in the highest registers the tone does not spin out long enough because of the tremendous tension: one has to use more bow. And it cuts the hairs: there is a little surface nap on the bow-hairs which a wire string wears right out. I had to have my four bows rehaired three times last season—an average of every three months. But all said and done it has been a Godsend to the violinist who plays in public. On the wire A one cannot get the harmonics; and the aluminum D is objectionable in some violins, though in others not at all.[22]

A Victor Immortal

[T]he manner in which the masterly playing of the artist has been caught in its perfection and preserved for all time is one of the triumphs of science.

— Victor Record Catalogue for January 1909
advertising Maud Powell's records

IN NOVEMBER OF 1904, MAUD BECAME the first instrumentalist to record for the Victor Talking Machine Company's prestigious Red Seal label (the celebrity artist series).[1] The phonograph had been improving steadily since Edison had built the first device to record and transmit sound in 1877. In the 1890s, the limited responsiveness of the phonograph lent itself primarily to the recording of brass bands, the human voice (in comedy routines, etc.), and the piano. At the turn of the century, recording ventured into opera—by 1910 preserving for all time the semblance of the voices of such giants as Melba, Nordica, Calvé, Plançon, Chaliapin, Adelina Patti, Eames, and Caruso. Enrico Caruso made his first disk records in 1902, just two years ahead of Maud. By that time the cylinder was beginning to give way to Emile Berliner's mass-produced disk which revolved at approximately 78 revolutions per minute. By 1911, the disk had captured the art of such pianists as Hofmann, Pugno, de Pachmann, Backhaus, and Paderewski.

All during the period in which Maud Powell was actively making records (1904 through 1919), the technology remained limited in duration of the record (2'50" maximum for a ten-inch disk, 4'50" maximum for a twelve-inch disk) and the quality of sound reproduction. Recordings were made acoustically then and did not progress to electrical transmission (by microphone) until 1925.

The technology limited recordings of the violin literature to short pieces; an entire concerto, or even an uncut movement of a concerto or sonata, exceeded its capabilities. Further, the mechanical contrivances used to record the music were awkward enough to disconcert anyone. Artists were placed in an acoustically "dead" room and forced to play into a large funnel, which looked like the gaping mouth of a dragon, ready to swallow the protagonist who dared perch so near its forbidding jaws. Yet the nearer the artist could stand to it, the better the recording!

Maud, who always suffered from pre-performance stage fright, once declared, "I am never as frightened as I am when I stand in front of that horn to play." She said it was the hardest thing to remember that every sound is recorded. Once she ruined a record by exclaiming "Ye Gods!" after she finished a piece in which she was disgusted with her work. She was horrified when the record was tried and her own voice wheezed out at the conclusion. She was not the only artist to experience this terror. Maud once regaled a reporter with the tale of the American opera singer Louise Homer's first encounter with the machine. Frightened "almost to death," the contralto exclaimed at the conclusion of her song, "I never sang so rotten in my life." Maud's imitation of the way the Victor recording squeaked out that line had the reporter in stitches.[2]

Even if one could overcome nervous fright, other dangers lurked within the recording studio. The concert artist accustomed to applause at the conclusion of his work had to learn to stifle the natural outflow of energy upon completing the recorded selection. Maud found that no other experience quite equaled the awful sensation of the silence accompanying recording except, perhaps, playing in a church where applause was forbidden. For her, applause was a welcome and necessary ingredient to fulfillment of the musical experience, a view she forcefully expressed in a letter she wrote in 1907 to the editor of *Musical America*:

> Although Mr. Joseph Bennett, the veteran critic of the London *Daily Telegraph*, is a very dear friend of mine, I cannot help disagreeing with him on the objections he takes to applause given by the public to an artist after a satisfying performance. Speaking from

the artist's standpoint, well-earned applause is like nectar from the gods and invariably incites to better efforts and more inspired results. Speaking as a listener, I confess to wanting to show my appreciation in hand-clapping and "bravos." Tense nerves and concentration of attention, in both performer and listener, must seek relief in some way. A sympathetic understanding is established between artist and audience in the course of a solo, the artist giving of his best to his listeners, they in turn giving him absorbed attention, and often an indescribable something which inspires him to outdo himself. Why should the mutual sympathy and understanding cease abruptly with the close of the solo? What is to become of the emotional exaltation engendered? Why should it not have vent?

I played last Sunday at divine service in a little country church. The oppressive silence which continued after each solo, was most painful, and I walked from the platform like a guilty culprit condemned in the presence of a great gathering of my fellow beings.

Playing into a talking-machine is even worse. It hears and records on the plate of its memory, but makes no sign, either of approval or disapproval. When the solo is finished, the receiving funnel looks at one blankly and the artist spoils record after record by ejaculating in the moment of nerve relaxation, "Heavens, take it away!" "Let me have air." etc.[3]

Despite the difficulties involved, Maud recognized the potential importance of the phonograph in elevating the musical taste of the public. Because of this, no matter how limited the technology, the American violinist determined at the outset to play only music which met the highest artistic standards. Although she could only play short classical works and honed-down movements of violin concertos and sonatas, her artistry, conveyed through even this crude medium, helped to revolutionize American musical taste. In addition, she set in a lasting medium a standard for violin playing which endures to this day. Public taste was altered permanently because for the first time, people who did not normally have access to live concerts could hear the highest artistry in their own homes. As one wag put it, "People who can turn on Kreisler and Maud Powell and Caruso in their own parlors are not going to listen to a diet of uninterrupted trash, just because a neighbor's daughter can play it herself."[4] Jim Cartwright, a prominent classical record dealer and collector, has written that he is "amazed at how well her art comes through" even the primitive medium of a circa 1905 Victor Talking Machine with outside wooden horn. He comments: "No wonder her records sold so well!"⁵

With her fine musical intelligence, Maud deftly shortened the score of any music which exceeded the strict time limitations, always careful to preserve its musical essence. In her first recording sessions on November 4 and 8, 1904, she set a standard for repertoire and violin playing from which she never swerved, recording the final movement of Mendelssohn's E minor violin concerto (with piano accompaniment) as well as Vieuxtemps' *St. Patrick's Day* and *Polonaise*, Sarasate's *Zigeunerweisen*, and Wieniawski's *Faust Fantasie* with impeccable taste and command over her instrument. Upon hearing a tape of some of her recordings, Yehudi Menuhin made the following observations: "The recordings reveal a remarkable violinist playing with great dash and style and cultivated musicianship in the manner of the period, that is, without exaggerated vibrato, but so incredibly disciplined and clean, with the authority of the great traditions of the German and French schools."⁶

Added to her concert appearances throughout America, the phonograph contributed enormously to making Maud Powell's name a household word. Over the years, her name stood with those of Caruso, Melba, Kreisler, and Paderewski — emblazoned across the country as the "Victor Immortals."

Many of Maud's recordings won first prizes at the Buffalo, St. Louis, and Portland Expositions, while her rendition of *Souvenir* by Franz Drdla, recorded in 1907, became the "best seller" of all violin recordings, European and American. Her beautiful *Méditation* from the opera *Thaïs* by Massenet was a close second.

Maud Powell's recorded legacy is extensive in repertoire and in number because she made recordings nearly every year up to the time of her death.⁷ Alternately made in New York City and Camden, New Jersey, most of the recordings featured George Falkenstein at the piano, although some were made with pianists Arthur Loesser and Waldemar Liachowsky. The recording technology made large-scale orchestral accompaniment unfeasible and thus prevented the recording of concertos with orchestra. At most, as in some of Maud's records, a string quartet might accompany the artist.

Within two years of her first recording, the Victor phonograveur invited Maud back to the Camden laboratory, where he surprised her with the improvement that had been made in reproducing the character of the violin tone. She was so impressed that she asked to be allowed to remake all of her earlier recordings by the improved process. When in 1910 Maud recorded Wieniawski's *Caprice Valse*, the touted "genius phonograveur of the day" C. G. Child wrote: "I think the *Caprice Valse* is the most delicate and dainty violin solo that we have ever recorded, and the interpretation is simply charming. Everyone who has heard it is fascinated with the record."[8]

In a 1915 interview, Maud was asked to reflect on her recordings and their impact on American musical taste:

> In the quarter of New York that is richest in tradition there is a house which is a "home" to Maud Powell—at least for a few weeks in the year. To meet and talk to this famous woman is a thing of joy, for she greets her guests with the charming simplicity of the really great. . . .
>
> "You, no doubt, have some personal favorites among your Victor records. Which are they?" . . .
>
> "I like—*Deep River*," said Mme. Powell, in the tone which indicates mental stock-taking.
>
> "*Deep River*? Why?"
>
> "I like it musically. I like it as a tune; it is well harmonized and I consider it one of my best records from the point of view of recording. The phrasing is good, and I feel that I was at my best in it. Then, too, it's a real American tune. A man I met in Texas, who had lived in New Orleans in the 70's, told me that he had heard it sung, with a slight variation of rhythm, by the darkies who loaded the cotton schooners."
>
> "Then, I like the Tenaglia Aria, too. Let me see—oh, yes—that's listed as *Have Pity Sweet Eyes*. You see, to speak of the *Tenaglia Aria* doesn't convey much and people like some sort of suggestion from the title."
>
> "Do you feel that this aria is a 'find'? That is, is it something like—oh, say the Raff Cavatina? Something that everybody can and will enjoy?"
>
> "Oh, no," said Mme. Powell. "It isn't superficial enough for that!" and she laughed with the glee of a wood elf. "Oh, no—but it takes the listener into a few moments of serious enjoyment through its simplicity and nobility—like a perfect Greek statue or a lovely bit of architecture.
>
> "Oh, the old writers wrote marvelous things, didn't they? Things that last to this day and—like the old painters—it seems to me that they must have worked with a touch of religious ardor. I don't believe,

for instance, that those wonderful cathedrals could have been built in a day like this, do you? Why, we have no reverence for *anything*! "That reminds me. A woman friend of mine says she 'hates' the violin. What she means is that she is afraid of it emotionally. Isn't that rather typically American?"

Mme. Powell got up and for a moment or two was very evidently looking for something, then she said:

"I wanted to show you a book of wild flowers—painted for me. These little things! The beauty of them is enough to make one weep or sing—but—people don't see them. We are too busy playing the game of life to really *live*, and for us pleasure is a synonym for excitement. Our music is *ragtime*, which sometimes tickles the rhythmic sense, but more often merely assaults the ears, and vulgar songs of the day, with their unspeakable words! People don't seem to realize that there is much more beauty in quiet music and in classical music if they'll only get familiar with it. That it's more beautiful and—lasts longer."

"Lacking the inspiration of an audience, how can you manage to put so much emotional force into a record like—well, say the Sibelius *Valse Triste*?"

Mme. Powell laughed, and then she said: "Just nervousness! Making a record is the most nervous work I've ever done in my life! I'm as limp as a rag when it's over."

"Just nervousness?"

"Yes, I think so. But of course, being an artist means that your nervousness goes into the right channels and accomplishes the thing you want to do. There's a ghastly feeling that you're playing for all the world and an awful sense that what is done *is* done."

"You watch that awful face at the window, waiting for the raising of the eyebrows which tells you to begin, and then (laughing heartily), for the life of you, you don't know whether you can put your finger on the right note or not! I assure you there is no chance of being bored!"

"Violin records seem wonderfully satisfying. Why should they be?"

"I do think that the violin or the string quartette too, perhaps, does more to cultivate taste. It's freer from the 'feet of clay.' You are not required to listen to words or speculate on accompanying dramatic action and all that. The music is more impersonal than when you listen to a voice. It makes its own appeal and there are not extraneous distractions. A song from opera is less complete in form because it is related to the context, both of music and action, but with us — the things that we play must be complete in themselves."

"Will you tell me another record that you personally like?"

"As a crisp and scintillating piece of violin work I like Hubay's *Hejre Kati*, and I think it's a wonderful achievement in recording."

"How much of the original brilliance is lost in the Victrola reproduction?"

"Practically none; there may be a little less of — well — shall we say string elasticity? That seems to express what I mean. I've heard people say that the Victrola doesn't sound like the violin, but d'you know, to me it sounds *exactly* like the violin. I think perhaps people have to learn how to listen. You can get behind all the mechanical part and listen subjectively."

"Is there another record?"

"Yes, the Bach *Bourrée*. I like it for its rhythm. One man, by the way, who doesn't know anything about classical music, says it's my best record — Bach, if you please! Then, too, there's a lovely aesthetic effect in going from the B minor of the *Bourrée* into the F major *Menuett* of Gluck. The first C in the menuett gives me untold satisfaction. It's wonderful, and the transition is *so* simple. It occurs, of course, in the interval between the end of the bourree and the beginning of the menuett."

"By the way, I wish people wouldn't play my record of the Mendelssohn Concerto so fast. It loses all the nuances, all the rhythmic charm, and sounds — stupid.

"Once, when I was on a concert tour, I went into a store where they happened to be playing it. I was rather 'on edge' with the strain of concert work, so I went to the young man at the Victrola and said, 'Won't you please play that a little slower?' He told me the Victrola was playing at the right speed, but I said, 'Well, but you're playing that in G, and it's written and played in E.' Then Mr. Turner came up and said, 'Since this is the lady who made the record she *may* be right, you know'; then, of course, the poor boy wilted — but it does spoil the record to play it so fast." . . .

"How much of the musical development is due to the Victrola?"

"Ah! It's hard to say too much about the influence of the Victrola — it is a real, a vital and indeed a national influence. Why, do you know, out in Montana I saw a man get off the train who looked like a tramp. He had a big sack over his shoulder containing records which we ourselves had seen him select in a Victrola shop. He must have had a hundred dollars' worth — and he was going to carry them ten miles!"

A famous critic has said concerning Maud Powell: "There is at least one woman that can fiddle with the best of the men and at the same time express herself clearly and forcibly in writing." He meant in talking, too.

I had had a delightful morning and was by no means ready to leave, but Mme. Powell had been practising when I called, and even an interviewer must be reasonable; but — there was no difficulty in remembering what she had said, even in the roar of the city streets.[9]

Countless individual lives must have been inspired and enriched by Maud Powell's disembodied art. Her recordings made a profound impression on Yehudi Menuhin, who still remembers his love for her recording of *The Swan* which he heard as a little boy.[10] An accomplished amateur violist responded in the following way to an article on Maud Powell's life published with her picture in 1980:

> You would have little idea of what it meant to me to see, for the first time, a picture of Maud Powell, and to read of her magnificent accomplishments in the violin world. It was like opening a door into a sun-lit room — that chamber having been obscure and in shadow since I was a boy of ten years, when I first heard the golden tones of her violin on a 1916 recording. All my life that moment of time has remained in my memory — even now, at the good age of seventy-five I hear the seamless flow of her double-stopping in thirds — but alas what it was she was playing I do not know — all that remained with me all these years has been the exquisite beauty of that sound — heard but once — but engraved forever on the "tabula rasa" of my mind.[11]

22

Musical Exploration in South Africa, 1905

Music is the universal language of mankind. . . .

— Henry Wadsworth Longfellow

ON HER SECOND TOUR OF ENGLAND WITH SOUSA'S BAND, from January to May of 1905, Maud repeated her personal triumph of two years earlier. Estelle Liebling's companionship eased the typically demanding tour schedule, although they toured only the British Isles this time.

Max Liebling, Estelle's father, contributed an elaborate *Fantasia on Sousa Airs* for solo violin with band accompaniment. One could hear snatches of the *Washington Post March* peeping out of the virtuoso solo which abounded in technical difficulties. Critics wrote that the selection gave "Miss Powell one more opportunity of demonstrating her exceptional executant powers," and that was a "thing to enthuse over."[1]

Throughout the tour, English critics viewed Maud's violin playing as "*the* event of the program" and noted respectfully that she "is an artist of rare culture and richly endowed with musical temperament."[2]

No sooner had the Sousa tour ended than Maud embarked on an ambitious tour of South Africa, at the head of her own concert company.[3] Apart from Camilla Urso's tour ten years earlier, it was the first time an American musician had toured that country. Maud left England on May 6 for South Africa with a soprano, a tenor, a bass singer, a pianist, and a cellist — all English with the exception of one Boer. The brilliant young cellist, May Mukle, is the only company

[222]

member whose identity is known. Born in 1880 in London, of an English mother and a German father, by the age of eleven she could support herself with concert engagements. After studying under Signor Pezze at the Royal Academy of Music, Mukle was early recognized as the equal of Pablo Casals.[4] With the aid of a magnificent Montagnana instrument, her playing was "beautifully controlled," her "tone mellow and of considerable power."[5] Her repertoire covered the literature of the instrument, and in 1922 she gave the first performance of Ernest Bloch's *Schelomo* with Sir Henry Wood conducting.

Mukle once related how she and Maud had first met:

> I first met Maud Powell at an "At Home" in London . . . . Although I had never actually known what she was like, or even whether she had ever been in England, such was my ignorance, yet I knew immediately I heard her that this must be the Maud Powell about whom I had heard so much, for she played unaccompanied Bach and certainly I had never liked him so much before or ever thought that his music could mean so much. To say that I fell in love with Maud Powell's playing is putting it mildly, and after her first number I *had* to go up to her and, to use an Irishism, ask if I might speak to her. My joy can easily be imagined when several years later I was engaged to play on her South African tour, and so learned to know her personally. Night after night, and we played forty-two concerts in seven weeks, I listened to her from the wings, and I think that she is less variable in her concert pitch of performance than any other artist I have ever traveled with during my sixteen years of public life.[6]

On May 30, the day they arrived in Cape Town, the company gave their first concert before an enthusiastic audience at the Good Hope Theatre. The South Africans were surprised to hear an American violinist play as beautifully as the European violinists whom they had heard perform. The *Cape Times'* critic wrote: "Her technic is clear and fluent, and her tone and style are remarkable for their purity and breadth. She played last night a variety of works, and proved at once and beyond a doubt the truth of the claims that have been put forward on her behalf."[7] Maud's "apparently limitless" power of execution was "manifest indeed." Even after hearing four nights of performances in Cape Town, the *Cape Times'* critic admitted, "Not once has her performance lost its interest and we must own to a distinct and unmistakable desire for more."[8] For every piece she played, a double encore was demanded.

Maud related that the normally stolid Boers, who nearly matched the English in numbers, listened passively and with apparent disinterest. But when the music ended, they applauded vigorously, stamping on the floor and insisting on encores, with canes and umbrellas if necessary.

After their performance in Johannesburg, the *Transvaal Leader* reported: "Last night's concert was a splendid success—in so far as the premiere violinist of the world was concerned, a great triumph. . . . Her playing was a revelation. Such perfection in tone production, such command of her instrument, such graceful execution, and . . . such a sweet voiced instrument, are given to few women to possess, and no living woman is endowed with the power to produce the same magnificent breadth of tone, the same grand artistic sum, as that achieved by the fair American."[9]

The *Rand Daily Mail* more fully described the effect of that concert:

> Of Maud Powell, it must at once be said that she quickly played herself into the hearts of her listeners. Carried onward by the stream of melody they knew nothing of the lapse of time. All too suddenly the solos seemed to end, so real was the influence which the gifted violinist exerted. Throughout, her playing was magnificent, her execution of the first order. Possessing an exquisite style and a lovely Guarnerius instrument, she secured a complete conquest, her right to the position of a great artist being readily recognized by the audience.
>
> One could not wish for more finished technic. Harmonics and double stopping were splendid, and some beautiful staccato and pizzicato effects were attained. Piece after piece was played with a fluency and ease that held the listeners altogether delighted. So much, in short, were they under the influence of the music that at any unaccompanied passage the proverbial pin might have been heard to drop. The bow was indeed wielded by a master hand, and the general pleasure was not marred by the slightest straining after effect on the part of the artist.[10]

The company progressed from one triumph to another until the original twenty-five engagements expanded to forty-two, due to the re-engagements requested in all the large towns. Lasting eight weeks, the tour included concerts in Pearl, Worcester, Beaufort West, Kimberley, Bloemfontein, Kroonsted, Johannesburg, Krugersdorp, Potchefstrom, Pretoria, Boksburg, Standerton, Ladysmith, Pietermaritzburg, Durban, East London, Queenstown, King Williamstown, Grahamtown, and Port Elizabeth. All the reviews spoke of Maud's performance in superlatives; their general tenor is suggested by Durban's *Natal Mercury*: "Maud Powell ranks among the greatest of living violinists, and her playing last night was a revelation. The violin was made to sing the music with all the wealth of expression of the human voice and an artistic finish that only a few artists ever attain."

As a musical country, Maud found South Africa "surprising": "At times I marveled at the numbers which received most applause, Beethoven or Brahms in one town, and again only a few miles away Paganini or Wieniawski."[11]

Maud's enterprising spirit warmed to the novel adventure of touring in a strange country. All her senses were invigorated by the various cultures she encountered. Her native curiosity combined with her sensitivity to conditions resulting from the tragic Boer War, concluded only three years previously, helped her to expand her inner resources and grow more broadly and deeply as a human being. Everywhere she went, she snapped photographs of the landscape and people she came to know and appreciate. The people of South Africa received the American violinist warmly. In a brief interview account of her experiences, Maud reveals in a small way the acuity of her observations and her unpretentious delight in the hospitality of her hosts:

"South Africa, taken as a whole, is a splendid country, very much in the rough, of course, as to dwellings and city improvements, but settled throughout with a most hospitable, wholesouled and music loving population of Boers and Britons . . . and, although I gave forty-two concerts, my whole trip was made so restful that I feel in the best of health and spirits for my coming tour of my own country and Canada.

"Traveling throughout the country is not very comfortable, partly on account of the ravages made in the traffic facilities by the war. However, the railroad officials made it as easy as possible for me by the granting of a private car, which I was informed was an unusual privilege in that country.

"The railway, by the way, is of the primitive, narrow gauge sort, built on the stage coach principle. When you come to a hill it just climbs up and down, as tunnels or cuttings are undreamed of. There are no trestles or bridgework for the small streams, so the longest way 'round them is the shortest way across.

"At my concerts the Boers showed much enthusiasm and afterwards seemed to vie with each other in offering hospitalities. In all the large towns the Mayors seem to represent the people socially as well as politically, and everywhere they seemed eager to show their country and extend courtesies to me and my party.

"In Natal, where the scenery is wonderfully beautiful, we were taken on a 30 mile drive in a government mule wagon, to see Howick Falls, which are 364 feet high, and drop with a terrific roar. My snapshot of the falls illustrates their size in July — the South African winter time — when it is the dry season. At other seasons, I was told, it is a much bigger waterfall. At Kimberley we were conducted in great state through the De Beers diamond mines and through the 'Ferruna Deep' gold mines, at Johannesburg. In the former the laborers, convicts for the most part, picked the diamonds out of the running sluice every other minute. It was a tempting spectacle.

"I hugely enjoyed Pietermaritzburg, which is by far the prettiest town in South Africa, and contains some magnificent public buildings. I also like Durban, which, though a more pretentious town, is not so distinctive in progressive characteristics, as it is largely a winter resort only.

"A quaint custom in both Pietermaritzburg and Durban is the use of those jolly little 'rickshas. It was a novel sensation to me to step into a 'ricksha in my evening dress, valuable fiddle in hand, and to be trotted off to the concert. This sort of conveyance seemed rather romantic and delightful on those wonderful starlit nights I spent under the Southern Cross.

"The townspeople of Ladysmith were more than cordial in their reception of me. All around were evidences of the terrors of war, in the demolition of portions of some of the fine buildings. Even the Town Hall did not go unscathed, its pretty little clock tower having been partly destroyed by a Boer shell. But the citizens don't dwell much on that topic, and it was only called to my attention when in my appreciation of their putting a billboard on the Town Hall announcing my concert, I had remarked, 'Just fancy any other country advertising my appearance on its Town Hall!' It was a generous compliment. At Ladysmith we also visited the surrounding battlefields, which gave us more of an idea what hardships the Ladysmith settlers had to undergo during the war." "What did you bring back in the way of souvenirs, Miss Powell?" queried the interviewer.

"Well, in addition to more than 200 photographs, I secured a specimen of a Kaffir piano, which must be seen to be appreciated, as it beggars description."[12]

The American visitor did not fail to make contact with and to observe the life of the black Africans, noting unhappily that these people were not admitted to her concerts.

South Africa, like many other countries, excludes the aborigines from theatres and concert halls, so my knowledge of them was gained elsewhere than in my audiences. Can you imagine any ignorant man here in this city standing for hours under a hotel window to hear me play? Yet that happened in Johannesburg, Pietermaritzburg and every other African city that I visited. I noticed it first in Johannesburg one morning while I was practicing. Glancing out of the window I spied a Kaffir in wide-mouthed, wide-eyed bronze nudity listening.

I was careful not to let him see me and watched to see how long he would listen. He stood there immovable two hours or more, absolutely enraptured, yet he lived in a kraal and was elaborately costumed when he had on a few strings of beads. Again, just outside Pietermaritzburg we passed a Kaffir boy playing most wonderfully on a mouth organ. He did not stop as we approached, but turned softly aside to let the "white gods" pass.[13]

Maud made a special effort to absorb the music and art of the black Africans and generally study their culture and way of life, and it was from this that she derived the greatest benefit:

As a trip, . . . it was splendid, and helped me a great deal. You see I believe that the breadth of a musician's art depends largely upon the psychological knowledge he possesses, and that such knowledge is only gained by a deep and conscientious study of self. These South Africans gave me a view of life which I think has brought a new note into my playing. I have felt it since I returned. There, existence is so raw, so uncultivated. The people are like the country, a vast waste of kopjes and plains. It was almost primitive man of which I had a glimpse.[14]

And in another vein:

> An American trying to play or sing ragtime is insufferably vulgar. I do not mean that ragtime is vulgar, I mean it is vulgar when we try to play it. Under a white hand ragtime degenerates into a poor imitation of sounds that are wonderful when made by a primitive race.
>
> We white of North America are touched heavily with the Puritan spirit, we cannot be spontaneous, we lack the emotional abandon that comes so easily to natural, primitive people. I have suffered from it myself. Until I went to South Africa, I never fully understood what a handicap this was, and is, to all Americans with Puritan ancestry.[15]

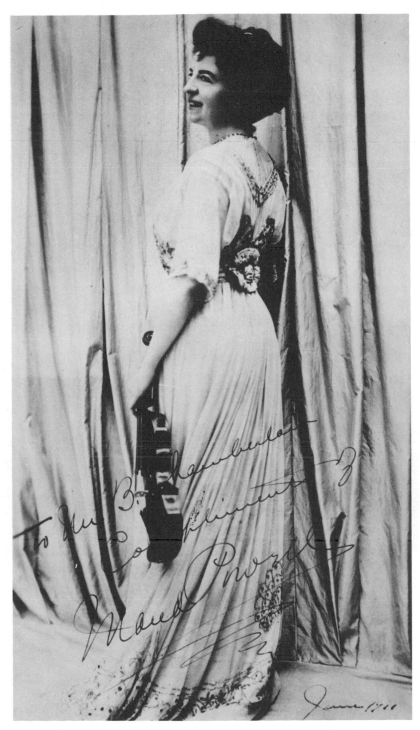

Maud in a 1910 photo autographed in 1911 to Mr. B. Chamberlain.

Maud performing with the Bellingham (Washington) Orchestra, Mrs. Davenport-Engberg, conductor, on January 24, 1913. Godfrey Turner is standing on the right. The man on the left is probably Mrs. Davenport-Engberg's husband, who managed the orchestra. The photographic composition is characteristic of Sunny's sense of humor.

These photos by Sunny are symbolic of the fun-filled atmosphere surrounding the Norfolk (Connecticut) Festival in June 1911. *This page, top, l to r:* Maud, Mrs. Bassett, Mrs. Arthur

s, soprano Louise Homer, Mrs. William Cook, and Mrs. Paul Morgan; *bottom, l to r:* tralian pianist Ernest Hutcheson, tenor George Hamlin, American pianist Franklin ett, conductor Dr. Arthur Mees, Worcester Festival president William Cook, past presi-, Paul Morgan, and American composer Arthur Farwell. *This page, top,* Maud's friends e June 1910 Norfolk Festival, *l to r:* English composer Samuel Coleridge-Taylor, George lin, Maud, Mrs. Arthur Mees, Gertrude May Stein, Franklin Bassett, Dr. Arthur Mees; m, soprano Alma Gluck and Maud at Norfolk in June 1911.

Victor Supremacy

The world's famous singers

The world's famous instrumentalists

The world's famous bands and orchestras

The world's famous comedians

The Victrola is all artists and all instruments in one. It gives you the actual tones of the renowned singers and instrumentalists of the world. It is the genius, the power, the beauty of every voice and every instrument. It is the supreme musical instrument of all time.

Victor dealers everywhere

Ask your nearest dealer for demonstration

Victrola the greatest of all musical instruments

$15 to $400

. . . ng page, Victor advertisement. In 1904 Maud became the first instrumentalist to record
. . . *Victor* Talking Machine Company. *Above,* Sunny, left, and Maud, holding "Nipper,"
Victor representatives, about 1918.

Maud, about 1913, holding her Guadagnini.

23

The Musician's Musician

*Listen to Maud Powell's violin. If you want to be transported to
a heaven of delight by the pathos of a simple sweet song, —if
you want to feel the uplift which an evening of aesthetic enjoyment gives, or if you want to feel a thrill of patriotism because a
great, modest, unaffected, true and vibrant talent has been born
in the Western Hemisphere—in short, if you want to find out
how much can be got out of a fiddle, go—listen to—Maud
Powell.*

—*Victor Talking Machine Company*

MAUD POWELL'S REAPPEARANCE ON THE AMERICAN concert platform was
eagerly greeted by critics and audiences alike. Her reputation for dis-
cernible growth in her art with each passing year led them to expect
from her a very special musical experience. With her musical instincts
so sure and her technical perfection unquestioned, she was to them a
"comfortable artist" in whom they could trust implicitly.

The blend of "poise, dignity, sincerity, intelligence, graciousness
and patience" in her personality combined with her "flawless" violin
art enabled her to treat a "legion of her admirers" to an afternoon of
music in Mendelssohn Hall "that will not soon be forgotten."[1] The
recital given January 11, 1906, featured Richard Strauss's Sonata in
E-flat Major as well as works by Bach, Corelli, Rust, Farwell, Paganini,
Dvořák, Reger, and Wieniawski. The critic Richard Aldrich noted
that "her playing is that of a ripe and thoroughly equipped artist,
one who has known and felt the significance of the music she plays.
What she does is for the music itself, and not at all for the exploitation of herself, and needs no assistance of any interest outside of it."[2]

[229]

One musical observer pointed out that the violinist's programs reflected her personal study of the violin literature, old and new, unbounded by tradition. The programs she offered indicated progress for the artist and, as a matter of course, informed the audiences that heard her. Maud consciously strived to educate her audiences in the history of violin playing and composition through her program choices and her program notes. In this regard, the writer for the *Evening Sun* paid her tribute as a "serious artist, an interpreter, not a gymnast," following the Mendelssohn Hall recital.

> This American woman stands at the head of her profession today. . . . Maud Powell is the Sembrich of the violin. If she wound up a regular musical art program . . . with Wieniawski's waltz caprice and Paganini's *Witches' Dance*, it was not to show she could do the tricks like Kubelik and Marie Hall — she can, though — but rather for the very good reason that those composers have a place in history. Paganini "treats the violin with supreme daring," as Liszt the piano and Berlioz the orchestra. Not Paganini but Corelli was the first great violinist. From Corelli's *Variations Sérieuses* to Dvořák's *Humoresque*, Miss Powell hitched her fiddle strings to a series of masterpieces which to music lovers and students are meat and drink, not to say cigars and repartée. From a Bach allegro to a Richard Strauss sonata, the music was played for music's sake. There was a new romance of H. H. Huss, and there were such practical jokes as a scherzo by Germany's new Max Reger and three little Indian songs of a Thunder God, a Spirit and an "Ichibuzzhi," harmonized by Arthur Farwell. The violinist made the antique Corelli seem the most alive.[3]

The versatility of Maud's mind and art were distinctive traits amid a sea of violinists whose performances made little distinction between music of different styles and periods. After hearing a recital in 1907 which ranged from Arensky's concerto to Mozart's *Rondo* in G Major (from the Haffner *Serenade*), and from Wieniawski and Dvořák to Corelli and Couperin, Boston critics wrote: "No American violinist comparable with Mme. Powell in mastery of her instrument as a medium of expression, in grasp of the intellectual content of her music, in resiliency to its qualities of poetry and imagination and in differentiation of his characteristic traits has yet served her art as has she."[4] "She comprehends alike the noble serenity, the classic spirit of the old Italians, the romanticism of later writers for virtuosos, the restlessness of the ultra-moderns in thought and expression. She is not an exponent or an interpreter of only one school."[5]

Gustav Saenger, the violinist, pedagogue, composer, conductor, and editor of *The Musical Observer*, explained the historical importance of this development in the August 1913 issue:

> [T]oday Wieniawski is succeeded by the *modern virtuoso* who in one recital program covers the entire history of violin music from Tartini to Brahms and Tschaikowsky, and who . . . plays each work with distinctness, character and proper artistic interpretation. The list of modern players who can be placed in this class is not a very large one. Such names as Kreisler, Ysaÿe, Thomson, Zimbalist, Elman and Flesch are uppermost in our minds when we try to mention the biggest, and it is just here that we are enabled to place Maud Powell, just where she belongs — *right at the top-notch of the representative list of masculine players and equal to any of them in the artistic rendition of every important classic or modern work of which the literature of the violin may boast.*

Boston critic H. T. Parker further explained Maud's allure for discriminating music lovers: "Mme. Powell's [art] happens to be of a pure, unforced, almost severe integrity, and it is so impersonal that her listeners hear the violinist only as the potent and absorbing voice of the music. Ysaÿe persuades by a personal weight; Kreisler allures by a romantic charm; Thomson impresses by a commanding mental force; youth plays in Mischa Elman. . . . In Mme. Powell, on the other hand, are the power and the fascination of an almost disembodied artistry. There is the music, the violin — and a transporting pleasure."[6]

It was the uniqueness of Maud Powell's art which enabled her to present the music she did to American audiences and gain acceptance for it. One observer remarked: "From almost its beginning her career as a performer was successful, brilliant, impressive. However, it was not so much her performances themselves but rather their nature, which gave her the exceptional standing she soon won and then held so long."[7] Behind the technique and musicianship loomed an imposing intellect, broad humanity, and deep spirituality, which formed the substratum of her character. These qualities were fused almost volcanically through the imposition of discipline over a spirited temperament and then were projected through the music like molten lava poured into a mold, red-hot with fire but fitted to form —

the essence of art. This artist first sought truth and then gave expression to it, as one close friend observed upon her death:

> Gifted with an uncommon degree of mentality and deep seriousness of purpose, Maud Powell devoted herself to the highest ideals in art and never permitted her remarkable technical gifts on the violin to overshadow her desire to be first and foremost always the faithful interpreter voicing the message of the composer. She went deeply into the study of harmony, composition, and musical history, and kept abreast of the times also in her reading and in special scientific research. Her mind reached out in all directions and touched every subject. She was a savant but not a pedant. A broad humanity and a native sense of humor tinged all her thought and speech and put her close to her audiences. She was idolized by her friends. Musicians admired her virile style, her big tone, her commanding personality, her authoritative readings.[8]

Students, critics, and musicians (including Schradieck, Spalding, Parlow, Auer, Kreisler, Kubelik, Ysaÿe, Reményi, Gerardy, Saint-Saëns, Grainger, Dvořák, Bruch) were drawn to her recitals by her magnetic art, leading one observer to comment that no other artist had so many friends among the cultured and discriminating populace. At a New York recital in April of 1906, Maud's performances of unaccompanied Bach "proved sublime feats of pure violin playing." "The violinists present were spellbound and others were impressed that something out of the ordinary was happening," reported the critic for *The Musical Courier*. Albert Spalding reportedly once said that Maud Powell produced the most beautiful tone of all the great violinists of her day, especially when she played on the G string.[9] Maud's musicianship moved critic W. J. Henderson to pen the following parody of Leigh Hunt's "Abou Ben Adhem," published in *Musical America* in December 1905:

> Abou Maud Powell, may her tribe increase,
> Awoke one night from a deep dream of peace,
> And saw within the moonlight in her room,
> Making it green, just like a bank in bloom,
> A critic writing phrases worn and old.
> Exceeding praise had made Maud Powell bold,
> And to the presence in the room she said,
> "What writest thou?" The vision raised its head,
> And with a look of secrecy and stealth

Answered, "The names of those who get the wealth."
"And is mine one?" she faltered. "Nay, not so,"
Replied the scribbler. Maud then spake more low,
But cheerily still, and said, "Before we part
Write me as one who doth respect her Art."
The critic wrote and vanished. The next night
He came again with a great awakening light
And showed the names whom love of Art had blessed:
And lo! Maud Powell's name led all the rest.

Maud's enthusiasm for her art and her dauntless spirit continually led her to explore the limits of the violin literature and of her instrument. In 1907 James Huneker, another New York critic, observed: "Of Maud Powell there is this to be said: She has fulfilled her early promise. She is a mature *artiste*, one who will never be finished because she will always study, always improve. A Joachim pupil, she is nevertheless a pupil of Maud Powell, and her playing reveals breadth and musicianship, beauty of tone and phrasing."[10]

Perhaps more than any other violinist up to that time, Maud expanded the violinist's repertoire by programming and promoting works of both early and modern composers. She probably knew more composers, both European and American, personally and had a larger repertoire than any other violinist.[11] During her career Maud gave the American premieres of fourteen violin concertos, as well as innumerable other works. In doing so, especially through her premieres of the Tchaikovsky, Dvořák, and Sibelius concertos, she also pioneered the development of new violin technique.

Maud recovered and revived works by Corelli, Tartini, and Vivaldi, modernizing them slightly. She gave the American premiere of Locatelli's Sonata in F Minor. With Sam Franko as violist, Maud also shared in the American revival of Mozart's Sinfonie Concertante in E-flat in Franko's concert series devoted to early music.

If she could not find exactly what she wanted for her programs, Maud resorted to transcriptions. She once observed that "Transcriptions are wrong, theoretically; yet some songs, like Rimsky-Korsakov's *Song of India* and some piano pieces, like the Dvořák *Humoresque*, are so obviously effective on the violin that a transcription justifies itself."[12] Maud's own excellent transcriptions, listed in the appendix, indicate that she might have composed some fine original music.

It was strange that so original a musician did not compose, other than a cadenza to the Brahms violin concerto. But Sunny observed that "her ideals were so high and her idea of what the music worth while should be, that she did not begin what she did not feel sure could be carried through to a great result." Nevertheless, her transcriptions were original and considered to be "as fundamentally right as many an adaptation of folk-tunes that has been issued under the adapter's name."[13] The original manuscript of Maud's transcription "Nobody Knows the Trouble I See" reveals her dedication to musical integrity. In the final form she had simplified a number of chords in her persistent effort to keep the harmonization from obscuring the soul of the song.

Maud's "splendidly effective" transcription "Deep River," based on Coleridge-Taylor's piano setting of the Negro spiritual, was hailed in 1911 by Henry Krehbiel as "far and away the most effective bit of music based on American folksong which has yet been offered to the public, and the audience heard it with delight not unmixed with surprise."[14] The violinist asked not to be given credit for the piece and attributed its effectiveness to the beauty of Coleridge-Taylor's setting, which she diffidently said she "only recast . . . in great haste."

In contemplating the use of octaves in transcriptions, she observed: "[T]hough they are supposed to add volume of tone they sound hideous to me. I have used them in certain passages of my arrangement of *Deep River* but when I heard them played, promised myself I would never repeat the experiment. Wilhelmj has committed even a worse crime in taste by putting six long bars of Schubert's lovely *Ave Maria* in octaves. Of course they represent skill; but I think they are only justified in show pieces."[15]

She delighted in the transcriptions of her violinist friends, of Americans Arthur Hartmann, Francis MacMillen, and Sol Marcosson, as well as those by Kreisler, Joachim, and other Europeans.

In explaining some of the reasons for her untiring search for new works, Maud expressed her views forcefully during an interview in 1912:

> What are we poor violinists to do? The literature for the violin is so poor. The critics in Berlin recently jumped on Elman because he performed the Tschaikowsky concerto. "Is he going to play this forever?" they asked. But what is there? Even the good violin works

are usually not the great works of the composers. The Brahms concerto is inferior to the symphonies, the Tschaikowski concerto is inferior to the symphonies. Perhaps the Beethoven isn't. And Mendelssohn's concerto is assuredly better than his symphonies, a master work for the violin that, but so hackneyed! Even in my recent trip to Florida they asked me not to play it—and the request came from a Mendelssohn club!

Occasionally one can play Goldmark, but it is not the composer at his best as he is in *The Queen of Sheba* or *Sakuntala*. I like Wieniawski's concerto with the gypsy finale, but the middle movement I could never play in public if I had rehearsed it that same day. It is the kind of music you must be fresh for, or it bores you to do it. Vieuxtemps is almost dead, and de Bériot quite. Still, there is one movement of a de Bériot concerto which I nearly always play at concerts on shipboard. It goes very well without an accompaniment.[16]

Maud steadfastly sought out new music. Her keen artistic vision enabled her to see clearly the merits of a new concerto like Tor Aulin's in C Minor, Op. 14. She called it "essentially a violinist's concerto— written for violinists by one who is himself no mean performer on the king of instruments. Tor Aulin's message may not be profound or perhaps of paramount importance, yet it is, in view of the paucity of good violin works in the larger forms, distinctly worth while."[17]

For the 1905–06 season, Maud prepared two new violin concertos for their first American hearing. She performed the concerto written by Russian composer Anton Arensky (1861–1906) with Modest Altschuler and the Russian Symphony Orchestra on December 30 and 31, 1905. A pupil of Arensky, Altschuler was the Russian immigrant cellist and conductor who had organized the Russian Symphony Orchestra in New York in 1903. Maud apparently had played Arensky's A minor concerto in Europe, although it was not published until 1902. She may have met the composer in St. Petersburg in 1903 during the Sousa tour, or she may have learned of the concerto from Rimsky-Korsakov, who she knew in Europe.

In a concert in Carnegie Hall featuring all new Russian music, the Arensky concerto was received as "a melodious and effective concerto" though "not very deep or important from a musical point of view." The critics observed that it did not promise to become a standard part of the repertoire.[18] Although Maud was fully aware of its limitations, she believed it served well in a recital program:

This work should be given the qualifying title of Concerto de Salon, inasmuch as the graces and intimacies of its style and content appear to far better advantage with pianoforte accompaniment than with the heavier, more unwieldy setting of the orchestra score. This composition conveys no especially profound message, but is nevertheless sufficiently rich in pleasant melodic invention and rhythmic charm to make it worth while as a number for recital programs. It is cleverly constructed, commanding the respect and approval of the musician.[19]

Characteristically, Maud played the Arensky throughout the season, giving the new work a chance to be judged by more than one hearing.

On April 2, 1906, Maud gave the world premiere of a concerto composed by Henry Holden Huss and dedicated to her. She was assisted by Modest Altschuler and the Russian Symphony Orchestra in a concert sponsored by the New Music Society of America, which had been expressly formed to give new American works a hearing. This was the second time Maud had given the world premiere performance of a concerto composed by an American and dedicated to her. That evening the works of George W. Chadwick, George S. Smith, and F. S. Converse were also featured.

Since 1891, the year Maud had brought forward Shelley's violin concerto, American composition had not made much audible progress. After the concert, one critic expressed the continuing dilemma of the American composer: "The American composer is still a student of European methods and manners. He is exercising himself in the technic of the conservatory of experience. He has almost nothing to say and almost no way of saying it. There is every evidence of apprenticeship in his work, not a single flash of mastery."[20] Huss's concerto, like Shelley's, failed because it was not skillfully orchestrated. The enthusiasm greeting the performance was credited to the player and not to the composition.[21] Modest Altschuler unabashedly announced that Maud Powell was "the greatest violinist America has given to the world. Miss Powell's virtuosity is a compound of masculine virility and feminine delicacy hallowed with the soundest musicianship."[22]

In the spring of 1906, Maud began studying the Sibelius Violin Concerto in D Minor. Since it had been completed so recently, in 1905, she had never heard it played, nor had anyone else in America, until she herself played it. When she initially discovered the score, its first "hearing" was through the artist's peculiar gift, the mind's ear, which hears the music as it is read by the eye, the gift of hearing a concert without a note being played. She once described the effect of that silent concert on its distinguished audience of one:

> I unearthed that . . . accidentally, among a pile of other things. I became interested the minute I saw the first theme. My interest increased by leaps and bounds. I was delighted with the way the theme was developed in the cadenza. "If this sort of thing can only continue," I exclaimed as I turned to the second movement. I read it through and "this will go beautifully" I decided when I pictured to myself its effects with orchestra. "Now for the last movement." Of course that, being the last movement, must show some falling off. But on the whole I was thrilled by that concerto, thrilled by its themes. . . .[23]

Maud immediately made arrangements to present the Finnish composer's work to America. The revised concerto had been premiered only a short time before, on October 19, 1905, by Carl Halir at the Berlin Singakademie with Richard Strauss conducting. As she worked on the music, Maud reflected on the roots of her pioneer spirit:

> I never was so thoroughly convinced in heredity as I am when thinking over my own case. My [uncle] was one of the most noted explorers in this country, his scenes of operation being around the canyons of Colorado. My father showed the same tendency to delve and to depart from accepted paths in the educational world. He was noted, in a pedagogic way, for his exploration. I never am so happy as when working out something which I never heard before and which under ordinary circumstances is practically unknown, then comes that feeling of exploration and I love new and undiscovered country. I have worked with this concerto for over six months. I never play it without finding something which I never dreamed of before.[24]

Her joy was complete when she took something new to her audiences: "Then with a discriminating audience it is an inspiration to watch the awakening interest, the dawning understanding, then the quick delight, which is what the performer strives so hard after."[25]

The Sibelius concerto was one of those "impossibly difficult" works which required more than one hearing to be appreciated. Glowing with excitement, Maud said: "It is a gigantic, rugged thing, an epic really. . . . It is on new lines and has a new technique. O, it is wonderful."[26]

Sibelius recognized the risk the violinist was taking in presenting his work to the American public. Just before the concert, the Finnish composer sent Maud his picture, endorsing it: "To the Violin Queen, Miss Maud Powell, with gratitude—Jean Sibelius."[27]

The concert took place in Carnegie Hall on November 30, 1906, and was repeated the following evening. The Russian conductor Wassily Safonoff led the one hundred members of the New York Philharmonic. The next day's reviews give a variety of perspectives on the Sibelius concerto's dramatic United States premiere:

> Miss Powell played Sibelius's new concerto with splendid enthusiasm and devotion. It is [her] distinction that she has always had the courage to seek out and present modern works of promise, to enlarge the repertory of the solo violinist who plays concertos with orchestra. The repertory is limited and is indefinitely repeated by less adventurous artists than she, who prefer to be sure of their success with the old than to tempt fortune with the new. It is the more to be regretted that in this work she was working against odds too great—odds that the composer himself has set up against her by the paucity of ideas, its great length and almost unrelieved sombreness of mood. . . .
>
> Miss Powell was warmly greeted and her admirable playing was recognized by applause that was meant for her.
>
> — Richard Aldrich, *New York Times*

A brave and unselfish artist is Miss Powell. It was she who introduced Tschaikowsky's concerto to Americans. . . . The Tschaikowsky concerto is a stock piece of most virtuosi now, and its technical difficulties no longer excite the special wonder or the ire of critics. It is now Mr. Sibelius's turn. The Finnish composer has put out his dragnet and captured a multitude of curiosities in the way of difficulties never seen before. . . . All the heights of the violin are furiously scaled in this new concerto, and all its most lugubrious depths explored. . . . Mme. Powell played with astonishing verve and as if there were no mysteries in the score for her.

—H. E. Krehbiel, *New York Tribune*

This concerto is of the Finns, finny. It is of the North, rugged. It is of the Russ, rude. It is of the fiddle, technical. It is almost everything except beautiful. . . . It is bitter as gall and savage as wilderness. Nevertheless in so far as the technics of the violin are concerned it is ultra sophisticated. . . .

The first movement of this concerto is enough to appall almost any violinist. Now, every one who knows anything knows that Maud Powell is the last of players to seek out a medium for bald technical display. She is too true an artist for that. She must have found something else in this extraordinary concerto to induce her to master its frightful passages. She played it superbly. Her tone was full and brilliant. Her style had virility and breadth and dash. Her finger work was admirable and her bowing glorious. But why did she put all that magnificent art into this sour and crabbed concerto?

— W. J. Henderson, *New York Sun*

It is probably the most difficult of all concertos, but Miss Powell played it so fluently, so brilliantly, that this fact was not patent to the casual hearer. The enthusiasm with which she played it also indicated that there was more musical substance to it than a first hearing might indicate. Certainly the composer can thank his stars that it was Miss Powell who introduced this work to America; no other living violinist, unless it be Fritz Kreisler, could have made so much of it. It was admirable violin playing, from every point of view—why dwell on details? When Maud Powell plays, one thinks not of bowing and fingering, of staccato or legato, of harmonics or double stops, of trills—though they be, as hers are, Melba-like in their perfection; one thinks only of the music. Like a great actor, she makes one forget the player in the art. . . . [W]hether she can make it popular remains doubtful. Its rugged Northern character, its lack of sensuous beauty and smoothness—though there are lovely, calm moments—will stand in its way.

—Henry T. Finck, *New York Evening Post*

It was a new departure in solo repertory. Forbidding in its true Finnish darkness of outlook, the music was rhapsodic and epic by turns, the solo persistently set off against a Greek chorus of cellos, a background of mysterious deep horns or an uplifting choir of wood voices. Here is one of the few concertos that speak. And here was a performer of skill and devoted intelligence, who threw herself into the hard work with amazing self-abandon. Jan of Helsingfors will not soon hear his own work better played. Safonoff shook Miss Powell by the hand.

—William B. Chase, *New York Evening Sun*

The audience let loose with a great ovation in spite of the strangeness of the work. Camille Saint-Saëns, who had sat in the box on the right side listening "most attentively," was among those who applauded the most heartily. Safonoff was overcome with admiration for the violinist. "What an artist! I do not say this for convention, but from my heart," he wrote of her shortly thereafter, perhaps with the Sibelius concerto still ringing in his ears.[28] Following the second concert, the conductor wrote Maud a note:

> Hotel Netherland, New York
>
> Dear Miss Powell—I wish to express to you my warmest admiration for your superb playing of the Sibelius concerto with the New York Philharmonic Orchestra yesterday. To conquer these almost insurmountable difficulties of technic and interpretation requires really an unusually artistic force. With all sincerity,
>
> W. Safonoff
>
> December 2, 1906[29]

After this memorable musical event, the critics again noted growth in Maud Powell's art. She was said to be "at the very zenith of her artistic maturity," as they ranked her with the best violinists of the day. It was an observation the critics continued to make every year until her death. But in 1906 the latest word was: "Her tone has taken on a lovely lyric quality which it did not formerly possess, and she proclaims her message in the large style and impressive utterance of one for whom the violin has no secrets, and who searches the music she plays with a clear and commanding intellect."[30]

Maud was thoughtful about her art and when asked to reflect on its demands and limitations, she responded simply but with great feeling:

> Mme. Powell, how far do you think an artist may go in the matter of personal interpretation?
>
> Only so far as to make every little point tell; interpretation should never be a cloak for personal display.
>
> Do violinists ever feel that they cannot interpret the work of some certain composer?
>
> Not unless they're afflicted with spiritual laziness. Of course, there are always some composers whose work seems to lie more particularly within one's own taste and capabilities. Musicians ought to

be able—as an actor is—to associate themselves with the spirit of a composition. Many a time I've given a composition the benefit of the doubt and delved into it till I found the hidden treasure.

How do you think the technique of the modern violinist probably compares with that of Paganini?

We have to express more. In fact, I think too much is asked of the violinist—it would almost seem as though the orchestra is the solo instrument of the day; the violin is really a singing instrument, and it *has* its limitations, you know![31]

If the New York critics thought that the Finnish composer's violin concerto would be consigned to oblivion, they did not figure on Maud Powell's determination and her great love for the work. Nor did they possess her musical insight. With daring spirit, Maud set out to present in Cincinnati, Chicago, and Boston the concerto that had won her heart.

In Chicago she played it on January 25 and 26, 1907, with Frederick Stock, who had succeeded Thomas as the conductor of the Chicago Symphony Orchestra. The reviews the following day indicate that New York critics had failed to understand the work. W. L. Hubbard of the *Chicago Tribune* could not resist speculating that the quality of the orchestra might have made all the difference:

> Maud Powell—"our" Maud Powell . . .—scored a triumph yesterday. . . . She played for the first time here a composition which is one of the most difficult in all violin literature and at the same time one of the most original. And she played it superbly. There are extremely few of her brother artists who could compass its technical intricacies with such surety and seeming ease as she did, and still fewer of them who could interpret it with such masterful skill . . . .
>
> [T]he [New York] critics were at a loss just what to say. Either because of the unusualness of the work itself, or possibly because of the presentation by the orchestra having been inadequate, they seemed to have failed utterly to grasp the musical content of the composition. Certainly had they heard a performance as complete in note and spirit as was the one Miss Powell and Mr. Stock and his men gave, they could not have failed to discover the striking originality and the inherent musical strength that lie in this greatest of the talented Finnish composer's creations. It must have been that the performance there was inadequate as regards the orchestral part.
>
> The Thomas Orchestra patrons received the new concerto with unmistakable approval. . . . [A]nd when after hearty recalls for Miss

Powell she came back, and it was seen that the last movement was to be repeated, everybody smiled with satisfaction. Many gladly would have heard the entire concerto a second time. . . .

It is a work of true significance . . . and the performance was truly masterly. Miss Powell is such a comfortable artist. There is nothing of pose or virtuoso affectation and airs about her. She loves the work she is doing, and her heart, soul and mind are wholly in it. The public and the concert surroundings are forgotten, and only the task at hand claims her attention.

She showed keenest pleasure in the splendid work the orchestra did, and there was such fine sympathy between her and Mr. Stock and every one of the men in the orchestra that the performance took on the nature of a triumph for all concerned. Of her individual work no words too high in praise can be spoken. She commands a technic which places her among the foremost of the world's violinists, and yet so subservient is this technic made to musical expression and meaning that it is wholly lost sight of. She is a virtuoso in technic and ability, but an artist and unfailing musician—a great one—in spirit. . . . It was an afternoon long to be remembered.

Another critic, O. H. Hall, congratulated Sibelius upon having Maud Powell introduce his work because "few are so gifted with such clearness of artistic vision as she." The orchestra members swelled the ovation given by the audience: "Added to this was a resounding chorus of bravos from the men of the orchestra, a spontaneous tribute to the greatness of one artist from a band of brother artists. Miss Powell turned to them and very graciously insisted upon their rising and sharing in her triumph, but they chivalrously declined the honor."[32]

The artist's presence onstage evoked a magic force as elemental as the music itself:

Maud Powell . . . now at the height of her artistic career, svelt of figure, swaying to the rhythmic moods of this strange and at times almost savage music, swept her bow fearlessly and faultlessly through its amazing difficulties and gave it a strength and sincerity of interpretation that was as agreeable as it was astonishing. Her very enthusiasm in the interpretation of the work impresses that repeated hearings might reveal more charm; for she has evidently studied the intent of the composer for something more than a sensational showing in the mere mastery of his dazzling difficulties.

Her virtuosity was not only apparent in her bowing, fingering and technical accomplishments, but in the beautiful singing quality

of her tone, warm and sparkling with magnetic vitality. The striking, original composition, racked by the vigor of the northland, has
feverish moods fierce with the fire of the gypsy Czardas, weird, witch-
ing and involved, and is intensely violinistic. Miss Powell was at all
times equal to the titanic task imposed, for the tournies of technic,
remarkable as they were had an artistic alpha and omega in the
soothing, savage and brilliant melodies that flow from her facile fingers, interpreting every phase of the composer's strange and varie-
gated imagery in music.

The members of the orchestra followed with wonder at her amazing performance and Director Stock led his men along with unwavering and unusual nervous force. . . .

[S]he returned and repeated the entire last movement with a
power and brilliancy that even surpassed her previous performance.[33]

A reporter for *The Musical Courier* wired back to New York: "Great
success for Maud Powell in the Sibelius concerto with the Theodore
Thomas Orchestra. Veritable ovation."[34]

When Maud brought the Sibelius concerto to Boston, she had
been absent for six years. The audience welcomed the artist warmly
as she appeared with Dr. Karl Muck and the Boston Symphony Orchestra on April 19 and 20. The concerto, strange as it sounded on first
hearing, was greeted with both critical and popular acclaim. Critics
described it as "music that has made a concerto eloquent with emotions and poignant of mood as are few concertos, old or new," and as
a "symphonic poem with a violin obligato."[35]

The critics were as keenly observant of the violinist as of the
music. In Boston, which still had the highest artistic standards, Maud
was recognized as being in a class by herself, to be measured, according to the critics, by standards which she herself had set:

She has been Maud Powell, the violinist, and a violinist who has
sought not to glorify herself, but to unfold as clearly and to express
as fully as lay within her powers the music that she was playing. She
has never cultivated amplitude, elasticity and fineness of technique
for their own sake, though she has long since attained them. Steadily
they have been to her first the foundation, and then the medium,
of expression. She has emphasized neither a dazzling brilliance nor
a large sonority of tone, though both are now within her powers.
She has chosen rather to make her tone the characteristic and the
eloquent voice of her music. Behind her playing lie the faculties of

intellect that grasp the form and the substance of music and search and adjust its design and proportions. Side by side with them stand the faculties of imagination that discover and feel its moods, emotions and individual accent; while of both intellect and imagination are the fusing and communicating faculties that weld together all these things and impart them to her hearers. She does more: she brings them to life; for the distinctive trait of Mme. Powell's mind, fancy, and artistry is their nervous vitality. It is that at bottom which has set her so often to the discovery and the trial of new concertos and smaller pieces; which has spurred her, as in this very concerto by Sibelius that she played yesterday, to the conquering of strange technical difficulties and intricacies and to the winning of obscure and evasive imaginings; and which in all things has kept her alert, eager, unsatisfied . . . .

—H. T. Parker, *Boston Evening Transcript*[36]

No mere virtuoso greedy for popular favor would choose this concerto for personal display. Madame Powell has never been in the habit of setting applause traps. I know of no violinist now before the public who is better entitled to respect and admiration. In whatever she has undertaken in the course of her long and honorable career, she has been true to herself and to art in its highest form. No merchant ever trafficked in her heart. To speak of her mechanism at this late day would be an impertinence, for her abilities have long been recognized by two continents.

The greater the task to which she devotes herself, the more quickly do her skill, her brains, her soul respond. It is enough to say that her performance of this exceedingly difficult concerto was worthy, both in mechanism and in aesthetic and emotional quality, of the high ideal which she has had steadily before her. . . . [T]he composer was glorified and the occasion made memorable.

— Philip Hale, *Sunday Herald*, Boston[37]

Maud never gave up on the Sibelius violin concerto and played it again on tour in 1911 and 1912. Her performances with the New York Philharmonic on March 14 and 17, 1911, received mixed reviews. Henry Krehbiel remained unconvinced of the concerto's value, a factor which colored his view of the performance:

Whether or not the composition really deserves as much artistic devotion as its difficulties exact is a question which seemed as difficult to answer yesterday as it did four and a half years ago. . . . Miss Powell attacks its technical difficulties with her habitual daring, and overcame them successfully but not without some sacrifice of that tonal euphony of which she has such perfect control when her mind and heart are set on something more, and better than technical brilliancy.[38]

The critic for *Musical America*'s March issue seemed more convinced of the concerto's value:

> Maud Powell brought her flashing and scintillating technic to bear upon the Sibelius concerto, and her capacity for the production of clear, well shaded, and penetrating tone. Moreover, she brought also an intelligence capable of dealing with the musical thought-images of this Strindberg of music, who grips and bites at every bar. . . . The violin part makes every imaginable kind of demand upon the artist, and Miss Powell had no difficulty in rising through a technical into an interpretative plane.
>
> The adagio is a song from the depth of the heart, and gave the violinist opportunity to display the richness of her lower tones. The dazzling success of the violinist was supported by an intimate and well balanced reading of the orchestral part by the conductor. Miss Powell was presented with roses, and had many recalls.

A year later, Maud played the Sibelius concerto with the Boston Symphony at the request of "critics and public, both."

Boston critic Philip Hale wrote: "It is granitic music, and what beauty there is in it is the beauty that may be associated with desolate moor and a threatening sky, while the rebellious sun sinks slowly behind a bank of clouds. . . . Miss Powell, as before, overcame the technical difficulties with consummate ease, and played with the conviction and the authority that have ranked her high in the list of violinists."[39] The critic for *Musical America* (March 16, 1912) called it "one of the few great violin concertos in existence," adding that Maud's performance was "masterly from every point of view" and that the violinist was "now at the zenith of her splendid powers."

Asked in 1911 to reflect on the critical treatment of the Sibelius concerto, Maud responded: "Oh, yes! I know that there are only a few who have agreed with me in my estimate. But there are also a few more people who, if they have not given in to it with all their hearts, are following close behind me, as it were. But, after all, they liked it very much in Chicago and in Boston. It simply isn't a thing you get fully at first hearing."[40] She had as much confidence in its future as she did in the Tchaikovsky concerto, as one reporter discovered in 1908:

> I was led to Mme. Powell's apartments by the magic tones of her violin and for a moment I listened through the open transom to the wonder interpretation of some colossal composition. "Won't you tell me what you were playing?" I asked her after the greetings had been exchanged.
>
> "Did you like it? It is one of the things I love most to do, Tschaikovsky's Concerto. I introduced it into this country in 1888, playing it in New York. The public scarcely accepted it at first, but now it is in every violinist's repertoire. Sibelius' Concerto, another composition which I introduced two years ago in New York, isn't yet accepted by as many people as I have fingers," and she indicated by spreading each of her hands. . . . [41]

As she spoke of the Sibelius concerto, the reporter noted that "her face lighted up as only the face of an artist can when discussing the thing most loved."

After her death, a critic for the Brooklyn *Eagle* reflected:

> Years ago, when Sibelius was an unknown name in this country, Miss Powell, as she was then, played his exacting violin concerto at a special concert in Carnegie Hall. So far as anybody could guess from the state of musical taste at the time the work would be useless for her concert repertory and it seemed unlikely that she would have occasion to repeat it. Yet for that single performance she memorized that long composition in an unfamiliar style. That was Maud Powell. She was never content to play anything until she had put the best of herself into it and until she had brought the best out of it which her strong musical intelligence and great patience could fathom.[42]

In March 1911, Maud was delving into another monumental violin concerto when a reporter for *Musical America* called at her Gramercy Park apartment:

> I found Maud Powell at the piano busily communing with a score of the new Elgar violin concerto, intent upon determining whether the composition or her judgment were at fault. Beside her stood a great heap of music surmounted by Brahms's D Minor Violin Sonata and close at hand was a miniature full orchestral score of the aforesaid Elgar.
>
> Affectionately wrapped up in silken covers lay the violin. . . .

Miss Powell admits that she does not know just what to say about the Elgar. "I know that it is cleverly made, beautifully scored and all that sort of thing. But, somehow or other, I can't rid myself of the idea that it is 'made' music. Take this sequence which you find near the beginning as an example. It is the sort of thing any small writer or any beginner would write.

"Then the themes don't seem to please me—and, after all, they are the things that count. Now, it may be that my judgment is wrong, but I felt very different about the Sibelius concerto when I came across that for the first time. . . .

"[In spite of the critical treatment of the Sibelius] I wish the Elgar were something like it. I can't bring myself to believe that it is, in spite of the disposition abroad at present to look upon the latter as in the same category with the Brahms."[43]

The English composer's concerto had been written in 1909–10, and the American violinist was contemplating giving its first performance in the United States. But it was not to be. Maud related:

I had a bitter experience in regard to the Elgar concerto; Carl Stoeckel wanted the work performed for the first time in America at the Norfolk Festival, and I wrote Sir Edward Elgar offering him $500 for the first performing rights. I also invited him to be the guest of honor at the festival. The letter was answered by his publishers, who demanded $1000 for the performing rights to the work. I told Mr. Stoeckel, who, of course, would have been willing to pay this amount if the work had been worth it, by no means to consider it. . . . It is an empty, pompous work . . . .[44]

Elgar had written the concerto for Fritz Kreisler, who premiered it to mixed critical comment on November 10, 1910, with the composer conducting the Philharmonic Society of London. Albert Spalding eventually introduced it to America, where it received the most severe criticism in its early days.[45] Yehudi Menuhin, one of the first American artists to play the work successfully, has commented that it is "English to the point of being almost unexportable," which may explain the difficulty Maud and the American critics had with the work.[46] The melodic line of the concerto resembles the intonation and rhythmic patterns of British speech and in that sense it appears unviolinistic despite the composer's own mastery of the instrument. Nevertheless, it is difficult to understand why Maud did not respond soulfully to the tender intimacy and nostalgic lyricism of the work as well as to the intense, almost elegiac passion underlying its formal restraint.

For once, a new concerto's inherent beauty eluded the usually prescient violinist. But where one concerto fell, another arose to take its place in her ever-expanding repertoire. Max Bruch had just completed his *Concertstück*, written for and dedicated to Willy Hess, who had succeeded Carl Halir at the Berlin Hochschule. The composer sent the manuscript to Maud in May 1911, requesting that she give the world premiere.

The master wrote her a lovely letter in English, saying that he was most happy that an artist of such distinction should introduce his work. He wrote that he remembered distinctly the deep impression she had created in Berlin some years before in the very early days of what had become one of the greatest careers of the musical world, and he recalled the letter that he had given her to Dr. Hans Richter. He added that he was getting to be such an old man that he could not think of coming to America, something he would gladly do to hear her play this work, "but, I know that some day you will come again to Germany and play once more for your old master."[47]

Maud performed the Bruch *Concertstück* in F-sharp Minor on June 8, 1911, at the Norfolk Music Festival with Dr. Arthur Mees conducting. Although the concerto was well received, the violinist recognized its shortcomings: "The Bruch concerto is only moderately satisfactory. . . . [T]he unfortunate lack of a third movement has proved a drawback. Then the slow movement is lacking in contrast. I think the slow movement Bruch wrote in England, and the first movement when he was 20 years old. He simply put them together. Their publication is recent, but not their inspiration, I am sure."[48] Maud had written Bruch, asking him to compose a third movement for the concert piece, but he refused.

On June 16, 1911, just eight days after its world premiere performance, Maud recorded part of Bruch's *Concertstück*. Shocked, Bruch reportedly wrote to a friend, " . . . and she appears to have played the Adagio, shortened by half, into a machine (!!) I really gave her a piece of my mind about this."[49] The recording was never released.

Maud introduced the Bruch *Concertstück* to New York in recital on October 31, 1911. However, her rendition of the Mozart *Rondo* in G Major (from the Haffner *Serenade*) overshadowed the Bruch as she "imparted to the audience a sense of the incomparable grace of Mozart."[50] One critic ventured, "Not Zimbalist tonight, nor Kubelik and our own Spalding, lately heard (playing the Rondo), with their priceless foreign 'Strads,' can play the real Mozart like that."[51] W. J. Henderson reported in the *New York Sun* for November first:

> There was a startling change in the musical atmosphere. At once it seemed as if Papageno himself had sprung upon the stage and filled the auditorium with the sunlight of good humor. . . . Miss Powell's performance was one to cherish in the memory. Such exquisite phrasing, such dainty accentuation, such captivating humor and such flawless clearness and incisiveness of enunciation combined to make her presentation of the charming little work the gem of the recital.

The last full-scale concerto which Maud introduced to the world was the Coleridge-Taylor Violin Concerto in G Minor. It originated at the 1910 Norfolk Music Festival, where the English composer conducted his own works and Maud luxuriated among the listeners. He dedicated his concerto to the American violinist, who performed it at the Norfolk Festival on June 4, 1912.[52] Maud described it as "pretty, melodious music — like a bouquet of flowers," but she also recognized its limitations. While Coleridge-Taylor's gift for melody was brilliant, he seemed to lack the power to develop and sustain his themes through a lengthy work like the concerto.

The "First American of the Bow" won recognition for her versatile musicianship and artistic vision as she continually brought new music before the public. In tribute, New York critic Emilie Frances Bauer wrote that "Maud Powell is more than an artist, she is a great intellectual power in the musical world; she is a musician in whom honesty and reverence give her playing a nobility that is as sweeping as it is rare. No one has more authority or command over the instrument."[53]

24

Trailblazing in the West

They have yarns
Of a skyscraper so tall they had to put hinges
On the two top stories so to let the moon go by, . . .
Of the herd of cattle in California getting lost
in a giant redwood tree that had hollowed out. . . .

— Carl Sandburg

THE 1906–07 CONCERT SEASON HAD BEEN UNUSUALLY FULL for Maud. In August, Ysaÿe had canceled all his tour dates in the United States. Maud graciously agreed to fill as many of these as she could. She then postponed her own plans to return to Europe to May 1907, when she was to appear with the great orchestras of London. Asked in January to accept also the American engagements of the ailing Belgian violinist César Thomson, the American artist was forced to abandon all plans to return to Europe that year. With her discovery of the Far West as fertile ground for pioneer work in music, the American violinist's art was never again to be heard in Europe. Maud forsook Europe's age-old cultural comforts for the challenge of the raw, uncultivated American continent.

Perhaps then, it was fitting that Maud learned of Joseph Joachim's death on August 15, 1907, and of Dancla's that same year, rending the last link between Maud and her oldest European masters. Only the year before, Joachim had sent his favored pupil a photograph portrait commemorating his seventy-fifth birthday. It was inscribed: "with kindest greetings to Maud Powell, Joseph Joachim, Berlin, July 5th 1906."[1]

[250]

Fittingly, Maud opened the season which inaugurated her work in the Far West with acts of commemoration and of courage and compassion. Arriving in Worcester, Massachusetts, for the Golden Jubilee of the Worcester Music Festival, the violinist was accosted by a young immigrant boy as she alighted from the train. All tagged and labeled as was customary, he extended a piece of paper bearing in Russian the name and address of a relative. Upon translation, Maud asked the waiting cab driver where the street was. Informing her that it was in the slums, he warned that it would be dangerous for her to go there. Since Maud was a Powell, the news only aroused her spirit of adventure. She swept her charge into the cab and off they went, finding a colony of Russian immigrants who were expecting the lad. Maud related, "It was exciting, for I expected all sorts of things to happen, but was determined to see the thing through."[2]

The next day, perhaps remembering her debut with Joachim, the American violinist gave a memorable performance of the Bruch Concerto in G Minor: "Miss Powell could no doubt play the Bruch concerto backward, if she were not, by far, too musical to do such an inartistic thing. It is to her credit, therefore, that she made the dear old familiar number sound almost as though each measure were a separate and new source of musical joy to her soul. . . . The adagio of the concerto was fiddle-song of the most moving kind, and the scintillant finale fairly leaped and glinted under the player's confident fingers and bow."[3] Although another critic praised the concerto performance as "artistic in the highest conception of the term," he wrote that "it hardly approached in nobility the Bach which she played so magnificently unaccompanied after insistent and untiring recalls."[4]

The *Musical Courier* critic noted, "Miss Powell is in rare form nowadays, and the audiences who are to meet her again this winter will marvel at the added daring and insouciance of her technic and the deeper beauty which of late has crept into her tone."[5] The high-spirited violinist's playing was invigorated by the prospect of new worlds to conquer. From October through December of 1907, Maud's tour would take her through the Midwest, the Far West and the Southwest. While it is important to note that Maud had been at least as far west as Colorado in previous years (perhaps as early as 1887), the Far West only recently had been opened to *organized* touring.

For the past ten years, the Los Angeles impresario L. E. Behymer had been developing "The Great Philharmonic Course" through which he sponsored tours of individual artists and even the Chicago Symphony Orchestra throughout southern and northern California, Arizona, and New Mexico. (Oakland, San Francisco, and Berkeley were under the management of another.) Behymer was also the manager of the Los Angeles Symphony Orchestra, then in its eleventh season. For the Philharmonic Course, Behymer engaged Maud Powell, Johanna Gadski, Herbert Witherspoon, Ignace Paderewski, Josef Hofmann, Teresa Carreño, Lillian Blauvelt, Fritz Kreisler, Louise Homer, Harold Bauer, and Jan Kubelik, among whom the large and small cities could select under a lyceum-type arrangement. Beginning with the 1907 season, the enterprising Behymer organized a separate entity called "The Great Western Lyceum and Musical Bureau" to manage concert appearances from just west of Colorado's eastern border to the Pacific Coast. Extensive musical courses were booked by this organization for Denver, Salt Lake City, Ogden, Colorado Springs, Butte, Helena, Boise, Spokane, Portland, Seattle, Victoria and Vancouver, B.C., Tacoma, Eugene City, Sacramento, San Jose, and many other smaller cities throughout the West. Maud Powell was booked solid by Sunny on these two circuits and for additional engagements in other places along the route.

For the niece of John Wesley Powell, it was the adventure of a lifetime, and for the granddaughter of Joseph Powell, it was the opportunity for pioneer missionary work which would claim the rest of her life. Proceeding by train, the western tour opened in Helena, Montana, on October 15, worked its way west to Seattle and Portland, down the Pacific Coast to San Diego, and then skipped to Denver after four nights and three days on the train.

No one ever derived more pleasure from a tour of the western states than did Maud Powell. She was in her element, bringing a new standard for violin playing and music to audiences varying widely in sophistication. Everywhere she went, she reportedly created a deeper impression than any of her predecessors. Playing in churches, theaters, opera houses, and even a skating rink, Maud stirred the musical interest of every town in which she appeared. For the first time, these audiences were hearing an American violinist of the first rank, and both Portland and Los Angeles critics noted that few artists had made a more favorable impression on the musical life of their respective cities.

Mishaps were a normal part of the tour's excitement. In Portland, inexperienced draymen were too intimidated by the size of the Weber concert grand to move it to the Heilig Theatre. Not realizing the importance of the particular instrument for the concert, a new assistant shipping clerk resourcefully had the name of the Chickering, then upon the Heilig stage, covered with lampblack. That evening, as Maud's accompanist played, the lampblack came off in liberal quantities, much to the merriment of all concerned. For once, Maud made an exception to her usual practice of writing a letter of commendation and acknowledgment to the house management.

Maud's spirit was invigorated rather than exhausted by the arduous tour. When she returned to New York, after playing her way east, she was "radiating with inspiring enthusiasm" as she related what she had learned from the people of the West:

"I have come back a better American than I was before," began Miss Powell, who seemed to have brought with her the breeziness of the West. "In the first place, the pioneer instinct in me is very strong, as my father was a pioneer in educational work, and my grandfather conspicuous in the opening up of the West.

Then the spontaneous enthusiasm of the people out there is delightful. They absolutely refuse to accept Eastern verdicts without testing them for themselves. In their attitude towards music, as in everything else, they have the courage to be themselves. They are fresh, wholesome, receptive, responsive; they insist upon thinking independently at all costs, and they want only the best. Unfortunately they have been deceived a good deal by managers who have taken out artists of the second and third rank—or perhaps a little *passé*—and advertised them as stars of the first magnitude, charging high fees for them. And these people arrange their programs on the theory that they must cater to a taste that is not capable of appreciating what the Easterners demand. It is a great mistake, and the Westerners have been disappointed so often in the extravagant claims made by managers that they are now strictly on their guard when new attractions are announced.

"Here is an indication of their progressiveness musically. In Colorado Springs, which is not a very large place, they have a very energetic Women's Musical Club, and when I was there I visited the ex-president. She casually mentioned that she was studying some of Vincent d'Indy's songs, and when the present president called I found she was working up songs by Debussy and Reger for one of their meetings.

"Throughout my trip I played the same programs I do in the East. For instance, I would open with Grieg's Sonata in G major, op. 13, for violin and piano, follow it with Vieuxtemps's Concerto, op. 31, and later play a group of smaller numbers; or beginning with the Schütt Suite, I would play the Arensky Concerto, and so on. The only numbers I had that could be considered as in any way of a 'popular' nature were three arrangements of *St. Patrick's Day*, *The Arkansas Traveler* and *Dixie*, which I used as encores. But they are such excellent arrangements — the *Dixie* being quite worthy of Paganini — that I should not hesitate to play them anywhere. But I must say the regular program numbers were just as keenly appreciated as they were. One number I invariably had to repeat was Schumann's *Traumerei*.

"That reminds me of a pretty incident in Seattle. There being no large concert hall there, our concert was given in the Dreamland Rink — a huge place — and it was packed [1,700 people]. Mattresses were placed against the windows to keep out the noise of the trolleys, and the evening was one of the most successful of the whole tour. The people seemed to be so absorbed in the music it was inspiring to play for them. When I played the *Traumerei* with muted strings there was not a sound in the place except the ticking of the clock, and the manager climbed up on a chair and stopped it. Wasn't it thoughtful? After the concert, by the way, they went to work there and organized a symphony orchestra to have for the succeeding concerts in the same course — Paderewski, Gadski, Kubelik and Witherspoon are some of the artists engaged. So if I gave them the impetus to form an orchestra, that was a little bit of pioneer work, wasn't it?

"Another point that interested me mightily was Ogden, Utah. It is quite a large city and though they have had lecture courses, I was the first musical attraction they had ever had. The concert was held in the Weber Stake Academy, which had no piano. They didn't realize till the last minute that I would need one, and after skirmishing around the town they found there was not a grand in the place. However, they succeeded in borrowing an upright. Then when I explained I would require a music stand, too, they bought one, and after the concert, which was a fine success, they came to me and said, 'Miss Powell, we now have a music stand to begin with, and when you come again we will have a grand piano for you.'

"One thing that was particularly pleasing was the appreciative attitude of the managers and committees. When they took pains to thank me personally for the pleasure they had derived from my concert, it added a friendly touch even to financial relations. One of the most graceful compliments that I received was a remark the managers in one of the larger towns made — 'Miss Powell, this is not the best concert we have ever had; it is the first.'

"In Salt Lake City, by the way, we attended the funeral service of a Mormon bishop. The music was simple but beautiful."[6]

Maud's tour of the West was followed by a tour of the extreme Southwest, with appearances in Dallas and San Antonio, Texas, in mid-December. While in Arkansas on December 22, 1907, Maud wrote enthusiastically to American violinist Arthur Hartmann, who had toured parts of the West the year before, "Aren't those Westerners splendid people to play for! I delight in them." Maud returned to New York in January to greet May Mukle on her arrival from England.

Maud and Sunny were the first to entice the young English cellist to the United States. Sunny had Mukle booked solid from January through May of 1908, with ten recitals in New York City — a record for a foreign artist. The tour included symphony and recital appearances jointly with Maud and separately in the principal cities of the East and Midwest, including Montreal, Quebec, Chicago, Buffalo, Pittsburgh, Detroit, and Oberlin, Ohio.

Mukle was knocked down by some toughs pushing through streets crowded with New Year's Eve celebrants, but although one of her eyes had been badly injured, the cellist appeared, patched Wotan-like, for her New York debut in Mendelssohn Hall on January 5. She clearly matched her violinist counterpart in sheer courage and determination, as well as in the sterling character of her art. The English cellist played Valentini's Sonata in E Major, Tchaikovsky's *Variations on a Rococo Theme*, Op. 33, and brought forward Howard Brockway's *Suite* for cello and piano with the American composer at the piano.

When she began to play, Mukle took her audience by surprise. The immense poise of the big, black-eyed artist veiled her great emotional depth. One critic reported: "[S]he proved to be not only a player of brilliant virtuosity but, as well, an interpreter of convincing emotional depth, unusual versatility of style and expression and a masterly sense of musical values. Of singular beauty at all times was

the tone she produced, whether in its sonorous breadth and reso-
nance, or in its subtle shading and variety of coloring."[7]

Maud Powell stood sponsor for Mukle that night, playing Bach's
Sonata in E Major for violin and harpsichord with George Falkenstein
in a manner "thoroughly consistent with this artist's unimpeachable
musicianship. It was a broad, authoritative reading, lucid in design,
of exquisite finish of phrasing and richness of tone and full-blooded
vitality."

At the conclusion of the concert, Mukle joined Powell and
Falkenstein in Arensky's Trio in D Minor. Thereafter, the critics heralded Mukle as the "Maud Powell of the Cello."

Maud and May Mukle created a precedent that season with a
performance of the Brahms Double Concerto in A Minor, Op. 102,
for violin and cello with orchestra. Premiered in 1887 in Cologne by
Joseph Joachim—for whom it was written—and cellist Robert
Hausmann, with Brahms conducting, the concerto had never before
been played in America with two women soloists.

Maud soon drew Mukle into her musical pioneer work. With
May's pianist sister Anne Mukle Ford joining them from England,
they formed the Maud Powell Trio and toured the American continent during the 1908–09 season.

The three musicians, accompanied by Sunny for most of the
tour, were booked for individual appearances with orchestra and for
recitals sponsored by music clubs in addition to their Trio work. The
tour of the West was tightly scheduled from November 13 through
December 16, averaging one concert every two days, in sixteen cities
(in only five of which Maud had played previously)—Butte and Missoula, Montana; Victoria and Vancouver, B.C.; Seattle and Tacoma,
Washington; Forest Grove, Portland, Hood River, and Salem, Oregon; Santa Barbara, Los Angeles, and San Diego, California; Phoenix, Arizona; Denver and Colorado Springs, Colorado.

Although Maud and her associates were facing many audiences
which had rarely, or never, heard chamber music played on such an
exalted level, the violinist refused to lower the artistic standards to
which she adhered in New York and Boston. Consequently, in addition to the Chaminade Trio in A Minor and Schuett's new *Walzer-
marchen*, the ensemble's repertoire included Beethoven's *Archduke*
Trio in B-flat, Op. 97, and Arensky's Trio in D Minor, Op. 32. For
her solo repertoire, Maud played Wieniawski's Concerto in D Minor,

Op. 22, Vieuxtemps' Concerto in D Minor, and Locatelli's Sonata in D Major as well as numerous short pieces, while May Mukle offered Boccherini's Sonata in A Major, Lindner's *Tarantella*, and several shorter pieces. Anne Ford contented herself with the accompaniments to the solo numbers as well as her part in the trios. When she did play solo, she rendered pieces by Chopin and Grieg. Despite the close spacing of the concerts, throughout the tour no two programs were ever exactly alike.

Their New York debut was praised for the Trio's "perfect ensemble," their "smoothness of execution," and the "delightful spirit imparted to the music."[8] Krehbiel noted with approval the "finished style and fine, sonorous tone" of Powell and Mukle.[9] Henry Finck wrote that pianist Anne Ford was "perhaps the most remarkable score reader in America" and a "good ensemble player."[10]

It was clear that Maud had put together a superior ensemble with which to tour—a practice not often followed by concert artists. Westerners were quick to appreciate Maud's determination to bring them the best in chamber music. They recognized that she did not fear to associate with other artists of the first rank. That May Mukle should share solo honors with the older, better-known violinist revealed Maud's deep-seated generosity and belief in her own high artistic purpose.

Western audiences had already learned to trust Maud's artistic integrity. They could expect the calibre of her program and her musical associates to match her own performances. In Seattle, one critic reflected, "It is one of the gloriously enjoyable traits of the violinist that she maintains consistently her high altitude of artistic endeavor in every phrase, even throughout such a long and trying program. . . ."[11]

In places like Seattle, Portland, and Los Angeles, where she had appeared only once before, the mere announcement of the violinist's appearance with her Trio was enough to fill the house. The news spread more by word of mouth than by advertisement—an artist's sweetest compliment. In Los Angeles, critics reported that for a second time, with an audience "large for a Los Angeles musical event," Maud "carried all before her." In Portland, Wallace Graham wrote: "I have never heard any other great artist hold the attention of a Portland audience to such a marked degree, with the exception of the great artist [contralto Ernestine] Schumann-Heink. For ease and gracefulness and musicianly interpretation, Maud Powell's playing cannot be surpassed. I have heard the three great European lady violinists, Lady Hallé, Wietrowitz and Soldat-Roeger, and, with the possible exception of Lady Hallé, when she was at her best, I have never heard a lady violinist the equal of our own American Maud Powell."[12]

The fact that she was an American meant a great deal. As a Portland critic revealed: "It is particularly pleasant to know that this celebrated violinist is a native American — one of us. She shows it not only in her winning stage personality but in her good sense in selecting such a representative programme. . . . It is also noteworthy that hers is not an inherited art — not bought with somebody else's money, but bequeathed to her as a talent to be answered for, and tempered by hard, faithful study."[13]

At a time when travel was difficult, accommodations poor, and performing conditions often primitive, Maud's effort to reach people all over the United States intensified their esteem. She and her Trio were given receptions in nearly every town, effusive demonstrations of appreciation and goodwill which exacted from the artist a handshake and a hundred words of advice or encouragement on musical matters. Maud avoided any pre-concert receptions but graciously enjoyed post-concert functions. "I wait for that until after the recital. . . . Then I am pleased to see people. In fact I need to; it affords a sort of outlet to the extra supply of magnetism and vitality left over from the recital proper."[14]

In Los Angeles, Maud received a festive welcome from the Celtic Club, of which she had been made the only woman member the year before. Two hundred members entertained her at a banquet where many complimentary speeches were given and then answered by Maud's rendition of *The Last Rose of Summer*.

Midwesterners were equally appreciative of the effort Maud made to reach them. On their return east, the Trio played in several small towns in Iowa and Illinois. They had been traveling with their own concert grand piano as Maud had learned from the previous tour that such an instrument was not always available. In Arlington, Iowa, no one had ever seen a grand piano before. The "Grand Opera House" was nothing more than a small corrugated iron shed, dimly lit by oil lamps — a virtual "tank," according to Sunny. The manager of the "Opry House" who was also the local postman, "did the thing up brown." He met the members of the company in a borrowed auto-mobile. As Sunny related: "He had a wonderful manner and we were friends at once. There was not enough room in the car, so he sat on my lap and gave directions to the chauffeur to stop at the 'Waldorf Astoria.' "[15]

The Trio was then piloted through the muddy streets to the con-cert hall, where the whole town waited expectantly. But the piano had to be moved first and it was not a simple task. Sunny related: "We carry a full size Steinway concert piano and as this particular engagement was one of the last of the season we had it boxed. When it was taken to the Opera House a crowd watched and followed the wagon. The expressman and carpenter were wonderful. They said 'there wasn't goin' to be no bills"—they considered it an honor for the lady to come into the town and play." In a tribute to Sunny's wonderful disposition, the local manager afterward wrote to a New York trade paper advising managers who wanted a good "attraction," to engage Maud Powell, if "only for the pleasure of meeting her magnificent husband!"[16]

In spite of its lack of sophistication, the audience reportedly gave respectful and appreciative attention to a concert of strictly first-class chamber music. It was just such experiences what warmed Maud to her self-expressed aim to "cultivate a keener, higher, more wide-spread appreciation of good music."

Returning to New York in advance of the Trio, Sunny described to music reporters the nature of their audiences:

> The musical situation in the Far West is really not understood in the East. . . . The remarkable appreciation of the highest form of the severest classical musical literature is astounding, and the manner in which audiences turned out to hear Mme. Powell and her associates, the tremendous enthusiasm displayed wherever the organization appeared, and the interest shown in the selection of the works pre-sented, told a story of remarkable musical development in that part of the country that would surprise Eastern musical authorities.[17]

The three musicians arrived back in New York only a day or two before Christmas. Maud was to play before the National Music Teachers' Association in Washington, D.C., on December 30, and within a matter of days, they were on the road again for a tour of New York, Illinois, Ohio, Michigan, Kentucky, Tennessee, Minnesota, North

Dakota, Manitoba, Wisconsin, Nebraska, and New Jersey—all within a two-month period. The Trio's schedule was so full that they were engaged to play in Chicago on the afternoon of January 4 and then in Milwaukee that evening. In addition to Minneapolis and St. Paul, the tour schedule included such out-of-the-way places as Winnipeg, Manitoba; and Fargo, Grand Forks, and Bismarck, North Dakota.

Perhaps no reviews better expressed the Maud Powell Trio's triumph during the entire 1908–09 season than the surprisingly sophisticated notices from Winnipeg, which ten years earlier had hosted a trio composed of Eugène Ysaÿe, Jean Gerardy (cello), and Alme Lachaume (piano). Some excerpts follow:

> —The smoothness of their execution, the brilliancy and illuminative quality of their interpretation, the fine spirit with which they played, not alone from the standpoint of technical excellence, but from their charming demeanor toward their admirers—all was delightful. There was feeling, heart, intellect and graciousness in their execution of an exacting programme. . . .

> —The ensemble playing was well-nigh perfect. . . . There was continuity of style throughout. Each part duly sustained the other, keeping the thread of the subject forever unbroken. The Maud Powell Trio reminded me very much of the Joachim quartette which appeared for several seasons at the Queen's hall, London, England, where the above features of perfect ensemble playing were conspicuous throughout and the four played as one.

> — the absolute ensemble, the purity of tone, and the brilliancy of the execution. . . . What strikes me is the ensemble. Each instrument keeps its own place, and the combined effort of the three produces a harmony which comes pretty near to perfection.

The critics were also delighted with Maud's individual performances:

> —[Maud Powell's] playing was a model of correct phrasing, clearness of tone, technique of very highest standard, combined with true intonation. . . . [T]he apparent ease with which she surmounted the greatest technical difficulties, were amongst the many indications she displayed of the true virtuoso.

> — She is a wonderfully versatile artist. . . . [S]he gave evidence that she is equally at home in pieces which call for breadth of treatment and dignity of style, as well as the more brilliant and bravura order of violin playing. This last was exemplified to a great degree in her

performances of the Devil's Trill, Valse Caprice, and Bazzini's Witches' Dance, where she simply toyed with whole passages of left hand pizzicato. . . . These three compositions I have heard performed by Joachim, Lady Hallé, Carrodus, and others, but Maud Powell's rendering, in my opinion, compared easily with the very best. It was a performance worthy of her great teacher, Joachim.

— Before . . . [Maud Powell's] playing the critic's voice is dumb; one can only humbly bow before so heaven-sent a gift and be grateful for being allowed to share in its glory and bask in its beauty.

— What impressed me most . . . was the musician's oneness with her instrument. In her hands it became a living thing "filled with spirit, fire and dew." . . . It was a vivid, magnetic, inspiring performance.

One reviewer declared: "Miss Mukle is a cellist worthy to appear upon the same programme with Miss Powell, which is saying multum in parvo."[18]

In the audience that night was the American violinist Louis Persinger (1887–1966), who had come to Winnipeg to teach for a few months. A pupil of Ysaÿe, Persinger had been the concertmaster of the opera orchestra in Brussels and then of the Bluthner Orchestra in Berlin. (He would later become the concertmaster and assistant conductor of the San Francisco Orchestra and the teacher of Menuhin and Ricci.) Persinger wrote: "It is a very great pleasure for me to add my name to the many, many others who have been entranced by the golden tones of Mme. Powell's violin. Artists endowed with such gifts as she showed . . . are certainly few and far between. . . . Mme. Powell has that all-compelling temperament and virtuosity, and above all, a most beautiful, rich tone which made the slow movements particularly beautiful to me; wherever there was a phrase to be 'sung,' Mme. Powell's violin simply rang with melody."

For the remainder of the season, March and April, the Trio grew into the Maud Powell Quartet, taking on Louis Green, second violin, and Jacob Altschuler, violist. The quartet was booked in a dozen cities east of Cincinnati, giving an opening concert in the New German Theater in New York on Sunday, March seventh. Additional players joined the quartet in a performance of Beethoven's septet.

On April 28, 1909, May Mukle and Anne Ford sailed for England. Of Mukle it was said that there probably never had been an artist who gained a larger circle of admirers in two seasons. The Maud Powell Trio had been responsible for some of the best chamber music heard on tour during the 1908–09 season. The excellent reviews and audience response certainly gave credence to one critic's claim that there had been "no such trio since the days (1901–02) of the Kreisler-Gerardy-Hofmann combination."

Sadly for the American public, Maud never again toured at the head of a chamber music ensemble; her solo engagements mounted steadily up to the last year of her life.

To the astonishment of her friends in the East, Maud headed West for a third consecutive season. From January to April 1910, the intrepid violinist crisscrossed the continent in a fourteen-week tour, playing in all the larger towns in North Dakota, Montana, Idaho, Washington, British Columbia, Oregon, and California, and in cities throughout the Midwest. Skeptical East Coast observers failed to see the value of Maud's missionary labors in the West. They felt that her talents were being wasted there. After all, she could have all the engagements she might ever desire in the East. They did not understand the allure of these pioneering adventures, but the Westerners who heard her understood what this master of the bow who called herself a "westerner" was doing for them and came to revere her for it.

In Anaconda, Montana, her appearance was hailed as "the greatest musical treat in the history of the city," while in Spokane, it was "one of the notable musical events of the year." In Walla Walla her performance "far surpassed Leonora Jackson," the only other violinist of note who had performed there, while in Bellingham, it was a "great honor" to hear the "greatest woman violinist in the world" in their own city.

Maud's obvious love for her countrymen and her appreciation and respect for their varied occupations, as well as their capacity to appreciate music, won her theirs in return. When Maud and Sunny visited the reduction works associated with the great Anaconda copper mine, the violinist remarked, "It's something to keep anybody's head down to the regular hat size to see what men are doing in an institution like this." This respect both induced trust from her audiences and compelled her to offer them nothing but the best. To the people of Anaconda, she brought the Mendelssohn concerto and the Franck sonata, while to others in Great Falls, Montana, and Tacoma,

Washington, she brought such music as the Grieg Sonata in G Minor and the Tchaikovsky concerto. One Anaconda resident proudly confided, "I've been hoping for years to hear Maud Powell on the violin, and now I've my chance at last, and right at home."

Sunny tried to explain the artist's approach to an incredulous New York reporter for *Musical America*:

> Miss Powell's programs are the same quality for these audiences as for the city ones. . . .
>
> The program begins with something heavy—a movement of the Tschaikowsky concerto, for instance—and ends with some fireworks of the Wieniawski type. Owing to the fact that many persons in these remote localities own talking machines, they have become familiar with much good music and we often have requests for such and such a classic that these people have learned to love through the medium of the phonograph. These are the people who are willing to pay almost anything to hear an artist like Miss Powell, and in such cases we can ask prices that would be considered prohibitive in this very city, in Boston, in Philadelphia, in San Francisco or anywhere else. In San Francisco, you know, you cannot make a cent if there is any other attraction, theatrical or musical, occupying attention at the same time. It is distinctly a "one audience" town.[19]

In proselytizing for America's musical growth, Maud and Sunny were quite willing to jar East Coast critics, reporters, musicians, and music lovers out of their smug contempt for the less refined civilization of the rest of the country. On this western tour, Sunny experimented with ticket prices to prove that people in the West were willing to pay to hear good music, perhaps even more than New Yorkers. Not only would the large receipts make more money available to the local sponsor for future concerts, but they might also encourage other top-quality artists to go to these out-of-the-way places. Thus began the experiment of charging three dollars a seat in western towns of one or two thousand. The reporter to whom Sunny related this experiment asserted that a "beggarly array of empty seats" would greet *any* artist who dared do such a thing in New York.

After astonishing the reporter with news of the large audiences Maud drew in spite of such rates in regions almost unexplored by musicians, and of her "phenomenally successful" tour in general, Sunny shrewdly drove home the message:

It is a mistake and an absurd one . . . that musicians should have to confine themselves to the beaten track, visiting only the large cities and ignoring those which lie between. These are the very places in which people are hungry for music—good music, I mean—and they are willing to do anything, to pay any price to hear it. Of course, it must not be thought that they will one and all welcome you with open arms and crowded houses; as yet the proportion is about equal in that respect. But you must see for yourself and you can easily tell after one visit whether it will be worth your while to stop at that place again on your next trip. It cannot be denied that the arrangements for dramatic and musical functions in these wayside towns are exceedingly crude as yet.

We visited one place in Montana where there was a really beautiful little new theater. The manager paid little attention to its appearance, however, and the place was hopelessly dirty. There were plenty of stage hands—all of whom had to be remembered by the visiting artists but there was not a single man of them willing to handle a broom. Miss Powell actually ruined one of her gowns in walking across the stage. The crowd that filled the place was a pretty wild looking one and it did not seem as though it were of the kind to absorb any amount of aesthetic enjoyment.

There was a cowboy, who took a seat as near the door as possible so that he could get out without too much noise. Well, not only did he stay till the very end, but all the rest of that curious audience let it be known in a very emphatic way that they had enjoyed themselves more than they had in a good, long time . . . .

Some of the musical clubs out West are doing much good for the propagation of the love for music, but there are also many others which are musical only in name and which are as good as useless as far as art is concerned. Still the general outlook is favorable and the possibilities for musicians in these little and apparently insignificant cities are more than they seem at first glance.

The experiment included lowering prices as well. In Seattle and Olympia, the most expensive seats were $1.50. In all cases, tickets were offered over a range of prices, for example, 50 cents to $1.50.

While in the domain of John Wesley Powell, Maud visited the Grand Canyon and paid homage to her famous uncle by descending the gorge's depths on a mule. Enjoying the adventure "to the utmost," she insisted that the contemplation of the marvelous sights and peculiar beauty of the region always inspired her with greater artistic impulses than she had ever known.

One reason Maud was one of the best-loved artists in America was that she never thought of herself as being any different from anyone else — and was horrified when anyone else did. She once reflected:

> The American public loves to think that the artist is a human being, although some people do not think so. I had one woman say to me: "Isn't it funny, you send your laundry out just like the rest of us!" "You do take toast and coffee for breakfast, don't you?" How absurd such remarks are! Why should one's talent make him different from the rest of the people? It is the artist's duty to reach his audience. The real difference may be shown in his work, but not in his ways. It is dreadful to go through life without being understood.[20]

When Maud arrived in Yakima, Washington, she discovered to her delight that David Warfield was playing in *The Music Master* at the Yakima Theater that night. Arriving late, she naturally found the house sold out. Undaunted, she cheerfully climbed the long outside stairway to the gallery and jostled for her place among the "sheep herders, mill hands and government ditch laborers" to witness the great actor at work. When a local reporter finally cornered her for an interview, he observed:

> [T]he thought was impressed home more clearly than ever that the greater people are in reputation and fame the more simple, natural and unassuming they are. The culture, travel, and association they have had broadened them so that they have love in their hearts for everyone and a great kindliness towards all humanity. The great ones do not need to hold aloof in order to create impressions by their reserve; they have their gifts in hand, and no matter what some think, all have to recognize at some time or other their talent and supremacy.[21]

At the start of her Yakima Theater recital, the great violinist revealed more than her artistic supremacy; circumstances provoked her to an unusual revelation of her human qualities as well. Maud was "vexed" that the programs were late and reportedly said so in a short speech in which she announced her first selection, the Vieuxtemps Concerto in D Minor. The *Morning Herald* critic observed with amusement that "her vexation rather marred the first movement, but in the second temper had given place to temperament and the finale was magnificent."[22]

Maud's arrival in Los Angeles for her concert on March 22, 1910, was heralded with much enthusiasm and anticipation: "[I]n Powell we have a sure, calm joy, for we know her already as the very finest woman player who has ever appeared here. Her last recitals here created as much of a furore as may be fomented in our quiet and dignified audiences. She compelled at once by her delightful personality, her great warm tone and her exquisite artistry—a finished and temperamental matter, in which the writer believes no living violinist surpasses her."[23]

In a recital featuring the Tchaikovsky concerto and the Schubert Duo in A Major, Maud, as "charming as ever in person," was greeted by a highly enthusiastic audience which filled Simpson Auditorium. By this time, Los Angeles audiences had heard both Kreisler and Mischa Elman, the young Russian pupil of Auer who first enraptured American audiences in 1908 at the age of sixteen. The *Los Angeles Times* critic nevertheless asserted on March 23, "Maud Powell is the equal of any violin player alive, regardless of sex":

> This statement is made in full consideration of those two marvels, Fritz Kreisler and Mischa Elman. While Miss Powell has not the big tone of Kreisler, nor the marvel-voice of Elman—a gift of nature . . . she reaches the heart with more unvarying certainty than either of these two players. And that is the test of a great violinist, as it is the test of any great artist.
>
> Kreisler is the sort of man to give you one colossal interpretation—his Bach Chaconne, for instance, which he plays like a veritable Apollo—and then an uninteresting bewilderment of technical stuff, such as, alas, made up the major portion of his last programme here. Elman's tone enthralls, enthralls to such an extent that sometimes you forget his immature renditions—translations which will not compare to Miss Powell's.
>
> So there you have the three: Kreisler, who once in awhile comes through with something which absolutely no other could produce; Elman, with his sublime voice and immaturity, and Miss Powell, who, in general effectiveness, equals either of them, bringing mind as well as sentiment to bear upon her bow translations, and throwing around the compositions of all the schools the wonderful luster of combined emotion and brain.

Maud's choice of accompanist revealed in another way her respect for her western audiences. Vladimir Liachowsky was a Russian who had studied with Artur Schnabel (one of the greatest pianists of the day) and who had come to America originally with Elman. Sunny explained the importance to the violinist of his gifts:

> It is impossible to travel with any but an accompanist of the very highest rank . . . for no other could ever undertake successfully the difficult piano versions of the orchestral portions of concertos—to mention only one type of composition. Now it would have been quite impossible for us to have presented, for instance, that of Tschaikowsky, . . . which . . . [is] scored so heavily, had it not been for the exceptional ability of Mr. Liachowsky. Most persons on tours of this kind overlook the fact that the accompanist is very often quite as important as the soloist, and therefore, when they reach Chicago they make the foolish move of engaging an inefficient one. Such a proceeding foredooms the artist to failure. [24]

In San Francisco, reporters noted that the class of works presented by Maud Powell was seldom heard at public concerts because the "average solo violinist does not bring along a pianist of sufficient musicianship to make it possible." Only Ysaÿe and Lachaume had presented recitals of matching calibre. [25] In three recitals plus a concert appearance before the St. Francis Musical Art Society, given March 27, 29, 31, and April 3, Maud offered concertos by Tchaikovsky, Mendelssohn, and Vieuxtemps and sonatas by Schubert, Locatelli, Tartini, and Franck, along with a host of shorter works.

This was the first time Maud Powell had appeared in San Francisco because of her inability to match schedules with the local impresario in previous years. Kreisler, Ysaÿe, and Elman had all been there before her, a rare occurrence in an American city. Earlier that season, Kreisler had been asked by the local manager what he might expect of Maud Powell. Kreisler assured him that he might be very proud to announce Powell. [26] He need not be afraid to promise his public one of the world's greatest artists, adding "and I do not mean for a woman. Any man might be proud to play with the tone and power of Miss Powell." To his credit, Kreisler let it be known that musicians like Ysaÿe, Thomson, and Thibaud called her a "brother artist," emphasizing, "she just happens to be a woman."

It might seem strange that a foreign musician was called upon to vouch for the foremost American violinist, but women violinists of Maud Powell's rank simply did not exist. The warm-hearted Kreisler thought that the great physical endurance required was the primary reason that feminine musicians of that class were such a "terrifically sad minority." He mused: "I have heard but two women . . . whom I consider masters of the bow. One of these is Maud Powell, the other Lady Hallé. . . . There may be others, but I do not happen to have heard them or had personal evidence of their skill."[27]

Although devastated by an earthquake in 1906, the rebuilt San Francisco was highly cultured by 1910. As a subscriber to the Great Philharmonic Course, the city had heard some of the world's finest violinists and pianists, as well as the Flonzaley Quartet and the New York Symphony conducted by Walter Damrosch. These Californians never accepted an artist on someone else's recommendation, no matter how impeccable the source. It was a trait which Maud Powell respected, appreciated, and even defended, for she formed her own impressions in exactly the same original manner:

> Those who sit calmly in so artistically cosmopolitan a center as New York are scarcely qualified to form ideas concerning Western conditions. . . . There is an atmosphere of smugness here-abouts that prevents one from acquiring the proper conception of the way things progress out there. Hearing as much music as we hear in New York and hearing it under the conditions we do makes it all but impossible for one who has not seen things on the spot to understand just how matters are developing.
>
> The fact is they have their own standards, their own very particular ideals in the West and they do not necessarily coincide with those that prevail here. I feel convinced that the proper place to look for the great American composers and works of the future will be the West. It may seem curious to those who imagine that artistic appreciation and culture are confined to the East to learn that the Eastern opinion of an artist counts for very little in the estimation of those who patronize musical functions in the West. They accept or reject the artist according to their ideas of him. The newcomer must make his own way, must definitely prove his capabilities before he can hope for anything resembling a following.
>
> In San Francisco, for example, it is necessary for the newly arrived artist to give two or three concerts if he hopes to profit financially. Comparatively few will attend the first, irrespective of what his success in other quarters may have been. If he pleases at this first appearance a very much larger gathering will be at his subsequent ones. But unless the musician who has not yet proved his case has made arrangements for more than one hearing his efforts are scarcely likely

to be particularly remunerative. On the other hand, there are many local artists in those parts who are looked upon with the highest favor and of whom Easterners have heard nothing.[28]

The skepticism of the local manager in San Francisco was so great that Sunny could not resist having some fun with him. When the manager grumbled, "If you say this woman is so good, why do you play all those dinky little towns?" Sunny shot back, "To make money to play in the big ones!"

The manager's worries were over after the first recital. The review in the *San Francisco Examiner* the next day was headlined "Violin Crown Falls Upon Maud Powell; Pronounced Greatest American Wielder of Bow; Thrills Garrick Audience." Thomas Nunan wrote for the *Examiner* on March 28: "The very best thing the United States of North America can say in regard to its instrumental production in music is that this is the native land of Maud Powell, the violinist."

The critic for the *Chronicle* of the same day gives us an idea of how Maud Powell appeared to San Franciscans hearing her in person for the first time:

> When Miss Powell came upon the stage for the first movement of the Tschaikowsky concerto, the audience saw a tall, frail-looking woman, graceful and charmingly unaffected. It did not seem that she could have a huge tone or any of the masculine musical attributes accredited to her. But with the first quiver of the strings in that beautiful work of the Russian composer, the hearts of her hearers at once were thrilled with the beauty of her tone, the appeal of her warm and soulful expression, the sublimity of her musical conception and her wondrous brilliancy and fire. She does not play for display. Simply she presents the beauty in the music for its own sake. She features the composer, not herself. She wins you, and at once you have placed her upon a pedestal, and you keep her there.

The gates of San Francisco had opened to the strains of Maud Powell's fiddle. Walter Anthony, the critic for the *San Francisco Call*, revealed how the greatness of her art had silenced the initial skepticism which had greeted her arrival in that city: "To say that she plays as well as a man, would be to flatter all the men in the world."

25

Courage

Poetry ought to have a mother as well as a father.
—*Virginia Woolf*

SOMETIME AROUND THE TURN OF THE CENTURY, New York critic Henry T.
Finck had written that Maud Powell "has no superior among living
violinists." Contemplating that statement in 1913, Gustav Saenger,
violinist, pedagogue, composer, conductor, and editor of *The Musical Observer*, wrote for his journal:

> [I]t still holds good. Maud Powell, to-day, stands at the very top of
> her profession, worthy to be ranked as one of the greatest living
> violin soloists. . . . Her bowing is as decisive, as energetic and as
> firm as any other great player's has ever been, and her interpretation
> of whatever she plays is the very essence of artistic culture and refine-
> ment. This is where her womanliness stands her in good stead. In
> all the years I have heard her play, I have never heard her rasp, nor
> force her violin more than was absolutely necessary. She never for-
> gets that it is a violin she is playing, and no matter how delicate,
> how passionate or how strong her tone may be, it is always a beau-
> tiful, sympathetic and luscious *violin tone*. And this is certainly
> more than some of our famous men players can boast of all the
> time.

By the turn of the century, Maud was ranked among the greatest
violinists in the world. Despite the recognition of her status, however, she faced resistance to the idea of a woman violin virtuoso
throughout her entire career. She continually reached out with her
art, daring to play the most demanding music and to uphold her art

before dubious conductors and critics as well as skeptical managers and audiences.

Even as late as 1904, men were the measure of her art, as if women were incapable of possessing certain qualities in their own right. W. J. Henderson probably thought that he was bestowing the ultimate accolade when he wrote: "She played yesterday not like a woman, but like a man, with splendid tone, with brilliant mastery of the fingerboard, with a certainty of technique that was most notable, and with beautiful intelligence and breadth of style."[1]

When Maud performed the Beethoven violin concerto with the Chicago Symphony on April 22 and 23, 1904, the *Chicago Tribune* critic commented that it is "a number usually not heard with pleasure from a woman." Ironically, it was her last appearance with Theodore Thomas, who, in his genial, fatherly way, presented Maud Powell to his orchestra as *his* "musical grandchild." At one with her great-souled friend in feeling deeply the spirit of the music, the American violinist gave the noble work a performance which was "all that the most critical could demand."[2] The skeptical *Tribune* critic was won over:

> Yesterday, however, no indulgence had to be asked because of the sex of the player. Miss Powell draws a bow as steady and true as does any one of her masculine colleagues, and her good left hand has all the swiftness, all the surety and all the technical cunning that any one of theirs can display. And mentally her grasp of the musical and emotional contents of the mighty work impressed as just as clear, just as powerful as the most persistent stickler for virility in Beethoven interpretation could ask. It was a performance in all ways satisfying, technically, musically, and interpretatively, and coming from a woman it was unique. The audience was genuinely enthusiastic, and an encore—a short work in sustained style for violin alone and of rare beauty—was given in truly masterly fashion.

Maud's sex never limited her choice of repertoire. The adventurous violinist chose to render the Brahms Violin Concerto in D, Op. 77, with Frederick Stock and the Chicago orchestra on February 21 and 22, 1908. Ten years after the composer's death, the music was still hardly accepted and was rarely performed by a woman. In 1900 W. J. Henderson had severely criticized Leonora Jackson, a Joachim pupil who had won the Mendelssohn Prize, for making her New York debut with it.[3] Writing in 1908, a Chicago critic described the concerto as one of the most "difficult, significant and imposing" of all modern virtuoso pieces for the violin.

Maud loved the Brahms and composed a cadenza for the first movement that reveals her understanding of its musical depths. That this woman had the work well in hand surprised another critic: "Miss Powell showed her capacity for drawing the bow . . . and after the first lone cadenza which showed her mettle she steadily advanced the work. The ardent tone of the second movement found her surprisingly unfailing in the revelation of its breadth and warmth and the big, rushing octave passages of the final movement were carried with a sureness, solidity and authority delightful and convincing in all the exacting phases of the Brahms composition."[4] He admitted that there was "no feminine violinist before the public today that could handle and more truthfully interpret a work of this magnitude."

Chicago critic W. L. Hubbard, who understood Maud better, wrote with elation but not surprise:

> Of the playing of Maud Powell only words of unqualified and seemingly extravagant commendation can be spoken. She played the concerto of Brahms as one would expect it to be played by an artist who, as technician, interpreter and musician, stands without a superior on the concert platform today.
>
> She is a doer of big things, and nothing that she has done has surpassed in magnificent authority, solidity, artistry and supreme beauty the reading she gave to this most exacting and most difficult of violin concertos. It was an achievement even greater than was her presentation of the Sibelius concerto and that was a masterpiece.[5]

The orchestra members, all male, joined in the applause until she was forced to play Bach's *Prélude* as an encore.

When the violinist returned to Chicago the following year (1909) to play the Beethoven violin concerto, critics wrote that she had proved conclusively her right to rank among the world's greatest violinists, so nearly perfect was her performance.

> Repose, dignity, authority were combined with humor, grace and the purest beauty. Here is indeed a noble art. It unites the masculine qualities of strength and musical bigness with a truly feminine tenderness. It compasses a range of tone color that exhausts the possibilities of the violin. It is supported by a technical command of the instrument that is complete. . . .

[Her interpretation] was fully in accord with the best Beethoven traditions, yet it escaped all hint of the academic, because it was vital every moment — vital with the force of personality. Whether in the serene beauty of the allegro, the intimate poetry of the larghetto or the exuberant humor of the finale, it was ever the quality of a sincere and personal address to the hearer that made her playing of such superlative significance.[6]

Orchestra and audience enthusiasm, exceeding any so far that season, forced the reluctant violinist to play Bach's Air on the G String as an encore. The enthusiasm led one critic to comment:

Violinists come and violinists go, but there is always one whose appearance is eagerly welcomed by patrons of the Theodore Thomas Orchestra, and it is scarcely necessary to state that Maud Powell retains her place in the affections of discriminating audiences. On each occasion of her playing further reason is given to excite admiration for the gifted woman who has reached a plane to which only three or four of her contemporaries have climbed. Great is the art, one indeed closely allied to genius that can present the most sublime of all violin concertos, that of Beethoven, but Miss Powell knows no limitations, hence she can and does play this work with the utmost distinction. She produces a certain quality of tone which is absolutely to be associated with herself. There is a peculiarly "speaking" characteristic in Miss Powell's playing, the master mind guiding the fingers.[7]

Maud Powell may have been "at the zenith of her art," as this critic wrote, but when she returned to New York the following month, she had to prove herself again. Maud was engaged for several performances with the New York Philharmonic, which had acquired a new conductor the year before. Gustav Mahler was not looking forward to her appearance because he doubted that a woman could perform the great concertos of Mendelssohn and Beethoven that Maud was to play.[8]

In their first concert together, Maud performed the Mendelssohn concerto at the Brooklyn Academy of Music, which was crammed with enthusiastic Brooklynites. To them, the most important service performed by Mahler that night was "that he brought back to us that lovely violinist, Maud Powell, who has been too long absent from our local concerts." According to one witness, "Her performance aroused a storm of applause, and the artist was recalled so many times as to prove that Mr. Mahler could not do a more popular thing than to re-engage her for one of the later Brooklyn concerts."[9] The Bohemian conductor had to confess that Maud's performance had converted him.[10]

The New York critics give the best description of Maud's reception when she performed the Mendelssohn and Beethoven concertos with Mahler and the New York Philharmonic on December 29 and 31, 1909, respectively:

> That the queen of violinists should have received a rousing welcome goes without saying. She was in splendid form, and played with all the beauty of tone, technical assurance, elegance of style, and emotional expressiveness of which she is past mistress. Few among even the greatest masters of the instrument can rival her accuracy of intonation, or the wonderful purity of her harmonics. Her delivery of the cadenza in the first movement [of the Mendelssohn concerto] was nothing short of wonderful. . . .
>
> — *Musical America*

> Most of the audience knew the Mendelssohn concerto by heart, but every note last night was welcome, coming from Maud Powell's magic fingers and bow. Like Paderewski's reading of Mendelssohn, hers vivifies melodies which are apt to seem a trifle hackneyed, but are clothed with new life and meaning when she plays them. They were replete with poetry, with melting tenderness, and yet full of spirit and rhythm. Her playing is intensely feminine, yet it does not lack the big qualities that the great violinists among men have been noted for. Once more Miss Powell has proved that she is the woman highest up in the violin world.
>
> —Henry T. Finck, *New York Evening Post*

> There was an uncommon pleasure . . . in the appearance of Miss Maud Powell. . . . Her playing of Mendelssohn's concerto was not a routine delivery of music long known and sucked dry. It was animated by the charm and vital freshness that have kept the piece alive so long. . . . Miss Powell played it with a beautiful tone, clear, round, peculiarly searching and expressive in quality and with much élan and rhythmical forcefulness. It was playing that delighted the fancy and warmed the heart. Not the least beautiful factor in this performance was the orchestral accompaniment, played as if it were really an integral musical portion of the composition signifying something.
>
> —Richard Aldrich, *New York Times*

Her playing stood forth by individuality of tone so complete as to tempt one to say, as of a human voice, that one would recognize the sound of that violin if one were to hear it again. It stood forth even more by the quality of attack, by the litheness that seemed to be a characteristic of the player herself. It was, in a word, vivid in all the sorts of color. . . .

—William B. Chase, *New York Evening Sun*

Miss Powell's playing of the Mendelssohn concerto was a real delight. Perhaps she has given us a little more tone at times, but she has never produced any purer or more beautiful. Nor has she at any time excelled the smoothness and classic elegance of style with which she delivered the fluent melodies of Mendelssohn's composition. Her performance was worthy of her high position among the artists of the violin.

—W. J. Henderson, *New York Sun*

New York has not enjoyed for many weeks performances as satisfying as those of Maud Powell. . . . Miss Powell . . . again proved herself an artist of the rarest qualities, and it is not saying too much to state that only upon the rarest occasions is a violinist of this rank heard. Miss Powell is no newcomer and what she has accomplished is a matter of history on both continents, but what she does at the present time is of the utmost significance because in every detail of her great work she shows steady improvement and greater breadth. Thus the Mendelssohn concerto . . . was a greater Mendelssohn than we usually hear because it had the advantage of an interpretation of a great artist. . . . But it was in the Beethoven concerto that Miss Powell arose to her full height, not alone as executant but as interpreter. She protected the broad classic line, she expressed the noble message with the dignity of a great artist and the intelligence of a great musician.

— *The Music News*

Miss Powell's playing of the [Beethoven] concerto was poetically conceived and artistically carried out. . . . [I]t had breadth and warmth of expression and nobility of style. . . . She made an uncommonly deep impression on the audience and was many times recalled.

—Richard Aldrich, *New York Times*[11]

Also deeply impressed, Mahler promptly engaged Maud to play the Sibelius concerto the next season. Critic Henry T. Finck made an American celebration out of Mahler's conversion: "Gustav Mahler remarked the other day that he had not come across the Atlantic, as some had intimated, to teach Americans, nor, he added, had he come here to be taught. Yet he has learned one thing—the important fact that America harbors a violinist of the fair sex who could not be duplicated in Europe. He . . . was as much pleased on discovering her rare musicianship as the Philharmonic audiences were to hear again this queen of violinists, who has been devoting most of her time during the last two years to playing in the middle and far West."[12]

For all the pioneering work of Camilla Urso and Maud Powell in laying to rest the damning epithet "plays well, for a woman," the prejudice against women players simply would not die. In 1913 the women's suffrage movement was in its last push toward ultimate victory. However, only the year before, Maud had felt it necessary to give a blistering answer to *The New Music Review*'s seemingly innocent brief report of one man's bias:

> We heard a distinguished violinist say not long ago that only one female fiddler had pleased him—and he had heard many. This woman was Teresina Tua. She fascinated him and compelled his admiration and respect, because she played like a woman and did not attempt to be virile, did not anxiously strive to "play like a man." To him the other women were unsexed without arriving at man's stature.
>
> It was Saint-Saëns, who said, with regard to Augusta Holmes: "Women are curious when they seriously concern themselves with art: they seem desirous first of all to make one forget they are women, and to show an overflowing virility, without dreaming that it is precisely this preoccupation which betrays the woman.[13]

Maud Powell's truly angry response was addressed as a personal letter to a personal friend, Philip Hale, the Boston critic and editor of *The New Music Review*. It was such good copy, however, that Hale could not resist publishing it. Although he did not reveal her name, the intellect and temperament of the artist were unmistakably emblazoned in every word, and it was soon reprinted in numerous music journals which named the violinist as its author:

> Why these cavillers confine their criticisms to fiddlers is more than I can understand. Is Mme. Carreño a Rubinstein or Mme. Bloomfield-Zeisler a Paderewski? Methinks not. Furthermore, Mme. Carreño doesn't try to be virile—she obeys the inner impulse. Mme. Zeisler doesn't try to be electric—she just *is*. Mme. [Urso] was the

sincerest of artists—and never tried to ape "mere man." No one would have admitted sooner than she that she was not a Joachim; but she could play a downward scale without his flop in changing positions and she could draw a steadier bow than he. Moreover, her ear remained true to the last. Lady Hallé was a cross old patch, but it is safe to say that any woman playing as well as she did must have been sincere and have had convictions. She was not a Vieuxtemps, but she played better than any local man in London, when I lived there. Miss Parlow is far and away more interesting than the Spaldings, MacMillens and their ilk. Whether it is all imitation in her case, as she says in her interviews, and as her St. Petersburg colleagues declare (perhaps through jealousy!) and whether she will develop on individual lines, still remains to be seen. Teresina Tua was the most delightful and fascinating woman violinist I ever heard; but she was much too pretty and fascinating to keep up the grind. It is doubtful whether her talent could ever have developed much beyond the Bruch G Minor Concerto, Mendelssohn E Minor Concerto and Vieuxtemps Polonaise stage.

What we women lack in art is that infinite and wonderful tenderness that speaks through the tone of Ysaÿe and Kreisler. We mother the whole race, our children, fathers, brothers and husbands—and with quick intuition the stranger at our door—but the quality does not as yet express itself in art. The lack, however, is not in the fiddling tribe alone, and why should we bear the brunt of that everlasting and overworked criticism? It would be a lark if the men could occasionally read our innermost thoughts when they are chanticleering around. I certainly think we are more clearly aware of our shortcomings than they are. And oh! our sorriest wail! the question of health and physical endurance! They little know how much more it costs us in will power to achieve than it does them. And then the discomfort of our clothes, the time and trouble it takes to keep oneself looking respectable, etc., etc., etc.[14]

Hale commented: "There is an old Bohemian proverb: To some God gave brains; to others, to play on the fiddle. There is at least one woman that can fiddle with the best of the men and at the same time express herself clearly and forcibly in writing."

Maud reflected on what a woman paid to follow "art," in "The Price of Fame," published in 1908. Styled as advice to young women considering a career in music, its tone reflects the suffering that lay behind her own success. Although it concludes positively, several paragraphs are particularly poignant:

Shall I tell you a secret? Most of the women violinists, the best ones, hate their instruments. Madame Urso was bitter but brave; Lady Hallé is (and I have this on the authority of a manager who traveled on tour with her) cranky and ill-tempered. Poor Arma Senkrah committed suicide. Teresina Tua, the most fascinating talent of them all, got into some sort of trouble while in her fresh, beautiful womanhood and lost most of her artistic cunning and her adorableness quite suddenly. I verily believe I am the only woman who, having stuck to her fiddle unflinchingly, has preserved the remnants of a sweet sanity. And I wouldn't bank heavily on my nerves or temper either! But I would not undo my life, and it is a satisfaction to assert that the professional woman generally keeps her poise, her technic, her memory and her hearing, longer than her masculine rival; and while she may not take the inspired flights of the greatest geniuses, she nevertheless preserves a higher average of excellence. I am often asked how it is that I almost invariably play well, and I believe it is because I am more willing than men are to live as even and quiet a life as possible.

Nor am I satisfied to rest on my laurels. My *confrères* and my public have been good enough to maintain that I hold the premiere place among women violinists. To continue to be worthy of that confidence is a heavier responsibility than the original building-up of this reputation. The work, the study, the courage, the patience, the self-denial must go on to the end.

Although Maud was accepted easily in music circles and by the public as the greatest American violinist without sex distinction, the thoughtful artist still had an abiding dislike for being referred to as a "famous woman violinist." She once remarked that, "It seems to imply that there is something unusual in a woman achieving distinction of any kind."[15] Actually, a good many women violinists came along who played with distinction, but in the end, Maud outdistanced them with the depth and breadth of her musicianship as well as the extent and impact of her career.[16] (W. J. Henderson wrote, "Our own Maud Powell is easily the first player among women and pretty near the top among men.")

Few of her female contemporaries or immediate successors managed to negotiate the physical demands of touring or survive the marriage bond as solo artists. Although Nettie Carpenter (b. 1865) won the first prize for violin at the Paris Conservatoire in 1884, her public career did not really survive her marriage in 1891. The career of Madge Wickham, Maud's classmate in Berlin, also ended with her marriage. The American-born (1864), European-trained Arma Senkrah (Harkness) ended her promising career with her marriage in 1888 and committed suicide in 1900. Leonora Jackson, born in Boston in 1879, made her New York debut in 1900 but cut short her fine career with her marriage in 1907. Teresina Tua retired from the concert stage when she married following her 1887 American tour. She returned to the stage from time to time, but devoted much of her life to teaching in Italy. Marie Hall (1884–1956), who studied under Sevčik in Prague, became the first British female violinist to achieve an international reputation. By 1902 she was one of the leading virtuoso performers in Europe. She married in 1911, however, and gradually disappeared from the concert platform.

Among those few whose marriages did not prevent a public career, Gabrielle Wietrowitz and Marie Soldat turned to teaching and quartet playing. Although Geraldine Morgan, Maud's classmate in Berlin and Leipzig, continued making solo appearances after her debut in 1892, she largely devoted her talents to establishing the Joseph Joachim School of Violin Playing, based at Carnegie Hall. In addition, she eventually formed the Morgan String Quartet, which performed in New York City at the turn of the century.

Only Camilla Urso and Lady Hallé seemed to sustain solo careers over a long period of time, although Kathleen Parlow, who came along later and was a pupil of Henry Holmes in San Francisco and then of Leopold Auer at the St. Petersburg Conservatory (1906–07), had a distinguished solo career from her New York debut in 1910 into the late 1920s. From 1929 on she devoted her talents primarily to teaching.

Among those who rose to public distinction as violinists but who were not generally soloists were many students of Julius Eichberg, appointed director of the Boston Conservatory in 1868. Lillian Shattuck, who was first violin in the first all-female quartet (the Eichberg Quartette, 1878–1890s), established herself as a string teacher in Boston. Edith Lynwood Winn, with whom Maud formed an enduring friendship, became a prominent violin teacher and an effective writer and advocate for women musicians. Olive Mead (1874–1946) concertized as a soloist for a number of years before forming the Olive Mead Quartet, which performed regularly in New York City from 1903 to 1917.

Quite a few female violin aspirants were coming up behind them. Between 1870 and 1910, the percentage of women in music and music teaching in America had risen from thirty-six to sixty-one percent, and many of these were violinists. There were few career choices in those days. Beginning in the late nineteenth century, a number of amateur and professional women's orchestras were formed to provide outlets for the increasing numbers of accomplished female string players. With the exception of harpists, women were largely barred from membership in the major professional symphony orchestras. In 1925, Alfred Hertz, conductor of the San Francisco Symphony, became one of the first to hire female string players.

When in 1913 *Musical America's* editor John C. Freund advocated opening orchestra jobs to women, he solicited Maud's views. He received by telegram the response he had undoubtedly expected from the woman he called "a master mind as well as a great musician with an international reputation":

> Of course women should play in symphony and other orchestras, if they want the work. Wanting the work implies measuring up to the standards of musical and technical efficiency, with strength to endure well, hours of rehearsing and often the strain of travel, broken habits and poor food. Many women are amply fitted for the work; such women should be employed on an equal footing with men. I fail to see that any argument to the contrary is valid. But if they accept the work they should be prepared to expect no privileges because of their sex. They must dress quietly and as fine American women they must uphold high standards of conduct. [17]

Freund supported her remarks, writing: "You see how sensibly she talks. She claims for women no privileges whatever on account of her sex, and there she takes ground that is unassailable. Capacity is not a thing of sex. Capacity has no sex. . . . If it be said that should women invade the orchestra and concert field or the theaters, they will take the bread from the mouths of some of the men, I reply, 'They will not do it where the men are competent, and if they do it where the men are not competent the public and my ears will benefit.' " [18]

In spite of the probity of Freund's argument, conductors of established symphony orchestras remained convinced that whatever happened on the level of staff musicians, admission of a woman as concertmaster or conductor of an orchestra would cause rioting both on and off stage. In 1916 Joseph Stransky, conductor of the New York Symphony, said he would not object to women players, but "they would have to be better players than the men who apply for the same positions."[19]

The height of the women's suffrage movement must have been a difficult time for Maud.[20] New York City witnessed a great suffragette parade in the spring of 1912 and later the arrival of Emmeline Pankhurst, the English suffragette, to speak in Madison Square Garden on October 21, 1913. These events made the musical world more keenly aware of Maud's achievements in a field still dominated by men. Interviewers increasingly focused on her womanhood, forcing her to speak her mind on women's rights.

Maud had won her way in her profession, not as a novelty, merely a child prodigy, or a freak of nature, but as a whole human being who expressed through her art the entire gamut of human emotions. She never thought of herself or her art in terms of masculine or feminine — only as human. Her pursuit of her art had always been devoid of artificial or external considerations, being impelled by something within. Boston critic H. T. Parker observed that Maud had "quietly waived aside the indulgences that rise almost spontaneously to meet her sex" and "gained and held her position by sheer artistic probity."[21]

She had battled prejudice all her life, from the boys who tagged and ridiculed her as she carried her fiddle along the streets of Aurora and Chicago, to the initial scorn of conductors such as Mahler and Richter, to the petty provincialism of small-town managers. By her example and her writings, she had long advocated the right of the female musician to take her place alongside the men in her profession. But on the question of the right to vote, the great artist was at times, and for complex reasons, ambivalent.

Maud had associated with suffragettes a great deal and had been instrumental in bringing the English suffragettes to America. However, their mode of operation under Emmeline Pankhurst and the Women's Social and Political Union (founded in 1903), which Maud had witnessed in England, had left its mark. "When . . . the English suffragettes introduced militant methods I was repelled and ashamed. What I abhorred was their lack of sportsmanship. They didn't 'play fair.' Witness the famous House of Commons incident, in which they did not keep their word."[22] No matter how right the cause, Maud could not sanction unfair means to gain a just end.

There were two other dominant experiences which influenced Maud's thinking, her relationships with her father and her husband. Both men had subordinated their self-interest to the advancement of this extraordinary woman in music. Bramwell Powell was a kind, tolerant man who, with his unusual foresight and intelligence, believed in the full development of the human being without regard to sex. He had led a broken and lonely personal life as a result of his wife's ambition and his daughter's gifts, but he never complained and pursued his own career with characteristic excellence. Maud was almost too keenly aware of his sacrifice for her sake.

Maud's perfect match with Sunny, combined with her father's example, probably weakened the sense of injustice she might have felt in connection with the legal handicaps facing a married woman. Although the marriage meant that Sunny could pursue his chosen career as a concert manager, he tailored his schedule to his top artist, his wife, and subordinated his personal life to the demands of her career.

Although Sunny knew his wife's thinking very well in most cases, he misjudged the complexity of her emotions and thinking on the subject of votes for women. In an interview with a reporter, he denigrated the women's suffrage movement in England, implying that it constituted merely a collection of unattractive spinsters. But Maud took up the subject "very seriously," speaking "very intelligently" about it in a revealing interview:

> "I grew up in the suffragette atmosphere. My mother and her friends, I knew already then, had the best husbands that there were. They were chivalrous and supportive in every way but on this point, they differed. The three suffragettes liked to discuss these matters very much while their husbands were present (Susan Anthony who was single was able to say whatever she wanted to without any husband to consider) which made me very upset when I was a young woman. It bothered me so much that a lot of the nice evenings that could have been so pleasant were ruined by these bloody debates and this is the first reason why I am not for women's right to vote.
>
> "And then I also think about it this way—what can a woman gain by voting? What can the country gain? To answer the second question first, if the good votes win, the bad votes will win too. So

why make a bad thing worse? The woman herself does not need the right to vote. Please understand me right, the urge for the woman to get out of her present sphere into a simple humanity does not require the right to vote. We have not yet in the whole East of America the right to vote for women, although there is so much which has changed in her favor.

"My own career might be an example to my way of thinking. I earned a name for myself and a fortune through my playing even if I am of the weaker sex.

"In the world of art and everyday life, the concept of male and female changed drastically in favor of the woman. Both concepts are important in terms of marriage, career and emotional thinking and have become indispensable."

After a little pause, Maud Powell said, "Maybe my point of view is not authoritative. I was very lucky in my life—lucky as an artist and lucky in marriage."

In a whispered tone, so he who was in the other room could not hear it—"Really, I have a jewel of a husband—made for an artist. The husbands of a lot of women who forget the meal because of study and practicing could learn from Mr. Turner. He is never upset about it. He never reproaches me. He never nags. He shares my love and enthusiasm for music. He is my best adviser, my best friend. That's why my life is so complete and happy."[23]

If Maud was not wholeheartedly in favor of women's suffrage, she was certainly not opposed to it. Her considerable powers of observation enabled her to see injustice even if she had largely overcome it in her career and it was completely absent in her personal life. In an interview published on the very day Emmeline Pankhurst addressed her American counterparts in Madison Square Garden (October 21, 1913), Maud gave expression to the deep humanity which formed the substratum of her art, indicating that the greatest art is androgynous, transcending sexual distinctions:

In the world's orchestra Maud Powell is one of the first violins simply because she is so much more than a violinist. When a famous European musician cried out in amazement, "You play like a man!" he missed the fact that in her womanhood was the source, not the limitation of her art.

She came in out of the rain, on an autumn day recently, laid off her wraps, and talked to the wood fire. She talked of militancy in politics and peace in art, of American music and of greatness in women.

"Militancy? I loathe it. But the women in England live in a pitiful isolation. The men have little to do with them in any way that will help the sexes to understand each other. A few clever hostesses attract swarms of men. At the other extreme the athletic young girls with their flat heels have a certain rough-and-tumble outdoor relation with men. But as for the genuine friendship, real comradely exchange of ideas and points of view, common enough here, you will find little of it in England. The result is bad."

"You are not opposed to woman suffrage?"

"Certainly not. I don't have any particular desire for the vote, but the withholding of it seems unfair. It is true that a good many women are not ready for it. But many men are quite as unfit."

"Do you think the women who have won artistic distinction have helped to encourage the others in their progress toward greater freedom?"

"It may be so. After my concerts women have told me they were glad I was one of them."

But Mme. Powell hastened to disclaim artistic supremacy for her sex.

"There are few women that equal the greatest men in the field of art. Women have a genius for mothering. But they seldom carry over the greatness of their motherhood into the field of art. They have not been interested—have not thrown their whole natures into artistic forms of expression. There is something of the man, too, in the greatest woman, as there is of the woman in the greatest man. You find that in the tenderness that is in Ysaÿe's playing at times."

This reference was characteristic. There is no jealousy in Mme. Powell's heart. She loves the praise of excellence as much as she hates the flattery of pretentious mediocrity. She recalled with reverently grateful memory the playing of Camilla Urso. . . .

She spoke of the pleasure the recorded playing of her fellow artists gave her—Kreisler's, for example. She greatly admires his art, though she does not accept his view of woman suffrage.[24]

During the First World War, women were involved in every aspect of the war effort. In the end, their valiant work, combined with Maud's innate sense of justice, thoroughly convinced the violinist of the soundness of "votes for women." Maud described her conversion in an article written in December 1917:

Then came the war. The women of England, including the hysterical suffragettes, faced the situation squarely and bravely. They gave up their men-folk, and turned heroically to the tasks that hitherto had been performed chiefly by masculine hands, masculine brains. They commanded the respect and admiration of the whole world. I, for one, reversed my judgment of that same hysterical element, and forgave.

And what is it we are working for, paying for, our men fighting for? A world democracy, to be sure. But the word democracy gives the woman suffragist pause, for it is borne in upon her consciousness of right and justice that democracy is not altogether what it purports to be when such a large proportion of the adult population has no voice in the conduct of the government — is denied representation in fact. Now this representation and all it implies should be *thrust* upon us as a matter of duty, not handed over in gingerly spirit as a mere privilege. Then we must be educated to our new responsibilities. We must learn, learn, learn, in order to meet intelligently new conditions arising out of this frightful world-upheaval. By the way, talk with almost any Englishwoman and with all her pretty, feminine ways, one is abashed before her knowledge of state affairs. With new duties, new emergencies we shall acquire undreamed of strength and prowess. For such is woman's nature. And we shall be the better mothers, the better home keepers for our larger vision and wider capabilities. We shall bring up better men children, demanding from them, as from our husbands, higher ideals and cleaner activity. Goodness knows, the world of politics needs a house cleaning. Let us live up to the proverb of the new broom. Moreover, let us not fail to renew the broom whenever it shows the least sign of wear.

Thus it is that the war and some of its consequences have brought about my complete conversion to woman suffrage. Women are fitter than some of us thought. There is no turning back now, for we are being swept onward by a great tidal wave of world change, a change that makes for bigger thought, deeper feeling and more rugged action.[25]

When New Yorkers went to the polls in November of 1919, after women had won the right to vote in that state in 1917, Maud Powell was among them. A picture of her casting her first ballot was prominently displayed in the newspapers. While Congress approved the Nineteenth Amendment to the Constitution, which gave women the right to vote nationally in 1919, Maud Powell did not live to see its ratification on August 26, 1920. However, her mother, an unwavering supporter of the cause, without whose courage Maud well might not have developed her native gifts, survived another five years, long enough to exercise her newly-won right.

Maud in 1916.

A RECORD PROGRAM!

Every Number a Maud Powell Victor Record

Carnegie Hall

57th Street and 7th Avenue

Monday Evening
January 8, 1917

Violin Recital by

Maud Powell

Assisted by

Arthur Loesser, Pianist

The program numbers will be chosen from the list of
Maud Powell's Victor Records

Select your two favorite Maud Powell records from the list on following
page, write them in the space provided on the Post Card attached, sign and mail
to her manager. YOUR VOTE will help decide the making of the program.

SEATS NOW ON SALE

*Box Office Prices 25c., 50c., 75c., $1.00
First Tier Box Seats $1.50*

This page, top, front of card mailed to patrons announcing Maud's Victor record recital; *bottom,* autographing her records in the fall of 1916. *Facing page, top,* Arthur Loesser, Maud's pianist, 1915–17; *bottom,* Arthur and Maud on tour (man at left unidentified).

This page, l to r: Sunny, unidentified person, pianist Arthur Loesser, Maud, and other members of her party descending into the Grand Canyon on Bright Angel Trail in 1916. *Facing
page,* Maud in 1918 at the Grand Canyon memorial dedicated in May 1918 to her uncle
John Wesley Powell, the canyon's first explorer.

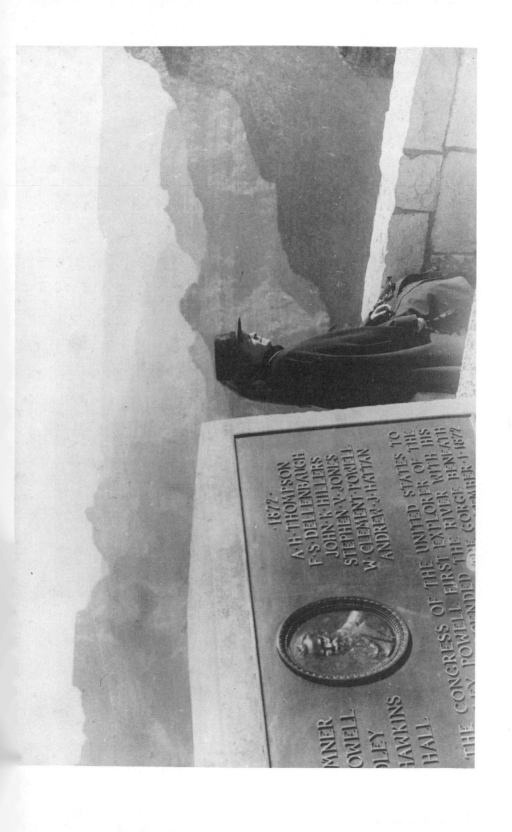

This page, Maud in Hawaii in January 1916. *Facing page,* on the steps
of Ottawa, Illinois,' $250,000 high school where Maud gave the open-
ing concert in its 1,000-seat auditorium: *l to r,* John Hoff, director of
music for Ottawa Public Schools and conductor of the orchestra and
chorus; Riva Bayne, music teacher; Maud; Charles H. Kingman, high
school principal; Arthur Loesser; Dr. A. J. Roberts, member, board of
trustees.

acing page, top left, Sunny's hijinks, Mount Vernon, N.Y., about 1904–08; *right,* Maud's aunt Kitty (Henrietta Love), her cousin Mabel Love, and Maud; *bottom,* outing n Mount Willard, White Mountains, N.H., about 1915 or 1916, *back row, l to r:* unny, Maud, Edna Speier, Aurin Moody Chase, Alan Mesbitt; *front row, l to r:* Donald hase, Lucy Chase, Ellen Chase, Aurin Chase, Jr. *This page,* Billy (back), Sunny, and aud engaging in some trick photography at their Great Neck home after 1908.

Maud at her home in Gramercy Park, about 1918–19.

Educator of a Nation

I have undertaken, not to see differently from others, but to look further than others, and whilst they are busy for the morrow only, I have turned my thoughts to the whole future.

— *Alexis de Tocqueville*

FROM 1910 UNTIL THE END OF HER LIFE, Maud Powell's concert dates on tour increased in number each year. The increase reflected a musical awakening in America stimulated in large part by the violinist herself. Believing deeply that it was her mission to plant the seeds for cultivation of the highest music by her countrymen, she gave increasing attention to the needs of small towns in remote areas. In articles and interviews, she continually gave prescriptions for nurturing music in these places, based on her personal observations.

The formation of town music clubs linked to the National Federation of Music Clubs was of vital importance to this work. Maud offered some advice on how to begin:

> It makes such a difference if there is a leading thought in a town. Even one person can do so much. Just suppose you went to stay in some little place, quite asleep on the subject of music. You would at once do something to stir them up; it might be a very simple thing at first. You might only call some of the people together once a week to listen to phonograph records. Then you might start a little music club, and before long you would suggest having a few artists come during the season, to play and sing for them. And so the good work begins and goes on. The artists need not be of the highest or most expensive; many of the humbler sort are doing splendid work in just this way. They are filling the great need — the need to make the people know and love good music. For example, I know

and love the César Franck Sonata. When we play that in a music center, we know there will be a number in the audience who are familiar with it and admire it. How much greater sympathetic response would the artists secure, if all, or nearly all of the listeners understood the work. So it is understanding of what good music is that we are trying to spread as we travel the length and breadth of the land.[1]

The best contribution Maud could make to these initial efforts was to appear under the auspices of the local music club. The personal example and encouragement of a magnetic, first-class artist served to stimulate local interest in music more than any other single action. In Maud Powell's case, each performance reflected her personal interest in and response to the community in which she appeared:

> I like to feel the pulse of a town where I am to play, even if it be quite a small place. How can this be done when one remains but a few hours or a day? It is not so difficult. Soon after I arrive, I go for a walk, for I need fresh air after a night of railway travel. I explore the little town, its shop windows and principal streets. I drop into the music store, too, get acquainted with the proprietors, tell them who I am, ask about the victrola and the records. Then I meet the club people and others whom it is necessary for me to know. By the time the concert is to begin, I have a pretty good idea of the temper of that town and its people. When I go before them, I play as though that were the one concert of my life.[2]

Sunny ingeniously advertised Maud's willingness to appear anywhere she was needed through the music magazines, like John C. Freund's *Musical America* and *The Musical Courier*, to which local music clubs subscribed. Maud further manifested her interest in the progress and work of the clubs by appearing at the annual meetings of the National Federation of Music Clubs. She even participated in local club meetings as she toured. In Hobart, Oklahoma, she gave her personal approval to the Library and Music Club's plan to "bring one artist of Maud Powell's rank to Hobart each season, and to make it the musical event of this part of the state." She offered her assistance in securing an artist for the next season.[3]

While Maud's appearance was ideal for boosting a town's musical awareness, a club might well doubt whether it could afford to have her come. Understanding this, Sunny went out of his way to ensure the concert's financial success for the small-town club. Although we do not know how Maud's fee was adjusted for the small towns, Sunny once emphasized: "She is no sightseer. . . . I am a firm believer in making money for the local manager, which can only be accomplished by the fairest treatment."[4]

In 1913, the artist's fee in one small town was $300, which the concert receipts easily covered. On her 1910 tour to the West Coast, tickets to Maud Powell's concerts in such places as Olympia and Seattle, Washington, ranged from fifty cents to $1.50, while in New York during the 1906–07 season, New York Philharmonic ticket prices ranged from seventy-five cents to $2.00. In Tacoma, Washington, the local newspaper noted that ticket prices for Maud Powell's recital were considerably lower than usual for performances of this kind.

Each summer, Maud planned her programs for the coming season and wrote all her own program notes. When she originally launched her mission to appear in small towns in remote areas, she was impressed by her audiences' need for advance preparation. As she related in 1915,

> I have found that in some of the smaller towns and in places where the percentage of cultivated musicians in the audience is apt to be small, the public want me to talk from the stage about the compositions I am to play. In many cases this sugar-coats the pill for them. The old belief that "classical music" is a fundamentally dull thing out of which one can get no pleasure is still broadly prevalent. However, it is remarkable how a little information about the works to be played — just enough to help them form mental pictures — will improve the attitude of the hearers and gain their sympathy.
>
> Yet I entertain an abiding dislike for the spoken word in a musical performance of any kind — it disrupts the existing mood and makes it vastly difficult to reestablish it — and so I have adopted the expedient of employing program notes. These are of the utmost usefulness, I find. I recall the difficulty I had not long ago to win the consent of certain persons in charge of a concert of mine to the inclusion of a Bach piece in my program. Bach, they argued, must necessarily be beyond the grasp of my hearers. And yet when their programs had given them a certain amount of information about the composition, they received it with every sign of pleasure.[5]

Sunny sent the programs ahead so that music lovers unfamiliar with the programmed music could procure the scores and derive the fullest educational benefit from the violinist's appearance. It worked. Maud found that:

> In many places they make it their business to "study up" my recitals beforehand. They have their Victor machines, they provide themselves with records of the various numbers on the program, and they post themselves on the lives of the composers and the characteristics of the compositions. They study these matters diligently before the concert takes place, and their talking machines afford them private rehearsals, one might say, so that the enjoyment derived from the actual concert is two-fold.[6]

Maud's recital work and interest in each town inspired the formation of a number of symphony orchestras, including those in Seattle (formed in 1907) and Bellingham, Washington (1912), as well as the development of many more. Her willingness to go out of her way (sometimes retracing her steps) to perform with fledgling orchestras like those in Seattle, Bellingham, St. Paul (formed in 1908), and Minneapolis (1903) attracted public attention to the orchestras' work and encouraged the musicians to aspire to an ever higher program standard.

Maud's experience in San Antonio was typical. Her friend of long standing, Mrs. Eli Hertzberg, president of the San Antonio Symphony Society, not only introduced a promising violin student to the great artist over lunch, but she arranged for the orchestra to hold a private rehearsal in Maud's honor as well. The violinist was too tightly scheduled to play with the young orchestra of twenty-nine strings plus wind and percussion instruments, but she scribbled out a gracious note of encouragement on her way back to the West Coast:

> I am most interested in the career of the San Antonio Orchestra and want to thank you for giving me the privilege of hearing a private rehearsal. I hope the citizens of San Antonio will realize the cultural as well as the business value of having a real Symphony Orchestra. It should be made a civic institution, along with good schools, good pavements, good policing, good systems of parks and sanitation; all those things in fact that make a man proud of his home town.
>
> In your young conductor, Mr. Blitz, you have a talent and a personality of real force. He will lead the orchestra on righteous musical paths, straight to the desired goal. He has gift, training, personality magnetism and those painstaking qualities that a musi-

cal conscience gives. I am glad he plays the cello for it is essential that a conductor understand the use of the bow. The bowed instruments or stringed instruments, as they are more often called, form the very backbone of the orchestra. I am looking forward with interest to hearing again the orchestra when I come to San Antonio next time.[7]

The Bellingham orchestra was formed under the leadership of Mrs. Davenport-Engberg, who had studied violin in Berlin with Willy Hess. The orchestra's formation was sparked by the announcement that Maud Powell would be coming to the town of 30,000 to play in 1912. One year later, Maud described the drama behind that historic occasion:

> Fancy a place so remote having an orchestra! Well, it is due entirely to the efforts of Mrs. Davenport-Engberg and it has been in existence more than a year. When Mrs. Engberg understood I was to play there last year she set about establishing an orchestra, her own violin pupils forming a nucleus. She had no easy task before her. At that time not a soul in Bellingham had any idea of what a viola was. Mrs. Engberg industriously set about teaching some of her pupils the viola. Gradually other instrumentalists were secured. A flutist was found and in order that his sojourn in Bellingham would be assured the resourceful organizer of the orchestra procured him eleven pupils. Picture to yourself a town of that rank with eleven people busily learning to play the flute!
>
> Well, they rehearsed ceaselessly. As the time drew near they practised the piece I was going to play with them. Their concertmaster played the solo part. Nervousness was naturally aroused to a high pitch when I appeared to rehearse with them. "Now if you make a single mistake at the performance," Mrs. Engberg flatly told her players, "I solemnly vow to run right out through the door at the back of the platform." "Very well," answered a voice in the orchestra, "but you won't be able to get through for the crowd!" But the concert went off most creditably.[8]

Composed of about forty-five players, roughly half of whom were women, it was the first mixed orchestra to be conducted by a woman.

The following year, Maud reinforced the town's support for the orchestra by playing with it and pointing out its significance to the community: "Bellingham is very fortunate, indeed, in having the splendid symphony orchestra that Mrs. Davenport-Engberg has made possible, not only from a musical point of view, but also taken from a publicity and advertising standpoint. . . . There is nothing that will give a city better publicity and standing than prestige along musical lines, and right here in your pretty little city you have headed in the right direction in that respect. . . . "⁹ The violinist expressed surprise at the degree of success achieved by the young orchestra and pointed out that not one city on the coast of twice its size could boast of such an organization.

Maud understood how important it was to give the right encouragement and how much her personal encouragement meant. She noted that the ensemble "had improved wonderfully": "They asked me if I were pleased. 'Pleased,' I answered, 'why I am thoroughly amazed!' So I was. But my saying so delighted them beyond all words. And now, through the work and devotion of one woman [Mrs. Davenport-Engberg] that town has an orchestra on which it may well pride itself."¹⁰

Maud Powell was the first artist of her rank to play with the orchestra. In 1913 there was still virgin timber along most of the highway from Seattle north to Bellingham, near the Canadian border, and few artists braved the hazards of travel to get there. In one instance, Emilio de Gogorza, the famous Spanish baritone, turned back to Seattle after a mudslide on the Great Northern Railway delayed his arrival.

Nothing deterred Maud, who got a kick out of other musicians' reactions to touring "off the beaten track." She sent *The Musical Courier* the following amusing story about the French Band, which had been touring the same part of the country as the famed violinist:

> When the French Band was in the State of Washington... the members were pretty well tired out after their long journey of one night stands, but everything changed to a rosy atmosphere—at least for a second or two—when they received the itinerary for the last week to find that, instead of being booked for six concerts, they had only five on the list, the sixth night reading 'Pullman.' Their delight took a sudden drop, however, when it was explained that 'Pullman' did not mean a rest on the sleeper, but another concert in the city of Pullman, Wash.

Maud Powell's legendary devotion to her musical pioneer work and her standing as an artist combined to make her the most sought-after musician in America. Some said only Lillian Russell and David Warfield could vie with her in popular esteem throughout the country. Knowing that Maud was never patronizing and sensing her openness and sympathy, it was only natural for Mrs. Engberg to seek the famous artist's aid and friendship.

One of the first days they spent together was in the company of Mrs. C. X. Larrabee, a superb pianist. According to Mrs. Engberg's son, "Maud Powell was politically congenial at first, but thawed to adolescent enthusiasm on several occasions, particularly when she played my mother's Amati—an instrument which had an immense full tone."[11] The women played the Sarasate duet for two violins and recorded it on an old Edison phonograph (wax cylinder record), which pleased Maud.

According to Mrs. Engberg's son, Maud was "such a lovely person—graceful and considerate." She sensed the struggle within her pioneering sister, and through the years encouraged Davenport-Engberg to continue her lonely work. Paul Engberg recounts: "To show you how good she was—when my mother deprecated the work she was doing, and not being able to follow her career out in the 'sticks' M. P. said, 'I'll trade places with you.' Ten years later my mother became the first woman conductor of a major professional orchestra, the Seattle Symphony, and she attributed her long conversations with M. P. for her perseverance in the face of discouraging odds."[12]

For the country's musical awakening and advancement, Maud gave credit to the women who were actively involved in hundreds of local musical organizations. Returning from a Maine-to-Texas tour in 1911, Maud commented, "The women are making the musical wheels revolve." But the reporter pointed out that her view was not in accord with some other theories then current. "[S]he smiled blandly and insisted even more firmly that the women of America deserved the largest slice of credit. . . . "

> Maybe not in New York . . . but then you know that you can't judge by this city. As long as women continue to spend their money on those absurd and hideous Spring bonnets one cannot look to them for undivided support of artistic matters.
>
> Besides that, New York is full of *nouveaux riches* and is *so* different from the rest of the country!

But get outside of it and you will find that women are not wasting their money on their Spring hats. They deserve a tribute for encouraging not only music but every form of culture. They have formed their art clubs and societies and in little, out-of-the-way localities you find that they can discuss the art of Botticelli and have on the walls of their houses reproductions of the great masterpieces of painting rather than the cheap chromos one might be inclined to expect.

They have their musical organizations, they arrange and patronize the concerts of the great artists. They insist upon their husbands accompanying them and if the latter don't want to they drag them there by the scruff of the neck.

If in New York the men decline to attend musical functions the reason is simply that they are worn out by working. And why must they work so much? To make money to satisfy their wives' extravagance. When women take it into their heads to become less extravagant the men will find more opportunity to patronize concerts.[13]

Luring the American male into the concert hall was a problem everywhere, although it was particularly acute in the heartland. The common association of women and German immigrant musicians with musical endeavor induced the disdain of the self-made American man. As Maud observed:

Musical progressiveness is not equally distributed. I find many of the newer Western communities more prone to advance than some of those in the Middle West such as Kansas and Iowa, which are inclined to be a little sluggish. And the motive force for such advancement lies largely, as has been so often pointed out, in the activity of the women's clubs. They are indefatigable in their energy. The men are still somewhat slow. And it is characteristic of existing conditions that one should sometimes hear the surprised exclamation, "Oh! look at the men," when some of them are seen at a concert. That is one of the peculiar, one of the amazing problems of our national life, the solution of which we have not yet found! Why should it be that so many persons cannot bring themselves to look upon a taste for music as something compatible with distinctly masculine likings?[14]

Maud herself was credited with doing much to break down these prejudices. When wives dragged their husbands along to her concerts, she wooed them and won them with her clever programming and spirited playing. The artist described one such conversion to a reporter:

> A touching episode happened at one of the concerts I gave in the South. A farmer and his family were in the audience. He was a strikingly handsome, though uneducated man and had gone along with his people largely for the reason that he would be needed to drive them back home again.
>
> After the recital there was the usual crowd on the stage to greet me with the usual kind of compliments. But what this man said to me meant more than all the applause I received during the course of the evening. He managed to stutter and stammer that a certain part of the program had meant so much to him that it seemed to him joyful, sorrowful and a multitude of other things which he simply could not express, much as he tried. When he finally stopped I gathered that he meant to tell me that the music represented to him an epitome of life. The piece in question was the first movement of the Tschaikovsky concerto.[15]

As a thoroughgoing American, Maud understood the character of her countrymen well enough to know what musical qualities appealed to them and which puzzled them. Asked to comment on the development of public taste, Maud observed:

> Oh—I think the public still rather likes to be dazzled; but it seems to differ somewhat in different communities. Some like the brilliant things, some the emotional, and some the spirituelle-dainty. It's largely a question of putting them in the right mood. A great deal depends on the art of compiling programs—I mean that things must be led up to properly; creating the proper contrasts and so on. The American public doesn't like long, meandering introspective things, but they like things with a definite idea; things that are short and can be grasped in their entirety. They think rather too much about just going from one bar to another and enjoying it as they go along, instead of thinking of a composition as a whole.[16]

Eventually, the violinist wrote out her own prescription for the reluctant male concert-goer on how to enjoy music.[17] In doing so, she made a practical appeal to the male intellect, based on her view that the appeal of music to women is more through the emotions and less through the mind, while to men it is more through understanding and less through feeling.

Maud began with the proposition that all thoughtful listening proceeds from the assumption that the master of musical composition knows his subject and speaks well and hence is worth listening to. The tunes of the masters are just as pleasure-giving as the tunes of the street and "vastly more interesting," while "their charm sinks deeper and lasts longer."

Instead of submitting passively to a "conglomeration of sound," one should "listen for something definite." Maud suggested listening "to the rise and fall of the music—the sky line, as it were—as you might listen to an orator speaking in a foreign tongue." She suggested that a piece of music has all the elements of a peroration: the introduction of the subject, its elaboration, the occasional rising to a climax with a contrasting quiet, level stretch, forceful repetition ("with an imaginary pounding on the desk"), dramatic pauses. Finally, the listener will sense the "coda" that builds to a huge close impressing with its finality or that drops to "an ultimate whisper that leaves one wondering where the music ends and one's soul begins."

Further, Maud urged the concert-goer to listen for rhythm. "Music at its very source is based on the rhythmic or periodic principle. It has pulse and is one manifestation of the great rhythmic scheme of things, which controls all, from the solar system down to man's heartbeat." He should be able to discern whether he can count four or three or six or eight or whether he can walk, march, dance, run, sway, rock, or float to its measure.

In the alternative, Maud urged the listener to "try to catch the spirit of the music, grave, gay, noble, or trifling." To let it suggest colors or pictures, perhaps stirred by a title, could also be helpful in grasping the music.

The musician emphasized the value of "constant repetition of the same piece to familiarize the listener with its character." "Familiarity with worth-while music steadily increases one's enjoyment in it."

The musical form or structure of music, according to the violinist, "is only rhythm elaborated, or rhythm in a large sense." While Maud felt structure could be easily discerned in simple compositions, the real stumbling block for many in her estimation was harmony. "The mass of sound is in fact too complex." To sort it out, Maud suggested following a single voice as it "finds its place in each successive chord throughout a song" and then choosing still another inner voice to follow. Finally, one should follow "two or more inner voices as they weave their way in and out through successive chords. . . . Presently the listener, who is now really learning to listen, will sense one chord melting into another. Let him seize on this perception and repeat it. For, lo, there is the secret—further revelations will come now that the magic key is found."

Maud's recital programming often made it easier for the uninitiated to grasp the musical idea. She sometimes performed as a group shorter pieces which represented various types of music. For instance, she would group dances or pieces demonstrating the importance of rhythm, like Beethoven's Minuet in G, Dvořák's Slavonic Dance in A, Brahms' Hungarian Dance in E Minor, Sarasate's Spanish Dance, *Zapateado*. Or she would group études or studies for unaccompanied violin by Paganini or Fiorillo or give an example of preludes by Bach and Fiorillo. Sometimes she would play a group of American compositions. At other times she would group together pieces representing a particular period or style of violin composition, such as those by Corelli, Tartini, Nardini, and Locatelli. She would also group together songs, including pieces like "Deep River," which brought home the beauty of pure melody.

These "groups" of music were only on the latter half of the program, however. Maud first exposed her audiences to a concerto and then a sonata, or two sonatas of impeccable quality, and even slipped in such classics as Mozart's *Rondo* from the Haffner *Serenade*. She did not withhold display pieces like Wieniawski's *Faust Fantasie*, Hubay's *Hejre Kati*, or Vieuxtemps' *Polonaise* from her audiences. She reveled in them as much as she believed that they too served an educational function, demonstrating another style and period of composition. However, she saved them until the latter portion of the program.

It could not have been easy for an artist of Maud Powell's calibre to continually confront musical ignorance and attempt to transform it into musical awakening and enlightenment. The confrontation could be comical, disheartening, or uplifting, depending on the circumstances. While touring in the South, she was informed that she had been the second great musical attraction that year. The previous one had been an "Italian orchestra." "I was puzzled and asked the woman for particulars, thinking she might, perhaps, refer to the French orchestra from the New Orleans Opera. I learned that the 'Italian orchestra' consisted of three young men with a harp, a sort of mandolin and a banjo!"[18]

Sometimes, if some members of the audience were familiar with violin playing at all, it was of the fiddling variety or purely pyrotechnical. However by 1915 Maud noted with relief: "Only now and then do I encounter such strange notions of what constitutes good violin playing as the one I met with a year or so ago, when a man once asked me why I put off my real violin playing till the end of the recital—that is, when I played a brilliant technical showpiece. He freely admitted that he had never known one who did anything but tricks of that sort on a violin."[19]

Only slowly were American audiences in remote areas becoming used to hearing a single artist in recital as opposed to the familiar miscellaneous concerts, composed of several performers presenting a varied program of vocal and instrumental music and even comedy routines. Maud Powell was one of the first to give purely instrumental recitals and was largely responsible for the acceptance of this mode of performance. Not only was the concert more satisfying, but with Sunny's innovative management, sponsoring organizations found that "one good artist costs less and makes more money for them in the end than four or five mediocre ones," as Maud put it. In a statement which reveals the care Maud took in preparing every last detail of her recitals, she described a stagehand's response to this concert format:

> During the afternoons we visit the theatre, my husband and I, to try to find a simple set for the stage. I don't want a deep set, and I want one as subdued in color as possible. I find that the background makes a difference, even if the audience does not know that it does. Once recently my husband, during one of these afternoon visits, heard one of the stage hands ask another if Miss Powell did "nothing but fiddle the whole evening." The answer was yes, and the questioner didn't seem overpleased.
>
> It is true, however, that during my concerts the stage hands are the most alert listeners. They stand or sit in the wings the whole evening without moving. In the West I have sometimes seen cowpunchers or cowboys enter and take seats in the back of the hall. They expect to get bored and have to leave. But they stay through the concert and then ask for more. It is surprising how much this public cares for good music.[20]

It took an unusual artistic force to overcome the expectations of listeners like these. Yet, invariably, Maud Powell cast a spell over her auditors with the magic of her bow and the magnetic force of her personality. Sometimes she had to call on her sense of humor to win over a particularly nervous or stiff audience:

A sense of humor . . . relieves tension. In small places it has helped tremendously that way in more than one case. You know the towns where the local club has taken a chance in bringing an artist to their midst, by the evening of the concert, usually the music lovers are all wound up and fearful as to the result of their efforts. It is a frequent occurrence to see a pretty girl and her best young man seated in the front row, very stiff and erect and thoroughly self conscious. Well, then, in such a case, when I see the first number does not relax them, I determine to do so by hook or by crook. I do not approve of an artist speaking to her audience, because it breaks the thread of thought, but when the thread is the wrong kind, then I do. An occasional remark such as "the worst will soon be over" has worked wonders.[21]

The artist once commented on the importance of audience response to the recitalist:

Do I always play the piece the same way? No, I do not, never twice in just the same way. . . . The environment is always different, so am I, so are the people, the weather, my mood; the violin, too, has moods sometimes. So you see how impossible for a violinist above all others, to play twice in exactly the same way. This does not mean I have no plan of interpretation, for of course I have; everything is carefully thought out. When that is all done there is still leeway for variety and the unforeseen.

Am I conscious of the audience? Yes, very much so; I do not see how it is possible for an artist not to be, if he is awake to the conditions and influences that surround him. So much depends on the audience. Some sit perfectly still, like wooden images; you feel as though you were playing to a stone wall, so unresponsive are they. Such an audience is a great strain on the player; it takes so much out of him. I feel perfectly exhausted after encountering this kind. On the other hand, a receptive audience never wearies me; I could play twice a day to such houses and never feel the effort. It is unexplainable, this mysterious *rapport* between player and listener. Two or three receptive ones in an audience help the player amazingly; they are able, sometimes, to enthuse a non-responsive crowd.

Especially so if they sit near the front, and have sympathy and knowledge. If they *know* when the piece is well played they show their appreciation by some demonstration at the close. The stolid people about them may look and wonder why they are clapping; but if they keep it up this very fact may arouse the others. Hand clapping is one way in which an audience can show its appreciation, one way in which it can respond and give out. That is what we musicians want, to take the people out of their self consciousness, to call forth response to what we ourselves are giving out to our listeners. Viewed in this light, applause has a deeper meaning than is sometimes considered.[22]

Audiences in these small towns still had much to learn about concert-going. If some did not know how to appreciate the music or enjoy the experience, others did not know anything about concert manners. Those music patrons who were more advanced rejoiced when Maud Powell quietly, unostentatiously, but nonetheless firmly, rebuked ill-mannered listeners. When one couple near the front continued their amusing intermission discussion after the program had resumed, the artist was annoyed, as were nearby patrons. Maud played two pieces and began the third of the set, but when the annoyance continued, the artist quietly dropped her bow, advanced a step and said, "If you don't like the concert, won't you please go to the box office and get your money back?" Whereupon her accompanist picked up the program and the concert continued — with quiet in the front row.

Sometimes, Maud's patience and resourcefulness were sorely tested by thoughtless auditors:

> I realize that a Brahms sonata is a pretty heavy dose for some audiences and on a certain occasion I arranged to place some light and simple pieces immediately after one of these so that the hearers would [not] feel altogether disconcerted. Before beginning I noticed a baby in the audience. It was "goo-gooing" considerably and I had my misgivings as to what might happen during the Brahms sonata. Strangely enough it kept remarkably quiet and the sonata went off well. Then I started Schumann's *Traumerei*. No sooner had I played the first ten bars than there arose loud "goo-goos" from the baby. I was disconcerted and I stopped and addressed the audience, telling them that I had them in the hollow of my hand and did not want to lose them, that the baby was undoubtedly a dear one but that I

could not continue while it "goo-gooed." Still the mother did not make the slightest attempt to leave. I played a little further and the same performance began again. I came to an abrupt halt in anger and told the audience very emphatically that the concert hall was not a nursery.

Then the mother took the hint, got up and left and the audience broke into applause. I played the rest of the music, still trembling with rage though fortunately I managed to control my bow.[23]

Sometimes unbounded audience enthusiasm taxed the performers unreasonably. The audience commonly demanded an encore after each selection, thus doubling the concert fare. The Powell Trio's Los Angeles appearance prompted the *Los Angeles Evening News* to devote a two-column editorial to the bad manners of the "concert hog." Six of eight numbers were "encored insistently and the artists forced to respond with additional contributions before the entertainment could proceed."[24]

During Maud's first appearance with the Seattle Symphony Orchestra in 1908, enthusiasm threatened to overwhelm her art. The audience seized the first breathing space in Saint-Saëns' *Introduction and Rondo Capriccioso* to burst into spontaneous applause and continued to seize such opportunities, a response which the press thought "must have been a pleasure to Maud Powell." In fact, it must have been difficult for her to continue. The artist had to play numerous encores for an audience which felt "as if her violin were simply an instrument, a speaking thing with a mind and a great, passionate heart—a thing which interprets rather than which plays."[25]

One of the problems confronting Maud as she toured was finding suitable concert halls in which to perform. The local "opry house," the Y.M.C.A. auditorium, churches, and even the modern theaters too often presented atmospheric or scheduling problems. Unexpected difficulties could ambush the artist who dared concertize off the beaten track:

> I had an experience once in a town in Montana which illustrates the disadvantage sometimes experienced in giving a recital in a local theater. I had been announced to give a recital on this occasion and on the arrival of my party in the city we inspected the theater. The building had been erected only a few years, but the stage had been used as a roller skating rink to which the children of the city had free access when no performance was being given. The place had

apparently never been cleaned. The floor was littered with waste paper, discarded programs, peanut shells and various kinds of debris. We were discouraged. My manager decided to postpone the recital until the next night and forthwith took a half page advertisement in the local paper announcing the postponement and assuring the patrons of the concert that they would be able to attend without fear of soiling their garments. He then hired a force of men to give the theater a house-cleaning such as it had never had. They got together two great stacks of dirt and refuse, which were piled in the corners and covered with canvas. The next night we were greeted by a large audience which contained a number of persons who had never dared to enter the building because of its unsanitary condition. Its appearance on the night of my recital was a revelation to them.[26]

The plucky American noted happily that "there are some notable exceptions in many of our cities." In place of the local theater, Maud forthrightly recommended the local high school auditorium. She pointed out: "In most cities it has the right atmosphere, its acoustics are good and it is kept far cleaner than the average privately owned hall or theater."[27]

In later years, in the larger cities Maud played recitals on a stage occupied by several hundred listeners, an arrangement to which she strongly objected:

> The audience's place is in the auditorium. . . . There the privilege is theirs to criticise everything about the player from the manner of holding the violin to her gown. But I object to it at close range. To begin with, scores of people on the stage exhaust an artist's magnetism — literally constitute a tremendous extra drain on it and impose an increased nervous tension. They also attract the attention of those in the body of the house to themselves, they become self-conscious, their applause distracts and seems forced. Their presence on the stage puts an end to the illusion and atmosphere which every artist, whether actor, singer or player should create. They see the mechanism which should be hidden and mysterious. I went through such an experience on my tour and shall not go through others.[28]

This disadvantage at the 4,300-seat Cleveland Hippodrome was offset by its "perfect" acoustics, which Maud observed "play a greater part in the success of a public concert than most people realize." In the Hippodrome, Maud explained, "the artist has those wonderful silences through which his slightest tones carry clearly and sweetly. I have played not only solos, but chamber music in this hall, and was always sorry to stop playing."[29]

Clearly, Maud did everything she could to improve concert conditions in America by enlarging and educating audiences and encouraging the genesis and development of musical activities in each community. Beyond that, she devoted considerable energy toward nurturing aspiring American musicians who, in their turn, would rise to the expanding opportunities and obligations of their profession and meet the needs of increasingly sophisticated audiences. She knew that her mission was to inspire and teach, but she could never confine herself to a small circle of violin pupils. The world was forever her classroom and all the people her students.

Riding Circuit for Her Faith

A POWERFUL EDUCATIONAL FORCE ON THE CONCERT PLATFORM, Maud instinctively responded to the needs of students and teachers who were in the audience. On her 1907 tour of California, one of Maud's concerts was attended by a large group of students from a music academy headed by Katherine Tingley.

At the concert one could feel that the artist was both pleased and inspired by the large group of Point Loma students in the pit, and, filling the boxes on the left, the enthusiastic glowing faces of the younger violin pupils. . . .

These students were not announced, but something of the quality of their tense interest, their musicianly appreciation, must have reached Maud Powell as she played. She looked up and smiled again and again as those young enthusiasts applauded, and then — which proved that she knew that *they* knew — she came out and played a Fiorillo *Etude* (the simple and golden 35th, the first part), something never heard outside of a classroom. . . . Maud Powell played it — and how we sat and listened! And back of the smile upon her lips, as she looked up at the boxes at the close, was a merry smile in the eye which said plainly, "Sh-h! This is our secret!"

One scarcely wishes to speak of her work in music critic fashion; of her bow technique, the *spiccato* that was ethereal in its softness and purity, the *staccato volant* that seemed not to have been created but born spontaneously from sheer, winged joy in life; the *legato* of which no one could say of a single tone, "This is its beginning and this its ending," so golden was the fashioning of it, so tender and indefinable the leaving of each tone, so perfect was the mastery of the bow at those critical places which mark the beginning and the leaving off of the noble, sustained stroke; so classic and simple in poise and sweep was the bow arm, so complete was her mastery of all left-hand technique. One did not need to ask, "Who was her teacher?" There was that in her work, individual as it was, which proclaimed the touch of the greatest of modern masters.[1]

What teaching Maud did, she did on the wing, listening with infinite patience in the towns she visited to young people aspiring to musical careers. The great violinist's advice was eagerly sought by students, and she willingly and forthrightly delivered her prescriptions under a variety of circumstances.

The distinguished violinist Louis Kaufman wrote that his career was made possible by "the good advice of Maud Powell, who had graciously listened to me after one of her Portland concerts."[2] Maud told his father that the boy "had talent but was poorly trained." Kaufman (b. 1905) related, "I always appreciated the honesty and frankness of Maud Powell towards my efforts and she strongly urged my father to send me to New York as soon as possible for serious study." As a young child, Kaufman was taken by his father to practically every concert of the notable violinists who visited his native Portland. He heard Kreisler, Elman, Heifetz, Zimbalist, Spalding, and Powell, who was "much admired" and whose example remained fixed forever in his mind: "I still have vivid memories of her tall statuesque appearance, and even though we always sat in the balcony of the local auditorium, her tone was very bright and clear. I was impressed by her dash and brilliance. There was no trace of a dull academic approach. . . . I remember her impeccable intonation, an unusual control of the left hand and a supple and powerful bow arm. . . . "

The respected violin teacher Karl V. Brown sought Maud Powell's advice when, as a youth, he encountered her on a train:

I walked more than three miles from our farm home to the railroad station of the branch line of the C. and O.R.R.: then transferred to the main line to Charleston and walked across the city to the "Opera House" for a thrilling evening. After I was seated on the train for the return home Miss Powell and her accompanist Francis Moore entered the same car where I was seated. There was only one empty seat left. Miss Powell was seated and Mr. Moore was left standing. I signaled to him that I would share my seat with him. When he saw that I had one of the programs in my hand he asked how far I had traveled and when I gave him the information, he said that Miss Powell should know about it and he introduced me to her. She was very charming and chatted like an old friend. When she learned that I was interested in learning to play the violin she suggested [I] would become a good orchestra violinist or a teacher. She said that the virtuoso stage was reached through early training and much hard work.[3]

Maud fervently endorsed teachers whose pupils gave evidence of sound training. In December 1912, she wrote a letter in support of Henri Ern, a classmate of hers in Berlin who had opened a studio in Chicago. He had taught Florence Hardeman, a fine violinist, and became the teacher of José Figueroa of the distinguished Figueroa family of musicians from Puerto Rico. Her letter reads:

> I cannot speak too highly of Mr. Ern's musicianship. His pupil, Miss Hardeman, showed most convincingly that she had been carefully, conscientiously and rightly taught. If all the violin talent I have found scattered over the States could be so well nurtured, we should soon become a musical nation.
>
> Please use my name in as forcible a way as you like in Mr. Ern's behalf. I should be only too happy if it could be of real use to him.[4]

She signed off, "In haste but earnestly."

Maud even judged violin and piano competitions sponsored by the National Federation of Music Clubs. Listening to the contestants unseen behind a screen convinced Maud and her fellow judges that there was no sex distinction in music.[5]

Precious time which Maud might otherwise have spent getting badly-needed rest was cheerfully devoted to teaching a nation how to study and teach music. Always interested in and enthusiastic about the advancement of musical understanding among the American people, she nevertheless saw clearly the shortcomings of American cultivation and appreciation of her art form. Sometimes the awkwardness and misdirection of American attempts to master the violin brought forth outcries of frustration from the native artist. Because the technology disallowed sonatas and concertos, her own recordings were working against all she had sought to convey through her careful programming. Maud vented her frustration in a letter to Edith Winn, describing a scene which was too often repeated:

> A student of the violin, seventeen years old, who has studied five years, and who has plenty of talent, producing a pleasing tone, played to me yesterday, and what do you think she played? A Ser-

enade by Drdla! And then she asked me if I thought she could some day become a player like Maud Powell if she went on working!

There is that deplorable tendency in America to study amateurishly and yet have artistic aspirations. Teachers and parents have no high standards. The great aim seems to be to play something pleasing. This girl, like many others, was striving to play rubato and badly imitating artistic subtleties before she had learned to enunciate clearly a simple line of melody. Training on the Handel Sonatas, David or De Bériot Concertos, Kreutzer and Rode Concertos, and others, was what she ought to have had. If we could only institute an educational branch in the talking machines, it might help some. These young players think that because our artists do short encore numbers for the machines, — like *Traumerei*, Dvořák's *Humoreske*, or Saint-Saëns' *Le Cygne*, that they must make these their life study or at least daily food. If they could but realize that these trifles are but as tiny petals of small flowers that grow in season on the musical tree, and that this tree of musical knowledge takes a long time to grow and must be watched and nurtured and trained for years before it reaches dignified stature, we might hope for better things artistically.[6]

The American tendency to be in a hurry, which Joachim noted, worked at cross-purposes to any artistic development. Maud understood only too well just how much patience and hard work were required to play an instrument well:

Too many Americans who take up the violin professionally do not realize that the mastery of the instrument is a life study, that without hard, concentrated work they cannot reach the higher levels of their art. Then, too, they are too often inclined to think that if they have a good tone and technic that this is all they need. They forget that the musical instinct must be cultivated; they do not attach enough importance to musical surroundings: to hearing and understanding music of every kind, not only that written for the violin. They do not realize the value of *ensemble* work and its influence as an educational factor of the greatest artistic value. . . .

No student who looks on music primarily as a thing apart in his existence, as a bread-winning tool, as a craft rather than an art, can ever mount to the high places. So often girls [who sometimes lack the practical vision of boys], although having studied but a few years, come to me and say: "My one ambition is to become a great *virtuoso* on the violin! I want to begin to study the great concertos!"

And I have to tell them that their first ambition should be to become musicians—to study, to know, to understand music before they venture on its interpretation. Virtuosity without musicianship will not carry one far these days. In many cases these students come from small inland towns, far from any music center, and have a wrong attitude of mind. They crave the glamor of footlights, flowers and applause, not realizing that music is a speech, an idiom, which they must master in order to interpret the works of the great composers.[7]

How well Maud Powell knew that unremitting mental and physical discipline was the foundation for her art—one which could be neglected by even the veteran artist only at her peril.

[W]ithout a technic more than adequate for the music being studied, a rapid development of interpretative power is difficult. I like to compare the violinist, in the development of his technic, with the baseball player or the golf player. To both, "good form" is a sine qua non. Without technic every exciting moment of the game finds the contestant undone. But a ball playing technic is the end of all—the final test. In the life of the artist technic is necessary, but not for itself; he needs technical accomplishment to enable him not alone to meet the excitement of a public performance with equanimity, he needs it also so that while his spirit may soar to the clouds and like Prometheus bring down fire from heaven to mortals, his fingers and bow may remain on the terra firma of his instrument to faithfully interpret the inspired message.[8]

The daughter of Bramwell Powell also understood that the discipline of mind and self were the principal objects of education in the broadest sense, a discipline one could learn as easily from instruction in music as in any other field. Noting that "[t]here is in America a growing tendency upon the part of the younger generation to disregard all forms of discipline," Maud recognized that "insisting upon attendance at lessons has as much moral influence as it has musical advantage." Like her father before her, Maud believed that the process of learning to play a musical instrument was invaluable to the development of the responsible and well-rounded adult, regardless of the ultimate musical attainment.

Asked to comment on the general education necessary for serious violinists, Maud reflected a moment and then replied very earnestly:

The more education in all fields the better it is for the musician. But the musical education and especially the acrobatic, physical (technical) part of that education must begin very young indeed and take first place. The first object of education, viz., discipline of mind and self, can be achieved through specialized training. Then, as the pupil grows older and stronger, information should be acquired to the utmost extent commensurate with health and strength.[9]

Another reporter disclosed more of Maud's thinking:

Upon being questioned about the place of the violin in a general musical education, Madame Powell gave it the prominence it deserves, but no more. She thinks every singer should learn to play for the resultant ear training. Singers who have not learned the instrument when young were not urged to take it up, but they should hear every good violinist possible to learn more about phrasing. In turn every violinist should listen to excellent singers in order to learn breathing, to make melodies sing. "All my life I've tried to sing on the violin." She then spoke of the exquisite singing of Sembrich and Blauvelt, both of whom play the violin, and mentioned other singers who listen to the playing of violinists whenever the opportunity offers.[10]

For music students caught up in the music they are producing, she had this warning:

Music is so utterly self-satisfying that one occasionally forgets to be expressive in a way that shall convey the meaning of the composer to all hearers. By this I mean that while one may personally feel the emotion latent in the composition and enjoy the task of performing the work one may forget to play it in a way that will convey this emotion to the most uninformed listener. To accomplish this end musicians should cultivate the habit of listening to themselves, to hear their own playing objectively. This is a thing that is by no means as easy as it seems, but the importance of which cannot be over estimated.[11]

The violinist prescribed further precautions:

The very first thing in playing in public is to free oneself of all distrust in one's own powers. To do this, nothing must be left to chance. One should not have to give a thought to strings, bow, etc. All should be in proper condition. Above all the violinist should play with an accompanist who is used to accompanying him. It seems superfluous to emphasize that one's program numbers must have been mastered in every detail. Only then can one defy nervousness, turning excess of emotion into inspiration.[12]

When in July 1909 *The Etude* dedicated an entire issue to "Woman's Work in Music," Maud Powell was asked to edit the violin department, the first time a woman had done so in the twenty-six years of the publication's existence. The American artist took advantage of the opportunity to encourage young women to study the violin seriously and to guide them with words of advice about violin study, advice which stands impeccable to this day. "The American Girl and Her Violin" vividly reveals the devotion, discipline, enthusiasm, and genius behind the musician's art. [13]

Not every girl could reach the virtuoso stage, but Maud held out the promise of "beautiful work, honorable work, work that is needed and wanted" by "quiet workers of honest endeavor, with high ideals and adequate equipment." To the girl who is "ambitious and alive with interest" for her work, "there is promising art-soil throughout the length and breadth of this big land of ours, from which a rich harvest may be reaped." But "a healthy seed" must be planted with care and "the young shoot . . . watched and nurtured with intelligence, faith and enthusiasm."

Maud Powell then revealed the true secret of her personal power and success—courage as well as intelligence, faith, and enthusiasm—the thoroughly positive attitude with which she lived her life and which pervaded her existence:

> Take heart, young musician—you who are too conscious of your limitations. Beethoven himself hath said: "The barriers are not erected that shall say to talent, 'Thus far and have no further.' " Cultivate courage. Have a oneness of purpose. Keep at it. Go on trying. I have heard a pupil play, and play creditably, a piece full of difficulties that she had utterly balked at in the beginning. Her imagination had magnified the difficulties out of all proportion, and had diminished her own powers of achievement in inverse ratio. Try! You do not know what you can do till you have tried. I am always disappointed in the girl who, on being introduced to me after a concert, says, "Oh, Miss Powell, I feel as if I never could touch the violin again—it seems so hopeless now." Much more to my liking is the girl who says, in a scarcely audible voice and with upper lip aquiver, "Oh, I feel as though I could do *anything* now—I just feel inspired!" Of *course*, enthusiasm is going to help you along. There are plenty of hard places to be conquered, but enthusiasm will make them easier. Indeed, enthusiasm is an asset that will be valu-

able throughout your life, and if you want your career to count for something, remember that it is she of the abiding faith and unquenchable enthusiasm whose work "tells" in the long run. As for opportunity, apathy will prevent you from seeing it, and a lack of courage from seizing it; and before that psychological moment arrives, which may mean an important turning point in your career, your apathetic and timid attitude of mind will have interfered with your progress and kept you in a state of unpreparedness. Then your rival, perhaps someone with less talent than yourself, but with a saner, stronger character, will perceive the opportunity, make the most of it and leave you and your duller companions wondering discontentedly why some people have so much better luck than others.

The violinist followed her spiritual advice with some very specific points on how to practice:

I. *Concentrate*. Concentrate your thoughts on your work, completely and absolutely. One hour of absorbed practice is worth forty of the casual sort.

II. *Play in tune*. The worst of all violinistic crimes is to be untrue in pitch.

III. *Practice scales religiously*. Play them slowly and with perfect evenness, both as to fingering and bowing.

IV. *Practice slowly* all difficult or intricate passages; also, jumps, trills, spiccato, staccato, arpeggios, etc.

V. *Practice long bows* slowly, slowly, slowly. Draw out the tone. Pull it and spin it, weave it, but never press it out or squeeze the string. By *pressing* the string with the bow you can check the natural vibration, and without changing the position of the left hand the smallest fraction, you can actually lower the pitch of the note you are producing.

VI. *Memorize everything*, including scales, etudes, pieces and difficult passages in chamber music.

VII. *Keep in mind the structure* of the composition while practicing separate phrases, difficult passages, etc. Do not let your playing or your memory become "patchy" — keep each measure mentally in its place; that is, in a correct relation, structurally, to the whole.

VIII. *"Vorspielen."* This German word means "to play before." Play your studies or pieces over in their entirety before any long-suffering friend who will listen. You will be amazed at the sore spots that will reveal themselves, and will make it your business to heal them as quickly as possible.

IX. *Hear other violinists.* You will listen in spite of yourself. Then *apply that kind of listening* to your own work. There will be more surprises in store for you.

X. *Love your instrument as yourself.* But love your art more than either. Keep the fires of enthusiasm burning. Nothing was ever accomplished without faith and enthusiasm.

Another list of pointers followed close behind her ten practice rules: Listen to every great artist; Don't hurry; Don't drag; Don't blur the passage work; Don't scratch; Don't play absent-mindedly or carelessly; Don't leave the hair at either the point or nut of the bow unused, thereby curtailing possibilities in phrasing; Don't leave out the accents and other marks of interpretation; Don't forget that rhythm is the first and most vital element in all arts, and most obviously so in music; Don't lose your poise; Don't overdo the vibrato; Vary the vibrato in keeping with the style and period of the piece; Don't alter the composer's meaning, especially in the classics, unless on the very best authority. Here, she paused to elaborate on a subject dear to her heart:

And let me say right here that the dictums of cultivated talent are safer to follow than the unreflecting outbursts of genius. Young Elman, for instance, is a law unto himself. I sat spellbound one afternoon listening to his Tschaikowsky Concerto. No one approaches him, it seems to me, in that school of composition. But the distortion of tempi and the liberties taken with text were bad models for an imitator, whether artist or pupil. With all my admiration for the amazing, the unaccountable genius of the boy, I cannot bring myself to accept his interpretation of the Beethoven Concerto. Beethoven is scarcely a vehicle for emotional self-expression. Rather is this concerto an art expression of perfect line, perfect poise, perfect beauty; a noble thought, nobly conceived, a thing for all time, pure, true, complete, like the best Greek statuary and to be approached only in a spirit of complete self-abnegation. Now, the fullness, the vitality of self-expression of this gifted boy, the lovely cheek of his artistic unconsciousness, are glorious. We of Anglo-Saxon origin know little of spontaneity of expression as exemplified in the Slavic and Latin races. When we cultivate spontaneity it is apt to be superficial. Our artistic emotions are not aroused within us creatively. Artistic self-expression is not a necessity. We are stirred from without and not within (artistically), and we are forever suffering intense and absurd self-consciousness in art, as in other matters. We have a horror of being sentimental or ludicrous. The young girl actually blushes when her teacher tries to induce her to play with "expression." There is a diffidence that stands between ourselves and our means of expression.

Then, the "don'ts" continued: Don't become an abject slave to "playing in" your fingers with scales, but don't play to have a good time merely; Keep your critical self always alert and watchful; Don't practice seventeen hours a day, nor even seven (three hours is sufficient); Don't forget to *think* out your interpretation away from your instrument; Don't get discouraged; Don't get in a rut, but don't leave technic to the chance of the moment; Don't expect your teacher to do your work for you.

Maud emphasized that "on *you*, the *you* that is within you, depends your success." One must keep the limelight of criticism focused on oneself. "It is stagnation to be satisfied. The artistic spirit never ceases to reach out for greater perfection."

The rapidity with which Maud Powell memorized music was considered awesome by those who knew her. When asked to explain how she committed music to memory, she answered "by ear." Pressed to say whether she could call off the individual notes if necessary, she looked at her interrogator with surprise and responded, "Why, indeed no; I try to get just as far away from the printed page as is possible." "But suppose you forget?" he insisted. "But I do not forget," she replied. "But suppose you should, if you could not call up the printed page and its individual notes, what would you do?" her questioner insisted. She shrugged and said, "Well, I don't know what on earth I would do."[14] (Maud could, in fact, write out the music from memory.)

In concentrating on the rapidity with which she was known to memorize a work, her interviewer had lost sight of the thoroughness with which she grasped a piece of music in its entirety, making her musical memory virtually infallible. In a brief article designed to assist other musicians in memorizing, Maud revealed the determination and intellect which backed her work:

> Some musicians visualize the score as they memorize, others get the composition by ear almost unconsciously, still others pack away the matter in their brain cells by rote, i.e., repetition and sequence. The chief things are thought, work and determination.

One should understand the composition structurally, harmonically and aesthetically before beginning to memorize. A good plan is to practice mentally, away from the instrument, associating the correct fingering, the right speed and tonal quality with each note as it is played. Also remember the relation of each note to the whole phrase and the relation of each phrase to the whole musical structure.

Rely on repetition till the fingers move subconsciously in spite of nervousness or temporary aberration of mind. Before playing a composition in public, try it on the dog — otherwise — long-suffering friends. In any event, if you decide to learn a piece, no matter how short or unimportant, learn it, that's all, and don't give up till you've got it.[15]

Perhaps the truest explanation for Maud's infallible memory was that she simply saw beyond the notes to the music itself, a trait she revealed while advising young people on violin study in "The American Girl and Her Violin":

Notes and rests, with expression marks, are mere symbols by means of which the composer tries to express an abstract musical idea in black and white. These symbols are wholly inadequate to express the real essence of music. The student should, after studying the notes and signs thoroughly, and reading the composer's printed intentions with perfect accuracy, try to make of the music an abstract essence, as the composer first conceived it — a disembodied, impalpable sequence of musical sound.

Maud further advised students to memorize everything, including scales, etudes, pieces, and difficult passages in chamber music, in order to develop their musical memory. But above all, she stressed Bach:

Memorize Bach — and more Bach. If you play the piano, memorize Bach on the piano. He is complex, intellectual, full of musical fibre, and should be daily food. He is more than food; he is an intellectual tonic. And you will find that all others will seem easy after Bach. But guard against the stiff wrist in the right hand and against stiff wrist and fingers in the left. He demands strength in the right arm, which stiffens your bowing if you are not careful. And he keeps your left hand so much in one position that you will lose elasticity in both wrist and fingers if you do not conscientiously guard against the tendency to tighten muscles. You must constantly think of *flexible firmness* when you play Bach.

Maud was so interested in violin study that she prepared her own book of exercises for violinists, the fate of which is unknown. She also advocated the recording of violin exercises for students' use.

Beyond the purely technical, Maud was concerned that the American artist develop as a true *American* virtuoso, not as a mere reflection of some European school of violin playing. An American musician had a duty, in her mind, to reflect the unique wellsprings of his country's greatness and to reach out to his fellow countrymen to lift them to ever-broadening horizons: "Yet an artist must be a virtuoso in the modern sense to do his full duty. And here in America that duty is to help those who are groping for something higher and better musically; to help without rebuffing them."[16]

She found the fulfillment of this ideal frustrated by the absence of inner depth:

> Our artists in various fields are clever, sprightly, full of technique. Some of them are trying to do the real thing, and I feel like taking an axe to get it out of them! There is more of liveliness and high spirits than of spirituality. We don't live deeply enough. We depend too much on the big outer stimulus — like a baseball game — to rouse us. . . .
>
> I sometimes think America needs a stroke that will humble her pride — bitter hardship like national defeat or the burden of heavy debt. We must be turned away from these things that we possess to a deeper inner life.
>
> The Civil War and the long strain of the years that led to the break produced the New England poetry and the melodies of Stephen Foster. I do not mean that the artist himself must go out and fight. But he expresses his generation. And this generation has not suffered.[17]

Ever present in Maud's ideal was her concern for assimilation and synthesis. Asked to explain her ideal to a reporter for *Musical America* in early 1916, Maud gave oral expression to an ideal she herself personified:

> What is my ideal? Ah, there, you ask a big question! One should have all the schools at one's command. Especially is this true of the American artist, for the American — above all others — must be eclec-

tic in taste and take from all other nations in spirit, he must use his "melting pot," so to speak. He must be analytical first, then synthetic, building his structure out of component parts of all nations, all classes, all schools, all styles; then he must combine them in such beautifully adjusted and well chosen proportions that the result is a satisfying and well nigh perfect whole.

Maud had great hopes for the development of what she called the "American School of Violin Playing":

I think there is a tremendous amount of talent here in America, but there is also a lack of self-reliance among the young students, and a woeful lack of confidence in American teachers. Americans are too apt to think it necessary to go abroad to study, whereas, I believe that it is possible to get the real foundation necessary to a musician who would be an artist, in our own Country. The advantages of European study, and these are the only advantages in my mind, are the opportunities one has there of hearing so much music that is fine, and in discussing music with other students. The American people, those who patronize music, I mean, are much to blame for this sentiment for having too little confidence in their own judgment, they feel that artists must have the European stamp before they can be considered worth hearing. The people must be educated, musically educated, so that art, true art, will be appreciated and understood, and consequently patronized, whether it be a home product or the result of foreign study. For this reason, I believe it will be a great many years before we have a real artistic appreciation, and before we develop an American School — but it is sure to come, for we have splendid material with which to work. The great financial genius of the American people naturally checks the development of artistic sentiment, but though latent, it is nevertheless there, and will be brought out. The time will come when there will be even more reason than there was in the Eighties for the question so frequently asked while in Europe: "Why do you come over here to finish your studies; why not continue in your own Country?"[18]

Maud Powell's advice to aspiring violinists was in keeping with her vision of America's musical destiny. To Edith Winn, she gave expression to her faith in and hope for the future of American violin playing as well as American composition:

The best points of all schools should be assimilated. It is clearly a case of Zangwill's idea of the melting pot. What sort of school will be boiled down ultimately, only time will tell. We are critical and analytical, and it is to be hoped, synthetic. Why should we not build up a school of our own? I mean a school of playing, not composition, though I also believe we may and should have a school of composition. That may not take rank with the Russian, German, French or Italian conviction of expression, but shall be a lower form, reaching all degrees of people and culture. The greatest good for the greatest number. Valuable in a larger artistic sense to the race in general than to the small cultured musical world.[19]

A woman of broad experience and profound insight and learning, Maud understood America's musical development in terms of the character of the American people and their advancement along scientific, educational, and other artistic lines. As the First World War loomed over Europe, threatening to destroy the old order, Maud saw increasingly that America's unique qualities offered hope for the evolution of an authentic school of art, literature, music, which, in its democratic rather than aristocratic nature, would be universal, a reflection of America's "melting pot" origins or character.

This new "finding ourselves" musically is not a mere passing phase. The question is so large and involves so many interlocked developments in other arts and sciences, to say nothing of our national soul awakening, that it were impossible to go into the subject thoroughly in a few words. I venture to hazard, however, that music will be democratized and brought to the great public more than the world has dreamed of heretofore. The process will not so much benefit music per se, as it will benefit that same great public. America has been the land of opportunity for untold thousands of emigrants who have come to us from all quarters of the earth. Their children have received, in most instances, a pretty good common school education and have gone out into the world to succeed better than they could have hoped to succeed in the old country. What has this done to us as a nation? We are quick, brainy, full of mental vitality and nervous energy; we are straightforward, democratic, practical. We have amazing inventiveness and have established institutions for the benefit of the great public. We have most of the virtues that one might care to enumerate—but not for one moment can we pride ourselves on being cultured. (The reader must not confuse culture with obnoxious "Kultur," which is another thing altogether.) Now I feel that as we have raised standards of education, and of opportunity for the masses in this great democracy of ours and have given every man a chance to live and to have his say in the government, so shall music in its process of democratization gain a great vitality and make a new place for itself in the world. It will become a necessary part of the people's individual life, their family life, their civic and national life. What the art gains in this evolution of robustness it will lose in distinction and "apartness." It will be democratic—not aristocratic. It will be cast in trenchant, unfurbelowed workday form. It will strike between the eyes and find its way straight to elemental reaction in the heart—as Sousa's marches find their way thither through the toes!

Out of all this, in good time, say in several generations, we shall probably evolve a real school of national art, literature and music. Why think about that now? Such things must come, evolve, normally—else they are likely to be artificial and unlasting.[20]

To parents and students alike, Maud gave practical advice concerning musical careers. In 1911 she wrote her prescriptions forthrightly, in American terms, putting the subject on a thoroughly practical plane.

First of all, she advised, a successful career is to be measured entirely by "the attainment of the end in view." But in establishing the standard, one must take into account the American environment. The "American mind is essentially practical, above whatever artistic instincts it may possess. The duty of developing a talent for the good of the race does not appeal to the American mind in its present stage of artistic advancement." As Americans, "our standard must be the economic one: . . . how to earn a good living with the violin." Maud acknowledged that this was making a "commercial question out of an artistic pursuit," but she countered with the fact that "business methods are necessary to keep art on its feet." She knew that "our wonderful but intensely practical country will never develop the arts except on a sound businesslike basis."

The violinist bemoaned the prevailing ignorance concerning the life of the professional musician. It was a mistake to think that a musician's life is easy and enjoyable. "Enjoyable it is for those who love their art for its own sake, but easy—never." She wrote that she worked harder "today than . . . when I was a student," and that this was "the common experience of all artists."

Maud believed that it was possible to make a good living with the violin provided that ambitions squared with talent and circumstances. Avenues of income were open to the teacher and the orchestra player, but Maud added this warning to the would-be virtuoso: "[B]eware the long, hard road that lies between gifted youth and the virtuoso estate! I have traveled it. I know every obstacle. For every step forward I have paid heavy toll. Let me reckon the cost for you in time, money, mental wear and tear and physical stress and put the matter squarely before you, pupil or parent—to decide whether the prize is worth the struggle."

Maud, who was paying the virtuoso's cost in her own substance, set forth the prerequisites: real talent, strength of character, endless patience, courage, stamina, good nerves, a strong physique, a parent or relative willing to sacrifice everything else in life to look after the pupil during the preparation period, and money enough to sustain the study period and then to launch the young artist's career.

Even with all these qualities, "the reward is by no means in sight," Maud wrote feelingly. "You are in the position of a man who has toiled and slaved, stripped himself, his family, his friends—for what? A ticket in a lottery. After you have spent your youth in the sweatshop of art, you are quite likely to be snubbed by the public." An artist with a flawless technique and wonderful artistic development may not be able to "swell box-office receipts by a single dollar" for lack of that elusive quality—magnetism. "The great public is moved by human qualities more than by art qualities," she warned. And magnetism is "something money cannot buy nor any teacher impart."

Maud further warned against making false comparisons in evaluating talent at an early age, reminding parents that artists such as Kreisler were playing the big concertos at twelve. Even prodigies might not realize the promise of their early youth, for "success is as much a question of character as of talent. Precocity is a foe of self-control and leads many to abandon the rigorous self-denial that is inseparable from the virtuoso career."

To be successfully launched on a career, the artist must understand his function. "The general public goes to concerts in search of entertainment and not education," Maud cautioned. "It seeks the stimulus of agreeable music, agreeably performed, and it is not particularly interested in art." The young concert artist must adapt his programs accordingly. "After he has convinced the public that it is a pleasure to listen to him, he can lead them by gradual stages to the higher phases of his art." On the other hand, bidding for "cheap applause" buries his chances of ever becoming a "real artist."

Even with a successful launching, Maud knew that a living income was not possible for at least two or three years. "Meanwhile, the expenses keep up. In fact, they never end." Then, too, the hard work is endless: "Even when the success is lasting, the hard work and self-denial must go on relentlessly. From the sweatshop of preparation, the virtuoso passes on to complete slavery in the house of art. Where one is wholly and sincerely in love with his art, there is compensation. But the artist must find his reward elsewhere than in cold cash." Maud once wrote that she had lived a rich life, but that "no business man could consider for a moment that the investment has proved a financial success." One had to bear in mind that "art was created for the artist and not for the public."

Maud was more encouraging about the life of the orchestra player. The income compared favorably with the average professional's income, but there were other rewards as well. She viewed the good orchestra player as an artist, and "in the estimation of thinking musicians, he ranks far higher than the mediocre virtuoso, while he performs a far greater service for his art." Maud took the opportunity at this point in her article to "record her astonishment at what seems to be an almost national aversion to learning instruments of reed and brass. Somewhere, possibly, in this country, there is a native-born oboe player, but I have never met him." She encouraged Americans to take up these instruments, saying that they offered the possibility of a good income and year-round employment.

Maud specifically encouraged women to enter the orchestral field, noting the opportunities with women's orchestras and observing that the door to all-male orchestras was now slightly cracked. Even musicians' unions and the public were not putting up any bars. She had spoken with women violinists in hotel and restaurant orchestras in the Northwest and found them earning good money.

Maud's last word to the American parent was that "a musical talent is not a thing to be stifled or rooted out. It ought to be encouraged and developed along common-sense lines." She firmly believed that "wherever that is done, a musical education will prove to be a commercial asset."[21]

Not everyone could have a career in music, but in Maud's view that did not deny them the opportunity to grace their lives with music. Amateur music makers had just as important a role to play as did professionals in expanding musical culture throughout the land by enlarging the circle of good listeners. Maud stressed the importance of music in the home as a means of cultivating appreciation for music, and as end in itself—for the joy that it can bring to the less gifted music-lover. She could not over-emphasize the importance of good listeners:

> Music can hardly be said to exist if it lies dormant in the printed page. To become a living, vital thing with influence, it must be heard. *There must be listeners.* The artist, by his very nature, sensitive, emotional, longing to make propaganda for the true and beautiful, should find sympathy, encouragement and an answering enthusiasm in his fellow-beings. If he can convey but a hint of the secret that the masters have revealed to him through the printed page, he does not live in vain. Oh, the misery of having something of infinite, though perhaps esoteric, beauty fall on ears that do not understand! And then to hear the uncultured listener affirm somewhat proudly and defiantly that he knows nothing whatever about music—but he knows what he likes! Such a soul is a sealed book. Little do people realize what joys lie in store for them if they would seek and humbly prepare their minds with a little study.[22]

Maud Powell refused to despair of America's improvement along those lines. One alert reporter spotted a good story behind the shudder which rippled down the famous violinist's spine as she attended a concert at Carnegie Hall during which listeners clapped too soon. The reporter must have known that there was never better copy than when Maud was aroused to speak, since she skillfully drew from the artist a wonderful expression of frustration, insight, hope, wonder, and faith in America's musical future. The violinist's original thinking is evident in every line:

AMERICA IS IN NEED OF MORE AMATEUR MUSICIANS,
WHO WOULD IN TURN STIMULATE NATIVE ARTISTS

An Intelligent Audience That Knows When to Clap and When to Keep Its Hands in Its Muff Has Yet to Be Developed in This Country, Says Maud Powell

"America needs trained audiences, not more trained musicians," declares Maud Powell, who has been facing audiences pretty much all over this terrestrial ball for something over thirty years and ought to know. She was getting her wraps on in Carnegie Hall after a symphony concert to which she had listened luxuriously from a seat in row J, where she had been (though little she kenned!) under observation all the afternoon by the reporter, off duty and enjoying a seat in row K which the music critic didn't happen to want that day. And every time some enthusiastic listener who loved the music not wisely but too well burst into a frenzied kid glove pattycaking at least three beats too early the reporter had observed a shudder go through the listener in row J, or a pained look pass between Mme. Powell and Godfrey Turner, her husband. Once the reporter was quite sure she heard a low moan escape the violinist. And so of course after the concert instead of rushing out to catch the first bus the reporter hung over the seat in front and asked for remarks on audiences.

Thereupon the violinist [made the foregoing remarks and continued]:

"American audiences do not keep pace with the increase in the number and quality of native artists. Musicians sorely need the stimulation of intelligent listeners."

"Go on!" begged the reporter.

"The American audience," began the artist once more, the light of battle in the piercing Powell eyes that are exactly as dark in reality as they are in the pictures in the record catalogue. But there was H. Godfrey Turner . . . holding her coat patiently all the while and reminding her that the janitor wanted to lock up the hall, so the meeting was adjourned to the studio down on Gramercy Park.

"Isn't it remarkable that even a New York audience is still untrained?" said Mme. Powell sadly. "One hears the well seasoned audience of our most famous string quartet applauding in the wrong places time after time, wholly mistaking the architecture of the composition. Only the other day I watched Paderewski use a prodigious amount of will power and obvious dramatic force of attitude indicating suspense in order to prevent the usual large number of musically ignorant hero worshippers present from ruining the wonderful impressiveness of a long pause.

"There is a psychological moment when the last breath of tone passes into nothingness, then a psychological instant before the soul of one who understands music could react in physical applause; not to have that sense of proportion, that instinct, shows a listener to be hopelessly inartistic and listening to a name rather than to the music, attending the concert or opera because it is the proper thing to do.

"Now I believe that America needs more amateur musicians, and especially more amateurs in chorus singing and ensemble playing. It is a silly notion that the cultivation of music is worth while only when one shows enough talent for public performance. Music in the home is a wonderful influence, and the possession of a machine is not enough, though personally I believe a good phonographic instrument is about as necessary in a home as a furnace or a bath tub. Think what it means, especially to children, to hear the world's best compositions recorded by the world's greatest artists over and over until they are thoroughly familiar.

"But putting disk records on a machine never gives one quite the same feeling for music that performing oneself does. I shall never forget the thrill of playing with a little amateur orchestra in the little Illinois town where I grew up. Self-expression is one of the fundamental needs of human life, and self-expression in music is bound to be a joy to all who will give themselves to it. It is a shame that so many girls who have had musical advantages give up their music entirely when they marry. Then, if ever, they should develop what abilities they may possess, and as their children grow up make music a strong factor in the life of the home. Perhaps the streets and the cheap motion picture theatres would be less popular with the young if there were more music and laughter in their homes. Folks need all those means of expression—singing, whistling, dancing, shouting, laughing, playing together—and home life would be a sweeter thing if each family would organize itself into a troupe of performers for its own amusement.

"Music would become a bond, a resource against the deadly ennui of 'nothing to do at home,' a pleasure, a luxury and a necessity. I believe as much in emotional training as in moral training, and music is the best emotional instructor, bringing out the very finest that is in the individual."

"Do you have dreadful experiences with the uncultured audiences out in the wilds west of Hoboken?" Mme. Powell was asked.

"The hotels are not all that a mortal could ask," replied the lady pensively, as though too poignant memories of small town hostels still lingered. "But some of the audiences in the smallest towns are the most wonderful. When they *do* like music, and have only [word illegible] depend upon it they are an audience that warms the cockles of one's heart. Oh, I do not despair about America at all.

"I as an American understand better than do foreign artists who have not lived here the marvelous possibilities of the American temperament, the tremendous growth of musical appreciation, already achieved throughout this big country and its possibility of greater growth in the future. Where others damn, I marvel at what has already been done and look forward hopefully to the future.

"American children of to-day are having musical advantages that the last generation did not dream of, and to-morrow's children will have even better chances. Some day—I am certain of it—American audiences will know what music means and exactly when to applaud!"[23]

Maud with her Guadagnini in 1918.

Top, Maud practicing on the porch of The Knoll, built in the spring of 1915 in Whitefield, N.H. The notes on the clef represent the pitches to which the violin strings are tuned. *Bottom,* inside The Knoll.

op, Maud working on her transcriptions; *bottom,* friends at The Knoll: *l to r,* Irene Frank, . E. Kellner, Maud, tenor Riccardo Martin, conductor Adolf Schmid, Sunny's secretary lna Speier, Maud's pianist Axel Skjerne.

Top, Maud "inspiring Tom Gogue, comedian, with a rendition of 'Molly on the Shore' while he digs a ditch at her camp in New Hampshire"; *bottom,* Maud washing her hands in a puddle at The Knoll, September 3, 1919.

Maud at The Knoll, September 3, 1919: *top left*, with Edna Speier; *top right*, with Sunny; *bottom*, at work and at play.

Top, Maud in her Gramercy Park apartment, *left*, at work in 1918; *right*, engaged in thera-peutic bed-making, November 1, 1917; *bottom*, playing ball with Sunny in Gramercy Park, spring 1919.

Maud at home in Gramercy Park in 1918 before a music case containing orchestra parts. The painting of the Grand Canyon is by Frederick S. Dellenbaugh, a member of John Wesley Powell's exploring expedition between 1870 and 1874.

Maud's portrait in oils by Nicholas R. Brewer, painted in the spring of 1918. The portrait's whereabouts are unknown.

Champion of American Composers

*America demands a poetry that is bold, modern, and all-
surrounding and Kosmical, as she is herself.*

— Walt Whitman

HENRY FINCK, THE NEW YORK CRITIC, once observed that probably no
American woman traveled as many miles between October and May
as did Maud Powell—nor did any other musician. When she set out
on her annual tour in October 1912, it was to fulfill more engagements than ever before. By that time, Maud had introduced to the
American public more new music than any other musician. She was
constantly growing in her art while steadily reaching out to an ever-
wider audience.

John C. Freund called this musician a "Musical Pioneer of Vital
Influence." In essence, she was a traveling educational institution,
lifting her audiences to an ever higher appreciation for her art. Her
technique, her musicianship, her versatility, her programming, her
personality—all combined to set a new standard for violin playing and serve as a model for the next generation of violinists and
musicians.

Nowhere were these contributions and personal qualities more in
evidence than during the three recitals Maud delivered that season to
San Franciscans who packed the hall to hear her. These recitals, given
December 12, 14, and 15 in the Scottish Rite Auditorium, provided
Maud with an opportunity to indulge in the masterful programming
for which she was famous. For the first concert, given on a Thursday,
her program was as follows:

Concerto, G minor (first time). . . . . Coleridge-Taylor
    (Dedicated to Mme. Powell)
Sonata. . . . . Nardini
Sonata, D minor, Op. 108. . . . . . . Brahms
Serenade . . . . Schubert
Scherzo "Marionettes" . . . . Gilbert
    (first time) (Dedicated to Mme. Powell)
Liebeslied . . . . Kreisler
Caprice (first time) . . . . Ogarew
Berceuse. . . . . Cui
Polonaise, D major . . . . Wieniawski

The second concert was arranged for Saturday afternoon in order to give students and teachers in the surrounding area an opportunity to hear Maud. The literature on this program was especially tailored for their educational benefit:

Symphonie Espagnole, Op. 21. . . . . Lalo
Sonata, E major . . . . Bach
    (for violin and piano)
Rondo (from the Haffner Serenade). . Mozart
Minuet . . . . Mozart
Scherzo Caprice (first time) . . . . . . Grasse
    (Dedicated to Maud Powell)
Hungarian Dance, A major . . . . . . Brahms-Joachim
Fantasie de Faust . . . . Wieniawski

For the third concert, on Sunday, Maud programmed the following:

Concertstück, F sharp minor, Op. 84 . Bruch
(a) Air. . . . . Tenaglia (1600?)
(b) Praeludium and Allegro . . . . . Pugnani/Kreisler (1727)
Sonata, G minor, Op. 13 . . . . Grieg
Deep River (first time) . . . . Coleridge-Taylor
    (Arranged by Mme. Powell)
Up the Ocklawaha (first time) . . . . Marion Bauer
    (Dedicated to Mme. Powell)
Minute Waltz. . . . . Chopin-Powell
Minuet . . . . Beethoven
Scènes de la Czarda . . . . Hubay

The audience which jammed into Scottish Rite Hall for the first concert gave Maud a long demonstration of welcome even before she

played. Through a program considered to be of "immense proportions," the violinist aroused her audience to "great enthusiasm."
Critics readily believed that few other violinists were capable of sustaining the listeners' interest through such a heavy program: "Notably, her numbers, less well played or lacking magnetism in the player,
would have proved taxing to the listener, as three heavy classics were
projected in succession and were tests of physical endurance aside
from their artistic qualifications."[1] Nevertheless, critic Walter Anthony
wrote that the program

> should have tempted to attendance every violin student in San
> Francisco. Music lovers who missed it forfeited just so much of grace
> which, like a blessing lost, or a benediction foregone, will not be
> made up to them.
>
> If you find this something superlative, I answer that superlative
> music may only be spoken of in corresponding terms, and last night's
> was a superlative program. I deem absence an irremediable loss to
> any whose soul reacts in pleasure to the charms of music.[2]

Maud's programming received more attention and especial praise
in reviews of her second recital, designed with students and teachers
in mind:

> From Lalo's "Symphonie Espagnole" and Bach's sonata in E major,
> it is a far cry, but the marvelous ingenuity of Madame Powell in the
> selection of numbers constructed a bridge over which her hearers
> were so gradually transported by her supreme art that the contrast
> was less abrupt, and the entire program seemed blended into one
> glorious symphony.
>
> Full opportunity did this wonderful artist grant herself to exhibit
> her great versatility. Entirely unaffected, and positively sure of her-
> self at all times, each succeeding number served its purpose in dis-
> playing the perfect technic, the wonderful tone power and the almost
> magic execution of one of the greatest instrumentalists of today.[3]

The three recital programs for San Francisco were unique in that
each one included music by an American composer, dedicated to
Maud. She always loyally played worthwhile American compositions
consistent with her concert requirements. Edwin Grasse was just one
of the numerous young musicians the great violinist befriended. Blind
since his birth in 1884 in New York City, Grasse was remarkably
gifted as a violinist and pianist and had an "exceptional creative gift"

as a composer. He had studied with Carl Hauser in New York and César Thomson in Brussels and then made his American debut in 1903, playing the Brahms violin concerto. Grasse was "adopted" by the Turners, and Sunny managed his concert career. His *Scherzo* was so well received in San Francisco that one critic asked for its repetition in the third concert. Maud happily obliged. During the previous season, Maud had played his "fascinating and clever study" *Wellenspiel*.

Maud described Marion Bauer's *Up the Ocklawaha* as a "new work which is of an elaborate nature, although it is not a suite and it is not a rhapsody or fantasy. I would almost call it a tone picture, taking into consideration the story that called it into being."[4] The violinist had commissioned the work as a result of a memorable trip up Florida's Ocklawaha River—the only means of getting from one city to another during a tour—and she called Bauer's composition "as good a piece of programme music as has ever been penned."

Maud and Marion Bauer had probably met in New York, perhaps through Henry Holden Huss, with whom Bauer had studied before going abroad. Born in 1887 in Walla Walla, Washington, Bauer joined her oldest sister, Emilie Frances, a pianist and music critic, in New York after graduation from high school. In 1906, she went to France to study with pianist Raoul Pugno, and while there, studied harmony with Nadia Boulanger. Boulanger, then still in her teens, was to become the midwife to American music, teaching composition to so many American composers who ultimately gained recognition for their works, including Virgil Thomson, Roy Harris, Walter Piston, and Aaron Copland.[5] Marion Eugenie Bauer believed that she was this eminent French musician's first American pupil.

Maud well understood the evolution of American music in her time, since she knew intimately the composers who were setting the pace.[6] The predominance of the German influence, in the mold of Beethoven and Brahms, was manifest in the works of the composers representing the old New England School—Chadwick, Paine, and Parker. Edward MacDowell (1861–1908), a fine pianist and the first internationally recognized American composer, represented another aspect of the German–New England School tradition. He received most of his musical education in Germany, and his compositions veered from the classic German Romantic tradition to embrace the Wagnerian emphasis on the rich harmony and more elongated forms of the tone-poem. A personal friend of the MacDowells for years, Maud contributed regularly to the MacDowell Society, formed to perpetuate the performance of the composer's works upon his death.

The influence of French composers, such as Saint-Saëns, d'Indy, Fauré, Debussy, and Ravel, was evident in music composed by Maud's old friend John Alden Carpenter (1876–1951) as well as in the work of the younger Grasse and Bauer. There were other trends in American composition, though perhaps of much less significance. The works of Arthur Farwell, the Midwestern composer who followed Dvořák's advice, were influenced by American Indian melodies.

Still, American composers had yet to find their way to authentic musical expression reflecting the American experience. But in 1911 Maud was optimistic and pointed to current trends as promising:

> Almost half a century has elapsed since the close of the Civil War, and in that period our country has undergone an expansion in the commercial arts that is without parallel in history; but we struck no new note in music until the last decade brought into vogue the reigning vulgarity of ragtime. Frown on it as we may, we must confess in the end that it has distinct individuality of rhythm. And that is a great deal; for rhythm stands at the root of all musical structure. But, above and beyond the vital importance of its structural quality, it has a soul of its own. It is a perfect expression in musical terms of our nervous vitality and of our national swagger, of the slapdash, devil may care, get there or bust method of the American. . . .
>
> It is only in this country we hear the assertion that there is no such thing and never can be any such thing as characteristically American music. Europeans enjoy our ragtime and Sousa marches more than most of us would believe. And they are no more at a loss to classify them than we are to detect a Scottish ballad.
>
> But we have in view a higher achievement in American music than this. It will be attained only when our composers realize the value of the material afforded by the history, the literature, the folklore, and the wonderful natural beauties of their own country. Of such material there is an abundance and a variety to create the poetic mood, which will induce the vitalizing and transforming touch of artistic inspiration. Music thus created will be characteristically American in content as well as expression. It will be genuine American music.[7]

The prescient violinist did all she could to foster and encourage American composers. When someone once commented on the number of American works on her programs, the artist responded with some puzzlement: "It has been noted that a number of American compositions are to be found on my programs, and I expect to carry this still further, but that is certainly not new. If anyone looks into the old programs he will find the first violin concerto written by Henry Holden Huss, and one by Harry Rowe Shelley, and there was a time when I was more interested in what our country could produce than in what was regarded as popular accepted repertory."[8] Again in the last year of her life, Maud emphasized her dedication to the cause of the American composer:

> You must not think that I have played only foreign music in public. I have always believed in American composers and in American composition, and as an American have tried to do justice as an interpreting artist to the music of my native land. Aside from the violin concertos by Harry Rowe Shelley and Henry Holden Huss, I have played any number of shorter original compositions by such representative American composers as Arthur Foote, Mrs. H. H. A. Beach, Victor Herbert, John Philip Sousa, Arthur Bergh, Edwin Grasse, Marion Bauer, Cecil Burleigh, Harry Gilbert, A. Walter Kramer, Grace White, Charles Wakefield Cadman and others. Then, too, I have presented transcriptions by Arthur Hartmann, Francis MacMillan and Sol Marcosson, as well as some of my own.[9]

Although few American composers had attempted writing violin concertos, or even sonatas, the smaller violin works which they composed represented attempts to come to grips with the instrument which meant progress along the evolutionary lines Maud knew inevitably must come. In her annual New York recital in October 1913, Maud featured five American compositions, presenting them as a group:

Up the Ocklawaha River (New) . . . . Bauer
Scherzo, Marguerite (New). . . . . . . Grasse
The Avalanche (New) . . . . Cecil Burleigh
    (from Suite, Rocky Mountain Sketches)
    (from manuscript)
Evening, a Reverie (New) . . . . Arthur Bergh
Scherzo, Marionettes . . . . Gilbert

The artist even recorded Gilbert's Scherzo *Marionettes*, which a New York critic called "thoroughly spontaneous and musical," a boost for which the composer could hardly have hoped.

Cecil Burleigh (1885–1980, Wyoming, N.Y.) was a violinist-composer who Maud and Sunny visited in New York. A half-century later he remembered vividly that Maud expressed her interest in his music, especially in the slow movement of his first violin concerto and *Avalanche* from the *Rocky Mountain Suite*. Burleigh considered her interest in performing his works a "great honor" coming from "one of the truly great violinists of her time."[10] Maud was one of the first to perform Burleigh's Violin Concerto in E-Minor, after Burleigh premiered it himself in 1916. It was largely due to Maud's interest and that of Arthur Farwell that his work gained recognition. As a result, Albert Spalding, a fine young American violinist, played some of Burleigh's works during his European tour in 1913.

It was not surprising then that so many American composers dedicated works to Maud. In 1912, W. H. Humiston (b. 1869, Marietta, Ohio)—a pianist and conductor who studied with MacDowell and became assistant conductor of the New York Philharmonic after 1916—dedicated his *Suite for Violin and Orchestra in F-sharp Minor* to the great violinist. Similarly, Gaylord Yost, a composer-violinist at the Indianapolis Conservatory of Music, dedicated *Danse Characteristique* to Maud. Her reply, written in 1913, indicates the pleasure with which she received the new music: "Thank you for the dedication of that little 'Danse Characteristique' with the dainty first theme and that lovely middle bit so dear to the heart of the fiddler because of the double stopping and the 3–2 rhythm. I expect to use it this winter. Again my best thanks."[11]

When asked why she played so many American works, the violinist replied:

> I have been criticised for this . . . but I invariably say that American artists owe it to their country to play the best examples of American music. How can we expect to have any national music, if someone does not play these works publicly? Foreign artists come over here and take enormous sums of money out of the country. They have not really served us vitally. They are not in sympathy with our institutions. They rarely play works by American composers. I must try to do what I can for American music.[12]

No matter how firmly committed Maud Powell was to promoting American compositions, she still required that the music meet a certain standard: "I do not believe in playing things just because they are American, if they do not happen to be good music. There is no use in that. The standard must be rigidly preserved. But any American music that attains the standard of value set by the world's classics ought to be frequently presented. There are many exquisite works by American composers."[13]

Asked to reflect on her personal predilections as far as modern music was concerned, Maud responded thoughtfully:

> I like everything that is good. We are born ahead of our time, I believe, but we are born with the power to see and hear ahead also. . . . You may say . . . that I am still on the lookout for good novelties and am gratified to find works of considerable value coming from our own composers. They are going to be better and better as time goes on and with the larger encouragement. I find as I grow older that works have to get a firm hold of me in order to make it possible for me to learn them.[14]

Maud Powell's unquenchable faith in the creative genius of the American people served as an inspiration to aspiring composers and musicians alike. She eschewed false comparisons between European cultural developments and American progress. The American temperament was, in her view, unique and for that reason held within it possibilities all its own for the development of a truly American musical culture:

> The American . . . begins at twenty-five, where others have left off. He is progressive, and he lives in an energetic world. I do not believe that this American rush is detrimental to musical development. It is true that no European could live in it, but it is part of the American who is unusually cultured and advanced in thought and he is built to endure it; there is something in the air that invigorates people to a point where they can accomplish great things through the exhilaration they receive.[15]

Later she said, for the *Minneapolis Journal*,

> At the present time we have nothing in America which could really be called a national school of composition. We have no distinctive utterance in invention or style. Speaking broadly of the nation at large, we are still in the ragtime stage—the first rung of the ladder

of our musical expression. But the trend of the times is changing fast. One fact might be mentioned as an indication of the trend of public sentiment which is the great arbitrator of every change. The amount of money spent on music in this country every year is a splendid criterion of our intentions and ambitions and speaks well for our future development.[16]

Until the end of her life, Maud continued to place on her programs new compositions which had captured her heart and imagination. For helping and encouraging American composers, music critics and musicians everywhere honored the First American of the Bow.

Following her third recital in December 1912, San Francisco critic Walter Anthony's tribute expressed the sentiments of a city that placed her among the "select few of the world's great artists" which it claimed as its "musical favorites": "It is not the gallantry of Kreisler, Ysaÿe, Marteau, or Kocián that gives Maud Powell a seat amongst them as one of the world's greatest violinists. . . . Wherever violin playing is comprehended in its higher aspects, Maud Powell's name is known and her artistry reflects credit on her native land, too often despised by the musically richer lands of Europe."[17]

The critic for the *San Francisco Bulletin* wrote: "I can't think . . . of any other musician who holds the important position in the musical annals of America that Maud Powell may claim. She is by temperament, style and genius American in her art. Her finely consistent career, that of a great artist who always upholds the dignity of her profession . . . honors the history of American music. Such an artist as Maud Powell makes America's claim in music a serious one. That is before she draws her bow across that wonderful violin of hers."[18]

Retreat and Restoration

*When I'm playful I use the meridians of longitude and parallels
of latitude for a seine, and drag the Atlantic Ocean for whales.
I scratch my head with the lightning and purr myself to sleep
with the thunder.*

— *Mark Twain, 1883*

AT FORTY-FIVE, MAUD WAS BEGINNING TO FEEL THE STRAIN of her relentless
touring schedule. Consequently, when Maud, Sunny, and Harold
Osborn Smith, Maud's accompanist, set off for Honolulu after San
Francisco, pleasure was to predominate over work.[1] She was scheduled to give two recitals, on December 27, 1912, and January 2,
1913.

From the first, the musical adventurer was entirely enchanted by
Hawaii:

> If you are ever looking for an ideal place in which to be lazy I can
> recommend that one above all others. . . . In the first place it has a
> climate which does not vary more than ten degrees throughout the
> entire year. And the people have such a delightful way of accom-
> plishing things and yet of not living constantly under a nervous ten-
> sion in order to do so. The manner in which they treated us was
> charming beyond description. No sooner did we land than they had
> thrown huge garlands about our necks and we were obliged to pass
> through the streets with them on. And there were feasts and ban-
> quets without number. At some of these we ate native food in
> native fashion seated at the table wearing long flower garlands and
> eating without knives or forks.[2]

By the time of her recital, the violinist was captivated by the magical islands. She uncharacteristically ran onstage at the conclusion of her accompanist's piano solo and threw a large green lei around his neck, to the audience's delight.

Maud luxuriated in the charms of native Hawaiian culture and the beautiful setting. When she was not swimming in the ocean, shopping for special souvenirs, or feasting on the ambrosial cuisine, the violinist could be found listening with profound attention to the music of the native Hawaiians:

> The music of the natives must be heard performed by them to be appreciated. Its main charm lies in its rendering. On paper it is unimpressive and of little value. But in playing it the Hawaiian musician, like the Hungarian gypsy introduces effects that are not to be reproduced on paper. They have a curious way of varying the rhythmic plan of a piece by improvising a bar here and another there when one least expects it. Moreover, there are other decorative features that defy reproduction in black and white. There is a lovely lazy charm to Hawaiian rhythms. But all of this music would quite lose its point if played by any but native artists and on anything but their own instruments.
>
> The music itself is apt to be sentimental and the words often vulgar. To appreciate it you must hear it under the proper circumstances. Its fascinations from the musician's point of view lie mainly in the elaborateness of its rhythmic effects.
>
> The Hawaiians are instinctive musicians. I remember having once heard a band of players perform a piece which their conductor had written only that afternoon. They were given only the melody and obliged to improvise their own accompaniments. One of them, I remember, played a dominant chord where a tonic should have been. I shall never forget the angry glances this drew from the others—glances which expressed the sentiment "You fool!" more emphatically than ever could have words.[3]

This experience with Hawaiian music broadened Maud's musical vision and served to deepen her ever-growing art.

Perhaps as importantly, Maud's encounter with Hawaii's seductive charms quieted her nerves and released the tension built up over the course of her tour. How much Hawaii's lazy charms meant to her can be gauged from her expression of pleasure at the prospect of returning for two recitals in December 1915:

I shall go sea-bathing on Christmas Day . . . and revel in the sunshine and the rain of the place. One takes both with the best grace in the world. Everything in Hawaii has the gentleness of a caress — the waves of the ocean, the sun, the rain. Nobody could ever think of raising an umbrella if, on riding out, he were caught in a shower; nor should I bother to shut my window as I should here if a little rain were to wet me. Even the waves of the ocean have a tenderness about them. And to hear the natives sing and play their music, especially by moonlight, is an experience not easily to be forgotten.[4]

Asked by the local newspapers to give them her impressions of Hawaii as she was about to leave in 1912, Maud graciously responded with a poem:

> A many hued jewel set in a sapphire sea.
> Where the winds and the waters caress and coax the soul to
>   gladness.
> Where good-fellowship reigns supreme and June abides alway.
> Where earth, with artless charm, plays at being heaven.
> Where I have left a throb of my heart and where I shall return
>   some day to find it in the gentle custody of the
> Hawaiian muse of rhythm and sweet melody.
> Aloha nui![5]

Unfortunately, Hawaii's restful charms were not powerful enough to endure for the rest of the tour as Maud played her way back east.

Maud's return to New York to play the Tchaikovsky concerto with the New York Philharmonic on March 6, 1913, became something of an American celebration. Year by year, as she toured the country combating musical ignorance with her luminous bow, Americans became more keenly aware of the significance of Maud Powell's pioneering work to the cultural growth of the country. Americans had come to appreciate the high musical standards, unwavering artistic excellence, and personal integrity and grace of America's First Violinist. She had served to raise her nation's cultural standing abroad, but even more importantly, she had given these Americans self-respect and pride in what they could achieve and a deep confidence in their own cultural future.

The artist appeared onstage directly after Dvořák's *My Home-Land* overture in a "vivid gown of gold over rose." Her slender and attractive appearance belied the fact that this woman had been a performing artist for nearly thirty of her forty-five years. The audience gave a "tumultuous reception" to the "greatest of American violinists" not only as a tribute to her art but as a sort of "welcome home" ovation. It was her first New York appearance of the season, and critics hailed her performance of the Tchaikovsky concerto as the twenty-fifth anniversary of its introduction, by Maud, to American audiences.

The critic for *Musical America* described the historic performance:

> It may well be questioned whether at any time during that quarter of a century Miss Powell has played this Concerto with more consummate artistry, with a greater wealth of tonal beauty, a deeper insight into its poetic significance and a more eloquent communication of these emotional contents than she did last week. In the heartfelt song of the Canzonetta she attained soulfulness of utterance that was positively tear-compelling in its sheer loveliness. That movement marked the climax of the performance which, on the whole, fairly touched the high-water mark of violin playing. The first movement was given with a fine buoyancy of spirit, impeccable technic and intonation. The cadenza was a brilliant feat.[6]

The applause was "deafening" and Maud was forced to return to the stage almost a dozen times, at first walking, then running, as she returned again and again to bow to both audience and orchestra.

The veteran critics Aldrich, Krehbiel, and Henderson were more critical in their comments, perhaps as a result of their close friendship with the artist, keen observation of her art through the years, and deep appreciation for the heights to which Maud Powell could soar.[7] Aldrich welcomed the violinist's appearance, noting that she played the concerto with great "sweep and energy" though "perhaps she has played with greater smoothness and mellowness of tone on some other occasions, but scarcely with more power." Both Aldrich and Krehbiel agreed that the orchestra's accompaniment was "faulty" and "clumsy." But Krehbiel and Henderson also wrote that Maud's performance was "impetuous" at times and lacked "polish." She did not "disclose the elegance of style, that artistic repose and breadth of interpretative thought which we have been accustomed to expect from her in the past," Henderson reported. He declined to speculate on the causes which "operated to take the polish away temporarily from this admirable artist's playing." But Krehbiel was less restrained, perhaps because he knew Maud Powell's mettle so well. In his crusty but caring way, he put his finger on the trouble. He wrote, "[W]henever she returns to us after an absence spent in missionary labors in far-away communities the wish always rises that she had rested a while and recovered some of her old artistic spirit before playing again in the metropolis." Henderson, for his part, merely expressed the wish that "Mme. Powell will stay here till she resumes her older and more beautiful style."

What had happened? As her critic friends knew, Maud was tired. The constant traveling, practicing, and performing along with the bad food, uncomfortable hotels, inclement weather, social demands, writing, studying—all amounted to an incredible strain on both mind and body. Sunny said that he tried to see to it that his wife never played more than three concerts a week and that she arrived no later than twelve o'clock on the day of the concert. But the tour schedule was packed with grueling activity. It was not unusual for the artist to arrive in town on the day, sometimes the evening, of her scheduled recital, give the performance, and then leave that same night or early the next morning for her next appearance.

The violinist was always scribbling postcards to family and friends, signing off "in haste." One short letter indicates more clearly some of the hectic nature of her tour schedule:

THE WEST HOTEL
ABSOLUTELY FIREPROOF
MINNEAPOLIS, MINNESOTA

Nov. 1909 Monday

My dear Mrs. Phelps,

I have not been able to get you on the phone so am sending this as an outline of my itinerary. If I can catch the 10:50 out of Grand Forks after the concert, I shall do so. In any event, even if I come on the 10:50 the next night I shall be here in time for rehearsal on Thurs. morning. I plan to leave on the 3 o'clock for Cedar Falls so will not have my trunk sent from the station. I'd better come straight to the West and then if I may, come to you on my return from Cedar Falls, which would be at 5:05 on Saturday afternoon. The only time I see for "tea" would be after the concert on Sunday yet that is a good deal for one day. Mr.

Turner wires that I may go to Fairboult on *Monday*, so you see I hardly know where I am "at."

Excuse my scribble—I have been writing programs and program notes all afternoon. Yesterday, I slept and rehearsed, else I should have tried to see you. I am getting my trunk out now, and shall rehearse again this evening with Mr. Eisner before taking our train to Grand Forks. I hope there will be no more blizzard!

With warmest regards to you both.

> Yours sincerely,
> Maud Powell[8]

Then, too, Maud suffered inordinately from nervousness prior to every performance. Although her nervous energy was transformed into inspiration once she began playing, the physical toll was incalculably high. "Rest" was not a word in her vocabulary. Sunny once declared that she only practiced three to four hours a week while on tour but admitted that "mentally she never stops."[9]

No matter what the hardship, Maud was always intent on giving her best performance, knowing that in many cases there were people in the audience who had never before heard a great artist or the music she presented. It was her way of doing justice to the composer, her art, and her audiences and was indicative of the humility with which she approached her work. An interview reveals Maud's sensitivity to her audiences:

> Is it true that each of your recitals is an "event" with you as it is with the musical public? . . .
>
> Most emphatically it is. I always try to put myself in the place of the audience. They have been thinking and planning for my appearance for weeks, sometimes for months. Should I not in turn give them the very best I have? I always do and they invariably repay me with appreciation both personal and general.

Even though Maud acknowledged the toll exacted on her energies for her adherence to this high standard, she who admitted, "I play the fiddle because I have to" could not alter her nature:

> I have often been urged, and sometimes have on my own part half resolved not to put forth in a certain recital the full emotional and psychic force which I am capable of giving out. But once on the

stage and launched upon the music, I have to perform, I realize that I must throw myself into the necessary spirit whatever labor it entails and give my best. The strain, to be sure, may be terrific, but if I don't go through it I am not doing what my audience has the right to expect.[10]

Maud Powell prided herself on never disappointing an audience throughout her career—a commitment which eventually cost her her life.

Maud stayed in New York during most of March 1913 (not exactly resting since she played in several other concerts), but then swept back out to the Midwest to complete her season's tour. She apparently had recovered her polished style, since the Chicago critics reported, "Her playing of the Tschaikovsky concerto [with the Chicago Symphony April 18 and 19] was the red letter event of the day and in all points it seems to have grown in grace and beauty through the mellowing years."[11] Hailing her as a prophet, the *Chicago Tribune* critic noted that she was honored with one of the greatest houses before which the Chicago Symphony had ever performed. She was recalled so many times that she was forced to give an encore.

However, while concertizing in Illinois, Maud was stricken with appendicitis. She had played a recital just two days before the required operation. Her next engagement was only a few days later, on May 5, in Grand Rapids, Michigan, but by the time she reached there, she had a dangerously high fever and was "far from being in good health." Sunny put her straight to bed, and early in the afternoon her physician warned, "If you play tonight, I'll not answer for the consequences. You'll do it at the risk of your life." Suffering extreme pain from peritonitis, Maud was nevertheless determined to fulfill her concert commitment.

The plucky artist gave a full recital that night which "illustrated her ability to the full satisfaction of her audience." The critics, unaware of just how sick she was, hailed her as "an artist with a clear vision, an apostle of pure music." Her "phenomenal" art appeared "peculiar, exalted and without alloy." She had enthralled her audience with "never failing artistry" and succeeded in "conveying a great message."[12] Adversity apparently brought out to a greater degree Maud's unusual mettle. Only a true artist could become so absorbed in the music that extreme physical pain could be forgotten. Once the music stopped, Maud immediately returned to the hotel and went straight to bed, the pain returning in all its fury.

Within forty-eight hours, Maud was scheduled to appear with orchestra at the Syracuse Music Festival.[13] Although she was tempted to cancel her engagement, someone who did not understand the situation wired that the non-appearance of two scheduled artists had severely disappointed the festival committee. Suffering greatly by this time and still dangerously ill from the post-operative infection, the violinist wired back that she was coming. She requested the directors to engage a doctor for her, as she was coming with a trained nurse in attendance.

On the train, an English baronet gave up his stateroom for Maud's comfort. Sunny's alarm at the situation was manifested in his engagement of a closed hack with a horse so aged that it could not possibly go fast enough to jolt her while making the trip from the hotel to the arena. Sunny supported his wife as far as the steps of the platform, and with the nurse within easy call, Maud Powell mounted the platform.

Her single concession to her infirmity was to play only the first movement of the Coleridge-Taylor violin concerto for which she was billed. She had arrived too late for any rehearsal and the conductor had had a chance merely to glance over the score, which was still in manuscript, yet the performance went off well. In response to congratulations, the violinist gave conductor Wallace Goodrich all the credit, saying, "He played that concerto; I didn't."

Maud also played a group of solos which included *Slumber Song* by Syracuse organist James Percy Davis, a characteristically generous gesture. For a short while after playing her program, Maud said she felt better and was moved to play an encore. Such extravagance took its toll.

The next morning, Sunny chatted with concerned reporters while Maud rested, mentioning that his wife had performed a similar feat during a serious illness in the previous year. He said he had made reservations on a train leaving Syracuse the next morning and that if nothing happened to prevent it, he would take her home to New York to rest. Her tour had ended. Outwardly, he assured them that she had probably not suffered any ill effects from her efforts; inwardly, he may have had his doubts. His wife was as dear to him as his own life and he was deeply concerned.

Maud remained ill through June, which forced her to cancel her promised recital at the New York Music Teachers' Association meeting in Saratoga. In early July she underwent another operation, after which she convalesced rapidly, claiming she had not felt so well for five years.

To provide some respite from touring life, Maud and Sunny eventually built a summer home just outside of Whitefield, New Hampshire, where they spent their most halcyon days.[14] The Turners first came to Whitefield on the recommendation of two New York critics, William B. Chase, whose family farm was there, and Henry T. Finck, who had a summer camp on nearby Forest Lake.

For their first three summers there, 1912–14, the Turners lodged at Locust Cottage, a summer boarding house run by Ina and Edmund Parker in connection with their farm. The peaceful green which surrounded her and the cool, bracing air were gentle palliatives for Maud's overwrought nerves.

Happily, the relaxed, friendly atmosphere also released Sunny's clown personality. The neighborhood children remembered Sunny as a "tall reserved Englishman with a rare sense of humor." He delighted in observing the town's affairs and once hilariously involved himself in the frugal spirit of New England life. One morning, one of Ina Parker's fresh breakfast doughnuts slipped off the "table girl's" tray to the floor. Embarrassed, she kicked it under the door. As the plate was passed around, Maud remained discreet but Sunny slyly "turned an eye to the door and meekly asked for the one on the floor."[15]

While Sunny charmed the local children with his antics, he once confessed that all his clowning was designed to relax his wife by dissolving into laughter the tension caused by her work. One of the children observed, "He was a real tonic for her and she enjoyed him ever so much."

The Chase, Burns, and Parker children all called Maud "Madam Powell," since she was "a very distinguished looking lady and we kids were in awe of her." But as far as they could see, she dressed in ordinary clothing like the other guests.

By the summer of 1914, Maud and Sunny had become so attached to the place that they purchased one acre of land on a knoll just across from Locust Cottage. There, on Parker Road, they built their summer cottage in the spring of 1915. From the outside, the home looked like a bungalow with its large, sloping roof and broad porch from which there was a wonderful view of the White Mountains. It was larger on the inside than it first appeared. Of Maud's design, "The Knoll," as she and Sunny affectionately christened it, blended with the landscape on the outside while inside it was simplicity itself.

The main room was a large music/living room in which Maud placed her Steinway grand piano, which she had sent up from New York. The walls and floors were finished with natural pine, giving the home a clean, fresh appearance. The living room was furnished with soft grey Navajo rugs which blended beautifully and restfully with the natural wood. Over against the wall by the windows sat a large backless couch. One could lean back comfortably on its big colorful pillows.

A round hutch table stood cozily next to the large stone fireplace with its birch log mantelpiece. To the left of the fireplace was a small, crowded office crammed with storage shelves and Edna Speier's office equipment. The Turners' bedroom was next to the office, opening onto the living room, and there was a small loft above.

Edna Speier, who served as the Turners' secretary and housekeeper, stayed with them. The Turners treated her like a daughter. Edna often talked of Maud Powell as a fabulous person, almost a god, and said that Maud and Sunny were extremely good to her.

The accompanist for the inevitable summer practice sessions lodged in a room next to the small garage. Sunny hung a sign over the door reading: "Fiddle Dee Dee." Automobiling was one of the Turners' favorite diversions. Sunny's automobile savvy enabled him to convey Maud on tour sometimes in gypsy-like fashion. When showing the accompanist his summer quarters, Sunny protected his prize position as chauffeur by intoning, "Don't think . . . just because you live next to the garage, that you are the chauffeur; you're only the accompanist."[16]

Maud and Sunny planted a flower garden and landscaped the house. Maud did not raise vegetables, but she did grow herbs. The flower garden was her particular delight since she was a serious botanist. She also had a knack for discovering four-leaf clovers. Sunny once exclaimed to a reporter: "God bless me . . . , I couldn't find a four leaf clover in six years with a microscope, but Miss Powell sees them by the score as she walks along, without looking for them. It is uncanny."[17]

Working in the flower bed took a toll on the violinist's hands, but she did not overly concern herself with that. One reporter who looked her up in her summer quarters found her washing her hands in the roadside puddle near her home by which Sunny had erected the sign: "Danger! Pud Muddle." Her response to his positive shock resulted in an interesting interview:

"What's a little clean mud?" remarked the famous American violinist. "You've got to eat a peck of it before . . . "

"That's all right for ordinary people," I said. "Violinists, I should think, would be more careful. Some insure their hands for thousands. They . . . "

Madame Powell rubbed her hands together.

"With the greatest respect, pish!" she said, "A little mud never hurt anybody."

"You wouldn't have caught Paganini doing it," I suggested.

"Paganini!" cried Madame Powell, wiping her hands on the front of her skirt and making for the house. "Come with me and I'll show you something. Paganini? What does anybody know about Paganini? Nobody living ever heard him play. You have to take his genius on hearsay."

"That is so," I agreed. "Paganini used to muffle himself up and look as consumptive as possible, and make a terrific fuss over the protection of his hands."

"Paganini must have been something of an advertising genius 100 years before press agents were invented," was Madame Powell's retort.

With that I went with her to the bungalow. . . . When I arrived I learned that Maud Powell, the American who has been called the only great woman violinist who ever lived, believes her hands were made to be used, not worshiped.

Any hour of the day she is ready to lay down her fiddle to take up the automobile spanner or the garden rake, or the dishcloth, or even the spade.[18]

Maud and Sunny, however, did employ John B. Burns as a gardener, who, joined by his son Clayton, plowed, planted, and hoed his way into the Turners' affections.

One summer, Maud experimented with a divining rod made of a crotched willow branch, finding water as her reward. Sunny, with his ever-ready camera in hand, recorded the successful experiment. It was a skill she needed when unusual heat and a drought parched the mountains in the summer of 1919. Maud reported merrily to the American violinist Arthur Hartmann: "We're digging for a spring, located with witch-hazel divining-rod, and have found beautiful water. I celebrated by playing 'Molly on the Shore' over the well to be, for the appreciative, red-headed Irish digger! Let us hope the Spring is to be a perpetual one in this day of the victorious 'Drys.' "[19]

Maud loved the country. Being near the mountains among the dark green of the towering pine trees, taking in the fresh air and the restful scenery, the simplicity of life, all allowed for a refreshing expansion of her inner being and rejuvenation of her spirit and health. She divided her time among visits with friends, long rambling country walks, sketching and painting, reading literature, studying music, and practicing.

Amid this peace, and the general hilarity provided by Sunny, life had its poignant moments. During her meanderings through the natural world, Maud's spirit of adventure was often gratified by unexpected encounters and new discoveries on which she sometimes mused: "Once while taking a long country walk, I stopped at a farm house to ask for a glass of water. An old man sat in the kitchen playing a violin. I questioned him regarding his instrument and finally took the violin and played for him. Tears of delight came to his eyes. He took the instrument, looked at it a moment tenderly, and then said, 'I will never touch it again.' "[20] It was perhaps one thing to play to the acclaim of thousands of people in a large concert hall; it was another to come to terms so directly with her power to move profoundly the inner spirit of another. Could the artist have been shaken by the realization that her spontaneous gift had altered forever the old man's delight in making music on his beloved fiddle?

Always athletically inclined, Maud played golf at the Crawford House in addition to the many hours she spent walking. The Turners often joined the Chase family in driving up Mt. Willard's carriage road or the south peak of Dalton Mountain for a picnic. Maud once climbed up Mt. Willard with the Chase children, picturesquely carrying a parasol and wearing the wrong kind of shoes. Sunny recorded the violinist's visit to the top of Mt. Washington with his camera.

Conversation reflected the dalliance of summer days, winding into local history and town news. Maud took an interest in everyone but herself, never discussing her tours and only rarely making a personal disclosure. Once, though, one of the Chase children heard her say that she just hated her name, "Maud," because it made her feel as though she were a mule!

When she crossed the pasture to Locust Cottage, Maud sought out the company of Ina Parker in the warmth of her kitchen, where the aging William Burns often commanded the attention of cottage guests as he spun out his tales of pioneer Whitefield. The violinist was interested in the Parker history and the old ways of doing things, relaxing in the friendly atmosphere of good conversation and gentle people. Everyone respected her silence about her work, recognizing her need to escape from it as much as possible during the summer months.

One of Maud's favorite haunts in the village square was Charles McIntyre's harness shop. In addition to its normal business, the shop offered checker games, stories, politicking, and gossip. Maud's simple, down-to-earth personality made her a welcome guest when she stopped by for one of her frequent early morning visits. Her favorite seat was on the leather stitching horse. Maud's friendship with Lyman McIntyre, the shop owner's son, carried over into correspondence while Maud was on tour.

Maud involved herself in the town's affairs whenever she thought she could make a contribution. Although normally discreet, she did write one blistering letter to the town officials concerning road conditions. It probably set some tongues wagging:

THE KNOLL
WHITEFIELD, N.H.

September 11, 1915

Mr. John Burns,
    Whitefield, N.H.

Dear Sir,

Before sending my cheque for taxes, permit me to protest in vigorous terms against the misuse of the funds collected for the improvement of the public highways. It is short sighted economy to do the work of road-building so badly that it has to be re-done at short intervals. For example: short boards were used on the small bridge over the ditch or stream between "The Knoll" and the railroad (on road running South to the Bethlehem road). The nails soon worked up, — a menace to tires. Later long boards were put in. Why were the long ones not used in the first place? The Bethlehem road along the Burns Pond is an insult, a scandal and a disgrace. It will have to be done over or the town will have suits for damages on its hands. The road by the Mountain View Hotel was a pig pen for automobilists. Why wasn't it done right in the first place? Wilful economy, or gross ignorance are the cause of all this. We pay double road tax, (in general taxes as well as the automobile license) and have to ride over the most damnable (there is no other word for it) roads that it has been our experience to traverse. Whitefield is a beautiful little town, but let me tell you gentlemen, that it is not as progressive as it should be. Good roads would bring more life, greater prosperity, better shops, more patronage. Having settled here, we have the interests of the little town at heart. I want my friends to come here and I do not want to be obliged to apologize to them for the existent conditions.

I would gladly give a concert next Summer for the improvement of the roads if I could be assured by a body of public spirited men that the funds accruing therefrom would be properly applied.

Yours very truly,
(signed) Maud Powell

Mr. Bray and Mr. Weeks will also receive the foregoing letter. M.P.[21]

We do not know whether the proffered concert was ever given. Neither do we know whether some town officials experienced a fleeting feeling of regret concerning Maud Powell's decision to make her summer home in Whitefield! It seems likely that nothing was done. During the next two summers, Maud and Sunny could be seen spreading cracked stone in some of the potholes near their home.

Above all, Maud found the atmosphere surrounding Whitefield singularly conducive to her work:

But oh, the summer—then I can work unrestrained. Up in the White Mountains, in our bungalow, I spend several months of the year. The joy of it, to be in the heart of nature, surrounded by all her loveliness, with time for work. I love it. When there, I can really work, with my mind fully on what I am doing. One can accomplish so much more under such conditions. I work four days a week there, not whole days of course, but perhaps from nine until one or two. I prepare the concert and recital programs for the coming season, though I generally have them pretty well laid out in mind before I go to the mountains, in order to know just what music to take with me.[22]

For all the neighbors' discretion, there was no question that Maud's presence aroused their curiosity and interest in her violin playing. One resident remembered seeing Maud and Sunny walking in town about the time he, then a teenager, was studying the violin. He recalled thinking, "Wouldn't it be wonderful to go to their cottage and hear her play!" Lacking courage, the young man played her records over and over again in proxy.

Not everyone was so intimidated, as Maud once related with great glee:

One morning, during a summer vacation in the mountains, while practicing with door and windows open, a young ragamuffin walked boldly in, and after criticizing my performance, wished to know whether I ever played in shows. When I told him I did, his opinion of me rose considerably. He asked me about my travels, manifesting much interest in everything I said, and finally closed the interview by asking if I knew "Jack the Ripper," evidently thinking that all celebrities must be mutually acquainted.[23]

The residents of nearby Locust Cottage could sit on their porch and hear "Madam" practicing for hours every day, as she invariably played with the windows wide open or even meandered out onto her spacious porch as she played. One of the "table girls" at Locust Cottage wrote: "Her violin music could be heard at any time of day according to her moods, — but more frequently after dinner (the noon meal). Another friend Anna of my age and I also a table girl, would hurry our clearing up duties, to sit under the shade of the Locust trees and listen to Miss Powell's violin music."

Maud's persistent practice was cause for an amusing incident which may very well have taken place at Whitefield:

Every morning she went through her customary exercises. Every morning a boy employed about the place "doing chores" passed her open window, and heard her working away at something which in the course of a few days he learned to identify. When he heard her playing it every morning for more than a week he could no longer contain himself, and as he passed the open window he shouted, "Aw, say, can't ye play it yit?"[24]

The violinist did not withhold her art from her neighbors. She often played for the Chase and Parker families and other neighbors in the evenings. Once, Maud ventured to play for a very old lady: "She told me she was 104 years of age. When I had finished playing some well known compositions, she said, 'What is it all for?' This query amused me much, for there are many people, and people not nearly as old as my interrogator, and having full possession of their senses, too, who seem to wonder much the same thing, although they do not have the courage to ask the question."[25]

No one was asking the question when Maud played at Ina Parker's birthday party. So deep an impression did Maud Powell's playing make that night, that some sixty-five years later, Mrs. Parker's niece remembered the scene:

> We young people at the house gave my Aunt a birthday party out in a grove of trees. We had a big bonfire and roasted marshmallows. There were a few special guests from the Mountain View Hotel there, invited by Madam Powell. They, the people from the Knoll were invited and I think now they had the affair all planned ahead. After the party Madam turned to me and said, "I've sent for my fiddle." She then stood under the trees by the fire and played for over an hour.

Some of the guests said that the performance that night was better than any they had attended in New York. The artist herself was struck by the magic of that performance and it remained for her, forever after, a cherished memory. She once spoke of that enchanted party:

> Then on another occasion, a moonlit night in the White Mountains, I was with a happy crowd in a forest, toasting marshmallows and popping corn over a huge bonfire which we had built in an ancient tree stump. Under the influence of the crackling fire, and the glinting rays of the harvest moon, we soon fell to musing. "Mildred" began to sing, in her clear sweet voice. Then someone else told a story and another repeated a poem. Two children stood up and sang a little duet. Meantime, I had asked my husband to fetch my violin from the cottage across the fields. Presently I found myself standing between the boles of a huge pine playing in the

weird fitful light of the dying fire, while even the children were hushed to an awed silence.[26]

That was Maud's way of thanking these kindly New Englanders for allowing her to share in the life of their community and renew her spirit in the peace and solitude of the country.

A Certain Perspective

The art of music was not born of the music of Nature; it was born of the pains and pleasures, the joys and sorrows of mankind.

If you would love the higher music, you must love the songs of the people. . . .

—*John Wesley Powell*

AFTER A THREE-WEEK TOUR OF THE MIDWEST in early October, Maud Powell (restored to health) returned to New York's Aeolian Hall for the opening recital of the season on October 21, 1913. She was greeted by a large audience which included New York's most distinguished musicians. Henry Schradieck was prominent among this "picked audience of representative violinists, music lovers and critics."

Appreciative throughout, the audience seized every opportunity "for giving to the distinguished artist flattering approval," leaving "no doubt as to her high artistic standing in the community."[1] The critics sensed in her interpretations new depth, and reported that "according to the general verdict, [she] never played better."

In fact, from season to season, this remarkable player seems to advance by leaps and bounds. While she commands a repertoire of practically every school and style, her interpretations are constantly gaining in breadth, in finish and exquisite clearness. She is a living example of that class of artist who never stands still, who is ever on the alert to penetrate deeper and deeper into the mysteries of her art.

She has mastered every conceivable form of classic expression and her understanding and interpretation of the entire modern repertoire is a most remarkable exposition of perfected violinistic achievement.

Recognized as "one of the greatest musical figures that this country has produced," Maud Powell was hailed as "a scholar and musician who has superb mastery of her instrument and tremendous musical intelligence." Underneath all that, the critic for *The Musical Leader* sensed something in Maud's character which enabled her art to touch a higher truth: "She has never played with more breadth, more beauty of tone and more insinuating grace, and [like Nellie Melba, the opera singer] offered . . . [another] example of the power of simplicity, of sincerity and of the highest musical proficiency. Greater enjoyment of violin playing will probably not fall to the lot of those who listen to music during a season."

Those who met Maud Powell always felt that they were in the presence of a very special human being with a "singularly loveable character." They were impressed by her simple, human, and unaffected personality. When asked by a reporter in Keokuk, Iowa, what it took to be an artist, she responded that she believed in the all-around development of mind and body, a thorough grounding in history, literature, poetry, the fine arts in general, and a lively interest in the every day affairs of life as absolutely necessary for a proper perspective. Perspective, she emphasized, was one of the first requisites of genuine musical interpretation. The reporter concluded that her delight in the simple things of life kept her "natural, sane, joyous and unspoiled."[2]

The spirited violinist had a good sense of humor and could always be enticed into trying the unconventional, as long as it promised fun and adventure. In Waukesha, Wisconsin, one man with a twinkle in his eye invited her to try her skill at the wheel of a racing car. With her hat firmly tied down and her full-length coat wrapped around her, Maud took a spin in the streamlined vehicle. On earning the violinist's approval and admiration, the vehicle was promptly christened the "Maud Powell Flyer" by its ecstatic owner.

Perspective kept her from taking herself too seriously. When the Irish policeman on duty around Portland's Heilig Theater requested "Molly on the Shore," the manager confidently relayed the request to Sunny. Meanwhile, he left the stage door open and busied himself inside so as not to notice the sergeant stepping inside for a moment.

Sunny "fixed it" with his wife and she gleefully announced that while "Molly" was not on the program, Grainger's rollicking bit of fun was called for. The violinist then played it "joyously" with real "Hooray for Auld Ireland" in it, to everyone's delight.

The simple things of life included heart-warming recitals and reunions with old friends in the cities of her childhood. Maud arrived in February of 1908 in a heavy snowstorm on the evening of her first concert in Peru. She was brought from the railway station to the Maze home in an open carriage drawn by two white horses, bundled under snow-white blankets trimmed in red. Once inside, she sat on the floor beside the fire to warm herself.

Turn Hall had been sold out, so every sort of carriage from the livery barns of two cities had been engaged before 7:30 that evening. Only horse-drawn vehicles could get through the huge drifts and the blinding snowstorm.

At Turn Hall, a magnificent floral tribute in the form of a music stand awaited Maud onstage. Maud wrote that no gift had been more "superb" nor had any "touched a more responsive heart-chord." Fittingly, the artist was introduced by the superintendent of Peru schools. As she came onstage, she received a rousing ovation and then began to play "Home Sweet Home." "And then, for nearly two hours . . . the audience was held in almost breathless silence, broken only by frequent bursts of applause, while the great violinist seemed to lose herself in her art and filled the hall with the ravishing music which has made her a world celebrity."[3]

An informal reception followed. Then Maud returned to the Maze home. Going to the bedroom where Frances Maze, an aspiring pianist, lay ill, the great artist played several pieces for the disappointed youngster who had had to miss the concert. That night, Maud carefully wrapped her Guadagnini in a blanket and took it to bed with her to protect it from the cold.[4]

The violinist later wrote a poignant letter of thanks to the people:

> The return to the city of my birth, the warm reception given me by the people of Peru, and of LaSalle and other neighboring towns, will live with me always as one of the most tender of memories. Many, many old friends of my grandparents, Mr. and Mrs. Wm. Paul, and of my dear father and mother, by coming to the concert through that terrible snow storm, showed a loyalty to them and to

me, which touched me inexpressibly. I only wish my father, who always loved Peru, could have felt the hand pressures and have seen the loyal glances of the eye that greeted his daughter after the program was played. It was very beautiful and sweet to hear Professor Hart's tribute to my father's memory, and to hear the same affectionate remembrance voiced by my friends whom I met afterwards. I wish my little mother could have been strong enough to come with me—how the occasion would have warmed her heart! Now, I want to return to Peru some day when I am "off duty" and when I may have more opportunity of getting acquainted with all the old, and new friends.[5]

Maud had the flowers carefully packed and sent east to her mother. She returned twice more, in 1910 and 1913, on both occasions giving recitals for the benefit of the Peru Hospital Fund.

Earlier in the 1907–08 season, Maud had visited her other hometown, Aurora. Arriving at noon on October 7, 1907, she and Sunny went directly to the home of her close friends Mr. and Mrs. T. N. Holden. They spent the afternoon enjoying a ride about the city and countryside. However, pleasure soon yielded to the ever-present demands of the violin, and plans for a gathering of old friends in the evening were postponed until the following evening so that Maud could devote the time to practice.

When she appeared before the hometown audience on October 8, her old friends saw her as a handsome woman, handsomely gowned, with a face of "fine character, showing indisputably the determination and perseverance behind the acquirement of her wonderful skill." They found that the "warmth and magnetism of Maud Powell's playing is something to hear, it cannot be described."[6] The "silence was absolute" as, spellbound, they were "held by the magic of her exquisite playing." An elderly German businessman was heard to confide: "Mein Gott, I nefer knew such beautiful sounds could come from a fiddle."[7]

The recital was given in the People's Church for the benefit of the School for the Deaf. The familiar surroundings warmed Maud's heart: "As she came to the front of the stage, looked about, a flood of memories came over her and she remembered that the first time she played Traumerei was in Aurora in the old Stein's orchestra. . . . The beautiful melody with all its pleading and delicacy was played in such manner as to bring forth a storm of applause, and in response

Traumerei was played again, if possible more beautifully than before."[8]

Gracious and smiling, the violinist was forced by the unbroken applause to extend the program with encore after encore. Later, old friends who found her in the dressing room, wrapping her violin in white silk, were received by the "same pleasant, laughing girl of old." She "expressed her deep pleasure in playing before Aurora people, inquiring anxiously whether the program [which included a Grieg sonata and a Vieuxtemps concerto] was too long."[9]

For Maud, who once said that she had no home due to her career, Peru and Aurora remained fundamental points of reference in which her being was grounded. In 1910, the rare opportunity to spend time with old friends again presented itself in both cities. Looking "immensely well" with her dark hair and brilliant dark eyes set off by a soft tan-colored gown, she spontaneously responded to their warm embrace at an afternoon tea held in conjunction with her appearance in Aurora. Almost instinctively, she reached for her fiddle and began to play small, lovely pieces which she normally did not play in public. "She played until it was suspected that there was a big, big lump in the throats of some people," one person reported.[10]

At another Aurora reception, she talked animatedly with some of the teachers who had known her father well. She was heard to remark wistfully, "My father had a heart of gold."[11]

At her earlier recital in Peru, Maud had been deeply moved by the presentation of a loving cup and pink chrysanthemums by two little girls on behalf of the citizens of Peru. Caught by surprise, she hesitated an instant, then impulsively stooped, gathered the two little girls into her arms, kissed them both, then bowed and hastened from the stage. Presently reappearing, she stepped to the front of the stage, saying, "Dear friends, I can only thank you with the fiddle." The sweet strains of "Home Sweet Home" swept over the audience as eyes grew dim with tears. At its conclusion, deeply moved herself, Maud quietly but candidly wiped the tears from her own eyes.[12]

Maud had a special gift for reaching children with her music, a gift she took time to utilize extensively during the last ten years of her life. As early as 1910, she began giving afternoon concerts to the children in the schools before her evening recital. The phonograph and the popularity of her recordings made such concerts possible by familiarizing children with the music she presented. When she played for 2,600 children in Kalamazoo, Michigan, who were prepared through the phonograph, Maud claimed she had one of the most attentive and appreciative audiences in her entire career: "Where at one time it was a bore it is now a pleasure for me to play to the children. They seem to understand with only slight elucidation, the expression of my art, the infinite depth of even the heaviest of my pieces."[13] In the late 1880s and throughout the 1890s Maud had played for children in the public schools in Washington, D.C., where her father had been superintendent.

In Hobart, Oklahoma, Maud's two appearances drew people from nearly every town and hamlet in southwest Oklahoma and the Texas Panhandle. In the afternoon, the artist played for 500–700 school children prepared by the Victrola. She was delighted to find that every school had its own phonograph and that the library not only had its own machine, but it loaned records to the schools as well. "Bravo!" Maud responded to the news, "that is an original and splendid idea indeed. I had not heard of that plan before. I am often asked such things by newspaper men and will be pleased to tell them about the Hobart plan."

Hobart was probably one of the smallest towns that had ever "had the pleasure of entertaining and hearing this wonderful musician." It was the first time the local music club had attempted to bring an artist of the first rank to that part of Oklahoma. Thanks to Sunny's management skills, the town was able to pay Maud a flat fee and still make a profit for the library.

The impression made by Maud Powell was long remembered. She provided a model for the children of which their parents wholeheartedly approved. They kept in their minds the image "of Maud Powell, a plain wholesome woman, a native, a true daughter of America, in a hall draped and massed with her country's flag, playing before a purely American audience, which she thoroughly understood and had immediately captured by her unassuming graces, upon her wonderful instrument as no other woman has ever played, and in a way that everyone appreciated and enjoyed her art. To many of the five hundred school children, . . . it was the occasion and opportunity of a life time."[14]

The decorations were furnished by the Dixie Store, which placed a large "Welcome Maud Powell" sign in a specially decorated display window. It caught Maud's eye as she was passing, so she stepped inside to purchase some ribbon while expressing her appreciation to the manager.

As she toured the country giving concerts in this fashion, people marveled at how Maud was able to reach these children and hold their attention for an hour. The violinist always charmed her young audience by describing each piece before she played it. Then too, there was the unaccountable force of her personality as she "sang on her violin with simple intensity," making one realize that the "charm of pure melody is the highest charm music attains." In Cedar Rapids, Iowa, one critic ventured to describe the allure of her playing: "[The music was] played with the emotion, the pulse, the vital something that reaches out and makes an audience breathe as one man, all in the bow, not in the swaying of body or the flourishing arm. She was there to give a message through the ears, and no trick for the eye was used to assist, all was in the music." In searching for the secret of her art, this critic recorded his impressions after visiting Maud:

> [B]ut we are sure that Powell and "sincerity" are now synonyms. She is an American woman who has achieved a position where her name is a household word over this vast country. Neither false advertising, nor spurious publicity, nor any of the illegitimate tricks that bring bubbles to the surface in our musical world, have played any part in her career, she has honestly won what her playing merited; therefore, when she said that her aim was to make others feel what she felt and especially when she then explained her feeling for her chosen art, we were aware of why America is proud of her. Madame Powell has a sensitive reverence for the truth and is keenly alive to the simplicity of truth in art. She instinctively enjoys form in all phases of art; the symmetry of architecture, the orderly unfolding of a plot, the arrangement of a poem, the design of a picture, and most of all, the intelligible unfolding of music are a part of the truth to her. She explained that form to her did not necessarily mean the old accepted forms which dominated what we call the classical period, for new forms may arise, composers may express themselves in a vital manner and not slavishly follow the old. There must be for her, however, those elements that make an orderly whole, and she believes in encouraging those men "who like torches, throw light ahead." She has faith in Sibelius, the new tone poet from the frozen north. She believes in many Americans, not always for what they really achieve, but for what they promise.

Rhythm is an element she believes to be another truth in art. We are frank to confess that while she made clear the meaning of her conception of "rhythm," we could not resist recalling her playing at the children's concert. All that she said about its importance, we could hear again in the simple melodies that pulsed with velvet vigor. It seemed as though her remarks were defining the charm, and withal the essence of her art. I could see that a mind so charged with the light of elemental truth could never carry any message that was abnormal to the public of this country; then I could understand why she has been such a force for good in America, and why her wanting to make others feel [w]hat she feels, makes an irresistible appeal that makes her soundly popular.[15]

How deeply Maud Powell touched the heart of American life can be judged by the following letter, written after the artist quietly worked a revolution in Kalamazoo. The letter subsequently was circulated to every school superintendent in the country:

Mr. H. Godfrey Turner, 1400 Broadway, New York City:

November 23, 1916

Dear Mr. Turner — Madam Powell has been here and gone. To say that both concerts were a success is to put it mildly. They were a success artistically, financially, physically and spiritually. Yesterday evening we had a large, sympathetic and appreciative audience. I think I have never been in so large an audience at a concert at any previous time when there was such appreciative silence. At the afternoon concert there were twenty-six hundred children and one hundred adults. We sold our house and must have refused a couple of hundred children and adults admission.

Madam Powell is a wonder. She is not only a great violinist but a woman of great personal charm and magnetism. She has a message that gets home to the hearts of men, women and children. It was wonderful to see her hold that vast audience of children for a concert for one hour and a quarter.

I dare say that few great artists would be willing to undertake it. Madam Powell was very gracious and generous in her praise of our preparation and arrangements for the concerts but we know perfectly well that no amount of previous preparation for a concert would have availed had not the musician entered into the spirit of the afternoon. She was the friend of the children the instant she appeared on the platform. The whole town is crazy about Madam Powell.

You will be interested to know that our Teachers' Club will clear $650.00 from the proceeds of these two concerts which for us, to use the common expression is "going some."

I shall often think of Madam Powell and the pleasure of meeting her and hope you will give her my kindest regards the next time you see her.

Very truly yours,
J. A. Starkweather

P.S.—I received last night from Madam Powell a telegram as follows:

Give my love to the children and tell them I shall not forget them.

Best wishes to the little ones.

Maud Powell
Arthur Loesser

It is being delivered to the children of the city this morning. It was a very sweet and gracious thing to do and you may rest assured that the children of Kalamazoo will not forget her.

I have been thinking this morning about the wonderful possibilities for the education of the coming generation. Madam Powell has in her the ability to reach children. It certainly is a rare gift and I firmly believe that there is no better way to make Americans appreciate good music than by the process of educating the children through concerts such as Madam Powell gave here Wednesday afternoon. If you can interest the teachers of the United States to cooperate with Madam Powell in children's concerts, ten years of such effort would make a remarkable difference in musical America.

I would appreciate very much an autographed photograph of Madam Powell if you have one you could send me.

With kindest regards, I am,

Very truly yours,
J. A. Starkweather[16]

If the children were transformed by Maud Powell's performances, the artist was even more so. The tale of Maud's experience with the children in her hometown gives some impression of the emotional impact the children made on her:

Miss Powell was scheduled to play with the Chicago Symphony Orchestra at the Aurora, Ill., Festival, on the evening of April 16, 1917. In the afternoon she went to Sylvandell, where the big festival was being held, to hear the children sing . . . . [The local newspaper reported:]

Maud Powell has played before great audiences in all the leading music centers of the world, but she never poured her very soul into her violin with more impassioned fervor than when, yesterday afternoon, she impulsively responded to the almost tearful appeal of the children of her old home town and won thereby a tribute that brought tears to her eyes. . . .

Sylvandell was crowded to the doors with public and parochial school pupils and adults gathered to hear the first of the two afternoon children's concerts by the Chicago Symphony Orchestra. . . .

As the applause from the last song died away Maud Powell, in street costume, emerged from the director's room to the left and walked upon the stage. The audience understood in a minute who the visitor was and a storm of applause greeted her in which the children on the platform joined. Bowing her acknowledgments, Miss Powell turned to the youthful singers. She told them that she had been greatly impressed by the letters written to her by Aurora public school pupils asking that she play for them at the afternoon concert, but that in justice to herself and her audience at the evening performance she could not do so. She said that she had not intended coming down at all in the afternoon, but could not resist the temptation to see the children and hear them sing. They had performed so splendidly, she said, that she wished to thank them and to urge them to continue their interest in music. Miss Powell then bowed and retired to the director's room, but the spontaneous appeal for her to play that came in another outburst of applause overwhelmed her.

The next number on the program was . . . *Meditation* from *Thaïs*, with violin obligato by Harry Weisbach, concert master of the orchestra. Miss Powell threw off her coat, seized Mr. Weisbach's violin and was out on the platform in a moment. The chorus of childish cheers mingled with the handclapping was silenced in a moment as Miss Powell spoke a few words to Director Frederick Stock. He smiled and bowed, lifted his baton, the orchestra began the opening bars and in another instant Miss Powell swung into the obligato.

The breathless audience clung to every note. Both soloist and orchestra played as though inspired. The walls of Sylvandell have echoed and will re-echo to the strains of masterly music, but never again to such as those. When the last notes died away the vast audience again gave vent to its feelings with cheers and terrific handclapping. . . .

[T]he same paper continued:

Well, the last symphony orchestral concert for the year has passed into history — Maud Powell came to her home town and today left for Superior, Wis., where she plays Wednesday evening.

She was feeling well and looked as she always looked with her pretty brown eyes and that mass of almost black hair. Those who were at Sylvandell yesterday and who possess the music machine record, the *Thaïs Meditation*, will never again play it without thinking of the excited girl, thrilled with the reception given her by that great audience of children, as she stood playing that beautiful melody. . . . Standing with Ruth Breyspraak, her eyes fell on the number which followed the singing . . . *Meditation*. Then it was that she ran out, snatching Concertmaster Harry Weisbach's "fiddle." "You don't belong to the union" called out an orchestra man jokingly. Later she sat in her pretty brown gown, with her little brown hat, gaily entwined in its scarf, shaking and spent and excited — the artist that she is, thrilled to the core of her being with the children's appreciation. Around her were equally temperamental women friends weeping with the sheer excitement of the occasion.

Then in the evening Maud Powell donned her lovely soft gown in its purple tints and came down and played for the great room filled with admiring grownups. . . .[17]

Of all her experiences as a touring artist, perhaps none appealed to the woman in Maud more than playing for the children of America. Maud did not just play for the children in advanced communities, but in out-of-the-way places as well, prosperous little towns like Hobart and severely deprived communities wherever they were found. Her big heart could be moved more by these children than almost any other audience in her vast experience. She once said to a reporter:

I'll not tell you of the high lights in my artistic career — of the moments sacred to the memory when inspiration came, when something within spoke, which was stronger and better than myself. But I will mention a few human occasions, when the woman and not the artist was predominant.

Once I played for a theater full of miners' children, children who had never seen a tree, nor a blade of grass, nor had they ever heard music before a little brave school teacher came to town one day and slaved thereafter heart and soul to open their minds to a perception of beauty. I told the children the story of each piece before I played it—invented it as I went along—and I consider it one of the triumphs of my life that I held them practically spellbound for forty-five minutes.[18]

Maud's willingness to forward the work of countless school teachers struggling against seemingly hopeless odds lifted many a teacher out of a morass of discouragement and rekindled the flame of inspiration. One letter from a teacher in Anaconda, Montana, written in 1910, survives as a touching and remarkable testament to the importance of Maud Powell's missionary labors:

My Dear Miss Powell—

I was greatly disappointed the morning after your concert here to find you had left for Missoula on the early train. I wanted to see you and again express our gratitude to you for giving the Anaconda Boys and Girls such a musical Feast. I cannot tell you the conditions existing here. No love of art. *No appreciation*— but *your* concert has left a wonderful impression upon the children and the following week I devoted to both programs— explaining the numbers as best I could and the children were as enthusiastic and seemed to realize what it means to be a truly great artist such as you are. Even the little Babes (six and seven yrs. of age) reproduced the "Haensel and Gretel" story to me— just as you told it to them. One of my 8th Gr. boys heard your evening Program and gave me a complete analysis of it in Class— as we had been studying Sonata, Concerto, Symphony Forms, theories, etc.

To me, Miss Powell, your coming repaid me for *all* the uphill struggles of my western experience—to know you and to hear you was a wonderful inspiration. We are all grateful to you and Mr. Turner and I hope when I have again taken up residence in my dear Chicago that I shall hear you often.

Believe me, gratefully,

Mabelle M. Shelton[19]

Maud Powell's deep appreciation for the patient, faithful efforts of music teachers led to her participation in the dedication of the Theodore Presser Home for Retired Music Teachers in Philadelphia in 1914. Rising from her seat on the platform, Maud gave the dedication with deep emotion:

> It gives me a thrill of pleasure to have a share in these dedication exercises to-day — to help dedicate this beautiful home, this flower of peace, this munificent gift of Mr. Theodore Presser to my brothers and sisters of the musical profession. It shall stand as an expression of gratitude — of recognition of work bravely and faithfully done. May it breathe of peace and contentment; of comfort, of hospitality and the restfulness that gentle surroundings bring.
>
> God bless its hospitable roof! God bless its munificent mission! God bless the noble founder and, above all, bless those who shall dwell within its hospitable doors, now and always![20]

The warm-hearted Powell was frequently moved to support charitable causes, giving concerts for wage-earners, hospitals, and schools, and to support music schools connected with various settlement houses. She became an Advisory Council member of the Brooklyn Music School Settlement. She supported the work of the Gramercy Neighborhood Music Committee, giving free concerts for the foreign-born and donating a violin to the committee to be awarded to the most deserving student in the orchestra at Public School 40.

Maud played some unusual concerts that further revealed her humanity. While she was working with great concentration on a concerto while on tour, oblivious to the heat of the summer day, a black child clad in ragged clothing darted through the open French window. In halting speech, the brave youngster asked for a lively tune to dance to. Maud cheerfully obliged with a jig and the child responded with a merry dance, lost in the magic of the moment. Suddenly overcome by shyness, the child darted away without a word. A few days later as Maud was practicing, the mysterious child returned and in seconds, before the artist realized her presence, was gone again. She had left a scepter of rose hollyhocks on the table, a floral offering the great-souled violinist long treasured.

An even more unusual appeal to her good nature once arrived in the form of a strange letter. Maud's fame made her the recipient of scores of letters from young and aspiring musicians seeking her advice and thanking her for the inspiration which her beautiful playing had given them. But this letter was different. It was written in pencil on the back of printed laundry lists and was a strange mixture of sense and nonsense. The writer was from Illinois and an inmate in an asylum. He had watched Maud's career for many years and knew many details concerning her work. He wrote that he looked forward to the time when she would come to his home and give recitals — for then would the souls of his friends be released from bondage. He and they had waited long months for her coming, he continued, and begged and prayed that she would no longer delay but come to them quickly and use her magic wand.

Maud always answered the letters she received. But this time no answer was required by post; Maud Powell answered in person! Unfortunately, nothing more is known of this story.

31

Mentor for Pianists

The United States themselves are essentially the greatest poem.

— *Walt Whitman*

EVER SEEKING TO ENCOURAGE TALENT, MAUD ALWAYS SELECTED a young pianist for her tours, knowing that she could offer him unparalleled experience and exposure.[1] She discovered Francis Moore, her accompanist between 1913 and 1915, in El Paso, Texas, while typically nosing into the town's musical life. The violinist found him to be a young man of "talent, brain and plenty of wholesome ambition." The El Paso–born Moore signed a three-year contract with Powell and set out to "prove that Texas can raise something besides 'Hogs and Hell!' "

Within two years, the recognition resulting from touring with Powell enabled him to settle in New York City as a musician and accompanist in great demand by the most distinguished artists. Maud did not stand in his way and at his request released him from the contract a year early.

Lacking an accompanist for the 1915–16 season, the famous violinist walked into the Institute of Musical Art (the forerunner of the Juilliard School of Music) and inquired as to who was good. Arthur Loesser was recommended in reply.

A native of New York City, Arthur Loesser had first come to public attention as a child prodigy when he played a recital in the Waldorf Astoria ballroom at the age of ten. Soon thereafter, he studied piano at the Institute with Sigismond Stojowski, a "very sensitive pianist" from whom he learned a great deal. Graduating with highest honors, he went abroad for a couple of years, making his European debut in Berlin in 1913. The war drove him back to America "with a very decided jerk." At that point, he met Maud Powell.

Notified of Maud's interest, the twenty-year-old pianist went to see her:

> [O]f course she wanted to know whether I could play and she placed before me what was regarded in those days as a modern piece of music. It was a Sonata for Violin and Piano by Vincent D'Indy, and I read it satisfactorily. I had played a good deal with violinists during my education. Some of the violinists who became quite eminent were classmates, schoolmates, friends of mine. There was Joseph Fuchs for example and Sascha Jacobson. . . . So, I was quite used to playing with violin, and Maud Powell engaged me and this was my great adventure in becoming acquainted with my own country. I managed to get west of the Hudson for the first time in my life. Oh, far west. Well, Ohio and Indiana—that was nothing. I got to Texas, Arizona and California, Oregon and Washington and even Hawaii. This was quite wonderful.[2]

Maud had recognized young Arthur's special qualities immediately. She had found a pianist capable of matching her musicianship measure for measure, a prospect which undoubtedly excited the older artist. She could play the sonata literature from Bach to d'Indy to her heart's content with a partner who had a twin artistic soul.[3] Louis Kaufman, violinist and life-long friend of Loesser's, believes it is "significant that Maud Powell had the taste and judgment to select this young colleague—out of a possible group of more experienced and well-known accompanists."[4]

But Arthur was young yet, and for all his precocity, there was a world of things he did not know about art and life. Under Maud Powell's tutelage, Loesser had a learning experience ahead of him which was to impress itself deeply upon him as an artist and as a person.

First of all, he was to have daily contact with an individual whose artistry was supreme; not only was she a violinist of the first rank, but a musician quite without peer as well. He was probably unaware of Maud's skill as a pianist which enabled her to judge his work and offer helpful suggestions. One reporter who came to pay his respects in 1915 recorded his impressions of her talent at that time:

If they could drop in upon her at her home unawares, they would experience a shock of pleasant amazement. The present writer, though already acquainted with her pianistic abilities, could not, as he stood outside the door of her Gramercy Park apartment, resist the impression that it was a pianist of pre-eminent abilities who played with such inspiring energy and breadth the exacting piano part of the D'Indy Violin Sonata. To hear her dissect and analyze such a work, playing a phrase here and a page there, is to obtain a glimpse of an extraordinary musical spirit served by a powerful and luminous intelligence.[5]

The rarely-attempted d'Indy sonata was to be played in her forthcoming New York recital, coupled with de Bériot's G major concerto, which by then had been relegated largely to the province of conservatory students. The artist's programming of the de Bériot concerto raised some eyebrows in sophisticated New York, but Maud defended her choice ably enough:

> And yet it is a work of solid and substantial musical qualities. . . . In practicing it, I have been repeatedly moved to exclamations of delight. After all, where are we to find good new concertos today? Consider, for one thing, how superior in musical substance is De Bériot by comparison with Paganini. I played Paganini last year because several musicians asked me to do so in order to show that I could cope with it. Yet my heart was not in it. It afforded me no musical satisfaction. Whenever I picture Paganini to myself, it is with a thought of his charlatanism. Now the De Bériot work may be hackneyed, but a good deal that is generally overlooked becomes apparent when it is properly played; that is to say, with the proper understanding of its style and interpretative traditions. As much is true of the Mendelssohn. I flatter myself on having the authoritative idea in both cases. A passage near the opening of the last movement, for instance, I play in a way not practised by the majority of artists. Yet I received the idea from Joachim who in turn had it from David; and in the case of De Bériot I obtained essential suggestions from Dancla.[6]

Among the smaller pieces on the program were Victor Herbert's *A la Valse*, Edwin Grasse's recently published *Polonaise*, and Percy Grainger's "Molly on the Shore," which Maud had asked the Australian composer to arrange for violin and piano.

On the evening of their New York recital, October 26, 1915, young Loesser learned that appearing with Maud Powell offered more exposure in one recital than some artists received in an entire season! Percy Grainger, in a box, reportedly heard his own music and saw the spread of its infectious humor to the faces of a surprised and delighted house. He joined in the reception held by Sunny and Maud after the recital. In addition to Grainger and the usual host of violinists and distinguished musicians, there was a full complement of New York critics in the audience, fifteen in all. Sunny wittily published excerpts of their remarks with the title "Fourteen to One," indicating the favor with which the recital was received by nearly all.

The "one" was Henry Krehbiel, who perceived that the artist's energy and enthusiasm overpowered the de Bériot concerto. Nevertheless, this distinguished critic, whose "admiration for Miss Powell's splendid skill . . . long ago grew into affection," wrote that the recital merited more than a triple asterisk for the performance of the rarely-heard d'Indy sonata, where she "did do her own rare musical instincts and abilities justice." He wrote, "It is a work of an unusual type, whose beauties do not disclose themselves either in the self-complacent player or to the careless hearer, but she and Mr. Loesser presented them clearly, forcibly and eloquently."[7] Arthur Loesser's contribution to the success of the sonata did not escape the perceptive Krehbiel's notice: "Peculiarly ingratiating was the tricksy and jocose second movement, in which Mr. Loesser's fine taste and ingenious skill, found full play. A young artist he, whom it is a pleasure to welcome to the concert platform."

W. J. Henderson enjoyed the de Bériot concerto's performance more than his colleague had: "Mme. Powell rendered it with a delightful spirit. The qualities of grace and elegance of finish she employed as required, as also much tonal beauty. Indeed the player seemed to be at her best last evening. Her sound musicianship, a gracious dignity and commanding interpretative power were features all effectively displayed to a large assemblage that gave full evidence of its pleasure."[8]

Most of the critics reiterated *The Musical Observer's* concise observations after the previous year's recital in which she had performed Vieuxtemps' Concerto in D Minor, Op. 31, and Richard Strauss's Sonata in E-flat Major, Op. 18: "Her playing once more revealed to us an artist von Gottes Gnaden [by the grace of God], and made all who were present realize that in Maud Powell we possess one of the greatest violinists of the present day."

Loesser's tour with Maud during the 1915–16 season was the beginning of a "wonderful, wonderful friendship" and a "real career." The disappointment caused by his abrupt return from Europe yielded to the wonders of America, whose treasures were opened to him by the First Lady of American Music.

As they toured from Boston to Honolulu and from Illinois to New Mexico, Sunny imparted his accumulated stage knowledge to the youngster until, at the age of twenty, Arthur Loesser had absorbed all the stage craft he needed for life. Sunny gave instructions on bowing and stage deportment. One handy suggestion was always to be sure that his white shirt cuffs were showing so that the ladies would know he had a shirt on! Sunny's own presence of mind made an indelible impression:

> In Hood River, Oregon, which was famous for its apples, at the concert at intermission time, down this aisle came a very nervous lady with a basket of apples to present to Madame Powell. Unfortunately, the basket was designed like a flower basket—the kind that is in the shape of a lily, with spreading out top—and by the time that she had presented it to Madame Powell and tried to make her speech—two apples fell off to the floor. It was large enough so that it had to sit there and after Maud Powell had graciously accepted it, [it was] left [on] the stage. After intermission it was Loesser's turn to play a solo and Godfrey Turner always went out to the stage to raise the lid. This particular time he walked out—looked at the basket, looked at each apple, picked an apple up in one hand, picked another in the other hand—stared at them and compared them and then took a gigantic bite out of one of them. It brought down the house—everybody who had been so nervous about this poor woman and felt so sorry for her—howled and laughed and he marched off the stage and then when they had all calmed down Arthur came out to play.

Arthur proved himself when the piano pedal fell off while he was playing one of his solos. Leaning over to look underneath the instrument, he suddenly became aware of the terrible silence in the audience. The thought occurred to him, "Why those poor people think I fainted." So he very quickly kicked the pedal. It fell down and he came up smiling, explaining to the audience, "You see, I didn't faint. The pedal broke and I have to get an instrument to get it fixed." With that, he went off stage, while the audience settled back in their seats reassured.

During their years of travel together (1915–18), Maud and Sunny took Arthur on a mule ride down the Grand Canyon's Bright Angel Trail, one of the pioneer violinist's favorite points of inspiration. It was one of her ingenious ways of broadening his education. With obvious pride, she told him: "You have to see this and you have to learn about it. It was my Uncle, Major Powell who went down the river. . . . " With that, she launched into a lengthy exposition of the importance of her Uncle Wes's explorations and theories which deeply impressed the youth. It was an experience for which Loesser always felt deeply indebted to Maud. He was touched that the great artist had done this for him, although she had no doubt enjoyed it as much as he.

It appears that Arthur was still learning stage deportment when they reached Portland, Oregon, in January 1916. One feature of the "genuine musical feast" was his "exceedingly automatic" acknowledgment of applause. Following Maud onto the stage, "he took exactly four steps forward, faced about to the right, threw a glance at the start to the left and bowed low. Then he waited as the violinist swished by him, paused a moment, reversed the former evolutions and disappeared in the wings."[9] It became most comical when the artists were recalled a dozen times or more after one selection. But the critic was quick to note "his technique was brilliant, remarkably clean, and the tone had the singing quality." Maud Powell had merely "improved with age," an observation which left nothing more to be said about Portland's favorite violinist.

Everywhere, the musicians were greeted by large crowds. Arthur expressed his amazement that their concert in Columbus, Ohio, could attract 3,500 people. A New York audience of 1,000 was unusual, and even at that, was usually "liberally papered" (with free tickets) even for recitals of the most distinguished artists. Of course, Maud Powell never "papered" her recitals, so this example of genuine interest in classical music was a revelation to him.

Arthur could not help but be impressed by Maud's reception in every city. Walter Anthony, the critic for the *San Francisco Chronicle*, wrote:

The pleasure one feels in admiring Maud Powell is such a satisfactory sentiment! It is unmarred by qualifications, mental reservations, and is free from "buts." She is not a great musician—for an American. She is a great musician. She is not a superb violinist—for a woman. She is a superb violinist. She stands before the American public and the music lovers of the world simply on her merits as a violinist-musician but she is not a mere abstraction. Hers is a personality with gifts singularly hers even in the company of the Elmans and the Kreislers.[10]

It was one thing to play when all was well, but Maud displayed her legendary courage and grit when she fell ill on tour, arising from a sickbed to play on a drafty stage in a recital sponsored by the Oakland Teachers' Association. The "lines of struggle" showed in her face that night, but she spoke through her violin in such a way that her audience was deeply moved: "With it she gives tongue to poetry of searching beauty. She speaks all languages. Humor is hers, and fancy. Pathos and tragedy are in her bow and violin. She knows the moods of all men and women, and can give them voice. Her violin has become for her a living soul."[11] She played the Wieniawski concerto and a Beethoven sonata that night.

Being introduced to American audiences by such an artist was an exhilarating experience for her young accompanist. Maud's audiences expected her to appear with a very fine pianist; it was one of the hallmarks of her performances. But one San Francisco critic expressed his surprise and delight in Loesser's unique qualities:

> The surprise of the afternoon was Arthur Loesser, the pianist. He is an artist from tip to toe, and he understands his particular position to a nicety. As accompanist he submerges himself to the guidance of the soloist and plays with a delicacy of touch and an understanding of the artist's ideas that is decidedly ingenious and masterly. As a soloist he displays the same delicacy of execution; however, with an increased firmness and reliance upon his own artistic intelligence. He has even the element of greatness because he possesses decided individuality of style and with added experience and a little more display of confidence in his stage deportment he will surely become one of the foremost pianists before the public.[12]

Touring with Maud also impressed more deeply on the young American the amazing variety, strength, and flexibility of the American culture. With Europe at war, America's growing musical public, which Maud was so much responsible for generating, could accommodate the influx of exiled musicians as well as the modern harmonies of the d'Indy sonata. In Los Angeles, where she played to a full house and "storms of applause," Maud was interviewed by a reporter who awaited her arrival, knowing she would have hopeful things to say about the advance of music in America.

I want to enjoy your out-of-doors right away, but I must have my daily rehearsal with my accompanist, Mr. Loesser. You know, we play the d'Indy Sonata to-night. How does it take? Well, differently in different localities. For instance, we played it in Boston at a moderate-priced concert for working people and it was heard with rapt attention. Then we played it in New York to a quite aristocratic audience, if you please, and many were bored and put in their time rattling their programs. So, you see, not quite all the musical appreciation is in "N' York."

I find a great and growing interest in music all over the country this year. In spite of the return of many American musicians from Europe and the coming of hundreds of Europeans, I think there will be plenty for all of us to do. And so much more concert-giving, possibly at lower admission prices, will result in a much larger concert-attending public in coming years.

And, then, another aid to the same end is the fact that the music recording and producing machines are making the public acquainted with a high class of compositions through the best obtainable artists. The artists of twenty years ago felt that most of their auditors were strangers to the player and to the composition; now the most of them have your work and your compositions in their own homes and woe be to you if you don't live up to your recorded reputation.

Besides this, so many of the public schools are adding what they call courses of "musical appreciation" that the youngsters are able to "talk back" at you when you speak of the themes of a sonata or the movements of a symphony.

Oh, yes, we are growing, and we have so many great artists in America that we are almost self-sufficient. Maybe some day we could be quite so if art were not as wide as the whole world. But as I am intensely an American, and not by adoption, either, I can't help enjoying the eagle's scream once in a while, you know.[13]

The war only made Americans more aware of the value of her art to their lives:

Among the world treasures now safely beyond the reach of European guns are Maud Powell's bow arm and the musical mind and human heart behind it. Her music is made in America. It is a native product, yet not limited by any narrow view of nationality. On her programs are the compositions of American, Finnish, German, French, Belgian composers. If the spirit of the sympathetic understanding that informs her art were the possession of statesmen and kings, there would be no war. She plays peace in a troubled world. [14]

Upon her return to New York, Maud gave a quick recap of the tour and its successes:

It has been a most delightful season. We began in October and are ending with the spring festival dates. Our first recitals were in New York, Boston and Cambridge, followed by a tour through Ohio, Kansas, Oklahoma and Texas to the Pacific Coast. We had huge audiences in all the California cities. But I am not going west of Colorado next season, although Mr. Behymer has written for return engagements.

We gave two recitals in San Francisco, and then went to Honolulu for the Christmas holidays, giving two recitals there also. Then we came back to the mainland, where the first appearance on our return was in Oakland, in the Municipal Auditorium, a beautiful building with excellent acoustics for so huge a place. From Oakland we went to Seattle, appearing with the Symphony Orchestra before the largest audience in the history of the organization, they told us. Then back to Portland, where the Heilig—the biggest theater in the city—was packed for the recital. Our trip took us Eastward from Portland, through Colorado, New Mexico, Texas, Oklahoma, Kansas, Michigan, Georgia and South Carolina. The latter part of the season was devoted to appearances in Ohio, Michigan, Wisconsin and Illinois, in the latter with the Chicago Symphony Orchestra. During the middle of April we were in Kansas. [15]

Maud had really relished the opportunity, which Loesser's ability made possible, to perform a larger number and variety of sonatas than ever before on tour. Her delight in this expansive programming also afforded Loesser a rare opportunity. He related: "She would usually start off with a concerto, with the orchestra part being reduced for the piano. Then would come a sonata—oh, we played many sonatas—Beethoven and Brahms, and all the well-known sonatas including the one by D'Indy which was regarded as modern in those days.

Then would come a group of solos by myself and then I believe she would finish off the program with some violin solos." In the absence of Sunny, Maud would quietly go to the piano and turn pages for young Arthur during his solo appearance, which critics noted was "a graceful thought many musicians might copy."

Upon her return, Maud spoke with a reporter about repertoire and interpretation as well as the importance of her splendid accompanist:

> "Criticism of the de Bériot piece was confined, I found, to before the recital. . . . The performance always seemed to justify the place I have given it on my programs. Among the smaller novelties that had success this year it must be conceded that Percy Grainger's *Molly on the Shore* achieved the greatest glory. It is a little classic and has come to stay."

Maud Powell is probably the only violinist who has successfully presented the d'Indy Sonata on recital programs. This exceedingly modern composition was given nine times during the present season. In all, six concertos and eight chamber music sonatas have figured on her 1915–1916 programs.

> "The success of a large sonata work," says the famous violinist, "depends upon the character of the pianist's playing. If it lies within the style and artistic sympathies of the pianist, then it is possible to give a convincing performance. I attribute to Arthur Loesser, the young pianist I introduced this season, the pleasure I have taken in sonata work and the great number I have been able to include in my programs.

> "To give successfully compositions like the sonatas of d'Indy, Brahms, Beethoven or Bach is making propaganda for serious music. The public must be coaxed into listening to the music and not to the artist. The task is not an easy one, for a good deal of mental projection is required in connection—or, I might say, collusion— with musical talent to guide an audience in this direction."

Mme. Powell is, perhaps, the only great violinist before the public who differentiates in styles of composition and their interpretation.

> "The Mozart Concerto and the Sonata by César Franck, if you wish examples," she replied to a query. "They are about as far apart in character as the two poles are geographically, and they must be played in their respective characters. A Hubay Hungarian Rhapsodie is in a class by itself, rhythmically as well as in style.

> "A simple song transcribed for violin must literally sing the words. It is absolutely necessary that each piece have its own

'atmosphere'—to use an overworked term. Not only must there be differentiation in style, but there must, for successful enunciation, be a special kind of technique as well."[16]

Viewing the pianist as an equal partner in making music, Maud once graphically demonstrated in an article she penned just why such a view was essential to bring out the full effect of a composition:

> Speaking of violin literature: it is always very helpful to young students, and, I may add also to audiences, to consider the pieces played as duets for piano and violin rather than as violin solos. Occasionally a composer writes a pure melody so complete in itself as to need no accompaniment. Such is perhaps Schumann's *Traumerei*, although even its beauty is enhanced by the lovely accompaniment. But more often the melody tells only half the story, as in characteristic pieces or so-called program music. A pretty characteristic piece that I often play is *At the Brook*, by Boisdeffre.
>
> Often when I am playing informally I describe the music in a few words. Of this composition I say something like this—"The piece I am to play now is really a duet, so you will have to listen very carefully to both parts. If you want to know where the brook is I think you will find it in the piano: *I* am just a little skiff floating on the surface, or perhaps a gleam of sunshine playing with the ripples." In other words, the piano part (I was going to say accompaniment, but the word is misleading) is so descriptive that the melody would be meaningless without it. . . .

Maud cited several other examples of the piano's contribution. Rimsky-Korsakov's *Song of India* (*Chanson d'Indoue*) "establishes a languorous mood through the mesmerizing influence of the monotonous piano part." In Saint-Saëns' *The Swan*, the "clever treatment" of the piano part suggests the "mirror-like yet plastic surface of water, thus throwing into relief the gentle melody of the violin which in imagination portrays the swan's graceful movements." The exaltation in Handel's *Largo* is created by the simple chords of the piano: "[T]hey move like Fate, itself, ever onward, inevitably, inexorably, to a definite goal, carrying a triumphant soul (the melody) with them."

Modern compositions presented more of a challenge to the violinist and pianist in terms of achieving a proper balance of parts:

> It is especially necessary in these days for violinists to develop a faculty of listening to the whole harmonic structure of compositions

in order to cultivate a sense of ensemble; for contemporary composers of music for violin and piano, more and more, rely upon the rich colorful complex harmonizations that have been developed within the past few years, for creating atmosphere; and unless one has learned to listen intelligently and can analyze the function that harmony plays, an adequate effective interpretation is impossible for the violinist will fail certainly to attain the balance of parts. Modern impressionistic music demands of the performer that he shall have power of visualization and a well-developed color sense. He must have in his own mind a clear concept of the picture the composer limns. Modern composers paint, as on canvas, with a broad brush and with bold color; and the artist must have the breadth of vision to see the work in its total effect. A good example of this type of music is Sibelius' Concerto (First Movement). This is a work to tax the technical resources of the artist and his imagination.

As a homely comparison, modern music for the violin and piano may well be likened to a complicated salad, in which the ingredients are so cleverly blended as to be undistinguishable except to an epicure. They defy analysis; they bear not the least resemblance to the simple salads of former days. To intelligently enjoy (analyze) these highly seasoned concoctions really demands an educated taste. To carry out the comparison — the simple salads are like the older classics, direct and simple in construction, with a simple well-defined interrelation of parts; modern music is highly seasoned and complex (full of bizarre chord combinations and weird harmonizations), and the enjoyment of it demands power of analysis, with a highly developed color sense.[17]

Not every talented pianist made a good accompanist. Maud discovered repeatedly that the self-sufficiency of the piano as a solo instrument tended to develop pianists with no real feeling for ensemble playing. This tendency was discouraging to her because she felt pianists (and violinists who paid all their attention to technique) were losing sight of the higher aspects of their art for which, after all, the true musician lived:

In general I have noticed that violinists are better musicians than pianists. The violinist, you see, has to play in quartets, he has to play in orchestras. The pianist does not and the moment the average pianist tries to accompany a violin piece disaster follows. They can play in time but for some mysterious reason they are not rhythmic. For all this I do not mean that musicians—pianists, violinists, or any others—should devote hours upon hours to mere technic. That is the fault of the pupils of Sevčik, of the Prague school of violin playing. They can play scales and trills, and have a nice, pleasant tone but they miss the higher aspects of their art. It goes without saying that an excess of technical drudgery will rob a player's work of precisely those elements required for its greatness and generality of appeal.[18]

Maud took particular delight in Arthur Loesser's abilities even though he could be irascible at times. She recognized his irascibility as growing pains and continued to endure it while ever expanding his opportunities. Loesser made his first recordings as Maud Powell's accompanist in the summer of 1916.

Their recording of Percy Grainger's rollicking "Molly on the Shore," made in June 1916, was a best-seller by fall. Not only did the recording provide Loesser with undreamed-of exposure, but Percy Grainger's name as a composer was thrust into the limelight. The Australian-born Grainger was only thirty-four at the time and had made his American debut as a pianist in recital on February 11, 1915.[19]

Loesser was not always outwardly appreciative of the opportunities Maud provided. The ease with which his piano mastery came to him did not prepare the immature twenty-one-year-old for the Victor Company's rejection of what must have been his first solo recording. Loesser's rebellion at the rejection apparently made him unpleasant company all during the recording session on June 20, 1916.[20] But Maud somehow understood and in her kind but straightforward way wrote a firm letter of advice, reprimand, and forgiveness which reveals her true humanity perhaps better than any other surviving written document.

THE KNOLL
WHITEFIELD, N. H.

Aug. 14, 1916

Dear Loesser,

Will you plan to do some rehearsing up here, beginning on Wednesday morning the 23rd. We will work hard for a week. Come on the night train, or if you prefer to see the country, leave New York on Tuesday morning, arriving here between seven and eight in the evening. We will pay the Railroad and put you up at Locust Cottage nearby. — And perhaps being near the end of the summer, consequently "pleite" (isn't that the word for "broke"!) you might not be averse to receiving a little cheque besides. Then you can rent a bicycle and go in for other terrible (?) extravagances while here.

Bring your sweet self along, not that contrary imp of deviltry that got into you at Camden and made them all hate you. (And incidentally spoiled my records.) You've got to learn something about psychic forces, if you want to get on in the world. And it was unkind, after I had managed to introduce you and give you a chance to make a little money and reputation by record-making, to be so hopelessly disagreeable. Do you know how I have reconciled Mr. Turner (and myself) to inviting you up here? By trying to realize the true psychology of the situation. You were disappointed that your record was not accepted. You thought you didn't care. But you did. And you got all nasty and defiant inside. Because you've got an acquisitive brain with a good memory you are unnaturally clever at storing away facts and figures and notes and things. But you are younger than other boys your age in your world-vision. Your talent is your capital — but of what earthly use is it if you don't make the world pay interest on it? You can't manage the world unless you cultivate judgment, for yours is not the talent to stir the emotions of the ignorant like Elman's. Your talent has all sifted through your brain, which is the true way after all, but now you must sift your brain through your heart by cultivating a sense of humanity in order to win the game of life.

I don't suppose I can make you understand, you are such a kid after all, but at any rate you can try to understand what I mean, and that it is meant for your good. Further, that I know that sweet self of yours back of all that unfortunate self-consciousness, and that I want to have your better self go on tour with us this winter (and incidentally come up here). I haven't a mirror in the music room. Please take your own photograph down from your dressing table (if you haven't already) and turn your mirror to the wall. You can shave and tie your scarf by a piece of glass 2 inches by four of the same! And don't indulge yourself by having an argument with somebody in order to avoid giving a little thought to what I have written. If you do argue I

shall be convinced that you must eventually be a criminal law-
yer instead of a musician!

Yours with affection,
Maud Powell[21]

Loesser must indeed have felt the affection communicated, for he
came to Whitefield, and in the fall they were on the road together.

If Arthur had not before fully comprehended the magnitude of
privilege that was his as Maud Powell's concert partner, Henry T.
Finck's review in *The Evening Post* following their recital in New
York's new Cort Theatre on October 24, 1916, could have enlightened him:

> Could it have been known in advance to the thousands of lovers
> of violin music how wonderfully Maud Powell—now fully restored
> to health—was going to play yesterday afternoon, Carnegie Hall, or
> even the Metropolitan Opera House, would have proved too small
> to hold the throngs that would have crowded the auditorium. Sel-
> dom if ever has an artist received more enthusiastic applause than
> was showered on her in the acoustically admirable Cort Theatre; and
> all of it was more than deserved. After such a demonstration of
> supreme artistry, it is not too much to say that Mme. Powell ranks
> second, and a very close second, to Fritz Kreisler, greatest of living
> violinists.
>
> Often has Maud Powell played well in this town, but perhaps
> never before has she played so that every bar from beginning to end
> was flawless and enjoyable. This was true even of the Scherzo
> Fantastique of Bazzini, with its bouncing bow staccatos and simul-
> taneous pizzicato and arco. The brilliancy and ease with which she
> executed these extremely difficult tricks could hardly have been sur-
> passed by their originator, Paganini; and one could understand why
> he—as was Mme. Powell yesterday—was so frenziedly applauded for
> them.
>
> In a Mozart rondo, written in 1776 for Elizabeth Haffner's wed-
> ding, Mme. Powell made further demonstrations of her virtuosity,
> taking it at a pace which recalled Wagner's remark that Mozart's fast
> movements could not be played too fast. Another miracle of agility
> was her playing of the final movement of the D minor sonata of
> Saint-Saëns—a sort of *moto perpetuo* that almost made one dizzy
> to listen to.

Yet these demonstrations of superlative virtuosity were the least part of the art of America's greatest violinist. It was her heart-playing that counted for most, and this reached its climax in her exquisitely tender rendering of Dvořák's deeply emotional "Songs My Mother Sang," one of the best hundred songs ever written, and which Mme. Powell herself has adapted for violin. Fritz Kreisler introduced a fragment of it in one of his Slavic pieces, but here is the whole song, at the beck and call of thousands of violinists who will soon be playing it—as they play the various Kreisler arrangements, including the charming Beethoven Rondino, which was one of yesterday's encores.

Much pleasure was given also by the "Plaisir d'Amour" of Martini, another of Maud Powell's own arrangements, and by Beethoven's Romance in G major, in which the double-stopping was exquisitely pure and ingratiating. . . .

Mme. Powell had to repeat the Dvořák song, and add several extras, among them Chopin's "Maiden's Wish" and Percy Grainger's "Molly on the Shore," which is another of the "best sellers" to-day. She played this delightfully tuneful piece in a way that made it the climax of the whole recital, to the huge delight of the audience.

Violinists often engage accompanists who are not equal to the higher flights. Not so Maud Powell. Arthur Loesser played with her the Arensky concerto in A minor, and the Saint-Saëns sonata, in a way that made one hope that Mme. Powell might next consider one of the Grieg sonatas, the most poetic of all works of their class.

Ironically, Loesser joined Maud later that season in one of the most unique recitals in music annals, Maud Powell's "Record Recital." Americans were crazy about the phonograph, and soon it was even more ubiquitous than Maud Powell in person. Everywhere the artist went, she was greeted with scores of requests to play favorite recordings as encores to her scheduled program.[22]

In response to popular demand, Maud decided to give in New York's Carnegie Hall on January 8, 1917, a recital programmed wholly from music she had recorded—something no artist had done before. Sunny sent out announcements listing forty-five records made by Maud for Victor. The recipients were asked to mark their first and second choices on a return post card. Maud then compiled a program of seventeen pieces from the marked favorites:

1. Concerto, No. 7, G major . . . . . De Bériot
2. (a) Love's Delight . . . . Martini (1706–1784)

(b) Tambourin . . . . Leclair (1697–1764)
(c) Bouree (unaccompanied) . . . . Bach (1685–1750)
(d) Minuet . . . . Mozart-Burmeister
　　　　　　　　　　　　　　　　(1756–1791)
(e) Finale from Concerto, Op. 64 . Mendelssohn (1809–1847)
3. Character Pieces:
　　(a) Deep River . . . . Coleridge-Taylor–Powell
　　　　　　　　　　　　　　　　(Religious melody, African)
　　(b) Zefir . . . . Hubay
　　(c) Kol Nidrei . . . . Max Bruch
　　　　　　　　　　　　　　　　(Religious melody, Hebrew)
　　(d) Farfalla (Fireflies) . . . . Sauret
　　(e) Twilight . . . . Massenet-Powell
　　(f) St. Patrick's Day . . . . Vieuxtemps
　　　　　　　　　　　　　　　　(Religious melody, Irish)
4. Dances:
　　(a) Valse Triste . . . . Sibelius
　　(b) Molly on the Shore . . . . Percy Grainger
　　(c) Gavotte (from Mignon) . . . . . Thomas-Sarasate
　　(d) Minute Waltz . . . . Chopin-Powell
　　(e) Polonaise . . . . Vieuxtemps

The program revealed the tremendous advance of musical taste in America. As one critic observed, only ten years earlier, "some of the compositions on the list would hardly have been known much less liked by the general public. Now they are household intimates."[23] That said a great deal for both the phonograph and Maud Powell's musical pioneer work.

The fact that the public had chosen the de Bériot Concerto No. 7 in G Major, the Mendelssohn concerto *Finale*, and the unaccompanied Bach *Bourée* gave some indication of the public's musical sophistication. The de Bériot concerto, which Maud recorded in 1915, was the first violin concerto recorded entire, with all three movements on separate disks, although each movement had to be shortened to meet technical limitations. The Mendelssohn concerto *Finale* had been one of the first of Maud's recorded efforts in 1904. The inclusion of three of the artist's own transcriptions among the highest ranking popular favorites must have been gratifying to Maud, especially since she had a special affection for "Deep River."

The audience which packed Carnegie Hall that night seemed to understand the significance of the event, but then settled back to enjoy the concert they had chosen, performed by an artist they loved. Although the same performance could have been heard anywhere, one critic observed, "Mme. Powell in life was more absorbing and vital than Mme. Powell of the talking machine." In "rare form," the artist reportedly "gave generously of her gifts and moved and thrilled in turn a large audience that demanded enough encores to make another goodly-sized program."[24]

Henry Krehbiel noted that in a program which ran through "an extraordinary list of moods and styles, . . . Miss Powell was at her best, playing with a warm tone, accurate intonation and finished style."[25] Another critic reported: "All that the popular violinist was heard in she played in masterly fashion. With admirable poise, with large, beautiful tone and majestic sweep, she held a secure grip upon her hearers, and their response was ample proof of the power of her appeal. Since the details of Mme. Powell's art are well known to concert-goers at this day, suffice it to say that the potency of her appeal remains undiminished."[26] Richard Aldrich concluded that, "If this was playing to the gallery, the upper parts of the hall paid the compliment back by thunderous applause."[27]

Thanks to the tutelage, exposure, and management provided by Maud and Sunny, Arthur Loesser was poised to strike out on his own by January 1919.[28] He went on to a distinguished career as a performer and pedagogue. After Maud died, Arthur composed a piece for violin and piano entitled "California," which he fittingly dedicated to the memory of Maud Powell.[29]

One of the last photo portraits taken of Maud, about May 1919.

AMER

Honestly,

when it comes to *Maud Powell* there are mighty few left with the old idea that men play better than women.

At this time,

more than ever, our *best* should be considered first.

S. Godfrey Turner

1400 Broadway, New York

acing page and above, left, Maud at U.S. Army Camp Upton, Long Island, one of the many military camps she visited during World War I, on May 27, 1918. *Top,* receiving a sson in surveying as Sunny looks on; *bottom,* "hats off" to the boys' favorite performer. *bove, right,* one of Sunny's ads appearing in October 1918.

This page, Maud was among the first women to exercise her newly-won right to vote in New York state in November 1919.

Facing page, top left, Axel Skjerne, Maud's pianist, 1917–20; *right,* Axel with Maud in Champaign, Ill., November 15, 1918 or 1919; *bottom,* Maud with Samuel Carr (left), president of the New England Conservatory, and George W. Chadwick, dean of American composers, at the Norfolk Festival, June 1918.

Representative of the critical acclaim she received throughout her career, Sunny's clever advertisement, *this page,* records the reception accorded Maud's Aeolian Hall recital with pianist Arthur Loesser on October 26, 1915. *Facing page,* Maud and her colleagues about 1918.

FOURTEEN
TO
ONE

DEUTSCHES JOURNAL
One may only add that the occasion served to renew her title to pre-eminent mastery.   Dr. Heinrich Moeller.

EVENING MAIL
Her concert last evening would have been amply worth while if only for the sake of hearing her play the d'Indy Sonata.   Sigmund Spaeth.

EVENING POST
A tone so velvety and rich that only a very small proportion of the greatest violinists possess it.   Henry T. Finck.

EVENING SUN
Returned this season in magnificent form.   W. B. Chase.

EVENING WORLD
The justly popular American violinist, because her skill and art have placed her in the front rank of public performers.   Sylvester Rawling.

GLOBE
Has little to fear from her rivals of the sterner sex.   Hugo Goerlitz.

HERALD
Gave her annual violin recital last night before a large aadience.   Edward Ziegler.

PRESS
Virtuoso skill and sterling musicianship revealed once more her unusual technical and artistic accomplishments.   Max Smith.

STAATS-ZEITUNG
One must almost believe that a man stands there giving of his best.   M. Halperson.

SUN
Sound musicianship, a gracious dignity and commanding interpretative powers were features all effectively displayed to a large assemblage that gave full evidence of its pleasure.   W. J. Henderson.

TIMES
Deeply impressed a large audience of the kind of listeners that count.   Richard Aldrich.

TRIBUNE
Unnecessarily and aggressively pugnacious.   H. E. Krehbiel.

BROOKLYN EAGLE
d'Indy Sonata .   It was the eloquent playing of an artist like Maud Powell that made it triumph.

BROOKLYN TIMES
Her playing seemed the very acme of her art.

BROOKLYN STANDARD-UNION
Before a crowded auditorium she demonstrated that her powers as a master of the violin are beyond gainsaying.

Mgr. H. GODFREY TURNER, 1400 Broadway, N. Y.

First page of the manuscript of Maud's cadenza for the first movement of the Brahms Violin Concerto in D Major.

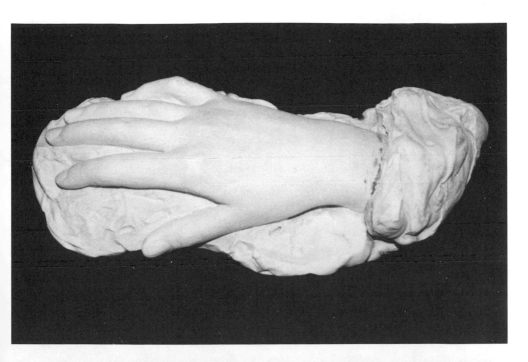

CARUSO   POWELL   WILLIAMS   PLANÇON   PATTI   TAMAGNO   GILIBERT   GERVILLE-RÉACHE

VICTOR IMMORTALS

Top, the plaster cast of Maud's right hand made by Warren B. Davis on April 6, 1893, for he 1893 World's Columbian Exposition held in Chicago.

One of the last photo portraits taken of Maud, about May 1919.

32

Playing for the Soldiers

And thou America,
Thy offspring towering e'er so high, yet higher
  Thee above all towering,
With Victory on thy left, and at thy right hand Law;
Thou Union holding all, fusing, absorbing, tolerating all,
Thee, ever thee, I sing.

— *Walt Whitman*

THE SUNSHINE SPREAD IN NEW YORK BY MAUD'S LIGHTHEARTED CONCERT
featuring her recorded favorites soon yielded to the shadow of war.
When Germany announced unrestricted submarine warfare on February 1, 1917, Americans were deeply aroused and divided by pre-
sentiments of American involvement in the European conflict. They
watched helplessly as the newspaper headlines reported President
Wilson's response to events inexorably drawing them into the holo-
caust. On February 3, the United States broke off diplomatic relations with Germany. In a matter of weeks, eight American vessels
were sunk and a German plot to involve America in a war with Mexico and Japan was revealed. On April 2, President Wilson, who had
labored valiantly for peace, asked Congress to declare war on Germany, which they did on Good Friday, April 6, 1917.

   Ever since German U-boats had sunk the British passenger ship
Lusitania on May 7, 1915, with the loss of more than 1,100 people,
128 of them Americans, sentiment in America had run strongly in
favor of England in the European war. Nevertheless, America's blood
attachment to both Germany and England ran strong enough to
split families on the issue, and the Powell-Turner family was no exception. Since the war had begun in that fateful summer of 1914, Maud

and Sunny had had a very personal interest in its outcome. Sunny's son by his previous marriage was serving in the Nineteenth Scotch Highlanders and had been awarded a military cross, while his nephew Herbert Marshall (the actor) lost a leg in the war. Maud's own sentiments were firmly on the side of England with its democratic traditions. She had always loathed German militancy. In 1915, she wrote to her cousin, "I don't want [my family's blood] Prussionized, thank you!" in spite of its German origin. But her brother favored Germany in the conflict: "And Billy, gentle Billy, is heart and soul for Germany in this terrible war. We keep off the subject entirely at Gt. Neck."[1]

The war which had been raging relentlessly in Europe since 1914 began to alter America's musical profile as numerous artists sought refuge in her broad peaceful land. Ysaÿe arrived in 1916. His estate in Ostend was in ruins, while his town house in Brussels was in German hands. The great violinist toured the United States to send money home to his beleaguered wife and children, who had taken refuge in London. In 1918, he became the conductor of the Cincinnati Symphony Orchestra and a teacher at the Cincinnati Conservatory of Music until July 1919, when he returned to Europe.

Jacques Thibaud, the distinguished French violinist, came to America for the 1917–18 season, his home in France demolished. Albert Spalding, the American violinist who had made his New York debut in 1908, enlisted in the army in 1917 but returned safely at the end of the war.[2] Fritz Kreisler, an Austrian citizen, served six weeks in the Austrian army but then returned to the United States upon his discharge.[3] Strong American sentiment against Kreisler forced him to withdraw from the concert platform for the 1917–18 season. Maud Powell willingly shouldered his canceled engagements whenever she could and donated all receipts to the American Red Cross.

Among the brilliant Russian pupils of Leopold Auer, the most eminent teacher at the St. Petersburg Conservatory, Efrem Zimbalist was already permanently settled in America. Mischa Elman, who had made his New York debut in 1908, had been touring Europe when the war broke out and immediately returned to the United States in 1914, becoming a U.S. citizen in 1923.

Both Leopold Auer and Jascha Heifetz fled the Russian Revolution in 1917. Heifetz made his sensational debut in Carnegie Hall on October 27, 1917, and became an American citizen in 1925.

Auer, trapped in Norway, where he had gone for a vacation in May 1917, made his way to New York's safe harbors by the next February. He gave recitals in the United States' principal cities and then took up teaching privately in New York. America's musical life was enriched immeasurably by the contributions of these Russian-Americans. But musical observers noted that "the vogue of the Russian violinists of the Auer tradition did not lessen Maud Powell's established popularity and she remained a favorite until her death."[4]

Removed as America was from the direct terror of the Great War, the people had no illusions about its dreadful consequences. Of the sixty-five million men mobilized around the world, more than half suffered injuries, and of those 8.5 million were killed, including 126,000 Americans. While the war decimated an entire generation of European manhood and uncounted civilians, the impact was less drastic on the other side of the ocean. But the entrance of the United States into the war abruptly jerked the country out of its insular pursuits and concerns and made the American people come to grips with the world's suffering.

Through this "soul-awakening," Maud saw good emerging in America. In October 1917, John C. Freund polled musicians on whether America's emergence as a leader in world politics would result in its assumption of "a new and comparatively more important place as a musical nation." Maud Powell responded with the intelligence, feeling, and vision for which she was famous:

> I dare hope. I dare believe, that out of this unspeakable war-hell, ultimate good will come. The end is not yet, and if we can but suffer the deprivation, biting sorrow and scorching anxiety of our allies, if we can go through the soul-searching process that the warring nations have experienced since 1914, then, and then only, can there be an American soul-awakening that shall lead the way to real achievement in the arts. What America has needed for many years is a real shaking up. Our smugness, our middle class thought, should be rooted out; our soul-deadening prosperity should quake in the balance. Nothing of any importance can be achieved in an environment of public content and self-approval, for under such conditions there can be born no public spirit that sighs for artistic satisfaction, and without a public, the artist's pot cannot boil, nor can his artistic spirit soar in flights of creative ecstacy. I do not hold with the idea that burdens of trouble and actual want or starvation give rise to art

genius. During dire trouble there is stagnation. Blind sorrow and devastating tragedy benumb the sensibilities—the creative powers are in abeyance. But nature has her own remedies. Hope steals in and offers solace. The tortured soul bursts its fetters, rises into finer ether, and straightway proceeds to create *new expression for its new estate*.

Let us hope that America will not be found wanting when the test comes, but will take her stand bravely with older nations, in the arts, as she has in invention, commerce and organizing ability. The time of trouble will help our pampered, restless women. Nobler outlets will be given their nervous energy. Where there are noble women, there are noble sons. When women's souls ache with a longing to express higher things—the infinite, the ineffable, the true—then will they give birth to sons of genius.[5]

Everyone played a part in the war effort. Maud was an initial member of the board of the Music Service League of America, which worked to provide hospitals, prisons, and army camps with phonographs and records. She continued her appointed rounds on tour, but then tripled her schedule by playing Kreisler's canceled engagements and by giving concerts in all the camps and armed services hospitals throughout the country. She observed, "Since I can't knit on account of having to be careful of my fingers and hands and am never long enough in one town to do Red Cross work, my chief joy in life is playing for the soldiers."[6]

Maud first began playing for the soldiers in 1917 under the auspices of the Young Men's Christian Association, which set up large "huts" or auditoriums for entertainment in the camps. Eventually, the War Department Commission on Training Camp Activities opened a whole series of "Liberty Theatres" in the camps, which Maud Powell toured tirelessly. Actors and managers contributed their services freely, while drama directors volunteered to coach the production of original plays by the soldiers. Isadora Duncan with her dancers, and musicians such as Schumann-Heink (three sons in the army), Geraldine Farrar, Alma Gluck, John McCormack, Efrem Zimbalist, Mischa Elman, and David Bispham (only son killed in England) offered their services to the commission as well.

Although she had been on the concert stage for nearly thirty-five years and had broken down almost every conceivable barrier to appreciation of her art, Maud found that she had not yet completed her musical pioneer work. Her first appearance in a Liberty Theatre at Camp Lewis in Tacoma, Washington, became known far and wide as the day "Maud Powell licked the prize fighter."[7]

On her initial rounds of the training camps, certain military officials doubted whether the boys could appreciate her refined art. Some who had ventured to take a chance on engaging the artist soon had misgivings and offered to help her out with a movie reel or two to increase interest. Appalled, Maud instantly refused.

At Camp Lewis, Maud was informed by Colonel Brayden that the admission fee for the boys was to be two dollars, whereupon the artist directly informed him that she had never charged a soldier anything to hear her and could not then. She related: "Colonel Brayden told me that I couldn't appear there for nothing because the camp needed funds and people usually played there on a percentage basis. The camp, he advised me, wanted 25 per cent of the takings." In the end, the men were charged twenty-five cents admission and the officers fifty.

When the colonel sent word to Washington that Powell was going to play, the "powers that be" were horrified. Maud related: "[T]he Colonel . . . was reprimanded from Washington, and told not to book any attractions that would be over the soldiers' heads. Can one blame him for being over-anxious as to how I would be received? He warned me not to be surprised if the boys walked out. I told him I was willing to take that chance."

To another reporter, Maud voiced her amazement at the attitude of official Washington: " 'But what could they have been thinking of!' exclaimed Madame Powell vehemently, when she told me this story the other day in her charming, restful studio in Gramercy Park, New York. 'They forgot that when we say "army" today, we mean something quite different than when we said it several years ago. They forgot that our army now is the very flower of the nation.' "

Well, the boys came. They came in droves, so that the theater, which was built on a slope and seated 4,200 men, was packed. There were no backs to the seats, so the crowded audience waited uncomfortably for fifty minutes for the concert to begin. Finally, some thoughtless officer, at the eleventh hour, informed the colonel that the concert might begin because the general (for whom they had been waiting) was not coming after all. One reporter described what happened next: "When Mme. Powell walked upon the stage she smiled charmingly as she plucked her fiddle strings, and said: 'It wasn't a woman, boys, who kept you waiting this time.' From then on, the audience was hers — one and all. Nor did the favor increase because of trivial selections, for there were none, but only such strictly concert numbers as Saint-Saëns' sonata for violin and piano, and the Mendelssohn concerto."

Asked what kind of program she gave, Maud answered:

> One of my regular ones. I began with the Mendelssohn concerto, which takes just thirty minutes. I concluded long ago that, if you are careful in the choice of a program, the classics will please everybody. Just give them something with a clean line, something that is filled with charm and with the delicate and brilliant passages. Once after I had played the Saint-Saëns sonata, a woman remarked to me that she had never before seen anything in the work. "Because," I replied, "there are many ways of playing it."
>
> Again people may not understand a work well enough to like it thoroughly, but they realize, nevertheless, that there is something sweeping and imaginative about it. You can tell by the way they listen.

Rather than being intimidated or overwhelmed, the men in the camp applauded madly for encore after encore.

Six weeks earlier, the prize fighter Willie Ritchey had drawn a tremendous crowd at the same prices, after having been heralded six months in advance. Maud Powell's concert had been advertised for only two days. "Well," she reported, laughing, "the place was packed, and I took in just three hundred more quarters than Ritchey did. That night Colonel Brayden gleefully sent this night letter to Washington: 'Powell licked Ritchey tonight.' "

As time went on, the government expressed utter amazement at Maud's success on the Liberty Theatre circuit. She drew the largest box office receipts of any artist on the circuit. In one week, her three appearances netted $1,000 for the government. By November 17, 1918, the greatest receipts of any Liberty Theatre had been with Maud and her violin as the only attractions. With sheer astonishment it was reported that "even before her tryout, Mme. Powell insisted that she would play nothing but good programs for the boys," and they came back again and again to hear everything from Beethoven to Sibelius. "We . . . were literally dumfounded at the reception she received, not only from the more intelligent officers, but also from the least educated of the men. Her receipts have been simply wonderful."

Vindicated, Maud Powell heartily enjoyed the last laugh over the doubting officials:

> "It is such a mistake to think that the boys in the camps do not want to see and hear good things. So fixed had become this idea that even the men were taking it for granted that all entertainment meant a big cast, lots of clothes, comedy or dancing. Without youth or beauty," said Mme. Powell smiling mischievously, "they wondered what a 'one-woman show' could do in the Liberty Theater. I heard stage-hands repeat such remarks myself," and here she laughed outright at the recollection, "and saw these same stage-hands listening in the wings until the last encore."[8]

Maud's gift for clever programming kept her listeners enthralled throughout an entire concert. She seemed to know just what to play in order to please her singular audiences in khaki, insightfully basing her programming on the universal appeal of music:

> It is just the same you see as with Bernhardt's acting. One does not need to understand French in order to appreciate the fineness of her performance and to realize what is going on. So, one need never have studied a note of music to respond to its appeal.[9]
>
> . . . .
>
> I remember when I was a young girl with my hair down my back, just starting on my professional career, that Theodore Thomas said to me: "Whatever you do, educate your public. Never cast aside your ideals. Play the little simple, tuneful things that you have perhaps outgrown yourself but which are delightful to your audiences, if you must, and you will never make a mistake. Never descend to playing the cheap music!" I have never forgotten this advice.[10]

So Maud reached out to the soldiers with the humanity of her art.

> I do not play to them as an artist to the public, but as one human being to another. Therefore, every one of the pieces I play must above all have human interest — an obvious appeal to some simple, fundamental emotion. Each one must be a complete mood in itself. Its instinct may be that of melody, as the Henselt *I Wish I Were a Bird*, or rhythm, as the minuets and gavottes of Mozart and Beethoven and the dances of Sarasate, which are immensely popular with the men; or that of power to create "atmosphere," or that of dazzling technical display, or that of humor or coquetry.

Variety is absolutely essential. Therefore I begin my programs with something big and majestic and straight-forward that comes right out and hits the listeners "between the eyes," as it were. [Such as the *Finale* to the Mendelssohn concerto or a movement from de Bériot's Concerto in G Major.] A piece that expresses a quiet, rather sentimental mood may come after this, and then something very sprightly and gay. They should not be long and named intelligently to stir the imagination of the listener. A little "story" background heightens the interest of the men.[11]

At Love Field, near Dallas, Texas, where the great violinist played for 700 soldiers crammed into the YMCA building, she reportedly won their hearts simply by being her "natural self, unconventional, without any formality." Little "gales of laughter" followed "her sallies and the wildest of applause," her music. Her playing, sympathy, enthusiasm, and evident pleasure in entertaining the soldiers won their hearts.

In Toronto's army camp, Maud saw demonstrated graphically the "futility of trying to interest any group of boys without considering their background." With amusement, Maud related to a reporter how she came to play to a "select" audience of a chosen few:

"I got to the enormous auditorium and I found about 400 soldiers scattered about in its vastness. It seemed rather hopeless, but I made up my mind to win the few even if I could not reach the many. I did not believe that the violin interested so few men, and the paucity of the audience seemed all the more strange as Ysaÿe had played there only a week before. Suddenly a thought occurred to me. I finished the number I was playing and asked the boys to tell me what Ysaÿe had had on his program the week before.

"And what do you suppose it was?"

Mme. Powell's eyes twinkled.

"Of all things in the world, the *Kreutzer Sonata*, which takes 45 minutes—nearly all of the allotted concert time—to play, and which Ysaÿe *rehearsed* on this occasion to the accompaniment of the camp piano—fancy the piano part of the *Kreutzer Sonata* on the camp piano—because he was to play it at a city concert a day or two later."

"The *Kreutzer Sonata* is a tremendous trial at times, even for the trained listener," I ventured.

"Of course, it is. And as very few Liberty Theatre auditors are up to it can you imagine the effect of such a recital as that upon the helpless Canadians? Is it any wonder that they did not flock to another violin concert?"[12]

Maud held her printed program down to an hour and ten minutes, but it was inevitably prolonged with requests from the boys for their phonograph favorites, such as *Méditation* from *Thaïs*, *Ave Maria*, *Traumerei*, *Souvenir*, and Dvořák's *Humoresque*. The artist explained:

> You see there are countless classic compositions that have no terrors for the general public which probably by this time regards them as popular music! After my regular program I ask the boys what they want me to play—what they would like to hear, and the number called is practically without exception something good. But this is largely due, I am sure to the influence of the talking machine. There is "one in every home" nowadays, and the violin records have made everyone familiar with the more celebrated "encore" numbers.[13]

She would close her program with community singing of such songs as "America," "Keep the Home Fires Burning," "Smiles," and "Hail, Hail" from *The Pirates of Penzance*, a songfest the artist enjoyed as fully as the soldiers. She would play a verse through as though someone were singing it and the boys then joined in the refrain. Her face aglow with enthusiasm, Maud recalled that "The perfect pitch, the heartiness and volume of the tone poured forth from 2,400 throats, the quick response to my wishes in the matter of pianissimo effects, crescendi, changing of tempi and climax building are not only amazing but thrilling."[14]

At Vancouver Barracks, Washington, Maud demonstrated her ability to deliver a profound human message in the simplest manner. Upon witnessing the men's eyes brighten, the "thousand smiles and a thunder of applause," an enchanted reporter spoke with "the first violin of the time" about her ability to reach her soldier audience: " 'I think it's jolly to be able to play for them,' is the way the first violin dismisses her gift. 'There is something about them, those clean cut American boys in their uniforms, that makes one feel it a little thing to be of service to them.' "[15]

The violinist began to view the standards of musical appreciation in the army camps to be "quite as high as they are in the average concert auditorium."[16] This tireless musical missionary was coming face to face with the results of her pioneering labors. These youths had grown up with Maud Powell just like they had with John Philip Sousa. They knew her and they trusted her implicitly, and she never let them down.

The great-hearted artist willingly endured danger and hardship to reach camps that were off the beaten track. Her impromptu agreement to perform at Camp Kearny near San Diego interrupted a planned rest over the Christmas holidays. During a harrowing fourteen-mile automobile ride in the moonlight over a narrow mountain pass, the plucky violinist recalled, "whatever nervousness we might have experienced was increased by the cheerful driver, who frequently turned his head to inform us that at this point a machine went off the road and was dashed to pieces on the rocks below, or at that point a man was killed."[17]

Fifteen hundred soldiers had been holding down their seats for two hours, while outside the hall, enough men to fill another large theater jostled for places near the windows. Maud's arrival was hailed with terrific vocal outbursts. The musical activities director had been busy all day answering the question, "Will it be the real Maud Powell?" It was.

Appreciation intensified as the violinist threw her "whole soul . . . in her work." At the close of the concert, "the men rose in a body and gave three mighty, deafening cheers." That was Maud's "greatest thrill" in playing for the soldiers. She once said, "I shall never forget that moment."[18]

Maud invariably played for the men in the base hospitals at the conclusion of her camp recitals. At Camp Lee, the boys were lying on cots in the open air, for it was a magnificent moonlit night. Those unable to be outside were moved near the windows. In the soft moonlight and the open air, the great violinist played to the pajama-clad throng which surrounded her. Then Maud led the boys in community singing and soothed for a time, with the mercy of her art, the pain spawned by a merciless war.

The stricken soldiers at Denver's General Hospital No. 21 were so cheered by the news of Maud Powell's forthcoming visit that they pestered the doctor for new bathrobes to look their best for the great lady. In their excitement, men so sick that they were assigned to private rooms insisted on sitting up for the concert. A little before three, Maud appeared, "herself all excitement."

At each ward door the musician stops. . . . Lifting her violin she plays—and as she plays each face before her becomes rigid with the intensity of listening. Boys in every attitude fill the ward. Attendants roll forward men in wheel chairs. On the window sills are crowded others. Many sit on the edges of their cots. Some stand about, heel-less slippers flapping as they move, bathrobes wrapped about them like classic togas. In the beds men lie flat or propped on elbow.[19]

When she left, the men remembered Maud for her gift of sympathy and courage more than for her art, "splendid as it was."

Maud's visits to the camps and hospitals paradoxically drained and restored her native vitality. She explained: "One is obliged . . . to pour out so much of one's inner self in order to reach the boys and make the best impression. But then, you see, the boys give you so much that it is all very illuminating."[20] She admitted that these experiences filled her with renewed enthusiasm for life that made her art even more human:

It is so moving just to watch the boys in the audiences, for so many of them are so wonderfully absorbed. The music seems to take them out of themselves absolutely, and as I watch their faces some of them seem to be seeing visions, and that is always moving to an artist. Others sit with their heads bowed, their faces in their hands, and seem to be asleep, although their enthusiasm at the end of the number tells a different story.[21]

. . . .

In the hospitals, looking down along the rows of cots, I would see all their eyes fixed on me, but they did not see me or know I was there. They were simply wrapped up in the music.[22]

Maud had hoped to rest in her home near Whitefield during the summer of 1918, but the demand for her in the army camps was simply too great. After a complete tour of the Liberty Circuit, the exhausted but determined violinist finally hung her hat on the front rack in her Gramercy Park apartment for a few weeks' rest in September. Over the past year, reporters had found it difficult to catch her in town. No sooner did she arrive in New York, it seemed, than she started off on another tour. Studying the "war map" in Sunny's office with its little flags marking all the places Maud had played for the troops, one reporter wrote, "It would be easier to say where she had not been, for the little flags that are thickly clustered upon the map cover nearly every State in the Union and mark twenty-six of the army camps east of the Mississippi, not to speak of those 'out west.' "[23]

A reporter who found her "in" at last asked if she would do it all over again. "No!" she exclaimed emphatically. "Not do it all over again, but keep on doing it. Each year at the first of June I am at my summer home, but now the summer is almost over and I have just finished touring the camps, and as soon as I have had a few weeks' rest I will begin again."[24]

Typically, Maud embraced the opportunity to proselytize on behalf of the soldiers, hoping to encourage other artists to follow her trail.

> "There has never been such a wonderful audience in the world . . . as the soldiers, because they are in such an extraordinary state of receptivity. They are all in tune. Everything they do, they do *en masse*. They have come together animated by the same noble purpose. It has lifted them out of the usual rut of life and placed them in an elevated frame of mind so that when the artist comes among them she finds them eager to drink in the beauty of what she offers."
>
> "So you see," interrupted Mr. Turner, . . . "it is wrong to think that our new army is not musical. The soldier at one camp who said he had heard Mme. Powell in his little home town in Montana not long before is just an instance of the numbers of young men in each camp who have been studying music or attending concerts before they were called to the colors."

The violinist continued:

> "In the [soldier audience] . . . there is an expectancy, an eager desire for something fine, born, as I said before, of their outlook on the serious aspect of life and their unity of spirit. Their eyes have a different expression. I face them as I play, and everywhere I see those wonderful, wonderful eyes. And the applause! It is a spontaneous, hearty outburst that rocks the roof. And when they cheer — well," said Mme. Powell, her deep brown eyes lit with enthusiasm, "it sends thrills all up and down here," and her slender fingers made wiggly, bird-like movements up and down the back of her neck.
>
> "Academic players and inexperienced players should not go into the camps. But," said Mme. Powell, and I believe that of her many

splendid qualities I was most impressed by her generosity in lauding others, "I do not necessarily mean by that the younger fiddlers. Some of them have wonderful dash and spontaneity and I love to listen to them. But the interest of the soldier is killed by anything which is badly done or is cold and studied. They love the kind of thing May Peterson did when she stayed over two and a half hours at a station filled with troop trains to walk up and down the cars singing little songs, and called a halt on her manager when he wished to announce that she was of the Metropolitan Opera Company. They would love an artist like Bert Williams, for he is a real artist," she added emphatically.

"So please," entreated Mme. Powell, as I was leaving, "make everybody understand that there is a big place in the Liberty Theaters for real art and artists. Make them understand that the boys in camp want good things — not elaborate, complicated, hard-to-understand performances, but the beautiful expression of a simple, human emotion."[25]

That summer, John C. Freund was moved to place Maud Powell's picture on the front cover of *Musical America* with the caption: "Long One of the Most Powerful Forces for Musical Advancement in America."[26]

"America's Own Violinist"

What shall be said to-day in celebration of her art, her intellect, her interpretations, her tone, her technique, her style, her abiding virtuosity, that shall not seem impertinent redundance? What commendation of her gifts more suggestive than the unvarnished assurance that they were as they have ever been?

— Musical America

THE FLAME OF MAUD POWELL'S ART NEVER BURNED BRIGHTER or with greater intensity than during her last touring years. She "delivered her important and luminous message like one inspired." In 1916, a New York critic wrote: "She never sinks beneath the level of greatness, though occasionally she transcends it. Here is an example and at the same time an inspirational incentive to the matured artist no less than the youthful aspirant."[1]

The same critic was no less impressed by the spirit which informed a New York recital given April 13, 1918:

> Any who doubt that she is to-day in the fullness of her powers should have heard her on this occasion to note the inspiring co-ordination of virtuosity with temperamental fervor and spiritual perception, to observe how subtly and nobly blended are guiding intelligence, imagination and sheer objective capacity to accomplish any effect desired. Such art unites in itself the freshness and vitality of inexhaustible youth with the rich intellectual and emotional deposits of mature experience.[2]

During the previous season, the virtuoso had "electrified and delighted" a great audience at the Peabody Conservatory. "It was a recital which will be forever remembered by those who heard it, for the art of Maud Powell is unforgettable," wrote one critic.

> When she last played here a few years ago, one would have said she was at the zenith of her power. But this was not so. There was unmistakable growth manifest yesterday, as if, with all the resources at her command, she finds no end to the heights she can attain. The grace and freedom of her bowing, her astounding vibrato, the authority of her phrasing, these were but a few of the things which the big audience beheld and wondered at. The tonal glory that came in blinding radiance from beneath her bow was nothing short of bewildering. The audience sat dazzled and amazed.[3]

A similar experience was reported in Cleveland in November of 1916, when Maud performed the Saint-Saëns B minor concerto with the Cincinnati Symphony Orchestra. The house was filled to capacity, with extra chairs in every space large enough to hold them. A critic reported:

> About fifteen years ago we all imagined that Maud Powell had ripened into artistic maturity. . . . [I]t seemed likely that she played as well as she ever would play.
> Three years ago, when she played at the Hippodrome, it was quite apparent that she had not halted in her development. Always a poet of the violin, she seemed to have probed to greater depths of feeling, which she amply communicated to her audience.
> And now, added to all of her excellent qualities, among which the technical must be included, glows the intellectual mind of a superb musician. The warm tone has not cooled one degree . . . ; Madam Powell stands as a remarkable mistress of the violin.
> I would prefer to call her a master of the instrument, but I recall that a critic once said that to say Maud Powell's violin playing is like a man's is to flatter all mankind.
> The audience received her enthusiastically, and after the long and difficult concerto, she responded with two encores, one of which was played with the orchestra's harpist as accompanist.
> The Cincinnati players acquitted themselves better than ever before in Cleveland. . . .
> But it was Maud Powell's night and she deserved the applause and welcome back that she received.[4]

The incomparable musician was received much the same everywhere. In Minneapolis, a large audience gathered to hear her "in the undiminished glory of her art."[5] In Seattle, this "genius," this "supreme artist . . . simply played upon the heartstrings of her audience." Seldom had they given themselves up "so completely to unrestrained appreciation."[6] They noted that the same prodigious technique had been enhanced by an added richness, a deeper tone quality, a sweetness that would linger in the hearts of the people for whom she played.

In Dallas, applause was "one of the outstanding features of the evening. Maud Powell's grip on her audience is best told by the fact that she was forced, literally forced, to give an encore after each group."[7] People from all over western Texas assembled to form one of the largest audiences in Abilene's history. The artist was greeted with a "storm of applause from a packed house where barely standing room was available and then—breathlessly they listened." The "matchless program" received a "quiet, reverent hearing."[8]

The Wichita Forum was filled with the largest audience the artist had yet commanded in that city. Maud was greeted "in extreme disregard of customary Wichita coolness to recital programs and she doubled her program with encores."[9]

In Denver, the violinist's ability to "reach out with her music and touch the soul of her hearer . . . found expression in rapt silence while she played, a furore of applause when she had finished a number."[10] Seattle's unusually large audience found Maud Powell "serene in the triumph of her magnetic art," as she played the Lekeu and Carpenter sonatas.[11]

In Portland, her "tremendous musicianship and incredible versatility" were given full sway in a program "destined for the people as well as the critics." "The performance was a series of masterpieces in arpeggios, double-stopping, harmonics and bowing; her playing is of an electric precision and bold coloring, at times sweeping to soul-stirring dynamics, not masculine but grandly feminine, and again portraying an underlying poetry that is charming and individual."[12]

At the Tacoma Theater, Maud, still and always the educator of a nation, paused frequently to address a group of young violin students who occupied a central section of the house, explaining the pieces on her program.[13]

Again at the Heilig Theater in Portland, the beloved artist's reception was "almost in the nature of a great family reunion, so much has she endeared herself to Portland music lovers."[14]

At the age of fifty, Maud Powell was an American institution, just like her friend John Philip Sousa. The war heightened Americans' deeply felt appreciation for both Maud's art and ideals. Her native American birth and sturdy American character had always aroused her auditors with patriotic fervor, but never more than during the Great War. As she toured throughout the country, Maud was embraced by the American public as "America's own violinist" and welcomed as "an old favorite." At times, her reception bordered on the blasphemous: "Los Angeles shares with all the rest of the world a keen interest to novelties. . . . We are, however, more loyal in our adoration of fixed idols than many a public, and we have not failed for years to bend the knee in homage to Maud Powell."[15]

Maud's own deeply felt patriotism manifested itself in her wartime repertoire. She continued to play numerous small works by American composers, but she steadfastly refused to play Kreisler's lovely short pieces although no personal animosity existed between the two artists. Maud felt that the war had heightened the need to bring what recognition she could to works by American composers as well as music which was particularly expressive of the American spirit. She frequently played her own arrangement of the songs "My Old Kentucky Home," "Old Black Joe," "Kingdom Comin'," and "Shine On" as an encore during the war years. She unfailingly announced that she was playing "Kingdom Comin' " in the spirit of prophecy, saying that the kingdom that was coming was a world democracy, adding emphatically, "It's *got* to come."

Music particularly expressive of the American spirit included her own arrangement of Coleridge-Taylor's piano setting of *Deep River*, Herman Bellstedt, Jr.'s *Caprice on Dixie* (for unaccompanied violin), and Henri Vieuxtemps' classic arrangement of *The Arkansas Traveler*. Maud took particular delight in *The Arkansas Traveler* and the charm of the country tale concerning its origins. The notes from which she spoke in presenting the piece to her audiences reveal her particular affection for the story and the music.[16]

Maud clearly never lost sight of the need of her civilian audiences to be transported from the very real horror of the war to a vision of the ideal. Hailed as a "seeress" who "dominates all," she reached out with her merciful art to uplift the spirits of her fellow countrymen: "Miss Powell in a striking gown of green and silver was the impersonation of a goddess of music, combining the human and divine in beautiful strains that spoke of uplift and freedom from all fetters of sordid worldliness. Even war was forgotten, while listening to the magic notes of the divinely played instrument, and nowadays it takes something mighty fine to make us forget war."[17]

For Maud a tour across the continent had become much like a royal progress as news of her most recent triumphs was flashed from city to city along the route. Maud sensed in these warm receptions a musical awakening due largely to the war's broadening influence. "Emotions are keener, and there is a deeper sense of values. People are beginning to need music," she reflected. This news was given thoughtful attention. Coming from Maud Powell, said the writer for *Musical America*, it had "all the weight of authority":

> For the great violinist knows how to interpret this nation's soul and its artistic manifestations. She has experienced, has viewed first hand the phenomena of its development for years. Wishes do not father her thoughts on the subject and there are elements in our cultural life she condemns unsparingly—elements which many do not find it in themselves to censure.
>
> Where the average musician is a superficial observer Maud Powell is a psychologist. Trifles she construes after a fashion that leads to potent truths. And numerous trifles, to the casual mind irrelevant, are to her lights whereby to see great issues. The spectacle of a man alone at a concert is of deeper import to her than to the average individual. The sight of two men in a Western town lured to the concert hall by the mere power of the music signifies something of an awakening. For men in this country do not attend musical functions alone unless musically inclined.
>
> "I have observed, moreover," she declares, "that men in many of these Western towns, like those in camps and in prisons listen with a look in their eyes that demonstrates how powerfully the music is exerting its effect. They look at the artist vacantly, as it were. The music, not the personality of the player, is absorbing them. Year by year the number of men not drawn to the concert by the mere necessity of accompanying the women folk thither has been increasing."[18]

The prescient artist predicted that the soldiers who were attending concerts in increasing numbers would exert powerful influence in the future.

Maud saw that theatrical managers had begun to take notice of the increased attendance at serious musical functions to the point of entering the field themselves. But she also recognized that some things had not changed so much:

> Of course, there is still the tendency to look upon a musical artist as "the show" — just as they look upon a circus, a play, a burlesque or vaudeville act. Also the demand for music which is beneath a serious artist's standard. There are limits to which a musician can go and others which he cannot pass without forfeiting a necessary self-respect. If I receive a request from some prosperous farmer for something I do not care to play, with the promise that he will attend the concert with his family at five dollars a ticket, I take the liberty of refusing his five dollars and declining his programmatic suggestion.[19]

Maud continued to believe that "one result of the war will be to bring us a greater self-knowledge, to the violinist as well as to every other artist, a broader appreciation of what he can do to increase and elevate appreciation for music in general and his Art in particular. And with these I am sure a new impetus will be given to the development of a musical culture truly American in thought and expression."[20]

Maud Powell had become an American legend, as truly as her Uncle John Wesley Powell, to whom a monument had been erected at the Grand Canyon. In 1918, Nicholas R. Brewer, a celebrated American portraitist and landscape artist, painted the famous violinist. In his career, he painted such notables as Ignace Paderewski and former Vice President Garner, but he won popular fame as the artist for the Cream of Wheat cereal box and town billboards throughout the country. Maud welcomed the four-day respite from her labors and captivated Brewer with her charm:

> At our first greeting I perceived the invigorating charm this woman possessed, which, coupled with her musical talent, made our acquaintance delightful.
>
> When it came to planning the picture she suggested my arranging an unconventional costume. From a chest I pulled a gown which

had belonged to a grand opera star. I had picked it up in New York for studio use because of its cut and color. She was charmed with it and soon put it on. Of course, the violin with its beautiful red color had to be in the picture. Seating herself on my Roman divan of purplish red, amidst pillows of varying tints, she fell into a characteristic pose, holding in her right hand the instrument which formed a centralizing note of color. I flung about her shoulders a long purplish gray scarf that streamed to her feet forming graceful lines and partly concealing her left arm.

With a temperament innately artistic, her sympathetic grasp of my requirements and her delightful conversation rendered the sittings a pleasure and the work a success. At every rest interval she seized her violin and played.[21]

Maud later wrote to Brewer: "People seem to like the portrait immensely. Even my maid said, 'Mrs. Turner, them photographs don't make you look graceful and *a lady* like the painting does,' which if you think it over is a tribute to the artist. Please don't belittle the compliment, for the truth comes from such people—I know I value their point of view."[22]

The portrait may not have revealed the toll which the violinist's unforgiving tour schedule had taken. It was more clear to her new accompanist, Axel Skjerne, a young Danish pianist who had settled in New York in 1916. When offered the position in the fall of 1918, he found the offer "too tempting" to turn down, lured by Maud's reputation and her plan to program the interesting and relatively recent sonatas by Carpenter, Lekeu, Milhaud, and Fauré, the violin concerto by Burleigh, and smaller works by White, Ravel, and Gretchaninoff—all new additions to Maud's ever-expanding repertoire. As Skjerne gamely accompanied Maud on a grueling tour, with a formidable number of cross-continent engagements, he grew to have a deep respect and abiding affection for this courageous musician. He said, "I adored her as the accomplished violinist that she was. She was among the first in the world."[23]

The raging flu epidemic and generally disturbed conditions attending the sudden cessation of the war in November had made concertizing more than the usual hardship in many ways. By spring the strain was beginning to show in Maud's behavior as reported by Skjerne in a newcomer's English:

We last night were placed on a disgraceful stage in a draft, . . . so I wonder how she in the world could get through her program in her light dress when my hands and the keys were as cold as ice. It was not lots of fun, but indeed there was chock full of people that we had to place three roads [rows?] upon the stage. Some lady who pretend to be a good friend of Mme. Powell after having just met each other en passant for some time ago which Mme. Powell hardly can recall, wanted to show up by arranging a reception after the concert here in the hotel without asking Mme. Powell, whom it was in honor to.

Almost the whole audience in their swellest dresses came to the reception. Everything was just what the hostess wanted but Mme. Powell's absence! [?] I triumphed that the very lady failed in her calculations! Can you fancy me standing up to deliver a speech to the whole party? It was not so bad, though. Was even surprised and proud after having finished to realize the impression it made on the attendants, by having explained very severely about the responsibility concerning Mme. Powell's health in not nearly having finished her tour and it was out of the question that she should come down![24]

In one city, a critic sensed that Maud was tiring as her recital progressed, although her art's "universal appeal," its "altruism and lack of tawdry display" were at once "dignified and compelling." He reflected that "Lofty thought and ideal have been Maud Powell's taskmasters, and were expressed in every lovely shade of tone color that came now gay, now plaintive and always beautiful from her violin but one does not feel that these have been easy taskmasters. . . ."[25]

Maud was aware of the physical toll exacted by her touring life. She had sought and found some relief in osteopathy. Formulated in 1874 by the American physician Andrew Taylor Still, the osteopathic view is that true health involves complete physical, mental, and social well-being rather than merely the absence of disease. Osteopathy stresses the treatment of the whole patient and the consideration of nutrition and mental factors in addition to physical symptoms. As an artist Powell could appreciate this holistic approach to health. Greatness in her discipline required a similar mental and physical approach in working out the relationship between technical detail and musical interpretation and inspiration until they came together in a perfect whole.

Osteopathy was not accepted by the medical establishment, yet Maud studied the issue carefully and concluded that the practice was sound. Characteristically, she then urged that osteopaths be permitted to treat hospitalized soldiers and gave a benefit recital for the New York Osteopathic Clinic which grossed over one-fourth of the clinic's annual costs — the greatest proceeds from any concert held in Aeolian Hall during the 1917–18 season.

Unfortunately, nothing could rescue Maud from her own incurably big heart which drove her to continually overdraw the well of her vital forces. Still on tour past the end of the season in June 1919, Maud gave a recital sponsored by the all-male Denver Press Club in which each of her numbers was "a thing perfect in itself, done with the generous outpouring of pure golden tone that is Powell's own particular gift."[26] Afterward Maud had planned to vacation in Yellowstone National Park, indulging in the rare luxury of actually lingering amid the scenic splendor of the American West. But American composer J. Rosamond Johnson, the director of the Negro Music School Settlement of 131st Street in New York City, sent out an urgent call for her incomparable aid. A year earlier, the war had forced the withdrawal of key financial support for the institution, and its programs were threatened.

Knowing of the violinist's interest in the Settlement and relying on her enormous popularity, Johnson appealed to her to give a benefit concert. Deeply moved, Maud cut short her vacation and recrossed the continent to appear on June 19 at the Metropolitan Baptist Church. It is somehow fitting that Maud Powell's last New York concert should be given under such circumstances:

> The great violinist, lavishing on the program the fullness of her ripest art, played a wide variety of music. . . . She did not hesitate to give her audience such stern stuff as the Lekeu Sonata (on top of Drdla's *Souvenir*), but the response it evoked and the intense absorption in which it was heard proved how completely she realized the assimilative capacity of her hearers.
>
> Through it all they listened as though their lives depended upon grasping the fullest meaning of the music. Not a sound broke from them, nor did an eye wander from the figure on the platform. A tumult of hand-clapping broke out at the end of each piece. . . .
>
> But the greatest moment of the evening came with the performance of the Negro folk-songs and spirituals. Here the audience

contributed almost as positive a share as the violinist. Lips moved that knew the words of *Deep River*, faces took on a visible emotion. It had always been one of Rosamond Johnson's wishes to hear *Nobody Knows the Trouble I've Seen* arranged for violin played by Mme. Powell. To surprise him she transcribed the piece on the train and then played it to the intense delight of everyone. The number will probably be a fixture, henceforth, in her repertoire. Mr. Johnson addressed the gathering during the evening and spoke feelingly of Mme. Powell's art and the music of his people which this art was now glorifying.[27]

Only a short time before, John C. Freund, the editor of *Musical America*, had pointed out the great debt that America owed Maud, whom he called "our most distinguished American violinist and the Grand Woman of American musical life for many years." As an old friend, he knew the price that this musical missionary and pioneer had paid to bring her art, in keeping with her high ideals and noble vision, before the American people:

> Few realize how much the cause of good music in this country has been aided by Mme. Powell. And how, especially in years gone by, when traveling was more difficult, hotels were poor, she stood the strain, never flinched, never disappointed her audience, was always good-natured, good-tempered, and always, indeed gave them her best.
>
> Do you wonder that wherever she goes, wherever her name is put up, it means a crowded house of enthusiasts, who welcome one whom they have learned to love and regard as an old and tried friend?[28]

34

"America's One Great Master of the Violin"

And before you know me gone
Eternity and I are one.

— William Dean Howells

IN THE LATE SUMMER OF 1919, MAUD RETREATED FROM THE CONCERT LIFE ONE last time to the cool, peaceful calm of the White Mountains. There she reveled in the natural surroundings but, as usual, did not leave music behind. She wrote to the American violinist Arthur Hartmann asking if she could borrow his copy of Breitkopf and Hartel's out-of-print edition of Hellmesberger's cadenzas for Bach's A minor concerto. Referring to Hartmann's transcription of Poldini's *Poupée Valsante*, Maud wrote: "I hope the sale of The Dancing (I mean 'waltzing') Doll has gone up. I have played it often this winter, with a little story to stir the imagination of the public."[1] Hartmann's transcription was the last Victor recording of Maud Powell's to be released.

For the coming season Maud was preparing the violin sonata of her old friend Henry Holden Huss and wrote him a lighthearted note concerning it. She also wrote the Italian-American violin teacher Pier A. Tirindelli that she was studying his violin concerto, as well as his other works.

Concert life in New York was returning to normal. Kreisler returned to both America's good graces and the concert stage with a recital in Carnegie Hall on October 27, 1919. Maud once more included his lovely transcriptions and original works in her programs. Ysaÿe had returned to his family in Europe in July. Spalding had returned to civilian life and resumed concertizing, and Thibaud was back in Paris. The many Russian violinists remained in America, however, which was to be permanently enriched by their adoption. In Heifetz's art, in particular, Maud recognized a worthwhile model for others to follow in seeking the path to true artistic greatness:

> Violin players to-day, generally speaking, group themselves in two classes, or schools. . . . One . . . is based on the theory that the performer of the music is of greater importance than the music itself. . . .
>
> The principles of the other class are founded in the belief that the power of the best music infinitely transcends the boldest flights of the virtuoso — that the function of the artist is purely interpretative: that the best he can do is to mirror faithfully the spiritual content of the music he plays. . . .
>
> One depends for effect upon personal display, the other upon musicianship plus vision. In the latter category are the world's greatest violinists, among whom, if I may judge by a single hearing, we shall include to-day Jascha Heifetz. All that Heifetz does apparently shows that he is more concerned with music than with his own self-exploitation. His tremendous vogue is due to sincerity of spirit joined to extraordinary ability.[2]

Maud Powell had been among the many violinists in the audience when the seventeen-year-old Heifetz made his debut in Carnegie Hall on October 27, 1917. It was reported that "No one . . . seemed more transported than Maud Powell, who stayed to applaud frantically till the very last encore."[3] The great Russian violinist never heard Maud perform, but he soon came to understand her contribution to America's cultural life. In 1979 Heifetz wrote that his students knew well who Maud Powell was and what she stood for.[4]

A new generation of violinists was coming forward as Maud began to see her own generation falter. The violinist keenly felt the passing of her dear friend Geraldine Morgan, who had "the most musical talent of all the girls I have known who played the fiddle."[5] Lillian Nordica, with whom Maud had given joint recitals in days long past, had died on May 10, 1914, during a world tour. Then, Henry Schradieck died on March 25, 1918, at the age of seventy-two.

Maud had weathered the years gracefully. Phillips Brooks once commented, "A woman may not be beautiful at twenty-five, but it is her own fault if she is not beautiful at fifty." Reflecting on that remark, Edith Winn wrote: "Miss Powell was a beautiful woman at fifty, especially as looked upon by her friends in and out of the profession. There was a poise that came with the years, a softening influence felt in her presence and in her low clear voice, that reflected the expansion of a noble soul."[6]

It is difficult to say what it is about the musician's art that transcends human limitations and touches a spiritual reality beyond the physical realm. Ordinary mortals guess; perhaps the musicians know, although they cannot express it in words. Maud Powell rarely spoke "of the moments sacred to the memory when inspiration came, when something within spoke, which was stronger and better than myself." Once, though, she ventured to describe this ecstatic state:

> I do not take as much comfort out of a recital where I am keyed up to the highest pitch, to uphold the standard of Art, as when I am playing for the love of music, to a great audience of men in khaki. They listen to Music, not to Art; their enjoyment of the music as music gives me infinite pleasure. I realize how this receptivity in the listeners reacts on the player, for I am quite taken out of myself, and am told afterwards that my playing was more spontaneous than I had dreamed. In fact, at such times, I scarcely realize I am in the body at all; I am just the avenue through which music itself is poured out to others.[7]

Certainly, everyone who heard Maud Powell play realized that her art came "von Gottes Gnaden."

Maud's absorption in the music made her oblivious to all physical discomfort, including even the pain of peritonitis. While her physical condition varied from glowing health to serious illness, she continued to play impeccably, everything subordinated to the demands of her art. What was it that drove her to play the violin without regard to the physical consequences implicit in the strain of excessive touring? Edith Winn believed it was Maud's faith and enthusiasm that kept her going: "Up to the time of her death, her bearing was as erect and her presence as youthful and vivacious as in early life, with the exception of the inevitable marks of passing years that no amount of enthusiasm nor ambition can quench. What was the secret of this youthfulness? I answer—unquenchable faith in her mission toward art. Her spirit kept her fresh for her work, and that spirit was born of lofty patriotism."[8]

Other interviewers inquired into this artistic mystery, but the violinist herself could not explain it satisfactorily. "I play my fiddle because I simply have to," she frequently replied. Maud responded to one reporter's query:

> "Is the fame a great artist gains really worth the struggle?" asked the interviewer, who had heard that Miss Powell once said it wasn't.
>
> "That isn't the question," she replied. "A business man would say 'no' for based on his standards there is not the financial returns proportionate to the absolutely hard work and sacrifices one has to make, although if one has the artist's instinct one cannot help playing or studying. There is nothing else to do. It is that inner feeling that gives the child the courage to work hard for a musical profession. There are so many people who study music simply for a commercial purpose, so many students are turned out each year to earn their living from their music when they really have no musical ability, and it is too bad. A musician must be born with the divine spark of music and it is the same in other professions. For success one must have a natural gift for one's work. Then if one has that feeling for an art or a profession nothing can keep him from it and the hardships of traveling, of living at hotels and other inconveniences are accepted as a matter of course without worry. If you worried about them you'd soon be worn to a frazzle."[9]

Maud knew well enough how the end would come for her. She probably had some inkling that her heart was not holding up to the strain of the last few years of unceasing travel and performance. If so, she never said anything about it, although she quietly made out her will on November 5, 1919.

In Emporia, Kansas, after the artist had played gloriously, arousing the enthusiasm of a large audience, she saw one of her friends for the last time. They met at a supper given by a few friends, including William Allen White, the renowned literary figure. Her old friend's knowledge that Maud had to arise early to continue her journey moved him to inquire whether the constant travel was not wearing upon her. Maud replied: "Well, you know, I do not feel it. I enjoy my work, I find my audiences so receptive and kindly, and then it is in the blood—I have what some people might call gypsy blood in me. I am a born nomad. I suppose that some day you will read in the paper that Maud Powell, while playing a Beethoven concerto, passed out. I expect to die with my violin in my hands."[10] And so it nearly was.

The tour began in October 1919, without a preliminary New York recital. Maud was in Saint Louis on Thanksgiving Day, November 27, for a concert to be given that night. A reporter caught her early in the afternoon at her hotel for an interview, during which Maud amiably acknowledged and encouraged local advances in music education and also noted the increasing numbers in the "bald-headed row" at classical music concerts. Her vision of America's musical future was as clear as ever: "I am not pessimistic. It is time for a further growth of culture, and I think we will have it. The hearts of the thousands of young men who fought over there desire something more satisfactory, something deeper than the surface of things, and the country which suffered with them will find it."[11]

Maud's performance at the Odeon Theatre was her first in St. Louis in over a decade. The newspaper report of the following day recorded the dramatic events of the concert that brought Maud Powell's career to a close:

> Mme. Maud Powell, internationally renowned as a violinist, is seriously ill at Barnes Hospital today, although showing distinct improvement since the afflicting scene of last night, when she fell unconscious upon the Odeon stage a moment after she had ended an intensely mournful rendition of the negro spiritual, *Nobody Knows de Trouble I've Seen.* . . .
>
> Dr. G. Canby Robinson . . . who was present at the concert and who took charge of Mme. Powell, issued the following statement this morning:
>
> "Mme. Powell is in a serious condition at Barnes Hospital, although she is distinctly better this morning than during the night. The attack that seized her during the concert was brought on by an acute gastric condition. A surgical operation is not contemplated."
>
> The violinist's husband and manager, H. Godfrey Turner, has been summoned from New York by telegram. There was some difference of opinion last night among the physicians in the audience who hastened to the violinist's side. One diagnosis was acute indigestion; another was heart trouble. . . .
>
> Mme. Powell, making her first visit here in 18 years, appeared on the Odeon stage for her Thanksgiving night concert. Those who had seen her in earlier days were struck by the strands of gray in her hair and by the wan, weary look of her face. She is 52 years old, and

has followed the exhausting profession of a concert artist for nearly 35 years. But her slender figure bore itself with queenly dignity; she was every inch the grand dame of the violin.

Her first selection was the popular Mendelssohn concerto in E minor, and violinists in the audience noticed that the performance was by no means equal to her former prowess. There was the same vigorous, masculine sweep of the bow, the same clear, sweet tone and much of the old feeling in emotional passages. But there were many lapses of intonation, and not a few blurs when the notes came fast. The applause, however, was in volume out of all keeping with the diminutive size of the audience, and Mme. Powell returned half a dozen times to bow her acknowledgements. She complained, according to her accompanist, Axel Skjerne, of the oppressive heat on the stage.

But she mustered all of her strength of will and body for the second number, the grave but gracious and charming Sonata in D minor, Op. 108, by Brahms, and bestowed upon it, by common consent, so masterly a performance that one wondered why the limitation of sex should be introduced into the advertisements naming her as "the foremost woman violinist." It was an interpretation of which most male violinists might be proud. Again there was explosive applause.

Either one of these numbers would have been considered a day's work by a soloist with the Symphony Orchestra. Yet Mme. Powell's program was but half finished when she returned to play her own arrangement of the negro plantation song, the words of which, by a strange and pathetic chance, are as follows:

> "Nobody knows de trouble I've seen,
> Nobody knows but Jesus;
> Nobody knows de trouble I've seen,
> Glory hallelujah!
> Sometimes I'm up, sometimes I'm down,
> Sometimes I'm almos' to de groun';
> Oh, nobody knows de trouble I've seen,
> Nobody knows but Jesus!
> If you get there before I do,
> Tell all my friends I'm coming too.
> Oh, nobody knows de trouble I've seen,
> Nobody knows but Jesus!"

By what was undoubtedly a heroic effort of volition, the artist played the number out to the very last note, with all its broad and unctuous melancholy. Then those familiar with her utter lack of mannerism were astonished to see her raise her eyes to the ceiling. She did not bow to the outburst of handclapping, but stood for a moment as if in a daze. But afterwards it was apparent that she was concentrating her last atom of strength to keep from dropping her precious Guadagnini violin.

She turned, reeled slightly and walked to the piano, upon which she carefully laid her violin. "My handkerchief, please," she gasped to her accompanist. She covered her face, turned her back to the audience and then slid down through Skjerne's outstretched arms to the floor.

From the audience came an exclamation of horror and pity; then all but a few who hastened behind the stage sat silent and motionless, as if stunned. Several men rushed upon the platform and tenderly carried off the rigid figure, in its brilliant gown of yellow satin. Soon afterwards C. M. Bergmann, manager of the concert, dismissed the audience.

There was no couch in the Odeon dressing rooms, so the violinist was laid upon the floor, upon a tarpaulin which had been stretched to protect the feathers in her train. Dr. Robinson and Dr. Arthur D. Froetz took her in charge. Deathly pallid, with a pulse scarcely perceptible, she lay unconscious for a quarter of an hour, while women friends wrung their hands and wept.

Then moans of pain showed that sensibility was returning, and one of the physicians approached with a hypodermic needle. "No morphine," gasped the stricken woman, pushing his hand away, and she whispered fearfully: "Is it my heart?" The collapse occurred at 9:25 p.m., and it was more than half an hour later when an ambulance arrived. At the hospital she sank into a semi-comatose condition.

Mme. Powell ate dinner at 2 p.m., according to Skjerne, and followed her customary practice, on days when she gives a concert, of taking only the lightest of lunches in the evening before going on the platform. He said that she had never suffered a similar attack before.[12]

It was fitting that the last concert given by Maud Powell, the first great American violinist, was on that peculiarly American holiday, Thanksgiving, that it took place in the heartland, and that the last music she performed was her own transcription of the deeply moving American Negro spiritual "Nobody Knows the Trouble I See." That she should strive for perfection to the last note in spite of imminent physical collapse was characteristic. "I knew I had six more notes to play," she later recalled, "and I played them. But the last one was not as long as it should have been."[13]

Sunny made haste to cancel a number of Maud's forthcoming engagements while his wife rested in the hospital. This heart attack Maud Powell survived, much to the relief of the musical world. News of her condition was instantaneously transmitted throughout the world and hundreds of floral arrangements were sent to her hospital room to speed her recovery. Maud jovially pointed out that it was quite a remarkable and not unpleasant experience to be dead for a day to know that people really thought so much of her!

The violinist rested through December but then began to feel that she was something of her old self again. She resumed her work in recording sessions on December 29 and 30 and was quite pleased with the results. The indomitable artist resisted all efforts by her family and friends to persuade her to give up her concert tours. When she proposed to resume her tour at the turn of the year, Sunny questioned its advisability but to no avail. He yielded to her strong will and printed her picture in *Musical America* on January 1, 1920, with the caption: "MAUD POWELL, who, restored to health, is resuming her concert tour with decided success." Another ad announced: "She will be on hand to fulfill her engagements with her accustomed spirit."

Maud had insisted on going to Uniontown, Pennsylvania, to fulfill her engagement there as promised. She had been looking forward to her visit, and Sunny accompanied her on the trip. On Tuesday evening, January 7, the party of three, Sunny, Maud and Axel Skjerne, ate dinner in the Titlow Hotel, after which Maud returned to her room to warm up for the concert. At about six-thirty, just prior to the scheduled concert in Penn Theatre, Maud collapsed without warning, falling to the floor. Sunny was at the theater supervising the stage arrangements. But Dr. A. E. Crow was summoned, probably by Skjerne, and upon finding her condition serious, the doctor secured a nurse and ordered the concert canceled at once.

The artist spent a restless night, with Sunny anxiously in attendance at her bedside. The poor man was beside himself with worry, but Maud seemed to be resting easily by morning. Before his wife regained consciousness, Sunny penned a letter to Edna Speier that began without salutation and ended without signature, the whole tenor of which indicates his extreme agitation and concern for his wife's life:

HOTEL TITLOW
UNIONTOWN, PA.

January 8, 1920

The dread morning has arrived. There is much to tell but I am too strung up to tell it. She had a restless night—vomited a great deal. It means the end for some time. The whole of this season must be cancelled—I *believe*. Keep all this to yourself as yet. Forgive me for sending such news. And forgive me for telling you that I too am very shaky. As soon as possible we will come home. Some sort of arrangement will have to be made of our affairs and we will all rest. We have driven too hard—and so often against odds. That you will stick as true as ever I know. I don't have to ask you.

God Bless.[14]

Regaining consciousness, Maud whispered to Sunny that she wanted to rest for the first time in her career. Immediately, Sunny wired cancellations across the United States.

Maud revived enough to converse with Dr. Crow when he called that morning and admitted that this attack meant a long rest for her until her strength was regained. But when Dr. Crow reached the hotel lobby, he was informed that he was wanted in Madam Powell's room at once. When he reached her bedside he found the artist slipping away, in spite of the application of a hypodermic by the nurse in attendance. Sunny, who had gone to the drug store for some medicine, reached her bedside before her life departed. It was eleven-thirty in the morning. The official cause of death was attributed to acute dilatation of the heart. Maud's accompanist described it more fittingly, "Her heart was worn out."

A number of local people called on Sunny and Skjerne to express their condolences, including local representatives of the Victor Company. Funeral arrangements were confused and awaited the arrival of Billy Powell from New York.

In the end, a private funeral was held on January 10 at Fresh Pond Crematory, without flowers, and the body was cremated in accordance with the artist's wishes, the ashes probably scattered on the Hudson River. The great violinist was buried before half the family was notified of the funeral arrangements.[15]

Sunny was almost completely paralyzed with grief, for Maud was the light of his life. On January 20, he wrote Burt Wells, a close friend in Denver, a letter which reveals the depth of his tragedy: "To you, of all men, there is much for me to say, if only the terrible thing in my mind would allow my brain to work. It is impossible for me to get on to any subject other than the one terrible thing that has happened. None of us knew until now, what she really was."[16] All he could think of was her recordings, which had become, with her passing, "Jewels in the national treasury." Did Sunny also remember that the last piece she played, her transcription "Nobody Knows the Trouble I See," was dedicated to him?

The musical world responded with scarcely less shock. Maud Powell was dead at the age of fifty-two.

Epilogue

It is a manifest understatement of the general emotion to chron-
icle the death of Maud Powell as a shock to music-lovers. It is
the truth so far as it goes, but it fails to express in anything like
its fullness the poignant and personal sense of loss which pro-
ceeds from the untimely taking-off of a supreme and unforget-
table artist.

—Musical America

WHERE OTHERS TAUGHT INDIVIDUALS, MAUD POWELL EDUCATED A NATION.
She could not be content with passing on her art through a few chosen individuals, endowing them with her particular view of music
and violin artistry. Her cosmic vision demanded that she reach thousands with her musical message.

She knew that she was born with a message to deliver, one that
she said "I must carry . . . as long as I am able." Those who saw
Maud Powell as a "prophet" understood that her art transmitted a
message charged with the light of elemental truth. The great woman
exhibited the simplicity, humility, and enthusiasm of one who has
communed with the Infinite in her art and felt deeply the experience
of life. That was why her performances were so often a "revelation"
and had about them the reverential quality of communal worship.
Through her art radiated her love for and commitment to the violin,
music, and humanity. That was why Maud Powell, as a human being,
was so revered and loved by the American people.

Many who knew Maud Powell called her a "prophet" or a "seeress"
partly because they saw that her powerful mind was attuned to the
future. Yet she never lost sight of the present, and part of her power
lay in the fact that she understood the past and knew where she

stood in the continuum. She was not overwhelmed or paralyzed by her vision as many others might be. Rather, she was extraordinarily equipped to take practical steps toward bringing that vision closer to reality.

The gift of vision combined with a gift for action and leadership were Powell family traits handed down from one generation to another. These gifts were perhaps heightened and tempered by the experience of the American West. The close correlation between cause and effect in a frontier society taught them to think ahead and to move toward their goals with practical wisdom. Both Maud's father and uncle had disciplined their minds and garnered their facts through patient and painstaking observation and experimentation in the human and natural world. They learned more from contemplation of their observations than from formal education, although books were studied hard when they could be found. In this way, the Powells developed highly original minds.

These keenly forged minds contemplated original approaches to the unprecedented challenges implicit in building a civilization in the New World. The Powells tackled questions of fundamental significance for the growing nation: how to spread the word of God; how to organize science to harness the West; how to educate the nation's children; how to raise women to full citizenship; how to instill a love for music and its cultural value. That they proceeded with their ideas and innovations with single-minded confidence, optimism, and enthusiasm illuminated their full embrace of life, uncautioned, untempered by advice found in books or the refinements of America's more urbane civilization in Eastern cities. A willingness to work so was not without a shrewd Western calculation of the quirks of nature itself or of the nature of human beings, for that matter; nor was it without a perspective that lent itself to humor, idealism, and generosity of spirit. But it had to be backed by intelligence, courage, and determination, and the inner strength to lead others toward a larger vision.

More than anything else, the Powell family inheritance was a sense of mission and duty to God. John Wesley's rule for Christian living which Joseph Powell instilled in his children informed the spirit that moved them. It demanded selfless devotion and personal discipline to:

> Do all the good you can,
> By all the means you can,
> In all the ways you can,
> In all the places you can,
> At all the times you can,
> To all the people you can,
> As long as ever you can.

It was this spirit which ennobled Maud Powell's life and exalted her art.

Only in America could such extraordinary devotion and faith, idealism, energy, vision, intelligence, character, and talent have reached such complete fulfillment with such far-reaching consequences for a nation and its people. Like the John Adams family, the Powells labored with future generations in mind and understood that the full fruits of their labors were to be gleaned by those who came after them. To labor for the future, not merely for the present, at great personal sacrifice, without complaint and without losing faith, ultimately tests the inner mettle of the human spirit. Maud Powell faced that challenge and guided America's early musical efforts very practically but with insight, idealism, and vision which was infused with indomitable personal faith and enthusiasm.

The silencing of Maud Powell's bow was a tragic loss to the musical world, but the stilling of Maud Powell's incandescent mind, electric energy, and magnetic personality was felt as a deep personal loss by thousands of people. The tributes and expressions of sympathy came pouring in, overwhelming Sunny, Billy, and Mrs. Powell. Along with Maud's family, the musical world was in shock:

> Untimely, indeed, is this great-souled woman's passing. She was still young, had barely turned fifty and in mental and physical alertness and initiative far out-distanced many persons half her age. It seemed to all who knew her that twenty more years could scarcely exhaust her dynamic energy and unfaltering, idealistic enterprise or tarnish the splendor of her art. . . .
>
> Maud Powell was a great violinist—the greatest this country has produced—and a great teacher, though not in any narrow pedagogical sense. . . . It is an open question whether in point of vital emotional insight and communication her interpretations of the great classics did not excel those of her one-time master, the mighty Joachim himself. Yet her musicianship, her command of the grand style, her

technical resource, the superb poise and breadth of her playing—
these things and more proclaimed her allegiance to the great instructors, who helped shape her art. Schradieck, Dancla, Joachim,
Léonard—names to conjure with in the history of modern violin
playing! Her musical taste was impeccable and her sympathies wide.
But she was the relentless foe of bad music, of vicious art in general.
She warred ceaselessly against it throughout her career and her successes were achieved exclusively in compositions artistically righteous
in her sight.

Never will the full measure of America's debt to Maud Powell
be fully known. But to the musical advancement of the country, so
evident now, she contributed incalculably. Where others taught individuals she taught a nation. There is probably no obscure community in this country that she has not visited and revisited. To the
musically unlettered she played irreproachable music—not works above
their dull comprehension, but compositions combining simplicity
and merit, that subtly united charm and educative value. She broke
down all artificial barriers and even addressed her audiences when
occasion demanded—either to explain the music and whet their
interest, or to rebuke them for unmannerly behavior in the concert
room. As time sped, she came to be known and loved. Ministering
as she did to the artistic good of America, she was still fully alive to
the nation's spiritual shortcomings. And spoke her mind on them
with salutary frankness. . . .

It seems impossible that this great and beautiful personality can
have gone from us! Come what other geniuses of the fiddle may,
the loss of Maud Powell is irreparable.

—Musical America[1]

Across the American continent and in foreign cities across the
ocean, concerts were given in memory of Maud Powell. In New York,
Maud's old friend Henry Holden Huss gave a concert in her honor
which featured the *Romanza in E* which he had written for and dedicated to Maud so many years ago. The program of the New York
Symphony Orchestra in the fifth and last of the concerts it had been
giving that season in high school auditoriums of the East Side, included
Beethoven's *Eroica* Symphony, the funeral march of which was played
in memory of Maud Powell. The concert was given at Stuyvesant
High School under the auspices of The Music League of the People's
Institute and the Gramercy Neighborhood Music Committee on March

13, 1920. The program recalled the violinist's last appearance for the Committee on May 16, 1919, and then paid her tribute:

> On this occasion that intimate spirit, which always characterized her playing, dominated the program, making the evening memorable.
>
>   To-night, with a deep sense of loss and sorrow, we honor the memory of Maud Powell. She was not only America's great master of the violin, but a woman of lofty purpose and noble achievement, whose life and art brought to countless thousands inspiration for the good and the beautiful.

Two months after Maud's death, Sunny was still reeling from the blow. He wrote Arthur Loesser: "No one quite understands what has happened to me. I cannot understand it myself." The tributes continued to pour in:

> The death of Maud Powell robs the musical world of one of the most capable and thoroughly artistic violin players of her time. She ranked with the very greatest exponents of her art, and upheld her high rank regardless of the marvelous array of astonishing violinists who visited the United States during her lifetime.
>
>   *— The Musical Observer*, January 1920

> [T]he world loses an imposing musical figure . . . . [She] was more than a violin virtuoso.
>
>   *— The Musical Courier*, January 15, 1920

> A great artist is dead. A true American has gone from our midst. A nature richly endowed with genius, character and spirit has gone to be with the Great Musician.
>
>   *— Morning Herald*, January 9, 1920

> Maud Powell was regarded by both American and European critics as the foremost woman violinist in the world and she is entitled to rank as one of the greatest musicians ever produced in the United States.
>
>   *— New York Times*, January 9, 1920

> From the circle privileged to know Mme. Powell personally, will be absent one whose kindliness, charm and great-heartedness, shown especially in her encouragement of the aspirants to greatness in her own line, cannot be replaced. . . . The musical world will miss an artist who for forty years has triumphed on the concert platforms of Europe, America and Africa, whose name was known from Boston to Johannesburg, from Petrograd to London. . . . Her own country

came to regard her as a unique and definite force in American music. For, not content with raising the ideal of the American virtuoso abroad and at home, her pioneer instinct led her to blaze a musical trail in her American concert programs.

— *Musical America*, January 17, 1920

Mrs. Powell and Billy, a bachelor, lived on at Great Neck. Maud's mother sadly made a beautiful "crazy quilt" from the richly colored velvets and satins of her daughter's concert gowns. She died at the age of eighty-one on February 2, 1925. Since May 1912, Billy had been the editor for the Commerce Clearing House, Inc., which was the Loose-Leaf Division of the Corporation Trust Company. When he died on March 6, 1935, at the age of sixty-four, the president of Commerce Clearing House, formerly Billy's assistant, wrote the following tribute:

> Our old chief has closed his service. Good mentor and friend, all of that and much more. No words at our command serve to describe our relationship or feelings. To us, in our innermost thoughts, he was "My Captain."
>
> This is no obituary—he wouldn't want any. But everyone in C.C.H. should respect his work as we do. While he did not invent loose-leaf service, he gave it character. His product was so good that it lived and prospered without sales effort. The C.C.H. services of today are built on the foundations he laid.
>
> He was thorough in all he did—the most thorough worker, the most thorough editor, the most thorough in agreement as well as in disagreement, thoroughly consistent, thorough in warding off friendships and thorough in subduing his natural brilliance. Having a keen sense of humor, he made it thoroughly dry. He died as he had lived, unostentatiously and ready for the last assignment. He was the last of the Powells and our world is poorer.[2]

Sunny never recovered from his loss. Henry Finck, who was among the friends who had given Sunny his cheery nickname, was keenly aware of this. Sometime after 1920, Finck described Sunny as the "funniest Englishman I have ever met," but then caught himself and added, "I should say, he was that before Maud died." Sunny continued with his management business, handling such artists as Arthur Loesser, Axel Skjerne, and Edwin Grasse, but his heart was not in it. Without Maud he did not prosper, and in his sixties Sunny was reduced to giving talks about his life with Maud Powell and the management business to supplement his income. He eventually sold Maud's piano, the Guadagnini and the Rocca, and her bows in order to meet his relatively simple needs.

Sunny was capably assisted in his work by the loyal Edna Speier, who undoubtedly provided him with much-needed emotional support. Edna, who was probably twenty years younger than Sunny, had loved Maud and Sunny as if they were her own parents. Eventually, because they lived and worked together when staying at The Knoll in Whitefield, propriety forced Edna and Sunny to marry, united by their love for Maud. Not entirely bereft of his sense of humor, Sunny placed an entry in the financial books of the business where Edna was sure to see it: "$20 for G. D. wedding ring."

Maud's estate had been willed to Sunny, who sent her entire music library to the Detroit Public Library. The vast collection contains an imposing range of music with Maud's own interpretive notations. In 1926, the Guadagnini was sold to Henry Ford and it now rests in the Henry Ford Museum.[3]

Sunny died on July 27, 1928, at the age of sixty-eight. Edna lived on, but eventually Maud's possessions and papers were scattered. The most substantial public collection of her papers is housed in the New York Public Library, where some of her scrapbooks and photographs can be found. The most substantial private collection of her papers is in the hands of the noted collector Harold Lineback in Saint Louis, who withheld his permission for their use in the preparation of this biography. The biography Sunny had planned to commission never materialized.

Perhaps the most poignant and most fitting tribute to Maud Powell was penned by Robert J. Cole:

> In whatever sky the younger stars now rising may shine at last, Maud Powell is yet America's one great master of the violin. Brilliancy of execution alone does not make a finished art. This woman laid first the foundations of character. She "scorned delights and lived laborious days." For a generation she has divided her time between almost continuous practice, study of music, public performances. She spared herself in nothing. Despising tricks, she paid the full price of high achievement, curbing an eager and impatient spirit to the sternest discipline.
>
> Respecting her own craft, she was a tireless propagandist of music in the broader sense. Her programmes were finely wrought with

treasure old and new. More than one young composer owed his first hearing to her. And a profound reverence, a true priestly power, informed her ministrations before the altar of supreme genius, like that of Beethoven.

Maud Powell was an American. She saw clearly the failures in our national art and the sources of such weakness. Referring once to successful American work in many fields, she said: "There is more liveliness and high spirits than of spirituality. We don't live deeply enough. We depend too much on the big outer stimulus—like a baseball game—to rouse us . . . . We must be turned away from the things that we possess to a deeper inner life."

Being a woman, she must needs find greatness in the expression of her womanhood. Those who said she "played like a man" were deceived by the courage and intensity of her attack. There was no imitation of masculinity. When Maud Powell played, her fiddle sang for the dumb fingers of old women sewing the years into the fabric of their patience; for the hand of the bride adorning herself for her husband; for the child who holds a first doll in the small circle of her arm; for the pioneer's wife, the sailor's and the soldier's; for the lonely woman unfulfilled.

America was richer for her life. And though the strings of her violin are silent, waiting in vain for the melodious marriage of the bow, all that she gave is not lost. For the lesson of her life is not limited to the violinist. Every honest craftsman may take inspiration from a career guided by so lofty a purpose, wrought out through such faithful apprenticeship, bestowing upon others an unshadowed service whose flower was beauty and truth.

—*New York Sun*, January 10, 1920

Appendices

A. VIOLIN CONCERTOS PREMIERED
IN AMERICA BY MAUD POWELL

January 19, 1889

Tchaikovsky Concerto in D, New York Symphony, Walter Damrosch, conductor.

March 26, 1890

Huss Romance and Polonaise for Violin and Orchestra (Dedicated to Maud Powell). World Premiere, Frank Van der Stucken, conductor, orchestra unknown.

February 14, 1891

Saint-Saëns Concerto No. 2 in C, Brooklyn Philharmonic, Theodore Thomas, conductor.

February 23, 1891

Shelley Concerto in G Minor (Dedicated to Maud Powell), World Premiere, C. Mortimer Wiske, probable conductor, orchestra unknown.

April 7, 1894

Dvořák Concerto in D Minor, New York Philharmonic, Anton Seidl, conductor.

Date unknown

Lalo Concerto in F Major, Theodore Thomas, conductor, orchestra unknown.

1894–95 season

Lalo Concerto Russe in G Minor, conductor, orchestra, and exact date unknown.

January 11, 1901

Rimsky-Korsakov *Fantasia Concertante on Russian Themes*, New York Philharmonic, Emil Paur, conductor.

December 30, 1905

Arensky Concerto in A Minor, Russian Symphony Orchestra, Modest Altschuler, conductor.

April 2, 1906

Huss Concerto in D Minor, Op. 12 (Dedicated to Maud Powell), World Premiere, Russian Symphony Orchestra, Modest Altschuler, conductor.

1906–07 season

Conus Concerto in E Minor, conductor, orchestra, and exact date unknown.

[425]

November 30, 1906	Sibelius Concerto in D Minor, New York Philharmonic, Wassily Safonoff, conductor.
November 21, 1909	Aulin Concerto in D Minor, Minneapolis Symphony, Emil Oberhoffer, conductor.
June 8, 1911	Bruch Concertstück, World Premiere, Norfolk (CT) Festival Orchestra, Arthur Mees, conductor.
June 4, 1912	Coleridge-Taylor Concerto in D Minor (Dedicated to Maud Powell), World Premiere, Norfolk (CT) Festival Orchestra, Arthur Mees, conductor.

B. MUSIC DEDICATED TO MAUD POWELL

Marion Eugenie Bauer	*Up the Ocklawaha*, Tone Picture for Violin, Op. 6 (New York: Arthur P. Schmidt, 1913).
Mrs. H. H. A. Beach	*Romance* for Violin and Piano, Op. 23 (Boston: Arthur P. Schmidt, 1893).
Herman Bellstedt, Jr.	*Caprice on Dixie*, for unaccompanied violin (Cincinnati: Herman Bellstedt, Jr., 1906).
Samuel Coleridge-Taylor	Violin Concerto in D Minor (1912).
Henri Ern	Minuet (manuscript, José Figueroa Papers, San Juan, Puerto Rico).
Harry Gilbert	Scherzo *Marionettes*.
Edwin Grasse	*Scherzo Caprice*.
W. H. Humiston	Suite for Violin and Orchestra in F Sharp Minor (New York: Breitkopf & Hartel, 1912).
Henry Holden Huss	Romance and Polonaise for Violin and Orchestra (1890); Violin Concerto in D Minor, Op. 12 (1906); *Romance* in E (New York: G. Schirmer, 1907).
Arthur Loesser	*California* (New York: Carl Fischer, 1923).
Harry Rowe Shelley	Violin Concerto in G Minor (1891).
Gaylord Yost	*Danse Characteristique* (1913).

C. MAUD POWELL'S TRANSCRIPTIONS AND COMPOSITIONS

TRANSCRIPTIONS

Beethoven	Minuet in G, No. 2 (New York: Breitkopf & Hartel, 1917).

Boccherini	Minuet (*Antique*).
Chopin	Waltz (Op. 64, No. 1) (Boston: G. Schirmer, 1910).
Coleridge-Taylor	*Deep River* (Dedicated to Mrs. Carl Stoeckel), (Boston: Oliver Ditson Company, 1905).
Couperin	*La Fleurie* (New York: G. Schirmer, 1906).
Debussy	Children's Corner Suite: *Golliwogg's Cake-Walk*.
Dvořák	*Songs My Mother Sang* (New York: Breitkopf & Hartel, 1917).
Foster	Plantation Melodies: *My Old Kentucky Home*; *Old Black Joe*; Work, *Kingdom Comin'*, Schoolcraft, *Shine On* (New York: Carl Fischer, 1919). (Recorded as *Four American Folk Songs*.)
Gluck	Melody from the opera *Orfeo* (Boston: G. Schirmer, 1910).
Jensen	*Serenata* (New York: Breitkopf & Hartel, 1918).
Johnson, J. R.	*Nobody Knows the Trouble I See* (Dedicated to H. Godfrey Turner) (New York: Oliver Ditson Company, 1921).
Martini	*Love's Delight* (*Plaisir d'amour*) (New York: Breitkopf & Hartel, 1917).
Massenet	*Twilight* (*Crépuscule*) (Edward Schuberth & Co., 1892).
Palmgren	*May Night*.
Rimsky-Korsakov	*Song of India* (*Chanson d'Indoue*) (New York: Breitkopf & Hartel, n.d.).
Sibelius	*Musette*.

ORIGINAL COMPOSITIONS

Cadenza for the first movement of the Brahms Violin Concerto in D Major, Op. 77 (manuscript, Detroit Public Library).

EDITION

Pietro Locatelli	Sonata in F Minor for Violin and Piano, Op. 6, No. 7; harmonized by L. A. Zellner; revised and edited by Maud Powell in 1919.

D. CHRONOLOGY OF RECORDING SESSIONS

4 November 1904	Neruda: Slavonic Cradle Song, Op. 11 Vicuxtemps: Polonaise, Op. 38 Vieuxtemps: Bouquet Américain, Op. 33: St. Patrick's Day
8 November 1904	Gounod-Wieniawski: Fantasie de Faust Mendelssohn: Violin Concerto in E Minor, Op. 64: Finale Sarasate: Zigeunerweisen, Op. 20
11 July 1907	Drdla: Souvenir Gluck-Powell: Orphée et Eurydice: Mélodie Mozart: Divertimento No. 17 in D Major, K. 334: Minuet François Schubert: The Bee; Chopin-Powell: Minute Waltz, Op. 64, No. 1
19 May 1909	Gluck-Powell: Orphée et Eurydice: Mélodie Massenet: Thaïs: Méditation Mendelssohn: Violin Concerto in E Minor, Op. 64: Finale Mozart: Divertimento No. 17 in D Major, K. 334: Minuet François Schubert: The Bee; Chopin-Powell: Minute Waltz, Op. 64, No. 1 Zarzycki: Mazurka, Op. 26
20 May 1909	Boisdeffre: Au bord d'un ruisseau (At the Brook), Op. 52 Drdla: Souvenir Gluck-Powell: Orphée et Eurydice: Mélodie Massenet: Thaïs: Méditation Mendelssohn: Violin Concerto in E Minor, Op. 64: Finale Neruda: Slavonic Cradle Song, Op. 11 François Schubert: The Bee; Chopin-Powell: Minute Waltz, Op. 64, No. 1 Vieuxtemps: Polonaise, Op. 38 Vieuxtemps: Bouquet Américain, Op. 33: St. Patrick's Day Zarzycki: Mazurka, Op. 26
25 May 1910	Debussy-Powell: Children's Corner Suite: Golliwogg's Cake-Walk Emmett-Bellstedt: Caprice on Dixie (unaccompanied) Hubay: Zephyr (Blumenleben), Op. 30, No. 5

	Sauret: Farfalla, Op. 40, No. 3 (Will-o'-the-wisp) Schubert: Ave Maria Schumann: Kinderscenen, Op. 15: Traumerei Lady John Scott: Annie Laurie (unaccompanied) Wieniawski: Violin Concerto No. 2 in D Minor, Op. 22: Second Movement—Romance
27 May 1910	Sauret: Farfalla, Op. 40, No. 3 (Will-o'-the-wisp) Schubert: Ave Maria Schumann: Kinderscenen, Op. 15: Traumerei Wieniawski: Capriccio Valse, Op. 7 Wieniawski: Violin Concerto No. 2 in D Minor, Op. 22: Second Movement—Romance
15 June 1911	Brahms-Joachim: Hungarian Dance Coleridge-Taylor–Powell: Deep River, Op. 59, No. 10 Grieg-Marcosson: To Spring, Op. 43, No. 6 Sarasate: Spanish Dance, Op. 26, No. 8 Vieuxtemps: Bouquet Américain, Op. 33: Arkansas Traveler
16 June 1911	Brahms-Joachim: Hungarian Dance Bruch: Konzertstück, Op. 84: Adagio (The Little Red Lark) Handel: Xerxes: Largo
12 October 1911	Brahms-Joachim: Hungarian Dance in D Minor Brahms-Joachim: Hungarian Dance in F Major; Hungarian Dance in A Major Raff: Cavatina, Op. 85, No. 3 Sarasate: Spanish Dance, Op. 26, No. 8 Vieuxtemps: Bouquet Américain, Op. 33: Arkansas Traveler
28 October 1911	Fiorillo: Prelude (unaccompanied) Handel: Xerxes: Largo Raff: Cavatina, Op. 85, No. 3 Saint-Saëns: Carnival of the Animals: Le Cygne Sarasate: Spanish Dance, Op. 26, No. 8 Sarasate: Zigeunerweisen, Op. 20 Vieuxtemps: Bouquet Américain, Op. 33: Arkansas Traveler
27 December 1911	Bach-Gounod: Ave Maria (with Alma Gluck, Sop.) Raff: Cavatina, Op. 85, No. 3 Vieuxtemps: Bouquet Américain, Op. 33: Arkansas Traveler

27 September 1912

Fauré: Berceuse, Op. 16
Gilbert: Marionettes—Scherzo
Hubay: Hejre Kati—Scènes de la Czarda
Moszkowski-Rehfeld: Serenata
Ogarew: Caprice, Op. 51, No. 2
Tenaglia: Air—Have Pity, Sweet Eyes
Wieniawski: Kujawiak, Op. 3, No. 2; Mazurka, Op. 19, No. 2

8 September 1913

Bach: Partita No. 1 in B Minor, BWV 1002: Bourrée (unaccompanied); Gluck: Minuetto
Boccherini-Powell: Quintet in E, Op. 13, No. 5: Tempo di Menuetto
Borowski: Adoration
Bruch: Kol Nidrei, Op. 47
Dvořák-Barth: Slavonic Dance No. 7 in A Major
Elgar: Salut d'amour, Op. 12
Saint-Saëns: Le Déluge, Op. 45: Prélude

9 September 1913

Bach: Partita No. 1 in B Minor, BWV 1002: Bourrée (unaccompanied); Gluck: Minuetto
Boccherini-Powell: Quintet in E, Op. 13, No. 5: Tempo di Menuetto
Dvořák-Barth: Slavonic Dance No. 7 in A Major
Elgar: Salut d'amour, Op. 12

24 June 1914

Boisdeffre: Au bord d'un ruisseau (At the Brook), Op. 52
Brahms-Joachim: Hungarian Dance No. 7 and Hungarian Dance No. 8 (or 9)
Danks: Silver Threads Among the Gold
Drdla: Souvenir
Mascagni: Cavalleria Rusticana: Intermezzo
Massenet-Powell: Crépuscule (Twilight); Sibelius-Powell: Musette, Op. 27
Offenbach: Les Contes d'Hoffmann: Barcarolle
Schmitt: Chanson à Bercer
Sibelius: Valse Triste, Op. 44
Thomas-Sarasate: Mignon: Gavotte

25 June 1914

Drdla: Souvenir
Handel: Xerxes: Largo
Offenbach: Les Contes d'Hoffmann: Barcarolle
Schubert: Ave Maria
Schumann: Kinderscenen, Op. 15: Traumerei
Wieniawski: Capriccio Valse, Op. 7

10 July 1914	Massenet: Thaïs: Méditation Offenbach: Les Contes d'Hoffmann: Barcarolle Schumann: Kinderscenen, Op. 15: Traumerei
18 June 1915	de Bériot: Violin Concerto No. 7 in G Major, Op. 76: First Movement — Allegro Maestoso Fernandez-Arbos: Tango Godard: Jocelyn: Berceuse Kneass: Ben Bolt, and Bull: Mt. Solitude Leclair: Tambourin Mendelssohn: Songs Without Words, No. 30, in A Major, Op. 62, No. 6: Spring Song Saar: Gondoliera Schubert: Rosamunde, Op. 26: Entr'acte III, in B-flat
21 June 1915	Mendelssohn: Songs Without Words, No. 30, in A Major, Op. 62, No. 6: Spring Song
5 June 1916	Beethoven-Powell: Minuet in G, No. 2 de Bériot: Violin Concerto No. 7 in G Major, Op. 76: Second Movement — Andante Tranquillo de Bériot: Violin Concerto No. 7 in G Major, Op. 76: Third Movement — Allegro Moderato Drdla: Guitarrero, Op. 88 Dvořák: Humoresque Dvořák-Powell: Songs My Mother Sang Gluck-Powell: Orphée et Eurydice: Mélodie Grainger: Molly on the Shore Herbert: Petite Valse Martini-Powell: Love's Delight Neruda: Slavonic Cradle Song, Op. 11 Sauret: Farfalla, Op. 40, No. 3 (Will-o'-the-wisp) Wieniawski: Capriccio Valse, Op. 7
6 June 1916	Bach: Sonata No. 3 in E Major: Second Movement — Allegro Bach: Sonata No. 3 in E Major: Fourth Movement Sarasate: Zigeunerweisen, Op. 20 Sauret: Farfalla, Op. 40, No. 3 (Will-o'-the-Wisp) Wieniawski: Capriccio Valse, Op. 7 Wieniawski: Violin Concerto in D Minor, Op. 22: Second Movement — Romance
20 June 1916	Beethoven-Powell: Minuet in G, No. 2 Drdla: Guitarrero, Op. 88 Dvořák: Humoresque Sarasate: Zigeunerweisen, Op. 20

6 June 1917	Foster: My Old Kentucky Home; Old Black Joe; Schoolcraft: Shine On; Work: Kingdom Comin' (arranged by Powell); Titled: "Four American Folk Songs" Leybach: Fifth Nocturne Puccini: La Bohème: Act I, Introduction; Act II, Musetta's Waltz; Act I, Bright Eyes as Yours; Titled: "La Bohème Potpourri"
7 June 1917	de Bériot: Violin Concerto No. 7 in G Major, Op. 76: Second Movement—Andante Tranquillo Cadman: Little Firefly (Wah Wah Taysee) Chopin-MacMillen: The Maiden's Wish; Massenet: Elégie Poldini-Hartmann: Poupée Valsante Rimsky-Korsakov–Powell: Sadko: Chanson d'Indoue
29 December 1919	D'Egville: Strathspey, Op. 27 (Dance Eccossaise) Mendelssohn: Songs Without Words, No. 30, in A Major, Op. 62: Spring Song Rimsky-Korsakov–Powell: Sadko: Chanson d'Indoue
30 December 1919	D'Egville: Strathspey, Op. 27 (Dance Eccossaise) Rimsky-Korsakov–Powell: Sadko: Chanson d'Indoue

E. DISCOGRAPHY: RECORDINGS OF MAUD POWELL

Listed here are both published and unpublished recordings by Maud Powell, all made for the Victor Talking Machine Company from 1904 through 1919. This discography is based on one compiled by Jim Cartwright which was first published in the "Discographic Data" section of one of his Immortal Performances record sales catalogues in 1982. His version was copyrighted in 1982 and 1987 (Jim Cartwright, Immortal Performances Classical Records and Tapes, 1404 West 30th Street, Austin, Texas 78703). For purposes of this book, however, the format has been altered.

All recordings are 78 rpm, ten- and twelve-inch disks, except for the Masters of the Bow (MB) and Pearl (GEMM) labels, which are 33 1/3 rpm. Matrix numbers with "B" prefixes indicate ten-inch disks; those with "C" prefixes indicate twelve-inch disks. It must be noted that many early Victor "78 rpm" records were actually recorded at speeds ranging from 75 to 81 rpm. For convenience, these are referred to as "78 rpm records" in this discography, following the common usage. Where more than one take is listed, the take that was published is italicized. A catalogue number in parentheses indicates that the number was assigned but the recording was not published. The absence of any catalogue number indicates that the recording was not published.

The single-face Victor recordings were coupled in 1923 and issued as double-face Red Seal records. Some of the Maud Powell 78s were issued in Europe by Victor's affiliated Gramophone (and Typewriter) Company, Limited, at first as G & T disks, and after 1909 with HMV labels. The Gramophone Company also began to issue double-face Red Seal records in 1923, and the most popular Maud Powell recordings were coupled.

Acknowledgment of Sources: Jim Cartwright, upon whose discography this one is based, gratefully acknowledges the following sources: Julian Morton Moses, *Collectors Guide to American Recordings*, the Listings Department of RCA, Jim Creighton, Ted Fagan, Dave Hermann, Alan Kelly, David Kirby, John Sam Lewis, William R. Moran, the collection of Mr. and Mrs. Laurance C. Witten II in the Historical Sound Recordings collection of the Yale University Library, and Miss Barbara Migurski, Assistant to the Curator for that collection.

Very special thanks to Jim Cartwright for so carefully compiling the Maud Powell discography and for reviewing my version of it. A native Texan, Mr. Cartwright studied music at North Texas State University, although he received his bachelor's degree in business administration. After service in the U.S. Army, he studied music and computer science at the University of Texas. Since 1971 he has owned and operated Immortal Performances Classical Records and Tapes in Austin, Texas. He is coauthor with Paul Worth of *John McCormack: A Comprehensive Discography* (Westport and London: Greenwood Press, 1986). He has published discographies of Ignace Jan Paderewski, Nellie Melba, Arturo Toscanini and the La Scala Orchestra, Arturo Toscanini and the Philharmonic Symphony Orchestra of New York, Amelita Galli-Curci, Leopold Stokowski and the Philadelphia Orchestra, and Alfred Hertz, among others, as supplements to his Immortal Performances record catalogues. He produces and hosts a weekly radio show, "Immortal Performances," featuring historic instrumental, orchestral, and vocal recordings.

My personal thanks also to William R. Moran, coauthor of *The Encyclopedic Discography of Victor Recordings*, vol. 1 (1983); vol. 2 (1986) (Westport and London: Greenwood Press), for so carefully reviewing this discography and for providing additional information.

		VICTOR RED SEAL		G & T OR HMV		
MATRIX-TAKE	DATE/PLACE/ACCOMPANIST	SINGLE FACE	DOUBLE FACE	SINGLE FACE	DOUBLE FACE	LP REISSUES
Bach: Partita No. 1 in B Minor, BWV 1002: Bourrée (unaccompanied); **Gluck:** Minuetto (George Falkenstein, piano)						
C-13731–1	8 September 1913	74357		2–07989	DB656	
–2	9 September 1913					
Bach: Sonata No. 3 in E Major: Second Movement — Allegro (Arthur Loesser, piano)						
B-17805–1	6 June 1916 New York City	64618		4–7981	DA345	
Bach: Sonata No. 3 in E Major: Fourth Movement (Arthur Loesser, piano)						
B-17806–1	6 June 1916 New York City	64619		4–7982	DB345	
Bach-Gounod: Ave Maria (with Alma Gluck, soprano) (George Falkenstein, piano)						
B-11418–1,	27 December 1911					
2,3						
Beethoven-Powell: Minuet in G, No. 2 (Arthur Loesser, piano)						
B-17793–1	5 June 1916 New York City	64620	804	4–7974	DA341	GEMM-101
–2,3	20 June 1916 Camden, NJ					
de Bériot: Violin Concerto No. 7 in G Major, Op. 76: First Movement — Allegro Maestoso (George Falkenstein, piano)						
C-16111–1	18 June 1915 New York City	74446	6378	2–07932	DB394	
de Bériot: Violin Concerto No. 7 in G Major, Op. 76: Second Movement — Andante Tranquillo (Arthur Loesser, piano)						
C-17791–1	5 June 1916 New York City	74492		3–07904	DB391	
–2	7 June 1917					
	George Falkenstein, piano					
de Bériot: Violin Concerto No. 7 in G Major, Op. 76: Third Movement — Allegro Moderato (Arthur Loesser, piano)						
C-17792–1	5 June 1916 New York City	74493	6257	3–07903	DB394	

Matrix-Take	Date/Place/Accompanist	Victor Red Seal Single Face	Victor Red Seal Double Face	G & T or HMV Single Face	G & T or HMV Double Face	LP Reissues
Boccherini-Powell: Quintet in E, Op. 13, No. 5: Tempo di Menuetto (George Falkenstein, piano)						
C-13727-1	8 September 1913	74354		3–07900	DB395	
-2	9 September 1913					
(Some Victor files show Take 2 as issued; others show Take 1 as issued and Take 2 as destroyed; however, copies marked Take 2 have been reported.)						
Boisdeffre: Au bord d'un ruisseau (At the Brook), Op. 52 (George Falkenstein, piano)						
B-7099–1,2,3	20 May 1909 Camden, NJ	64103				
(Take 1 with mute)						
Boisdeffre: Au bord d'un ruisseau (At the Brock), Op. 52 (Francis J. Lapitino, harp)						
B-14994-1	24 June 1914	64103	801	4–7967	DA343	MB-1005
Borowski: Adoration (George Falkenstein, piano)						
C-13733–1,2	8 September 1913					
(Some Victor books indicate Take 3 recorded on 9 September 1913.)						
Brahms-Joachim: Hungarian Dance (George Falkenstein, piano)						
B-10538–1,2	15 June 1911					
-3	16 June 1911					
Brahms-Joachim: Hungarian Dance in D Minor (Waldemar Liachowsky, piano)						
B-11087–1,2	12 October 1911 New York City					
Brahms-Joachim: Hungarian Dance in F Major: Hungarian Dance in A Major (Waldemar Liachowsky, piano)						
C-11088–1,2	12 October 1911 New York City					
Brahms-Joachim: Hungarian Dance in A Major; see **Brahms-Joachim**: Hungarian Dance in F Major						

MATRIX-TAKE	DATE/PLACE/ACCOMPANIST	VICTOR RED SEAL		G & T OR HMV		LP REISSUES
		SINGLE FACE	DOUBLE FACE	SINGLE FACE	DOUBLE FACE	
Brahms-Joachim: Hungarian Dance No. 7; Hungarian Dance No. 8 (or 9) (George Falkenstein, piano)						
C-15002–1,2	24 June 1914					
(Some Victor books indicate Take 2 recorded on 25 June 1914.)						
Bruch: Kol Nidrei, Op. 47 (George Falkenstein, piano)						
C-13729–1	8 September 1913	74355	6256	2–07999		MB-1005
Bruch: Konzertstück, Op. 84: Adagio (The Little Red Lark) (George Falkenstein, piano)						
B 10541–1,2	16 June 1911	(64208)				
Bull: Mt. Solitude; see **Kneass**: Ben Bolt						
Cadman: Little Firefly (Wah Wah Taysee) (George Falkenstein, piano)						
B-20023–1,2	7 June 1917	64705				MB-1005
Chopin-MacMillen: The Maiden's Wish; **Massenet**: Les Erinnyes: No. 3, Invocation (Elégie) (George Falkenstein, piano)						
C-20024–1,2	7 June 1917	74548	6257	2–07993	DB624	
Chopin-Powell: Minute Waltz, Op. 64, No. 1; see **François Schubert**: The Bee						
Coleridge-Taylor-Powell: Deep River, Op. 59, No. 10 (George Falkenstein, piano)						
C-10535–1,2	15 June 1911	74246	6253			
Danks: Silver Threads Among the Gold (George Falkenstein, piano)						
B-15003–1	24 June 1914	64459	808	3–7980		
Debussy-Powell: Children's Corner Suite: Golliwogg's Cake-Walk (George Falkenstein, piano)						
C 9013–1,2	25 May 1910 New York City					
Drdla: Guitarrero, Op. 88 (Arthur Loesser, piano)						
B-17795–1	5 June 1916 New York City	64621				
–2	20 June 1916 Camden, NJ		803	4–7971		

| Matrix-Take | Date/Place/Accompanist | Victor Red Seal | | G & T or HMV | | LP Reissues |
		Single Face	Double Face	Single Face	Double Face	
Drdla: Souvenir (George Falkenstein, piano)						
B-4669–1	11 July 1907 New York City	64074				
–2	20 May 1909 Camden, NJ	64074				
–3,4	24 June 1914					
–5	25 June 1914	64074	808	3–7964		
Dvořák: Humoresque (Arthur Loesser, piano)						
C-17797–1	5 June 1916 New York City	74494	6255	2–07949		
–2	20 June 1916 Camden, NJ					
Dvořák-Barth: Slavonic Dance No. 7 in A Major (George Falkenstein, piano)						
C-13730–1	8 September 1913					
–2	9 September 1913					
Dvořák-Powell: Songs My Mother Sang (Arthur Loesser, piano)						
B-17796–1	5 June 1916 New York City					
D'Egville: Strathspey, Op. 27 (Dance Eccossaise) (orch./Josef A. Pasternack)						
B-23558–1,2	29 December 1919					
–3,4	30 December 1919					
Elgar: Salut d'amour, Op. 12 (George Falkenstein, piano)						
B-13728–1	8 September 1913	64373				
–2,3	9 September 1913		802	4–7980	DA346	MB-1005
Emmett-Bellstedt: Caprice on Dixie (unaccompanied) (George Falkenstein, piano)						
B-9010–1,2	25 May 1910 New York City	64143				
Fauré: Berceuse, Op. 16 (George Falkenstein, piano)						
B-12394–1	27 September 1912 New York City					

MATRIX-TAKE	DATE/PLACE/ACCOMPANIST	VICTOR RED SEAL SINGLE FACE	VICTOR RED SEAL DOUBLE FACE	G & T OR HMV SINGLE FACE	G & T OR HMV DOUBLE FACE	LP REISSUES
Fernandez-Arbos: Tango (George Falkenstein, piano)						
C-16116–1,2,3	18 June 1915 New York City					
	(Some Victor books indicate Take 3 recorded 21 June 1915.)					
Fiorillo: Prelude (unaccompanied)						
B-11148–1,2	28 October 1911 New York City					
Foster: My Old Kentucky Home; Old Black Joe; **Schoolcraft:** Shine On; **Work:** Kingdom Comin' (arranged by Powell)						
	Titled: "Four American Folk Songs" (orch./Josef A. Pasternack)						
C-20014–1,2,3	6 June 1917	74547	6253	2–07997	DB390	
Gilbert: Marionettes-Scherzo (George Falkenstein, piano)						
B-12395-1,2	27 September 1912 New York City	64300				
Gluck: Minuetto; see **Bach:** Partita No. 1 in B Minor, BWV 1002: Bourrée						
Gluck-Powell: Orphée et Eurydice: Mélodie (George Falkenstein, piano)						
B-4670–1	11 July 1907 New York City	64075				
–2	19 May 1909 Camden, NJ					
–3	20 May 1909 Camden, NJ	64075				
–4	5 June 1916 New York City Arthur Loesser, piano	64075	807	4–7973		
Godard: Jocelyn: Berceuse (George Falkenstein, piano)						
B-16107–1,2	18 June 1915 New York City	(64435)				
Gounod-Wieniawski: Fantasie de Faust (with piano)						
B-1913–1	8 November 1904 New York City					

| Matrix-Take | Date/Place/Accompanist | Victor Red Seal | | G & T or HMV | | LP Reissues |
		Single Face	Double Face	Single Face	Double Face	
Grainger: Molly on the Shore (Arthur Loesser, piano)						
B-17789-1,2	5 June 1916 New York City	64611	811	4–7976	DA341	
Grieg-Marcosson: To Spring, Op. 43, No. 6 (George Falkenstein, piano)						
B-10536-1,2	15 June 1911	64264	810	4–7984	DA343	MB-1005
(Some Victor books indicate Take 2 recorded 16 June 1911.)						
Handel: Xerxes: Largo (George Falkenstein, piano)						
C-10540-1,2	16 June 1911	74412				
−3	25 June 1914		6249	2–07927	DB395	
with Rattay, Fruncillo, Levy, Bourdon (string quartet) and Conrad, tuba						
Handel: Xerxes: Largo (Waldemar Liachowsky, piano)						
B-11146-1,2	28 October 1911 New York City	64227	804			
Herbert: Petite Valse (Arthur Loesser, piano)						
B-17794-1	5 June 1916 New York City	64617		4–7977		
Hubay: Hejre Kati−Scènes de la Czarda (George Falkenstein, piano)						
C-12427-1	27 September 1912 New York City	74324	6258	2–07992	DB393	MB-1005
Hubay: Zephyr (Blumenleben), Op. 30, No. 5 ((George Falkenstein, piano)						
C-9012-1	25 May 1910 New York City	74188				
Kneass: Ben Bolt; **Bull:** Mt. Solitude (George Falkenstein, piano)						
C-16110-1	18 June 1915 New York City					
Leclair: Tambourin (George Falkenstein, piano)						
B-16108-1,2	18 June 1915 New York City	64520		4–7983		

MATRIX-TAKE	DATE/PLACE/ACCOMPANIST	VICTOR RED SEAL		G & T OR HMV		LP REISSUES
		SINGLE FACE	DOUBLE FACE	SINGLE FACE	DOUBLE FACE	

Leybach: Op. 52, Fifth Nocturne (Francis J. Lapitino, harp; orch./Josef A. Pasternack)

C-20015-1,2	6 June 1917	74531	6251	2-07995		

Martini-Powell: Love's Delight (Arthur Loesser, piano)

B-17790-1,2	5 June 1916 New York City	64615				

Mascagni: Cavalleria Rusticana: Intermezzo (George Falkenstein, piano)

B-14992-1,2	24 June 1914					

(Some Victor books indicate Take 2 recorded 25 June 1914.)

Massenet-Powell: Crépuscule (Twilight) (Francis J. Lapitino, harp); **Sibelius-Powell**: Musette, Op. 27 (George Falkenstein, piano)

C-14995-1	24 June 1914	74408		3-07906	DB642	MB-1005

Massenet: Les Erinnyes: No. 3, Invocation (Elégie); see **Chopin-MacMillen**: The Maiden's Wish

Massenet: Thaïs: Méditation (George Falkenstein, piano)

C-7098-1	19 May 1909 Camden, NJ	74135		2-07900		
-2	20 May 1909 Camden, NJ					

Massenet: Thaïs: Méditation (with Lapitino [harp], Fruncillo, Bourdon, Levy, Conrad [second violin, viola, and base])

C-15051-1,2	10 July 1914	74135	6255			

Mendelssohn: Songs Without Words, No. 30, in A Major, Op. 62, No. 6: Spring Song (George Falkenstein, piano)

B-16121-1	18 June 1915 New York City					
B-16121-2,3	21 June 1915 New York City					

Mendelssohn: Songs Without Words, No. 30, in A Major, Op. 62, No. 6: Spring Song (Francis J. Lapitino, harp)

B 23557-1,2	29 December 1919					

MATRIX-TAKE	DATE/PLACE/ACCOMPANIST	VICTOR RED SEAL		G & T OR HMV		LP REISSUES
		SINGLE FACE	DOUBLE FACE	SINGLE FACE	DOUBLE FACE	
Mendelssohn: Violin Concerto in E Minor, Op. 64: Finale (piano: 1904 unknown; 1909 George Falkenstein)						
C-1911–1	8 November 1904 New York City	85040				
–2	19 May 1909 Camden, NJ	74026				
–3	20 May 1909 Camden, NJ	74026	6252	2-07996	DB391	
Moszkowski-Rehfeld: Serenata (George Falkenstein, piano)						
B-12396–1	27 September 1912 New York City	64281	807	3-7965	DA346	MB-1005
Mozart: Divertimento No. 17 in D Major, K. 334: Minuet (George Falkenstein, piano)						
B-4668–1,2,3	11 July 1907 New York City	64073	805	4-7975		
–4	19 May 1909 Camden, NJ	64073	805	4-7975		
Neruda: Slavonic Cradle Song, Op. 11						
B-1898–1	4 November 1904 New York City with piano (unknown)	81051				
–2	20 May 1909 Camden, NJ George Falkenstein, piano	64027				
–3 (with mute)		64027				
–4	5 June 1916 New York City Arthur Loesser, piano	64027	809*	*47969		

*(labels of some copies erroneously show Falkenstein as accompanist)

Offenbach: Les Contes d'Hoffmann: Barcarolle (George Falkenstein, piano; Francis J. Lapitino, harp)						
B-14993–1	24 June 1914	64457	802	3-7978	DA344	
–2,3	25 June 1914	64457	802	3-7978	DA344	

| MATRIX-TAKE | DATE/PLACE/ACCOMPANIST | VICTOR RED SEAL | | G & T OR HMV | | LP REISSUES |
		SINGLE FACE	DOUBLE FACE	SINGLE FACE	DOUBLE FACE	
Offenbach: Les Contes d'Hoffmann: Barcarolle (with Lapitino [harp], Fruncillo, Bourdon, Levy, Conrad [second violin, viola, cello, and bass])						
B-15052–1,2	10 July 1914					
Ogarew: Caprice, Op. 51, No. 2 (George Falkenstein, piano)						
B-12399–1	27 September 1912 New York City	64301	806	4–7970	MB-1005	
Poldini-Hartmann: Poupée Valsante (George Falkenstein, piano)						
B 20026–1,2	7 June 1917	64734	806	4–7979		
Puccini: La Bohème: Act I, Introduction; Act II, Musetta's Waltz; Act I, Bright Eyes as Yours						
Titled: "La Bohême Potpourri" (orch./Josef A. Pasternack)						
C–20013–1,2	6 June 1917		(74546)			
Raff: Cavatina, Op. 85, No. 3 (Waldemar Liachowsky, piano)						
C–11090–1	12 October 1911 New York City					
–2	28 October 1911 New York City					
–3	27 December 1911	74283	6251	2–07991		MB-1005
	George Falkenstein, piano					
Rimsky-Korsakov–Powell: Sadko: Chanson d'Indoue (George Falkenstein, piano)						
B-20025–1	7 June 1917					
Rimsky-Korsakov–Powell: Sadko: Chanson d'Indoue (orch./Josef A. Pasternack)						
B-23559–1,2	29 December 1919					
–3,4	30 December 1919					
Saar: Gondoliera (George Falkenstein, piano)						
B-16109–1,2	18 June 1915 New York City	64521		4–7906		

MATRIX-TAKE	DATE/PLACE/ACCOMPANIST	VICTOR RED SEAL		G & T OR HMV		LP REISSUES
		SINGLE FACE	DOUBLE FACE	SINGLE FACE	DOUBLE FACE	
Saint-Saëns: Carnival of the Animals: Le Cygne (Waldemar Liachowsky, piano)						
B-11147-1,2	28 October 1911 New York City	64265	801			
Saint-Saëns: Le Déluge, Op. 45: Prélude (George Falkenstein, piano)						
B-13732-1	8 September 1913					
Sarasate: Spanish Dance, Op. 26, No. 8 (George Falkenstein, piano)						
C-10539-1,2	15 June 1911					
(Some Victor books indicate Take 2 recorded 16 June 1911.)						
Sarasate: Spanish Dance, Op. 26, No. 8 (Waldemar Liachowsky, piano)						
C-11089-1	12 October 1911 New York City					
−2	28 October 1911 New York City	74259	6254	3–07905		MB-1005
Sarasate: Zigeunerweisen, Op. 20 (with piano, unknown)						
B-1912-1	8 November 1904 New York City					
Sarasate: Zigeunerweisen, Op. 20 (piano, 1911 Waldemar Liachowsky; 1916 Arthur Loesser)						
B-11149-1	28 October 1911 New York City	64262		5–7969		
−2,3	6 June 1916 New York City					
−4	20 June 1916 Camden, NJ	64262*	811*			
*(The labels of some copies erroneously show Liachowsky as accompanist.)						
Sauret: Farfalla, Op. 40, No. 3 (Will-o'-the-wisp) (piano: 1910 George Falkenstein; 1916 Arthur Loesser*)						
C-9008-1	25 May 1910 New York City					
−2	27 May 1910 New York City	74183				
−3	5 June 1916 New York City					
−4	6 June 1916 New York City	74183	6258	2–07994	DB390	MB-1005
*(Victor books show Falkenstein, but probably in error)						

MATRIX-TAKE	DATE/PLACE/ACCOMPANIST	VICTOR RED SEAL		G & T OR HMV		LP REISSUES
		SINGLE FACE	DOUBLE FACE	SINGLE FACE	DOUBLE FACE	

Schmitt: Chanson à Bercer (George Falkenstein, piano)

B-15001–1	24 June 1914	64458		3–7981		

Schoolcraft: Shine On; see **Foster**: My Old Kentucky Home; Old Black Joe; **Schoolcraft**: Shine On; **Work**: Kingdom Comin' (arranged by Powell) Titled: "Four American Folk Songs"

Schubert, François: The Bee; **Chopin-Powell**: Minute Waltz, Op. 64, No. 1 (George Falkenstein, piano)

B-4671–1,2	11 July 1907 New York City	64076				
–2	[sic] 19 May 1909 Camden, NJ					
–3,4	20 May 1909 Camden, NJ	64076	810	4–7968	DA551	

(Take 4 with mute)

Schubert, Franz: Ave Maria (George Falkenstein, piano)

C-9014–1	25 May 1910 New York City					
–2	27 May 1910 New York City	74177				

Schubert: Ave Maria (Rattay, Fruncillo, Levy, Bourdon [string quartet], Lapitino, harp, and Falkenstein, piano)

C-15014–1	25 June 1914	74177	6249	2–07988	DB396	

Schubert: Rosamunde, Op. 26: Entr'acte III, in B-flat (George Falkenstein, piano)

C-16112–1	18 June 1915 New York City	74447		2–07940		

Schumann: Kinderscenen, Op. 15: Traumerei (George Falkenstein, piano)

B-9015–1	25 May 1910 New York City					
–2	27 May 1910 New York City	64134				

Schumann: Kinderscenen, Op. 15: Traumerei (Conrad, Fruncillo, Levy, Bourdon [string quartet], and Lapitino, harp)

B-15013–1,2	25 June 1914					
–3,4	10 July 1914					

Matrix-Take	Date/Place/Accompanist	Victor Red Seal		G & T or HMV		LP Reissues
		Single Face	Double Face	Single Face	Double Face	

Lady John Scott: Annie Laurie (unaccompanied)
B-9011–1   25 May 1910 New York City

Sibelius-Powell: Musette, Op. 27; see **Massenet-Powell**: Crépuscule (Twilight)

Sibelius: Valse Triste, Op. 44 (George Falkenstein, piano)
C-14999–1   24 June 1914   74402   6256   2-07919   DB396

Tenaglia: Air — Have Pity, Sweet Eyes (George Falkenstein, piano)
C-12397–1   27 September 1912 New York 74325   6378   2-07998
              City

Thomas-Sarasate: Mignon: Gavotte (George Falkenstein, piano)
B-15000–1   24 June 1914   64454   803   3-7979   DA344   MB-1005

Vieuxtemps: Bouquet Américain, Op. 33: Arkansas Traveler (George Falkenstein, piano)
B-10537–1   15 June 1911   (64211)
    –2,3   12 October 1911 New York City
             Waldemar Liachowsky, piano
    –4,5   28 October 1911 New York City
             Waldemar Liachowsky
    –6   27 December 1911
             George Falkenstein, piano

Vieuxtemps: Bouquet Américain, Op. 33: St. Patrick's Day (piano, 1904 unknown; 1909 George Falkenstein)
C-1897–1   4 November 1904   85039*
             New York City   74025
*(The first issue of 85039 erroneously listed Wieniawski as the composer.)
    –2   20 May 1909 Camden, NJ   74025   6254

MATRIX-TAKE	DATE/PLACE/ACCOMPANIST	VICTOR RED SEAL		G & T OR HMV		LP REISSUES
		SINGLE FACE	DOUBLE FACE	SINGLE FACE	DOUBLE FACE	
Vieuxtemps: Polonaise, Op. 38 (piano, 1904 unknown; 1909 George Falkenstein)						
B-1899-1	4 November 1904 New York City	81052 64028				
-2	20 May 1909 Camden, NJ	64028	809	4-7978		
Wieniawski: Capriccio Valse, Op. 7 (George Falkenstein, piano)						
C-9033-1	27 May 1910 New York City	74173		2-07990		
-2	25 June 1914 with orchestra					
-3	5 June 1916 New York City Arthur Loesser, piano					
-4	6 June 1916 New York City Arthur Loesser, piano	74173	6250			
Wieniawski: Kujawiak, Op. 3, No. 2; Mazurka, Op. 19, No. 2 (George Falkenstein, piano)						
C-12398-1,2	27 September 1912 New York City	74326	6250	3-07901	DB393	
Wieniawski: Violin Concerto No. 2 in D Minor, Op. 22: Second Movement—Romance (George Falkenstein, piano)						
C-9009-1,2	25 May 1910 New York City	74179				
-3	27 May 1910 New York City	74179				
-4	6 June 1916 New York City Arthur Loesser, piano	74179	6252	3-07902	DB656	
Work: Kingdom Comin'; see **Foster**: My Old Kentucky Home; Old Black Joe; **Schoolcraft**: Shine On; **Work**: Kingdom Comin' (arranged by Powell) Titled: "Four American Folk Songs"						
Zarzycki: Mazurka, Op. 26 (George Falkenstein, piano)						
B-7097-1	19 May 1909 Camden, NJ	64104	805	4-7972		
-2	20 May 1909 Camden, NJ				DA551	

Notes

ABBREVIATIONS

Grove's   *Grove's Dictionary of Music and Musicians.*
MLP   Mabel Love Papers, in the possession of Jean Holmes, Detroit, MI.
MPP Sketch   Minnie Paul Powell, biographical sketch of Maud Powell, manuscript in MLP.
NGGC   Neva Garner Greenwood Collection, Falls Church, VA.

Chapter 1
PIONEER HERITAGE

1. The records differ on the year of Maud Powell's birth. For 1867: Powell Family Bible, Baker University, Baldwin, Kansas; U.S. Census for 1880, National Archives, Washington, D.C.; Paris Conservatoire records. For 1868: Maud Powell's autobiographical data submitted to *Grove's Dictionary of Music and Musicians* (hereafter *Grove's*), manuscript in Mabel Love Papers in the possession of Jean Holmes, Detroit, MI (hereafter MLP). It is not known why Maud expressed confusion about her birthdate, but the correct year is undoubtedly 1867.

2. Peru (Inca Indian word for "wealth") was named in 1832 for the South American country which freed itself around that time from 300 years of Spanish domination. The description of Peru is based on "Peru, Illinois; Historical Program" (City of Peru, 1960); L. H. Shadensack, "Peru's Water Street a Century Ago, 1860–1880" (W. H. Maze Company); Nancy Chadbourne Maze, ed., *Peru, Illinois, Centennial Booklet; Tales and Pictures of Peru, 1835–1985* (Peru, IL, 1985). The assistance of Nancy Chadbourne Maze is gratefully acknowledged.

3. The story of the Bengelstraeters' emigration from Germany to LaSalle is based on MLP.

4. In later years, Waldemar Liachowsky, one of Maud's accompanists, wrote to Germany in behalf of Maud and her mother, seeking records of

[447]

the Bengelstraeter family. The marriage certificate recorded in the Protestant church register at Lüdenschied indicates that Peter Hermann Bengelstraeter from Lösenbach, thirty years old, son of Hermann Diedrich Bengelstraeter from Elspe, married on May 22, 1835, Wilhelmina Potthof, twenty years old, daughter of Hermann Heinrich Potthof from Lösenbach.

5. Letter from Carl Brune and A. Lamberti, friends of the family in Lösenbach, written presumably to Dr. Ruben B. Landon or the local attorney in LaSalle, Mr. John P. Thompson, November 23, 1849. Thompson became the children's legal guardian upon their parents' death.

6. William (Wilhelm) was born January 5, 1839; Wilhelmina, August 6, 1843; Henrietta (Kitty), October 8, 1845, according to their birth certificates and parish records. The gold for the farm was never found and was thought to have been buried with Wilhelmina, secured tightly in her petticoat.

7. Because there was no legal adoption procedure, adoption took the form of indenture. William Americanized his name to Streeter and later ran away and joined the Union Army; MLP.

8. Description of William Paul based on John Barron, "It was like this . . . ," *LaSalle News Tribune*, n.d., 1973; and handwritten description of William Paul dated October 1887, Public Library, Vineland, NJ.

9. Description of Caroline Paul based on obituary in MLP and handwritten description of William Paul dated October 1887, Public Library, Vineland, NJ.

10. The description of Minnie is based on MLP, photographs, and John Barron, "It was like this . . . ," *LaSalle News Tribune*, n.d., 1973.

11. "Maud Powell," Letters and Art, *The Literary Digest* 64 (31 January, 1920): 32–33.

12. Webster's son lived on a 659-acre tract of land owned by his father just west of Peru. Lincoln and Stephen A. Douglas stayed in Peru overnight prior to one of their famous senatorial debates of 1858, held in nearby Ottawa the next day.

13. William Culp Darrah, *Powell of the Colorado* (Princeton: Princeton University Press, 1951), 46. Information on the Peru schools is from Maze, ed., *Peru, Illinois, Centennial Booklet*, 35. W. B. Powell came to Peru from Hennepin, Illinois, where he had succeeded his war-bound brother John Wesley Powell as principal of the public schools on April 14, 1861.

14. The story of Joseph and Mary Powell's emigration and journey west is based on MLP and Darrah, *Powell of the Colorado*, chs. 1 and 2.

15. Darrah, *Powell of the Colorado*, 31–33.

16. MLP.

17. Minnie Paul Powell's biographical sketch of Maud Powell (hereafter MPP Sketch), MS in MLP.

Chapter 2
AURORA

1. For a general depiction of the progress of women in music in America, especially with regard to the violin, see Christine Ammer, *Unsung, A History of Women in American Music* (Westport, CT: Greenwood Press, 1980).

2. The description of Maud Powell's early life and education is based primarily on the following sources: Maud Powell's autobiographical sketch in manuscript, MLP; MPP Sketch; "Maud Powell's Big Success," *Aurora Daily Beacon*, 5 July 1907; "Girlhood of Maud Powell," *Aurora Beacon-News*, 25 July 1937, quoting the recollections of Charles Van Liew, graduate of East Aurora High School's Class of 1881, and of various other classmates and teachers, including Jennie Osborn, Sam Clark, Carolyn Coon, and Ada Foster; "Painting of Late Maud Powell, Famous Violinist, on Exhibition Today at the Conklin Galleries," *Aurora Beacon-News*, 28 December 1924; Maud Powell, "Struggles Which Led to Success; Miss Maud Powell, America's Most Distinguished Violinist," *The Etude* (October 1911); Maud Powell, "An Artist's Life," *The Musical Observer* (1918); John Barron, "It's Like This . . . ," *LaSalle News Tribune*, 25 February 1975 (reprint of letter from Martha Freeman Esmond to Julia Boyd of New York, May 17, 1891); Letter from John W. Plain to Eleanor Plain, August 29, 1960; Frederick Martens, *Violin Mastery* (New York: Frederick A. Stokes Company, 1919); "Maud Powell at Home," *New York Evening Sun*, 21 October 1913; "Maud Powell Concert," *Aurora Beacon-News*, 27 February 1895; Letter from Maud Powell to her cousin Mabel Love, 22 May 1915, MLP; "John Fauth's Recollections," *Aurora Beacon-News*, 12 August 1934; "Maud Powell Makes Big Hit," *Aurora Daily Beacon*, 9 October 1907. The assistance of the Aurora Public Library, the Aurora Historical Museum, and the late John Barron is gratefully acknowledged.

3. "Maud Powell's Big Success."

4. "Maud Powell's Musical Education," quoting "The Girl Who Wants To Be Great," *The Pictorial Review*, Neva Garner Greenwood Collection, Falls Church, VA (hereafter NGGC).

5. W. B. Powell had completed his master of arts degree at Lombard University in Galesburg, IL (June 17, 1868), before leaving Peru for Aurora in January 1870. Powell was superintendent of the Aurora Public Schools, East Side, from January 1, 1870, to June 30, 1885.

6. Descriptions of Aurora are taken from Vernon Derry, author and comp., *The Aurora Story* (Aurora Bicentennial Commission, 1976).

7. Van Liew in "Girlhood of Maud Powell."

8. Powell, "An Artist's Life."

9. Osborn in "Girlhood of Maud Powell."

10. Powell, "Struggles Which Led to Success."

11. Undated, untitled article, NGGC.

12. Coon in "Girlhood of Maud Powell."

13. Undated, untitled article in Aurora Historical Museum; John Barron, "It's Like This . . . ," *LaSalle News Tribune*, 25 February 1975.

14. *Aurora Daily Beacon*, 1 October 1907.

15. "Maud Powell's Musical Education."

16. Powell, "An Artist's Life."

17. MPP Sketch.

18. Martens, *Violin Mastery*, 184.

19. The description of Urso is based on Ammer, *Unsung*, 23–28.

20. "Maud Powell at Home."

21. Ammer, *Unsung*, 27.

22. The exact age at which Maud began violin and piano study is the subject of conflicting accounts. Primary deference has been given to Maud's own recollections and all other accounts reconciled with hers. Numerous reports in newspaper articles date the beginning of Maud's violin studies after Camilla Urso's appearance in Aurora. However, Maud's statements indicate that she had begun violin lessons earlier. More difficult to reconcile are Maud's recollections of her mother's determination to start her on the violin at the earliest possible age with her mother's own account of those early years, written in later life:

> Born of music loving parents . . . it was natural that in common with so many other American girls, she should, at an early age, begin piano study. At the age of seven she began her musical studies and within six months made her first public appearance, participating in a piano duet, although her little feet could not reach the pedals. She was far from being a prodigy, however, and was not so considered by her parents who only wished to give her the additional culture which the study of music secures. They had at that time no thought of preparing her for a professional musical career. It was some months after this first appearance before an audience other than the home circle, that the idea of teaching little Maud the violin and of making her an artist, first occurred to Mrs. Powell. The little daughter was taken one night to hear Camilla Urso, and manifesting great delight at the artist's power, it was determined to buy for her a violin. [MPP Sketch]

23. Untitled article, 1 May 1924, Detroit Public Library.

24. Powell's ideas on education pre-dated John Dewey's famous education tract, *School and Society* (1899), which expounded theories Powell had already articulated and put into practice. The description of W. B. Powell's educational approach is derived from the following sources: Letter from Ada Foster (former teacher) to "Now and Then," *Aurora Beacon-News*, 6 December 1931; R. Barclay, "Reading Profited from Two Aurorans," *Aurora Beacon-News*, 24 July 1971; "Now and Then," *Aurora Beacon-News*, 10 March 1929; Letter from Mrs. George Atherton to "Now and Then," *Aurora Beacon-News*, 3 December 1944; William Bramwell Powell, "The Educational Outlook," *Jour. of Proc. and Addresses*, National Education Association (1897): 154; William B. Powell, "Geographic Instruction in the Public Schools," *National Geographic*, 5 (January 31, 1894): 137; Emma J. Todd and William B. Powell, *How to Teach Reading* (Boston: Silver, Burdett & Company, 1899); William B. Powell, *How to See* (Philadelphia: Cowperthwait & Co., 1886); William B. Powell, "Methods of Teaching Music," *Jour. of Proc. and Addresses*, NEA (July 11–14, 1899): 987; "Superintendent Powell's Defense," *Washington Evening Star*, 27 June 1900; John W. Cook, "William Bramwell Powell," *Jour. of Proc. and Addresses*, NEA (June 27–July 1, 1904): 361; William B. Powell, "Medical Inspection of Schools," *Jour. of Proc. and Addresses*, NEA (July 7–12, 1898): 454; William B. Powell, "Industrial and Manual Training in the School Course," *Proc. of the International Congress of Education*, NEA (1894): 606.

25. Powell, "The Educational Outlook," 155.

26. Powell, "Geographic Instruction," 143. Powell urged his fellow educators to "Study the child, and see how he thinks." By studying the child, he pointed out, "We are learning what he ought to know; we are learning what he wants to know, and we are learning how he can know the most easily and the most naturally." Powell, "The Educational Outlook," 155.

27. Todd and Powell, *How to Teach Reading*, 10.

28. Powell, "Methods of Teaching Music," 987.

29. Powell, "Geographic Instruction," 143.

30. "Superintendent Powell's Defense."

31. Powell, "Methods of Teaching Music," 988.

32. Undated, untitled article in Aurora Historical Museum.

33. Powell incorporated his ideas in his textbooks: William B. Powell, *How to See* (Philadelphia: Cowperthwait & Co., 1886); *How to Talk* (Philadelphia: Cowperthwait & Co., 1882); *How to Write* (Philadelphia: Cowperthwait & Co., 1882); with Emma J. Todd, *The Normal Course in Reading* (Boston: Silver, Burdett & Co., 1888); also with

Emma J. Todd, *How to Teach Reading* (Boston: Silver, Burdett & Co., 1899); with Louise Connolly, *A Rational Grammar of the English Language* (New York: American Book Co., 1899); and William B. Powell, *A History of the United States for Beginners* (New York: The Macmillan Co., 1900). Powell's books concentrated on language lessons (using nature study for their substance) which Powell, in Peru, then Powell and Emma Todd, his assistant in Aurora, worked out in theory and tested in the classroom. There is a physical and intellectual beauty about Powell's books which is striking. They reveal his profound insight and genius and his love for his work.

34. The life of John Wesley Powell, Maud's brilliant uncle, is well documented in Darrah, *Powell of the Colorado*, and in Wallace E. Stegner, *Beyond the Hundredth Meridian* (Boston: Houghton Mifflin Company, 1954; rpt. ed., Lincoln: University of Nebraska Press, 1982). John Wesley Powell's contribution to American life, like that of his brother Bramwell and his niece Maud, is incalculable. He was especially noted for his "powerfully original and prophetic mind," traits which Bram shared and which were Maud's by inheritance. He rose to the rank of Major during the Civil War, losing his right arm in the Battle of Shiloh and making friends with General Ulysses S. Grant at Vicksburg.

35. From MPP Sketch.

36. Alexander Lehmann, "Sketch of William Lewis," *The Violinist*, 1902; "A Pioneer in the Violin Business in Chicago," *The Violinist*, June 1910.

37. Maud Powell to Mabel Love, 22 May 1915, NGGC.

38. MPP Sketch.

39. Powell, "Struggles Which Led to Success."

40. "Maud Powell's Big Success."

41. *Musical Record*, date unknown, NGGC.

42. Martens, *Violin Mastery*, 186.

43. Ibid.

44. "John Fauth's Recollections," "Now and Then," *Aurora Beacon-News*, 12 August 1934.

45. MPP Sketch.

46. Ibid., and Powell, "Struggles Which Led to Success."

47. Undated, untitled article in Aurora Historical Museum.

48. The streets were lighted with sixteen 2,000-candle-power electric arc lamps which were placed on high towers strategically located throughout the city; Derry, *The Aurora Story*.

49. Undated, untitled article, NGGC.

50. *Batavia News*, reported in the *Aurora Beacon-News*, 11 March 1881.

51. Maud Powell, "How Fashion Invades the Concert Stage," *Musical America*, 26 December 1908.

52. Van Liew in "Girlhood of Maud Powell."

53. Undated, untitled Aurora newspaper article, NGGC.

54. The bracelet was listed among the possessions in Maud Powell's estate after her death, indicating that she did indeed guard it carefully. Special thanks to Daniel A. Cerio, Esq., for his extraordinary efforts in obtaining Maud Powell's will and the papers filed by the Administrator of her estate in New York City.

55. Osborn in "Girlhood of Maud Powell."

56. Ada Foster to "Now and Then," *Aurora Beacon-News*, 6 December 1931.

Chapter 3
LEIPZIG, 1881–1882

1. Minnie Paul Powell to "Nellie," Ellen Powell Thompson, 22 July 1881, MLP.

2. The description of the Powell family trio settling in Leipzig is drawn from Letter from Minnie Paul Powell to her sister-in-law "Nellie," Ellen Powell Thompson, 22 July 1881, MLP.

3. "Von den Muttern beruhmter kinder," *Morgen Journal*, 26 May 1912, trans. by Ruth Eigenmann Figueroa.

4. Geraldine Morgan's father, John Paul Morgan, was the founder of the Oberlin Conservatory of Music and organist at Old Trinity Church. Her mother was a composer and translator of songs. Geraldine studied violin under Leopold Damrosch in New York. After Leipzig, she went on to Berlin to study eight years with Joseph Joachim. She was the first American to win the Mendelssohn Prize, in 1886. She made her American debut in 1892 with the New York Symphony in Bruch's G Minor Violin Concerto. She formed the Morgan String Quartet and became the founder and director of the Joachim School of Violin Playing based at Carnegie Hall. She continued her career as a soloist after her marriage until about 1910; she died in New York on May 20, 1918. Ammer, *Unsung*, 35.

5. Maud indicated that the Carpenters were in Leipzig at the same time she was; however, the Paris Conservatoire records indicate that Nettie Carpenter had been enrolled there from 1879 through 1882–83, when she was Maud's classmate. This may explain the confusion.

6. Minnie Paul Powell to "Nellie," Ellen Powell Thompson, 22 July 1881, MLP.

7. The visit to the conservatory and meeting with John Rhodes is described in Letter from Minnie Paul Powell to "Nellie," Ellen Powell Thompson, 22 July 1881, MLP.

8. For an excellent exposition on the evolution of violin playing, see Dominic Gill, ed., *The Book of the Violin* (New York: Rizzoli, 1984).

9. Schradieck's career and teaching approach are drawn from various sources: Robert Braine, "In Memoriam—Henry Schradieck," *The Etude*, June 1918; William W. Todd, "Henry Schradieck—An Appreciation," *The Violinist*, August 1916; "Henry Schradieck," *The Violinist*, 1918; Arthur M. Abell, "Henry Schradieck—In Memoriam," *The Musical Courier*, 1918.

10. Minnie Paul Powell to "Nellie," Ellen Powell Thompson, 22 July 1881, MLP.

11. The description of the beginnings of the Leipzig Conservatory and the musical atmosphere created by Mendelssohn is drawn from various sources: Dr. Herbert W. Wareing, "The Conservatory at Leipzig," *The Etude*, April 1911; Virginia O. Behrs, "Musical Leipzig of Yesterday," *The Etude*, July 1949; "The Royal Conservatory of Music at Leipzig," *The Musical Courier*, 19 August 1891; Helen Johnson, "The Joyous Mendelssohn," *The Musical Observer*, December 1947; "Ferdinand David," *The Musical Observer*, 1907.

12. "Biographical Sketches of Maud Powell, World-Famous Violinist, and Members of Her Family," compiled by an unknown resident of Peru, Illinois, in 1914, Peru Public Library; MPP Sketch.

13. Martha Freeman Esmond to Julia Boyd, 17 May 1891, printed in a Chicago newspaper, Herma Clark, "When Chicago Was Young," 1 October 1939. Also printed in John Barron, "It's Like This . . . ," *LaSalle News Tribune*, 25 February 1975.

14. Charles Van Liew, "Girlhood of Maud Powell."

15. Grace Greenwood, New York *Independent*, reprinted in the *Aurora Beacon-News*, date unknown, but it has to be before Maud's return to America in 1885 and after her tour of England in 1883; the article is in Aurora Historical Museum.

16. MLP.

17. Minnie Paul Powell to her sister, Henrietta "Kitty" Landon Love, 29 November 1881, Aurora Historical Museum.

18. Ibid.

19. Ibid.

20. Minnie Paul Powell to Henrietta "Kitty" Landon Love, 8 January 1882, MLP.

21. "Von den Muttern beruhmter kinder," *Morgen Journal*, 26 May 1912, trans. by Ruth Eigenmann Figueroa.

22. The description of the Gewandhaus Orchestra and Leipzig's musical life is drawn from several sources: Wareing, "The Conservatory at Leipzig"; "A Famous Musical Shrine," *The Etude*, February 1932; Max von Lewen Swarthout, "Letter from Leipzig," *The Violinist*, June 1903; "Leipzig as a Musical Center," *The Presto*, 28 December 1899.

23. Minnie Paul Powell to Henrietta Landon Love, 29 November 1881, Aurora Historical Museum.

24. Ibid.

25. Powell, "Struggles Which Led to Success."

26. MPP Sketch.

27. Maud Powell, "Women and the Violin," *The Ladies' Home Journal*, February 1896.

28. Ibid.

29. Ibid.

30. MPP Sketch.

31. The description of the Powells' life over the holidays is based on a letter from Minnie Paul Powell to her sister, Henrietta "Kitty" Landon Love, 8 January 1882, MLP.

32. Minnie Paul Powell to "Nellie," Ellen Powell Thompson, 24 February 1882, MLP.

33. Ibid.

34. Powell, "Struggles Which Led to Success."

35. Reprinted in undated, untitled article in Aurora Historical Museum.

36. Inscription No. 3390, Royal Conservatory for Music at Leipzig, School Report for Miss Maud Powell from Chicago.

37. MPP Sketch; Maud Powell, "Women and the Violin"; Foster, "Painting of Late Maud Powell."

Chapter 4
PARIS, 1882–1883

1. See, *Grove's*, 1926 ed., "Conservatoire de Musique"; "How the Paris Conservatoire was Conceived," *Musical America*, 11 August 1906; Moritz Moszkowski, "The Paris Conservatory of Music," *The Etude*, January 1910.

2. MPP Sketch; Maud Powell's autobiographical sketch for *Grove's*: "Examinations Rigid, Especially for Foreigners"; Moritz Moszkowski, "Methods and Customs of the Paris Conservatoire," *The Etude*, February 1910.

3. Maud Powell's autobiographical sketch for *Grove's* indicates there were eighty applicants for six vacancies, while MPP Sketch indicates eighty-three applicants for thirteen vacancies in the violin classes. We have used the numbers found in the Conservatoire's official records.

4. MLP.

5. The examination procedure is taken in part from André Benoist, "My First Day at the Conservatoire de Paris," *The Etude*, December 1948.

6. MPP Sketch.

7. Martens, *Violin Mastery*, 187.

8. Paris Conservatoire records.

9. The description of Charles Dancla is derived from the following: *Grove's*, 1926 ed., "Dancla"; "Charles Dancla," *The Etude*, March 1910; T. L. Phipson, "The Career of Charles Dancla," *The Strad*, 1897; Charles Dancla, *Notes et Souvenirs* (Paris: Société Anonyme de l'Imprimerie de Vaugirard, 189-).

10. Donald Jay Grout, *A History of Western Music* (New York: W. W. Norton, 1973), 650.

11. All quotations from Dancla and explanations of his views on music and teaching are from his memoirs, *Notes et Souvenirs*.

12. When Baillot died in 1842, Habeneck recommended that two French artists be chosen to replace him on the faculty of the Conservatoire—Alard and Dancla. Politics intervened and the Belgian artist Massart was chosen along with Alard. The injustice to Dancla, which he keenly felt, was rectified fifteen years later with his appointment to the faculty in 1857; Dancla, *Notes et Souvenirs*, 40–41.

13. Paris Conservatoire records. Nettie Carpenter (b. 1865, New York) went to Europe at an early age, playing in London at the age of twelve. At the Paris Conservatoire, she won the first prize for violin in 1884. She toured Europe and America with much success, until her career ended with her marriage to the English cellist Leo Stern in 1891; Ammer, *Unsung*, 36.

14. Paris Conservatoire records; Michele Maurin, Documentaliste, Paris Conservatoire, to Neva Garner Greenwood, 14 February 1981, NGGC.

15. Maud Powell's autobiographical sketch for *Grove's*; MPP Sketch.

16. Martens, *Violin Mastery*, 187–88.

17. The quotations which follow are from Dancla, *Notes et Souvenirs*, 15–17, 38, 60, 72–73.

18. Martens, *Violin Mastery*, 186.

19. Charles Dancla to Bertha Bucklin Chase, 18 October 1898, Lucy Chase Sparks Papers, Whitefield, NH.

20. Maud Powell to Frank Dossert, 24 July 1890, MLP.

21. MPP Sketch. Augustus George Heaton (b. 1844) eventually worked for the U.S. Capitol in Washington, D.C. The portrait he painted of Maud has not been located.

22. John Wesley Powell's biographer wrote of him: "[T]he process of self-education never stopped in him. He learned in his sleep. He learned

from every book, acquaintance, experience; facts stuck in his mind, and not like stray flies on flypaper but like orderly iron filings around magnetic poles, or ions around anode and cathode in an electrolytic bath." Stegner, *Beyond the Hundredth Meridian*, 124.

23. *American Register*, Paris, reprinted in undated, untitled article in Aurora Historical Museum.

24. Grace Greenwood, New York *Independent*, reprinted in the *Aurora Beacon-News*, date unknown, but it has to be before Maud's return to America in 1885 and after her tour of England in 1883; the article is in Aurora Historical Museum.

25. Paris Conservatoire records.

26. Maud Powell's autobiographical sketch for *Grove's*.

27. Powell, "Women and the Violin."

Chapter 5
ENGLAND, 1883–1884

1. Norman Foerster, ed., *American Poetry & Prose* (Boston: Houghton Mifflin Co., 1957), 803.

2. Maud Powell manuscript, MLP.

3. MPP Sketch.

4. Ibid.

5. *Grove's*, 1926 ed., "Santley."

6. *The Musical Standard* (London), reprinted in undated, untitled article in Aurora Historical Museum.

7. "Maud Powell Trio Concert," clipping in Maud Powell's scrapbook, New York Public Library.

8. *Galignani's Messenger* (London), Aurora Historical Museum.

9. *The Westminster and Chelsea News* (London), Aurora Historical Museum.

10. *The Buxton Advertiser* (London), Aurora Historical Museum.

11. *The Westminster and Chelsea News* (London), Aurora Historical Museum.

12. MPP Sketch.

13. Ibid.; Maud Powell's autobiographical sketch for *Grove's*.

14. John Barron, "It's Like This . . . ," *LaSalle News Tribune*, 25 February 1975.

15. Minnie Paul Powell to her sister Henrietta "Kitty" Landon Love, 24 September 1883, MLP.

16. Ibid.

17. See *Grove's*, 1926 ed., "Neruda"; Henry C. Lahee, *Famous Violinists* (Boston: L. C. Page and Company, 1899); Margaret Campbell, *The Great Violinists* (Garden City, NY: Doubleday, 1981).

18. MPP Sketch.

19. *The West Middlesex Advertiser* (London), Aurora Historical Museum.

20. MPP Sketch.

21. Sargent's portrait was presented to Joachim by the Right Honorable Arthur Balfour on May 16, 1904, at a large gathering of friends celebrating the Diamond Jubilee of Joachim's first appearance in England. In response, Joachim stated that he had always viewed England as his second home. The violinist played the Beethoven concerto that day with the Queens Hall Orchestra, conducted by Henry J. Wood. "Joseph Joachim Dying," *Musical America*, August 1907; D. Sanders, "The Joachim Jubilee of 1899" *The Musical Observer — New York*.

22. Maud Powell's autobiographical sketch for *Grove's*; 1st ed.

JOSE SHERRINGTON: Younger sister of Mme. Lemmens-Sherrington, born at Rotterdam October 27th, 1850; studied at Brussels under Madame Meyer-Boulard and Signor Chiriamonte, and soon showed a gift for florid singing, and a very fine shake. In 1871 she appeared in London and the Provinces, under the auspices of her sister. In 1873 made a tour in Holland, and then returned to [England], where she has since established herself as a concert singer, and is much in request. Though gifted with much dramatic talent, Miss Jose Sherrington has never appeared in public on the stage. Her voice is a good soprano reaching from A below the stave to E in alt.

Thanks to Peter Norris, Director of Music, The Yehudi Menuhin School, England, for providing this information.

23. *The Express* (Newcastle-on-Tyne), Aurora Historical Museum.

24. *Grove's*, 1926 ed., "Joachim."

25. Ibid.; "Musicians of the Day—Dr. Joseph Joachim," *The Musical Standard*, 24 March 1894.

26. *The Graphic*, March 1884. Outside of Berlin and Germany, Joachim's greatest influence was in England. The English public's admiration for him was joyfully commemorated when $6,000 was subscribed for a Stradivarius violin (the "Red" Strad) which was presented to him at the close of the Monday Popular Concerts in 1888.

27. *New Orleans Picayune*, 20 December 1896; Lady Hay was the wife of Sir John Hay.

28. "[I]n fact almost every well-known violin player had been to Berlin to seek his advice and instruction. . . . " Lahee, *Famous Violinists*, 252–53.

29. MPP Sketch.

30. Foster, "Painting of Late Maud Powell."

Chapter 6
BERLIN, 1884–1885

1. The portrayal of Joseph Joachim's life, his violin playing, his teaching approach, and the atmosphere at the Berlin Hochschule is based on the following sources: Andreas Moser, *Joseph Joachim* (London: P. Wellby, 1901); Chapin, *The Violin and Its Masters* (New York: Lippincott, 1969); *Grove's*, 1926 ed., "Joachim," "Joachim Quartet"; "The Teachers of Joseph Joachim," *The Musical Observer*; Lahee, *Famous Violinists*; I. Troostwyk, "Reminiscences of the Great Joachim by One of His Pupils," 14 January 1916; Sol Marcosson, "Some Reminiscences of Joachim," *The Violinist*, Vol. 8, October-May, 1909–10; Edith L. Winn, "Personal Reminiscences of Joseph Joachim," *The Musical Observer*, 1907; "Max Pilzer to Become Concert Soloist," *The Musical Courier*, 19 April 1917; "The Secret of Joachim's Playing," *Musical America*, 14 September 1907; Martens, *Violin Mastery*; H. M. Kennedy, "Two Interviews with Joachim," *The Violin World*, 15 August 1900; C. R. Drake, "The Passing of Joseph Joachim," *The Musical Standard*, October 1907; Edmund Severn, "The Influence of Joseph Joachim," NGGC; Edith L. Winn, "Joseph Joachim," *The Etude*, October 1907; "Joachim's Social Preferences and His Kindness to the Lesser Lights," *Musical America*, 14 September 1907.

2. *Grove's*, 1926 ed., "Joachim."

3. From "Violin Art in Germany, from Spohr to Joachim," *Violin Playing and Violin-Players*, 99–100, NGGC:

Spohr, the artist, the composer, was a fitting counterpart to Spohr the man. Possessed of the highest art ideals, and averse to everything not reconcilable with these ideals, the trivial ear-pleasing and public-catching never for an instant beguiled his muse away from the path that his strong individuality, and a certain uncompromising Teutonic obstinacy, had clearly marked out for it. Everything in his works, from his violin concertos or duets to his small pieces, is "gediegen" — scholarly, noble, masterly in form, melodious, pleasing and save for certain chromatic mannerisms, was interesting and original.

From this description, it is clear that Joachim felt Spohr's influence in his own approach to music.

4. From ibid., 100, David (1810–73):

. . . seems to have been possessed to a rare degree of the power of assimilating other influences without losing his own individuality. His style was a happy blend of lightness, elegance, and solidity. In his compositions he combined sound musicianship with graceful melodic invention and rhythmical piquancy. Distinguished equally as quartet player and soloist, at home in the deep waters of Bach and Beethoven, and in the surface rollers of the modern virtuosi, an unexcelled orchestral leader and inspiring teacher, David was indeed a very great power in his day.

5. "For several years he studied under David most of the classical works for the violin, such as the concertos of Mendelssohn, Beethoven and Spohr, and at the same time his general education was not neglected, so that by the time his student days were over he was not only a cultivated musician but a cultivated man." From "Musicians of the Day — Dr. Joseph Joachim," *The Musical Standard*, 24 March 1894.

6. "He evinced that thorough uprightness, that firmness of character and earnestness of purpose, and that intense dislike of all that is superficial or untrue in art which have made him not only an artist of the first rank but in a sense a great moral power in the musical life of our day." Robert Braine, Department for Violinists, *The Etude*, January 1910.

7. Foster, "Painting of Late Maud Powell."

8. Martha Wendt, "The Rise and Decline of Virtuosity in the Nineteenth Century as Traced Through the Art of Violin Playing," *American String Teacher*, Fall 1966:

> [T]he full development of all the powers of the violin, or virtuosity on this instrument, was only made possible with the ingenious modern bow designed by [François] Tourte [1747–1835]. He improved the construction of the bow by using the wood of a fine but strong texture, namely pernambuco. He bent the stick in the "reverse" direction, establishing correct proportions of curvature, height, length and weight. This bent elastic stick of the bow gives the modern player . . . the ability to execute every conceivable type of tone and bowing and thus "incalculable advantages over those of an earlier age."

9. Martens, *Violin Mastery*, 189–90.

10. For a delightful vignette of Paganini, his times, and his contributions to the violin art, see Yehudi Menuhin and Curtis W. Davis, *The Music of Man* (New York: Methuen, 1979), 165–70; see also Lahee, *Famous Violinists*, ch. 4.

11. "The Secret of Joachim's Playing," quoting Andreas Moser.

12. Lahee, *Famous Violinists*, 253–54. A contemporary observed: "He is no virtuoso in the ordinary sense, for he is far more, — before all he will be a musician"; ibid., 245.

13. Personal account of Joachim playing the Beethoven violin concerto at the age of twenty or twenty-two given by Arthur Abell in "Joseph Joachim, Nestor of Violinists," *The Musical Courier*, 28 June 1906:

[W]ith the first tones from his instrument I forgot everything else — the hall, the audience, even Herr Joachim himself. His nobility and fullness of tone, his finished technic, his spirit and conception, made undivided claim upon me. . . . I might describe the artist with the one word "inspired". . . . Yesterday for the first time a performance gave me an impression of perfection. The rendering was to the smallest detail a most true and most inspired reproduction of the work; every detail, even the big cadenza introduced into the first movement, appeared as a feature demanded by the inner nature of the thing. There was nothing slovenly, no vain virtuoso ornamentation; but every sforzato, crescendo or staccato was done complete justice. After the concert it occurred to me that the most wonderful part of the bravura had escaped me; double stopping, chromatic runs in octaves, and I know not what — but during the playing I took hardly any notice of that, for the virtuoso was absolutely merged in the artist, one completely covered up the other.

From Davol Sanders, "The Joachim Jubilee of 1899": "No other man has played Beethoven's master-work with such simplicity, with such *finesse*, with such purity of style and unaffected dignity." From "The Artistic Standards of Joseph Joachim," *The Musical Observer*: "Even the very best members of his calling had never attempted to do more than play the notes of the Beethoven Concerto correctly. Joachim, however, sought to bring to light all the hidden beauties of this sublime work. In his hands it received new life, making the hearer conscious of the sublime spirit a work can induce when reproduced with pure artistic conviction."

14. At nineteen, Joachim aspired to be a composer as well as a violinist and briefly joined Liszt in his enthusiasm for Wagner and the "new" music. Joachim's most famous and perhaps most enduring composition is his Hungarian Concerto for Violin and Orchestra. See Chapin, *The Violin and Its Masters* for an overview of the influence of Joachim and Schumann in the context of musical developments during the first half of the nineteenth century; see also Severn, "The Influence of Joseph Joachim," NGGC.

15. Foster, "Painting of Late Maud Powell."

16. Lahee describes the circumstances under which the first women were admitted to study with Joachim in *Famous Violinists*, 326–27.

17. Edith L. Winn, "Recollections of Joseph Joachim," *The Musical Observer*, 1907.

18. Maud Powell's autobiographical sketch for *Grove's*.

19. MPP Sketch.

20. "[H]e demands from his pupils the fullest reverence for their profession." Andreas Moser, "Joseph Joachim," NGGC.

21. Among his most famous pupils were Leopold Auer, Carl Halir, Willy Hess, Tivadar Nachez, and Carl Flesch. "He aimed to create not virtuosos among his pupils, but disciples to spread the gospel of true art and to deliver broadcast the great teachings which inspired him." Marcosson, "Some Reminiscences of Joachim."

22. Martens, *Violin Mastery*, 186–87.

23. Ibid., 185–86.

24. Ibid., 165: Tivadar Nachez said, "Yet if Joachim may be criticized as regards the way of imparting the secrets of technical phases in his violin teaching, as a teacher of interpretation he was incomparable! As an interpreter of Beethoven and of Bach in particular, there has never been any one to equal Joachim." From Lahee, *Famous Violinists*, 259: "Joachim is not a builder of technique or a teacher of beginners. Pupils who are accepted by him must be already proficient technicians."

25. Martens, *Violin Mastery*, 188–89.

26. Edith L. Winn, "Heinrich Jacobsen," *Musical Record and Review*, January 1902; Troostwyk, "Reminiscences of the Great Joachim." Joachim gave his former pupil and assistant teacher Heinrich Jacobsen credit for the advancement of many of his pupils, including Maud Powell, who studied with both men simultaneously.

27. H. M. Kennedy, "Two Interviews with Joachim," *The Violin World*, 15 August 1900.

28. Lahee, *Famous Violinists*, 259.

29. Drake, "The Passing of Joseph Joachim."

30. Winn, "Joseph Joachim."

31. "Joachim's Tribute to Maud Powell," *The Musical Courier*, August 1906.

32. All the records of the Berlin Hochschule pertaining to Maud Powell were apparently lost in World War II, but we do have a picture of Joachim's graduating class of 1885 in which Maud appears. Henri Ern, the teacher of the distinguished Puerto Rican violinist José Figueroa, was one of her classmates.

33. Emilie Frances Bauer, "Music in New York," *The Musical Leader and Concert-Goer*, 26 July 1906: " . . . Miss Powell thinks no more of preparing a new concerto than she does of playing an old one. The secret lies in the marvelous rapidity with which she grasps the work and also with her powers of memorizing which are regarded as abnormal by all who know her methods of study and practice." Maud Powell explains her approach to a new work in her own forthright and inimitable style in "The American Girl and Her Violin," *The Etude*, July 1909.

34. Powell, "Women and the Violin."

35. "Joachim's Tribute to Maud Powell." Their kinship in this regard is most clearly revealed by the way Joachim rips through the chords in his 1903 recording of Brahms' Hungarian Dance No. 1 (Pearl GEM 101) and Maud plays so zestfully Hubay's *Hejre Kati*, Op. 32, from *Scènes de la Czarda* in her recording of that piece (HMV 74324 and Discopaedia MB 1005). Maud's program note reads: "Hubay was a Hungarian violinist and composer who wrote with skill and fancy in the idiom of his chosen instrument. In the Hejre Kati he gives us typical dance rhythm of the Hungarian people—the melancholy introduction ('Lassu'), a rather material and middle movement and the well known 'Priska', the latter a lively movement which rushes along in mad excitement, till in the sheer nature of things it must come to a sudden breathless stop."

36. For the most insightful analysis of Joachim's contribution to the Brahms violin concerto, read Yehudi Menuhin's delightfully literary introduction to the facsimile publication of the autograph score of the Brahms violin concerto, published by the Library of Congress, Washington, D.C.

37. Severn, "The Influence of Joseph Joachim," 205. Ysaÿe (1858–1931) did not play the concerto publicly until 1903 or 1904. He did not feel comfortable with it until 1905, when he performed it with great success in Berlin. For an excellent account of Ysaÿe's struggle with the Brahms concerto, see Antoine Ysaÿe and Bertram Ratcliffe, *Ysaÿe* (reprint ed., St. Clair Shores, MI: Scholarly Press, 1978), 237–38.

38. Chapin, *The Violin and Its Masters*, 159.

39. See Severn, "The Influence of Joseph Joachim"; *Grove's*, 1926 ed., "Joachim Quartet"; Andreas Moser, "Joseph Joachim as a Quartet Player," *The Musical Observer*, 1907. Severn, who heard the Joachim Quartet in 1888, made the following observations about each player: Joachim—"the greatest violinist in musical history, who devoted himself to string quartet playing." Heinrich de Ahna, second violin—"an eminent violin soloist . . . . To hear the inter-play between two such great artists, each capable of answering the other in full, was a delight." Emanuel Wirth, violist—"probably the greatest quartet viola player that ever lived. . . . With Wirth it was not a question of virtuosity, although he was a master both as a violinist and a viola player; but such sincerity, and such tremendous emotional power, are not met with many times during the span of a human life." Robert Hausmann, cellist—"pupil of the great Muller and the greater Piatti, was an ideal quartet cellist, brought up under the very eyes of Joachim, who, in 1879, made him teacher at the Royal High School of Music in Berlin. . . . " Severn indicates that Wirth's viola and Hausmann's cello were Amatis, to which he attributed the quartet's "distinctive tone" in 1888. *Grove's* and others

indicate that the quartet eventually played with Stradivarius instruments exclusively.

40. The American Woman's Club was founded to protect American women students from harmful foreign influences. "Music Students Who Go Abroad," *The Musical Observer*, 1907; "Where American Music Students Meet in Berlin," *Musical America*, NGGC.

41. Foster, "Painting of Late Maud Powell."

42. MPP Sketch.

Chapter 7
THEODORE THOMAS'S MUSICAL GRANDCHILD

1. "Girlhood of Maud Powell."

2. John W. Cook, "William Bramwell Powell," *Journal of Proceedings and Addresses*, National Education Association (June 27–July 1, 1904).

3. Note dated 23 April 1885, printed in the *Aurora Beacon-News*, 25 April 1885.

4. *Aurora Daily Beacon*, 13 May 1885.

5. *Aurora Beacon-News*, 1885, reprinted in *The Musical Courier*, 10 May 1917.

6. *Aurora Daily Beacon*, 13 May 1885.

7. The history of Theodore Thomas and his orchestra is drawn from *Grove's*, 1926 ed., "Thomas" and "Symphony Concerts in the United States"; and Rose Fay Thomas, *Memoirs of Theodore Thomas* (New York: Moffat, Yard and Company, 1911). Quotations are from the latter source unless otherwise noted.

8. Thomas, *Memoirs*, 50.

9. The Belgian violinist Henri Vieuxtemps toured the United States that same year and observed the progress that had been made since his second American tour in 1857: "Everywhere societies and artistic associations had been formed and everywhere the taste for serious music was much developed." Article in NGGC.

10. Thomas, *Memoirs*, 67.

11. The pillars upon which Theodore Thomas built his orchestral programs were Wagner and Beethoven. Thomas explained these choices: "Beethoven is the nearest us in spirit; . . . he expressed more than any other composer; and . . . he has reached the highest pinnacle in instrumental music. . . . [H]e gives delight to the educated, and teaches the uneducated." Also "[Wagner] represents the modern spirit, and his effective scoring makes the desired climax. . . . Wagner excites his hearers, especially the younger generation, and interests the less musical." Unidentified article in NGGC.

12. Thomas, *Memoirs*, 86–87.

13. Ibid., 127. Chicago audiences had heard his great orchestra in concert since 1869. Previously, Chicago had its own Philharmonic Orchestra, composed of local musicians and conducted by Hans Balatka, with William Lewis often appearing as soloist. Chicago had two fine choral societies, the Beethoven and Apollo Clubs, which under Carl Wolfsohn and W. L. Tomlins, respectively, gave performances of some of the great choral literature every year.

14. Maud Powell manuscript, MLP.

15. Ibid.

16. Ibid.

17. *Chicago Tribune*, 31 July 1885.

18. *Chicago Daily News*, 31 July 1885.

19. *Chicago Tribune*, 31 July 1885.

20. *Chicago Daily News*, 31 July 1885.

21. *Chicago Tribune*, 31 July 1885.

22. *Chicago Daily News*, 31 July 1885.

23. *Aurora Daily Beacon*, October 1907.

24. Gustav Kobbé, "Maud Powell, An Appreciation," *The Musical Courier*, August 1913.

25. Maud Powell manuscript, MLP.

26. *Aurora Beacon-News*, 5 September 1937.

27. *New York Tribune*, 15 November 1885.

28. 16 November 1885.

Chapter 8
THE POWELL FAMILY IN WASHINGTON

1. Maud Powell, "The Price of Fame," *New Idea Woman's Magazine*, December 1908.

2. Bramwell Powell, distressed that the public schools educated only the upper 40–60 percent of the pupils, sought ways to eliminate barriers to the education of all students. For him, universal education was the principal means by which the working classes of people could be saved from the social ills of the day. He not only reformed the outdated curriculum but improved the physical circumstances under which learning occurred. He set about erecting new buildings and renovating old ones to house the growing school population, doing what he could to combine utility with comfort and ensuring that each classroom received proper light, ventilation, heating, and advantageous seating. He instituted medical inspections of schools and school children, hoping to prevent the sickness and disease which hinder learning. He knew that parents would learn through the education of their children. Acting on this, he edu-

cated the community on the fundamentals of healthful living by introducing manual training in cooking, sewing, domestic economy, etc., in
the higher grades. Manual training was viewed by Powell as a fundamental means of introducing each branch of knowledge. His emphasis
on dealing with the concrete prior to learning from symbols, designed
to enable the child to build knowledge from original perceptions, instilled
independence of mind and originality of perception. Exhibiting a peculiarly Western bias, he believed that where a child's hands, eyes, feet,
brain, and heart are trained in correlation, he becomes a whole human
being, healthy, intelligent, and industrious. He applied his theory to
mathematics, science, geography, history, and drawing by alloting time
in the school day to the child's manipulation, measurement, and even
manufacture of objects corresponding to the subject under study.

Powell firmly believed that both boys and girls should receive the
same course of study through the sixth year. But he perceived that at the
beginning of the seventh year, manual training would evolve naturally
into attempts at artistic effects and the use of tools, whereupon it would
lose its purely academic function. Consequently, Powell advocated its
continuance in the form of specialized training of the hands as produc-
ers, instead of as learners, and introduced sewing and cooking classes for
the girls and shop, using tools and machines, for the boys. In addition,
Powell devised a way to give students not bound for college a headstart
in the business world by organizing the first business high school in the
country. See William B. Powell, "Medical Inspection of Schools," *Jour.
Proc. and Addresses*, NEA (July 7–12, 1898): 454; William B. Powell,
"Industrial and Manual Training in the School Course," *Proc. of the
International Congress of Education*, NEA (1894): 606; William B. Powell,
"The Educational Outlook," *Jour. of Proc. and Addresses*, NEA (July
6–9, 1897): 154.

3. John W. Cook, President of the Northern Illinois State Normal
School, who was inspired by Powell and became his friend, wrote: "Mr.
Powell was first and last a schoolmaster. I have never known a man more
devoted to his profession. He gave himself to its duties with a passionate
absorption that left little thought or care for anything else. His industry
was tireless. Dr. Gregory would have said of him that he was at once
God-like and ox-like." John W. Cook, "William Bramwell Powell,"
Jour. Proc. and Addresses, NEA (June 27–July 1, 1904): 362.

4. William Paul Powell to Janet McWilliam, Supervising Principal,
Division 3, District of Columbia Public Schools, 14 May 1930, MLP.

5. For a description of the history and significance of John Wesley
Powell's work, see Darrah, *Powell of the Colorado*; Stegner, *Beyond the
Hundredth Meridian*; John Davis, "Biographical Memoir of John Wesley

Powell (1834–1902)," *National Academy of Sciences Biographical Memoirs* 8 (February 1915).

6. In his monograph "Lands of the Arid Region," Powell proposed a fivefold classification of the public lands: mineral, coal, irrigable, pasturage, and timber so that the government could more intelligently write laws governing the use of those lands. John Wesley Powell, "Report on the Lands of the Arid Region of the United States," 1st ed., 1877; 2d ed., 1879. Powell's proposals in the report were revolutionary and served as the blueprint for reform of public policy in dealing with the arid region.

7. MLP.

8. Darrah, *Powell of the Colorado*.

Chapter 9
MAUD POWELL ON HER OWN

1. Powell, "Struggles Which Led to Success."

2. Thomas, *Memoirs*, 153. In 1878, while making plans for the Cincinnati College of Music for which he became the director, Theodore Thomas wrote:

> I do not mean to say that no sincere musical work is done in America, on the contrary, we have many earnest musicians, and a number of able critics; but I speak now of the general average, the rank and file, of which the standard is deplorably low. Nor can it be otherwise so long as we have not a single endowed musical institution which can be regarded as on the same plane with our great universities, nor any well furnished public library of music and works on music for reference. Every European country has found it necessary to have such musical colleges, in order, first, to shape the taste of the people, and afterwards to emancipate them from foreign influences and develop national characteristics. America has, as yet, been too young to see the pressing need of such an institution, but it will come in time.

3. For information on significant violinists in America, see Lahee, *Famous Violinists*; Martens, *Violin Mastery*; Ammer, *Unsung*; Margaret Campbell, *The Great Violinists* (New York: Doubleday, 1981); Boris Schwarz, *Great Masters of the Violin* (New York: Simon and Schuster, 1983).

4. Lahee, *Famous Violinists*, 341–42.

5. Thomas, *Memoirs*, 31.

6. Martens, *Violin Mastery*, 190–91; Maud Powell manuscript, MLP.

7. Among the composers Paine educated were John Alden Carpenter, Arthur Foote, and George Chadwick, who became a faculty member of the New England Conservatory in 1882.

8. *The Musical Herald*, April 1887. Teresina Tua was born in 1867 and died in 1955.

9. Ibid.

10. Martens, *Violin Mastery*, 31.

11. Ibid.

12. H. Godfrey Turner to Burt Wells, Knight Campbell Music Company, Denver, Colorado, 20 January 1920, NGGC.

13. "Fiddle and The Fiddler," *New York Times*, 20 March 1898.

14. Powell, "Women and the Violin."

15. "Fiddle and The Fiddler."

16. Martens, *Violin Mastery*, 31.

17. Maud Powell, "What One's Art Should Mean," undated article, source unknown, MLP.

18. Edith L. Winn, "Maud Powell as I Knew Her—A Tribute," *The Musical Observer*, March 1920.

19. Powell, "The American Girl and Her Violin."

20. Winn, "Maud Powell as I Knew Her."

21. Charles F. Peters, "Little Glimpses of Famous Musicians," *The Bohemian*, May 1907.

22. Ibid.

23. Winn, "Maud Powell as I Knew Her."

24. Powell, "The American Girl and Her Violin."

25. Peters, "Little Glimpses of Famous Musicians."

Chapter 10
Music and Musicians

1. *The Oberlin Review*, 20 March 1888.

2. This dual use of an opera orchestra was the exception. Reflecting the puritanical constraints which proscribed drama (including opera) on or near the Sabbath, Americans developed a predilection for concerts as opposed to opera. Hence, orchestras, both professional and amateur, grew up largely independently of the opera house, a phenomenon much less common in Europe.

3. *The American Musician*, 14 April 1888.

4. *The Musical Leader and Concert-Goer*, 1906.

5. A German composer, conductor, and violinist, Leopold Damrosch came to New York in 1871 to become conductor of the Mannergesangverein Arion, a leading male chorus. A friend of Liszt, Berlioz, and Wagner, he founded and made a success of the Oratorio Society

(1874) and the German Opera, installed in the Metropolitan Opera (1884–85).

6. *New York Times*, 20 January 1889.

7. Ibid., 18 January 1890.

8. *Brooklyn Citizen*, 10 December 1894.

9. MLP.

10. With this remark William Fry, an American journalist-composer living in the first half of the nineteenth century, was refused permission by the director of the Paris Opera to present at his own expense an open rehearsal of his opera *Leonora*. H. Wiley Hitchcock, *Music in the United States: A Historical Introduction* (Garden City, NJ: Prentice-Hall, 1969), 48.

11. From Henry James, *Hawthorne*, written for the "English Men of Letters" series (London: Macmillan and Company, 1879).

12. See H. Wiley Hitchcock, *Music in the United States*, for a discussion of America's institutional foundations for music.

13. Maud Powell, "Musical Future of America," *The Violinist*, September 1911:

> Time was when the weird incantations, the battle songs, and the burial chants of the Indian were the characteristic music of the people who inhabited this country. They were not of our race, but their history is part of our history and the most romantic element of it. And their folk-lore and their music have been diligently collected and conserved for us.
>
> The Indian was an intensely musical being in his own uncivilized way; but the white man who displaced him was not. Our colonial forbears were psalm singers. The pioneers who opened up the wilderness were too busy even for that pious but unmusical diversion. Years passed before any phase of our national existence found musical expression. It was the negro, finally, another alien to our blood, who began to express the emotions of his primitive nature in song. The simplicity and originality of his melodic inspiration, springing from his unsophisticated nature, had an irresistible appeal and charm. He brought into manifestation a new and a characteristic musical idiom. But after the Civil War the unsophisticated negro became obsolete, and melodies like "Suanee River" disappeared with them.
>
> If it obliterated the melodious darky, that same Civil War furnished the first real inspiration to our native composers, patriotic songs, marching tunes, battle hymns, and songs of defeat and victory were turned out in endless profusion. Much of this was worthless and ephemeral; but there remains a fairly substantial residuum of crude, homely,

but stirring music, hallowed by patriotic associations, and valuable not only on that account, but because it is characteristically American in its musical idiom.

14. Letter dated 21 June 1890, MLP.

15. Maud Powell to Frank Dossert, 30 August 1890, Pittsfield, MA, MLP.

16. Letter dated 12 February 1891, MLP.

17. *New York Tribune*, 15 February 1891.

18. 15 February 1891; 14 February 1891.

19. Maud Powell program note, NGGC.

20. *New York Tribune*, 24 February 1891.

21. Henry E. Krehbiel, *Century Magazine*, September 1892. Details of Dvořák's life are drawn from the following: G. Overmyer, "Dvořák in the New World," *Musical America*, September 1941; R. J. Nicolisi, "Music in America," *The American Music Teacher*, April-May 1977; "Dr. Antonin Dvořák," *The Metronome*, November 1892; "Dvořák on Negro Melodies," *The Musical Record*, July 1893; "Highlights in the Life of Dvořák," *Etude*, 1924; "Antonin Dvořák," *Boston Musical Herald*, 1892; "Dvořák's Method of Teaching," *The Musical Standard*, 17 February 1894; *Grove's*, 1926 ed., "Dvořák."

22. "Dvořák on Negro Melodies." Dvořák was a demanding composition teacher. His advice (from "Dvořák's Methods of Teaching") would have pleased the Powells:

> If you write well by accident once you will be just as likely to write badly ten times. Have a reason for everything you do. Examine your reason from every point of view. Make up your mind as to the merit of a musical theme, its treatment and its accompaniment only after careful, thorough consideration. Then, having come to a decided opinion on the matter, set to work and write it out. You may find many things to change on further reflection, you may modify your work in many ways, but if your reasoning has been thorough you will find that the foundation, the kernel, of your work remains just the same. I have no patience with the people who write down the first idea that comes into their head, who accompany it with the harmonies that happen to suggest themselves at the moment, or combination of instruments, that catches their fancy, without any regard to effect! There would not be so much nonsense written if people thought more.

23. See Grout, *A History of Western Music*, 633–48.

24. Darrah, *Powell of the Colorado*, 394.

25. Dvořák never advocated wholesale incorporation of Negro and folk melodies into a composition. His point (in "Dvořák on Negro

Melodies") was that these tunes provided suggestions for melodies and rhythms on which the imagination might build:

These are the folk songs of America, and your composers must turn to them. All of the great musicians have borrowed from the songs of the common people. . . . In the negro melodies of America I discover all that is needed for a great and noble school of music. They are pathetic, tender, passionate, melancholy, solemn, religious, bold, merry, gay, or what you will. It is music that suits itself to any mood or purpose. There is nothing in the whole range of composition that cannot be supplied with themes from this source. The American musician understands these tunes, and they move sentiment in him. They appeal to his imagination because of their associations.

26. He backed up his example with a very influential and much-discussed article in *Harper's*, February 1895; cited in Hitchcock, *Music in the United States.*

27. *The Oberlin Review*, 18 November 1892.

28. Ibid.

29. MLP.

30. "Maud Powell," *The Musical Courier*, 27 July 1900.

Chapter 11
Worlds Apart

1. The portrait of Gilmore is drawn from the following sources: *Grove's*, 1926 ed., "Gilmore"; Hitchcock, *Music in the United States*; *The Musical Leader and Concert-Goer*, June 1906; T. L. Pittenger, "The Days of the Really Big Bands," Culver-Stockton College *Concept*, Fall 1967; D. K. Antrim, "The Immortal 'Pat,' " *The Etude*, January 1945; N. H. Quayle, "Sixty Years Since Gilmore," ibid., December 1952; G. R. Leighton, "Bandmaster Gilmore," ibid., April 1934; H. W. Schwartz, *Bands of America* (rpt. ed., New York: Da Capo Press, 1975).

2. As bandmaster for the Union Army, Gilmore's first experiment with giant-sized festivals took place in New Orleans during the Civil War, where he gathered the forces of 10,000 school children, 600 instruments, the combined batteries of thirty-six guns, and the united fire of three regiments of infantry to present "The Star-Spangled Banner" and other patriotic songs. He probably did more to win over the South to the Union cause on that occasion than the combined Union Army!

3. For the National Peace Jubilee, Gilmore enlisted Julius Eichberg, the director of the Boston Conservatory; Carl Zerrahn, one of the best-known orchestra leaders in Boston; Ditson, the music publisher; and Mason, the organ builder. He proposed construction of a four-acre struc-

ture which would seat 50,000 people, whom he envisioned listening to a chorus of 10,000 accompanied by an orchestra of 1,000 players (for which he inveigled Ole Bull to serve as concertmaster).

Since it was to be a *national* festival, Gilmore actively sought and received the participation of nearly every musical club and choral society in the land and bands from many communities. He even persuaded Boston public school officials to permit Julius Eichberg to train 20,000 school children to sing popular melodies at one of the performances, an experience which had educational value. In fact, Gilmore's "mad" grand design went far toward awakening and reviving interest in music throughout the United States, and in this sense he performed a very real service to the nation. Eight hundred choirs from Maine to California formed the grand chorus of 10,000, learning the numbers to be sung in accordance with detailed instructions for rehearsal provided by Eben Tourjee of the New England Conservatory. While these choruses were practicing works of Handel and Haydn as well as Mozart's *Twelfth Mass* and Gounod's "Ave Maria," picked bands were rehearsing daily. The Jubilee gave them the opportunity and incentive to study music of a much higher grade than they had attempted before and thus it was destined to leave behind a legacy of improved musical taste.

On June 15, 1869, shortly after Edward Everett Hale's opening prayer, the combined forces of orchestra and chorus let loose with Luther's "A Mighty Fortress Is Our God," overwhelming the crowd with the sound. But the undoubted hit of the entire event was the rendition of Verdi's "Anvil Chorus," in which the orchestra and chorus were joined by 100 red-shirted firemen swinging their hammers at the anvils before them, in perfect time. As the piece progressed, bells pealed and a whole battery of cannon were fired in awesome climax. The crowd went wild.

Gilmore dared to try to top the success of the 1869 National Peace Jubilee with an International Peace Jubilee he staged on June 17, 1872, in celebration of the termination of the Franco-Prussian War. He doubled the forces at his command to a chorus of 20,000 and an orchestra of 2,000, with the participation of bands from all over Europe. It was not as successful as his earlier event; even Gilmore had to admit that the gathered forces were too unwieldy to produce worthwhile results.

4. Leighton, "Bandmaster Gilmore."

5. *Chicago Times*, 17 May 1891. Campanini was an Italian operatic tenor (1846–96) who lived in New York from 1880 and enjoyed considerable popularity as a hard-working and extremely zealous artist. He was the leading lyric tenor at the Metropolitan Opera during its first season (1883).

6. *Chicago Tribune*, 16 May 1891; it was just this sort of thing that Theodore Thomas abhorred and which led him to rule that no encores would be given at his concerts. In his view, audience enthusiasm overstepped the bounds of good taste when it required repetition of every movement or piece on the program, since it lengthened concerts inordinately and taxed the musicians beyond reason, to say nothing of the effect on the music.

7. *Chicago Tribune*, 16 May 1891.

8. Martha Freeman Esmond to Julia Boyd, 17 May 1891.

9. "Miss Maud Powell," *American Art Journal* (9 January 1892).

10. See *Grove's*, 1926 ed., "New York Musical Societies."

11. Ysaÿe and Ratcliffe, *Ysaÿe*, 98–99.

12. The general account of the tour is taken from the report written for publication by one of the members of the Society, "The Arion Trip," *The Musical Courier*, July and August 1892. All quotations are from this source unless otherwise noted.

13. Frank Dossert's *Missa Solemnis* was performed under his direction in Vienna at a high mass during the tour. Its reception was so favorable that it was to be performed again in the fall when the orchestra of the court opera could assist.

14. American critics observed, "[The Society's] work bears about as much resemblance to the everyday Maennerchor as does the playing of an ordinary pianist when compared with that of a virtuoso." "The Arion Charity Concert," *The Musical Courier*, 2 November 1892.

15. *Neue Freie Press* (Vienna), 19 and 20 July 1892, trans. by Ruth Eigenmann Figueroa. Of particular interest to the music-loving public was the Steinway concert grand piano on which Rummel played. Noted particularly for its tone quality, it was called one of the "jewels" of the concerts and was afterward placed on display. Steinway and Sons had been an established piano manufacturer in New York since 1853 and had factories in Europe as well.

16. Ibid., 19 July 1892. Of course, the critic placed emphasis on her European training in explaining Maud Powell's gifts, failing altogether to mention the fact that she had received at least five years of training in America to her two years and four months of European instruction. Of all her teachers, Maud said she owed the most to her American master, William Lewis; see Martens, *Violin Mastery*, 186.

17. "Maud Powell Concert," *Aurora Daily Beacon*, 27 February 1895.

18. "Maud Powell, An American Violinist," *New Orleans Picayune*, 20 December 1896.

19. "Fiddle and The Fiddler."

20. *Neue Freie Press* (Vienna), 20 July 1892, trans. by Ruth Eigenmann Figueroa.

21. Ibid., 21 July 1892.

22. *The Monthly Musical Record*, London, 1 August 1892.

23. "The Arion Charity Concert," *New York Times*, 31 October 1892.

24. "Fiddle and The Fiddler."

25. MPP Sketch.

Chapter 12
MUSICAL VISIONS OF THE NEW WORLD

1. *New York Times*, 20 April 1891.

2. For a visual record of the 1893 World's Fair in Chicago, see *The Chicago World's Fair of 1893, A Photographic Record* (New York: Dover Publications, 1980).

3. See Thomas, *Memoirs*.

4. For the opening ceremonies on October 21, 1892, Thomas assembled a 5,500-voice chorus, 200 players in his orchestra, two large military bands, and two drum corps of fifty each to perform in a hall which was one mile in circumference and taller than the U.S. Capitol. The stage was equal in size to the entire New York Metropolitan Opera House. The hall was filled with "one solid, compact sea of humanity," as well as the President of the United States (Benjamin Harrison) for the opening ceremonies. Thomas performed works by the American composers Chadwick and Paine and then trained his forces on Handel's "Hallelujah" chorus. The cheer which rose from the deeply moved crowd was "strange and thrilling"; ibid., 381–83.

5. The cast, made on April 6, 1893, was donated by Marshall Howenstein to the University of Illinois at Urbana-Champaign.

6. Minnie Powell said: "Everyone played on the piano, and I was so tired of it that I made up my mind that my daughter should learn something different." "Fiddle and The Fiddler."

7. "What the War Showed Maud Powell," *Woman's Citizen*, 22 December 1917.

8. Around this time, the Metropolitan Opera began to include native American singers like Lillian Nordica, Louise Homer, Geraldine Farrar, Emma Eames, and Alma Gluck, all friends of Maud's.

9. Alfred Hertz, the conductor of the San Francisco Symphony, became one of the first to hire female string players in 1925. However, much earlier, in 1909, Maud wrote that Nora Clench sat at the first violin desk in the Buffalo Symphony Orchestra, under the conductorship of John Lund, "over a decade ago." By 1909, she reported, several women were playing in the Hartford Symphony Orchestra; Maud Powell, "The Amer-

ican Girl and Her Violin," *The Etude*, July 1909. See Ammer, *Unsung*; Ammer provides an excellent view of women's musical status at the time. See also Judith Alstadter, "Celebrating the 20th Century Woman in Music," *The Triangle of Mu Phi Epsilon* 79, no. 4 (1985): "In 1895, an anonymous writer in *Scientific American* claimed that women were physically incapable of sustaining the rigors of rehearsals and performance in symphony orchestras, and even if the concept of a mixed orchestra were not impossible on grounds of propriety, it would be so because women were capable of 'not more than a third of what men are able to do.' "

10. The eventual affiliation of the musicians' unions with the American Federation of Labor compelled them to accept qualified women as members. The Musicians' Union in New York joined the AFL in 1903.

11. The Fadette Women's Orchestra of Boston (1888–1920) was the only professional women's orchestra which competed directly and successfully with men's ensembles. It was founded and conducted by Caroline B. Nichols, a violinist and former pupil of Julius Eichberg. The Los Angeles Women's Symphony was founded in 1893 with twenty-five members and had expanded to seventy members by 1936. The Women's Philharmonic Society of New York supported a string orchestra and a chorus composed wholly of professional women musicians. Founded in 1899 by Melusina Fay Peirce, it had 200 members by 1910. Amy Fay, Melusina's sister, and sister-in-law to Theodore Thomas, was president of the Society when it honored Maud Powell. See Ammer, *Unsung*.

12. Ibid., 27.

13. See "Impressions of the Musical Congress," *The Music Review*, August 1893.

Chapter 13
THE MAUD POWELL STRING QUARTET, 1894–1898

1. Information on the members of the Quartet is from Overmyer, "Dvořák in the New World," 6; "A Society Event," *Elmira Daily Gazette and Free Press*, 10 December 1894.

2. The Kneisel Quartet was hailed in London in its first venture abroad in 1896 as the equal of the Joachim Quartet. See Lahee, *Famous Violinists*, 361–64. For more on the Eichberg Quartette, see Ammer, *Unsung*, 29–31.

3. Maud Powell to the Editor, *Musical America*, May 25, 1918.

4. "Violinists Shackled Cries Miss Powell," *New York Times*, 4 March 1912.

5. "Maud Powell's Quartet," ibid., 27 October 1894.

6. On this tour, Maud frequently played a new composition, *Polonaise*, by J. Miersch, the brother of the Quartet's cellist, an indication of her generosity.

7. "Maud Powell's Quartet," *New York Times*, 4 January 1895.

8. "Miss Powell's Violin Recital," *The Oberlin Review* (May 31, 1895).

Chapter 14
MISSIONARY FOR MUSIC

1. Winn, "Maud Powell as I Knew Her."

2. Maud Powell to Charles M. Faye, Los Angeles, 1908–09 tour, MLP.

3. Henry T. Finck, *The Golden Age of Music in New York* (Funk & Wagnalls, 1926; reprinted by Da Capo Press, 1971).

4. MPP Sketch.

5. Martens, *Violin Mastery*, 195–96.

6. Quotations here and in the next paragraph are from *The Musical Courier*, 18 April 1918.

7. *Daily Republican Herald* (Winona, MI), 11 December 1913.

8. Peters, "Little Glimpses of Famous Musicians."

9. Gustav Kobbé, "Maud Powell," *The Musical Leader and Concert-Goer*, April 1907.

10. See "Musical Critics of the New York Daily Press," *The Musical Leader and Concert-Goer*, January–June 1906.

11. Philadelphia press review, reprinted in *Elmira Daily Gazette and Free Press*, 10 December 1894.

12. Maud often played chamber music with Victor Herbert, who was a very fine cellist. At one luncheon party they played together with Max Fiedler, one of Herbert's rivals for appointment as conductor of the New York Philharmonic. Theodore Steinway was one of the contented listeners. E. N. Waters, *Victor Herbert, A Life in Music* (New York: MacMillan, 1955).

13. The reviews are reprinted in *The Musical Courier*, February 1898.

Chapter 15
CONQUERING EUROPE, 1898–1900

1. Henry Adams, *The Education of Henry Adams* (Boston: Houghton Mifflin, 1918), 363.

2. The Henschels probably introduced Maud to Clara Butt, whom New York critic Richard Aldrich called a "truly phenomenal" contralto and one of the rising English opera stars. In 1899 and 1900, Maud assisted Clara Butt in several recitals in St. James's Hall.

3. Reprinted in *New York Times*, 11 December 1898.

4. Ibid.

5. *Violin Times*, 15 December 1898.

6. Manuscript, MLP.

7. *The Musical Courier*, 27 July 1904.

8. *Musical America*, 6 May 1899.

9. *The Violinist*, January 1900.

10. In 1901, Queen Alexandra conferred upon Lady Hallé the title "Violinist to the Queen." Lady Hallé died in 1911.

11. The concerto was composed in 1880 and dedicated to Pablo de Sarasate, who produced it at a Chatelet concert in Paris on January 2, 1881.

12. *The London Musical Courier*, 16 March 1900.

13. *The Violin World*, 15 December 1900.

14. *The Strad*, September 1900.

15. *The Violin World*, 15 December 1900.

Chapter 16
TURNING POINT, 1901

1. When John Wesley Powell retired as President of the American Association for the Advancement of Science, he wrote a farewell address which exemplifies the great breadth, range, and depth of his intellect. In lyrical prose, he traced the "Evolution of Music from Dance to Symphony" with monumental probity. *Proceedings of the American Association for the Advancement of Science* (August 1889).

2. See Darrah, *Powell of the Colorado.*

3. In 1897, Powell said, "Twenty-five years ago the public schools educated only the upper 40, 50 or 60 percent of the pupils who were talented, and barred out by a system of examinations and promotions the 40 or 50 percent for whom really the public schools exist in this free nation, which is controlled by these people." Powell, "The Educational Outlook," 154–55.

In 1870, seven million students were enrolled in U.S. public schools, but average attendance was four million, averaging seventy-eight days of schooling annually. Only 80,000 students were in the high schools. By 1920, twenty-one million students were in the elementary schools and two million in the high schools.

In Washington, D.C., with a population of 230,000 in 1890, three high schools were built due to Powell's efforts. There were four high schools, a teaching body of 1,179, and a school term running from mid-September to June 20 by 1900. Powell also established there the first commercial high school in the United States. During his superintendency, the white high school enrollment grew from 745 pupils to 2,579, nearly a 250 percent increase. Attendance during the same period increased by over 50 percent while the city population increased 38 percent. The grammar schools too grew proportionally larger.

4. Senate Report 711, 56th Cong., 1st Sess.

5. In 1897, Powell observed, "Today the child learns in school to think and act and do—to create. The child has become a character. He has become an independent thinker. . . . I am talking from my own experience." Powell, "The Educational Outlook," 156.

6. Powell's eloquent defense is reported in *Washington Evening Star*, 27 June 1900.

7. Ibid. Upon his death in 1904, the Washington, D.C., Board of Education remembered Powell in a resolution which said he was "widely known" as an "eminent teacher, an able administrator, and a man of liberal views of education and was actively identified with every phase of the development of the public school system. . . . " Resolution adopted February 10, 1904.

In 1930, an elementary school was dedicated to William Bramwell Powell in the District and his portrait presented at the dedication by associates "who admired him as a man and acknowledged him as an educator far in advance of his time." Janet McWilliam, Supervising Principal, Div. 3, D.C. Public Schools, to William Paul Powell, 9 May 1930, MLP.

8. Maud Powell program note, NGGC.

9. Reviews of the concert are reprinted in *The Musical Courier*, January 1901.

10. "Some Tributes to Maud Powell," *The Musical Leader and Concert-Goer*, 1 November 1906.

11. For more information on the formation of American orchestras, see *Grove's*, 1926 ed., American Supplement, "The Opening of the Twentieth Century"; Hitchcock, *Music in the United States*. For more information on these violinists, see Schwarz, *Great Masters of the Violin*; Campbell, *The Great Violinists*; Ammer, *Unsung*; *Grove's*, 1926 ed. and American Supplement.

12. The Russian Symphony Orchestra, New York, 1904, Modest Altschuler, conductor; St. Louis, 1907, Max Zach, conductor; St. Paul, 1908, Walter Rothwell; Seattle Symphony, 1907, Kegrize; San Francisco, 1911, Henry Hadley; Kansas City, 1910, Carl Busch; Detroit, 1914, Weston Gales; Baltimore, 1916, Gustav Strube. The New York Philharmonic was endowed in 1911, the New York Symphony Society in 1914, and the Cincinnati Symphony Orchestra in 1915.

In opposition to the practice of hiring foreign musicians to form orchestras in America, the American violinist-conductor Sam Franko (1857–1937) established the American Symphony Orchestra (1894–99) to demonstrate that American musicians rivaled in quality their European counterparts.

13. Among the new violinists who were appearing were Jan Kubelik (1880–1940; in America 1902–03); the French master Jacques Thibaud (1880–1953; in America 1903, 1913); Fritz Kreisler (1875–1962; in America from 1901); Bronislaw Huberman (1882–1947; in America 1902); and Carl Flesch (1873–1944; in America 1913). Eugène Ysaÿe continued to tour the U.S. occasionally.

14. While assisting Madam Rosa Olitzka, a Metropolitan Opera star, in a recital in Mendelssohn Hall, New York, Maud played Tartini's sonata *Didone Abbandonata*, which Kreisler had played earlier that season. She reportedly played with "brilliancy and beauty" and aroused a "tumult" in the audience. The *Times*, 25 January 1901, reported, "Her performance of the Tartini sonata was distinguished by lovely purity of tone, impeccable technic, and high dignity of style. It was good, solid, musical violin playing, and was a genuine delight to hear."

15. *The Oberlin Review*, 28 February 1901.

16. José Figueroa in conversation with Karen A. Shaffer, June 19, 1987. Many thanks to Mr. Figueroa for our many conversations through which he has contributed enormously to my education in the history of violin playing.

17. Maud Powell, "Violin Interpretation," *The Etude*, August 1909. Before Ysaÿe, the great violinists, including Joachim, used a form of finger vibrato in which the pitch was subjected to only quite imperceptible oscillations, resulting in a "dry" tone. To vibrate on relatively unexpressive notes was regarded as inartistic. The violin pedagogue Carl Flesch believed Ysaÿe was the first to make use of a broader vibrato and to attempt to give life to passing notes. In his view, Kreisler extended this innovation by resorting to a still broader and more intensive vibrato, employing it even in the faster passages. Although Flesch viewed the continuous vibrato as Kreisler's most important technical attribute, he believed that it was the "inevitable result of his highly individual need for an increased intensity of expression." There is no evidence that Flesch ever heard Maud Powell perform. *The Memoirs of Carl Flesch*, centenary ed. (England, 1973), 120–21.

18. John Maltese in conversation with Karen A. Shaffer, June 13, 1987. My thanks to John Maltese for his lucid and perceptive observations on Maud Powell's violin playing. As a record collector, Mr. Maltese notes that the 78 rpm collections in every home contained at least one Maud Powell recording.

19. Albert Moglie in conversation with Karen A. Shaffer, November 16, 1982. My thanks to Albert Moglie for taking the time to reminisce

about Maud Powell, who sometimes came to him for violin and bow repairs.

20. *The Oberlin Review*, 28 February 1901.

21. *Pittsburgh Post*, reprinted in *The Musical Courier*, March 1901.

22. *Baltimore News*, reprinted, ibid.

23. *German Press* (Baltimore), reprinted, ibid.

24. *Baltimore News*, reprinted, ibid.

25. *Nashville American*, reprinted, ibid.

26. Reviews reprinted in *The Musical Courier*, April 1901.

27. *Boston Sunday Journal*, 14 April 1901.

28. Maud Powell to Theodore Thomas, 27 January 1901, Chicago Symphony Orchestra Archives.

29. *Chicago Tribune*, 20 April 1901.

30. "Noteworthy Personalities—Miss Maud Powell," *Music*, June 1901.

Chapter 17
AT HOME IN EUROPE, 1901–1902

1. In 1880, Theodore Thomas had been offered the position of conductor of the Philharmonic Society, but he declined in order to continue his work in America. Among the violinists whose names added to the lustre of the orchestra's history were Auer, Alard, de Bériot, Bull, David, Ernst, Spohr, Vieuxtemps, Viotti, Wieniawski, Joachim, Ysaÿe, and Wilhelmj, among the men, and Urso, Norman-Neruda, Tua, Soldat, and Wietrowitz, among the women.

2. Reprinted in *The London Musical Courier*, 26 October 1901.

3. A selection from many similar reviews, reprinted in *The Musical Courier*, 27 July 1904.

4. C. Fred Kenyon, "Interview with Miss Maud Powell," *The Musical Standard*, 1902, reprinted in *The Violin World*, 15 January 1902.

5. *The London Musical Courier*, 29 March 1902.

6. Theodore Thomas had met Saint-Saëns during his trip to Europe in 1880 and called him "a giant among pianists" after hearing him play his own Piano Concerto No. 4 in London. Thomas, *Memoirs*, 180, 191.

7. "Some Tributes to Maud Powell."

8. The conflict between Saint-Saëns and Nadia Boulanger in connection with the Prix de Rome competition of 1908 is told in Leonee Rosenstiel, *Nadia Boulanger, A Life in Music* (New York: W. W. Norton, 1982). Rosenstiel writes (p. 65) that Saint-Saëns had been heard to remark that "a woman composer was like a dog walking on its hind legs, a freak of nature, unnatural, and as a steady sight, unwelcome."

9. "Some Tributes to Maud Powell."

10. 20 September 1902.

11. *The Musical Courier*, 27 July 1904.

Chapter 18
STARS AND STRIPES ABROAD, 1903

1. In his memoirs, Sousa wrote, "Thomas was one of the greatest conductors that ever lived." John Philip Sousa, *Marching Along* (Boston: Hale, Cushman & Flint, 1928), 11.

2. The description of Sousa's musical predilections and style is largely drawn from Paul Bierly, *John Philip Sousa, American Phenomenon* (Englewood Cliffs, NJ: Prentice-Hall, 1973); Hitchcock, *Music in the United States*; Schwartz, *Bands of America*.

3. Richard Strauss was influenced by Sousa's instrumentation and the effects achieved with it; in 1900 the band had sixty-one members — thirty-six woodwinds, twenty-two brass, and three percussion.

4. Bierly, *John Philip Sousa*, 12.

5. Ibid., 119.

6. Sousa's was the first band to perform Liszt's *Hungarian Rhapsody* and Richard Strauss's *Don Juan*.

7. Sousa wrote, "High class compositions become popular because the real composer is always inspired." John Philip Sousa, "Music the American People Demand," *The Etude*, 1910.

8. Bierly, *John Philip Sousa*, 123.

9. One of the most important members of the band was August Helmecke, the bass drummer. Sousa declared that "my bass drummer has the spirit and soul of a great artist." When Sousa wrote a new march, he left the accents out of the score, knowing that "Gus" would know exactly where to put them in. Retiring after twenty-two years with Sousa, Helmecke served as the percussionist for the Metropolitan Opera Orchestra for several seasons. See August Helmecke, "How Sousa Played His Marches," *The Etude*, August 1950.

10. Arthur Pryor, the "Paganini of the Trombone," became Sousa's assistant conductor and after the 1903 tour organized his own band with Sousa's blessing. After Herbert L. Clarke's cornet solo at one concert, Saint-Saëns went to the stage and stated publicly that he had never heard such a magnificent performance on either a trumpet or cornet in all his eighty years. Bierly, *John Philip Sousa*.

11. Sousa, *Marching Along*, 245. Among the Sousa violin soloists over the years were Mary Gailey, Nicoline Zedeler, Florence Hardeman, Grace Jenkins, and Bertha Bucklin. Bucklin had studied with Dancla and had a successful, but brief, solo career, touring with Sousa in 1900.

12. Estelle Liebling's father, Max Liebling, was a pianist-accompanist for the great singers of the day in New York City. Estelle Liebling

(1880–1970) first studied piano in Berlin and then voice under Professor Niclas-Kempner and later, Madame Mathilda Marchesi in Paris. Possessing a voice "beautiful throughout its register," Liebling appeared with such artists as Lillian Nordica, Jean Gerardy, Jan Kubelik, and Joseph Hofmann and numbered Ignace Paderewski among her admirers. Liebling used her many talents as an opera singer, choral conductor, author, lecturer, composer, and arranger. Her book of cadenzas and her vocal arrangements of all the coloratura arias are only one concrete example of her contributions to the musical world. Retiring from the stage after her marriage, she soon established herself in New York City as a very great teacher, counting among her pupils the world-renowned Beverly Sills. The information on Liebling is based on a manuscript by Dorothy Miller and Sue Read in possession of Peter Greenough and Beverly Sills, whose gracious assistance is gratefully acknowledged.

13. Herman Bellstedt, Jr., of the Bellstedt and Ballenberg Band of Cincinnati, was a friend of Sousa's and a great German cornet soloist who had been a Sousa soloist. He was a prominent musical figure in Cincinnati, associated with the best in band, symphony, and opera.

14. Bierly, *John Philip Sousa*, 131.

15. Finck, *The Golden Age of Music*, 314.

16. The tour schedule was provided through the painstaking efforts of Paul Bierly, Sousa's biographer, who kindly sent the results of his research in this regard.

17. All reviews are from the Sousa Papers, U.S. Marine Library, Washington, D.C.

18. See Sousa, *Marching Along*, 234–36; *London Daily Telegraph*, 2 February 1903.

19. Jan A. Williams to Neva Garner Greenwood, 12 March 1979, NGGC.

20. Cities on the European leg included: Lille, Brussels, Ghent, Anvers, Liège, Cologne, Berlin, Konigsberg, St. Petersburg, Warsaw, Vienna, Prague, Dresden, Leipzig, Hamburg, Copenhagen, Kiel, Dortmund, and Amsterdam.

21. A sampling of Maud's press clippings indicates the level of her success: "Miss Powell played in a truly divine manner, her violin seeming indeed enchanted" — *Paris L'Eclair*. "A violinist of impeccable talent" — Lille, France, 2 May 1903. "Among the first violinists of the world, owing to the purity of her bowing and the exactness of her method" — *Le Progres du Nord*, Lille, 1 May 1903. "A wonderful violinist, with a surprisingly accurate technic and a warm and noble tone" — *Berlin Morgen Post*. An artist of the higher rank, manifesting masterful control of her instrument, while rendering in faultless manner one of the

most technically difficult selections of all violin literature. She combines a brilliant technic with a tone of rare purity and a phrasing of uncommon subtlety. Her success was tremendous and richly deserved" — *Journal de Liège*. "A wonderful artist, with dash, charm and stupendous technic" — *Brussels La Réforme*. "The enthusiasm reached its highest pitch after Miss Powell's solo" — *Dresden Zeitung*. "A beautiful tone and a splendid technic. She was received with a storm of applause" — *Dresden Deutsche Wacht*. "Miss Powell stands on the highest artistic plane, possessing a brilliant technic, true artistic feeling and the magnetic power to arouse enthusiasm in her auditors" — *Hamburger Nachrichten*. "A full, beautiful tone, exquisite style and a heavenly violin" — *Copenhagen Tidende*. "The artistic pinnacle of the whole evening's program" — *Copenhagen Middagsposten*.

22. MPP Sketch.

23. Finck, *The Golden Age of Music*, 314.

Chapter 19
A SUNNY PARTNER

1. Powell, "The Price of Fame."

2. Views of Mabel Love, Maud Powell's cousin, in conversation with Neva Garner Greenwood.

3. Marriage certificate, MLP.

4. "Music and Musicians," *New York Times*, 1 November 1911.

5. Mabel Love manuscript, MLP.

6. Finck, *The Golden Age of Music*.

7. "Struggles Which Led to Success."

8. *The Musical Standard*, April 1907.

9. Ibid.

10. Powell, "An Artist's Life."

11. Ibid.

12. Maud Powell, "Pitting American Violin Works Against the Foreign Product," *Musical America*, 14 October 1911.

13. *Musical America*, 12 May 1917.

14. *New York Evening Sun*, 11 January 1904.

15. Mabel Love conversation with Neva Garner Greenwood.

16. Powell, "How Fashion Invades the Concert Stage."

Chapter 20
A SUCCESSION OF FIDDLES

1. *Grove's*, 1926 ed., "Guarnerius," values a good "Joseph" from 150 to 600 pounds, according to size, power of tone, finish and condition. Joseph Guarnerius dedicated his violins to Jesus, inscribing each with

I.H.S. surmounted by the cross after his name, hence the appellation "del Gesu."

2. The "Messiah" Strad is currently in the Ashmolean Museum, Oxford.

3. "Maud Powell," *The Musical Courier*, 27 July 1904.

4. "Fiddle and The Fiddler."

5. For the qualities and characteristics of Joseph Guarnerius del Gesu violins, see Alfred, Arthur, and W. Henry Hill, *The Violin Makers of the Guarneri Family* (London: W. E. Hill and Sons, 1965); *Grove's*, 1926 ed., "Guarnerius"; and Yehudi Menuhin and Curtis W. Davis, *The Music of Man*, 113–14. Menuhin believes that the Guarneri del Gesu cannot be surpassed for the music of the Romantic repertoire.

6. "Fiddle and The Fiddler."

7. Powell, "The American Girl and Her Violin."

8. Ibid.

9. "Fiddle and The Fiddler."

10. Ibid.

11. Information on the Rocca is from the following sources: H. Godfrey Turner to Nathan E. Posner, who purchased the instrument from Turner on the date of the letter, 18 November 1924; Rembert Wurlitzer of New York, Certificate dated January 14, 1963, on instrument bearing Register No. 6057, issued upon purchase of the Rocca; Mrs. Rembert Wurlitzer to Neva Garner Greenwood, 28 January 1981, NGGC. The instrument is now in the possession of an amateur violinist in the U.S., and the crest on the tailpiece still bears Joseph Rocca's initials, G. R., and Maud Powell's name.

12. Certificate No. 1616 for Instrument No. 4667, issued by John Friedrich and Bro. (signed by Ernest N. Doring) to Henry Ford of Dearborn, MI, 1 February 1926. The Guadagnini, whose creator lived from 1711 to 1786, currently rests in the Henry Ford Museum, Dearborn, MI. More recently, the violin has been attributed to George Gemunder (1860–65) or John Frederick Lott (1840–60), Letter from Robert E. Eliason, Curator, Musical Instruments, Henry Ford Museum, to Karen A. Shaffer, 14 February 1983. One indication that it may in fact be a Guadagnini is Maud's statement that when the Guadagnini was found, it had the original short neck which had been nailed in with hand-wrought iron nails. A longer, modern neck was blocked on in its place, and other necessary changes were made to the instrument by Oswald Schilbach, the New York luthier.

13. There was a lawsuit filed by Schilbach against Maud Powell over the Guadagnini, but Maud had acted properly and won her right to keep the instrument. See *New York World*, 4 June 1908, for what is probably the most accurate account of events.

14. Martens, *Violin Mastery*. Schilbach had the Guarnerius up for sale in April 1907. After it was sold for $5,000, Maud battled briefly with New York customs officials. They instituted legal proceedings to recover duties on an instrument they claimed she had brought into the United States from England solely for the purpose of sale rather than for personal use. Upon receipt of a straightforward letter from the artist and protests by the musical world, customs officials dropped the case; *Musical America*, 8 October 1910. In 1911, Lyon & Healy was in possession of the Guarnerius. At one point it came into the possession of the Juilliard School of Music in New York, but its whereabouts since that time are unknown.

15. Martens, *Violin Mastery*, 194.

16. "Maud Powell Talks Violins," *The Musical Standard*, January 1908.

17. Martens, *Violin Mastery*, 194.

18. "Maud Powell Talks Violins."

19. *Oregon Journal*, 26 November 1908.

20. Karen A. Shaffer, conversation with luthier Albert Moglie, who personally saw and handled Maud Powell's violin and bows, Washington, D.C., 15 November 1982. The American violinist Aaron Rosand now performs with one of Maud Powell's Tourte (1747–1835) bows.

21. Bill Weaver, a Washington, D.C., luthier, clarified the progress of violin string making.

22. Martens, *Violin Mastery*, 194–95.

Chapter 21
A Victor Immortal

1. Other violinists, including Joachim, Kubelik, and Sarasate, had recorded in Europe prior to 1904.

2. *Atchison Daily Globe*, 6 November 1913.

3. Letter is dated 12 July 1907 and was published in *Musical America*, September 1907. It concludes: "No, Mr. Bennett is surely on the wrong tack. The Gloucester Festival Committee should have fewer soloists and shorter programs, then much irksome applause might be eliminated. And I know whereof I speak, for I have played on these very Gloucester Festival programs, which, like all English ballad concert programs, are of un-heavenly length."

4. Undated, untitled article, NGGC.

5. Jim Cartwright to Karen A. Shaffer, 18 June 1987.

6. Yehudi Menuhin to Karen A. Shaffer, 14 April 1981.

7. This volume includes a complete discography as Appendix D.

8. Undated, untitled article, NGGC.

9. "An Original Interview with Maud Powell," *The Music Lover*, August 1915.

10. Yehudi Menuhin to Neva Garner Greenwood, 24 May 1979.

11. Paul Keatley Stolz to Neva Garner Greenwood, 6 January 1981.

Chapter 22
MUSICAL EXPLORATION IN SOUTH AFRICA, 1905

1. *Sheffield Independent*, 5 April 1905.

2. Reviews are from the Sousa Papers in the U.S. Marine Library, Washington, D.C.

3. The account of the South Africa tour is based on *The Musical Courier* and *Musical America*, July, August, October, November 1905.

4. Information on May Mukle is derived from *Grove's*, 1926 ed., American Supplement, "Mukle"; "May Mukle's Brilliant Career," *Musical America*, 13 July 1907; Letter from Lyndon Marguerie (England) to Neva Garner Greenwood, NGGC. Marguerie studied cello with May Mukle, whose entire family was musical, her father being an organ builder who could improvise for hours on the piano or organ even though he had no formal training. Mukle completed her studies at the Royal Academy of Music by the age of seventeen, carrying away all honors, and became an Associate of that institution. She played throughout the world during her long lifetime and there was hardly a famous instrumentalist of her day with whom she did not play, including the cellist Pablo Casals and pianist Arthur Rubinstein. Vaughn Williams composed a suite of English folk tunes for her. For fifteen years, she ran the "Mainly Musicians Club" in the heart of London. She died in March 1963 at the age of eighty-three. Max Kalbeck in Vienna saluted Mukle around the turn of the century as "this woman Casals." A personal friend of Mukle's, Casals said "She was a fine person as well as a fine musician"; from explication of the May Mukle Prize, Royal Academy of Music, London.

5. Lyndon Marguerie to Neva Garner Greenwood, NGGC.

6. *Musical America*, November 1908.

7. 31 May 1905, reprinted in *The Musical Courier*, 12 July 1905.

8. *Musical America*, July 1905.

9. Reviews from 17 June 1905, reprinted in *The Musical Courier*, 16 August 1905.

10. Ibid.

11. Peters, "Little Glimpses of Famous Musicians."

12. *The Musical Courier*, October 1905.

13. "That Makes Rag-Time Music Successful," date and source unknown, Arthur Loesser Papers, Mrs. Arthur Loesser, Cleveland, OH.

14. Peters, "Little Glimpses of Famous Musicians."

15. "That Makes Rag-Time Music Successful."

Chapter 23
THE MUSICIAN'S MUSICIAN

1. *Musical America*, January 1906.
2. *New York Times*, 12 January 1906.
3. William B. Chase, *New York Evening Sun*, 17 January 1906.
4. H. T. Parker, *Boston Evening Transcript*, 24 April 1907.
5. Philip Hale, *Boston Herald*, 17 April 1907.
6. Parker, *Boston Evening Transcript*, 24 April 1907.
7. "Maud Powell Is Dead," *The Musical Courier*, 15 January 1920.
8. Ibid.
9. Karen A. Shaffer, conversation with Harold Lineback of Saint Louis, who knew Spalding personally.
10. James Huneker, "Heroes and Heroines of the Violin," *Everybody's Magazine*, May 1909.
11. Ysaÿe was especially noted for his large repertoire. It might have rivaled Maud's, but he did not play the music of American composers. In contrast, Maud kept up to date with contemporary European compositions in addition to promoting American composers' works. Her music library is housed in the Detroit Public Library.
12. Martens, *Violin Mastery*, 192.
13. H. Godfrey Turner, Introduction to "Nobody Knows the Trouble I See," Maud Powell transcription (Boston: Oliver Ditson Company, 1921).
14. *New York Tribune*, 1 November 1911; "Music and Musicians," *New York Times*, 1 November 1911. *Twenty-four Transcriptions of Negro Melodies for the Piano* by Coleridge-Taylor was an outgrowth of the composer's first visit to America around 1901.
15. Martens, *Violin Mastery*, 189.
16. *New York Times*, 4 March 1912. Maud Powell's program note for the Wieniawski Concerto in D Minor reads:

Wieniawski, born 1835, died 1880, was a virtuoso of the utmost distinction. Born in Poland, educated in Paris; he lived later in Brussels and taught there. He is looked upon as the greatest of the so-called Belgian school of violinists. He toured America in 1870 in company with Anton Rubinstein. It is related that they played the Kreutzer Sonata (Beethoven's opus 47) from memory. This is accounted a somewhat sensational achievement as chamber music is generally played from the printed page. Wieniawski's compositions for violin, written in virtuoso style, are well constructed, and show a nice sense of form, as well as keen appreciation of the possibilities and limitations of the instrument. For his time and style, his taste was impeccable.

17. Maud wrote a sort of program note on the Tor Aulin concerto which was published in the *Minneapolis Tribune*, 21 November 1909. See *Minneapolis Tribune*, 22 November 1909, for the review of the American premiere by Maud Powell with the Minneapolis Symphony Orchestra, Emil Oberhoffer conducting.

18. *New York Times*, 31 December 1905 and 1 May 1906.

19. Maud Powell program note, NGGC.

20. *New York Sun*, 3 April 1906.

21. Henry E. Krehbiel, *New York Tribune*, 3 April 1906.

22. "Some Tributes to Maud Powell."

23. Herbert F. Peyser, "Women Are Making Our Musical Wheels Turn, Says Maud Powell," *Musical America*, 1 April 1911.

24. *The Musical Leader and Concert-Goer*, December 1906.

25. Peters, "Little Glimpses of Famous Musicians."

26. "That Makes Rag-Time Music Successful."

27. *The Musical Courier*, November 1906.

28. *The Musical Leader and Concert-Goer*, December 1906.

29. *The Musical Courier*, December 1906.

30. Ibid.

31. "An Original Interview with Maud Powell."

32. *Chicago Daily Journal*, 26 January 1907.

33. *Chicago Daily News*, 26 January 1907.

34. 28 January 1907.

35. H. T. Parker, *Boston Evening Transcript*, 20 April 1907; Philip Hale, *Boston Sunday Herald*, 21 April 1907.

36. 20 April 1907.

37. 21 April 1907.

38. *New York Tribune*, 18 March 1911.

39. *Boston Herald*, 9 March 1912.

40. Peyser, "Women Are Making Our Musical Wheels Turn."

41. "That Makes Rag-Time Music Successful."

42. "Maud Powell," in "Letters and Art," *The Literary Digest*, 31 January 1920.

43. *Musical America*, 1 April 1911.

44. *New York Times*, 4 March 1912. Only four years later, Novello, the publisher, was making it known that the performing rights could be had without charge, except for the cost of hiring the score and parts.

45. Emery reports that "one of the oldest critics in America" (probably Krehbiel) wrote, "The concerto is for the most part merely notes,

notes, notes. The themes are inconspicuous; the development is as dull as it is pretentious; there is no emotional appeal; there is nothing sensuously beautiful or thoughtfully noble; the architecture is not impressive; the ornamentation is commonplace. The most interesting feature, the oasis, is the cadenza in the finale, and that is much too long." Frederic B. Emery, *The Violin Concerto* 1 (Chicago: The Violin Literature Publishing Company, 1928): 217–18.

46. Yehudi Menuhin, *Unfinished Journey* (New York: Alfred A. Knopf, 1977), 122. Menuhin comments: "If climate fashions music, Elgar's music . . . expresses the flexibility within restraint of a weather which knows no exaggerations except in changeableness; and the response to it of a people able to distinguish infinite degrees of gray in the sky and of green in the landscape, never taking to unseemly extremes."

47. "Maud Powell to Play New Bruch Concerto," *The Musical Leader*, 18 May 1911.

48. *Musical America*, 17 June 1911; *New York Times*, 4 March 1912.

49. See Wulf Konold, Note on Philips recording No. 9500 423.

50. *The Globe*, 1 November 1911.

51. "Music and Musicians," *New York Times*, 2 November 1911. Born in 1880 near Prague, Jan Kubelik first visited America in 1902–03. He studied under Sevčík at the Prague Conservatory. Efrem Zimbalist (b. 1889, Russia) had been a pupil of Leopold Auer. He made his New York debut in 1911, performing the Glazunov concerto with Josef Stransky and the New York Philharmonic to rave reviews.

52. For the story of the origin and world premiere of the Coleridge-Taylor violin concerto, see *The International Library of Music, Music Literature* 11 (New York: The University Society, 1936); *Grove's*, 1926 ed., "Taylor"; *The Music Student*, 1916–17; *New York Times*, 4 March 1912; *The Musical Leader*, 16 May 1912; *Morgen Journal*, 26 May 1917.

53. *New York Evening Mail*, 1 November 1911.

Chapter 24
Trailblazing in the West

1. *The Musical Courier*, August 1907.

2. "Miss Powell's Experience," 1907 newspaper clipping, NGGC.

3. *The Musical Courier*, October 1907.

4. Bach's *Prélude*, Sonata in E Major; *The Musical Leader and Concert-Goer*, October 1907.

5. *The Musical Courier*, October 1907.

6. "Maud Powell Champions the West's Taste for Music," *Musical America*, 14 December 1907.

7. *Musical America*, January 1908. Henry Finck wrote: "She has a remarkably large tone—her C string has the sonority of an organ pipe—and the tone is not only big, but luscious." *New York Evening Post*, 6 January 1908.

8. *New York Evening Post*, 26 October 1908.

9. *New York Tribune*, 26 October 1908.

10. *New York Evening Post*, 26 October 1908.

11. *Seattle Times*, 21 November 1908.

12. "Maud Powell Trio Returns from Tour," *Musical America*, 26 December 1908.

13. *The Oregonian*, 26 November 1908.

14. "Using Program Notes for Violin Recitals," *Musical America*, 16 December 1908.

15. See "Pioneer Work Done by the Powell Trio," *Musical America*, 1 May 1909; Gustav Saenger, "Maud Powell—An Appreciation," *The Musical Observer*, August 1913.

16. Ibid.

17. "Maud Powell Trio Returns from Tour."

18. All the Winnipeg reviews are in Maud Powell's scrapbook, New York Public Library.

19. *Musical America*, May 1910.

20. *The Musical Courier*, 18 April 1918.

21. *North Yakima Republic*, 9 February 1910.

22. *Yakima Washington Morning Herald*, 9 February 1910.

23. *Los Angeles Sunday Times*, 20 March 1910.

24. *Musical America*, May 1910.

25. *San Francisco Chronicle*, 27 March 1910.

26. *San Francisco Examiner*, 18 February 1910.

27. *The Metronome*, April 1910.

28. *Musical America*, 2 March 1913.

Chapter 25
COURAGE

1. *New York Sun*, 9 January 1904. Maud had played the Saint-Saëns Concerto in B Minor.

2. *Chicago Daily News*, 23 April 1904.

3. It should be remembered that Ysaÿe did not perform the Brahms violin concerto to his own satisfaction until 1905. Henderson claimed that Jackson had "no business to play the Brahms concerto for any one but a teacher." When she played it with the Chicago Orchestra later that month (January 1900), Theodore Thomas refused to re-engage her because she was not good enough. Generally, she was thought to be a fine vio-

linist and had a successful career, but at least at that point she had not mastered the concerto. Born in Boston in 1879, she ended her career prematurely with her marriage in 1907; see Ammer, *Unsung*, 36–37.

4. *Chicago Daily News*, 22 February 1908.

5. Reprinted in *Yakima Washington Morning Herald*, 8 February 1910.

6. *The Musical Leader and Concert-Goer*, December 1909.

7. Ibid., 11 November 1909.

8. *Musical America*, 8 January 1910.

9. *Brooklyn Daily Eagle*, 4 December 1909.

10. *Musical America*, 8 January 1910.

11. The reviews may be found as follows: *Musical America*, 8 January 1910; *New York Evening Post*, 30 December 1909; *New York Times*, 30 December 1909; *New York Evening Sun*, 30 December 1909; *New York Sun*, 30 December 1909; *The Music News*, January 1910; *New York Times*, 1 January 1910. In the Beethoven concerto, Maud used the Joachim cadenza in the first movement and also the last, with some modifications of her own.

12. *New York Evening Post*, 1 January 1910.

13. *The New Music Review*, January 1912.

14. Ibid., February 1912. Kathleen Parlow (b. 1890, Calgary, Alberta) received her early training in San Francisco from Henry Holmes. The first foreigner ever admitted to the St. Petersburg Conservatory, she studied with Leopold Auer in 1906–07. Auer considered her a genius. After her American debut in late 1910, Parlow won recognition as a distinguished violinist during her touring career, which ended in the late 1920s. From 1929 on, she devoted her talents primarily to teaching.

15. *Saint Paul Dispatch*, 15 April 1918.

16. See Ammer, *Unsung*, for an excellent review of American women violinists. Sources on European women violinists include: "European Women Violinists," *The Musical Standard*, July 1907; Lahee, *Famous Violinists*; Campbell, *The Great Violinists*. Because of the lack, until now, of accessible information on Maud Powell's life, many of Campbell's dates are inaccurate, as is the information concerning the disposition of Maud's Guadagnini violin after her death. I have attempted to set the record straight with regard to the Guadagnini in the notes to the Epilogue.

17. *Musical America*, 23 August 1913. John C. Freund (b. 1848, London) came to New York in 1871 and became the influential editor of *Musical America* in 1893. In 1913, he began a campaign for "the musical independence of the United States." He greatly admired Maud

Powell for the pioneer work she was doing and called her "an Artist of the Highest Ideals."

18. Ibid.

19. Ammer, *Unsung*.

20. See Eleanor Flexnor, *Century of Struggle* (Cambridge, MA.: The Belknap Press, 1975), for an excellent history of the American women's suffrage movement.

21. *Boston Evening Transcript*, 20 April 1907.

22. "What the War Showed Maud Powell."

23. "Ein Interview Mit Frau Maud Powell," *Morgen Journal*, trans. by Ruth Eigenmann Figueroa.

24. Robert J. Cole, "Maud Powell at Home," *New York Evening Sun*, 21 October 1913.

25. "What the War Showed Maud Powell."

Chapter 26
EDUCATOR OF A NATION

1. Powell, "An Artist's Life." Maud's program note for the Franck sonata read:

A brilliant critic has described Franck as "a Bach who had read the score of *Parsifal*." Religious devotion and the atmosphere of the church pervade the music of Franck as of Bach, yet the expression of dramatic force and emotional intensity of Franck is of the modern manner. And though Franck knew his Wagner, he broke new paths, branding the way for the younger generation. Indeed, he toiled without other recognition than the filial devotion of the young men who are today the leaders in the French school of composition. The Sonata, dedicated to Eugène Ysaÿe, is built upon slender and simple thematic material, but the harmonies are of the richest hue. While the development and transformation of motives into beautiful melodies, of short themes into magnificent movements fraught with emotional intensity, leads one to agree with d'Indy that "this sonata is a direct legacy from Beethoven."

2. Ibid.

3. *Hobart Daily Republican*, 27 March 1917. By July 1909, the National Federation of Music Clubs "offered a bureau of reciprocity, which published a list of members of all clubs in the federation who were willing to give recitals for either expenses only or a small fee; a program exchange, which made available to all clubs a well-prepared scheme of programs; a plan of study, making available programs of study of various aspects of music; a circulating library of scores; and a well-tested constitution and

bylaws prepared for new clubs. In addition, in 1907, the National Federation inaugurated a competition for American composers, offering cash prizes in three categories of composition." Ammer, *Unsung*, 230.

4. *Musical America*, Fall 1910.

5. "Using Program Notes for Violin Recitals," *Musical America*, 16 October 1915.

6. Ibid., 2 March 1913.

7. San Antonio newspaper clipping, 10 February 1918, NGGC. While preparing for Maud Powell's return in 1920, San Antonians received word of the violinist's sudden death.

8. *Musical America*, 29 March 1913.

9. *The Musical Observer*, March 1913.

10. *Musical America*, 29 March 1913.

11. Paul Engberg to Neva Garner Greenwood, 22 August 1979. Information on the friendship between Davenport-Engberg and Maud Powell was graciously provided by Mrs. Engberg's son Paul.

12. Ibid.

13. Peyser, "Women Are Making Our Musical Wheels Turn." See "Woman—The Potent Influence in Our Musical Life," *Musical America*, 8 October 1910.

14. *Musical America*, 2 March 1913.

15. Peyser, "Women Are Making Our Musical Wheels Turn."

16. "An Original Interview with Maud Powell."

17. Sigmund Spaeth, "Maud Powell . . . Tells . . . How to Enjoy Music," *New York Evening Mail*, reprinted in *Musician*, August 1917.

18. Peyser, "Women Are Making Our Musical Wheels Turn."

19. Peyser, "Using Program Notes for Violin Recitals."

20. *New York Times*, 4 March 1912.

21. *The Musical Courier*, 18 April 1918.

22. Powell, "An Artist's Life."

23. Peyser, "Women Are Making Our Musical Wheels Turn."

24. "Maud Powell Trio Returns From Tour," *Musical America*, 26 December 1908.

25. *Seattle Times*, 23 November 1908.

26. *Musical America*, 18 November 1916.

27. Ibid.

28. *Musical America*, 10 May 1919.

29. Martens, *Violin Mastery*, 193.

Chapter 27
Riding Circuit for Her Faith

1. "The Heart Touch in Music," *Century Path*, 24 November 1907.

2. Henry Roth, "Louis Kaufman," *The Strad*, June 1983; also Louis Kaufman to Karen A. Shaffer, 4 February 1985.

3. Karl V. Brown to Dr. and Mrs. Joseph Greenwood, 16 July 1977.

4. Special thanks to José Figueroa for this information.

5. Martens, *Violin Mastery*, 191.

6. Winn, "Maud Powell as I Knew Her."

7. Martens, *Violin Mastery*, 185.

8. Maud Powell, "Two Types of Violin Playing," *The Etude*, November 1918.

9. Winn, "Maud Powell as I Knew Her."

10. Undated, untitled article, NGGC.

11. Peyser, "Women Are Making Our Musical Wheels Turn."

12. Martens, *Violin Mastery*, 193.

13. See also Maud Powell, "Violin Interpretation," *The Etude*, August 1909, which is a continuation of her article "The American Girl and Her Violin."

14. R. Frederick Grover, "How to Memorize," *The Violinist*, ca. 1909.

15. Maud Powell, "Remarks on Memorizing," *The Violinist*.

16. Martens, *Violin Mastery*, 190.

17. Cole, "Maud Powell at Home."

18. MPP Sketch.

19. Winn, "Maud Powell as I Knew Her."

20. Maud Powell, "We Shall Evolve a Real School of National Art, Literature and Music," *Musical America*, 19 October 1918, p. 5.

21. Maud Powell, "The Violinist," *The Delineator*, October 1911.

22. Powell, "The American Girl and Her Violin."

23. Undated, untitled article, source probably *Musical America*, ca. 1916, NGGC.

Chapter 28
CHAMPION OF AMERICAN COMPOSERS

1. *San Francisco Chronicle*, 12 December 1912.

2. *San Francisco Call*, 13 December 1912.

3. *San Francisco Chronicle*, 13 December 1912.

4. *The Musical Leader*, 16 May 1912.

5. Rosenstiel, *Nadia Boulanger*.

6. See Hitchcock, *Music in the United States*; G. Hindley, ed., *Larousse Encyclopedia of Music* (Secaucus, NJ: Chartwell Books, 1976); Grout, *A History of Western Music*.

7. Maud Powell, "Musical Future of America," *The Violinist*, September 1911. Charles Ives (1874–1954), who is considered to be the first truly original and independent American composer, was working at his

music in obscurity while earning his living in the insurance business in Connecticut. Nearly all of his music was composed by 1915, but he never heard it performed by a full orchestra until he was seventy-one years old.

8. *The Musical Leader*, 16 May 1912.

9. Martens, *Violin Mastery*.

10. Jessica Burleigh (Mrs. Cecil Burleigh) to Neva Garner Greenwood, 1 September 1977, NGGC.

11. *The Musical Courier*, October 1913.

12. Winn, "Maud Powell as I Knew Her." The neglect of the American composer of violin music was pointed out by a writer for *Musical America* in 1918, reprinted in *The Literary Digest* (May 11, 1918):

> Violinists and pianists are, I say, the only ones who do not pay attention to American music for their instruments. I will confine my remarks to the violinists. There is no greater admirer of Fritz Kreisler than the present writer. Yet Mr. Kreisler, with all the success he has had in America and all the money he has made here, has done no American violin music, with the exception of Ernest Schelling's Concerto, which he performed several times last season. That can not be placed to his credit so much, for he and Mr. Schelling are known to be warm friends. Ysaÿe, to be sure, played Henry Holden Huss's fine Sonata in G Minor at a recital a few years ago. Has he played it since? Efrem Zimbalist gave a single performance of John Powell's excellent Concerto in New York, and also played Albert Spalding's "Alabama" at a Metropolitan Sunday night concert once. Is that a record to be proud of? And Mr. Kreisler has had dedicated to him a Sonata in D by Mortimer Wilson, one of the most learned of American composers, a pupil of Reger. This work, which the Boston Music Company thought enough of to spend its money to publish—and American music publishers are none too ready to make the outlay for long chamber-music compositions—deserved a hearing from Mr. Kreisler two years ago when it was published. It did not get it!
>
> Albert Spalding interested himself on his tours in his own compositions, and in one or two Cecil Burleigh pieces; Mischa Elman has played a piece or two by Rubin Goldmark this year, but that was his first American music in all his tours here. And this year Jascha Heifetz, the sensation of the violin world, plays us transcriptions by one Achron, plus the standard hackneyed violin repertoire. Max Rosen does the same. And so it will probably be until some one rises up and tells these violinists that they must wake, be progressive, play new music and investigate what American composers have written for the violin.

Maud Powell is credited with always giving her time generously for the American composer. . . .

13. *Baltimore Evening Sun*, 28 June 1918.

14. *The Musical Courier*, 18 April 1918.

15. *The Musical Leader*, 16 May 1912. The distinguished conductor Antal Dorati made an interesting observation, similar to Maud's, about the differences between the New World and the Old in his introduction to Elkhonon Yoffe's recent book *Tchaikovsky in America* (New York: Oxford University Press, 1986), 6:

> Speaking as a European who lived about one half of his life in the New World . . . and at least once a year still goes back and forth across the Atlantic Ocean, I can say that the difference between the two continents is enormous, and does not begin, but ends with the differences of their peoples. Indeed, the very air one breathes is different . . . , the light has different shades, the winds blow differently, the same fruits are of different taste, the behavior of animals is not the same, and the people, we humans, *Homo sapiens*, of the same races living on the two continents, differ from each other most profoundly in the way we live, in the way we think, in the way we feel.

16. *Minneapolis Journal*, 14 December 1913.

17. *Pacific Commercial Advertiser*, 20 December 1912.

18. 13 December 1912.

Chapter 29
Retreat and Restoration

1. Harold Osborn Smith was Maud's accompanist during the 1912–13 season, but very little is known about him.

2. "Go West, Young Musician! Maud Powell Advises," *Musical America*, 29 March 1913.

3. Ibid.; "Using Program Notes for Violin Recitals."

4. *Musical America*, 16 October 1915.

5. "Mme. Powell Wins Friends in Hawaii," *Musical America*, 25 January 1913.

6. "Powell Brilliant with the Philharmonic," *Musical America*, 15 March 1913.

7. Their reviews are in *New York Tribune*, 7 March 1913; *New York Sun*, 7 March 1913; *New York Times*, 7 March 1913.

8. Karen A. Shaffer Collection.

9. *Boston Herald*, 8 March 1912.

10. *Musical America*, 16 October 1915.

11. *Chicago Daily News*, 19 April 1913.

12. *Grand Rapids Herald*, 6 May 1913.

13. *Musical America*, 17 May 1913.

14. Maud's life in Whitefield, NH, is based largely on the reminiscences of Whitefield residents who gave very generous assistance in filling in the details. Gratefully acknowledged is the help of Lillian A. Burns and Lucy Chase Sparks, who gathered invaluable information which they provided in addition to their personal recollections. The following people contributed information used herein: Mrs. Willard R. Davis, Mrs. William A. Fagan, The Reverend Reginald W. Eastman, Mrs. Richard Morse, Aurin M. Chase, Ruth McIntyre, Mrs. Lola Brown. Sources for other Whitefield stories are Douglas McIntyre, *The Courier* (Littleton, NH), 4 September 1980; *The Musical Courier*, 16 and 30 August 1917; *Musical America*, 30 September 1916, 29 September 1917. All quotations are from these sources unless otherwise noted.

15. Thanks to Lillian A. Burns for the delightful poem "The Fallen Doughnut Story," the last lines of which are quoted in the text.

16. *The Musical Courier*, 3 July 1919.

17. Ibid.

18. Undated, untitled article, NGGC.

19. Maud Powell to the American violinist Arthur Hartmann 23 July 1919, MLP.

20. MPP Sketch.

21. Used with the permission of Lillian A. Burns.

22. Powell, "An Artist's Life."

23. MPP Sketch.

24. *The Etude*, May 1916.

25. MPP Sketch.

26. *Pacific Commercial Advertiser*, 7 December 1915.

Chapter 30
A CERTAIN PERSPECTIVE

1. For reviews, see *New York Tribune*, 22 October 1913; *New York Sun*, 22 October 1913; *New York Times*, 22 October 1913; *The Musical Leader*, October 1913. Her program included the Coleridge-Taylor violin concerto, a group of American compositions, works by Beethoven, Brahms, Dvořák, and Sarasate, and the Bach E Major Sonata for Violin and Piano. Maud's program note for the Bach Sonata reads:

The word Sonata brings to the mind of a musician the perception of the form or set of rules which the composer follows in writing a large classic work, such as a Symphony, Concerto or String Quartet. Like the quartet, the Sonata belongs to the chamber music form of composition. Chamber music, or concerted music for solo instruments, is classic in spirit and intimate in character. Originally intended for the players themselves or a few favored listeners, it has now found its way into the precincts of our modern concert rooms. Bach's music encompasses nearly every emotion and characteristic of every human experience. This particular Adagio is fraught with religious meaning and is as expressive as a Gothic Cathedral with the spirit of purity and exaltation that breathes through its columned aisles. The little Allegro is in direct contrast. It is full of humor and playful charm. One can easily imagine it being tinkled on an old spinet in the king's palace, of long ago, with worthy squires and dames in powdered perukes nodding their heads in pleased sympathy with the dainty rhythm.

2. Newspaper clipping, 13 October 1913, NGGC.

3. *Twin City News-Herald* (Peru, Illinois), February 1908.

4. My thanks to Nancy Chadbourne Maze for providing this information and for showing me the bedroom in the Maze home in which Maud Powell stayed.

5. Maud Powell to Editor, *Twin City News-Herald*, 20 February 1908. Thanks to Angie Ringsdorf and Mrs. Dellinger and her fifth-grade class, Northview School, and to the board of directors of the People's Hospital and administrator Ralph Berkeley for commemorating this event with a plaque hung in the hospital, Peru, IL.

6. *Aurora Daily Beacon*, 9 October 1907.

7. *Aurora Daily News*, 10 October 1907.

8. *Aurora Daily Beacon*, 10 October 1907.

9. Ibid.

10. Ibid., 9 November 1910.

11. *Aurora Beacon-News*, 18 November 1910.

12. *LaSalle News Tribune*, 5 November 1910.

13. *Daily Oklahoman*, 25 March 1917.

14. Hobart, OK, newspaper clipping, 27 March 1917, NGGC.

15. *The Republican* (Cedar Rapids), 1913.

16. *The Musical Courier*, 4 January 1917.

17. *The Musical Courier*, 10 May 1917.

18. *Pacific Commercial Advertiser*, 7 December 1915.

19. MLP.

20. See *Philadelphia Record*, 27 September 1914; *The Inquirer*, 27 September 1914; *The North American*, 27 September 1914; *Cleveland Press*, 13 December 1913; *Music Trade Review*, 3 October 1914.

Chapter 31
MENTOR FOR PIANISTS

1. Maud Powell's accompanists:

GEORGE FALKENSTEIN — Maud Powell performed with him in public on numerous occasions and he was her accompanist for most of her recordings.

MAURICE EISNER — 1907 tour of the Far West. From Champaign, IL; he became the director of the new Northwestern Conservatory of Music, Art and Expression in Minneapolis in 1906.

WALDEMAR LIACHOWSKY — 1909–10, 1910–11, 1911–12 tours; a pupil of Artur Schnabel, he originally came to the U.S. with Mischa Elman.

HAROLD OSBORN SMITH — 1912–13 tour.

FRANCIS MOORE — 1913–14, 1914–15 tours; from El Paso, TX.

ARTHUR LOESSER — 1915–16, 1916–17, 1917–18 tours.

AXEL SKJERNE — 1918–19, 1919–20 tours: Born in Copenhagen in 1891, he settled in New York in 1916; studied piano at the Royal Conservatory of Music and privately with Franz Neruda, Lady Hallé's brother; studied with Albert Jonas, a noted pianist and pedagogue; concert tour of Europe in 1912; performances were marked for their musical understanding, technical command, and artistic integrity.

2. All personal information about Arthur Loesser and his relationship with Maud Powell is from his own reminiscences and those of his wife, who graciously provided the information and some press reviews as well.

3. Maud's program note for the d'Indy Sonata in D Major, Op. 59, was as follows: "Two interesting facts stand out in d'Indy's early life. He was a pupil of Cesar Franck and he played drums in orchestra three years to learn instrumentation. A master in every sense, with strong intellect and a subtle critical faculty, his has undoubtedly been a strong influence in guiding the development of the modern school of composition in France. This sonata is a fair example of his best work, noble in conception and brilliant in mastery of the technique of composition."

4. Louis Kaufman to Karen A. Shaffer, 4 February 1985.

5. *Musical America*, 16 October 1915.

6. Ibid.

7. *New York Tribune*, 27 October 1915.

8. *New York Sun*, 27 October 1915.

9. Newspaper clipping, Arthur Loesser Papers, Mrs. Arthur Loesser, Cleveland, OH.

10. 13 December 1915.

11. Newspaper clipping, Arthur Loesser Papers.

12. Alfred Metzger, "Maud Powell a Peer among Violinists," *Pacific Coast Musical Review*, 16 December 1915.

13. *Musical America*, December 1915.

14. Newspaper clipping, Arthur Loesser Papers.

15. *Musical America*, 29 April 1916.

16. Ibid.

17. Powell, "Two Types of Violin Playing."

18. *Musical America*, 7 April 1917.

19. Grainger became a naturalized American citizen in 1918. Maud Powell's program note for "Molly" is as follows: "Percy Grainger, the young Australian pianist, who has become the vogue in the east, is intensely interested in the study of folk music. In this respect, in his personal appearance, he resembles his master, Grieg. In his indefatigable research throughout the Celtic Isle, Australia, South Africa and elsewhere he has made a collection of most interesting phonographic records of the songs of the people. Not the least fascinating of these is his setting of 'Molly,' slightly revised by Madam Powell with the composer's sanction."

20. Special thanks to William R. Moran for confirming this speculation. Mr. Moran is coauthor of *The Encyclopedic Discography of Victor Recordings, Matrix Series 1–4, 999*, vol. 1, 1983; vol. 2, 1986 (Westport and London: The Greenwood Press).

21. Arthur Loesser Papers.

22. A 1913 advertisement for the Victor Company read: "Talking Machines have come to be as necessary as the telephone and the electric light." The price for a machine was $75.

23. Newspaper clipping, Arthur Loesser Papers.

24. Ibid.

25. *New York Tribune*, 9 January 1917.

26. Newspaper clipping, Arthur Loesser Papers.

27. *New York Times*, 9 January 1917.

28. Sunny took care to advertise Arthur Loesser's critical acclaim through clever ads in *Musical America*.

29. My thanks to the distinguished violinist Josef Gingold, who so graciously provided this information, and to David Cerone, president of the Cleveland Institute for the Performing Arts, for confirming it.

Chapter 32
PLAYING FOR THE SOLDIERS

1. Maud Powell to Mabel Love, 22 May 1915, MLP.

2. See Albert Spalding, *Rise to Follow* (New York: Henry Holt and Company, 1943).

3. See Louis Lochner, *Fritz Kreisler* (reprint ed., Neptune City, NJ: Paganiniana Publications, 1981).

4. Undated, untitled article, NGGC.

5. *Musical America*, 20 October 1917.

6. *Saint Paul Pioneer Press*, 15 April 1918.

7. The Camp Lewis story is from *The Musical Courier*, 18 April 1918 and 2 January 1919; *Musical America*, 7 September 1918.

8. *Musical America*, 7 September 1918.

9. Ibid.

10. *Baltimore Evening Sun*, 28 June 1918.

11. *Musical America*, 7 September 1918.

12. Newspaper clipping, Arthur Loesser Papers.

13. *Baltimore Evening Sun*, 28 June 1918.

14. *The Musical Courier*, 2 January 1919.

15. *The Morning Oregonian* (Portland), 23 February 1918.

16. *Musical America*, 28 December 1918.

17. *The Musical Courier*, 18 April 1918.

18. Ibid., 10 January 1918.

19. Newspaper clipping, Arthur Loesser Papers.

20. Article, NGGC.

21. Ibid.

22. *The Spokesman Review* (Spokane), n.d., Arthur Loesser Papers.

23. *The Musical Courier*, 5 June 1919.

24. *Musical America*, 7 September 1918.

25. Ibid.

26. Ibid., 27 July 1918.

Chapter 33
"America's Own Violinist"

1. *Musical America*, 4 November 1916 (New York recital).

2. Ibid., 13 April 1918 (New York recital).

3. *Baltimore American*, 9 December 1916.

4. *Cleveland Leader*, 18 November 1916.

5. *Minneapolis Morning Tribune*, 16 April 1918.

6. Newspaper clipping, Arthur Loesser Papers.

7. *Dallas Morning News*, n.d., Arthur Loesser Papers.

8. Newspaper clipping, Arthur Loesser Papers.

9. *The Musical Courier*, March 1919.

10. *Denver Times*, 14 February 1919.

11. *Seattle Daily Times*, March 1919.

12. March 1919 article, NGGC.

13. Newspaper clipping, Arthur Loesser Papers.

14. Ibid.

15. *Los Angeles Examiner*, 7 January 1918.

16. Notes in Karen A. Shaffer Collection.

17. *San Francisco Examiner*, 12 January 1918; San Jose newspaper clipping, Arthur Loesser Papers.

18. *Musical America*, 10 May 1919.

19. Ibid.

20. Martens, *Violin Mastery*, 197.

21. Information on Nicholas Brewer and the story of Maud Powell's portrait was graciously provided by Barbara Brewer Peet, Mr. Brewer's daughter (he died in 1949). The quotation is from Nicholas R. Brewer, *Trails of a Paintbrush* (Boston: The Christopher Publishing House, 1938). The portrait was exhibited throughout the U.S. but its present location is unknown.

22. Maud Powell to Nicholas R. Brewer, 10 June 1918.

23. After Maud Powell died, Skjerne joined the faculty of Indiana University, where he chaired the piano department until 1927. In that year, he began his long association with the Oberlin Conservatory of Music. His students learned from him that "serious music was something to be experienced individually, to be respected, revered, studied full time and performed as the result of the most concentrated effort." Skjerne believed that musical understanding was achieved only through a selfless dedication to the mastering of the endless demands of both the instrument and the great music composed for it. Although he became a naturalized U.S. citizen, Skjerne was knighted in 1954 by King Frederick IX of Denmark for his promotion of Danish music in the United States. Always a man of cultural refinement, personal integrity, and high musical ideals, he died while vacationing in Jutland in 1968. Axel Skjerne's daughter, Ingeborg Freitag, graciously provided the information on her father.

24. *The Musical Courier*, 10 April 1919.

25. Newspaper clipping, Arthur Loesser Papers.

26. Katherine Anne Porter, unnamed Denver newspaper, 5 June 1919.

27. *Musical America*, 28 June 1919.

28. Ibid., 31 May 1919.

Chapter 34
"America's One Great Master of the Violin"

1. Maud Powell to Arthur Hartmann, 23 July 1919, MLP.

2. Powell, "Two Types of Violin Playing."

3. Herbert F. Peyser, *Musical America*, November 1917.

4. Jascha Heifetz to Neva Garner Greenwood, 12 March 1979.

5. Maud Powell to the Editor, *Musical America*, 25 May 1918.

6. Winn, "Maud Powell as I Knew Her."

7. Powell, "An Artist's Life."

8. Winn, "Maud Powell as I Knew Her."

9. Duluth, MI, newspaper, 8 December 1913.

10. Article in NGGC.

11. *St. Louis Democrat*, 28 November 1919.

12. *St. Louis Post-Dispatch*, 28 November 1919.

13. H. Godfrey Turner's Introduction to Maud Powell's transcription of "Nobody Knows the Trouble I See" (Boston: Oliver Ditson Company, 1921).

14. Maud Powell Papers, New York Public Library.

15. Mabel Love, Maud Powell's cousin, in a conversation with Neva Garner Greenwood, said Sunny was so distraught that he did not "act right." He neglected to place a notice of the funeral date in the paper and friends were not contacted.

16. Quoted in an article in NGGC.

Epilogue

1. 17 January 1920.

2. The article is in MLP. The crazy quilt made by Maud's mother is in my possession, having been lovingly cared for and given to me by Jean Holmes, niece of Mabel Love, Maud Powell's first cousin. It constitutes part of the Maud Powell collection in my possession which eventually will be placed in a public repository.

3. A little over a year after Maud Powell's death, the *New York Times* carried a story saying that Sunny had given her violin to Erika Morini, a sixteen-year-old Viennese violinist who made her Carnegie Hall debut in 1921. The claim was made that in her will, Maud had entrusted her violin to "a great artist," which, based on a reading of the actual will, was not the case. A subsequent press report ("The Truth—About Maud Powell's Violin," article in Henry Ford Museum) indicates that the precious Guadagnini was not in fact given to Morini. (In fairness to the young Morini, she may not have known of the claims being made in her behalf.) For more than three years, the violin was silent. Then, at the close of Renée Chemet's introductory American tour, Sunny presented the French violinist with the coveted fiddle, which she played for the first time before the American public when she returned to the United States in October 1923. M. Fournier, a Parisian authority on violins,

reported to Sunny that the Guadagnini instantly "doubled" Chemet's "talent." Chemet reported that the violin gave her the "throat of a Caruso!"

Harold Lineback, of St. Louis, MO, possesses important original documents, letters and photographs, pertaining to Maud Powell. Neva Garner Greenwood was permitted to see them briefly but was not given permission to work with them.

Illustration Credits

Credits for illustrations are listed section by section and by page within each section, reading from top to bottom and from left to right. Because the primary research for this biography was done by an amateur, not all photographic sources were clearly recorded. Every effort has been made to accurately credit the illustrations, but with Neva Greenwood's death it has been difficult to obtain all the correct information.

KEY:
HGT   H. Godfrey Turner
LC   Library of Congress
MLC   Mabel Love Collection
NGGC   Neva Garner Greenwood Collection
WPPC   William Paul Powell Collection

JACKET AND FRONTISPIECE: NGGC

SET I, following page 26.

1. Powell Family Bible, Baker Univ., Baldwin, KS, courtesy MLC.

2. Top photos, left and right, Powell Family Bible, Baker Univ., Baldwin, KS, courtesy MLC; bottom, courtesy Nancy Chadbourne Maze, Peru, IL.

3. Powell Family Bible, Baker Univ., Baldwin, KS, courtesy MLC; Powell Family Bible, Baker Univ., courtesy Laurens E. Whittemore, NJ; courtesy MLC.

4. Courtesy William Culp Darrah Collection, Gettysburg, PA.

5. *The Puritan*, October 1897, 34; *Harper's Weekly* XLIII, no. 2202, 212; *The Violinist*, 1902.

6. NGGC; courtesy Jean Holmes, Detroit, NGGC.

7. *The Violinist*, February 1918; NGGC; NGGC; NGGC.

8. Photo by Georg Brokesch, Leipzig, courtesy Aurora Historical Museum, Aurora, IL.

SET II, following page 74.

1. Courtesy N.Y. Public Library and James Persons Coll., Detroit.

2. Photo by A. Cax, Chicago, from Rose Fay Thomas, *Memoirs of Theodore Thomas* (New York: Moffat, Yard and Company, 1911); NGGC; NGGC.

3. Photo by Falk, N.Y.; NGGC; photo by Bain News Service, courtesy LC; photo by Moreno, N.Y., courtesy N.Y. Public Library and Univ. of Illinois Music Library, Urbana-Champaign.

4. Photo by Weismantet, N.Y., MLC; courtesy Aurora Historical Museum, Aurora, IL; courtesy Smithsonian Institution Archives No. 58254, U.S. Dept. of Interior, U.S.G.S. Photo File No. P10-HIST-108.

5. Painting by Stanley Meltzoff, copyright 1963, National Geographic Society, with permission.

6. Courtesy N.Y. Public Library.

7. Courtesy Laurens E. Whittemore, NJ.

8. Courtesy Dallas Public Library.

SET III, following page 148.

1. Photo by Aimé Dupont, N.Y., NGGC.

2. Photo by Aimé Dupont, N.Y., *The Puritan*, October 1897, 33; NGGC; courtesy LC.

3. Courtesy LC; courtesy U.S. Marine Band Library (?); NGGC; *The Musical Courier*, 1 May 1907.

4. Courtesy U.S. Marine Band Library; "Band Fan Newsletter," Winter 1975–76, Detroit.

5. Courtesy MLC; NGGC.

6. Photo by Hall, N.Y., Powell Family Bible, Baker Univ., Baldwin, KS, and WPPC, courtesy Jean Holmes, Detroit; courtesy Jean Holmes; *The Musical Courier*, 18 Oct. 1905, LC.

7. Courtesy U.S. Marine Band Library; *The Etude*; NGGC.

8. Courtesy Lucy Chase Sparks, NH, NGGC.

SET IV, following page 198.

1. Photo by Hall, N.Y., *Musical America*, 26 Dec. 1908, LC.

2. Peru Public Library, Peru, IL, and NGGC; courtesy Paul K. Engberg, Seattle.

3. *Musical America*, 7 Nov. 1908, LC; *Musical America*, 1 May 1909, LC.

4. Photo by WPP, WPPC, courtesy Jean Holmes, Detroit; WPPC, courtesy Jean Holmes.

5. All, WPPC, courtesy Jean Holmes, Detroit.

6. With permission, Collections of Greenfield Village and the Henry Ford Museum, Dearborn, MI; photo by Bushnell, Seattle, Chase Family Collection.

7. Both, with permission, Collections of Greenfield Village and the Henry Ford Museum, Dearborn, MI.

8. Photo by Schloss, N.Y., courtesy Aurora Historical Museum, Aurora, IL.

SET V, following page 228.

1. With permission, Collections of Greenfield Village and the Henry Ford Museum, Dearborn, MI.

2 and 3. *Musical America*, 29 March 1913, LC.

4. Both photos by HGT, *Musical America*, 17 June 1911, LC.

5. Photo by HGT; photo by HGT, *Musical America*, 17 June 1911, LC.

6. MLC.

7. MLC.

8. MLC.

SET VI, following page 286.

1. Photo by Bangs, N.Y., courtesy N.Y. Public Library.

2. MLC; photo by Bain News Service, LC.

3. Both photos courtesy Mrs. Arthur Loesser Collection, Detroit.

4. Photo by Emory C. Kolb, courtesy Mrs. Arthur Loesser Collection, Detroit.

5. Photo by Emory C. Kolb, NGGC.

6. *Musical America*, 12 Feb. 1916, LC.

7. *Musical America*, 18 Nov. 1916, LC.

8. Top photos, left and right, WPPC, courtesy Jean Holmes, Detroit; bottom, courtesy Chase Family Collection.

9. Photo by HGT, WPPC, courtesy Jean Holmes, Detroit.

10. Photo by Bain News Service, LC.

SET VII, following page 324.

1. Photo by Bushnell, Seattle, courtesy N.Y. Public Library.

2. Photo by HGT, courtesy Chase Family Collection; courtesy Chase Family Collection.

3. Photo by Photo Press Illus. Service, NGGC; photo by HGT, *Musical America*, 5 Oct. 1918, LC.

4. Photos by Bain News Service, taken 3 September 1919, LC.

5. Photos by Bain News Service, taken 3 September 1919, LC.

6. Photos by Bain News Service, *Musical America*, 28 December 1918; photo taken 1 November 1917, LC; photo taken in the spring of 1919, LC.

7. Photo by Bain News Service, *Musical America*, 28 December 1918.

8. Courtesy Barbara Brewer Peet.

Set VIII, following page 382.

1. Photo by Bushnell, Seattle, *Musical America*, 19 May 1919, LC, and WPPC.

2. Photos by Bain News Service taken 27 May 1918: Boston newspaper, 2 June 1918; *Musical Courier*, 2 Jan. 1919; *Cleveland Plain Dealer*, 18 Aug. 1918.

3. Photo by Bain News Service taken 27 May 1918, courtesy National Archives, U.S. War Dept. General Staff; *Musical America*, 19 October 1918, p. 91.

4. Courtesy Mrs. Ingeborg Freitag, N.Y.; courtesy Mrs. Ingeborg Freitag; photo by HGT, *Musical America*, 15 June 1918.

5. Photos by Bain News Service, November 1919, LC.

6. *Musical America*, 13 Nov. 1915, LC.

7. *The Story of the Wolfsohn Bureau* (New York, 1920).

8. Courtesy Detroit Public Library Music and Performing Arts Department.

9. Top photo by Marlys Scarbrough, Chief Circulation Clerk, Music Library; both, courtesy Univ. of Illinois, Urbana-Champaign.

10. Photo by Bushnell, Seattle, LC.

Acknowledgments

As I mentioned in the Preface, I have tried to acknowledge the contributions of many people through the notes to the text, but inevitably, some people have been overlooked. The research effort was so comprehensive that the proper acknowledgment of all those to whom we are indebted would require a miracle, especially since Neva Greenwood did not live to write down all the names of the people she wished to acknowledge. My sincerest apologies to anyone not mentioned directly or indirectly.

Warmest thanks to the relatives of Maud Powell who have been exceedingly helpful in providing what information and encouragement they could and who wholeheartedly entered into the spirit of this project: Jean and the late Carl Holmes; the late Mabel Love; Ruth and James Persons; Louise Davis; Mary Alice Roberts; Donald P. and Marjorie Schnacke; Laurens and the late Gladys Whittemore; the late Margaret Whittemore.

Gratefully acknowledged is the invaluable assistance of virtually hundreds of librarians too numerous to name personally. However, I would like to single out for special thanks the courteous and able staff in the Music Division of the Library of Congress, where the majority of Neva Greenwood's research and many hours of my own was done: Elmer Booze, Thomas Jones, Despina Kavadas, Rodney Mill, Geraldine Ostrove, Rudolph Parker, William Parsons, and Wayne Shirley. Also, my personal thanks go to George Hobart, Curator, Documentary Photographs, of the Photographic Division of the Library of Congress for uncovering previously undiscovered photographs of Maud Powell. I would also like to acknowledge the Newspaper and Periodical Division of the Library of Congress as a rich resource which I used extensively.

No researcher can ever say enough about the importance of the libraries we have in this country and the wonderful responsiveness of their staffs. Gratefully acknowledged is the courteous and able assistance of the staff members of the following libraries, which represent separately and together a monumentally rich resource: Public Libraries of Jefferson County, Birmingham, AL; Birmingham Public Library, AL; The University of Arizona Library; Phoenix Public Library, AZ; The Berkeley Public Library, Berkeley, CA; Burlingame Public Library, Burlingame, CA; Sherman-Grinberg Film Libraries, Inc., Hollywood, CA; Univ. of Calif. at Los Angeles Library; Univ. of Southern California, School of Performing Arts Library, Los Angeles, CA; City of Oakland Main Library, CA; Fargo Public Library, Santa Barbara, CA; Santa Barbara Public Library, CA; Sutro Library, San Francisco, CA; Denver Public Library, CO; Norfolk Library, CT; Otis Library, Norwich, CT; The American National Red Cross Library, DC; Nellie C. Carico, Historian, and George H. Goodwin, Jr., Chief Librarian, U.S. Geological Survey, U.S. Dept. of Interior; The Library of Congress, DC; Martin Luther King Memorial Library, DC; U.S. Marine Band Library, DC; Agnes Scott College Library, Decatur, GA; Division of Library Services, Dept. of Education, State of Hawaii; Hawaii Newspaper Agency Library; Aurora Public Library, Aurora, IL; The Joseph Regenstein Library, Univ. of Chicago; Chicago Public Library; Danville Public Library, IL; Peru Public Library, IL; Pontiac Public Library, IL; Rockford Public Library, IL; Southern Illinois Univ. Library; William McClellan, Director, and Jean Geil, Associate Music Librarian, Music Library, Univ. of Illinois at Urbana-Champaign; Indianapolis–Marion County Public Library, IN; Indianapolis County Public Library, IN; Indiana State Library; Albert A. Wells Memorial Library, Lafayette, IN; Cedar Rapids Public Library, IA; Clinton Public Library, IA; Cornell College, IA; University of Iowa Library; Keokuk Public Library, IA; Baker University Library, Baldwin, KS; Topeka Public Library, KS; Paducah Public Library, KY; Acadia Public Library, Crowley, LA; Louisiana State Univ. Library; New Orleans Public Library; Friend Memorial Public Library, Inc., Brooklin, ME; Portland Public Library, ME; Enoch Pratt Free Library, Baltimore, MD; Peabody Conservatory of Music Archives, Peabody Institute of Johns Hopkins Univ., Baltimore, MD; Attleboro Public Library, Attleboro, MA; Boston Public Library, MA; Isham Memorial Library, Harvard University, Eda Kuhn Loeb Music Library; Holyoke Public Library, MA; Williston Memorial Library, Mount Holyoke College, MA; Lynn Public Library, MA; Milton Public Library, MA; New Bedford Free Public Library, MA; James Duncan Phillips Library, Essex Institute, Salem, MA; Springfield City Library, MA; Worcester Public Library, MA; McKeldin Library, Univ. of Maryland; Willard Library, Battle Creek, MI; Agatha Pfeiffer Kalkanis, Chief, Music and Performing Arts Department, Detroit Public Library, MI; Duluth Public Library, MN; Minneapolis Public Library and Information Center; City of St. Paul Public Library, MN; Kansas City Public Library, MO; Mexico–

Audroin County Library, Mexico, MO; St. Louis Public Library, MO; The Silver Bow Public Library, Butte, MT; Whitefield Public Library, NH; New Brunswick Free Public Library, NJ; The Newark Public Library, NJ; Orange Public Library, NJ; Paterson Free Public Library, NJ; Brooklyn Public Library, N.Y.; State Univ. of New York at Buffalo Library; Buffalo and Erie County Public Library, NY; Steele Memorial Library, Elmira, NY; Great Neck Library, NY; Mount Vernon Public Library, NY; Eastman School of Music Library, NY; The Bettmann Archive, Inc., NY; The Juilliard School Library; Library and Museum of the Performing Arts, New York Public Library at Lincoln Center; New York Public Library; The Library, Onteora Club, Tannersville, NY; William B. Ogden Free Library, Walton, NY; White Plains Public Library, NY; The University Archives, Duke University, Durham, NC; Public Library of Cincinnati and Hamilton County, OH; Univ. of Cincinnati Library; Oberlin College Archives, OH; The Conservatory Library, Oberlin College, OH; Miami University Library, Oxford, OH; Toledo–Lucas Public Library, OH; Lawton Public Library, OK; Library Assn. of Portland, OR; The New Allentown Public Library, Allentown, PA; State Library of Pennsylvania; The Free Library of Philadelphia, PA; Combs Broad Street Conservatory Library; The Curtis Institute of Music Library, PA; Uniontown Public Library, PA; Providence Public Library, RI; York County Library, Rock Hill, SC; Corpus Christi Public Libraries, TX; Dallas Public Library, TX; San Antonio Public Library, TX; Trinity Univ. Library, San Antonio, TX; Bellingham Public Library, Bellingham, WA; Washington State Library, Olympia, WA; Washington State Univ. Library, Pullman, WA; Neill Public Library, Pullman, WA; Seattle Public Library, WA; Spokane Public Library, WA; Tacoma Public Library, WA; Yakima Valley Regional Library, WA; Beloit Public Library, Beloit, WI; Dane County Library Service, Madison, WI; Brewer Public Library, Richland Center, WI.

The contributions of the late John Barron of *The Daily News Tribune*, LaSalle, IL, who provided information on Maud Powell's early life are gratefully acknowledged. Special thanks also to the archival staff of the Aurora *Beacon-News*, IL; *Mexico Ledger*, Mexico, MO; and *The Seattle Times*, WA, for providing concert reviews and other articles pertaining to Maud Powell.

Particular appreciation goes to the staffs, employees, and directors of many historical museums, public and private associations, and corporations which provided a wealth of information: The American Bandmasters Association, WI; Frank E. Ford, President, Aurora Historical Society; John Jaros, Director, Aurora Historical Museum; Georgene Rieke, Librarian, Aurora Historical Museum; Greater Aurora Chamber of Commerce; Walter R. Benjamin Autographs, Inc.; Museum of Art, Carnegie Institute, Pittsburgh, PA; Carnegie Hall Corporation, NY; CBS Records, NY; The Art Institute of Chicago; Chautauqua Institution, NY; Colorado Historical Society; Columbia Artists Theatricals Corp., NY; James Creighton, Discopaedia Co., Canada; Detroit Historical Museum, MI; Dossin Great Lakes Museum, MI; Robert Eliason, Sarah Lawrence, Henry Ford Museum, Dearborn, MI; Carl Fischer, Inc.; Fort Hayes Alumni Assn., Fort Hayes Kansas State College; Iowa State Historical Department, Division of Historical Museum and Archives; Division of Historic Preservation, Indiana State Museum; Indianapolis Museum of Art; LaSalle County Historical Society; William Lewis & Son; The Long Island Historical Society, NY; Liberty Music Shop; Society for the Preservation of Long Island Antiquities, NY; U.S. Marine Corps Museums; Minneapolis Institute of Art; Institute for Studies in American Music, Univ. of Missouri at Kansas City Conservatory; National Archives and Records Service, Audiovisual Division, DC; Nipper Record Collectors; Oregon Historical Society; Pittsburg State University, Cecil and Eva Wilkinson Alumni Center, Pittsburg, KS; The Presser Foundation, PA; John Wesley Powell Memorial Museum, Page, AZ; Theodore Presser Co., PA; RCA Records, NY; Morton Savada, Records Revisited, NY; Minnesota Historical Society, St. Paul, MN; San Antonio Museum Association, Witte Memorial Museum, TX; National Portrait Gallery, Smithsonian Institution, DC; Arthur C. Caps, Soundtrack, MA; Steinway and Sons, NY; Tuesday Music Club, San Antonio, TX; Mrs. Lois T. Sarvis, San Antonio, TX; Mrs. Charles George, San Antonio, TX; National Park Service, U.S. Dept. of Interior, Grand Canyon National Park, AZ; Vineland Historical and Antiquarian Society, NJ; WVA Dept. of Culture and History, Charleston, WVA; Alumni Assn. Wichita State Univ., KS; The State Historical Society of Wisconsin, Madison, WI; National Woman's Party; Dept. of Veterans Affairs, Veterans Home of California; H. Wiley Hitchcock, Director, Institute for Studies in American Music, Brooklyn, NY; Robert Bein & Geoffrey Fushi, Inc., Rare Stringed Instruments, Chicago, IL; Irving Berlin Music Corp.; W. E. Hill and Sons, England; *The American String Teacher*, American String Teachers' Association; *Music Educators Journal*, Music Educators National Conference; *The New York Times Book Review*.

Many thanks as well to the cooperative staffs of many foreign state libraries, museums, universities, and orchestras: Gesellschaft der Musikfreunde, Vienna; Wiener Stadt–und Landesbibliothek; Wiener Philharmoniker; De Philharmonie, Antwerp; Opera National, Brussels; Edward Johnson Music Library, Univ. of Toronto, Canada; Vancouver Public Library, Canada; Winnipeg Library, Canada; Brighton Philharmonic Society; British Broadcasting Corporation; The British Library; Royal College of Music Library; Royal Academy of Music Library; Royal Liverpool Philharmonic Society; Theatre Museum, Victoria and Albert Museum; Etablissement Public du Music du XIXe Siècle, Paris; Ministère des Affaires Culturelles, Direction des Archives de France; Gurzenich-Orchester der Stadt Koln; Hochschule Für Musik, Leipzig; Hochschule der Kunste, Berlin; Breitkopf & Hartel Musikverlag, Leipzig; Breitkopf & Hartel Musikverlag, Weisbaden; Concertgebouworkest, Amsterdam; Rotterdams Philharmonischorkest; het Residentie-Orkest, The Hague; Filharmonisk Selskap, Oslo; Conservatoire National Superieur de Musique, Paris; Musée D'Orsay, Paris; Stockholms Konserthusstiftelse, Filharmonikerna; Welsh National Opera.

The following individuals have helped in so many different ways that it is best simply to list them, confident that they will remember in what ways they have helped and know that their assistance has been deeply appreciated: Mr. and Mrs. Charles M. Adams; Julia Adams-Stanley; Christine Ammer; Martin J. Anderson; Samuel Applebaum; Max Aronoff; Richard Barr; Carol Neuls-Bates; LeRoy Bauer; Amy Beamer; Robert Benedict; Gregor Benko; Paul E. Bierly; Martin Bookspan; Adrian Boult; Marilyn Lott Brewer; Janet Briggs; Frederick P. and Nancy Greenwood Brooks, Jr.; Joseph B. Browder; Karl V. Brown; Cecil and Jessica Burleigh; Lillian A. Burns; Richard and Barbara Butler; Louise G. Butter; Virginia Brown Camicia; Margaret Campbell; Mary Canberg; Arthur C. Caps; Nellie Carico; Virginia Carman; Jim Cartwright; Jeanette Casey, Chicago Public Library; Daniel A. Cerio; David Cerone; Evelina Chao; Aurin Chase; Stephen H. Clapp; Curtis G. Clever; Nancy Cluck; Rena N. Coen; Shirley Conklin; Louise Shelby Connor; Edwin Constant; Clifford Cook; Aaron Copland; Edgar A. Cosimi; Paul S. Cousley; Dolores C. Culver; James, Janet, Michael, and Julia Damron; William Culp Darrah; Dario D'Attili; Oliver Davies; Jeane Dawson; Margaret Dell; Vernon Derry; Mrs. Edward Dethier; Pamela DeWall; Frances Diehl; Mary Jane C. Due; Adele B. Durban; Reginald W. Eastman; Robert E. Eliason; Byrd Elliot; M. Josephine Elliott; Paul K. Engberg; Margaret K. Farish; Janice Fenimore; Ella Mae Ferris; Edith Fickensher; Arthur Fiedler; José Figueroa; José and Ruth Figueroa, Jr.; Mary Findley; Colleen Finks; Jacques Français; John Frazer; Ingeborg Freitag; Joseph Fuchs; Jane Fulcher; Samuel Gardner; Donald M. Garvelmann; Jody Gatwood; Mrs. E. Lawrence Gay; Josef Gingold; George Glatkauskas; Stanley J. Goodman; Robert Goralski; Gerald G. and Celinda P. Graf; William A. Graf; David N. Greene; Gary Greene; Mr. and Mrs. Peter B. Greenough; Neva Elizabeth Greenwood; Bud Gropper; Mariclaire Hale; Carol Hamilton; Virginia Harpham; Lucille Hastings; Patricia Hederman; Jascha Heifetz; Joanne Hildebrand; George Hobart; Eleanor and Christopher Hope; Bryan Horner; Marshall and Helen Howenstein; Charles and Laura Jean Hunt; Elizabeth Jackson; Patricia Johnston; Gary Karr; Louis and Annette Kaufman; Ms. Keller; Ruth Kemper; John Kendall; Robert H. Klotman; Joseph Koch; Louis Krasner; Judith K. Krier; William Kroll; Dr. and Mrs. Chin Fu Kwok; Lois Applebaum Leibow; Samuel and Leah Levy; J. Reilly Lewis; Harold Lineback; Mrs. Arthur Loesser; Werner Lywen; Joan Macfee; John Maltese; Leslie and Lyndon Marguerie; Timothy J. McCollum; Mary Alice McDonald; C. Douglas McIntyre; John K. Mattison; Nancy Chadbourne Maze; Frederick Meisel; Joyce Mellon; Yehudi Menuhin; Emerson Meyers; Muriel Mikelsons; Mr. and Mrs. William H. Moenig, Jr.; Wilda Moenig; Albert F. Moglie; Ellis O. Moore; Robert Moore; William R. Moran; Dick Mortensen; Alyce Mullen; Kurt Myers; Peter Norris; Brad O'Keefe; Julia F. Peacock; Helen Pearce; Barbara Brewer Peet; Elizabeth and William Perry Pendley, Jr.; Jack Pfeiffer; Jack S. Phelan; Melissa J. Pittard; T. L. Pittenger; the late Eleanore Plain; Harrison Potter; Sally West Potter; Steven and Rachael Price; Aaron Rosand; Gilbert Ross; Maria Safonoff; F. C. Schang; Nelson O. Schreiber; Dr. and Mrs. Boris Schwarz; John R. and Helen B. Shaffer; Karl R. and Patricia L. Shaffer; Oscar Shapiro; Billy J. and Georgie Shoger; Laura Sias; Robert and Gloria Simmons; Bruce H. Simpson; Jean Shaw Smith; Mac and Sylvia Smith; Lucy Chase Sparks; Diana Steiner; Isaac Stern; Paul K. Stolz; Benjamin Swalin; Howard Taubman; Millard Taylor; Studs Terkel; Virgil Thomson; William S. Timblin; Larry Turner; Lory Wallfisch; Marty Walter; Edward N. Waters; William Weaver; Beverly Zisla Welber; Jan A. Williams; Fredda Wines; Laura Woodside; Mrs. Rembert Wurlitzer; Marianne Wurlitzer.

Maud Powell Foundation
Acknowledgments

THE MAUD POWELL FOUNDATION is a Virginia corporation organized in 1986 for the purpose of educating the general public about the life of the American pioneer violinist Maud Powell and her contribution to American musical life and to the art of violin playing. The Foundation is also established to further Maud Powell's musical ideals. In keeping with its purposes, The Foundation has copublished this biography of Maud Powell with Iowa State University Press.

The Board of Directors of The Maud Powell Foundation wishes to thank the following for the time and energy that they have devoted to furthering its purposes: Joseph Burstein; Terry and Janice Crellin; Dolores C. Culver; Janet Damron; Floyd Esche, *LaSalle News Tribune*; Colleen

Finks; the Falls Church Music Club; Mary Ann Flandro; Dingwall Fleary and the McLean Orchestra; Henry Fogel, Executive Director, and staff, Chicago Symphony Orchestra; Ann French, Henry Ford Museum; Jody Gatwood; Linda Gilbert; Neva Elizabeth Greenwood; Daphne Kwok; Virginia Harpham; Eugenia Hartman; Patricia Hederman; Louise Henry; George Hobart; Natalie R. Howard and Richard G. Howe, Howe Brothers Publishing; Margaret Hunt; Louis and Annette Kaufman; Richard Kinney, Director, Iowa State University Press; Judith Kuzel, Assistant Head Librarian, and Becky Tatar, Aurora Public Library; LaSalle (IL) Women's Club; Marjory Levenson; Mary Elizabeth Lewis; John Maltese; Susan Manola; Nancy Chadbourne Maze; Mick McAllister; Mary Alice McDonald; Laurence M. McMurrin; Trudy McMurrin; Albert Mell, Editor, *Journal of the Violin Society of America*; John Melnick; Yehudi Menuhin; George and Irene Minich and family; Robert Moore; George Moquin, Executive Director, and Tuula Yrjö-Koskinen, Congress Coordinator, Maryland Summer Institute for the Creative and Performing Arts; Prescott Morgan; John Newsome and Elizabeth Auman, Music Division, Library of Congress; Brad Oldenburg; Fay Parker; Aaron Rosand; Angie Ringsdorf and Mrs. Dellinger's fifth-grade class, Northview School, Peru, IL; the Board of Directors, People's Hospital, Peru, IL; Margaret Schick; Hugh Schultz, Marketing Director, Iowa State University Press; Franco and Louise Sciannameo, *The Violexchange*; John R. and Helen B. Shaffer; Karl R. and Patricia L. Shaffer; Ruth Shirk; Joseph Silverstein; Gloria Simmons; Alice Thompson; Lory Wallfisch; Eric Wen, Editor, *The Strad*; Ann Wilkshire.

The Board of Directors of The Maud Powell Foundation wishes to thank the following:

BENEFACTORS

Frederick P. and Nancy G. Brooks, Jr.

Kenneth Brooks

Virginia Brown Camicia

Joseph A. Greenwood

Ruth and James Persons

John R. and Helen B. Shaffer

Karl R. and Patricia L. Shaffer

Ren and Bee Stelloh

Suzuki Association of the Greater Washington Area

CONTRIBUTORS

Mr. and Mrs. Earl C. Abbe, Craig Allen, David Allen, Scott G. Anderson, William M. Anderson III, Mrs. Henry Anderton, Dr. and Mrs. Carl Anthon, AT&T Foundation, Marilyn J. Baker and Ellis D. Lutz, Kay H. and Marian Barney, Richard L. Barr, Carol Neuls-Bates, LeRoy Bauer, Amy L. Beamer, Sharon N. Beauregard, Robert Benedict, Catherine W. Betts, A. Merrick Blamphin, Aileen L. Blyth, Mary Frances Boyce, David C. Branand, David A. Budd, Joseph Burstein, Mr. and Mrs. Oliver Caldwell, Mr. and Mrs. Arthur C. Caps, Peter J. Chang, Evelina Chao, Vera Chao, Ellis Chasens, Kenneth and Danna Chayt, Dr. and Mrs. Donald Chen, Eric and Linda Christenson, Carol J. Cochran, Patricia S. Cochran, Mrs. David W. Colby, Thomas D. Collins, C. C. Conrad, Jean Carrington Cook, Ray N. Cooley, Jr., Corning Glass Works Foundation, Edgar Cosimi, Mrs. Floyd Covington, Zera H. Crist, Dolores C. Culver, Carla Dale, James and Janet Damron, Carleton and Louise Davis, Douglas Powell Davis, Helen P. Davis, Louise Davis, Margaret J. and Jeannette Dell, Colleen and Dave Derby, Mrs. Edouard Dethier, Pamela DeWall, Hal Doersam, Virginia and Daniel DeSimone, Bertha T. Donahue, Marion E. Donnelly, Montrose Draper, Mr. and Mrs. Daniel A. Dreyfus, Paul Driessen and Dvorah Ann Richman, Mary Jane C. Due, Michael J. Duggan, Loraine E. Edwards, Byrd Elliott, Paul and Ann Elmquist, Mr. and Mrs. Allan B. Ensign, Sarah G. Epstein, José Figueroa, José and Ruth Figueroa, Jr., Mary Findley, E. J. and Harriet Finkel, Colleen and Mark Finks, William Foster, Sam and Mattilyn Fraser, Paul Frick, Genevieve D. Fritter, Wilbert G. Fritz, Emma Jean and Winfrey Garner, Winifred Garrigus, Mariana R. Gasteyer, John J. Gattuso, Paul, Sylvia and Will Gayer, Mrs. Charles George, Robert Gerle, Mary Alice Glover, Hugh Grabosky, Celinda P. Graf, Melissa Graybeal, Robert Greenler, Sumner and Grace Greenwood, Jane Hammer, E. Randolph Hansen, Jr., Virginia Harpham, E. C. Harris, Jr., Ann C. Hart, Eugenia and George Hartman, Evelyn Swarthout Hayes, O. E. and Martha Hedges, Jascha Heifetz, August and Margery Hoenack, Phyliss Hoffman, Jean R. Hollingsworth, Mr. and Mrs. Carl L. Holmes, Household International, Marshall Howenstein, Charles and Laura Jean Hunt, Margaret Hunt, Isabel C. Hutson, Winifred Hyson, Patricia B. Ingle, Lois S. Irion, Edithann Janetski, Harold H. Johnson and Betsy Ancker-Johnson, Edna Jorgenson, Gary Karr, Louis and Annette Kaufman, John and Catherine Kendell, Emily A. Kennedy, Louis Krasner, Harvey M. Krasney, Florence Kwok, Dave and Nancy Lamoreaux, L. Courtland Lee, Craig and Michaele Lemrow, Arthur and Marjorie Levenson, Mr. and Mrs. William Leverage, J. Reilly Lewis, Mary Elizabeth Lewis, Phyllis K. Lind, Mayda Low,

John Maltese, Susan Manning, Jean Mansuri, Cecelia Marony, Orlando Martino, Audrey M. Maxwell, Alan and Jackie Mayers, George and Nancy Maze, Anna McCormick, Doris McLaughlin, Elizabeth McMahan, Mary A. McReynolds, Edward D. and Portia K. Meares, John and Marjory Melnick, Yehudi Menuhin, Mrs. C. P. Miller, Jeffrey and Jane Milstein, Mrs. Marshall Minich, John and Rosemary Monagan, Elizabeth W. Moore, Alyce and Roy Mullen, Julia and Erwin Niemeyer, Mrs. Stuart Ogilvie, Brad O'Keefe, Seetar G. Pande, Thomas and Fay Parker, Judith Parkinson, Trudy and John Pearman, Barbara Brewer Peet, Samuel and Liza Peng, David W. Persons, James and Karen Pierce, Melissa J. Pittard, Margaret Powell, Matt Prestone, Mary A. Price, Patricia S. Pylypec, Henry and Constance Rachlin, Barbara Davis Radcliffe, Frank and Rowena Reynolds, Marian Rix, Jacob and Jean Robbins, Judith Robertson, Harriet Robnett, Glen E. Rogers, Aaron Rosand, Claude and Sheldon Rosenthal, Donald and Martha Ross, Mrs. Allie L. Rowe, Mr. and Mrs. Ernest B. Ryder, Leo and Carol Sade, Mary Sandford, Martha D. Schroeder, Joan and Steve Schuldenfrei, Karen A. Shaffer, Rebecca F. Shaw, Charlotte V. Shear, Billy J. and Georgie Shoger, Arlene Shrut, Bruce H. Simpson, William I. Slapin, Margaret K. Smagorinsky, Anne and Curt Smith, Cynthia Smith, Arnold A. Sposato, Kurt H. Stern, Dr. and Mrs. Paul K. Stolz, Cathleen D. Stone, Donald and Julia Strode, Roger J. and Susan G. Sullivan, Julia S. Summerson, Benjamin F. Swalin, Sheldon A. Taft, Eleanor Tarpley, Mary Tarpley, Mr. and Mrs. F. Alex Teass, Mrs. E. S. Thoreson, William S. Timblin, Margaret C. Tolson, Mrs. Howard E. Tompkins, Mrs. W. James Trott, Dr. Larry Turner, Mary S. Tuttle, Mary Tyson, Ted Venners, Vincent and Paulina Vlasic, Lory Wallfisch, Russell G. Wayland, June Whelan, Buel and Beverlee White, Martin A. White, Mildred W. Whitman, Gladys and Laurens E. Whittemore, Ruth D. Willers, Edward Wollenberg, Eleanor Woods, Margaret Wright, David Wu, John and Colleen Wulff, Eddie R. and Shirley Wyatt, Mary T. D. Young, Michael P. Zazanis, Frederick Zenone.

Index

MAUD POWELL, PIONEER AMERICAN VIOLINIST
was edited and produced for the Maud Powell Foundation
and Iowa State University Press by Trudy McMurrin,
assisted by the following professionals and suppliers,
all of Salt Lake City, Utah:

Disk correction: Janice Crellin

Typesetting and Composition: Type Center, Inc.

Photo layouts: Laurence M. McMurrin

Jacket design and title page: Scott Engen

Printing: Publishers Press

Binding: Mountain States Bindery

WordPerfect 4.2 was used to prepare the manuscript.